Lecture Notes in Artificial Intelligence 3244

Edited by J. G. Carbonell and J. Siekmann

Subseries of Lecture Notes in Computer Science

Shai Ben-David   John Case
Akira Maruoka (Eds.)

Algorithmic Learning Theory

15th International Conference, ALT 2004
Padova, Italy, October 2-5, 2004
Proceedings

 Springer

Series Editors

Jaime G. Carbonell, Carnegie Mellon University, Pittsburgh, PA, USA
Jörg Siekmann, University of Saarland, Saarbrücken, Germany

Volume Editors

Shai Ben-David
University of Waterloo, School of Conputer Science
Waterloo, Ontario, Canada
E-mail: shai@cs.uwaterloo.cs

John Case
University of Delaware
Department of Computer and Information Sciences
Newark, DE 19716, USA
E-mail: case@cis.udel.edu

Akira Maruoka
Tohoku University
Graduate School of Information Sciences
Sendai 980-8579, Japan
E-mail: maruoka@ecei.tohoku.ac.jp

Library of Congress Control Number: 2004113282

CR Subject Classification (1998): I.2.6, I.2.3, F.1, F.2, F.4, I.7

ISSN 0302-9743
ISBN 3-540-23356-3 Springer Berlin Heidelberg New York

Springer is a part of Springer Science+Business Media

springeronline.com

© Springer-Verlag Berlin Heidelberg 2004
Printed in Germany

Typesetting: Camera-ready by author, data conversion by PTP-Berlin, Protago-TeX-Production GmbH
Printed on acid-free paper   SPIN: 11326540   06/3142   5 4 3 2 1 0

Foreword

Algorithmic learning theory is mathematics about computer programs which learn from experience. This involves considerable interaction between various mathematical disciplines including theory of computation, statistics, and combinatorics. There is also considerable interaction with the practical, empirical fields of machine and statistical learning in which a principal aim is to predict, from past data about phenomena, useful features of future data from the same phenomena.

The papers in this volume cover a broad range of topics of current research in the field of algorithmic learning theory. We have divided the 29 technical, contributed papers in this volume into eight categories (corresponding to eight sessions) reflecting this broad range. The categories featured are Inductive Inference, Approximate Optimization Algorithms, Online Sequence Prediction, Statistical Analysis of Unlabeled Data, PAC Learning & Boosting, Statistical Supervised Learning, Logic Based Learning, and Query & Reinforcement Learning.

Below we give a brief overview of the field, placing each of these topics in the general context of the field. Formal models of automated learning reflect various facets of the wide range of activities that can be viewed as *learning*.

A first dichotomy is between viewing learning as an indefinite process and viewing it as a finite activity with a defined termination. Inductive Inference models focus on indefinite learning processes, requiring only eventual success of the learner to converge to a satisfactory conclusion.

When one wishes to predict future data, success can be enhanced by making some restrictive but true assumptions about the nature (or regularities) of the data stream. In the learning theory community, this problem is addressed in two different ways. The first is by assuming that the data to be predicted is generated by an operator that belongs to a restricted set of operators that is known to the learner a priori. The PAC model and some of the work under the Inductive Inference framework follow this path. Alternatively, one could manage without any such prior assumptions by relaxing the success requirements of the learner: rather than opting for some absolute degree of accuracy, the learner is only required to perform as well as any learner in some fixed family of learners. Thus, if the data is erratic or otherwise hard to predict, the learner can ignore poor accuracy as long as no member of the fixed reference family of learners can do no better. This is the approach taken by some Online Sequence Prediction models in the indefinite learning setting and, also, by most of the models of Statistical Learning in the finite horizon framework.

Boosting is a general technique that applies a given type of learner iteratively to improve its performance. Boosting approaches have been shown to be effective for a wide range of learning algorithms and have been implemented by a variety of methods.

A second dichotomy is between *Supervised* and *Un-Supervised* learning. The latter we refer to as *learning from Unlabeled Data*. In the first scenario, the data has the form of an example-label pairs. The learner is trained on a set of such pairs and then, upon seeing some fresh examples, has to predict their labels. In the latter model, the data points lack any such labeling, and the learner has to find some persistent regularities in the data, on the basis of the examples it has seen. Such regularities often take the form of partitioning the data into clusters of similar points, but in some cases take other forms, such as locating the boundaries of the support of the data generating distribution.

Many learning algorithms can be viewed as searching for an object that fits the given training data best. Such *optimization* tasks are often computationally infeasible. To overcome such computational hurdles, it is useful to apply algorithms that search for approximations to the optimal objects. The study of such algorithms, in the context of learning tasks, is the subject of our Approximate Optimization Algorithms session.

There is a large body of research that examines different *representations* of data and of learners' conclusions. This research direction is the focus of our Logic Based Learning session.

A final important dichotomy separates models of interactive learning from those that model passive learners. In the first type of learning scenarios the actions of the learner affect the training data available to it. In the Query Learning model this interaction takes the form of queries of certain (pre-indicated) type(s) that the learner can pose. Then the data upon which the learner bases its conclusions are the responses to these queries. The other model that addresses interactive learning is Reinforcement Learning, a model that assumes that the learner takes actions and receives *rewards* that are a function of these actions. These rewards in turn are used by the learner to determine its future actions.

August 2004

Shai Ben-David
John Case
Akira Marouka

Preface

This volume contains the papers presented at the 15th Annual International Conference on Algorithmic Learning Theory (ALT 2004), which was held in Padova (Italy) October 2–5, 2004. The main objective of the conference was to provide an interdisciplinary forum for discussing the theoretical foundations of machine learning as well as their relevance to practical applications. The conference was co-located with the 7th International Conference on Discovery Science (DS 2004) and the 11th Conference on String Processing and Information Retrieval (SPIRE 2004) under the general title "The Padova Dialogues 2004".

The volume includes 29 technical contributions that were selected by the program committee from 91 submissions. It also contains the invited lecture for ALT and DS 2004 presented by Ayumi Shinohara (Kyushu University, Fukuoka, Japan) on "String Pattern Discovery". Furthermore, this volume contains the ALT 2004 invited talks presented by Nicolò Cesa-Bianchi (Università degli Studi di Milano, Italy) on "Applications of Regularized Least Squares in Classification Problems", and by Luc De Raedt (Universität Freiburg, Germany) on "Probabilistic Inductive Logic Programming".

Additionally, it contains the invited lecture presented by Esko Ukkonen (University of Helsinki, Finland) on "Hidden Markov Modelling Techniques for Haplotype Analysis" (joint invited talk with DS 2004). Moreover, this volume includes the abstract of the joint invited lecture with DS 2004 presented by Pedro Domingos (University of Washington, Seattle, USA) on "Learning, Logic, and Probability: A Unified View".

Finally, this volume contains the papers of the research tutorials on *Statistical Mechanical Methods in Learning* by Toshiyuki Tanaka (Tokyo Metropolitan University, Japan) on "Statistical Learning in Digital Wireless Communications", by Yoshiyuki Kabashima and Shinsuke Uda (Tokyo Institute of Technology, Japan), on "A BP-Based Algorithm for Performing Bayesian Inference in Large Perceptron-like Networks", and by Manfred Opper and Ole Winther on "Approximate Inference in Probabilistic Models".

ALT has been awarding the *E. Mark Gold Award* for the most outstanding paper by a student author since 1999. This year the award was given to Hubie Chen for his paper "Learnability of Relatively Quantified Generalized Formulas", co-authored by Andrei Bulatov and Victor Dalmau.

This conference was the 15th in a series of annual conferences established in 1990. Continuation of the ALT series is supervised by its steering committee consisting of: Thomas Zeugmann (Hokkaido Univ., Sapporo, Japan), Chair, Arun Sharma (Queensland Univ.of Technology, Australia), Co-chair, Naoki Abe (IBM T.J. Watson Research Center, USA), Klaus Peter Jantke (DFKI, Germany), Roni Khardon (Tufts Univ., USA), Phil Long (National Univ. of Singapore), Hiroshi Motoda (Osaka University, Japan), Akira Maruoka (Tohoku Univ., Japan), Luc De Raedt (Albert-Ludwigs-Univ., Germany), Takeshi Shinohara (Kyushu Institute of Technology, Japan), and Osamu Watanabe (Tokyo Institute of Technology, Japan).

We would like to thank all individuals and institutions who contributed to the success of the conference: the authors for submitting papers, the invited speakers for accepting our invitation and lending us their insight into recent developments in their research areas, as well as the sponsors for their generous financial and logistical support.

We would also like to thank Thomas Zeugmann for assisting us via his experience in the publication of previous ALT proceedings, for providing the ALT 2004 logo, and for managing the ALT 2004 Web site. We are very grateful to Frank Balbach who developed the ALT 2004 electronic submission page.

Furthermore, we would like to express our gratitude to all program committee members for their hard work in reviewing the submitted papers and participating in online discussions. We are also grateful to the external referees whose reviews made a considerable contribution to this process.

We are also grateful to the DS 2004 chairs Einoshin Suzuki (PC Chair, Yokohama National University, Japan) and Setsuo Arikawa (Conference Chair, Kyushu University, Japan) for their effort in coordinating with ALT 2004, and to Massimo Melucci (University of Padova, Italy) for his excellent work as the local arrangements chair. Last but not least, Springer provided excellent support in preparing this volume.

August 2004   Shai Ben-David
                                                                John Case
                                                                Akira Maruoka

Organization

Conference Chair

Akira Marouka   Tohoku University, Sendai, Japan

Program Committee

Shai Ben-David   Univ. of Waterloo, Canada, Co-chair
John Case   Univ. of Delaware, USA, Co-chair
Nader Bshouty   Technion, Israel
Michael Collins   MIT, USA
Sanjoy Dasgupta   UC San Diego, USA
Peter Flach   Univ. of Bristol, UK
Steffen Lange   DFKI, Saarbrücken, Germany)
Jon Langford   TTI Chicago, USA
Gabor Lugosi   UPF, Barcelona, Spain
Rüdiger Reischuk   Univ. at Lübeck, Germany
Rocco Servedio   Columbia Univ., USA
Arun Sharma   Queensland Univ. of Technology,
                          Brisbane, Australia
Ayumi Shinohara   Kyushu Univ., Japan
Eiji Takimoto   Tohoku Univ., Japan
Sandra Zilles   Univ. Kaiserslautern, Germany

Local Arrangements

Massimo Melucci   University of Padova, Italy

Subreferees

Kazuyuki Amano   Jochen Nessel
Pedro Felzenswalb   Ryan O'Donnell
Kouichi Hirata   Daniel Reidenbach
Klaus P. Jantke   Yoshifumi Sakai
Adam Klivans   Gilles Stoltz
Stephen Kwek   Rolf Wiehagen
Martin Memmel

Sponsoring Institutions

Institute for Theoretical Computer Science, University at Lübeck
Division of Computer Science, Hokkaido University

Remembering Carl Smith, 1950–2004

Sadly, Carl Smith passed away 10:30PM, July 21, 2004. He had had a 1.5 year battle with an aggressive brain tumor. He fought this battle with calm optimism, dignity, and grace. He is survived by his wife, Patricia, his son, Austin, and his sister, Karen Martin.

Carl was very active in the algorithmic or computational learning communities, especially in the inductive inference subarea which applies recursive function theory techniques.

I first met Carl when I interviewed for my faculty position at SUNY/Buffalo in the Spring of 1973. He was then a graduate student there and told me he was interested in recursive function theory. After I joined there, he naturally became my Ph.D. student, and that's when we both began working on inductive inference. We spent a lot of time together, pleasantly blurring the distinction between the relationships of friendship and advisor-student.

After Buffalo, Carl had faculty positions at Purdue and, then, the University of Maryland.

Carl had a very productive career. He was a master collaborator working with many teams around the world. Of course he also produced a number of papers about inductive inference by teams — as well as papers about anomalies, queries, memory limitation, procrastination, and measuring mind changes by counting down from notations for ordinals. I had the reaction to some of his papers of wishing I'd thought of the idea. This especially struck me with his 1989 *TCS* paper (with Angluin and Gasarch) in which it is elegantly shown that the learning of some classes of tasks can be done only sequentially after or in parallel with other classes.

Carl played a significant leadership role in theoretical computer science. In 1981, with the help of Paul Young, Carl organized the Workshop on Recursion Theoretic Aspects of Computer Science. This became the well known, continuing series of Computational Complexity conferences. Carl provided an improvement in general theoretical computer science funding level during his year as Theory Program Director at NSF. He was involved, in many cases from the beginning, in the COLT, AII, ALT, EuroCOLT, and DS conferences, as a presenter of papers, as a member of many of their program committees and, in some cases, steering committees. He spearheaded the development of COLT's Mark Fulk Award for best student papers and managed the finances.

Carl was very likable. He had a knack for finding funding to make good things happen. He was a good friend and colleague. He is missed.

August 2004   John Case

Table of Contents

Statistical Supervised Learning

Statistical Analysis of Unlabeled Data

Online Sequence Prediction

Approximate Optimization Algorithms

Logic Based Learning

Query and Reinforcement Learning

TUTORIAL PAPERS

String Pattern Discovery

Ayumi Shinohara

Department of Informatics, Kyushu University 33, Fukuoka 812-8581, JAPAN
PRESTO, Japan Science and Technology Agency
ayumi@i.kyushu-u.ac.jp

Abstract. Finding a good pattern which discriminates one set of strings from the other set is a critical task in knowledge discovery. In this paper, we review a series of our works concerning with the string pattern discovery. It includes theoretical analyses of learnabilities of some pattern classes, as well as development of practical data structures which support efficient string processing.

1 Introduction

A huge amount of text data or sequential data are accessible in these days. Especially, the growing popularity of Internet have caused an enormous increase of text data in the last decade. Moreover, a lot of biological sequences are also available due to various genome sequencing projects. Many of these data are stored as raw strings, or in semi-structured form such as HTML and XML, which are essentially strings. *String pattern discovery*, where one is interested in extracting patterns which characterizes a set of strings or sequential data, has attracted widespread attentions [1,36,13,24,12,3,4,30]. Discovering a *good rule* to separate two given sets, often referred as *positive examples* and *negative examples*, is a critical task in Machine Learning and Knowledge Discovery. In this paper, we review a series of our works for finding best string patterns efficiently, together with their theoretical background.

Our motivations originated in the development of a machine discovery system BONSAI [31], that produces a decision tree over regular patterns with alphabet indexing, from given positive set and negative set of strings. The core part of the system is to generate a decision tree which classifies positive examples and negative examples as correctly as possible. For that purpose, we have to find a *pattern* that maximizes the goodness according to the entropy information gain measure, recursively at each node of trees. In the initial implementation, a pattern associated with each node is restricted to a *substring pattern*, due to the limit of computation time. In order to allow more expressive patterns while keeping the computation in reasonable time, we have introduced various techniques gradually [15,17,16,7,19,8,21,32,6,18]. Essentially, they are combinations of pruning heuristics in the huge search space without sacrificing the optimality of the solution, and efficient data structures which support various string processing.

S. Ben-David, J. Case, A. Maruoka (Eds.): ALT 2004, LNAI 3244, pp. 1–13, 2004.

In this paper, we describe the most fundamental ideas of these works, by focusing only on substring patterns, subsequence patterns, and episode patterns, as the target patterns to be discovered. We also show their learnabilities in the probably approximately correct (PAC) learning model, which are the background theory of our approach.

2   Preliminaries

For a finite *alphabet* Σ, let Σ^* be the set of all *strings* over Σ. For a string w, we denote by $|w|$ the length of w. For a set $S \subseteq \Sigma^*$ of strings, we denote by $|S|$ the number of strings in S, and by $||S||$ the total length of strings in S. Let $\mathcal{N}$ be the set of natural numbers.

We say that a string v is a *prefix* (*substring*, *suffix*, resp.) of w if $w = vy$ ($w = xvy$, $w = xv$, resp.) for some strings $x, y \in \Sigma^*$. We say that a string v is a *subsequence* of a string w if v can be obtained by removing zero or more characters from w, and say that w is a *supersequence* of v.

A *pattern class* is a pair $\mathcal{C} = (\Pi, m)$, where Π is a set called the *pattern set* and $m : \Sigma^* \times \Pi \to \{0, 1\}$ is the *pattern matching function*. An element $p \in \Pi$ is called a *pattern*. For a pattern $p \in \Pi$ and string $w \in \Sigma^*$, we say p of class $\mathcal{C}$ *matches* w iff $m(w, p) = 1$. For a pattern p, we denote by $L_{\mathcal{C}}(p) = \{w \in \Sigma^* \mid m(w, p) = 1\}$ the set of strings in Σ^* which p of class $\mathcal{C}$ matches.

In this paper, we focus on the following pattern classes, and their languages.

Definition 1. *The* substring pattern class *is defined to be a pair* $(\Sigma^*, substr)$ *where* $substr(w, p) = 1$ *iff* p *is a substring of* w. *The* subsequence pattern class *is a pair* $(\Sigma^*, subseq)$ *where* $subseq(w, p) = 1$ *iff* p *is a subsequence of* w. *The* episode pattern class *is a pair* $(\Sigma^* \times \mathcal{N}, epis)$ *where* $epis(w, \langle p, k \rangle) = 1$ *iff* p *is a subsequence of some substring* v *of* w *such that* $|v| \le k$.

Finally, the substring (subsequence, episode, reps.) *pattern language, denoted by* $L^{str}(p)$ ($L^{seq}(p)$, $L^{eps}(\langle p, k \rangle)$, *resp.), is a language defined by substring (subsequence, episode, resp.) pattern class.*

Remark that the substring pattern languages is a subclass of the episode pattern class, since $L^{str}(p) = L^{eps}(\langle p, |p| \rangle)$ for any $p \in \Sigma^*$. Subsequence pattern languages is also an subclass of the episode pattern class, since $L^{seq}(p) = L^{eps}(\langle p, \infty \rangle)$ for any $p \in \Sigma^*$.

3   PAC-Learnability

Valiant [35] introduced the *PAC-leaning model* as a formal model of concept learning from examples. An excellent textbook on this topic is written by Kearns and Vazirani [23]. This section briefly summarizes the PAC-learnability of the languages we defined in the last section.

For a pattern class $\mathcal{C} = (\Pi, m)$, a pair $\langle w, m(w, p) \rangle$ is called an *example* of a pattern $p \in \Pi$ for $w \in \Sigma^*$. It is called a *positive example* if $m(w, p) = 1$) and is called a *negative example* otherwise. For an alphabet Σ and an integer $n \geq 0$, we denote by $\Sigma^{[n]}$ the set $\{w \in \Sigma^* : |w| \leq n\}$.

Definition 2. *A pattern class $\mathcal{C} = (\Pi, m)$ is* polynomial-time learnable *if there exist an algorithm $\mathcal{A}$ and a polynomial $poly(\cdot, \cdot, \cdot)$ which satisfy the following conditions for any pattern $p \in \Pi$, any real numbers ε, δ $(0 < \varepsilon, \delta < 1)$, any integer $n \geq 0$, and any probability distribution P on $\Sigma^{[n]}$:*

(a) *$\mathcal{A}$ takes ε, δ, and n, as inputs.*
(b) *$\mathcal{A}$ may call EXAMPLE, which generates examples of the pattern $p \in \Pi$, randomly according to the probability distribution P on $\Sigma^{[n]}$.*
(c) *$\mathcal{A}$ outputs a pattern $q \in \Pi$ satisfying $P(L_{\mathcal{C}}(p) \cup L_{\mathcal{C}}(q) - L_{\mathcal{C}}(p) \cap L_{\mathcal{C}}(q)) < \varepsilon$ with probability at least $1 - \delta$.*
(d) *The running time of $\mathcal{A}$ is bounded by $poly(1/\varepsilon, 1/\delta, n)$.*

The PAC-learnability is well-characterized in terms of *Vapnik-Chervonenkis dimension* [10] and the existence of *Occam algorithm* [9,11].

Theorem 1 ([10,29]). *A pattern class $\mathcal{C} = (\Pi, m)$ is polynomial-time learnable if the following conditions hold.*

(a) *$\mathcal{C}$ is* polynomial dimension, *i.e., there exists a polynomial $d(n)$ such that $|\{L_{\mathcal{C}}(p) \cap \Sigma^{[n]} : p \in \Pi\}| \leq 2^{d(n)}$.*
(b) *There exists a polynomial-time algorithm called* polynomial-time hypothesis finder *for $\mathcal{C}$ which produces a hypothesis from a sequence of examples such that it is consistent with the given examples.*

On the other hand, the pattern class $\mathcal{C}$ is polynomial-time learnable only if there exists a randomized polynomial-time hypothesis finder for $\mathcal{C}$.

It is not hard to verify that all of substring languages, subsequence languages, and episode pattern languages are of polynomial dimension. Therefore the problem is whether there exists a (randomized) polynomial-time hypothesis finder for these classes. For substring languages, we can easily construct a polynomial-time hypothesis finder for it, since the candidate patterns must be a substring of any positive examples, so that we have only to consider quadratic numbers of candidates. Indeed, we can develop a linear-time hypothesis finder for it [15], by utilizing the data structure called *Generalized Suffix Tree*. See also our recent generalization of it for finding *pairs* of substring patterns [6]. On the other hand, the consistency problem for subsequence languages language is **NP**-hard [26,22, 27]. Thus we have the following theorem.

Theorem 2. *The substring languages is polynomial-time PAC-learnable. On the other hand, subsequence languages nor episode languages is not polynomial-time PAC-learnable under the assumption $\mathbf{RP} \neq \mathbf{NP}$.*

Query learning model due to Angluin [2], and identification in the limit due to Gold [14] are also important learning models. We discussed in [25], the learnabilities of finite unions of subsequence languages in these models.

4   Finding Best Patterns Efficiently

From a practical viewpoint, we have to find a good pattern which discriminate positive examples from negative examples. We formulate the problem by following our paper [15]. Let *good* be a function from $\Pi^* \times 2^{\Sigma^*} \times 2^{\Sigma^*}$ to the set of real numbers. We formulate the problem of finding the best pattern according to the function *good* as follows.

Definition 3 (Finding the best pattern in $\mathcal{C} = (\Pi, m)$ according to *good*).

Input: *Two sets $S, T \subseteq \Sigma^*$ of strings.*
Output: *A pattern $p \in \Pi$ that maximizes the value $good(p, S, T)$.*

Intuitively, the value $good(p, S, T)$ expresses the goodness to distinguish S from T using the rule specified by the pattern p. We may choose an appropriate function *good* according to each applications. For example, the χ^2 values, entropy information gain, and gini index are frequently used. Essentially these statistical measures are defined by the numbers of strings that satisfy the rule specified by p. Thus we can describe the measure in the following form:

$$good(p, S, T) = f(x_p, y_p, |S|, |T|),$$

where $x_p = |S \cap L_{\mathcal{C}}(p)|$ and $y_p = |T \cap L_{\mathcal{C}}(p)|$. When the sets S and T are fixed, the values $x_{\max} = |S|$ and $y_{\max} = |T|$ are unchanged. Thus we abbreviate the function $f(x, y, x_{\max}, y_{\max})$ to $f(x, y)$ in the sequel.

Since the function $good(p, S, T)$ expresses the goodness of a pattern $p \in \Pi$ to distinguish two sets, it is natural to assume that the function f satisfies the *conicality*, defined as follows.

Definition 4. *We say that a function f from $[0, x_{\max}] \times [0, y_{\max}]$ to real numbers is* conic *if*

- *for any $0 \leq y \leq y_{\max}$, there exists an x_1 such that*
  - $f(x, y) \geq f(x', y)$ *for any $0 \leq x < x' \leq x_1$, and*
  - $f(x, y) \leq f(x', y)$ *for any $x_1 \leq x < x' \leq x_{\max}$.*
- *for any $0 \leq x \leq x_{\max}$, there exists a y_1 such that*
  - $f(x, y) \geq f(x, y')$ *for any $0 \leq y < y' \leq y_1$, and*
  - $f(x, y) \leq f(x, y')$ *for any $y_1 \leq y < y' \leq y_{\max}$.*

Actually, all of the above statistical measures are conic. We remark that any convex function is conic. We assume that f is conic and can be evaluated in constant time in the sequel.

We now describe the basic idea of our algorithms. Fig. 1 shows a naive algorithm which exhaustively searches all possible patterns one by one, and returns the best pattern that gives the maximum score. Since most time consuming part is obviously the lines 5 and 6, in order to reduce the search time, we should (1) reduce the possible patterns in line 3 *dynamically* by using some appropriate pruning heuristics, and (2) speed up to computing $|S \cap L_{\mathcal{C}}(p)|$ and $|T \cap L_{\mathcal{C}}(p)|$ for each pattern p. We deal with (1) in the next section, and we treat (2) in Section 7.

```
 1   pattern FindBestPattern(StringSet S, T)
 2       double maxVal = −∞;
 3       pattern maxPat = null;
 4       for all possible pattern p ∈ Π do
 5           x = |S ∩ L_C(p)|;
 6           y = |T ∩ L_C(p)|;
 7           val = f(x, y);
 8           if val > maxVal then
 9               maxVal = val;
10               maxPat = p;
11       return maxPat;
```

Fig. 1. Exhaustive search algorithm for finding the best pattern in $\mathcal{C} = (\Pi, m)$

5   Pruning Heuristics

In this section, we introduce some pruning heuristics, inspired by Morishita and Sese [28], to construct a practical algorithm to find the best subsequence pattern and the best episode pattern, without sacrificing the optimality of the solution.

Lemma 1 ([15]). *For any patterns* $p, q \in \Pi$ *with* $L_{\mathcal{C}}(p) \supseteq L_{\mathcal{C}}(q)$, *we have*

$$f(x_q, y_q) \leq \max\{f(x_p, y_p), f(x_p, 0), f(0, y_p), f(0, 0)\}.$$

Lemma 2 ([15,16]). *For any subsequence patterns* $p, q \in \Sigma^*$ *such that* p *is a subsequence of* q, *we have* $L^{seq}(p) \supseteq L^{seq}(q)$. *Moreover, for* $l \geq k$, *we have* $L^{eps}(\langle p, l \rangle) \supseteq L^{eps}(\langle q, k \rangle)$.

In Fig. 2, we show our algorithm to find the best subsequence pattern from given two sets of strings, according to the function f. Optionally, we can specify the maximum length of subsequences. We use the following data structures in the algorithm.

StringSet Maintain a set S of strings.
  – **int** *numOfSubseq*(**string** p) : return the cardinality of the set $\{w \in S \mid p$ is a subsequence of $w\}$.

PriorityQueue Maintain strings with their priorities.
  – **bool** *empty*() : return **true** if the queue is empty.
  – **void** *push*(**string** w, **double** *priority*) : push a string w into the queue with priority *priority*.
  – (**string, double**) *pop*() : pop and return a pair (*string, priority*), where *priority* is the highest in the queue.

The next theorem guarantees the completeness of the algorithm.

Theorem 3 ([15]). *Let* S *and* T *be sets of strings, and* ℓ *be a positive integer. The algorithm FindMaxSubsequence(S, T, ℓ) will return a string* w *that maximizes the value good(w, S, T) among the strings of length at most* ℓ.

```
1   string FindMaxSubsequence(StringSet S, T, int maxLength = ∞)
2       string prefix, seq, maxSeq;
3       double upperBound = ∞, maxVal = −∞, val;
4       int x, y;
5       PriorityQueue queue;    /* Best First Search*/
6       queue.push(""", ∞);
7       while not queue.empty() do
8           (prefix, upperBound) = queue.pop();
9           if upperBound < maxVal then break;
10          foreach c ∈ Σ do
11              seq= prefix+ c;    /* string concatenation */
12              x = S.numOfSubseq(seq);
13              y = T.numOfSubseq(seq);
14              val = f(x, y);
15              if val > maxVal then
16                  maxVal = val;
17                  maxSeq = seq;
18*                 upperBound = max{f(x, y), f(x, 0), f(0, y), f(0, 0)};
19              if |seq| < maxLength then
20                  queue.push(seq, upperBound);
21      return maxSeq;
```

Fig. 2. Algorithm *FindMaxSubsequence*.

6 Finding Best Threshold Values

We now show a practical algorithm to find the best episode patterns. We should remark that the search space of episode patterns is $\Sigma^* \times \mathcal{N}$, while the search space of subsequence patterns was Σ^*. A straight-forward approach based on the last subsection might be as follows. First we observe that the algorithm *FindMaxSubsequence* in Fig. 2 can be easily modified to find the best episode pattern $\langle v, k \rangle$ *for any fixed threshold k*: we have only to replace the lines 12 and 13 so that they compute the numbers of strings in S and T that match with the episode pattern $\langle seq, k \rangle$, respectively. Thus, for each possible threshold value k, repeat his algorithm, and get the maximum. A short consideration reveals that we have only to consider the threshold values up to l, that is the length of the longest string in given S and T.

However, here we give a more efficient solution. We consider the following problem, that is a subproblem of *finding the best episode pattern*.

Definition 5 (Finding the best threshold value).

Input: *Two sets $S, T \subseteq \Sigma^*$ of strings, and a string $v \in \Sigma^*$.*

Output: *Integer k that maximizes the value $f(x_{\langle v,k \rangle}, y_{\langle v,k \rangle})$, where $x_{\langle v,k \rangle} = |S \cap L^{\mathit{eps}}(\langle v, k \rangle)|$ and $y_{\langle v,k \rangle} = |T \cap L^{\mathit{eps}}(\langle v, k \rangle)|$.*

For strings $v, s \in \Sigma^*$, we define the *threshold value* θ of v for s by $\theta = min\{k \in \mathcal{N} \mid s \in L^{\text{eps}}(\langle v, k \rangle)\}$. If no such value, let $\theta = \infty$. Note that $s \notin L^{\text{eps}}(\langle v, k \rangle)$ for any $k < \theta$, and $s \in L^{\text{eps}}(\langle v, k \rangle)$ for any $\theta \leq k$. For a set S of strings and a string v, let us denote by $\Theta_{S,v}$ the set of threshold values of v for some $s \in S$.

A key observation is that a best threshold value for given $S, T \subseteq \Sigma^*$ and a string $v \in \Sigma^*$ can be found in $\Theta_{S,v} \cup \Theta_{T,v}$ without loss of generality. Thus we can restrict the search space of the best threshold values to $\Theta_{S,v} \cup \Theta_{T,v}$.

From now on, we consider the numerical sequence $\{x_{\langle v,k \rangle}\}_{k=0}^{\infty}$. (We will treat $\{y_{\langle v,k \rangle}\}_{k=0}^{\infty}$ in the same way.) It follows from Lemma 2 that the sequence is non-decreasing. Moreover, remark that $0 \leq x_{\langle v,k \rangle} \leq |S|$ for any k. Moreover, $x_{\langle v,l \rangle} = x_{\langle v,l+1 \rangle} = x_{\langle v,l+2 \rangle} = \cdots$, where l is the length of the longest string in S. Hence, we can represent $\{x_{\langle v,k \rangle}\}_{k=0}^{\infty}$ with a list having at most $min\{|S|, l\}$ elements. We call this list *a compact representation of the sequence* $\{x\langle v, k \rangle\}_{k=0}^{\infty}$ (*CRS*, for short).

We show how to compute CRS for each v and a fixed S. Observe that $x_{\langle v,k \rangle}$ increases only at the threshold values of v for some $s \in S$. By computing a sorted list of threshold values of v for all $s \in S$, we can construct the CRS of $\{x_{\langle v,k \rangle}\}_{k=0}^{\infty}$. If using the counting sort, we can compute the CRS for $v \in \Sigma^*$ in $O(|S|ml + |S|) = O(\|S\|m)$ time, where $m = |v|$.

We emphasize that the time complexity of computing the CRS of $\{x_{\langle v,k \rangle}\}_{k=0}^{\infty}$ is the same as that of computing $x_{\langle v,k \rangle}$ for a single k ($0 \leq k \leq \infty$), by our method.

After constructing CRSs $\bar{x}$ of $\{x_{\langle v,k \rangle}\}_{k=0}^{\infty}$ and $\bar{y}$ of $\{y_{\langle v,k \rangle}\}_{k=0}^{\infty}$, we can compute the best threshold value in $O(|\bar{x}| + |\bar{y}|)$ time. Thus we have the following, which give an efficient solution to the finding the best threshold value problem.

Lemma 3. *Given $S, T \subseteq \Sigma^*$ and $v \in \Sigma^*$, we can finding the best threshold value in $O((\|S\| + \|T\|)|v|)$ time, where $\|S\|$ and $\|T\|$ represent the total length of the strings in S and T, respectively.*

By substituting this procedure into the algorithm *FindMaxSubsequence*, we get an algorithm to find a best episode pattern from given two sets of strings, according to the function f, shown in Fig. 3. We add a method $crs(v)$ to the data structure **StringSet** that returns CRS of $\{x_{\langle v,k \rangle}\}_{k=0}^{\infty}$, mentioned above.

By Lemma 1 and 2, we can use the value *upperBound* at $(x_{\langle v,\infty \rangle}, y_{\langle v,\infty \rangle})$ to prune branches in the search tree computed at line 20 marked by (*). We emphasize that the values at $(x_{\langle v,k \rangle}, y_{\langle v,k \rangle})$ is insufficient as *upperBound*. Note also that $x_{\langle v,\infty \rangle}$ and $y_{\langle v,\infty \rangle}$ can be extracted from $\bar{x}$ and $\bar{y}$ in constant time, respectively. The next theorem guarantees the completeness of the algorithm.

Theorem 4 ([16]). *Let S and T be sets of strings, and ℓ be a positive integer. The algorithm FindBestEpisode(S, T, ℓ) will return an episode pattern that maximizes $f(x_{\langle v,k \rangle}, y_{\langle v,k \rangle})$, with $x_{\langle v,k \rangle} = |S \cap L^{\text{eps}}(\langle v, k \rangle)|$ and $y_{\langle v,k \rangle} = |T \cap L^{\text{eps}}(\langle v, k \rangle)|$, where v varies any string of length at most ℓ and k varies any integer.*

```
1   string FindBestEpisode(StringSet S, T, int ℓ)
2      string prefix, v;
3      episodePattern maxSeq;  /* pair of string and int */
4      double upperBound = ∞, maxVal = −∞, val;
5      int k′;
6      CompactRepr x̄, ȳ;  /* CRS */
7      PriorityQueue queue;    /* Best First Search*/
8      queue.push("", ∞);
9      while not queue.empty() do
10        (prefix, upperBound) = queue.pop();
11        if upperBound < maxVal then break;
12        foreach c ∈ Σ do
13           v = prefix+ c;    /* string concatenation */
14           x̄ = S.crs(v);
15           ȳ = T.crs(v);
16           k′ = argmax_k{f(x_{⟨v,k⟩}, y_{⟨v,k⟩})} and val = f(x_{⟨v,k′⟩}, y_{⟨v,k′⟩});
17           if val > maxVal then
18              maxVal = val;
19              maxEpisode = ⟨v, k′⟩;
20(*)          upperBound = max{f(x_{⟨v,∞⟩}, y_{⟨v,∞⟩}), f(x_{⟨v,∞⟩}, 0),
                             f(0, y_{⟨v,∞⟩}), f(0, 0)};
21           if upperBound > maxVal and |v| < ℓ then
22              queue.push(v, upperBound);
23     return maxEpisode;
```

Fig. 3. Algorithm FindBestEpisode.

7   Efficient Data Structures to Count Matched Strings

In this section, we introduces some efficient data structures to speed up answering the queries.

First we pay our attention to the following problem.

Definition 6 (Counting the matched strings).

Input: A finite set $S \subseteq \Sigma^*$ of strings.
Query: A string $seq \in \Sigma^*$.
Answer: The cardinality of the set $S \cap L^{seq}(seq)$.

Of course, the answer to the query should be very fast, since many queries will arise. Thus, we should preprocess the input in order to answer the query quickly. On the other hand, the preprocessing time is also a critical factor in some applications. In this paper, we utilize automata that accept subsequences of strings.

In [17], we considered a subsequence automaton as a deterministic complete finite automaton that recognizes all possible subsequences of a set of strings,

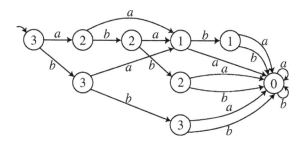

Fig. 4. Subsequence automaton for $S = \{abab, abb, bb\}$, where $\Sigma = \{a, b\}$. Each number on a state denotes the number of matched strings. For example, by traverse the states according to a string ab, we reach the state whose number is 2. It corresponds to the cardinality $|L^{\text{seq}}(ab) \cap S| = 2$, since ab is a subsequence of both $abab$ and abb, but is not s subsequence of bb.

that is essentially the same as the directed acyclic subsequence graph (DASG) introduced by Baeza-Yates [5]. We showed an online construction of subsequence automaton for a set of strings. Our algorithm runs in $O(|\Sigma|(m + k) + N)$ time using $O(|\Sigma|m)$ space, where $|\Sigma|$ is the size of alphabet, N is the total length of strings, and m is the number of states of the resulting subsequence automaton. We can extend the automaton so that it answers the above *Counting the matched strings* problem in a natural way (see Fig. 4).

Although the construction time is linear to the size m of automaton to be built, unfortunately $m = O(n^k)$ in general, where we assume that the set S consists of k strings of length n. In fact, we proved the lower bound $m = \Omega(n^k)$ for any $k > 0$ [34]. Thus, when the construction time is also a critical factor, as in our application, it may not be a good idea to construct subsequence automaton for the set S itself. Here, for a specified parameter *mode* > 0, we partition the set S into $d = k/mode$ subsets $S_1, S_2, \ldots, S_d$ of at most *mode* strings, and construct d subsequence automata for each S_i. When asking a query *seq*, we have only to traverse all automata similutaneously, and return the sum of the answers. In this way, we can balance the preprocessing time with the total time to answer (possibly many) queries. In [15], we experimentally evaluated the optimal value of the parameter *mode*.

We now analyze the complexity of *episode pattern matching*. Given an episode pattern $\langle v, k \rangle$ and a string t, determine whether $t \in L^{\text{eps}}(\langle v, k \rangle)$ or not. This problem can be answered by filling up the edit distance table between v and t, where only insertion operation with cost one is allowed. It takes $\Theta(mn)$ time and space using a standard dynamic programming method, where $m = |v|$ and $n = |t|$. For a fixed string, automata-based approach is useful. We use the Episode Directed Acyclic Subsequence Graph (EDASG) for string t, which was introduced by Troíček in [33]. Hereafter, let $EDASG(t)$ denote the EDASG for t. With the use of $EDASG(t)$, episode pattern matching can be answered quickly in practice, although the worst case behavior is still $O(mn)$. EDASG(t) is also useful to

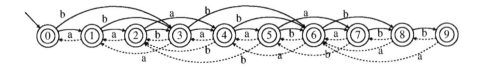

Fig. 5. *EDASG(t)* for *t* = *aabaababb*. Solid arrows denote the forward edges, and broken arrows denote the backward edges.

compute the threshold value θ of given v for t quickly in practice. As an example, *EDASG(aabbab)* is shown in Fig. 5. When examining if an episode pattern $\langle abb, 4 \rangle$ matches with t or not, we start from the initial state 0 and arrive at state 6, by traversing the forward edges spelling *abb*. It means that the shortest prefix of t that contains *abb* as a subsequences is $t[0:6] = aabaab$, where $t[i:j]$ denotes the substring $t_{i+1} \ldots t_j$ of t. Moreover, the difference between the state numbers 6 and 0 corresponds to the length of matched substring *aabaab* of t, that is, $6 - 0 = |aabaab|$. Since it exceeds the threshold 4, we move backwards spelling *bba* and reach state 1. It means that the shortest suffix of $t[0:6]$ that contains *abb* as a subsequence is $t[1:6] = abaab$. Since $6 - 1 > 4$, we have to examine other possibilities. It is not hard to see that we have only to consider the string $t[2:*]$. Thus we continue the same traversal started from state 2, that is the next state of state 1. By forward traversal spelling *abb*, we reach state 8, and then backward traversal spelling *bba* bring us to state 4. In this time, we found the matched substring $t[4:8] = abab$ which contains the subsequence *abb*, and the length $8 - 4 = 4$ satisfies the threshold. Therefore we report the occurrence and terminate the procedure.

It is not difficult to see that the EDASGs are useful to compute the threshold value of v for a fixed t. We have only to repeat the above forward and backward traversal up to the end, and return the minimum length of the matched substrings.

8   Concluding Remarks

In this paper, we focused on the pattern discovery problem for substring, subsequence, and episode patterns to illustrate the basic ideas. We have already generalized it for various ways: considering variable-length-don't care patterns [19] and their variation [32], finding correlated patterns from given a set of strings with numeric attribute values [8], and finding a boolean combination of patterns instead of single pattern [6,18]. We also show another data structure to support fast counting of matched strings [21,20], and application to extend BONSAI system [7].

Acknowledgments. The work reported in this paper is an outcome of the joint research efforts with my colleagues: Setsuo Arikawa, Satoru Miyano, Takeshi

Shinohara, Satoru Kuhara, Masayuki Takeda, Hiroki Arimura, Shinichi Shimozono, Satoshi Matsumoto, Hiromasa Hoshino, Masahiro Hirao, Hideo Bannai,
and Shunsuke Inenaga.

References

[1] R. Agrawal and R. Srikant. Mining sequential patterns. In *Proc. of the 11th International Conference on Data Engineering*, Mar. 1995.

[2] D. Angluin. Queries and concept learning. *Machine Learning*, 2(4):319–342, 1988.

[3] H. Arimura, S. Arikawa, and S. Shimozono. Efficient discovery of optimal word-association patterns in large text databases. *New Generation Computing*, 18:49–60, 2000.

[4] H. Arimura, H. Asaka, H. Sakamoto, and S. Arikawa. Efficient discovery of proximity patterns with suffix arrays (extended abstract). In *Proc. the 12th Annual Symposium on Combinatorial Pattern Matching (CPM'01)*, volume 2089 of *Lecture Notes in Computer Science*, pages 152–156. Springer-Verlag, 2001.

[5] R. A. Baeza-Yates. Searching subsequences. *Theoretical Computer Science*, 78(2):363–376, Jan. 1991.

[6] H. Bannai, H. Hyyrö, A. Shinohara, M. Takeda, K. Nakai, and S. Miyano. Finding optimal pairs of patterns. In *Proc. 4th Workshop on Algorithms in Bioinformatics (WABI2004)*, Lecture Notes in Computer Science. Springer-Verlag, 2004. (to appear).

[7] H. Bannai, S. Inenaga, A. Shinohara, M. Takeda, and S. Miyano. More speed and more pattern variations for knowledge discovery system BONSAI. *Genome Informatics*, 12:454–455, 2001.

[8] H. Bannai, S. Inenaga, A. Shinohara, M. Takeda, and S. Miyano. A string pattern regression algorithm and its application to pattern discovery in long introns. *Genome Informatics*, 13:3–11, 2002.

[9] A. Blumer, A. Ehrenfeucht, D. Haussler, and M. Warmuth. Occam's razor. *Inf. Process. Lett.*, 24:377–380, 1987.

[10] A. Blumer, A. Ehrenheucht, D. Haussler, and M. Warmuth. Learnability and the Vapnik-Chervonenkis dimension. *Journal of ACM*, 36:929–965, 1989.

[11] R. Board and L. Pitt. On the necessity of Occam algorithms. *Theoretical Computer Science*, 100:157–184, 1992.

[12] A. Califano. SPLASH: Structural pattern localization analysis by sequential histograms. *Bioinformatics*, Feb. 1999.

[13] R. Feldman, Y. Aumann, A. Amir, A. Zilberstein, and W. Klosgen. Maximal association rules: A new tool for mining for keyword co-occurrences in document collections. In *Proc. of the 3rd International Conference on Knowledge Discovery and Data Mining*, pages 167–170. AAAI Press, Aug. 1997.

[14] E. Gold. Language identification in the limit. *Information and Control*, 10:447–474, 1967.

[15] M. Hirao, H. Hoshino, A. Shinohara, M. Takeda, and S. Arikawa. A practical algorithm to find the best subsequence patterns. In *Proc. 3rd International Conference on Discovery Science (DS2000)*, volume 1967 of *Lecture Notes in Artificial Intelligence*, pages 141–154. Springer-Verlag, Dec. 2000. (Journal version is published in Theoretical Computer Science, Vol. 292, pp. 465–479, 2003).

[16] M. Hirao, S. Inenaga, A. Shinohara, M. Takeda, and S. Arikawa. A practical algorithm to find the best episode patterns. In *Proc. of The Fourth International Conference on Discovery Science (DS2001)*, Lecture Notes in Artificial Intelligence. Springer-Verlag, Nov. 2001.

[17] H. Hoshino, A. Shinohara, M. Takeda, and S. Arikawa. Online construction of subsequence automata for multiple texts. In *Proc. of 7th International Symposium on String Processing and Information Retrieval (SPIRE2000)*, pages 146–152. IEEE Computer Society, Sept. 2000.

[18] S. Inenaga, H. Bannai, H. Hyyrö, A. Shinohara, M. Takeda, K. Nakai, and S. Miyano. Finding optimal pairs of cooperative and competing patterns with bounded distance. In *Proc. 7th International Conference on Discovery Science (DS2004)*, Lecture Notes in Computer Science. Springer-Verlag, 2004. (to appear).

[19] S. Inenaga, H. Bannai, A. Shinohara, M. Takeda, and S. Arikawa. Discovering best variable-length-don't-care patterns. In *Proc. 5th International Conference on Discovery Science (DS2002)*, volume 2534 of *Lecture Notes in Computer Science*, pages 86–97. Springer-Verlag, 2002.

[20] S. Inenaga, M. Takeda, A. Shinohara, H. Bannai, and S. Arikawa. Space-economical construction of index structures for all suffixes of a string. In *Proc. 27th Inter. Symp. on Mathematical Foundation of Computer Science (MFCS2002)*, volume 2420 of *Lecture Notes in Computer Science*, pages 341–352. Springer-Verlag, Aug. 2002.

[21] S. Inenaga, M. Takeda, A. Shinohara, H. Hoshino, and S. Arikawa. The minimum dawg for all suffixes of a string and its applications. In *Proc. 13th Ann. Symp. on Combinatorial Pattern Matching (CPM2002)*, volume 2373 of *Lecture Notes in Computer Science*, pages 153–167. Springer-Verlag, July 2002.

[22] T. Jiang and M. Li. On the complexity of learning strings and sequences. In *Proc. of 4th ACM Conf. Computational Learning Theory*, pages 367–371. ACM Press, 1991.

[23] M. Kearns and U. Vazirani. *An Introduction to Computational Learning Theory*. MIT Press, 1994.

[24] L. Marsan and M.-F. Sagot. Algorithms for extracting structured motifs using a suffix tree with an application to promoter and regulatory site consensus identification. *J. Comput. Biol.*, 7:345–360, 2000.

[25] S. Matsumoto and A. Shinohara. Learning subsequence languages. In H. Kangassalo et al., editor, *Information Modeling and Knowledge Bases, VIII*, pages 335–344. IOS Press, 1997.

[26] S. Miyano, A. Shinohara, and T. Shinohara. Which classes of elementary formal systems are polynomial-time learnable? In *Proc. 2nd Workshop on Algorithmic Learning Theory (ALT91)*, pages 139–150, 1991.

[27] S. Miyano, A. Shinohara, and T. Shinohara. Polynomial-time learning of elementary formal systems. *New Generation Computing*, 18:217–242, 2000.

[28] S. Morishita and J. Sese. Traversing itemset lattices with statistical metric pruning. In *Proc. of the 19th ACM SIGACT-SIGMOD-SIGART Symposium on Principles of Database Systems*, pages 226–236. ACM Press, May 2000.

[29] B. Natarajan. On learning sets and functions. *Machine Learning*, 4(1):67–97, 1989.

[30] L. Palopoli and G. Terracina. Discovering frequent structured patterns from string databases: an application to biological sequences. In *Proc. 5th International Conference on Discovery Science (DS2002)*, volume 2534 of *Lecture Notes in Computer Science*, pages 34–46. Springer-Verlag, 2002.

[31] S. Shimozono, A. Shinohara, T. Shinohara, S. Miyano, S. Kuhara, and S. Arikawa. Knowledge acquisition from amino acid sequences by machine learning system BONSAI. *Transactions of Information Processing Society of Japan*, 35(10):2009–2018, Oct. 1994.

[32] M. Takeda, S. Inenaga, H. Bannai, A. Shinohara, and S. Arikawa. Discovering most classificatory patterns for very expressive pattern classes. In *Proc. 6th International Conference on Discovery Science (DS2003)*, volume 2843 of *Lecture Notes in Computer Science*, pages 486–493. Springer-Verlag, 2003.

[33] Z. Troníček. Episode matching. In *Proc. of 12th Annual Symposium on Combinatorial Pattern Matching*, volume 2089 of *Lecture Notes in Computer Science*, pages 143–146. Springer-Verlag, July 2001.

[34] Z. Troníček and A. Shinohara. The size of subsequence automaton. In *Proc. of 10th International Symposium on String Processing and Information Retrieval (SPIRE2003)*, volume 2857, pages 304–310. Springer-Verlag, 2003.

[35] L. G. Valiant. A theory of the learnable. *Communications of ACM*, 27:1134–1142, 1984.

[36] J. T. L. Wang, G.-W. Chirn, T. G. Marr, B. A. Shapiro, D. Shasha, and K. Zhang. Combinatorial pattern discovery for scientific data: Some preliminary results. In *Proc. of the 1994 ACM SIGMOD International Conference on Management of Data*, pages 115–125. ACM Press, May 1994.

Applications of Regularized Least Squares
to Classification Problems

Nicolò Cesa-Bianchi

Università di Milano, 20135 Milano, Italy,
`cesa-bianchi@dsi.unimi.it`

Abstract. We present a survey of recent results concerning the theoretical and empirical performance of algorithms for learning regularized least-squares classifiers. The behavior of these family of learning algorithms is analyzed in both the statistical and the worst-case (individual sequence) data-generating models.

1 Regularized Least-Squares for Classification

In the pattern classification problem, some unknown source is supposed to generate a sequence $\boldsymbol{x}_1, \boldsymbol{x}_2, \ldots$ of instances (data elements) $\boldsymbol{x}_t \in \mathcal{X}$, where $\mathcal{X}$ is usually taken to be $\mathbb{R}^d$ for some fixed d. Each instance $\boldsymbol{x}_t$ is associated with a *class label* $y_t \in \mathcal{Y}$, where $\mathcal{Y}$ is a finite set of classes, indicating a certain semantic property of the instance. For instance, in a handwritten digit recognition task, $\boldsymbol{x}_t$ is the digitalized image of a handwritten digit and its label $y_t \in \{0, 1, \ldots, 9\}$ is the corresponding numeral. A learning algorithm for pattern classification uses a set of *training examples*, that is pairs $(\boldsymbol{x}_t, y_t)$, to build a classifier $f : \mathcal{X} \to \mathcal{Y}$ that predicts, as accurately as possible, the labels of any further instance generated by the source. As training data are usually labelled by hand, the performance of a learning algorithm is measured in terms of its ability to trade-off predictive power with amount training data.

Due to the recent success of kernel methods (see, e.g., [8]), linear-threshold (L-T) classifiers of the form $f(\boldsymbol{x}) = \text{SGN}(\boldsymbol{w}^\top \boldsymbol{x})$, where $\boldsymbol{w} \in \mathbb{R}^d$ is the classifier parameter and $\text{SGN}(\cdot) \in \{-1, +1\}$ is the signum function, have become one of the most popular approaches for solving binary classification problems (where the label set is $\mathcal{Y} = \{-1, +1\}$). In this paper, we focus on a specific family of algorithms for learning L-T classifiers based on the solution of a regularized least-squares problem.

The basic algorithm within this family is the *second-order Perceptron algorithm* [2]. This algorithm works incrementally: each time a new training example $(\boldsymbol{x}_t, y_t)$ is obtained, a prediction $\widehat{y}_t = \text{SGN}(\boldsymbol{w}_t^\top \boldsymbol{x}_t)$ for the label y_t of $\boldsymbol{x}_t$ is computed, where $\boldsymbol{w}_t$ is the parameter of the current L-T classifier. If $\widehat{y}_t \neq y_t$, then $\boldsymbol{w}_t$ is updated and a new L-T classifier, with parameter $\boldsymbol{w}_{t+1}$, is generated. The second-order Perceptron starts with the constant L-T classifier $\boldsymbol{w}_1 = (0, \ldots, 0)$ and, at time step t, computes $\boldsymbol{w}_{t+1} = (aI + S_t S_t^\top)^{-1} S_t \boldsymbol{y}_t$, where $a > 0$ is a parameter, I is the identity matrix, and S_t is the matrix whose columns are the

S. Ben-David, J. Case, A. Maruoka (Eds.): ALT 2004, LNAI 3244, pp. 14–18, 2004.

previously *stored instances* $\boldsymbol{x}_s$; that is, those instances $\boldsymbol{x}_s$ ($1 \le s \le t$) such that $\text{SGN}(\boldsymbol{w}_s^\top \boldsymbol{x}_s) \ne y_s$. Finally, $\boldsymbol{y}_t$ is the vector of labels of the stored instances. Note that, given S_{t-1}, $\boldsymbol{y}_{t-1}$, and $(\boldsymbol{x}_t, y_t)$, the parameter $\boldsymbol{w}_{t+1}$ can be computed in time $\Theta(d^2)$. Working in dual variables (as when kernels are used), the update time becomes quadratic in the number of stored instances. The connection with regularized least-squares is revealed by the identity

$$\boldsymbol{w}_{t+1} = \underset{\boldsymbol{v} \in \mathbb{R}^d}{\arginf} \left(\sum_{s \in \mathcal{M}_t} (\boldsymbol{v}^\top \boldsymbol{x}_s - y_s)^2 + a \|\boldsymbol{v}\|^2 \right)$$

where $\mathcal{M}_t$ is the set of indices s of stored instances $\boldsymbol{x}_s$ after the first t steps.

Similarly to the classical convergence theorems for the Perceptron algorithm (see [1,6,7]), in [2] a theorem is proven bounding the number of updates performed by the second-order Perceptron on an arbitrary sequence of training examples. In the simplest case where the training sequence is linearly separable by some (unknown) unit-norm vector $\boldsymbol{u}$ with margin γ, the second-order Perceptron converges to a linear separator after at most

$$\frac{1}{\gamma} \sqrt{(a + \boldsymbol{u}^\top S\, S^\top \boldsymbol{u}) \sum_{i=1}^{d} \ln\left(1 + \lambda_i / a\right)}$$

many updates, where S is the matrix of stored instances after convergence is attained and $\lambda_1, \ldots, \lambda_d$ are the eigenvalues of $S\, S^\top$. The quadratic form $\boldsymbol{u}^\top S\, S^\top \boldsymbol{u}$ takes value in the interval $[\lambda_{\min}, \lambda_{\max}]$. This bound is often better than the corresponding bound $\sqrt{\sum_{i=1}^{d} \lambda_i} / \gamma$ for the Perceptron algorithm, where the dependence on the eigenvalues is linear rather than logarithmic. This advantage appears to be real as the second-order algorithm is observed to converge faster than the standard Perceptron on real-world datasets.

2   Application to Online Learning

Incremental algorithms, such as the second-order Perceptron, are natural tools in on-line learning applications (e.g., the real-time categorization of stories provided by a newsfeed). In these scenarios a stream of instances is fed into the learning algorithm which uses its current L-T classifier to predict their labels. Occasionally, the algorithm can query the label y_t of a selected instance $\boldsymbol{x}_t$ in order to form a training instance $(\boldsymbol{x}_t, y_t)$ which can be immediately used to improve its predictive performance. Hence, unlike the traditional learning setup, here the algorithm can selectively choose the instances to be used for training, but it has to do so while simultaneously minimizing the number of prediction mistakes over the entire sequence of instances, including those instances whose label has not been queried. The second-order Perceptron can be directly applied in this scenario by simply querying the label of an instance $\boldsymbol{x}_t$ with probability roughly proportional to $1/(1+|\boldsymbol{w}_t^\top \boldsymbol{x}_t|/C)$, so that the label of instances on which

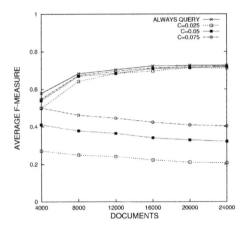

Fig. 1. Behaviour of the randomized second-order Perceptron for on-line learning on a newsstory categorization task based on the Reuters Corpus Volume 1. For each value of the parameter C a pair of curves is plotted as a function of the number of instances observed. The increasing curve is the average F-measure (a kind of accuracy) and the decreasing curve is the rate of labels queried. Note that, for the range of parameter values displayed, the performance does not get significantly worse as the parameter value decreases causing the label rate to drop faster. In all cases, the performance remains close to that of the algorithm that queries all labels (corresponding to the choice $C \to \infty$).

the current L-T classifier achieves a large margin $|w_t^\top x_t|$ have a small probability of being queried. (The empirical behaviour of this algorithm for different values of the parameter C is reported in Figure 1.) After this randomized step, if the label y_t is actually queried and $\text{SGN}(w_t^\top x_t) \neq y_t$, then the second-order update described earlier is performed. Surprisingly, the expected number of mistakes made by this randomized variant of the second-order Perceptron algorithm can be bounded by the same quantity that bounds the number of updates made (on the same sequence) by the standard deterministic second-order Perceptron using each observed instance for its training [5].

3   The Statistical Learning Model

Unlike the previous analyses, were no assumption is made on the way the labelled instances are generated, in *statistical pattern classification* instances x_t are realizations of i.i.d. draws from some unknown probability distribution on $\mathcal{X}$, and then binary labels $y_t \in \{-1, +1\}$ are random variables correlated to x_t via some unknown *noise model* specifying the conditional probability $\mathbb{P}(y_t = 1 \mid x_t)$. Hence, in this model a set $\mathcal{S}$ of training examples is a statistical sample and learning becomes equivalent to a problem of statistical inference. The goal in statistical pattern classification is to bound, with high probability with respect to the random draw of the training sample $\mathcal{S}$, the probability that the classifier,

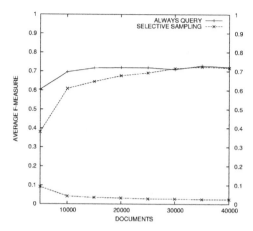

Fig. 2. Behaviour of the deterministic second-order Perceptron for on-line learning (called selective sampling in the legend) on the same newsstory categorization task of Figure 1. As in Figure 1, the increasing curve is the average F-measure and the decreasing curve is the rate of labels queried. Note that the label rate of the selective sampling algorithm decreases very fast and the performance of the algorithm eventually reaches the performance of the second-order Perceptron which is allowed to observe all labels.

generated by the learning algorithm run on $\mathcal{S}$, makes a mistake on a further random example drawn from the same i.i.d. source. This probability is usually called *statistical risk*. Building on the second-order Perceptron update bounds described above, holding for arbitrary sequences of data, it is possible to show that the risk of a L-T classifier generated by the second-order perceptron is bounded by

$$\frac{M_n}{n} + c\sqrt{\frac{1}{n}\ln\frac{n}{\delta}}$$

with probability at least $1 - \delta$ with respect to the random draw of a training sample of size n. Here $c > 0$ is a universal constant and M_n is the number of updates performed by the second-order Perceptron while being run once on the training sample. This bound holds for *any arbitrary* probability distribution on $\mathcal{X}$ and *any arbitrary* noise model.

Within the statistical learning model, the randomized step in the on-line learning scenario (where the algorithm queries the labels) is not needed anymore. Indeed, by assuming a specific noise model, different label-querying strategies for the second-order Perceptron can be devised that improve on the empirical performance of the randomized rule. In particular, assume for simplicity that instances $\boldsymbol{x}_t$ are arbitrarily distributed on the unit sphere in $\mathbb{R}^d$, and assume some unit-norm vector $\boldsymbol{u} \in \mathbb{R}^d$ exists such that $\mathbb{P}(y_t = 1 \mid \boldsymbol{x}_t) = (1 + \boldsymbol{u}^\top \boldsymbol{x}_t)/2$. Then, it can be shown that the L-T classifier computed by the second-order Perceptron is a statistical estimator of $\boldsymbol{u}$ (which is also the parameter of the Bayes optimal classifier for this model) [3]. This can be used to devise a querying strategy based on the computation of the confidence interval for the estimator. In practice, the randomized querying rule introduced earlier is replaced by a deterministic rule prescribing to query the label of $\boldsymbol{x}_t$ whenever $|\boldsymbol{w}_t^\top \boldsymbol{x}_t| \leq c\sqrt{(\ln t)/N_t}$, where c is some constant (the choice $c = 5$ works well in practice) and N_t is the number of labels queried up to time t. The empirical behavior of this deterministic version of the second-order Perceptron for on-line applications is depicted in Figure 2. Theoretical bounds for this specific algorithm proven in [3] show that, under additional conditions on the distribution according to which instances are drawn, the rate of queried labels decreases exponentially in the number of observed instances, while the excess rate of mistakes with respect to the Bayes optimal classifier grows only logarithmically in the same quantity.

The fact that, under the linear noise model described above, the L-T classifier learned by the second-order Perceptron estimates the parameter of the model can be also used to apply the second-order algorithm to the task of hierarchical classification, a variant of the classification task in which the labels given to instances are union of paths taken from a fixed taxonomy imposed on the set $\mathcal{Y}$ of class labels. Some preliminary results in this direction are shown in [4].

References

[1] H.D. Block. The Perceptron: A model for brain functioning. *Review of Modern Physics*, 34:123–135, 1962.

[2] N. Cesa-Bianchi, A. Conconi, and C. Gentile. A second-order Perceptron algorithm. In *Proceedings of the 15th Annual Conference on Computational Learning Theory*, pages 121–137. LNAI 2375, Springer, 2002.

[3] N. Cesa-Bianchi, A. Conconi, and C. Gentile. Learning probabilistic linear-threshold classifiers via selective sampling. In *Proceedings of the 16th Annual Conference on Learning Theory*, pages 373–386. LNAI 2777, Springer, 2003.

[4] N. Cesa-Bianchi, A. Conconi, and C. Gentile. Regret bounds for hierarchical classification with linear-threshold functions. In *Proceedings of the 17th Annual Conference on Learning Theory*. Springer, 2004.

[5] N. Cesa-Bianchi, C. Gentile, and L. Zaniboni. Worst-case analysis of selective sampling for linear-threshold algorithms. Submitted for publication, 2004.

[6] A.B.J. Novikoff. On convergence proofs of Perceptrons. In *Proceedings of the Symposium on the Mathematical Theory of Automata*, volume XII, pages 615–622. 1962.

[7] F. Rosenblatt. The Perceptron: A probabilistic model for information storage and organization in the brain. *Psychological Review*, 65:386–408, 1958.

[8] B. Schölkopf and A. Smola. *Learning with kernels*. MIT Press, 2002.

Probabilistic Inductive Logic Programming

Luc De Raedt and Kristian Kersting

Institute for Computer Science, Machine Learning Lab
Albert-Ludwigs-University, Georges-Köhler-Allee, Gebäude 079,
D-79110 Freiburg i. Brg., Germany
{deraedt,kersting}@informatik.uni-freiburg.de

Abstract. Probabilistic inductive logic programming, sometimes also called statistical relational learning, addresses one of the central questions of artificial intelligence: the integration of probabilistic reasoning with first order logic representations and machine learning. A rich variety of different formalisms and learning techniques have been developed. In the present paper, we start from inductive logic programming and sketch how it can be extended with probabilistic methods.

More precisely, we outline three classical settings for inductive logic programming, namely *learning from entailment*, *learning from interpretations*, and *learning from proofs or traces*, and show how they can be used to learn different types of probabilistic representations.

1 Introduction

In the past few years there has been a lot of work lying at the intersection of probability theory, logic programming and machine learning [40,15,42,31,35,18,25,21, 2,24]. This work is known under the names of statistical relational learning [14, 11], probabilistic logic learning [9], or probabilistic inductive logic programming. Whereas most of the existing works have started from a probabilistic learning perspective and extended probabilistic formalisms with relational aspects, we will take a different perspective, in which we will start from inductive logic programming and study how inductive logic programming formalisms, settings and techniques can be extended to deal with probabilistic issues. This tradition has already contributed a rich variety of valuable formalisms and techniques, including probabilistic Horn abduction by David Poole, PRISMs by Sato, stochastic logic programs by Eisele [12], Muggleton [31] and Cussens [4], Bayesian logic programs [22,20] by Kersting and De Raedt, and Logical Hidden Markov Models [24].

The main contribution of this paper is the introduction of three probabilistic inductive logic programming settings which are derived from the learning from entailment, from interpretations and from proofs settings of the field of inductive logic programming [6]. Each of these settings contributes different notions of probabilistic logic representations, examples and probability distributions. The first setting, probabilistic learning from entailment, combines key principles of the well-known inductive logic programming system FOIL [41] with the

S. Ben-David, J. Case, A. Maruoka (Eds.): ALT 2004, LNAI 3244, pp. 19–36, 2004.

naïve Bayes' assumption; the second setting, probabilistic learning from interpretations, incorporated in Bayesian logic programs [22,20], integrates Bayesian networks with logic programming; and the third setting, learning from proofs, incorporated in stochastic logic programs [12,31,4], upgrades stochastic context free grammars to logic programs. The sketched settings (and their instances presented) are by no means the only possible settings for probabilistic inductive logic programming. Nevertheless, two of the settings have – to the authors' knowledge – not been introduced before. Even though it is not our aim to provide a complete survey on probabilistic inductive logic programming (for such a survey, see [9]), we hope that the settings will contribute to a better understanding of probabilistic extensions to inductive logic programming and will also clarify some of the logical issues about probabilistic learning.

This paper is structured as follows: in Section 2, we present the three inductive logic programming settings, in Section 3, we extend these in a probabilistic framework, in Section 4, we discuss how to learn probabilistic logics in these three settings, and finally, in Section 5, we conclude. The Appendix contains a short introduction to some logic programming concepts and terminology that are used in this paper.

2   Inductive Logic Programming Settings

Inductive logic programming is concerned with finding a hypothesis H (a logic program, i.e. a definite clause program) from a set of positive and negative examples P and N. More specifically, it is required that the hypothesis H *covers* all positive examples in P and none of the negative examples in N. The representation language chosen for representing the examples together with the *covers* relation determines the inductive logic programming setting [6]. Various settings have been considered in the literature, most notably learning from *entailment* [39] and learning from *interpretations* [8,17], which we formalize below. We also introduce an intermediate setting inspired on the seminal work by Ehud Shapiro [43], which we call learning from *proofs*.

Before formalizing these settings, let us however also discuss how background knowledge is employed within inductive logic programming. For the purposes of the present paper[1], it will be convenient to view the background knowledge B as a logic program (i.e. a definite clause program) that is provided to the inductive logic programming system and fixed during the learning process. Under the presence of background knowledge, the hypothesis H together with the background theory B should cover all positive and none of the negative examples. The ability to provide declarative background knowledge to the learning engine is viewed as one of the strengths of inductive logic programming.

---

[1] For the learning from interpretations setting, we slightly deviate from the standard definition in the literature for didactic purposes.

2.1 Learning from Entailment

Learning from entailment is by far the most popular inductive logic programming systems and it is addressed by a wide variety of well-known inductive logic programming systems such as FOIL [41], PROGOL [30], and ALEPH [44].

Definition 1. *When learning from entailment, the examples are definite clauses and a hypothesis H covers an example e w.r.t. the background theory B if and only if $B \cup H \models e$.*

In many well-known systems, such as FOIL, one requires that the examples are ground facts, a special case of definite clauses. To illustrate the above setting, consider the following example inspired on the well-known mutagenicity application [45].

Example 1. Consider the following facts in the background theory *B*. They describe part of molecule 225.

```
molecule(225).                          bond(225,f1_1,f1_2,7).
logmutag(225,0.64).                     bond(225,f1_2,f1_3,7).
lumo(225,-1.785).                       bond(225,f1_3,f1_4,7).
logp(225,1.01).                         bond(225,f1_4,f1_5,7).
nitro(225,[f1_4,f1_8,f1_10,f1_9]).      bond(225,f1_5,f1_1,7).
atom(225,f1_1,c,21,0.187).              bond(225,f1_8,f1_9,2).
atom(225,f1_2,c,21,-0.143).             bond(225,f1_8,f1_10,2).
atom(225,f1_3,c,21,-0.143).             bond(225,f1_1,f1_11,1).
atom(225,f1_4,c,21,-0.013).             bond(225,f1_11,f1_12,2).
atom(225,f1_5,o,52,-0.043).             bond(225,f1_11,f1_13,1).
...
ring_size_5(225,[f1_5,f1_1,f1_2,f1_3,f1_4]).
hetero_aromatic_5_ring(225,[f1_5,f1_1,f1_2,f1_3,f1_4]).
...
```

Consider now the example mutagenic(225). It is covered by the following clause

```
mutagenic(M) :- nitro(M,R1), logp(M,C), C > 1 .
```

Inductive logic programming systems that learn from entailment often employ a typical separate-and-conquer rule-learning strategy [13]. In an outer loop of the algorithm, they follow a set-covering approach [29] in which they repeatedly search for a rule covering many positive examples and none of the negative examples. They then delete the positive examples covered by the current clause and repeat this process until all positive examples have been covered. In the inner loop of the algorithm, they typically perform a general-to-specific heuristic search employing a refinement operator under θ-subsumption [39].

2.2 Learning from Interpretations

The learning from interpretations settings [8] has been inspired on the work on boolean concept-learning in computational learning theory [47].

Definition 2. *When learning from interpretations, the examples are Herbrand interpretations and a hypothesis H covers an example e w.r.t. the background theory B if and only if e is a model of B ∪ H.*

Herbrand interpretations are sets of true ground facts and they completely describe a possible situation.

Example 2. Consider the interpretation I which is the union of B

```
{father(henry,bill),    father(alan,betsy),    father(alan,benny),
father(brian,bonnie),   father(bill,carl),     father(benny,cecily),
father(carl,dennis),    mother(ann,bill),      mother(ann,betsy),
mother(ann,bonnie),     mother(alice,benny),   mother(betsy,carl),
mother(bonnie,cecily),  mother(cecily,dennis), founder(henry).
founder(alan). founder(an). founder(brian). founder(alice).
```

and $C = \{\text{carrier(alan)}, \text{carrier(ann)}, \text{carrier(betsy)}\}$. It is covered by the clause c

```
carrier(X)  :- mother(M,X),carrier(M),father(F,X),carrier(F).
```

This clause covers the interpretation I because for all substitutions θ such that $body(c)\theta \subseteq I$ holds, it also holds that $head(c)\theta \in I$.

The key difference between learning from interpretations and learning from entailment is that interpretations carry much more – even complete – information. Indeed, when learning from entailment, an example can consist of a *single* fact, whereas when learning from interpretations, all facts that hold in the example are known. Therefore, learning from interpretations is typically easier and computationally more tractable than learning from entailment, cf. [6].

Systems that learn from interpretations work in a similar fashion as those that learn from entailment. There is however one crucial difference and it concerns the generality relationship. A hypothesis G *is more general than* a hypothesis S if all examples covered by S are also covered by G. When learning from entailment, G is more general than S if and only if $G \models S$, whereas when learning from interpretations, when $S \models G$. Another difference is that learning from interpretations is well suited for learning from positive examples only. For this case, a complete search of the space ordered by θ-subsumption is performed until all clauses cover all examples [7].

2.3   Learning from Proofs

Because learning from entailment (with ground facts as examples) and interpretations occupy extreme positions w.r.t. the information the examples carry, it is interesting to investigate intermediate positions. Ehud Shapiro's Model Inference System (MIS) [43] fits nicely within the learning from entailment setting where examples are facts. However, to deal with missing information, Shapiro employs a clever strategy: MIS queries the user for missing information by asking her for the truth-value of facts. The answers to these queries allow MIS to reconstruct the trace or the proof of the positive examples. Inspired by Shapiro, we define the learning from proofs setting.

Definition 3. *When learning from proofs, the examples are ground proof-trees and an example e is covered by a hypothesis H w.r.t. the background theory B if and only if e is a proof-tree for H ∪ B.*

At this point, there exist various possible forms of proof-trees. In this paper, we will – for reasons that will become clear later – assume that the proof-tree is given in the form of an and-tree where the nodes contain ground atoms. More formally:

Definition 4. *t is a proof-tree for T if and only if t is a rooted tree where for every node n ∈ t with children child(n) satisfies the property that there exists a substitution θ and a clause c such that n = head(c)θ and child(n) = body(c)θ.*

Example 3. Consider the following *definite clause grammar*.

```
sentence(A, B) :- noun_phrase(C, A, D), verb_phrase(C, D, B).
noun_phrase(A, B, C) :- article(A, B, D), noun(A, D, C).
verb_phrase(A, B, C) :- intransitive_verb(A, B, C).
article(singular, A, B) :- terminal(A, a, B).
article(singular, A, B) :- terminal(A, the, B).
article(plural, A, B)   :- terminal(A, the, B).
noun(singular, A, B) :- terminal(A, turtle, B).
noun(plural, A, B)   :- terminal(A, turtles, B).
intransitive_verb(singular, A, B) :- terminal(A, sleeps, B).
intransitive_verb(plural, A, B) :- terminal(A, sleep, B).
terminal([A|B],A,B).
```

It covers the following proof tree *u* (where abbreviated accordingly):

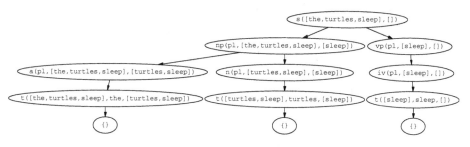

Proof-trees contain – as interpretations – a lot of information. Indeed, they contain instances of the clauses that were used in the proofs. Therefore, it may be hard for the user to provide this type of examples. Even though that is generally true, there exist specific situations for which this is feasible. Indeed, consider tree banks such as the UPenn Wall Street Journal corpus [27], which contain parse trees. These trees directly correspond to the proof-trees we talk about. Even though – to the best of the authors' knowledge (but see [43,3] for inductive logic programming systems that learn from traces) – no inductive logic programming system has been developed to learn from proof-trees, it is not hard to imagine an outline for such an algorithm. Indeed, by analogy with the learning of tree-bank grammars, one could turn all the proof-trees (corresponding to positive examples) into a set of ground clauses which would constitute the initial theory. This theory can then be generalized by taking the least general generalization (under θ-subsumption) of pairwise clauses. Of course, care must be taken that the generalized theory does not cover negative examples.

3 Probabilistic Inductive Logic Programming Settings

Given the interest in probabilistic logic programs as a representation formalism and the different learning settings for inductive logic programming, the question arises as to whether one can extend the inductive logic programming settings with probabilistic representations.

When working with probabilistic logic programming representations, there are essentially two changes:

1. clauses are annotated with probability values, and
2. the covers relation becomes a probabilistic one.

We will use $\mathbf{P}$ to denote a probability distribution, e.g. $\mathbf{P}(x)$, and the normal letter P to denote a probability value, e.g. $P(x = v)$, where v is a state of x. Thus,

> *a probabilistic covers relation takes as arguments an example e, a hypothesis H and possibly the background theory B. It then returns a probability value between 0 and 1. So, $covers(e, H \cup B) = \mathbf{P}(e \mid H, B)$, the likelihood of the example e.*

The task of probabilistic inductive logic programming is then to find the hypothesis H^* that maximizes the likelihood of the data $\mathbf{P}(E \mid H^*, B)$, where E denotes the set of examples. Under the usual i.i.d. assumption this results in the maximization of $\mathbf{P}(E \mid H^*, B) = \prod_{e \in E} \mathbf{P}(e \mid H^*, B)$.

The key contribution of this paper is that we present three probabilistic inductive logic programming settings that extend the traditional ones sketched above.

3.1 Probabilistic Entailment

In order to integrate probabilities in the entailment setting, we need to find a way to assign probabilities to clauses that are entailed by an annotated logic program. Since most inductive logic programming systems working under entailment employ ground facts for a single predicate as examples and the authors are unaware of any existing probabilistic logic programming formalisms that implement a probabilistic covers relation for definite clauses in general, we will restrict our attention in this section to assign probabilities to facts for a single predicate. Furthermore, our proposal in this section proceeds along the lines of the naïve Bayes' framework and represents only one possible choice for probabilistic entailment. It remains an open question as how to formulate more general frameworks for working with entailment (one alternative setting is also presented in Section 3.3).

More formally, let us annotate a logic program H consisting of a set of clauses of the form $p \leftarrow b_i$, where p is an atom of the form $p(V_1, ..., V_n)$ with the V_i different variables, and the b_i are different bodies of clauses. Furthermore, we associate to each clause in H the probability values $\mathbf{P}(b_i \mid p)$; they constitute the conditional probability distribution that for a random substitution θ for which $p\theta$ is ground and true (resp. false), the query $b_i\theta$ succeeds (resp. fails) in the knowledge base B. [2] Furthermore, we assume the prior probability of p is given as $\mathbf{P}(p)$, it denotes the probability that for a random substitution θ, $p\theta$ is true (resp. false). This can then be used to define the covers relation $\mathbf{P}(p\theta \mid H, B)$ as follows (we delete the B as it is fixed):

$$\mathbf{P}(p\theta \mid H) = \mathbf{P}(p\theta \mid b_1\theta, ..., b_k\theta) = \frac{\mathbf{P}(b_1\theta, ..., b_k\theta \mid p\theta) \times \mathbf{P}(p\theta)}{\mathbf{P}(b_1\theta, ..., b_k\theta)} \qquad (1)$$

Applying the naïve Bayes assumption yields

$$\mathbf{P}(p\theta \mid H) = \frac{\prod_i \mathbf{P}(b_i\theta \mid p\theta) \times \mathbf{P}(p\theta)}{\mathbf{P}(b_1\theta, ..., b_k\theta)} \qquad (2)$$

Finally, since we can $P(p\theta \mid H) + P(\neg p\theta \mid H) = 1$, we can compute $P(p\theta \mid H)$ without $P(b_1\theta, ..., b_k\theta)$ through normalization.

Example 4. Consider again the mutagenicity domain and the following annotated logic program:

$(0.01, 0.21) : \mathtt{mutagenetic(M)} \leftarrow \mathtt{atom(M, \_, \_, 8, \_)}$
$(0.38, 0.99) : \mathtt{mutagenetic(M)} \leftarrow \mathtt{bond(M,, A, 1), atom(M, A, c, 22, \_), bond(M, A,, 2)}$

where we denote the first clause by $\mathbf{b_1}$ and the second one by $\mathbf{b_2}$, and the vectors on the left-hand side of the clauses specify $P(b_i\theta = true \mid p\theta = true)$ and $P(b_i\theta = true \mid p\theta = false)$. The covers relation assigns probaility 0.97 to example 225 because both features fail for $\theta = \{\mathtt{M} \leftarrow 225\}$. Hence,

$$P(\, \mathtt{mutagenetic}(225) = true, \mathbf{b_1}\theta = false, \; \mathbf{b_2}\theta = false)$$
$$= \; P(\, \mathbf{b_1}\theta = false \mid \mathtt{muta}(225) = true \,)$$
$$\cdot \, P(\, \mathbf{b_2}\theta = false \mid \mathtt{muta}(225) = true \,)$$
$$\cdot \, P(\, \mathtt{mutagenetic}(225) = true \,)$$
$$= 0.99 \cdot 0.62 \cdot 0.31 = 0.19$$

---

[2] The query q succeeds in B if there is a substitution σ such that $B \models q\sigma$.

and $P(\text{mutagenetic}(225) = false, \text{b}_1\theta = false, \text{b}_2\theta = false) = 0.79 \cdot 0.01 \cdot 0.68 = 0.005$. This yields

$$P(\text{muta}(225) = true \mid \text{b}_1\theta = false, \text{b}_2\theta = false\}) = \frac{0.19}{0.19 + 0.005} = 0.97 .$$

3.2 Probabilistic Interpretations

In order to integrate probabilities in the learning from interpretation setting, we need to find a way to assign probabilities to interpretations covered by an annotated logic program. In the past few years, this question has received a lot of attention and various different approaches have been developed such as [38]. In this paper, we choose Bayesian logic programs [21] as the probabilistic logic programming system because Bayesian logic programs combine Bayesian networks [37], which represent probability distributions over propositional interpretations, with definite clause logic. Furthermore, Bayesian logic programs have already been employed for learning.

The idea underlying Bayesian logic programs is to view ground atoms as random variables that are defined by the underlying definite clause programs. Furthermore, two types of predicates are distinguished: deterministic and probabilistic ones. The former are called *logical*, the latter *Bayesian*. Likewise we will also speak of Bayesian and logical atoms. A Bayesian logic program now consists of a set of of Bayesian (definite) clauses, which are expressions of the form $\text{A} \mid \text{A}_1, \ldots, \text{A}_n$ where A is a Bayesian atom, $\text{A}_1, \ldots, \text{A}_n$, $n \geq 0$, are Bayesian and logical atoms and all variables are (implicitly) universally quantified. To quantify probabilistic dependencies, each Bayesian clause c is annotated with its conditional probability distribtion $\text{cpd}(c) = \mathbf{P}(\text{A} \mid \text{A}_1, \ldots, \text{A}_n)$, which quantifies as a macro the probabilistic dependency among ground instances of the clause.

Let us illustrate Bayesian logic programs on Jensen's stud farm example [19], which describes the processes underlying a life threatening heridatary disease.

Example 5. Consider the following Bayesian clauses:

$$\text{carrier}(X) \mid \text{founder}(X). \tag{3}$$
$$\text{carrier}(X) \mid \text{mother}(M, X), \text{carrier}(M), \text{father}(F, X), \text{carrier}(F). \tag{4}$$
$$\text{suffers}(X) \mid \text{carrier}(X). \tag{5}$$

They specify the probabilistic dependencies governing the inheritance process. For instance, clause (4) says that the probability for a horse being a carrier of the disease depends on its parents being carriers.

In this example, the `mother`, `father`, and `founder` are logical, whereas the other ones, such as `carrier` and `suffers`, are Bayesian. The logical predicates are then defined by a classical definite clause program which constitute the background theory for this example. It is listed as interpretation B in Example 2.

The conditional probability distributions for the Bayesian clause are

$P(\texttt{carrier}(\texttt{X}) = true)$
0.6

$\texttt{carrier}(\texttt{X})$	$P(\texttt{suffers}(\texttt{X}) = true)$
$true$	0.7
$false$	0.01

$\texttt{carrier}(\texttt{M})$	$\texttt{carrier}(\texttt{F})$	$P(\texttt{carrier}(\texttt{X}) = true)$
$true$	$true$	0.6
$true$	$false$	0.5
$false$	$true$	0.5
$false$	$false$	0.0

Observe that logical atoms, such as $\texttt{mother}(\texttt{M}, \texttt{X})$, do not affect the distribution of Bayesian atoms, such as $\texttt{carrier}(\texttt{X})$, and are therefore not considered in the conditional probability distribution. They only provide variable bindings, e.g., between $\texttt{carrier}(\texttt{X})$ and $\texttt{carrier}(\texttt{M})$.

By now, we are able to define the covers relation for Bayesian logic programs. A set of Bayesian logic program together with the background theory induces a Bayesian network. The random variables $\mathbf{A}$ of the Bayesian network are the Bayesian ground atoms in the least Herbrand model I of the annotated logic program. A Bayesian ground atom, say $\texttt{carrier}(\texttt{alan})$, influences another Bayesian ground atom, say $\texttt{carrier}(\texttt{betsy})$, if and only if there exists a Bayesian clause c such that

1. $\texttt{carrier}(\texttt{alan}) \in body(c)\theta \subseteq I$, and
2. $\texttt{carrier}(\texttt{betsy}) \equiv head(c)\theta \in I$.

Each node $\mathbf{A}$ has $\text{cpd}(c\theta)$ as associated conditional probability distribution. If there are multiple ground instances in I with the same head, a *combining rule* combine$\{\cdot\}$ is used to quantified the combined effect. A combining rule is a function that maps finite sets of conditional probability distributions onto one (*combined*) conditional probability distribution. Examples of combining rules are *noisy-or*, and *noisy-and*, see e.g. [19]

Example 6. The Stud farm Bayesian logic program induces the following Bayesian network.

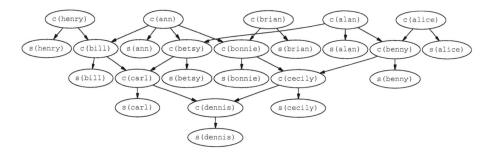

Note that we assume that the induced network is acyclic and has a finite branching factor. The probability distribution induced is now

$$\mathbf{P}(I|H) = \prod_{\text{Bayesian atom } \mathsf{A} \in I} \text{combine}\{\text{cpd}(c\theta) \,|body(c)\theta \subseteq I, head(c)\theta \equiv \mathsf{A}\}. \quad (6)$$

From Equation (6), we can see that an example e consists of a **logical part** which is a Herbrand interpretation of the annotated logic program, and a **probabilistic part** which is a partial state assignment of the random variables occuring in the logical part.

Example 7. A possible example e in the Stud farm domain is

{carrier(henry) = *false*, suffers(henry) = *false*, carrier(ann) = *true*, suffers(ann) = *false*,   carrier(brian) = *false*, suffers(brian) = *false*, carrier(alan) =?,   suffers(alan) = *false*, carrier(alice) = *false*, suffers(alice) = *false*, ...}

where ? denotes an unobserved state. The covers relation for e can now be computed using any Bayesian network inference engine based on Equation (6).

3.3   Probabilistic Proofs

The framework of stochastic logic programs [12,31,4] was inspired on research on stochastic context free grammars [1,26]. The analogy between context free grammars and logic programs is that

1. grammar rules correspond to definite clauses,
2. sentences (or strings) to atoms, and
3. derivations to proofs.

Furthermore, in stochastic context-free grammars, the rules are annotated with probability labels in such a way that the sum of the probabilities associated to the rules defining a non-terminal is 1.0 .

Eisele and Muggleton have exploited this analogy to define stochastic logic programs. These are essentially definite clause programs, where each clause c has an associated probability label p_c such that the sum of the probabilities associated to the rules defining any predicate is 1.0 (though less restricted versions have been considered as well [4]).

This framework now allows to assign probabilities to proofs for a given predicate q given a stochastic logic program $H \cup B$ in the following manner. Let D_q denote the set of all possible ground proofs for atoms over the predicate q. For simplicity reasons, it will be assumed that there is a finite number of such proofs and that all proofs are finite (but again see [4] for the more general case). Now associate to each proof $t_q \in D_q$ the value

$$v_t = \prod_c p_c^{n_{c,t}}$$

where the product ranges over all clauses c and $n_{c,t}$ denotes the number of times clause c has been used in proof t_q. For stochastic context free grammars, the values v_t correspond to the probabilities of the derivations. However, the difference between context free grammars and logic programs is that in grammars two rules of the form $n \to q, n_1, ..., n_m$ and $q \to q_1, ..., q_k$ always 'resolve' to give $n \to q_1, ..., q_k, n_1, ..., n_m$ whereas resolution may fail due to unification. Therefore, the probability of a proof tree t in D_q

$$P(t \mid H, B) = \frac{v_t}{\sum_{s \in D_q} v_s} .$$

The probability of a ground atom is then defined as the sum of all the probabilities of all the proofs for that ground atom.

Example 8. Consider a stochastic variant of the definite clause grammer in Example 3 with uniform probability values for each predicate. The value v_u of the proof (tree) u in Example 3 is $v_u = \frac{1}{3} \cdot \frac{1}{2} \cdot \frac{1}{2} = \frac{1}{12}$. The only other ground proofs s_1, s_2 of atoms over the predicate sentence are those of sentence([a, turtle, sleeps], []) and sentence([the, turtle, sleeps], []). Both get value $v_{s_1} = v_{s_2} = \frac{1}{12}$, too. Because there is only one proof for each of the sentences, $P(\text{sentence}([\text{the, turtles, sleep}], [])) = v_u = \frac{1}{3}$.

At this point, there are at least two different settings for probabilistic inductive logic programming using stochastic logic programs. The first actually corresponds to a learning from entailment setting in which the examples are ground atoms entailed by the target stochastic logic program. This setting has been studied by Cussens [5], who solves the parameter estimation problem, and Muggleton [32,33], who presents a preliminary approach to structure learning (concentrating on the problem of adding one clause to an existing stochastic logic program).

In the second setting, which we sketch below, the idea is to employ learning from proofs instead of entailment. This significantly simplifies the structure learning process because proofs carry a lot more information about the structure of the underlying stochastic logic program than clauses that are entailed or not. Therefore, it should be much easier to learn from proofs. Furthermore, learning stochastic logic programs from proofs can be considered an extension of the work on learning stochastic grammars. It should therefore also be applicable to learning unification based grammars.

4   Probabilistic Inductive Logic Programming

By now, the problem of probabilistic inductive logic programming can be defined as follows:

> **Given**   – a set of examples E,
>   – a probabilistic covers relation $P(e \mid H, B)$,
>   – a probabilistic logic programming representation language, and
>   – possibly a background theory B.
>
> **Find**   the hypothesis $H^* = argmax_H P(E \mid H, B)$.

Because $H = (L, \lambda)$ is essentially a logic program L annotated with probabilistic parameters λ, one distinguishes in general two subtasks:

1. *Parameter estimation*, where it is assumed that the underlying logic program L is fixed, and the learning task consists of estimating the parameters λ that maximize the likelihood.
2. *Structure learning*, where both L and λ have to be learned from the data.

Below, we briefly sketch the basic parameter estimation and structure learning techniques for probabilistic inductive logic programming. A complete survey of learning probabilistic logic representations can be found in [9].

4.1   Parameter Estimation

The problem of parameter estimation is thus concerned with estimating the values of the parameters λ^* of a fixed probabilistic logic program L that best explain the examples E. So, λ is a set of parameters and can be represented as a vector. As already indicated above, to measure the extent to which a model fits the data, one usually employs the likelihood of the data, i.e. $P(E \mid L, \lambda)$, though other scores or variants could – in principle – be used as well.

When all examples are fully observable, maximum likelihood reduces to frequency counting. In the presence of missing data, however, the maximum likelihood estimate typically cannot be written in closed form. It is a numerical optimization problem, and all known algorithms involve nonlinear optimization The most commonly adapted technique for probabilistic logic learning is the Expectation-Maximization (EM) algorithm [10,28]. EM is based on the observation that learning would be easy (i.e., correspond to frequency counting), if the values of all the random variables would be known. Therefore, it first estimates these values, and then uses these to maximize the likelihood, and then iterates. More specifically, EM assumes that the parameters have been initialized (e.g., at random) and then iteratively performs the following two steps until convergence:

E-Step: On the basis of the observed data and the present parameters of the model, compute a distribution over all possible completions of each partially observed data case.

M-Step: Using each completion as a fully-observed data case weighted by its probability, compute the updated parameter values using (weighted) frequency counting.

The frequencies over the completions are called the *expected counts*.

4.2   Structure Learning

The problem is now to learn both the structure L and the parameters λ of the probabilistic logic program from data. Often, further information is given as well. It can take various different forms, including:

1. a *language bias* that imposes restrictions on the syntax of the definite clauses allowed in L,
2. a *background theory*,
3. an *initial hypothesis* (L, λ) from which the learning process can start, and
4. a scoring function $score(L, \lambda, E)$ that may correct the maximum likelihood principle for complex hypthesis; this can be based on a Bayesian approach which takes into account priors or the minimum description length princple.

Nearly all (score-based) approaches to structure learning perform a heuristic search through the space of possible hypotheses. Typically, hill-climbing or beam-search is applied until the hypothesis satisfies the logical constraints and the score(H, E) is no longer improving. The logical constraints typically require that the exammples are covered in the logical sense. E.g., when learning stochastic logic programs from entailment, the example clauses must be entailed by the logic program, and when learning Bayesian logic programs, the interpretation must be a model of the logic program.

At this point, it is interesting to observe that in the learning from entailment setting the examples do have to be covered in the logical sense when using the setting combining FOIL and naïve Bayes, whereas using the stochastic logic programs all examples must be logically entailed.

The steps in the search-space are typically made through the application of so-called refinement operators [43,36], which make perform small modifications to a hypothesis. From a logical perspective, these refinement operators typically realize elementary generalization and specialization steps (usually under θ-subsumption).

Before concluding, we will now sketch for each probabilistic inductive logic learning setting a structure learning algorithm.

4.3   Learning from Probabilistic Entailment

One promising approach to address learning from probabilistic entailment is to adapt FOIL [41] with the conditional likelihood as described in Equation (2) as the scoring function $score(L, \lambda, E)$ (see N. Landwehr, K. Kersting and L. De Raedt, forthcoming, for more details).

Given a training set E containing positive and negative examples (i.e. true and false ground facts), this algorithm computes Horn clause features $b_1, b_2, \ldots$ in an outer loop. It terminates when no further improvements in the score are obtained, i.e, when $score(\{b_1, \ldots, b_i\}, \lambda_i, E) < score(\{b_1, \ldots, b_{i+1}\}, \lambda_{i+1}, E)$, where λ denotes the maximum likelihood parameters. A major difference with FOIL is, however, that the covered positive examples are *not* removed.

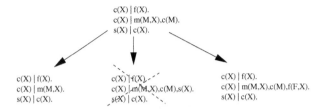

Fig. 1. The use of refinement operators during structural search within the framework of Bayesian logic programs. We can add an atom or delete an atom from the body of a clause. Candidates crossed out illegal because they are cyclic. Other refinement operators are reasonable such as adding or deleting logically valid clauses.

The inner loop is concerned with inducing the next feature b_{i+1} top-down, i.e., from general to specific. To this aim it starts with a clause with an empty body, e.g., `muta(M)` ←. This clause is then specialised by repeatedly adding atoms to the body, e.g., `muta(M)` ← `bond(M, A, 1)`, `muta(M)` ← `bond(M, A, 1)`, `atom(M, A, c, 22, _)`, etc. For each refinement b'_{i+1} we then compute the maximum-likelihood parameters λ'_{i+1} and $score(\{b_1, \dots, b'_{i+1}\}, \lambda'_{i+1}, E)$. The refinement that scores best, say b''_{i+1}, is then considered for further refinement and the refinement process terminates when $score(\{b_1, \dots, b_{i+1}\}, \lambda_{i+1}, E) < score(\{b_1, \dots, b''_{i+1}\}, \lambda''_{i+1}, E)$. Preliminary results with a prototype implementation are promising.

4.4   Learning from Probabilistic Interpretations

SCOOBY [22,20,23] is a greedy hill-climbing approach for learning Bayesian logic programs. SCOOBY takes the initial Bayesian logic program $H = (L, \lambda)$ as starting point and computes the parameters maximizing $score(L, \lambda, E)$. Then, refinement operators generalizing respectively specializing H are used to to compute all legal neighbours of H in the hypothesis space, see Figure 1. Each neighbour is scored. Let $H' = (L', \lambda')$ be the legal neighbour scoring best. If $score(L, \lambda, E) < score(L', \lambda', E)$ then SCOOBY takes H' as new hypothesis. The process is continued until no improvements in score are obtained.

SCOOBY is akin to theory revision approaches in inductive logic prorgamming. In case that only propositional clauses are considered, SCOOBY coincides with greedy hill-climbing approaches for learning Bayesian networks [16].

4.5   Learning from Probabilistic Proofs

Given a training set E containing ground proofs as examples, one possible approach combines ideas from the early inductive logic programming system GOLEM [34] that employs Plotkin's [39] least general generalization (LGG) with bottom-up generalization of grammars and hidden Markov models [46]. The resulting algorithm employs the likelihood of the proofs $score(L, \lambda, E)$ as the scoring function. It starts by taking as L_0 the set of ground clauses that have been used in the proofs in the training set and scores it to obtain λ_0. After initialization, the algorithm will then repeatedly select a pair of clauses in L_i, and replace the pair by their LGG to yield a candidate L'. The candidate that scores best is then taken as $H_{i+1} = (L_{i+1}, \lambda_{i+1})$, and the process iterates untill the score no longer improves. One interesting issue is that strong logical constraints can be imposed on the LGG. These logical constraints directly follow from the fact that the example proofs should still be valid proofs for the logical component L of all hypotheses considered. Therefore, it makes sense to apply the LGG only to clauses that define the same predicate, that contain the same predicates, and whose (reduced) LGG also has the same length as the original clauses. More details on this procedure will be worked out in a forthcoming paper (by S. Torge, K. Kersting and L. De Raedt).

5   Conclusions

In this paper, we have presented three settings for probabilistic inductive logic programming: *learning from entailment, from interpretations and from proofs.* We have also sketched how inductive logic programming and probabilistic learning techniques can – in principle – be combined to address these settings. Nevertheless, more work is needed before these techniques will be as applicable as traditional probabilistic learning or inductive logic programming systems. The authors hope that this paper will inspire and motivate researchers in probabilistic learning and inductive logic programming to join the exciting new field lying at the intersection of probabilistic reasoning, logic programming and machine learning.

Acknowledgements. The authors would like to thank Niels Landwehr and Sunna Torge for interesting collaborations on probabilisitc learning from entailment and proofs. This research was supported by the European Union under contract number FP6-508861, *Application of Probabilistic Inductive Logic Programming II.*

References

[1] S. Abney. Stochastic Attribute-Value Grammars. *Computational Linguistics*, 23(4):597–618, 1997.

[2] C. Anderson, P. Domingos, and D. Weld. Relational Markov Models and their Application to Adaptive Web Navigation. In D. Hand, D. Keim, O. Zaïne, and R. Goebel, editors, *Proceedings of the Eighth International Conference on Knowledge Discovery and Data Mining (KDD-02)*, pages 143–152, Edmonton, Canada, 2002. ACM Press.

[3] F. Bergadano and D. Gunetti. *Inductive Logic Programming: From Machine Learning to Software Engeneering.* MIT Press, 1996.

[4] J. Cussens. Loglinear models for first-order probabilistic reasoning. In K. Laskey and H. Prade, editors, *Proceedings of the Fifteenth Annual Conference on Uncertainty in Artificial Intelligence (UAI-99)*, pages 126–133, Stockholm, Sweden, 1999. Morgan Kaufmann.

[5] J. Cussens. Parameter estimation in stochastic logic programs. *Machine Learning*, 44(3):245–271, 2001.

[6] L. De Raedt. Logical settings for concept-learning. *Artificial Intelligence*, 95(1):197–201, 1997.

[7] L. De Raedt and L. Dehaspe. Clausal discovery. *Machine Learning*, 26(2-3):99–146, 1997.

[8] L. De Raedt and S. Džeroski. First-Order jk-Clausal Theories are PAC-Learnable. *Artificial Intelligence*, 70(1-2):375–392, 1994.

[9] L. De Raedt and K. Kersting. Probabilistic Logic Learning. *ACM-SIGKDD Explorations: Special issue on Multi-Relational Data Mining*, 5(1):31–48, 2003.

[10] A. Dempster, N. Laird, and D. Rubin. Maximum likelihood from incomplete data via the EM algorithm. *J. Royal Stat. Soc.*, B 39:1–39, 1977.

[11] T. Dietterich, L. Getoor, and K. Murphy, editors. *Working Notes of the ICML-2004 Workshop on Statistical Relational Learning and its Connections to Other Fields (SRL-04)*, 2004.

[12] A. Eisele. Towards probabilistic extensions of contraint-based grammars. In J. Dörne, editor, *Computational Aspects of Constraint-Based Linguistics Decription-II*. DYNA-2 deliverable R1.2.B, 1994.

[13] J. Fürnkranz. Separate-and-Conquer Rule Learning. *Artificial Intelligence Review*, 13(1):3–54, 1999.

[14] L. Getoor and D. Jensen, editors. *Working Notes of the IJCAI-2003 Workshop on Learning Statistical Models from Relational Data (SRL-03)*, 2003.

[15] P. Haddawy. Generating Bayesian networks from probabilistic logic knowledge bases. In R. López de Mántaras and D. Poole, editors, *Proceedings of the Tenth Annual Conference on Uncertainty in Artificial Intelligence (UAI-1994)*, pages 262–269, Seattle, Washington, USA, 1994. Morgan Kaufmann.

[16] D. Heckerman. A Tutorial on Learning with Bayesian Networks. Technical Report MSR-TR-95-06, Microsoft Research, March 1995.

[17] N. Helft. Induction as nonmonotonic inference. In R. Brachman, H. Levesque, and R. Reiter, editors, *Proceedings of the First International Conference on Principles of Knowledge Representation and Reasoning (KR-1989)*, pages 149–156, Toronto, Canada, May 15-18 1989. Morgan Kaufmann.

[18] M. Jaeger. Relational Bayesian networks. In D. Geiger and P. Shenoy, editors, *Proceedings of the Thirteenth Annual Conference on Uncertainty in Artificial Intelligence (UAI-97)*, pages 266–273, Providence, Rhode Island, USA, 1997. Morgan Kaufmann.

[19] F. Jensen. *Bayesian networks and decision graphs*. Springer-Verlag New, 2001.

[20] K. Kersting and L. De Raedt. Adaptive Bayesian Logic Programs. In C. Rouveirol and M. Sebag, editors, *Proceedings of the Eleventh Conference on Inductive Logic Programming (ILP-01)*, volume 2157 of *LNCS*, Strasbourg, France, 2001. Springer.

[21] K. Kersting and L. De Raedt. Bayesian logic programs. Technical Report 151, University of Freiburg, Institute for Computer Science, April 2001.

[22] K. Kersting and L. De Raedt. Towards Combining Inductive Logic Programming and Bayesian Networks. In C. Rouveirol and M. Sebag, editors, *Proceedings of the Eleventh Conference on Inductive Logic Programming (ILP-01)*, volume 2157 of *LNCS*, Strasbourg, France, 2001. Springer.

[23] K. Kersting and L. De Raedt. Principles of Learning Bayesian Logic Programs. Technical Report 174, University of Freiburg, Institute for Computer Science, June 2002.

[24] K. Kersting, T. Raiko, S. Kramer, and L. De Raedt. Towards discovering structural signatures of protein folds based on logical hidden markov models. In R. Altman, A. Dunker, L. Hunter, T. Jung, and T. Klein, editors, *Proceedings of the Pacific Symposium on Biocomputing*, pages 192 – 203, Kauai, Hawaii, USA, 2003. World Scientific.

[25] D. Koller and A. Pfeffer. Probabilistic frame-based systems. In C. Rich and J. Mostow, editors, *Proceedings of the Fifteenth National Conference on Artificial Intelligence (AAAI-1998)*, pages 580–587, Madison, Wisconsin, USA, July 1998. AAAI Press.

[26] C. Manning and H. Schütze. *Foundations of Statistical Natural Language Processing*. The MIT Press, 1999.

[27] M. Marcus, M. Marcinkiewicz, and B. Santorini. Building a large annotated corpus of English: The Penn TREEBANK. *Computational Linguistics*, 19(2):313–330, 1993.

[28] G. McKachlan and T. Krishnan. *The EM Algorithm and Extensions*. John Eiley & Sons, Inc., 1997.

[29] T. M. Mitchell. *Machine Learning*. The McGraw-Hill Companies, Inc., 1997.

[30] S. Muggleton. Inverse Entailment and Progol. *New Generation Computing Journal*, 13(3–4):245–286, 1995.

[31] S. Muggleton. Stochastic logic programs. In L. De Raedt, editor, *Advances in Inductive Logic Programming*, pages 254–264. IOS Press, 1996.

[32] S. Muggleton. Learning stochastic logic programs. *Electronic Transactions in Artificial Intelligence*, 4(041), 2000.

[33] S. Muggleton. Learning structure and parameters of stochastic logic programs. In S. Matwin and C. Sammut, editors, *Proceedings of the Twelfth International Conference on Inductive Logic Prgramming (ILP-02)*, volume 2583 of *LNCS*, pages 198–206, Sydney, Australia, 2002. Springer.

[34] S. Muggleton and C. Feng. Efficient induction of logic programs. In S. Muggleton, editor, *Inductive Logic Programming*, pages 281–298. Acadamic Press, 1992.

[35] L. Ngo and P. Haddawy. Answering queries from context-sensitive probabilistic knowledge bases. *Theoretical Computer Science*, 171(1–2):147–177, 1997.

[36] S. Nienhuys-Cheng and R. de Wolf. *Foundations of Inductive Logic Programming*. Springer-Verlag, 1997.

[37] J. Pearl. *Reasoning in Intelligent Systems: Networks of Plausible Inference*. Morgan Kaufmann, 2. edition, 1991.

[38] A. Pfeffer. *Probabilistic Reasoning for Complex Systems*. PhD thesis, Stanford University, 2000.

[39] G. Plotkin. A note on inductive generalization. In *Machine Intelligence*, volume 5, pages 153–163. Edinburgh University Press, 1970.

[40] D. Poole. Probabilistic Horn abduction and Bayesian networks. *Artificial Intelligence*, 64(1):81–129, 1993.

[41] J. Quinlan and R. Cameron-Jones. Induction of logic programs: FOIL and related systems. *New Generation Computing*, 13(3–4):287–312, 1995.

[42] T. Sato. A Statistical Learning Method for Logic Programs with Distribution Semantics. In L. Sterling, editor, *Proceedings of the Twelfth International Conference on Logic Programming (ICLP-1995)*, pages 715 – 729, Tokyo, Japan, 1995. MIT Press.

[43] E. Shapiro. *Algorithmic Program Debugging*. MIT Press, 1983.

[44] A. Srinivasan. *The Aleph Manual*. Available at
      `http://www.comlab.ox.ac.uk/oucl/~research/areas/machlearn/Aleph/`.

[45] A. Srinivasan, S. Muggleton, R. King, and M. Sternberg. Theories for mutagenicity: A study of first-order and feature based induction. *Artificial Intelligence*, 85(1–2):277–299, 1996.

[46] A. Stolcke and S. Omohundro. Inducing Probabilistic Grammars by Bayesian Model Merging. In R. Carrasco and J. Oncina, editors, *Proceedings of the Second International Colloquium on Grammatical Inference and Applications (ICGI-94)*, number 862 in LNCS, pages 106–118, Alicante, Spain, September 21-23 1994.

[47] L. G. Valiant. A theory of the learnable. *Communications of the ACM*, 27(11):1134–1142, November 1984.

Appendix: Logic Programming Concepts

A first order *alphabet* is a set of predicate symbols, constant symbols and functor symbols. A *definite clause* is a formula of the form $A \leftarrow B_1, ..., B_n$ where A and B_i are logical atoms. An atom $p(t_1, ..., t_n)$ is a predicate symbol p/n followed by a bracketed n-tuple of terms t_i. A term t is a variable V or a function symbol $f(t_1, ..., t_k)$ immediately followed by a bracketed n-tuple of terms t_i. Constants are function symbols of arity 0. *Functor-free* clauses are clauses that contain only variables as terms. The above clause can be read as A if B_1 and ... and B_n. All variables in clauses are universally quantified, although this is not explicitly written. We call A the *head* of the clause and $B_1, ..., B_n$ the *body* of the clause. A *fact* is a definite clause with an empty body, ($m = 1$, $n = 0$). Throughout the paper, we assume that all clauses are *range restricted*, which means that all variables occurring in the head of a clause also occur in its body. A *substitution* $\theta = \{V_1 \leftarrow t_1, ..., V_k \leftarrow t_k\}$ is an assignment of terms to variables. Applying a substitution θ to a clause, atom or term e yields the expression $e\theta$ where all occurrences of variables V_i have been replaced by the corresponding terms. A *Herbrand interpretation* is a set of ground facts over an alphabet A. A Herbrand interpretation I is a model for a clause c if and only if for all θ such that $body(c)\theta \subseteq I \rightarrow head(c)\theta \in I$; it is a model for a set of of clauses H if and only if it is a model for all clauses in H. We write $H \models e$ if and only if all models of H are also a model of e.

Hidden Markov Modelling Techniques for Haplotype Analysis*

Mikko Koivisto, Teemu Kivioja, Heikki Mannila, Pasi Rastas, and
Esko Ukkonen

Department of Computer Science and HIIT Basic Research Unit
P.O. Box 68 (Gustav Hällströminkatu 2b)
FIN-00014 University of Helsinki, Finland
Firstname.Lastname@cs.helsinki.fi

Abstract. A hidden Markov model is introduced for descriptive modelling the mosaic–like structures of haplotypes, due to iterated recombinations within a population. Methods using the minimum description length principle are given for fitting such models to training data. Possible applications of the models are delineated, and some preliminary analysis results on real sets of haplotypes are reported, demonstrating the potential of our methods.

1 Introduction

Hidden Markov models (HMMs) have become a standard tool in biological sequence analysis [8,2]. Typically they have been applied to modelling multiple sequence alignments of protein families and protein domains as well as to database searching for, say, predicting genes.

In this paper we introduce HMM techniques for modelling the structure of genetic variation between individuals of the same species. Such a variation is seen in so–called haplotypes that are sequences of allelic values of some DNA markers taken from the same DNA molecule. The single nucleotide polymorphisms (SNPs) are important such markers, each having two alternative values that may occur in haplotypes of different individuals. The SNPs cover for example the human genome fairly densely. The variation of haplotypes is due to point mutations and recombinations that take place during generations of evolution of a population. Studying the genetic variations and correlating them with variations in phenotype is the commonly followed strategy for locating disease causing genes and developing diagnostic tests to screen people having high risk for these diseases.

Several recent studies have uncovered some type of block structure in human haplotype data [1,10,4,18,11,6]. However, the recombination mechanism as such does not necessarily imply a global block structure. Rather, at least in old populations one expects to see a mosaic–like structure that reflects the recombination

---

* A research supported by the Academy of Finland under grant 201560

S. Ben-David, J. Case, A. Maruoka (Eds.): ALT 2004, LNAI 3244, pp. 37–52, 2004.

history of the population. Assume that the haplotypes of an observed population have developed in generations of recombinations from certain 'founder' haplotypes. Then the current haplotypes should consist of conserved sequence fragments (possibly corrupted by some rare later mutations) that are taken from the founder sequences. Our goal is to uncover such conserved fragments from a sample set of haplotypes.

Unlike most earlier approaches for analyzing haplotype structures, the model class introduced here has no bias towards a global block structure. Our model is an acyclic HMM, capable of emitting equal length sequences. Each state of the model can emit a sequence fragment that is to be put into some specific location of the entire sequence. As the location is independent of the locations of other states, the madel has no global block structure. The hidden part of each state represents a conserved fragment, and the transitions between the states model the cross–overs of recombinations. We distinguish a general variant whose transition probabilities depend on both states involved, and a 'simple' variant whose transition probabilities depend only on the state to be entered.

For selecting such a HMM for a given training data we suggest a method based on the minimum description length principle (MDL) by Rissanen [12,13] which is widely used in statistics, machine learning, and data mining [9,5]. An approximation algorithm will be given for the resulting optimization problem of finding a model with shortest description in the proposed encoding scheme. The algorithm consists of two parts that are iterated alternatingly. The greedy part reduces the set of the conserved fragments, and the optimizer part uses the usual expectation maximization algorithm for finding the transition probabilities for the current set of fragments.

Our idea of block–free modeling has its roots in [17] which gave a combinatorial algorithm for reconstructing founder sequences without assuming block structured fragmentation of the current haplotypes. In probabilistic modelling and using MDL for model selection we follow some ideas of [6]. Unfortunately in the present block–free case the optimization problem seems much harder. Recently, Schwartz [14] proposed a model basically similar to our simple model variant. However, his method for model selection is different from ours. A non–probabilistic variant of our model with an associated learning problem was introduced in [7].

The rest of the paper is organized as follows. In Section 2 we describe the HMMs for modelling haplotype fragmentations. Section 3 gives MDL methods for selecting such models. Section 4 discusses briefly the possible applications of our models. As an example we analyze two real sets of haplotypes, one from lactose tolerant and the other from lactose intolerant humans. Section 5 concludes the paper.

We assume basic familiarity with HMM techniques as described e.g. in [2].

2   Fragmentation Models

2.1   Haplotype Fragmentation

We want to model by a designated HMM the haplotypes in a population of a species of interest. The haplotypes are over a fixed interval of consecutive genetic markers, say m markers numbered $1, 2, \ldots, m$ from left to right. The markers may be of any type such as biallelic SNPs (single nucleotide polymorphisms) or multiallelic microsatellite markers. The alleles are the possible alternative 'values' a marker can get in the DNA of different individuals of the same species. A biallelic SNP has two possible (or most frequently occurring) values that actually refer to two alternative nucleotides that may occur in the location of the SNP in the DNA sequence. Hence each marker i has a corresponding set A_i of possible alleles, and each haplotype over the m markers is simply a sequence of length m in $A_1 \times \ldots \times A_m$.

Our HMM will be based on the following scanario of the structure of the haplotypes as a result of the microevolutionary process that causes genetic variation within a species. We want to model the haplotypes of individuals in a population of some species such as humans. Let us think that the observed population was founded some generations ago by a group of 'founders'. According to the standard model of DNA microevolution, the DNA sequences of the current individuals are a result of iterated recombinations of the DNA of the founders, possibly corrupted by point mutations that, however, are considered rare. Simply stated, a recombination step produces from two DNA sequences a new sequence that consists of fragments taken alternatingly from the two parent sequences. The fragments are taken from the same locations of the parents as is their target location in the offspring sequence. Hence the nucleotides of the parent DNA shuffle in a novel way but retain their locations in the sequence.

The haplotypes reflect the same structure as they can be seen as subsequences obtained from the full DNA by restriction to the markers. So, if haplotype R is a recombination of haplotypes G and H, then all three can be written for some $c \geq 0$ as

$$R = G_1 H_1 G_2 H_2 \cdots G_c H_c$$
$$G = G_1 G_1' G_2 G_2' \cdots G_c G_c'$$
$$H = H_1' H_1 H_2' H_2 \cdots H_c' H_c$$

where $|G_i| = |H_i'| > 0$ for $1 \leq i \leq c$, and $|G_i'| = |H_i| > 0$ for $1 \leq i < c$ and $|G_c'| = |H_c| \geq 0$. Haplotype R has a cross-over between markers i and $i+1$ if the markers do not belong to the same fragment G_j or H_j for some j.

Assume that such recombination steps are applied repeatedly on an evolving set of sequences, starting from an initial set of founder haplotypes. Then a haplotype of a current individual is built from conserved sequence fragments that are taken from the haplotypes of the founders. In other words, each haplotype has a *parse*

$$f_1 f_2 \cdots f_h$$

where each f_i is a contiguous fragment taken from the same location of some founder haplotype, possibly with some rare changes due to point mutations. This parse is unknown. Our goal is to develop HMM modelling techniques that could help uncovering such parses as well as conserved haplotype segments.

To that end, we will introduce a family of HMMs whose states model the conserved sequence fragments and the transitions between the states model the cross-overs. The conserved fragments in the models will be taken from the sequences in $A_1 \times \cdots \times A_m$. The parameters of the HMM will be estimated from a training data that consists of some observed haplotypes in the current population. We will apply the minimum description length principle for the model selection to uncover the fragments that can be utilized in parsing several different haplotypes of the training data. Our model does not make any prior assumption on the distribution of the cross-over points that would prefer, say, a division of the haplotypes into global blocks between recombination 'hot spots'.

2.2   Model Architecture

A hidden Markov model $M = (F, \epsilon, W)$ for modeling haplotype fragmentation consists of a set F of the *states* of M, the *error parameter* $\epsilon \geq 0$ of M, and the *transition probabilities* W between the states of M.

Each state $f \in F$ is actually a haplotype fragment by which we mean contiguous segment of a possible haplotype between some *start marker* and some *end marker*, that is, f is an element of $A_s \times \cdots \times A_e$ where $1 \leq s \leq e \leq m$. We often call the states f the *fragments* of M. The start and end markers of f are denoted by $s(f)$ and $e(f)$, respectively.

The *emission probabilities* $P(d|f)$ of state (fragment) f give a probability distribution for fragments $d \in A_{s(f)} \times \cdots \times A_{e(f)}$ when the underlying founder fragment is f. This distribution will include a model for mutation and noise rates, specified by the noise parameter ϵ. It is also possible to incorporate a model for missing data which is useful if the model training data is incomplete. We adopt perhaps the simplest and most practical alternative, the missing–at–random model. Let us write $f = f_s \cdots f_e$ and $d = d_s \cdots d_e$. Assuming that the markers are independent of each other we have

$$P(d|f) = \prod_{i=s}^{e} P(d_i|f_i),$$

where we define

$$P(d_i|f_i) = \begin{cases} 1 & \text{if } d_i \text{ is missing} \\ 1 - \epsilon & \text{if } d_i = f_i \\ \epsilon/(|A_i| - 1) & \text{otherwise.} \end{cases}$$

We assume that a value for ϵ is a given constant and do not consider here its estimation from the data. Therefore we omit ϵ from the notation and denote a fragmentation model just as $M = (F, W)$.

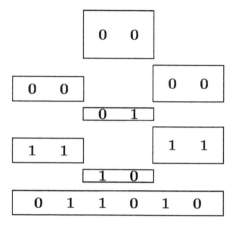

Fig. 1. A simple fragmentation model for haplotypes with 6 binary markers

Model M has a transition from state f to state g whenever f and g are adjacent, that is, if $e(f) + 1 = s(g)$. If this is the case, the transition probablity $W(f, g)$ is defined, otherwise not. The probabilities of the transitions from f must satisfy $\sum_{g \in F} W(f, g) = 1$.

A transition function W defined this way has the drawback of fairly large number of probabilities to estimate. Therefore we consider the following simplified version. A fragmentation model is called *simple* if all probabilities $W(f, g)$ for a fixed g but varying f are equal. Hence g is entered with the same probability, independently of the previous state f. Then we can write $W(f, g) = W(g)$, for short. A simple fragmentation model is specified by giving the fragments F, the transition probability $W(g)$ for each $g \in F$, and the error parameter ϵ. From now on, in the rest of the paper, we only consider the simple fragmentation models.

An example of a simple fragmentation model over 6 (binary) markers is shown in Figure 1. The fragments for the states are shown inside each rectangle, the height of which encodes the corresponding transition probability. For example, each of the three states whose start marker is 1 have transition probability $1/3$, and the three states with start marker 3 have transition probabilities $2/3$, $1/6$, and $1/6$. When $\epsilon = 0$ this model generates haplotype 000000 with probability $1/3 \cdot 2/3 \cdot 1/2 = 1/9$ (the only path emitting this sequence with non-zero probability goes through the three states with fragment 00), and haplotype 111111 with probability 0.

2.3 Emission Probability Distribution

Let us recall how a hidden Markov model associates probabilities to the sequences it emits. A *path* through a simple fragmentation model $M = (F, W)$ over m markers is any sequence $(F_1, \ldots, F_h)$ of states of M such that $s(F_1) = 1$, $e(F_i) +$

$1 = s(F_{i+1})$ for $1 \leq i < h$, and $e(F_h) = m$. Let π be the set of all paths through M.

Consider then the probability of emitting a haplotype $H = H_1 \cdots H_m$. Some allele values may be missing in H. The probability that H is emitted from path $(F_1, \ldots, F_h)$ is

$$P(H, (F_1, \ldots, F_h)|M) = \prod_{i=1}^{h} W(F_i)P(H_{s(F_i)} \cdots H_{e(F_i)}|F_i)$$

which simply is the probability that the path is taken and each state along the path emits the corresponding fraction of H, the emission probabilities being as already defined. The probability that M emits H is then

$$P(H|M) = \sum_{(F_1, \ldots, F_h) \in \pi} P(H, (F_1, \ldots, F_h)|M). \tag{1}$$

3   MDL Method for Model Selection

3.1   Description Length

Let D be our training data consisting of n observed haplotypes $D_1, \ldots, D_n$ over m markers. The minimum description length (MDL) principle of Rissanen considers the description of the data D using two components: description of the model M and description of the data D given the model. Hence the total description length for the model and the data is

$$L(M, D) = L(M) + L(D|M)$$

where $L(M)$ is the length of the description of M and $L(D|M)$ is the length of the description of D when D is described using M.

The MDL principle states that the desired descriptions of the data are the ones having the minimum length $L(M, D)$ of the total description. For a survey of the connections between MDL, Bayesian statistics, and machine learning see [9,5].

To apply this principle we have to fix the encoding scheme that will give $L(M)$ and $L(D|M)$ for each particular M and D.

The model $M = (F, W)$ can be described by telling what are the fragments F_i in F and where they start. The transition probabilities $W(F_i)$ should also be given. The error parameter ϵ is assumed constant and hence it needs not to be encoded.

To encode fragment F_i we use

$$L(F_i) = \sum_{j=s(F_i)}^{e(F_i)} \log |A_j| + \log m$$

bits where $\log |A_j|$ bits are used for representing the corresponding allele of F_i, and $\log m$ bits are used for $s(F_i)$. The probabilities $W(F_i)$ are real numbers.

Theoretical arguments [5] indicate that an appropriate coding precision is obtained by choosing to use $\frac{1}{2} \log n$ bits for each independent real parameter of the model; recall that n is the size of training data D. In our case there are $|F| - t$ independent probability values where t denotes the number of different start markers of the fragments in F. One of the probabilities $W(F_i)$ for fragments F_i with the same $s(F_i)$ namely follows from the others as their sum has to equal 1. Thus the total model length becomes

$$L(M) = \sum_{i=1}^{|F|} L(F_i) + \frac{|F| - t}{2} \log n$$

$$= \sum_{i=1}^{|F|} (\sum_{j=s(F_i)}^{e(F_i)} \log |A_j| + \log m) + \frac{|F| - t}{2} \log n. \qquad (2)$$

Using the relation of coding lengths and probabilities [5], we use

$$L(D|M) = - \log \prod_{i=1}^{n} P(D_i|M) = - \sum_{i=1}^{n} \log P(D_i|M) \qquad (3)$$

bits for describing the data D, given the fragmentation model M. Here probabilities $P(D_i|M)$ can be evaluated using (1).

We are left with designing an algorithm that solves the MDL minimization problem. One has to find an $M = (F, W)$ for a fixed error parameter ϵ that minimizes $L(M) + L(D|M)$ for a given data D.

3.2   Greedy Algorithms for MDL Optimization

As solving the MDL optimization exactly in this case seems difficult we give a greedy approximation algorithm. The algorithm has to solve two tasks that are to some degree independent. First, one has to find a good fragment set F for the model. Note that the model length $L(M)$ depends only on F (and on n). Second, for a fixed F one has to find a good W such that $L(D|M)$ is minimized.

Let us consider the second task first. Given F and D, we will use the well-known expectation maximization (EM) algorithm for finding W that gives (locally) maximum $P(D|M)$ from which we get minimum $L(D|M)$; see e.g. [2, pp 63–64]. The EM algorithm, delinated as Algorithm 1 below, starts with some initial W and then computes the expected number of times each state of the model with the current W is used when emitting D. These values are normalized to give updated W. The process is repeated with the new W until convergence (or a given number K of times). When converged, local maximum likelihood estimates for W have been obtained.

Algorithm 1. EM–algorithm for finding W for a model $M = (F, W)$.

1. Initialize W somehow.

2. (E–step) For each training data sequence $D_i \in D$ and fragment $f \in F$, compute $q_i(f)$ as the probability that M emits $D_{i,s(f)} \cdots D_{i,e(f)}$ from f. This can be done using the standard Forward and Backward algorithms for HMMs.

3. (M–step) For each fragment f, let $q(f) \leftarrow \sum_{i=1}^{n} q_i(f)$. Finally set

$$W(f) \leftarrow \frac{q(f)}{\sum_{f' \in F(s(f))} q(f')}$$

where $F(s(f))$ denotes the subset of F that consists of all fragments having the same start marker as f.

4. Repeat steps 2 and 3 until convergence (or until a given number of iterations have taken).

We will denote by $EM(F)$ the W obtained by Algorithm 1 for a set F of fragments.

To analyze the running time of Algorithm 1, assume that we have precomputed the probabilities $P(D_{i,s(f)} \cdots D_{i,e(f)}|f)$ for each $f \in F$ and $D_i \in D$. Then the Forward and Backward algorithms in step 2 just spend a constant time per each fragment when they scan F from left to right and from right to left, respectively. This happens for each D_i. Hence step 2 needs time $O(n|F|)$. This obviously dominates the time requirement of step 3, too. So we obtain the following remark.

Proposition 1. *Algorithm 1 (EM algorithm) for* $M = (F,W)$ *takes time* $O(Kn|F|)$ *where* K *is the number of iterations taken.*

Let us then return to the first task, selecting fragment set F. According to our definition of fragmentation models, set F should be selected from the set of all possible fragments of the sequences in $A_1 \times \cdots \times A_m$. As this search space is of exponential sixe in m, we restrict the search in practice to the fragments that are present in D. Let us denote as $\Phi(D) = \{D_{i,j} \cdots D_{i,k} \mid D_i \in D, 1 \le j \le k \le m\}$ the initial set of frgments obtained in this way. Then $|\Phi(D)| = O(nm^2)$.

We select F from $\Phi(D)$ using a simple greedy strategy: delete from $\Phi(D)$ the fragment whose elimination maximally improves the score $L(M) + L(D|M)$. If a fragment is deleted, then one has to remove also all other fragments that the deletion makes isolated. A fragment is isolated if no path through the model can contain it, which is easy to test. Repeat deletions until the score does not improve. The remaining set of fragments is F. This method is given in more detail as Algorithm 2.

Algorithm 2. Basic greedy MDL learning

Notation: $M(-f) =$ the model that is obtained from the current model $M = (F,W)$ by deleting fragment f and all fragments that become isolated as a side–effect of the removal of f from F and by updating W by Algorithm 1 such that $L(D|M(-F))$ is minimal.

1 Initialize $M = (F, W)$ as $F \leftarrow \Phi(D)$; $W \leftarrow EM(\Phi(D))$
2 Return Greedy(M) where procedure Greedy is as follows.

procedure Greedy(M), where $M = (F, W)$
    do
        $L \leftarrow L(M) + L(D|M)$
        $\Delta \leftarrow \max_{f \in F}(L - [L(M(-f)) + L(D|M(-f))])$
        $f_\Delta \leftarrow \arg\max_{f \in F}(L - [L(M(-f)) + L(D|M(-f))])$
        if $\Delta > 0$ **then** $M \leftarrow M(-f_\Delta)$
    until $\Delta \leq 0$
    return M
end Greedy

To implement Algorithm 2 efficiently one has to precompute the coding lengths of all the fragments in $\Phi(D)$. This can be done in time $O(|\Phi(D)|)$ as the length only depends on the location of the fragment but not on the content. Then $L(M)$ can be evaluated for any $M = (F, W)$ in time $O(|F|) = O(|\Phi(D)|)$. Training a new $M(-f)$ by Algorithm 1 can be done in time $O(Kn|F|) = O(Kn|\Phi(D)|)$ where K is the parameter limiting the number of iterations. To find Δ and f_Δ in procedure Greedy, a straightforward implementation just tries each $f \in F$, taking time $O(Kn|\Phi(D)|^2)$. This will be repeated until nothing can be deleted from the set of fragments, i.e., $O(|\Phi(D)|)$ times. The total time of Algorithm 2 hence becomes $O(Kn|\Phi(D)|^3) = O(Kn^4 m^6)$.

As Algorithm 2 can be practical only for very small m and n, we next develop a faster incremental version of the greedy MDL training. This algorithm contructs intermediate models using the initial segments of the sequences in D, in increasing order of the length. A model, denoted M_{j+1} for the initial segments of length $j + 1$ will be constructed by expanding and retraining the model M_j obtained in the previous phase for the initial segments of length j.

Let $\Phi_j(D) = \{D_{i,k} \cdots D_{i,j} \mid D_i \in D, 1 \leq k \leq j\}$ be the set of fragments of D that end at marker j. To get M_{j+1}, fragments $\Phi_{j+1}(D)$ are added to M_j and then the useless fragments are eliminated as in Algorithm 2 by procedure Greedy to get M_{j+1}. Adding the fragments in such smaller portions to the optimization leads to a faster algorithm.

A detail needs additional care. Adding $\Phi_{j+1}(D)$ alone to the set of fragments may introduce isolated fragments that have no possibility to survive in the MDL optimization because they are never reached although they could be useful in encoding the data. To keep the new set of fragments connected we therefore also add fragments that bridge the gaps between the old fragments inherited from M_j and the new fragments in $\Phi_{j+1}(D)$. We use the following bridging strategy that by adding only the shortest bridges keeps the number of bridging fragments relatively small. We say that the set $\gamma(F)$ of the *gaps* of a fragment set F consists of all pairs (k, h) of integers such that $k - 1 = e(f)$ for some $f \in F$ but there is no $f \in F$ such that $k \leq e(f) \leq h$. Then define $\Phi_j(D, F) = \Phi_j(D) \cup \{D_{i,k} \cdots D_{i,h} \mid D_i \in D, (k, h) \in \gamma(F), h < j\}$. Now, we add for the new round the set $\Phi_{j+1}(D, F_j)$ where F_j is the fragment set of M_j.

Algorithm 3. Incremental greedy MDL learning

Notation: Procedure Greedy as in Algorithm 2.

1. Initialize $M = (F, W)$ as $F \leftarrow \emptyset$; $W \leftarrow \emptyset$
2. **for** $j \leftarrow 1, \ldots, m$ **do**

$$(F, W) \leftarrow \text{Greedy}(F \cup \Phi_j(D, F), EM(F \cup \Phi_j(D, F)))$$

3. **return** $M = (F, W)$.

For a running time analysis of Algorithm 3 assume that the greedy MDL optimization is able to reduce the the size of the fragment set in each phase to $O(mn)$. This is a plausible assumption as the size of D is mn. Then the size of each $F \cup \Phi_j(D, E)$ given to procedure Greedy in step 2 stays $O(mn)$. Hence Greedy generates $O(m^2n^2)$ calls of Algorithm 1, each taking time $O(Kmn^2)$. This is repeated m times, giving altogether $O(m^3n^2)$ calls of Algorithm 1 and total time $O(Km^4n^4)$ for Algorithm 3.

Adding new fragments into the optimization in still smaller portions can in some cases give better running times (but possibly at the expense of weaker optimization results). One can for example divide $\Phi_j(D)$ into fractions $\Phi_{k,j}(D)$ consisting of equally long fragments which start at marker k and end at j. The greedy MDL optimization is performed after adding the next $\Phi_{k,j}(D)$ and the necessary bridging fragments.

4   Using the Fragmentation Models

Once we have trained a model M, the numerous possibilities of applying such an HMM become available. We delineate here some of them.

1. Parsing haplotypes. Given some haplotype H, the path through M that has the highest emission probability of H is called the *Viterbi path* of H. Such a path can be efficiently found by standard dynamic programming, e.g. [2]. The fragments on this path give a natural parsing of H in terms of the fragments of M. The parse is the most probable decomposition of H into conserved pieces as proposed by M. Such a parse can be visualized by associating a unique color with each fragment of M, and then showing the parse of H with the colors of the corresponding fragments. Using the same color for conserved pieces seems a natural idea, independently proposed at least in [15,17].

2. Cross–over and fragment usage probabilities. The probability that M assigns a cross–over between the markers i and $i+1$ of haplotype H can be computed simply as the fraction between the probability of emitting H along paths having a cross–over in that point and the total probability $P(H|M)$ of emitting H along any path. Similarly, the probability that a certain fragment of M is used for emitting H is the fraction between the emission probability of H along paths containing this fragment and $P(H|M)$.

3. Comparisons between populations and case/control studies. Assume that we have available training data sets D^i from different populations. Then the corresponding trained models M^i can be used for example for classifying new haplotypes H on the basis of emission probabilities $P(H|M^i)$. The structure of the models M^i may also uncover interesting differences between the populations. For example, some strong fragments may be characteristic of a certain population but missing elsewhere. Also, the average length of the fragments should be related to the age of the population. An older population has experienced more recombinations, hence its fragments should be shorter on average as those of a younger population.

To demonstrate our methods we conclude by analyzing two real datasets related to the lactase nonpersistence (lactose intolerance) of humans [16]. Lactase nonpersistence limits the use of fresh milk among adults. The digestion of milk is catalyzed by an enzyme lactase (also called lactase–phlorizin hydrolase or LHP). Lactase activity is high during infancy but in most mammals declines after the weaning phase. In some healthy humans, however, lactase activity persists at high level throughout adult life, and this is known as lactase persistence. People with lactase nonpersistence have a much lower lactose digestion capacity than those with lactase persistence. A recent study [3] of a DNA region containing LCT, the gene encoding LHP, revealed that in certain Finnish populations a DNA variant (that is, an SNP), C/T_{-13910}, almost 14 kb upstream from the LCT locus, completely associates with verified lactase nonpersistence.

The datasets we analyse consist of haplotypes over 23 SNP markers in the vicinity of this particular SNP. The first dataset D_+, the persistent haplotypes, consists of 38 haplotypes of lactase persistent individuals, and the second dataset D_-, the nonpersistent haplotypes, consists of 21 haplotypes of lactase nonpersistent individuals. We trained models for datasets D_-, D_+, and $D_+ \cup D_-$ using Algorithm 3 with $\epsilon = 0.001$ and $K = 3$ iterations of the EM algorithm. Figures 2, 3, and 4 show the result. The fragments are shown as colored rectangles. Their height encodes the transition probability somewhat differently from the encoding used in Fig. 1. Here the height of fragment f gives the value $\tilde{W}(f) = q(f)/n$ where $q(f)$ is as in Algorithm 1 after the last iteration taken, and n is the number of haplotypes in the training data. Hence the height represents the avarage usage of f when the model emits the training data. The measure $\tilde{W}(f)$ describes the importance of each fragment for the training data better than the plain transition probability $W(f)$.

We observe that the model for persistent haplotypes has on average longer fragments than the model for nonpersistent haplotypes. This suggests, consistently with common belief, that lactase persistence is the younger of the two traits. When analyzing the Viterbi paths in the model for $D_+ \cup D_-$, we observed that all such paths for persistent haplotypes go through the large fragment in the middle of the model (number 4 from the top), while none of the Viterbi paths for the nonpersistent haplotypes includes it.

We also sampled two thirds of D_+ and D_- and trained models for the two samples. Let M_+ and M_- be the two models obtained. We then com-

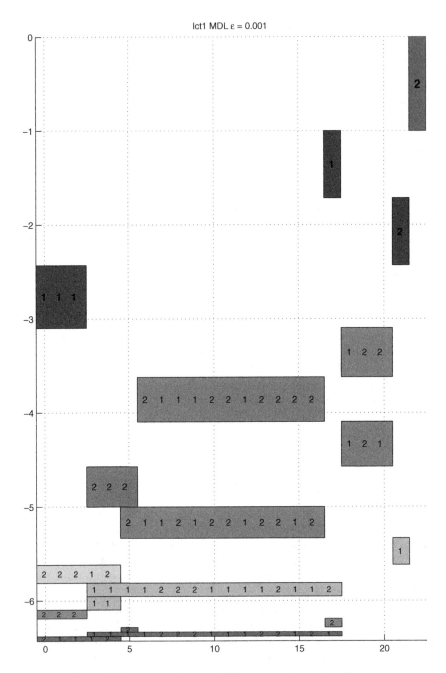

Fig. 2. A fragmentation model for nonpersistent haplotypes.

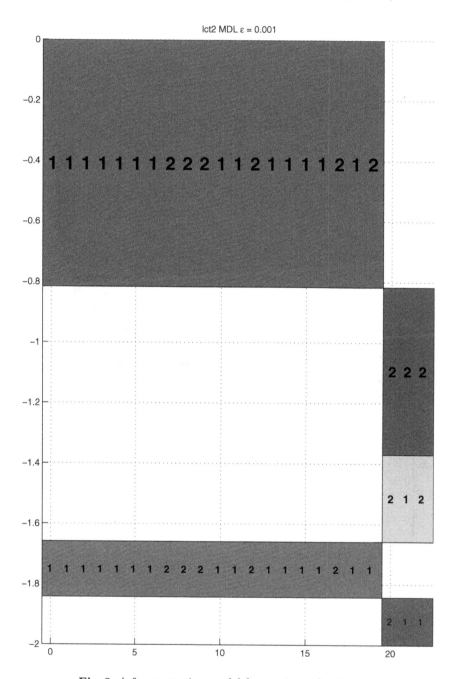

Fig. 3. A fragmentation model for persistent haplotypes.

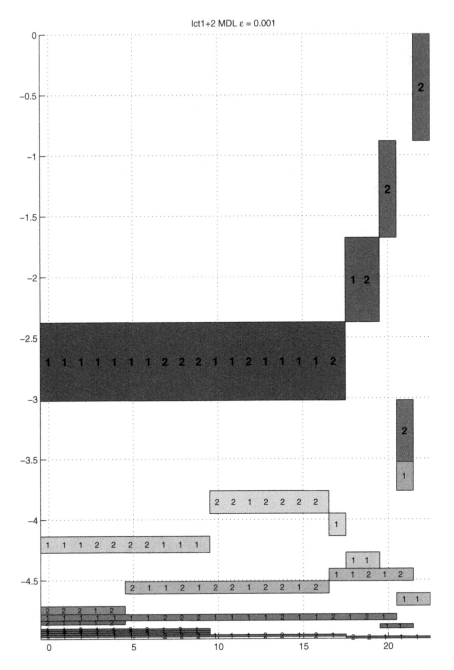

Fig. 4. A fragmentation model for the union of persistent and nonpersistent haplotypes

puted for all test haplotypes H outside the training samples the quantity $Q(H) = \log_{10} P(H|M_+)/P(H|M_-)$. One obviously expects that $Q(H) > 0$ when H is a persistent haplotype and $Q(H) < 0$ otherwise. Satisfyingly we found out in this experiment, that $Q(H)$ varied from 6.0 to 11.8 for persistent test haplotypes and from -2.6 to -44.7 for nonpersistent test haplotypes.

5 Conclusion

While our experimental evaluation of the methods suggests that useful results can be obtained in this way, many aspects still need further work. More experimental evaluation on generated and real data is necessary. We only used the simple models but also the general case should be considered. The approximation algorithm for the MDL learning seems to work quite robustly but theoretical analysis of its performance is missing. Also faster variants of the learning algorithm may be necessary for larger data. It may also be useful to relax the model such that the fragments of the model are not required to cover the haplotypes entirely but small gaps between them are allowed.

References

[1] M. Daly, J. Rioux, S. Schaffner, T. Hudson, and E. Lander. High–resolution haplotype structure in the human genome. *Nature Genetics* 29: 229–232, 2001.

[2] R. Durbin, S. R. Eddy, A. Krogh, and G. Mitchison. *Biological Sequence Analysis: Probabilistic Models of Proteins and Nucleic Acids.* Cambridge University Press 1998.

[3] N. S. Enattah, T. Sahi, E. Savilahti, J. D. Terwilliger, L. Peltonen, and I. Järvelä. Identification of a variant associated with adult–type hypolactasia. *Nature Genetics* 30: 233-237, 2002.

[4] S. B. Gabriel, S. F. Schaffner, H. Ngyen, J. M. Moore *et al.* The structure of haplotype blocks in the human genome. *Science* 296: 2225–2229, 2002.

[5] M. H. Hansen and B. Yu. Model selection and the principle of minimum description length. *Journal of the American Statistical Association* 96: 746–774, 2001.

[6] M. Koivisto, M. Perola, T. Varilo, W. Hennah, J. Ekelund, M. Lukk, L. Peltonen, E. Ukkonen, and H. Mannila. An MDL method for finding haplotype blocks and for estimating the strength of haplotype block boundaries. In: *Proc. Pacific Symposium on Biocomputing*, 502–513, World Scientific 2003.

[7] M. Koivisto, P. Rastas, and E. Ukkonen. Recombination systems. In: *Theory is Forever – Essays dedicated to Arto Salomaa, LNCS* 3113: 159–169, 2004.

[8] A. Krogh, M. Brown, I. S. Mian, K. Sjölander, and D. Haussler. Hidden Markov models in computational biology: Applications to protein modeling. *J. Mol. Biol.* 235: 1501-1531, 1994.

[9] M. Li and P. Vitanyi. *An Introduction to Kolmogorov Complexity and its Applications.* Springer–Verlag 1997.

[10] N. Patil, A. J. Berno, D. A. Hinds, W. A. Barrett *et al.* Blocks of limited haplotype diversity revealed by high–resolution scanning of human chromosome 21. *Science* 294: 1719–1723, 2001.

[11] M. S. Phillips, R. Lawrence, R. Sachidanandam, A. P. Morris, D. J. Balding *et al.* Chromosome–wide distribution of haplotype blocks and the role of recombination hot spots. *Nature Genetics* 33: 382–387, 2003.

[12] J. Rissanen. Modeling by shortest data description. *Automatica* 14: 465–471, 1978.

[13] J. Rissanen. Stochastic complexity. *J. Royal Statistical Society* B 49: 223–239, 1987.

[14] R. Schwartz. Haplotype motifs: An algorithmic approach to locating evolutionarily conserved patterns in haploid sequences. *Proc. Computational Systems Bioinformatics (CSB'03)*, 306–314, IEEE Computer Society 2003.

[15] R. Schwartz, A. G. Clark, and S. Istrail. Methods for inferring block–wise ancestral history from haploid sequences: The haplotype coloring problem. *WABI 2002, LNCS* 2452, 44–59.

[16] D. M. Swallow. Genetics of lactase persistence and lactose intolerance. *Annu. Rev. Genet.* 37: 197–219, 2003.

[17] E. Ukkonen. Finding founder sequences from a set of recombinants. *WABI 2002, LNCS* 2452, 277–286.

[18] K. Zhang, M. Deng, T. Chen, M. S. Waterman and F. Sun. A dynamic programming algorithm for haplotype block partition. *PNAS* 99: 7335–7339, 2002.

Learning, Logic, and Probability:
A Unified View

Pedro Domingos

Department of Computer Science and Engineering
University of Washington
Seattle, WA 98195, U.S.A.
pedrod@cs.washington.edu
http://www.cs.washington.edu/homes/pedrod

AI systems must be able to learn, reason logically, and handle uncertainty. While much research has focused on each of these goals individually, only recently have we begun to attempt to achieve all three at once. In this talk, I describe Markov logic, a representation that combines the full power of first-order logic and probabilistic graphical models, and algorithms for learning and inference in it. Syntactically, Markov logic is first-order logic augmented with a weight for each formula. Semantically, a set of Markov logic formulas represents a probability distribution over possible worlds, in the form of a Markov network with one feature per grounding of a formula in the set, with the corresponding weight. Formulas and weights are learned from relational databases using inductive logic programming and iterative optimization of a pseudo-likelihood measure. Inference is performed by Markov chain Monte Carlo over the minimal subset of the ground network required for answering the query. Experiments in a real-world university domain illustrate the promise of this approach.

This work, joint with Matthew Richardson, is described in further detail in Domingos and Richardson [1] and Richardson and Domingos [2].

References

[1] Domingos, P., & Richardson, M.: Markov logic: A unifying framework for statistical relational learning. In *Proceedings of the ICML-2004 Workshop on Statistical Relational Learning and its Connections to Other Fields*, Banff, Alberta, Canada (2004). http://www.cs.washington.edu/homes/pedrod/mus.pdf
[2] Richardson, M., & Domingos, P.: *Markov Logic Networks*. Technical Report, Department of Computer Science and Engineering, University of Washington, Seattle, Washington, U.S.A. (2004).
http://www.cs.washington.edu/homes/pedrod/mln.pdf

S. Ben-David, J. Case, A. Maruoka (Eds.): ALT 2004, LNAI 3244, p. 53, 2004.
© Springer-Verlag Berlin Heidelberg 2004

Learning Languages from Positive Data and Negative Counterexamples

Sanjay Jain[1*] and Efim Kinber[2]

[1] School of Computing, National University of Singapore, Singapore 117543.
sanjay@comp.nus.edu.sg
[2] Department of Computer Science, Sacred Heart University, Fairfield,
CT 06432-1000, U.S.A.
kinbere@sacredheart.edu

Abstract. In this paper we introduce a paradigm for learning in the limit of potentially infinite languages from all positive data and negative counterexamples provided in response to the conjectures made by the learner. Several variants of this paradigm are considered that reflect different conditions/constraints on the type and size of negative counterexamples and on the time for obtaining them. In particular, we consider the models where 1) a learner gets the least negative counterexample; 2) the size of a negative counterexample must be bounded by the size of the positive data seen so far; 3) a counterexample may be delayed. Learning power, limitations of these models, relationships between them, as well as their relationships with classical paradigms for learning languages in the limit (without negative counterexamples) are explored. Several surprising results are obtained. In particular, for Gold's model of learning requiring a learner to syntactically stabilize on correct conjectures, learners getting negative counterexamples immediately turn out to be as powerful as the ones that do not get them for indefinitely (but finitely) long time (or are only told that their latest conjecture is not a subset of the target language, without any specific negative counterexample). Another result shows that for behaviourally correct learning (where semantic convergence is required from a learner) with negative counterexamples, a learner making just one error in almost all its conjectures has the "ultimate power": it can learn the class of all recursively enumerable languages. Yet another result demonstrates that sometimes positive data and negative counterexamples provided by a teacher are not enough to compensate for full positive and negative data.

1 Introduction

Defining a computational model adequately describing learning languages is an important long-standing problem. In his classical paper [Gol67], M. Gold introduced two major computational models for learning languages. One of them, learning from texts, assumes that the learner receives all positive language data,

---

* Supported in part by NUS grant number R252-000-127-112.

S. Ben-David, J. Case, A. Maruoka (Eds.): ALT 2004, LNAI 3244, pp. 54–68, 2004.

i.e., all correct statements of the language. The other model, learning from informants, assumes that the learner receives all correct statements of the languages, as well as all other (incorrect) statements, appropriately labeled as incorrect, that can be potentially formed within the given alphabet. In both cases, a successful learner stabilizes at a correct description of the target language, i.e., a grammar for the target language. J. Barzdin [B̄74] and J. Case and C. Smith [CS83] introduced a different, more powerful model called *behaviorally correct* learning. A behaviorally correct learner almost always outputs conjectures (not necessarily the same) correctly describing the target language. An important feature of all these models is that they describe a process of learning in the limit: the learner stabilizes to the correct conjecture (or conjectures), but does not know when it happens. The above seminal models, doubtless, represent certain important aspects of the process of learning potentially infinite targets. On the other hand, when we consider how a child learns a language communicating with a teacher, it becomes clear that these models reflect two extremes of this process: positive data only is certainly less than what a child actually gets in the learning process, while informant (the characteristic function of the language) is much more than what a learner can expect (see for example, [BH70,HPTS84, DPS86]).

D. Angluin, in another seminal paper [Ang88], introduced a different important learning paradigm, i.e., learning from queries to a teacher (oracle). This model, explored in different contexts, including learning languages (see, for example, [LNZ02]), addresses a very important tool available to a child (or any other reasonable learner), i.e., queries to a teacher. However, in the context of learning languages, this model does not adequately reflect the fact that a learner, in the long process of acquisition of a new language, potentially gets access to all correct statements. (Exploration of computability via queries to oracles has a long tradition in the theory of computation in general [Rog67,GM98], as well as in the context of learning in the limit [GP89,FGJ+94,LNZ02]. Whereas in most cases answers to queries are sometimes not algorithmically answerable - which is the case in our model, or computationally NP or even harder - as in [Ang88], exploring computability or learnability via oracles often provides a deeper insight on the nature and capabilities of both).

In this paper, we combine learning from positive data and learning from queries into a computational model, where a learner gets all positive data and can ask a teacher if a current conjecture (a grammar) does not generate wrong statements (questions of this kind can be formalized as *subset queries*, cf. [Ang88]). If the conjecture does generate a wrong statement, then the teacher gives an example of such a statement (a negative counterexample) to the learner. In our main model, we assume that the teacher immediately provides a negative counterexample if it exists. However, in many situations, a teacher may obviously need a lot of time to determine if the current conjecture generates incorrect statements. Therefore, we consider two more variants of our main model that reflect this problem. In the first variant, the teacher is not able to provide a negative counterexample unless there is one whose size does not exceed the size of the longest statement seen so far by the learner. In the second variant (not considered in this version due to space restrictions), the teacher may delay providing a negative counterexample. Interestingly, while the former model is shown to be weaker than the main model, the latter one turns out to be as powerful as the main model (in terms of capabilities of a learner; we do not discuss related complexity issues – such as how providing counterexamples quickly may speed up convergence to a right conjecture)!

Our goal in this paper is to explore the new models of learning languages, their relationships, and how they fair in comparison with other popular learning paradigms. In particular, we explore how quality and availability of the negative counterexamples to the conjectures affects learnability. Note that learning from positive data and a finite amount of negative information was explored in [BCJ95]. However, unlike arbitrary negative counterexamples in our model, negative data in [BCJ95] is *preselected* to ensure that just a small number of negative examples (or, just one example) can greatly enhance capabilities of a learner. [Shi86] and [Mot92] also considered restricted models of learning from negative examples.

The paper is structured as follows. In Section 2 we introduce necessary notation and basic definitions needed for the rest of the paper. In particular, we define some variants of the classical Gold's model of learning from texts (positive data) and informants (both positive and negative data), **TxtEx** and **InfEx**, as well as its behaviorally correct counterpart **TxtBc** and **InfBc**.

In Section 3 we define our three models for learning languages from texts and negative counterexamples. In the first, basic, model, a learner is provided a negative counterexample every time when it outputs a hypothesis containing elements not belonging to the target language. The second model is a variant of the basic model when a learner receives the least negative counterexample. The third model takes into account some complexity constraints. Namely, the learner receives a negative counterexample only if there exists one whose size is bounded by the size of the longest positive example seen in the input so far. (In the full version of the paper we consider also a model which slightly relaxes the constraint of the model three: the size of the negative counterexample must be bounded by the value of some function applied to the size of the longest positive example in the input.)

Section 4 is devoted to **Ex**-style learning from positive data and negative counterexamples: the learner eventually stabilizes to a correct grammar for the target language. First, in order to demonstrate the power of our basic model, we show that any indexed class of recursively enumerable languages can be learned by a suitable learner in this model. Then we show that the second model is equivalent to the basic model: providing the least negative counterexample does not enhance the power of a learner. Our next major result (Theorem 4) is somewhat surprising: we show that there is a class of languages learnable from informants and not learnable in our basic model. This means that sometimes negative counterexamples are not enough - the learner must have access to all statements not belonging to the language! (This result follows from a more general result for

Bc-style learning in Section 5). In particular, this result establishes certain constraints on the learning power of our basic model. The proof of this result employs a new diagonalization technique working against machines learning via negative counterexamples. We also establish a hierarchy of learning capabilities in our basic model based on the number of errors that learner is allowed to have in the final hypothesis. Then we consider the model with restricted size of negative counterexamples (described above). We show that this model is different and weaker than our basic model. Still we show that this model is quite powerful: firstly, if restricted to the classes of infinite languages, they are equivalent to the basic model, and, secondly there are learnable classes in these models that cannot be learned in classical **Bc**-model (without negative counterexamples) - even if an arbitrary finite number of errors is allowed in the correct conjectures. Corollary 2 to the proof of Theorem 7 shows that there exists an indexed class of recursively enumerable languages that cannot be learned with negative counterexamples of restricted size (note that all such classes are learnable in our basic **Ex**-style model as stated in Theorem 1).

Section 5 is devoted to our **Bc**-style models. As in the case of **Ex**-style learning, we show that providing the least negative counterexample does not enhance the power of a learner. Then we show that languages learnable in our basic **Bc**-style model (without errors) are **Bc**-learnable from informants. In the end we establish one of our most surprising results. First, we demonstrate that the power of our basic **Bc**-style model is limited: there are classes of recursively enumerable languages not learnable in this model if no errors in almost all (correct) conjectures are allowed. On the other hand, there exists a learner that can learn all recursively enumerable languages in this model with at most one error in almost all correct conjectures! Based on similar ideas, we obtain some other related results - in particular, that, with one error allowed in almost all correct conjectures, the class of all infinite recursively enumerable languages is learnable in the model with restricted size of negative counterexamples. To prove these results, we developed a new type of learning algorithms, where a learner makes deliberate error in its conjectures to force a teacher to answer questions not directly related to the input language. In contrast to the case with no errors, we also show that when errors are allowed, **Bc**-learning from informants is a proper subset of our basic model of **Bc**-learning with errors and negative counterexamples (Corollary 4).

We also considered variants of the basic model when negative counterexamples are delayed or not provided at all (in the latter case the learner just gets the answer "no" if a current conjecture is not a subset of the input language; this model corresponds to learning with restricted subset queries [Ang88]). We showed that, surprisingly, both these variants are equivalent to the basic model! In other words, in the subset queries about the conjectures, the learner does not even need counterexamples - just the answers "yes" or "no" are enough (of course, the lack of counterexamples may delay convergence to the right conjecture, but we do not address this issue). To prove these results, we developed and employed for our model a variant of *stabilizing/locking sequence* [JORS99]. This topic is handled in the full version of the paper.

2   Notation and Preliminaries

Any unexplained recursion theoretic notation is from [Rog67]. The symbol N denotes the set of natural numbers, $\{0, 1, 2, 3, \ldots\}$. Cardinality of a set S is denoted by card(S). $L_1 \Delta L_2$ denotes the symmetric difference of L_1 and L_2, that is $L_1 \Delta L_2 = (L_1 - L_2) \cup (L_2 - L_1)$. For a natural number a, we say that $L_1 =^a L_2$, iff card($L_1 \Delta L_2) \leq a$. We say that $L_1 =^* L_2$, iff card($L_1 \Delta L_2) < \infty$. If $L_1 =^a L_2$, then we say that L_1 is an a-variant of L_2.

We let $\{W_i\}_{i \in N}$ denote an acceptable numbering of all r.e. sets. Symbol $\mathcal{E}$ will denote the set of all r.e. languages. Symbol L, with or without decorations, ranges over $\mathcal{E}$. By χ_L we denote the characteristic function of L. By $\overline{L}$, we denote the complement of L, that is $N - L$. Symbol $\mathcal{L}$, with or without decorations, ranges over subsets of $\mathcal{E}$. By $W_{i,s}$ we denote the set W_i enumerated within s steps, in some standard method of enumerating W_i.

We now present concepts from language learning theory. A *text* (see [Gol67]) is a mapping from N to $N \cup \{\#\}$. We let T range over texts. content(T) is defined to be the set of natural numbers in the range of T (i.e. content(T) = range(T) $- \{\#\}$). T is a *text for* L iff content(T) $= L$. That means a text for L is an infinite sequence whose range, except for a possible $\#$, is just L. Intuitively, $T(i)$ represents the $(i+1)$-th element in a presentation of L, with $\#$'s representing pauses in the presentation. $T[n]$ denotes the finite initial sequence, $T(0), T(1), \ldots, T(i-1)$, of T of length n. A finite sequence is an initial sequence of a text (i.e., it is a mapping from an initial segment of N into $(N \cup \{\#\})$). The *content* of a finite sequence σ, denoted content(σ), is the set of natural numbers in the range of σ. The empty sequence is denoted by Λ. The *length* of σ, denoted by $|\sigma|$, is the number of elements in σ. So, $|\Lambda| = 0$. For $n \leq |\sigma|$, the initial sequence of σ of length n is denoted by $\sigma[n]$. We let σ, τ, and γ range over finite sequences. We denote the sequence formed by the concatenation of τ at the end of σ by $\sigma\tau$. SEQ denotes the set of all finite sequences.

We say that a recursive function I is an informant for L iff for all x, $I(x) = (x, \chi_L(x))$. Intuitively, informants give both all positive and all negative data on the language being learned. $I[n]$ is the first n elements of the informant I.

A language learning machine (from texts) is a computable mapping from SEQ into N. One can similarly define language learning machines from informants. We let $\mathbf{M}$, with or without decorations, range over learning machines. $\mathbf{M}(T[n])$ (or $\mathbf{M}(I[n])$) is interpreted as the grammar (index for an accepting program) conjectured by the learning machine $\mathbf{M}$ on the initial sequence $T[n]$ (or $I[n]$). We say that $\mathbf{M}$ converges on T to i, (written: $\mathbf{M}(T){\downarrow} = i$) iff $(\forall^\infty n)[\mathbf{M}(T[n]) = i]$. Convergence on informants is similarly defined.

There are several criteria for a learning machine to be successful on a language. Below we define some of them. All of the criteria defined below are variants of the **Ex**-style and **Bc**-style learning described in the Introduction; in addition, they allow a finite number of errors in almost all conjectures (uniformly bounded, or arbitrary).

Definition 1. [Gol67,CL82] Suppose $a \in N \cup \{*\}$.

(a) **M TxtEx^a**-*identifies an r.e. language* L (written: $L \in \mathbf{TxtEx}^a(\mathbf{M})$) just in case for all texts T for L, $(\exists i \mid W_i =^a \text{content}(T))$ $(\forall^\infty n)[\mathbf{M}(T[n]) = i]$.

(b) **M TxtEx^a**-*identifies a class* $\mathcal{L}$ *of r.e. languages* (written: $\mathcal{L} \subseteq$ **TxtEx^a(M)**) just in case **M TxtEx^a**-identifies each language from $\mathcal{L}$.

(c) **TxtEx^a** $= \{\mathcal{L} \subseteq \mathcal{E} \mid (\exists \mathbf{M})[\mathcal{L} \subseteq \mathbf{TxtEx}^a(\mathbf{M})]\}$.

Definition 2. [CL82] Suppose $a \in N \cup \{*\}$.

(a) **M TxtBc^a**-*identifies an r.e. language* L (written: $L \in \mathbf{TxtBc}^a(\mathbf{M})$) just in case for all texts T for L, $(\forall^\infty n)[W_{\mathbf{M}(T[n])} =^a L]$.

(b) **M TxtBc^a**-*identifies a class* $\mathcal{L}$ *of r.e. languages* (written: $\mathcal{L} \subseteq$ **TxtBc^a(M)**) just in case **M TxtBc^a**-identifies each language from $\mathcal{L}$.

(c) **TxtBc^a** $= \{\mathcal{L} \subseteq \mathcal{E} \mid (\exists \mathbf{M})[\mathcal{L} \subseteq \mathbf{TxtBc}^a(\mathbf{M})]\}$.

One can similarly define learning from informants, resulting in criteria **InfEx^a** and **InfBc^a**. We refer the reader to [Gol67,CL82,JORS99] for details.

For $a = 0$, we often write **TxtEx, TxtBc, InfEx, InfBc** instead of **TxtEx^0, TxtBc^0, InfEx^0, InfBc^0**, respectively.

$\mathcal{L}$ is said to be an *indexed family* of languages iff there exists an indexing $L_0, L_1, \ldots$ of languages in $\mathcal{L}$ such that the question $x \in L_i$ is uniformly decidable (i.e., there exists a recursive function f such that $f(i, x) = \chi_{L_i}(x)$).

3   Learning with Negative Counterexamples

In this section we define three models of learning languages from positive data and negative counterexamples. Intuitively, for learning with negative counterexamples, we may consider the learner being provided a text, one element at a time, along with a negative counterexample to the latest conjecture, if any. (One may view this negative counterexample as a response of the teacher to the *subset query* when it is tested if the language generated by the conjecture is a subset of the target language). One may model the list of negative counterexamples as a second text for negative counterexamples being provided to the learner. Thus the learning machines get as input two texts, one for positive data, and other for negative counterexamples. We say that $\mathbf{M}(T, T')$ converges to a grammar i, iff for all but finitely many n, $\mathbf{M}(T[n], T'[n]) = i$.

First, we define the basic model of learning from positive data and negative counterexamples. In this model, if a conjecture contains elements not in the target language, then a negative counterexample is provided to the learner. **NC** in the definition below stands for negative counterexample.

Definition 3. Suppose $a \in N \cup \{*\}$.

(a) **M NCEx^a**-*identifies a language* L (written: $L \in \mathbf{NCEx}^a(\mathbf{M})$) iff for all texts T for L, and for all T' satisfying the condition:

$T'(n) \in S_n$, if $S_n \neq \emptyset$ and $T'(n) = \#$, if $S_n = \emptyset$,
where $S_n = \overline{L} \cap W_{\mathbf{M}(T[n],T'[n])}$

$\mathbf{M}(T,T')$ converges to a grammar i such that $W_i =^a L$.

(b) $\mathbf{M}$ $\mathbf{NCEx}^a$-*identifies a class* $\mathcal{L}$ of languages (written: $\mathcal{L} \subseteq \mathbf{NCEx}^a(\mathbf{M})$),
iff $\mathbf{M}$ $\mathbf{NCEx}^a$-identifies each language in the class.

(c) $\mathbf{NCEx}^a = \{\mathcal{L} \mid (\exists \mathbf{M})[\mathcal{L} \subseteq \mathbf{NCEx}^a(\mathbf{M})]\}$.

We also define two variants of above definition as follows:

— the learner gets least negative counterexample instead of any counterexample. This criteria is denoted $\mathbf{LNCEx}^a$.

— the negative counterexample is provided only if there exists one such counterexample $\leq$ the maximum positive element seen in the input so far (otherwise the learner gets $\#$). This criteria is denoted by $\mathbf{BNCEx}^a$. (Essentially S_n in the definition of $T'(n)$ in part (a) is replaced by $S_n = \overline{L} \cap W_{\mathbf{M}(T[n],T'[n])} \cap \{x \mid x \leq \max(\text{content}(T[n]))\}$).

Similarly, we can define $\mathbf{NCBc}^a$, $\mathbf{LNCBc}^a$ and $\mathbf{BNCBc}^a$ criteria of inference.

The $\mathbf{BNC}$ model essentially addresses some complexity constraints. In the full paper, we also consider generalization of $\mathbf{BNC}$-model above where we consider negative counterexamples within a recursive factor h of the maximum positive element seen in the input so far.

It is easy to see that $\mathbf{TxtEx}^a \subseteq \mathbf{BNCEx}^a \subseteq \mathbf{NCEx}^a \subseteq \mathbf{LNCEx}^a$. All of these containments will be shown to be proper, except the last one.

4   Ex-type Learning with Negative Counterexamples

We first show that every indexed family can be learned using positive data and negative counterexamples. This improves a classical result that every indexed family is learnable from informants. Since there exist indexed families not in $\mathbf{TxtEx}$, this illustrates a difference between $\mathbf{NCEx}$ learning and learning without negative counterexamples.

Theorem 1. *Suppose $\mathcal{L}$ is an indexed family. Then $\mathcal{L} \in \mathbf{NCEx}$.*

We now illustrate another difference between $\mathbf{NCEx}$ learning and $\mathbf{TxtEx}$ learning. Following result does not hold for $\mathbf{TxtEx}$ [Gol67] (for example, $\{F \mid F$ is finite $\} \cup \{L\} \notin \mathbf{TxtEx}$, for any infinite language L).

Theorem 2. *Suppose $\mathcal{L} \in \mathbf{NCEx}$ and L is a recursive language. Then $\mathcal{L} \cup \{L\} \in \mathbf{NCEx}$.*

The above result however doesn't generalize to taking r.e. language (instead of recursive language) L, as witnessed by $\mathcal{L} = \{\{A \cup \{x\}\} \mid x \notin A\}$, and $L = A$, where A is any non-recursive r.e. set. Here note that $\mathcal{L} \in \mathbf{TxtEx}$, but $\mathcal{L} \cup \{L\}$ is not in $\mathbf{NCEx}$.

The following theorem shows that using least negative counterexamples, rather than arbitrary negative counterexamples, does not enhance power of a learner - this is applicable also in case when a learner can make a finite bounded number of mistakes in the final conjecture.

Theorem 3. *Suppose* $a \in N \cup \{*\}$. *Then,*
  (a) $\mathbf{NCEx}^a = \mathbf{LNCEx}^a$.
  (b) $\mathbf{LNCEx}^a \subseteq \mathbf{InfEx}^a$.

The next result is somewhat surprising. It shows that sometimes negative counterexamples are not enough: to learn a language, the learner must have access to *all* negative examples. (In particular, it demonstrates a limitation on the learning power of our basic model).

Theorem 4. $\mathbf{InfEx} - \mathbf{NCEx}^* \neq \emptyset$.

We now show the error hierarchy for **NCEx**-learning. That is, learning with at most $n+1$ errors in almost all conjectures in our basic model is stronger than learning with at most n errors. The hierarchy easily follows from the following theorem.

Theorem 5. *Suppose* $n \in N$.
  (a) $\mathbf{TxtEx}^{n+1} - \mathbf{NCEx}^n \neq \emptyset$.
  (b) $\mathbf{TxtEx}^* - \bigcup_{n \in N} \mathbf{NCEx}^n \neq \emptyset$.

As, $\mathbf{TxtEx}^{n+1} \subseteq \mathbf{BNCEx}^{n+1} \subseteq \mathbf{NCEx}^{n+1} \subseteq \mathbf{LNCEx}^{n+1}$, the following corollary follows from Theorem 5.

Corollary 1. *Suppose* $n \in N$. *Then, for* $\mathbf{I} \in \{\mathbf{NCEx}, \mathbf{LNCEx}, \mathbf{BNCEx}\}$, *we have* $\mathbf{I}^n \subsetneq \mathbf{I}^{n+1}$.

Now we demonstrate yet another limitation on the learning power of our basic model when an arbitrary finite number of errors is allowed in the final conjecture: there are languages learnable within the classical **Bc**-style model (without negative counterexamples) and not learnable in the above variant of our basic model.

Theorem 6. $\mathbf{TxtBc} - \mathbf{NCEx}^* \neq \emptyset$.

We now turn to the model where size of negative counterexamples is restricted: **BNCEx**. We first show that there are classes of languages learnable in our basic model that cannot be learned in any of the models that use negative counterexamples of limited size.

Theorem 7. $\mathbf{NCEx} - \mathbf{BNCBc}^* \neq \emptyset$.

However, the following theorem shows that if attention is restricted to only infinite languages, then **NCEx** and **BNCEx** behave similarly.

Theorem 8. *Suppose* $\mathcal{L}$ *consists of only infinite languages. Then* $\mathcal{L} \in \mathbf{NCEx}^a$ *iff* $\mathcal{L} \in \mathbf{BNCEx}^a$.

Proof. (sketch) As $\mathbf{BNCEx}^a \subseteq \mathbf{NCEx}^a$, it suffices to show that if $\mathcal{L} \in \mathbf{NCEx}^a$ then $\mathcal{L} \in \mathbf{BNCEx}^a$. Suppose $\mathbf{M}$ $\mathbf{NCEx}^a$-identifies $\mathcal{L}$. Define $\mathbf{M}'$ as follows. $\mathbf{M}'$ on the input text T of positive data for an infinite language L behaves as follows. Initially let Cntrexmpls $= \emptyset$. Intuitively, Cntrexmpls denotes the set of negative counterexamples received so far. Initially let NegSet $= \emptyset$. Intuitively, NegSet denotes the set of grammars for which we know a negative counterexample. For $j \in$ NegSet, $ncex(j)$ would denote a negative counterexample for j. For ease of presentation, we will let $\mathbf{M}'$ output more than one conjecture (one after another) at some input point and get negative counterexamples for each of them. This is for ease of presentation and one can always spread out the conjectures.

Stage s (on input $T[s]$)
1. Simulate $\mathbf{M}$ on $T[s]$, by giving negative counterexamples to any conjectures $j \in$ NegSet by $ncex(j)$. Other grammars get $\#$ as counterexample.
2. Let S be the set of conjectures output by $\mathbf{M}$, in the above simulation, on initial segments of $T[s]$, and let k be the final conjecture.
3. If $k \notin$ NegSet, output a grammar for $\bigcup_{i \in S-\text{NegSet}} W_i$,
   Otherwise (i.e., if $k \in$ NegSet), output a grammar for $[(W_k - \text{Cntrexmpls}) \cup \bigcup_{i \in S-\text{NegSet}} W_i]$.
4. If there is no negative counterexample, then go to stage $s+1$.
5. Else (there is a negative counterexample), output one by one, for each $i \in S - \text{NegSet}$, grammar i. If a negative counterexample is obtained, then place i in NegSet and define $ncex(i)$ to be this negative counterexample. (Note that since $\mathbf{M}'$ is for $\mathbf{BNCEx}$-type learning, negative examples received would be $\leq \max(\text{content}(T[s]))$, if any).
   Update Cntrexmpls based on new negative counterexamples obtained.
6. Go to stage $s+1$.
End Stage s.

Suppose T is a text for an infinite language $L \in \mathcal{L}$. Then, based on conjectures made at step 3 and 5, and the negative counterexamples received, one can argue that for all but finitely many stages, answers given in step 1 to machine $\mathbf{M}$ are correct. (Since, one would eventually place any conjecture of $\mathbf{M}$ on text T, which enumerates a non-subset of L, in NegSet due to steps 3 and 5). Thus, for all but finitely many stages, the grammar output in step 3 would be correct (except for possibly a errors of omission by the final grammar of $\mathbf{M}$), and $\mathbf{M}'$ $\mathbf{BNCEx}^a$-identifies L. ∎

Our next result shows that the model $\mathbf{BNCEx}$, while being weaker than our basic model, is still quite powerful: there are classes of languages learnable in this model that cannot be learned in the classical $\mathbf{Bc}$-style model even when an arbitrary finite number of errors is allowed in almost all conjectures.

Theorem 9. $\mathbf{BNCEx} - \mathbf{TxtBc}^* \neq \emptyset$.

Note that the diagonalizations in Theorems 7 and 9 can be shown using indexed families of languages. Thus, in contrast to Theorem 1, we get

Corollary 2. *There exists an indexed family not in* $\mathbf{BNCBc}^*$.

5   Bc-Type Learning with Negative Counterexamples

In this section we explore **Bc**-style learning from positive data and negative counterexamples. First we show that, for **Bc**-style learning, similarly to **Ex**-style learning, our basic model is equivalent to learning with the least negative counterexamples.

Proposition 1. *(a)* **NCBc** = **LNCBc**.
  (b) **LNCBc** ⊆ **InfBc**.

Our next result shows that, to learn a language, sometimes even for **Bc**-style learning, positive data and negative counterexamples are not enough - the learner must have access to all negative data. In particular, limitations on the learning power of our basic **Bc**-style model are established.

Theorem 10. **InfEx** − **NCBc** ≠ ∅.

Proof. Let $\mathcal{L} = \{L \mid (\exists e)[\min(L) = 2e] \wedge$
  (i) $[L = W_e$ and $(\forall x \geq e)[L \cap \{2x, 2x + 1\} \neq \emptyset]]$.
  OR
  (ii) $(\exists x > e)[L \cap \{2x, 2x + 1\} = \emptyset, \wedge (\forall y > 2x + 1)[y \in L]]$
  $\}$
It is easy to verify that $\mathcal{L} \in$ **InfEx**. A learner can easily find e as above, and whether there exists $x > e$ such that both $2x, 2x + 1$ are not in the input language. This information is sufficient to identify the input language.
  We now show that $\mathcal{L} \notin$ **NCBc**. Intuitively, the idea is that a learner which learns a language satisfying clause (ii) above, must output infinitely many grammars properly extending the input seen upto the point of conjecture. By repeatedly searching for such input and conjectures, one can identify one element of each such conjecture as negative counterexample, allowing one to construct W_e as needed for clause (i) as well as diagonalizing out of **NCBc**. Note that we needed a pair $\{2x, 2x + 1\}$, to separate (i) from (ii) as one of the elements may be needed for giving the negative counterexamples as mentioned above. We now proceed formally.
  Suppose by way of contradiction that machine **M NCBc**-identifies $\mathcal{L}$. Then by the Kleene Recursion Theorem [Rog67] there exists a recursive function e such that W_e may be defined as follows.
  Initially, let $W_e = \{2e, 2e+1\}$ and σ_0 be such that content$(\sigma_0) = \{2e, 2e+1\}$. Intuitively Cntrexmpls denotes the set of elements frozen to be outside the diagonalizing language being constructed. Initially, Cntrexmpls = $\{x \mid x < 2e\}$. Intuitively, NegSet is the set of conjectured grammars for which we have found a negative counterexample (in Cntrexmpls). Initially let NegSet = ∅. $ncex(j)$ is a function which gives, for $j \in$ NegSet, a negative counterexample from Cntrexmpls. For the following, let γ_τ be a sequence of length $|\tau|$ defined as follows. For $i < |\tau|$,

$$\gamma_\tau(i) = \begin{cases} ncex(\mathbf{M}(\tau[i], \gamma_\tau[i])), & \text{if } \mathbf{M}(\tau[i], \gamma_\tau[i]) \in \text{NegSet}; \\ \#, & \text{otherwise.} \end{cases}$$

(where the value of NegSet is as at the time of above usage).

Let $x_0 = 2e + 2$. Intuitively, x_s is the least even element greater than $\max(\text{content}(\sigma_s) \cup \text{Cntrexmpls})$. Also we will have the invariant that at start of stage s,

(i) every element $< x_s$ is either in $\text{content}(\sigma_s)$ or Cntrexmpls and

(ii) $\text{content}(\sigma_s)$ consists of elements enumerated in W_e before stage s.

Go to stage 0.

Stage s

1. Dovetail steps 2 and 3 until step 2 or 3 succeed. If step 2 succeeds before step 3, if ever, then go to step 4. If step 3 succeeds before step 2, if ever, then go to step 5.

   Here we assume that if step 3 can succeed by simulating $\mathbf{M}(\tau, \gamma_\tau)$ for s steps, then step 3 succeeded first (and for the shortest such τ), otherwise whichever of these steps succeeds first is taken. (So some priority is given to step 3 in the dovetailing).

2. Search for a $\tau \supseteq \sigma_s$ such that
   $$\text{content}(\tau) \subseteq \text{content}(\sigma_s) \cup \{x \mid x \geq x_s + 2\},$$
   $\mathbf{M}(\tau, \gamma_\tau) \notin \text{NegSet}$ and
   $W_{\mathbf{M}(\tau, \gamma_\tau)}$ enumerates an element not in $\text{content}(\tau)$.

3. Search for a $\tau \subseteq \sigma_s$ such that $\mathbf{M}(\tau, \gamma_\tau) \notin \text{NegSet}$ and $W_{\mathbf{M}(\tau, \gamma_\tau)}$ enumerates an element not in $\text{content}(\sigma_s)$.

4. Let τ be as found in step 2, and $j = \mathbf{M}(\tau, \gamma_\tau)$, and z be the element found to be enumerated by W_j which is not in $\text{content}(\tau)$.
   Let $\text{NegSet} = \text{NegSet} \cup \{j\}$.
   Let $\text{Cntrexmpls} = \text{Cntrexmpls} \cup \{z\}$.
   Let $ncex(j) = z$.
   Let x_{s+1} be the least even number $> \max(\text{content}(\tau) \cup \{x_s, z\})$.
   Enumerate $\{x \mid x_s \leq x < x_{s+1}\} - \{z\}$ in W_e.
   Let σ_{s+1} be an extension of τ such that $\text{content}(\sigma_{s+1}) = W_e$ enumerated until now.

   Go to stage $s + 1$.

5. Let τ be as found in step 3, and $j = \mathbf{M}(\tau, \gamma_\tau)$, and z be the element found to be enumerated by W_j which is not in $\text{content}(\sigma_s)$.
   Let $\text{NegSet} = \text{NegSet} \cup \{j\}$.
   Let $\text{Cntrexmpls} = \text{Cntrexmpls} \cup \{z\}$.
   Let $ncex(j) = z$.
   Let x_{s+1} be the least even number $> \max(\{x_s, z\})$.
   Enumerate $\{x \mid x_s \leq x < x_{s+1}\} - \{z\}$ in W_e.
   Let σ_{s+1} be an extension of σ_s such that $\text{content}(\sigma_{s+1}) = W_e$ enumerated until now.

   Go to stage $s + 1$.

End stage s

We now consider the following cases:

Case 1: Stage s starts but does not finish.

In this case let $L = W_e \cup \{x \mid x \geq x_s + 2\}$. Note that, due to non-success of steps 2 and 3, the negative information given in computation of γ_τ based on NegSet is correct. Thus, for any text T for L extending σ_s, for $n > |\sigma_s|$, $\mathbf{M}(T[n], \gamma_{T[n]}) \in$ NegSet or it enumerates only a finite set (otherwise step 2 would succeed). Thus, $\mathbf{M}$ does not **NCBc**-identify L.

Case 2: All stages finish.

Let $L = W_e$. Let $T = \bigcup_{s \in N} \sigma_s$. Note that T is a text for L. Let Cntrexmpls denote the set of all elements which are ever placed in Cntrexmpls by the above construction. Note that eventually, any conjecture j by $\mathbf{M}$ on (T, γ_T) which enumerates an element not in L, belongs to NegSet, with a negative counterexample for it belonging to Cntrexmpls (given by $ncex(j)$). This is due to eventual success of step 3, for all $\tau \subseteq T$, for which $\mathbf{M}(\tau, \gamma_\tau) \not\subseteq L$ (due to priority assigned to step 3).

If there are infinitely many $\tau \subseteq T$ such that $\mathbf{M}(\tau, \gamma_\tau) \not\subseteq L$, then clearly, $\mathbf{M}$ does not **NCBc**-identify L. On the other hand, if there are only finitely many such τ, then clearly all such τ would have been handled by some stage s, and beyond stage s, step 3 would never succeed. Thus, beyond stage s computation of $\mathbf{M}(\tau, \gamma_\tau)$, as at stage s step 2, is always correct (with negative counterexamples given, whenever necessary), and step 2 succeeds infinitely often. Thus again infinitely many conjectures of $\mathbf{M}$ on (T, γ_T) are incorrect (and enumerate an element of $\overline{L}$), contradicting the hypothesis.

From above cases it follows that $\mathbf{M}$ does not **NCBc**-identify L. Theorem follows. ∎

Our next result shows that all classes of languages learnable in our basic **Ex**-style model with arbitrary finite number of errors in almost all conjectures can be learned without errors in the basic **Bc**-style model. Note the contrast with learning from texts where $\mathbf{TxtEx}^{2j+1} - \mathbf{TxtBc}^j \neq \emptyset$ [CL82].

Theorem 11. $\mathbf{NCEx}^* \subseteq \mathbf{NCBc}$.

Next theorem establishes yet another limitation on the learning power of our basic **Bc**-style learning: some languages not learnable in this model can be **Bc**-learned without negative counterexamples if only one error in almost all conjectures is allowed.

Theorem 12. $\mathbf{TxtBc}^1 - \mathbf{NCBc} \neq \emptyset$.

Now we turn to **Bc**-style learning with limited size of negative counterexamples. First, note that Theorem 9 gives us: $\mathbf{BNCEx} - \mathbf{TxtBc}^* \neq \emptyset$. In other words, some languages **Ex**-learnable with negative counterexamples of limited size cannot be **Bc**-learned without negative counterexamples even with an arbitrary finite number of errors in almost all conjectures.

On the other hand, as Theorem 7 shows, some languages learnable in our basic **Ex**-style learning with negative counterexamples cannot be learned in **Bc**-model with limited size of negative counterexamples even if an arbitrary finite number of errors is allowed in almost all conjectures.

Now we establish one of our most surprising results: there exists a **Bc**-style learner with negative counterexamples, allowing just one error in almost all conjectures, with the "ultimate power" - it can learn the class of all recursively enumerable languages!

Theorem 13. $\mathcal{E} \in \mathbf{NCBc}^1$.

Proof. First we give an informal idea of the proof. Our learner can clearly test if a particular $W_s \subseteq L$. Given an arbitrary initial segment of the input $T[n]$, we will want to test if content$(T[n]) \not\subseteq W_s$ for any r.e. set $W_s \subseteq L$, where L is a target language. Of course, the teacher cannot directly answer such questions, since W_s might not be the target language (note also that the problem is undecidable). However, the learner finds a way to encode this problem into a current conjecture and test if the current conjecture generates a subset of the target language. In order to do this, the learner potentially makes one deliberate error in its conjecture! We now proceed formally.

Define **M** on the input text T as follows. Initially, it outputs a grammar for N. If it does not generate a negative counterexample, then we are done. Otherwise, let c be the negative counterexample. Go to stage 0.

Stage s
1.   Output grammar s. If it generates a negative counterexample, then go to stage $s + 1$.
2.   Else,
        For $n = 0$ to ∞ do:
            Output a grammar for language X, where X is defined as follows:

$$X = \begin{cases} \emptyset, & \text{if content}(T[n]) \not\subseteq W_s; \\ W_s \cup \{c\}, & \text{otherwise.} \end{cases}$$

        If it does not generate a negative counterexample, then go to stage $s + 1$,
        Otherwise continue with the next iteration of For loop.
      EndFor
End stage s

We now claim that above **M** **NCBc**^{1}-identifies $\mathcal{E}$. Clearly, if $L = N$, then **M** **NCBc**^{1}-identifies L. Now suppose $L \neq N$. Let c be the negative counterexample received by **M** for N. Let j be the least grammar for L, and T be a text for L. We claim that all stages $s < j$ will finish, and stage j will not finish. To see this consider any $s < j$.

Case 1: $W_s \not\subseteq L$.

In this case note that step 1 would generate a negative counterexample, and thus we will go to stage $s + 1$.

Case 2: Not Case 1 (i.e., $W_s \subseteq L$ but $L \not\subseteq W_s$).

In this case, let m be least such that content$(T[m]) \not\subseteq W_s$. Then, in the iteration of For loop in step 2, with $n = m$, the grammar output is for $\emptyset$. Thus, there is no negative counterexample, and algorithm proceeds to stage $s + 1$.

Also, note that in stage $s = j$, step 1 would not get a negative counterexample, and since $c \notin L$, every iteration of For loop will get a negative counterexample. Thus, $\mathbf{M}$ keeps outputting grammar for $W_j \cup \{c\}$. Hence $\mathbf{M}$ **NCBc**^{1}-identifies L. Thus, we have that $\mathbf{M}$ **NCBc**^{1}-identifies $\mathcal{E}$. ∎

Since $\mathcal{E} \in \mathbf{InfBc}^*$, we have

Corollary 3. *(a)* **NCBc**^{1} = **InfBc***.
(b) For all $a \in N \cup \{*\}$, **NCBc**^{a} = **LNCBc**^{a}.

The following corollary shows a contrast with respect to the case when there are no errors in conjectures (Proposition 1 and Theorem 10). What a difference just one error can make! Using the fact that $\mathbf{InfBc}^n \subsetneq \mathbf{InfBc}^*$ (see [CS83]), we get

Corollary 4. *For all $n > 0$,* $\mathbf{InfBc}^n \subsetneq \mathbf{NCBc}^n = \mathbf{NCBc}^1$.

The ideas of the above theorem are employed to show that all infinite recursively enumerable languages can be learned in our basic **Bc**-style model with negative counterexamples of limited size allowing just one error in almost all conjectures. Note that, as we demonstrated in Corollary 2, contrary to the case when there are no limits on the size of negative counterexamples, such learners cannot learn the class of all recursively enumerable languages.

Theorem 14. *Let $\mathcal{L} = \{L \in \mathcal{E} \mid L$ is infinite $\}$. Then $\mathcal{L} \in \mathbf{BNCBc}^1$.*

As there exists a class of infinite languages which does not belong to $\mathbf{InfBc}^n$ (see [CS83]), we have

Corollary 5. *For all $n \in N$,* $\mathbf{BNCBc}^1 - \mathbf{InfBc}^n \neq \emptyset$.

Thus, $\mathbf{BNCBc}^m$ and $\mathbf{InfBc}^n$ are incomparable for $m > 0$. The above result does not generalize to $\mathbf{InfBc}^*$, as $\mathbf{InfBc}^*$ contains the class $\mathcal{E}$.

Based on the ideas similar to the ones used in Theorem 13, we can show that all classes of languages **Bc**^{n}-learnable without negative counterexamples can be **Bc**-learned with negative counterexamples of limited size when one error in almost all conjectures is allowed.

Theorem 15. *(a) For all $n \in N$,* **TxtBc**^{n} ⊆ **BNCBc**^{1}.
(b) **TxtEx*** ⊆ **BNCBc**^{1}.

Similarly to the case of **Ex**-style learning, **BNCBc** and **NCBc** models turn out to be equivalent for the classes of infinite languages.

Theorem 16. *Suppose $\mathcal{L}$ consists of only infinite languages. Then $\mathcal{L} \in \mathbf{NCBc}$ iff $\mathcal{L} \in \mathbf{BNCBc}$.*

We now mention some of the open questions regarding behaviourally correct learning when the size of the negative counterexamples is bounded.
Open Question: Is **BNCBc**^{n} hierarchy strict?
Open Question: Is **TxtBc*** ⊆ **BNCBc**^{1}?

References

[Ang88]   D. Angluin. Queries and concept learning. *Machine Learning*, 2:319–342, 1988.

[B74]   J. Bārzdiņš. Two theorems on the limiting synthesis of functions. In *Theory of Algorithms and Programs, vol. 1*, pages 82–88. Latvian State University, 1974. In Russian.

[BCJ95]   G. Baliga, J. Case, and S. Jain. Language learning with some negative information. *Journal of Computer and System Sciences*, 51(5):273–285, 1995.

[BH70]   R. Brown and C. Hanlon. Derivational complexity and the order of acquisition in child speech. In J. R. Hayes, editor, *Cognition and the Development of Language*. Wiley, 1970.

[CL82]   J. Case and C. Lynes. Machine inductive inference and language identification. In M. Nielsen and E. M. Schmidt, editors, *Proceedings of the 9th International Colloquium on Automata, Languages and Programming*, volume 140 of *Lecture Notes in Computer Science*, pages 107–115. Springer-Verlag, 1982.

[CS83]   J. Case and C. Smith. Comparison of identification criteria for machine inductive inference. *Theoretical Computer Science*, 25:193–220, 1983.

[DPS86]   M. Demetras, K. Post, and C. Snow. Feedback to first language learners: The role of repetitions and clarification questions. *Journal of Child Language*, 13:275–292, 1986.

[FGJ⁺94]   L. Fortnow, W. Gasarch, S. Jain, E. Kinber, M. Kummer, S. Kurtz, M. Pleszkoch, T. Slaman, R. Solovay, and F. Stephan. Extremes in the degrees of inferability. *Annals of Pure and Applied Logic*, 66:231–276, 1994.

[GM98]   W. Gasarch and G. Martin. *Bounded Queries in Recursion Theory*. Birkhauser, 1998.

[Gol67]   E. M. Gold. Language identification in the limit. *Information and Control*, 10:447–474, 1967.

[GP89]   W. Gasarch and M. Pleszkoch. Learning via queries to an oracle. In R. Rivest, D. Haussler, and M. Warmuth, editors, *Proceedings of the Second Annual Workshop on Computational Learning Theory*, pages 214–229. Morgan Kaufmann, 1989.

[HPTS84]   K. Hirsh-Pasek, R. Treiman, and M. Schneiderman. Brown and Hanlon revisited: Mothers' sensitivity to ungrammatical forms. *Journal of Child Language*, 11:81–88, 1984.

[JORS99]   S. Jain, D. Osherson, J. Royer, and A. Sharma. *Systems that Learn: An Introduction to Learning Theory*. MIT Press, Cambridge, Mass., second edition, 1999.

[LNZ02]   S. Lange, J. Nessel, and S. Zilles. Learning languages with queries. In *Proceedings of Treffen der GI-Fachgruppe Maschinelles Lernen (FGML), Learning Lab Lower Saxony, Hannover, Germany*, pages 92–99, 2002.

[Mot92]   T. Motoki. Inductive inference from all positive and some negative data. unpublished manuscript, 1992.

[Rog67]   H. Rogers. *Theory of Recursive Functions and Effective Computability*. McGraw-Hill, 1967. Reprinted by MIT Press in 1987.

[Shi86]   T. Shinohara. *Studies on Inductive Inference from Positive Data*. PhD thesis, Kyushu University, Kyushu, Japan, 1986.

Inductive Inference of Term Rewriting Systems from Positive Data

M.R.K. Krishna Rao

Information and Computer Science Department
King Fahd University of Petroleum and Minerals,
Dhahran 31261, Saudi Arabia.
krishna@ccse.kfupm.edu.sa

Abstract. In this paper, we study inferability of term rewriting systems from positive examples alone. We define a class of simple flat term rewriting systems that are inferable from positive examples. In flat term rewriting systems, nesting of defined symbols is forbidden in both left- and right-hand sides. A flat TRS is simple if the size of redexes in the right-hand sides is bounded by the size of the corresponding left-hand sides. The class of simple flat TRSs is rich enough to include many divide-and-conquer programs like addition, doubling, tree-count, list-count, split, append, etc. The relation between our results and the known results on Prolog programs is also discussed. In particular, flat TRSs can define functions (like doubling), whose output is bigger in size than the input, which is not possible with linearly-moded Prolog programs.

1 Introduction

Starting from the influential works of Gold [6] and Blum and Blum [4], a lot of effort has gone into developing a rich theory about inductive inference and the classes of concepts which can be learned from both positive (examples) and negative data (counterexamples) and the classes of concepts which can be learned from positive data alone. The study of inferability from positive data alone is important because negative information is hard to obtain in practice –positive examples are much easier to generate by conducting experiments than the negative examples in general. In his seminal paper [6] on inductive inference, Gold proved that even simple classes of concepts like the class of regular languages cannot be infered from positive examples alone. This strong negative result disappointed the scientists in the field until Angluin [1] has given a characterization of the classes of concepts that can be infered from positive data alone and exhibited a few nontrivial classes of concepts inferable from positive data. This influential paper inspired further research on the inductive inference from positive data. Since then many positive results are published about inductive inference of logic programs and pattern languages from positive data (see a.o., [10,2,3,11,8]). To

S. Ben-David, J. Case, A. Maruoka (Eds.): ALT 2004, LNAI 3244, pp. 69–82, 2004.

the best of our knowledge, inductive inference of term rewriting systems from positive data has not been studied so far.

In the last few decades, term rewriting systems have played a fundamental role in the analysis and implementation of abstract data type specifications, decidability of word problems, theorem proving, computability theory, design of functional programming languages (e.g. Miranda), integration of functional and logic programming paradigms, etc. In particular, term rewriting systems are very similar to functional programs and any learning results on term rewriting systems can be transfered to functional programs.

In this paper, we propose a class of simple flat term rewriting systems that are inferable from positive examples. In flat TRSs, nesting of defined symbols is forbidden in both left- and right-hand sides. A flat TRS is simple if the size of redexes in the right-hand sides is bounded by the size of the corresponding left-hand sides. This condition ensures that the reachability problem over flat terms is decidable. We prove this result by providing an algorithm to decide whether a flat term t reduces to a term u by a simple flat TRS R or not.

Simple flat TRSs have a nice property that the size of redexes in a derivation starting from a flat term t is bounded by the size of the initial term (actually, the size of redexes in t) and the size of the caps of intermediate terms in a derivation $t \Rightarrow^* u$ starting from a flat term is bounded by the size of the cap of the final term, where cap of a term is defined as the largest top portion of the term containing just constructor symbols and variables. These properties guarantee that we only need to consider rewrite rules whose sides are bounded by the size of the examples in learning simple flat TRSs from positive data.

The class of simple flat TRSs is rich enough to include many divide-and-conquer programs like addition, doubling, tree-count, list-count, split, append, etc. The relation between our results and the known results on Prolog programs is discussed in a later section. In particular, flat TRSs can define functions (like doubling), whose output is bigger in size than the input, which is not possible with linearly-moded Prolog programs. On the other hand, flat TRSs do not allow nesting of defined symbols in the rewrite rules, which means that we cannot define functions like quick-sort, that can be defined by a linearly-moded Prolog program.

The rest of the paper is organized as follows. The next section gives preliminary definitions and results needed about inductive inference. In section 3, we define the class of simple flat TRSs and establish a few properties about intermediate terms in derivations of these systems over flat terms. In section 4, we prove decidability of $t \Rightarrow^*_R u$ and then the inferability of simple flat TRSs from positive data is established in section 5. The final section concludes with a discussion on open problems.

2 Preliminaries

We assume that the reader is familiar with the basic terminology of term rewriting and inductive inference and use the standard terminology from [7,5] and [6, 10]. In the following, we recall some deifinitions and results needed in the sequel.

The alphabet of a first order language L is a tuple $\langle \Sigma, \mathcal{X} \rangle$ of mutually disjoint sets such that Σ is a finite set of function symbols and $\mathcal{X}$ is a set of variables.. In the following, $\mathcal{T}(\Sigma, \mathcal{X})$ denotes the set of terms constructed from the function symbols in Σ and the variables in $\mathcal{X}$. The size of a term t, denoted by $|t|$, is defined as the number of occurrences of symbols (except the punctuation symbols) occurring in it.

Definition 1. A *term rewriting system* (TRS, for short) $\mathcal{R}$ is a pair (Σ, R) consisting of a set Σ of function symbols and a set R of rewrite rules of the form $l \rightarrow r$ satisfying:
(a) l and r are first order terms in $\mathcal{T}(\Sigma, \mathcal{X})$,
(b) left-hand-side l is not a variable and
(c) each variable occuring in r also occurs in l.

Example 1. The following TRS defines multiplication over natural numbers.

$$a(0, y) \rightarrow y$$
$$a(s(x), y) \rightarrow s(a(x, y))$$

$$m(0, y) \rightarrow 0$$
$$m(s(x), y) \rightarrow a(y, m(x, y))$$

Here, a stands for addition and m stands for multiplication. □

Definition 2. A *context* $C[, \ldots,]$ is a term in $\mathcal{T}(\Sigma \cup \{\Box\}, \mathcal{X})$. If $C[, \ldots,]$ is a context containing n occurrences of $\Box$ and $t_1, \ldots, t_n$ are terms then $C[t_1, \ldots, t_n]$ is the result of replacing the occurrences of $\Box$ from left to right by $t_1, \ldots, t_n$. A context containing precisely 1 occurrence of $\Box$ is denoted $C[\ ]$.

Definition 3. The *rewrite relation* $\Rightarrow_{\mathcal{R}}$ induced by a TRS $\mathcal{R}$ is defined as follows: $s \Rightarrow_{\mathcal{R}} t$ if there is a rewrite rule $l \rightarrow r$ in $\mathcal{R}$, a substitution σ and a context $C[\ ]$ such that $s \equiv C[l\sigma]$ and $t \equiv C[r\sigma]$.
We say that s *reduces to* t in *one rewrite* (or reduction) *step* if $s \Rightarrow_{\mathcal{R}} t$ and say s *reduces to* t (or t is reachable from s) if $s \Rightarrow_{\mathcal{R}}^* t$, where $\Rightarrow_{\mathcal{R}}^*$ is the transitive-reflexive closure of $\Rightarrow_{\mathcal{R}}$). The subterm $l\sigma$ in s is called a *redex*.

Example 2.   The following derivation shows a computation of the value of
term $m(s(s(0)), s(s(s(0))))$ by the above TRS.

$$m(s(s(0)), s(s(s(0)))) \Rightarrow a(s(s(s(0))), m(s(0), s(s(s(0)))))$$
$$\Rightarrow a(s(s(s(0))), a(s(s(s(0))), m(0, s(s(s(0))))))$$
$$\Rightarrow a(s(s(s(0))), a(s(s(s(0))), 0))$$
$$\Rightarrow s(a(s(s(0)), a(s(s(s(0))), 0)))$$
$$\Rightarrow s(s(a(s(0), a(s(s(s(0))), 0))))$$
$$\Rightarrow s(s(s(a(0, a(s(s(s(0))), 0)))))$$
$$\Rightarrow s(s(s(a(s(s(s(0))), 0))))$$
$$\Rightarrow \cdots \Rightarrow s(s(s(s(s(s(0))))))$$

This is one of the many possible derivations from $m(s(s(0)), s(s(s(0))))$. Since
the system is both terminating and confluent, every derivation from this term
ends in the final value $s(s(s(s(s(s(0))))))$.   □

Remark 1. The conditions (b) left-hand-side l is not a variable and (c) each
variable occuring in r also occurs in l of Definition 1 avoid trivial nonterminating
computations. If there is a rewrite rule $x \to r$ with a varible left-hand-side is
present in a TRS, every term can be rewritten by this rule and hence no normal
form exist resulting in nonterminating computations. If the right-hand-side r
contains a variable y not present in the left-hand-side l of a rule $l \to r$, then the
term l can be rewritten to $C[l]$ (substitution σ replacing the extra-variable by l)
resulting in ever growing terms and obvious nontermination.

Definition 4. Let U and E be two recursively enumerable sets, whose elements
are called *objects* and *expressions* respectively.

  - A *concept* is a subset $\Gamma \subseteq U$.
  - An *example* is a tuple $\langle A, a \rangle$ where $A \in U$ and $a =$ **true** or **false**. Example
    $\langle A, a \rangle$ is *positive* if $a =$ **true** and *negative* otherwise.
  - A concept Γ is *consistent* with a sequence of examples $\langle A_1, a_1 \rangle, \ldots, \langle A_m, a_m \rangle$
    when $A_i \in \Gamma$ if and only if $a_i =$ **true**, for each $i \in [1, m]$.
  - A *formal system* is a finite subset $R \subseteq E$.
  - A *semantic mapping* is a mapping Φ from formal systems to concepts.
  - We say that a formal system R *defines* a concept Γ if $\Phi(R) = \Gamma$.

Definition 5. A *concept defining framework* is a triple $\langle U, E, \Phi \rangle$ of a universe
U of objects, a set E of expressions and a semantic mapping Φ.

Definition 6. A class of concepts $C = \{\Gamma_1, \Gamma_2, \ldots\}$ is an *indexed family of*
recursive concepts if there exists an algorithm that decides whether $w \in \Gamma_i$ for
any object w and natural number i.

Here onwards, we fix a concept defining framework $\langle U, E, \Phi \rangle$ arbitrarily and only consider indexed families of recursive concepts.

Definition 7. A *positive presentation* of a nonempty concept $\Gamma \subseteq U$ is an infinite sequence $w_1, w_2, \ldots$ of objects (positive examples) such that $\{w_i \mid i \geq 1\} = \Gamma$.

An *inference machine* is an effective procedure that requests an object as an example from time to time and produces a concept (or a formal system defining a concept) as a conjecture from time to time. Given a positive presentation $\sigma = w_1, w_2, \ldots$, an inference machine IM generates a sequence of conjectures $g_1, g_2, \cdots$. We say that IM *converges to* g on input σ if the sequence of conjectures $g_1, g_2, \ldots$ is finite and ends in g or there exists a positive integer k_0 such that $g_k = g$ for all $k \geq k_0$.

Definition 8. A class C of concepts is *inferable from positive data* if there exists an inference machine IM such that for any $\Gamma \in C$ and any positive presentation σ of Γ, IM converges to a formal system g such that $\Phi(g) = \Gamma$.

We need the following result of Shinohara [10] in proving our result.

Definition 9. A semantic mapping Φ is *monotonic* if $R \subseteq R'$ implies $\Phi(R) \subseteq \Phi(R')$. A formal system R is *reduced w.r.t.* $S \subseteq U$ if $S \subseteq \Phi(R)$ and $S \not\subseteq \Phi(R')$ for any proper subset $R' \subset R$.

Definition 10. A concept defining framework $C = \langle U, E, \Phi \rangle$ has *bounded finite thickness* if

1. Φ *is monotonic* and
2. *for any finite set $S \subseteq U$ and any $m \geq 0$, the set $\{\Phi(R) \mid R$ is reduced w.r.t. S and $|R| \leq m\}$ is finite.*

Theorem 1. (Shinohara [10])
If a concept defining framework $C = \langle U, E, \Phi \rangle$ has bounded finite thickness, then the class

$$C^m = \{\Phi(R) \mid R \subseteq E, |R| \leq m\}$$

of concepts is inferable from positive data for every $m \geq 1$.

3   Simple Flat Rewrite Systems

In the following, we partition Σ into set D of defined symbols that may occur as the outermost symbol of left-hand-side of rules and set C of constructor symbols that do not occur as the outermost symbol of left-hand-side of rules.

Definition 11. (flat terms and systems)

- A term t in $\mathcal{T}(\Sigma, X)$ is *flat* if there is no nesting of defined symbols in t.
- A TRS R is *flat* if left-hand sides and right-hand sides of all the rules in it are flat.
- The cap of a term t in $\mathcal{T}(D \cup C, X)$ is defined as
  $cap(t) = \square$ if $root(t) \in D$, and
  $cap(t) = f(cap(t_1), \ldots, cap(t_n))$ if $t \equiv f(t_1, \ldots, t_n)$ and $f \notin D$.
- The multiset[1] of maximal subterms with defined symbol roots in a term $t \in \mathcal{T}(D \cup C, X)$ is defined as
  $Dsub(t) = \{t\}$ if $root(t) \in D$, and
  $Dsub(t) = Dsub(t_1) \cup \ldots \cup Dsub(t_n))$ if $t \equiv f(t_1, \ldots, t_n)$ and $f \in C$.
- We write $t \preceq u$ if $cap(t)$ is a subcap of $cap(u)$, that is, we can obtain $cap(u)$ from $cap(t)$ by substituting some holes in $cap(t)$ by contexts. In other words, $cap(t)$ is a top portion of $cap(u)$.

Definition 12. A flat rewrite rule $l \to r$ is *simple* if $|l\sigma| \geq |s\sigma|$ for every $s \in Dsub(r)$ and every substitution σ. A flat term rewriting system R is *simple* if it contains finitely many rules and each rule in it is simple.

The above condition ensures that no variable occurs more often in a subterm of the right-hand side with defined symbol root than its occurrences in the left-hand side. This is formalized by the following lemma.

Lemma 1. Let t and s be two terms. Then, $|t\sigma| \geq |s\sigma|$ for every substitution σ if and only if $|t| \geq |s|$ and no variable occurs more often in s than in t.

Proof sketch: If-part. Induction on number variables in $Domain(\sigma)$.

Only-if-part. When σ is the empty substitution, $|t\sigma| \geq |s\sigma|$ implies $|t| \geq |s|$. We can prove by contradiction that no variable occurs more often in s than in t if $|t\sigma| \geq |s\sigma|$ for every substitution σ. $\qquad\square$

It is easy to check (syntactically) whether a given TRS is flat or not.

Theorem 2. It is decidable in linear time whether a given TRS is simple flat or not.

Proof: Follows from the above lemma. $\qquad\square$

Remark 2. Simple flat TRSs have some similarities to the length-bounded elementary formal systems [10]. Length-bounded elementary formal systems (LB-EFS) are logic programs such that the sum of the arguments of body atoms is bounded by the sum of the arguments of the head. However, there are some significant differences between them.

---

[1] Multisets allow repetitions of elements and the multiset $\{1, 1, 2\}$ is different from the multiset $\{1, 2\}$. Here, $\cup$ stands for the multiset union.

(a) Elementary formal systems only have constants and function symbols of arity one, where as simple flat TRSs have function symbols of arbitrary arity,

(b) Simple flat TRSs in with an additional condition $|l\sigma| > |s\sigma|$ *for every $s \in$ Dsub(r) and every substitution σ* are terminating, whereas LB-EFS with similar condition can be nonterminating. For example, the elementary formal system with clauses

$$p(f(X)) \leftarrow p(x)$$
$$p(a) \leftarrow$$

is length-bounded, but has an infinite SLD-derivation starting from an initial query $\leftarrow p(Y)$.

It may be noted that the above LB-EFS terminates for all ground queries (though loops for nonground queries). In this sense, LB-EFSs are good for checking (whether an atom is in the least Herbrand model) but not good for computing, as computing involves variables in the queries and LB-EFS can be nonterminating for nonground queries even with the additional condition that body atoms are strictly smaller than the head. In contrast, Simple flat TRSs with such additional condition are good for both checking and computing as they are terminate for every term (ground as well as nonground).

A nice property of simple flat TRSs is that the sum of the sizes of arguments of defined symbols in any derivation is bounded by the maximum sum of the sizes of arguments of the defined symbols in the initial term. This in turn ensures that it is decidable whether a term t reduces to a term u by a simple flat system or not. These facts are established in the following results.

Lemma 2. Let R be a simple flat TRS and t be a flat term such that n is greater than the size of every term in $Dsub(t)$. If $t \Rightarrow_R u$ then n is greater than the size of every term in $Dsub(u)$. Further, u is also a flat term and $t \preceq u$.

Proof : Let $l \rightarrow r$ be the rule and σ the substitution applied in $t \Rightarrow_R u$ (say at position p). That's, $t \equiv C[l\sigma]$ and $u \equiv C[r\sigma]$ for some context C. It is clear that $Dsub(u) = (Dsub(t) - \{l\sigma\}) \cup Dsub(r\sigma)$. Since R is a simple flat TRS, $|l\sigma| \geq |s\sigma|$ for every $s \in Dsub(r)$ and hence n is greater than the size of every term in $Dsub(u)$.

Since $t \equiv C[l\sigma]$ is flat, no defined symbol occurs in σ and hence $r\sigma$ is flat because r is flat. Therefore, $u \equiv C[r\sigma]$ is flat.

It is easy to see that $cap(u) \equiv cap(t)[cap(r\sigma)]_p$ and hence $t \preceq u$.   □

The following theorem states the above fact for any term reachable from t.

Theorem 3. Let R be a simple flat TRS and t be a flat term such that n is greater than the size of every term in $Dsub(t)$. If $t \Rightarrow_R^* u$ then n is greater than the size of every term in $Dsub(u)$. Further, u is also a flat term and $w \preceq u$ for every term w in $t \Rightarrow_R^* w \Rightarrow_R^* u$.

Proof : Induction on the length of the derivation $t \Rightarrow_R^* u$ and Lemma 2. □

The above theorem essentially says that the size of $Dsub$-terms of intermediate terms is bounded by the size of $Dsub$-terms of the initial term and the size of caps of intermediate terms is bounded by the size of the cap of the final term.

4   Decidability of $t \Rightarrow_R^* u$

In this section, we prove that it is decidable whether a flat term t reduces to a term u by a simple flat system R or not, by providing a decision procedure for this problem. Throughout this section, we only consider flat terms and simple flat systems.

In our decision procedure, we use left-to-right reduction strategy and keep track of reductions which did not increase the cap (for loop checking). The intermediate terms are annotated with this information, i.e., we consider tuples of the form $\langle v, V \rangle$, where v is a term and V is a set of redexes. The following definition gives next possible terms to consider.

Definition 13. A tuple $\langle w, W \rangle$ is a possible successor to a tuple $\langle v, V \rangle$ in reaching a term u if

1. $v \Rightarrow_R w$ by an application of rule $l \rightarrow r$ at position p with substitution σ,
2. p is the leftmost redex position in v such that $v/p \not\equiv u/p$, i.e., the subterms at position p in u and v differ.
3. $w \preceq u$,
4. $r\sigma \not\equiv l\sigma$ and $r\sigma \notin V$ — loop checking,
5. $W = \phi$ and $root(r)$ is a constructor symbol OR
   $W = \phi$ and $r\sigma \equiv u/p$ OR
   $W = V \cup \{l\sigma\}$, $r\sigma \not\equiv u/p$ and $root(r)$ is a defined symbol.

The set of all successors of $\langle v, V \rangle$ is denoted by $NEXT(\langle v, V \rangle, u)$.

Condition 2 ensures that the reduction is applied at the leftmost position that needs to be reduced. Condition 3 ensures that the reduction contributes to the cap of u and does not add any constructor symbols not in the cap of u. Condition 4 ensures that same redex does not appear repeatedly at the same position (loop checking). Condition 5 is about book-keeping. If $root(r)$ is a constructor symbol or $r\sigma \equiv u/p$, it is clear that no more reductions take place at p in w (but reductions may take place below or to the right of p). Therefore, there is no need for any more loop checking at position p and hence W is set to ϕ. In the other case, $l\sigma$ is added to W.

Example 3. Consider the following simple flat system.

$$a(0, y) \rightarrow y$$
$$a(s(x), y) \rightarrow s(a(x, y))$$
$$b \rightarrow f(b)$$
$$b \rightarrow f(f(b))$$
$$b \rightarrow g(b, b)$$
$$b \rightarrow c$$
$$c \rightarrow b$$
$$c \rightarrow c$$
$$c \rightarrow d$$

$NEXT(\langle f(b), \phi \rangle, f(f(f(b)))) = \{\langle f(f(b)), \phi \rangle, \langle f(f(f(b))), \phi \rangle, \langle f(c), \{b\} \rangle\}$. Note that 5th rule cannot be applied in computing $NEXT$ as $f(g(b, b)) \not\leq f(f(f(b)))$, i.e., due to condition 3. When 6th rule is applied, the redex b is saved for loop checking as the right-hand side has a defined symbol as root.

$NEXT(\langle f(f(b)), \phi \rangle, f(f(f(b)))) = \{\langle f(f(f(b))), \phi \rangle, \langle f(f(c)), \{b\} \rangle\}$.
Note that 4th rule cannot be applied due to condition 3.

$NEXT(\langle f(c), \{b\} \rangle, f(f(f(b)))) = \phi$ because 7th rule and 8th rule cannot be applied due to condition 4 (loop checking) and 9th rule cannot be applied due to condition 3.

$NEXT(\langle a(s(0), s(0)), \phi \rangle, s(s(0))) = \{ \langle s(a(0, s(0))), \phi \rangle \}$.
$NEXT(\langle s(a(0, s(0))), \phi \rangle, s(s(0))) = \{ \langle s(s(0)), \phi \rangle \}$.

$NEXT(\langle a(s(0), s(0)), \phi \rangle, s(s(s(0)))) = \{ \langle s(a(0, s(0))), \phi \rangle \}$.
$NEXT(\langle s(a(0, s(0))), \phi \rangle, s(s(s(0)))) = \{ \langle s(s(0)), \phi \rangle \}$.
$NEXT(\langle s(s(0)), \phi \rangle, s(s(s(0)))) = \phi$.   □

Lemma 3. $v \Rightarrow_R w$ for every $\langle w, W \rangle$ in $NEXT(\langle v, V \rangle, u)$.

Proof: Straightforward from Definition 13.   □

The following function checks whether a flat term t reduces to a term u by a simple flat system or not. Here, $\langle u, - \rangle$ stands for any tuple with u as the first element and $\langle u, - \rangle \in S$ is true if there is a tuple in S with u as the first element.

function REACHABILITY-CHECK(R, t, u);
begin
    if $t \not\leq u$ **then** Return(no);
    $Queue := \{\langle t, \phi \rangle\}$;
    while $Queue \neq \phi$ **do**
        begin
            Let $\langle v, V \rangle$ be the first element of $Queue$;

$$\textbf{if } u \equiv v \textbf{ then } \text{Return}(\textbf{yes});$$
$$Queue := (Queue - \{\langle v, V \rangle\}) \cup NEXT(\langle v, V \rangle)$$
   end;
  Return(**no**);
end;

The above function is exploring the search space of terms derivable from t in a breadth-first fashion (data structure QUEUE) looking for u. The search space is constructed conservatively by creating only potential intermediate terms leading to u and using loop checking.

We prove the correctness of this decision procedure, in rest of this section.

Lemma 4. $t \Rightarrow^*_R w$ for every $\langle w, W \rangle$ added to $Queue$ during the execution of REACHABILITY-CHECK(R, t, u).

Proof: Follows from Lemma 3 and noetherian induction.   □

The following theorem proves termination of REACHABILITY-CHECK.

Theorem 4. If R is a simple flat TRS and t and u are two flat terms, the function call REACHABILITY-CHECK(R, t, u) terminates.

Proof: Consider a tuple $\langle w, W \rangle$ added to $Queue$ in the function call REACHABILITY-CHECK(R, t, u). By Lemma 4, $t \Rightarrow^*_R w$. Let n be the smallest integer greater than the size of every term in $Dsub(t)$. By Theorem 3, n is greater than the size of every term in $Dsub(w)$. Further, $w \preceq u$ by condition 3 of Definition 13, and hence the size of $cap(w)$ is bounded by the the size of $cap(u)$. Therefore the set of distinct tuples that are added to $Queue$ is finite as both Σ and R are finite.

Since we are following left-to-right reduction strategy and using loop checking, no tuple is added to $Queue$ more than once. In every iteration of **while** loop, one tuple is deleted from $Queue$ and hence REACHABILITY-CHECK(R, t, u) terminates.   □

We need the following results about left-to-right derivations.

Definition 14. A derivation $t_1 \Rightarrow t_2 \Rightarrow \cdots \Rightarrow t_n$ is a left-to-right derivation if there is no $j \in [2, n-1]$ such that reduction $t_{j-1} \Rightarrow t_j$ takes place at position p_1 and reduction $t_j \Rightarrow t_{j+1}$ takes place at position p_2 such that p_2 is to the left of p_1.

Lemma 5. If t_1, t_2 and t_3 are flat terms such that $t_1 \Rightarrow_{p_1} t_2 \Rightarrow_{p_2} t_3$ and p_2 is to the left of p_1, then there is a term t'_2 such that $t_1 \Rightarrow_{p_2} t'_2 \Rightarrow_{p_1} t_3$.

Proof : Let C be the context obtained from t_1 by replacing the subterms at positions p_1 and p_2 by holes, and $u_1 \equiv t_1/p_1$, $u_2 \equiv t_1/p_2$, $v_1 \equiv t_2/p_1$, $v_2 \equiv t_3/p_2$. It is easy to see that $t_1 \equiv C[u_1, u_2] \Rightarrow_{p_2} t_2' \equiv C[u_1, v_2] \Rightarrow_{p_1} t_3 \equiv C[v_1, v_2]$.   □

Lemma 6. If R is a simple flat TRS and t and u are flat terms such that $t \Rightarrow_R^* u$, then there is a left-to-right derivation from t to u.

Proof: We can obtain a left-to-right derivation from t to u by repeatedly applying Lemma 5.   □

Lemma 7. If R is a simple flat TRS and t, w and u are flat terms such that $t \Rightarrow_R^* w \Rightarrow_R^* u$ is the shortest left-to-right derivation from t to u, then $\langle w, - \rangle$ is added to *Queue* during the execution of REACHABILITY-CHECK(R, t, u).

Proof : Induction on the length l of the derivation $t \Rightarrow_R^* w$.

Basis : $l = 0$. In this case, $w \equiv t$ and $\langle t, \phi \rangle$ is added to *Queue* in the initialization statement.

Induction step : Consider the previous term w' in $t \Rightarrow_R^* w' \Rightarrow_R w \Rightarrow_R^* u$. By the induction hypothesis, $\langle w', - \rangle$ is added to *Queue*. Since REACHABILITY-CHECK(R, t, u) terminates, $\langle w', - \rangle$ is replaced by $NEXT(\langle w', - \rangle, u)$. As $w \preceq u$ (by Theorem 3) and $t \Rightarrow_R^* u$ is the shortest derivation (i.e, no looping), it is clear that $\langle w, - \rangle \in NEXT(\langle w', - \rangle, u)$ and hence $\langle w, - \rangle$ is added to *Queue*.   □

The following theorem establishes the decidability of $t \Rightarrow_R^* u$.

Theorem 5. If t and u are two flat terms and R is a simple flat TRS, it is decidable whether $t \Rightarrow_R^* u$ or not.

Proof : Since REACHABILITY-CHECK is terminating, it is enough to show that REACHABILITY-CHECK(R, t, u) returns 'yes' if and only if $t \Rightarrow_R^* u$.

If-case : If $t \Rightarrow_R^* u$, it follows by Lemma 7 that $\langle u, - \rangle$ is added to *Queue*. It will eventually become the first element and REACHABILITY-CHECK(R, t, u) will return 'yes'.

Only-if-case : REACHABILITY-CHECK(R, t, u) returns 'yes' only if $\langle u, - \rangle$ is a member of *Queue*. If $\langle u, - \rangle$ is a member of *Queue*, $t \Rightarrow_R^* u$ by Lemma 4.   □

5   Inferability of Simple Flat TRSs from Positive Data

In this section, we establish inductive inferability of simple flat TRSs from positive data.

Definition 15. Let SF be the set of all simple flat rules, FT be the cartesian product of the set of all flat terms (with the same set) and Φ be a semantic mapping such that $\Phi(R)$ is the relation $\{(s,t) \mid s \Rightarrow_R^* t\}$ over flat terms. The concept defining framework $\langle FT, SF, \Phi \rangle$ is denoted by **SFT**.

Lemma 8. The class of rewrite relations defined by simple flat TRSs is an indexed family of recursive concepts.

Proof: By Theorem 5, it is decidable whether $t \Rightarrow_R^* u$ for any simple flat TRS R and flat terms t and u. By Theorem 2, it is decidable whether a TRS is simple flat or not. Since Σ is finite, we can effectively enumerate all simple flat TRSs – listing the TRSs of size n before those of size $n+1$, where size of a TRS is defined as the sum of the sizes of all the left- and right-hand side terms in it. $\square$

The following theorem plays the predominant role in proving our main result.

Theorem 6. The concept defining framework **SFT** $= \langle FT, SF, \Phi \rangle$ has bounded finite thickness.

Proof: Since Φ is the rewrite relation, it is obviously monotonic, i.e., $\Phi(R_1) \subseteq \Phi(R_2)$ whenever $R_1 \subseteq R_2$.

Consider a finite relation $S \subseteq FT$ and a TRS $R \subseteq SF$ containing at most $m \geq 1$ rules such that R is reduced w.r.t. S. Let n_1 be an integer such that $n_1 \geq |s|$ for every term s in $\{s \in Dsub(t) \mid (t,u) \in S\}$ and n_2 be an integer such that $n_2 \geq |cap(u)|$ for every $(t,u) \in S$.

By Theorem 3, $n_1 \geq |w'|$ and $n_2 \geq |cap(w)|$ for every term $w' \in Dsub(w)$ such that $t \Rightarrow^* w \Rightarrow^* u$ and $(t,u) \in S$. That's, every redex in $t \Rightarrow^* u$ is of size $\leq n_1$ and the cap of every term in $t \Rightarrow^* u$ is of size $\leq n_2$. Since R is reduced w.r.t. S, every rule in R is used in derivations of S. Hence, $n_1 \geq |l|$ and $n_2 \geq |cap(r)|$ for every rule $l \rightarrow r \in R$.

Since Σ is finite, there are only finitely many simple flat TRSs containing at most m rules of the form $l \rightarrow r$ such that $n_1 \geq |l|$ and $n_2 \geq |cap(r)|$ (except for the renaming of variables). Therefore, the set $\{\Phi(R) \mid R$ is reduced w.r.t. S and contains at most m rules$\}$ is finite. Hence, the concept defining framework $\langle FT, SF, \Phi \rangle$ has bounded finite thickness. $\square$

From this Theorem, Lemma 8 and Theorem 1, we obtain our main result.

Theorem 7. For every $m \geq 1$, the class of simple flat TRSs with at most m rules is inferable from positive data.

The above result essentially means that there is an inductive inference machine that can effectively produce an equivalent simple flat TRS R' given any enumeration of the set of pairs of flat terms (s,t) such that s reduces to t by the target simple flat TRS R.

6   Discussion

In this paper, we study inductive inference of term rewriting systems from positive data. A class of simple flat TRSs *inferable from positive data* is defined. This class of TRSs is rich enough to include divide-and-conquer programs like addition, doubling, tree-count, list-count, split, append, etc. To the best of our knowledge, ours is the first positive result about inductive inference of term rewriting systems from positive data. The closest publication we know on this problem is Mukouchi et.al. [9], which deals with pure grammars like PD0L systems. These systems are TRSs with function symbols of arity at most one, and a restriction that the left-hand side of each rule is a constant (function of arity zero). This stringent restriction makes it very difficult to express even simple functions like addition in this class.

To motivate an open problem for further study, we compare simple flat TRSs with linearly-moded Prolog programs of [8]. The class of linearly-moded programs is the largest class of Prolog programs known to be inferable from positive data. The classes of simple flat TRSs and linearly-moded Prolog programs are incomparable for the following reasons.

1. Linearly-moded Prolog programs only capture functions whose output is bounded by the size of the inputs. Functions like addition, list-count, split, append, quick-sort have such a property. But functions like multiplication and doubling are beyond linearly-moded programs as the size of their output is bigger than that of the input. The following program computes the double of the list (output contains each element of the input twice as often).

    > Moding: double(in, out)
    > double([ ],[ ]) ←
    > double([H|T], [H, H|R]) ← double(T, R)

    This program is not linearly-moded w.r.t. the above moding[2] as the size of the output is twice the size of the input. In contrast, the following TRS for computing the double of a given list is simple flat.

    > double([ ]) → [ ]
    > double([H|T]) → [H, H|double(T)]

    This shows that there are functions that can be computed by simple flat TRSs but not by linearly-moded Prolog programs.

---

[2] However, it is linearly-moded w.r.t. the moding double(in, in), in which case this program can be used for checking whether a list L2 is the double of another list L1, but not for computing the double of a given list. Also see Remark 2, point (b).

2. The standard Prolog program for quick-sort is linearly-moded, but it is beyond simple flat TRSs as it involves nesting of defined symbols (partition inside the quick-sort and quick-sort inside append). This shows that there are functions that can be computed by linearly-moded Prolog programs but not by simple flat TRSs.

In view of this incomparability of the simple flat TRSs and linearly-moded Prolog programs, it will be very useful to work towards extending the frontiers of inferable classes of rewrite systems and characterize some classes of TRSs having the expressive power of both simple flat TRSs and linearly-moded Prolog programs, and yet inferable from positive data.

Acknowledgements. The author would like to thank King Fahd University of Petroleum and Minerals for the generous support provided by it in conducting this research.

References

[1] D. Angluin (1980), *Inductive inference of formal languages from positive data,* Information and Control **45**, pp. 117-135.

[2] H. Arimura, T. Shinohara and S. Otsuki (1994), *Finding Minimal Generalizations for Unions of Pattern Languages and Its Application to Inductive Inference from Positive Data,* Proc. of STACS'94, LNCS **775**, pp. 649-660.

[3] H. Arimura and T. Shinohara (1994), *Inductive inference of Prolog programs with linear data dependency from positive data,* Proc. Information Modelling and Knowledge Bases V, pp. 365-375, IOS press.

[4] L. Blum and M. Blum (1975), *Towards a mathematical theory of inductive inference,* Information and Control **28**, pp. 125-155.

[5] N. Dershowitz and J.-P. Jouannaud (1990), *Rewrite Systems,* In J. van Leeuwen (ed.), *Handbook of Theoretical Computer Science,* Vol. B, pp. 243-320, North-Holland.

[6] E.M. Gold (1967), *Language identification in the limit,* Information and Control **10**, pp. 447-474.

[7] J.W. Klop (1992), *Term Rewriting Systems,* in S. Abramsky, D. Gabby and T. Maibaum (ed.), *Handbook of Logic in Computer Science,* Vol. 1, Oxford Press, 1992.

[8] M. R. K. Krishna Rao (2000), *Some classes of prolog programs inferable from positive data,* Theor. Comput. Sci. **241**, pp. 211-234.

[9] Y. Mukouchi, I.Yamaue, M. Sato (1998), *Inferring a Rewriting System from Examples,* Proc. of DS'98, LNCS **1532**, pp. 93-104

[10] T. Shinohara (1991), *Inductive inference of monotonic formal systems from positive data,* New Generation Computing **8**, pp. 371-384.

[11] Takeshi Shinohara, Hiroki Arimura (2000), *Inductive inference of unbounded unions of pattern languages from positive data,* Theor. Comput. Sci. **241**, pp. 191-209.

On the Data Consumption Benefits of Accepting Increased Uncertainty

Eric Martin[1], Arun Sharma[2], and Frank Stephan[3]

[1] School of Computer Science and Engineering, National ICT Australia,[†]
UNSW Sydney, NSW 2052, Australia
emartin@cse.unsw.edu.au
[2] Division of Research and Commercialisation, Queensland University of Technology,
2 George street, GPO Box 2434, Brisbane QLD 4001, Australia
Arun.Sharma@qut.edu.au
[3] School of Computing, National University of Singapore, Singapore 117543
fstephan@comp.nus.edu.sg

Abstract. In the context of learning paradigms of identification in the limit, we address the question: why is uncertainty sometimes desirable? We use mind change bounds on the output hypotheses as a measure of uncertainty, and interpret 'desirable' as reduction in data memorization, also defined in terms of mind change bounds. The resulting model is closely related to iterative learning with bounded mind change complexity, but the dual use of mind change bounds — for hypotheses and for data — is a key distinctive feature of our approach. We show that situations exists where the more mind changes the learner is willing to accept, the lesser the amount of data it needs to remember in order to converge to the correct hypothesis. We also investigate relationships between our model and learning from good examples, set-driven, monotonic and strong-monotonic learners, as well as class-comprising versus class-preserving learnability.

Keywords: Mind changes, long term memory, iterative learning, frugal learning.

1 Introduction

Human beings excel at making decisions based on incomplete information. Even in situations where access to larger sets of data would result in a definitely correct hypothesis, they might not wait to receive the complete information which would allow them to conclude with certainty that their decision is definitely the best. They often propose a hypothesis having received little or no evidence, knowing that this hypothesis might not be correct and could be revised; they

---

[†] National ICT Australia is funded by the Australian Government's Department of Communications, Information Technology and the Arts and the Australian Research Council through Backing Australia's Ability and the ICT Centre of Excellence Program.

S. Ben-David, J. Case, A. Maruoka (Eds.): ALT 2004, LNAI 3244, pp. 83–98, 2004.

then gather a few more data and propose another and hopefully better hypothesis. Making imperfect decisions, but making them now and in the near future, is better than having to wait an unknown and possibly very long time to make the perfect decision. From a logical point of view, human beings draw uncertain and nonmonotonic inferences on the basis of few assumptions when they could make deductions on the basis of much larger sets of premises. From the point of view of Inductive inference, they accept to change their hypotheses (execute a mind change) when they could learn the underlying concept with certainty (without any mind change) if they waited to receive a larger set of data.

Let us illustrate these considerations with an example. Take a class $\mathcal{L}$ of languages (nonempty r.e. subsets of the set $\mathbb{N}$ of natural numbers) and a text t for a member L of $\mathcal{L}$ (so every positive example—member of L—occurs in the enumeration t while no nonmember of L—negative example—occurs in t). A learner M (algorithmic device that maps finite sequences of data to hypotheses, represented as r.e. indexes) that successfully Ex-identifies L in the limit from t (outputs as hypothesis an r.e. index for L in response to all but finitely many initial segments of t) will often find that many elements in t are useless at the time they are presented to it. For example, assume that $\mathcal{L}$ is the set of all nonempty final segments of $\mathbb{N}$. If 7 is the first natural number that occurs in t then M will likely conjecture that $L = \{7, 8, 9, \ldots\}$. If 11 is the next natural number that occurs in L then 11 will be seen as useless and can be forgotten. Only a natural number smaller than 7 will, in case it occurs in t, be used by M. We follow the line of research based on limiting the long term memory [3,4,6,13,14]. We propose a model where the learner can decide to either remember or forget any incoming datum, based on previously remembered data. The learner can output conjectures using only the data it has recorded. It could for instance remember at most three data, in which case it could output at most four hypotheses—one before the first datum is presented, and one after the presentation of each of the three data. More generality is achieved by assuming that the learner has an ordinal data counter, that can store values smaller than a given ordinal α. When it sees a new datum, the learner can either memorize it and decrease the value of its data counter, or decide not to use that datum and leave the value of the data counter unchanged. The basic idea is that learning incurs a cost whenever the learner considers that a piece of information is relevant to the situation and should be memorized; we propose to capture this cost by down-counting an ordinal counter. This forces learners to make a restrictive or frugal use of data.

In this paper we start investigating why a learner would accept to give up certainty for uncertainty, or a low degree of uncertainty for a higher degree of uncertainty. As a measure of uncertainty, we take mind change bounds on the output hypotheses (in a model where outputting a new hypothesis requires to decrease the value of an ordinal counter), rather than probabilistic accuracy on the output hypotheses. The main reason for thinking of uncertainty in terms of mind change bounds is that we measure the benefit of additional uncertainty—frugal use of data—in terms of ordinals, and it is natural to use a common 'unit of measure.' Hence we can think of learners as being equipped with two kinds of ordinal counters: a hypothesis counter that measures uncertainty, and a data counter that measures the cost of keeping track of information.

Section 2 describes the framework, which is basically a model of iterative learning with at most α mind changes, but where α is interpreted as an upper bound on the number of data that can be remembered and used rather than an upper bound on the number of mind changes as to what could be the target concept. Section 3 contains the conceptually most interesting result in the paper, that determines the exact tradeoff between frugal use of data consumption and degree of uncertainty for a particular class of languages to be learnt. Intuitively, the more mind changes the learner is willing to accept, the lesser the amount of data it needs to remember in order to converge to the correct hypothesis. This section also exhibits a class of languages that can be learnt by learners making frugal use of data if data come from fat texts (where positive examples occur infinitely often), but not if data come from arbitrary texts. Section 4 investigates some of the relationships between our framework and learning paradigms with more restrictive learners. In particular, it is shown that frugal use of data is a weaker concept than learnability by consistent and strong-monotonic learners, but not weaker than learnability by consistent and monotonic learners. Section 5 investigates some of the relationships between our framework and learning paradigms with more restrictive learning criteria. In particular, it is shown that class-comprising learnability from good examples, but not class-preserving learnability from good examples, is a weaker concept than frugal use of data. We conclude in Section 6.

2   Model Description

The set of rational numbers is denoted $\mathbb{Q}$. We follow the basic model of Inductive inference as introduced by Gold [8] while applying some notation from our previous work [17,18]. $\mathcal{D}$ denotes a recursive set of data. This set can be assumed to be equal to $\mathbb{N}$ and code, depending on the context, natural numbers, finite sequences of natural numbers, finite sequences of ordinals, etc. We usually do not make the coding explicit. We denote by $\sharp$ an extra symbol that represents an empty piece of information. Given a set X, the set of finite sequences of members of X is denoted $X^\star$; the concatenation of two members σ, τ of $X^\star$ is represented by $\sigma \star \tau$, just written $\sigma \star x$ in case τ is of the form (x). Given a member σ of $(\mathcal{D} \cup \{\sharp\})^\star$, we denote by $\mathrm{cnt}(\sigma)$ the set of members of $\mathcal{D}$ that occur in σ. Given a sequence t whose length is at least equal to an integer n, and given $i \leq n$, $t[i]$ represents the initial segment of e of length i and if $i < n$, $t(i)$ represents its $(i+1)$st element. The cardinality of a finite set D is denoted $|D|$.

We fix an acceptable enumeration $(\varphi_e)_{e \in \mathbb{N}}$ of the unary partial recursive functions over $\mathcal{D}$. For all $e \in \mathbb{N}$, W_e denotes the domain of φ_e, and D_e denotes the finite set whose canonical index is e (i.e., $D_e = \emptyset$ if $e = 0$ and $D_e = \{x_0, \ldots, x_n\}$ if $e = 2^{x_0} + \ldots + 2^{x_n}$ for some $n, x_0, \ldots, x_n \in \mathbb{N}$ with $x_0 < \ldots < x_n$). The symbol $\mathcal{L}$ refers to a class of r.e. subsets of $\mathcal{D}$, representing the class of languages to be learnt; hence $\mathcal{L}$ is a class of sets of the form W_e for e ranging over a particular subset of $\mathbb{N}$. A member σ of $(\mathcal{D} \cup \{\sharp\})^*$ is said to be *consistent in* $\mathcal{L}$ iff there exists $L \in \mathcal{L}$ with $\mathrm{cnt}(\sigma) \subseteq L$. A *text* for a member L of $\mathcal{L}$ is an enumeration t of $L \cup \{\sharp\}$ where each member of L occurs at least once; t is said to be *fat* if every member of L has infinitely many occurrences in t. A *learner* is a partial computable function from $(\mathcal{D} \cup \{\sharp\})^*$ into $\mathbb{N}$. Learnability means Ex-identification (in the limit): for all $L \in \mathcal{L}$ and for all texts t for L, the learner has to output on cofinitely many strict initial segments of t a fixed $e \in \mathbb{N}$ such that $W_e = L$.

We first define the key notion of memory function.

Definition 1. A *memory function* is defined as a partial recursive function h from $(\mathcal{D} \cup \{\sharp\})^*$ into $(\mathcal{D} \cup \{\sharp\})^*$ such that $h(()) = ()$ and for all $\sigma \in (\mathcal{D} \cup \{\sharp\})^*$:

- for all $\tau \in (\mathcal{D} \cup \{\sharp\})^*$ with $\sigma \subseteq \tau$, if $h(\sigma)$ is undefined then $h(\tau)$ is undefined;
- for all $x \in \mathcal{D} \cup \{\sharp\}$, $h(\sigma \star x)$ is undefined, or equal to $h(\sigma)$, or equal to $h(\sigma) \star x$.

Let Z be the range of h except $()$ and given $\sigma, \tau \in Z$, let $R(\sigma, \tau)$ hold iff $\tau \subset \sigma$. The *ordinal complexity of* h is undefined if (Z, R) is not well founded and is equal to the length of (Z, R) otherwise.[1]

Definition 2. Let a learner M be given.

Given a memory function h, we say that M has h-*memory* iff M can be represented as $g \circ h$ for some partial recursive function g.

The *data consumption complexity of* M is defined and equal to ordinal α iff α is the least ordinal such that M has h-memory, for some memory function h whose ordinal complexity is equal to α.

When it faces an incoming datum d, a learner that has h-memory for some memory function h will either decide not to memorize d, or memorize d for ever—the learner cannot memorize d for some time and then forget it.

Definition 3. Let a learner M be given. Let Z be the set of all $\sigma \in (\mathcal{D} \cup \{\sharp\})^*$ such that $M(\sigma)$ is defined. Given $\sigma, \tau \in Z$ let $R(\sigma, \tau)$ hold iff there is $\eta \in Z$ with $\tau \subseteq \eta \subseteq \sigma$ and $M(\sigma) \neq M(\eta)$. The *mind change complexity of* M is undefined if (Z, R) is not well founded, and equal to the length of (Z, R) otherwise.

We will often write 'DC complexity' for 'data consumption complexity,' and 'MC complexity' for 'mind change complexity.' If M Ex-identifies $\mathcal{L}$ and if the mind change complexity of M is equal to ordinal α, then M Ex-identifies $\mathcal{L}$ with less than α mind changes, that is, with at most β mind changes if α is of the form $\beta+1$ and with no mind change if $\alpha = 1$. Note that if α is a limit ordinal, then Ex-identifying $\mathcal{L}$ with less than α mind changes is not expressible as Ex-identifying $\mathcal{L}$ with at most β mind changes for some β.

---

[1] Assuming that (Z, R) is well founded, and denoting by ρ_R the unique function from Z into the class of ordinals such that $\rho_R(x) = \sup\{\rho_R(y) + 1 : y \in X, \ R(y, x)\}$ for all $x \in X$, the length of (Z, R) is defined as the least ordinal not in the range of ρ_R.

Remark 4. In the definitions above, and in case (Z, R) is well founded, one can furthermore define the *effective* length of (Z, R) as the least ordinal α such that there exists a recursive well-ordering $\sqsubseteq$ of Z that is isomorphic to $\{\beta : \beta < \alpha\}$, with $\sigma \sqsubset \tau$ whenever $R(\sigma, \tau)$; note that σ, τ might be equivalent with respect to $\sqsubseteq$ if they are not strictly ordered by R. Since Z is a subset of a recursively enumerable tree and R is compatible with $\{(\sigma, \tau) : \sigma, \tau \in (\mathcal{D} \cup \{\sharp\})^\star, \sigma \supset \tau\}$, the restriction of the Kleene-Brouwer ordering of a tree is always such an ordering, and so the effective length of (Z, R) is defined whenever the length of (Z, R) is defined. The effective length of (Z, R) yields the notions of effective data consumption complexity and mind change complexity, in the respective definitions. The effective mind change complexity is equivalent to the traditional one [1, 7,12,10,20] defined by ordinal counters; the noneffective version is used in our previous studies of the noneffective setting [17,18]. In [1] it is observed that any learner which makes on all texts only finitely many mind changes has an effective mind change complexity, that is, the effective mind change complexity is defined whenever the noneffective one is defined. The results in this paper hold for both the effective and the noneffective versions of mind change and data consumption complexities. Note that both the notions of data consumption complexity and of mind change complexity are defined 'externally,' without requiring the learner to explicit update an ordinal counter, hence avoiding the issues related to programs for the ordinals. More precisely, these externally defined notions provide a lower bound on the ordinal given by a learner that explicitly updates an ordinal counter, using a particular program for the ordinals.

Definition 5. A learner whose MC complexity is defined is said to be *confident*. A learner whose DC complexity is defined is said to be *frugal*.

In the literature, a confident learner is usually defined as a learner that converges on any text, whether this text is or is not for a member of the class $\mathcal{L}$ of languages to identify in the limit. We use the term 'confident' in the definition above relying on the fact (see [1]) that Ex-identification with a bounded number of mind changes if equivalent to Ex-identification by a confident learner.

3   DC Complexity Versus MC Complexity

We first state a few obvious relationships.

Property 6. *If the DC complexity of a leaner M is defined and equal to ordinal α, then the MC complexity of M is defined and at most equal to $\alpha + 1$.*

Remember the definition of an iterative learner:

Definition 7. A learner M is said to be *iterative* iff it is total and there exists a total recursive function $g : \mathbb{N} \times (\mathcal{D} \cup \{\sharp\}) \to \mathbb{N}$ such that for all $\sigma \in (\mathcal{D} \cup \{\sharp\})^\star$ and $x \in \mathcal{D} \cup \{\sharp\}$, $M(\sigma \star x) = g(M(\sigma), x)$.

Coding data into hypotheses immediately yields the following properties.

Property 8. *Let a nonnull ordinal α be given. If some iterative learner whose MC complexity is equal to α Ex-identifies $\mathcal{L}$, then some learner whose DC complexity is at most equal to α Ex-identifies $\mathcal{L}$.*

Property 9. *Let an ordinal α be given. If some learner whose DC complexity is equal to α Ex-identifies $\mathcal{L}$, then some iterative learner whose MC complexity is at most equal to $\alpha + 1$ Ex-identifies $\mathcal{L}$.*

The notion of data consumption complexity does not collapse to any ordinal smaller than ω_1^{ck}, the first nonrecursive ordinal:

Proposition 10. *For all any recursive ordinal α, $\mathcal{L}$ can be chosen such that:*

- *α is the least ordinal such that some learner whose DC complexity is equal to α Ex-identifies $\mathcal{L}$;*
- *α is the least ordinal such that some learner whose MC complexity is equal to α Ex-identifies $\mathcal{L}$;*
- *some learner whose DC and MC complexities are equal to α Ex-identifies $\mathcal{L}$.*

Proof. It suffices to define $\mathcal{L}$ as the class of all sets of the form $\{\gamma < \alpha : \gamma \geq \beta\}$ for β ranging over the set of ordinals smaller than a given nonnull ordinal α. (What is really considered here is a class of sets of codes of ordinals, for an appropriate coding of the ordinals smaller than α. We do not explicit the coding in order not to clutter the argument.) The optimal learner memorizes a datum iff it is an ordinal β smaller than all ordinals seen so far; the conjecture is $\{\gamma < \alpha : \gamma \geq \beta\}$.
□

The next proposition captures the fundamental idea that in some sense, a learner can be better and better off in terms of frugal use of data if it is keen to accept higher and higher degrees of uncertainty:

Proposition 11. *For all nonnull $k \in \mathbb{N}$, $\mathcal{L}$ can be chosen such that:*

- *for all $h < k$, some learner whose DC is $\omega \times (k - h)$ Ex-identifies $\mathcal{L}$ with at most h mind changes, and no learner whose DC is smaller than $\omega \times (k - h)$ Ex-identifies $\mathcal{L}$ with at most h mind changes—in particular, some learner whose DC is $\omega \times k$ Ex-identifies $\mathcal{L}$ with no mind change, and no learner whose DC is smaller than $\omega \times k$ Ex-identifies $\mathcal{L}$ with no mind change;*
- *some learner whose DC is $2k$ Ex-identifies $\mathcal{L}$ with at most k mind changes, and no learner whose DC is smaller than $2k$ Ex-identifies $\mathcal{L}$.*

Proof. For all $n \in \mathbb{N}$, let I_n and J_n be the two subsets of $\mathbb{N}$ of cardinality $n + 3$ such that $\{I_n : n \in \mathbb{N}\} \cup \{J_n : n \in \mathbb{N}\}$ is a partition of $\mathbb{N}$ and for all $n \in \mathbb{N}$, the members of I_n are smaller than the members of J_n, and the members of J_n are smaller than the members of I_{n+1}. Hence $I_0 = \{0, 1, 2\}$, $J_0 = \{3, 4, 5\}$, $I_1 = \{6, 7, 8, 9\}$, $J_1 = \{10, 11, 12, 13\}$, etc. Let a nonnull $k \in \mathbb{N}$ be given. Define $\mathcal{L}$ to be the class of all unions of k disjoint sets of the form I_n or

$(I_n \setminus \{\min(I_n) + m\}) \cup \{\min(J_n) + m\}$ with $n \in \mathbb{N}$ and $m < n + 3$. For instance, if $k = 1$ then $\mathcal{L}$ contains $\{0, 1, 2\}$, $\{3, 1, 2\}$, $\{0, 4, 2\}$ and $\{0, 1, 5\}$.

Note that if a learner M gets a datum x from a member L of $\mathcal{L}$, then M can determine the unique $n \in \mathbb{N}$ such that $x \in I_n \cup J_n$, and M knows that precisely $n + 3$ members of $L \cap (I_n \cup J_n)$ will eventually occur in the text t for L it is presented with. Since k is fixed, it follows that M can Ex-identify $\mathcal{L}$ with no mind change. Let $L \in \mathcal{L}$ be such that for all $n \in \mathbb{N}$, $J_n \cap L = \emptyset$. Let X be the set of all $\sigma \in (\mathcal{D} \cup \{\sharp\})^*$ that are consistent in $\mathcal{L}$. Let Y be the set of all $\sigma \in X$ such that for all $n \in \mathbb{N}$ and $m < n + 3$, if $\min(J_n) + m$ occurs in $\mathrm{cnt}(\sigma)$ then all members of $I_n \setminus \{\min(I_n) + m\}$ occur in $\mathrm{cnt}(\sigma)$ before the first occurrence of $\min(J_n) + m$ in $\mathrm{cnt}(\sigma)$. Given $Z \in \{X, Y\}$, let h_Z be the (unique) memory function such that for all $\sigma \in (\mathcal{D} \cup \{\sharp\})^*$, $h_Z(\sigma) = \mathrm{cnt}(\sigma)$ if $\sigma \in Z$, and $h_Z(\sigma) = \uparrow$ otherwise. It is immediately verified that both h_X and h_Y have ordinal complexity equal to $\omega \times k$. Finally, if a learner M having h-memory Ex-identifies $\mathcal{L}$ with no mind change, then h necessarily extends h_Y, because for all $\sigma \in Y$, M has to remember all members of $\mathrm{cnt}(\sigma)$. We conclude that some learner whose DC is $\omega \times k$ Ex-identifies $\mathcal{L}$ with no mind change, but no learner whose DC is smaller than $\omega \times k$ Ex-identifies $\mathcal{L}$ with no mind change.

Let a learner M have the following property when processing a text t for a member L of $\mathcal{L}$. For all $n \in \mathbb{N}$, if $I_n \cap L$ is nonempty then M remembers (1) the first member of $I_n \cup J_n$ that occurs in t and (2) the (unique) member of J_n that occurs in t, if such is the case. Obviously, M can have a data complexity of $2k$. Moreover, M can Ex-identify $\mathcal{L}$ with at most k mind changes: it suffices to make the first guess when data from k sets of the form $I_n \cup J_n$ have been observed, conjecturing that L contains I_n if some member of I_n but no member of J_n has been observed, and conjecturing that $(I_n \setminus \{\min(I_n) + m\}) \cup \{\min(J_n) + m\}$ is included in L if $\min(J_n) + m$ has been observed. Clearly, M does not Ex-identify $\mathcal{L}$ with less than k mind changes. Finally, it is easy to verify that a learner whose data complexity is smaller than $2k$ cannot Ex-identify $\mathcal{L}$.

The remaining part of the proposition is proved using a combination of the previous arguments. □

The notion of data consumption complexity is very restrictive, but becomes more general when learning from fat texts:

Proposition 12. *It is possible to choose $\mathcal{L}$ such that:*
- *some learner whose DC complexity is ω Ex-identifies $\mathcal{L}$ from fat texts;*
- *no frugal learner Ex-identifies $\mathcal{L}$ from texts.*

Proof. Suppose that $\mathcal{L}$ consists of the set $2\mathbb{N}$ of even numbers and every set of the form $D \cup \{2x + 1\}$ where $|D| = x$ and $D \subseteq 2\mathbb{N}$.

Assume that the learner sees $\sigma \in (2\mathbb{N} \cup \{\sharp\})^*$. Let $y = 2|\mathrm{cnt}(\sigma)| + 1$. The learner has to memorize $\mathrm{cnt}(\sigma)$ since it cannot exclude that the set to be learned is $\mathrm{cnt}(\sigma) \cup \{y\}$ and the current text is $\sigma \star y \star \sharp^\infty$. Thus the learner cannot be frugal.

A learner that learns from fat text can have a memory function h that extracts from any σ the first odd number $2x + 1$ – if there is any – and then the first occurrences of up to x many even numbers after the first occurrence of $2x+1$. The hypothesis of the learner on input σ is $2\mathbb{N}$ if $h(\sigma) = ()$ and $\text{cnt}(h(\sigma))$ otherwise. The learner succeeds because fat texts enable to delay the reading of the members of D after it has seen $2x + 1$, whenever the set to be learnt is of the form $D \cup \{2x + 1\}$. □

The next proposition gives other relationships between data consumption complexity, mind change complexity, and learning from fat texts.

Proposition 13. *For all recursive ordinals α, $\mathcal{L}$ can be chosen such that:*
- *some learner whose DC and MC complexities are equal to α Ex-identifies $\mathcal{L}$;*
- *some nonfrugal learner whose MC complexity is equal to 1 Ex-identifies $\mathcal{L}$;*
- *some learner whose DC complexity is equal to $\alpha+1$ and whose MC complexity is equal to 1 Ex-identifies $\mathcal{L}$ on fat texts;*
- *no frugal learner whose MC complexity is smaller than α Ex-identifies $\mathcal{L}$.*

Proof. Let a recursive ordinal α be given. Suppose that $\mathcal{L}$ consists of the following, for any $n > 0$, nonempty decreasing sequence $(\alpha_1, \ldots, \alpha_n)$ of ordinals smaller than α, and increasing sequence $(q_1, \ldots, q_n)$ of rational numbers:
- all nonempty initial segments of $((\alpha_1, q_1), \ldots, (\alpha_n, q_n))$;
- all rational numbers at least equal to q_n.

A learner that only remembers sequences of the form $((\alpha_1, q_1), \ldots, (\alpha_n, q_n))$ and outputs an index for $\{((\alpha_1, q_1), \ldots, (\alpha_n, q_n))\} \cup \{q \in \mathbb{Q} : q \geq q_n\}$ for the longest such sequence, will clearly have data consumption complexity equal to α, and can Ex-identify $\mathcal{L}$ with less than α mind changes, but cannot do any better.

A learner that only remembers sequences of the form $((\alpha_1, q_1), \ldots, (\alpha_n, q_n))$ and rational numbers smaller than any rational number remembered before will wait till both (α', q) and q are observed for some α' and q, thanks to which it can Ex-identify $\mathcal{L}$ with no mind change. On the other hand, considering texts that start with decreasing sequences of rational numbers that are long enough, it is easily verified that this learner has undefined data consumption complexity.

On fat texts, a learner can Ex-identify $\mathcal{L}$ with no mind change by only remembering sequences of the form $((\alpha_1, q_1), \ldots, (\alpha_n, q_n))$, followed by a rational number that also occurs last in the (necessarily) longest remembered sequence of the previous form. Such a learner will clearly have DC complexity equal to $\alpha + 1$.

The last claim of the proposition is easily verified. □

When $\mathcal{L}$ is an indexed family, it is sometimes essential to have a partial memory function as opposed to a total one:

Proposition 14. *It is possible to choose $\mathcal{L}$ such that:*
- *$\mathcal{L}$ is an indexed family;*
- *there exists a frugal learner that Ex-identifies $\mathcal{L}$;*
- *for all total computable memory functions h and frugal learners M, if M has h-memory then M does not Ex-identify $\mathcal{L}$.*

Proof. Define $\mathcal{L}$ to be the set of all sets of the form $\{(x,0),\ldots,(x,y)\}$ where $x, y \in \mathbb{N}$ and there exists $e \leq x$ with $\varphi_e(x)$ being defined and at least equal to y. Clearly, $\mathcal{L}$ is an indexed family. Define a learner M as follows. Supposed that M has memorized $((x, y_1),\ldots,(x, y_k))$ for some $k, y_1,\ldots, y_k \in \mathbb{N}$ with $y_1 < \ldots < y_k$ and is presented with (x, y). If $y \leq y_k$ then M discards (x, y). If $y > y_k$ then M tries to compute $\varphi_0(x),\ldots,\varphi_x(x)$. In case one computation eventually converges and its output is at least equal to y then M remembers (x, y); otherwise M discards (x, y). The hypothesis output by M is $\{(x,0),\ldots,(x,y)\}$ with (x, y) being the pair remembered last. It is easily verified that M has data consumption complexity bounded by $\omega \times \omega$, and that M Ex-identifies $\mathcal{L}$.

Let a total memory function h and a frugal learner M be such that M has h-memory. For all $x \in \mathbb{N}$, let $\widehat{h}(x)$ be the least $y > 0$ such that

$$h((x,0),\ldots,(x,y)) = ((x,0),\ldots,(x,y-1)).$$

Let e be an index for $\widehat{h}$. Put:

$$L_1 = \{(e,0),\ldots,(e,\widehat{h}(e))\} \text{ and } L_2 = \{(e,0),\ldots,(e,\widehat{h}(e)-1)\}.$$

Then L_1 and L_2 both belong to $\mathcal{L}$. But it follows immediately from the definition of $\widehat{h}(x)$ that M will not correctly converge on both $(e,0),\ldots,(e,\widehat{h}(e)),\sharp,\ldots$ (text for L_1) and $(e,0),\ldots,(e,\widehat{h}(e)-1),\sharp,\ldots$ (text for L_2). □

4   Relationships with Some Restricted Learners

In this section, we will investigate how some of the usual restrictions on learners [19] affect the notion of data consumption complexity. Whether it can be enforced that every hypothesis is consistent with the data seen so far (consistency), whether it can be enforced that every hypothesis extends the previous hypothesis (monotonicity), whether it can be enforced that every hypothesis equals the previous hypothesis H in case all data seen so far are consistent with H (conservativeness), are among the questions that have received a lot of attention, see for example [2,11,13,16,19,21].

Definition 15. A learner M is said to be *consistent* iff for all $L \in \mathcal{L}$ and $\sigma \in (L \cup \{\sharp\})^*$, $M(\sigma)$ is the index of a set that contains all data that occur in σ.

Definition 16. A learner M is said to be *conservative* iff for all $\sigma \in (\mathcal{D} \cup \{\sharp\})^*$ and members x of $\mathcal{D} \cup \{\sharp\}$, if $M(\sigma)$ is defined and is the index of a set that contains x then $M(\sigma \star x)$ is defined and equal to $M(\sigma)$.

Definition 17. Let a learner M be given.
  (a) M is said to be *strong-monotonic* iff for all $L \in \mathcal{L}$, texts t for L and $i, j \in \mathbb{N}$ with $i < j$, if $M(t[i])$ and $M(t[j])$ are both defined then $W_{M(t[i])} \subseteq W_{M(t[j])}$.
  (b) M is said to be *monotonic* iff for all $L \in \mathcal{L}$, texts t for L and $i, j \in \mathbb{N}$ with $i < j$, if $M(t[i])$ and $M(t[j])$ are both defined then $W_{M(t[i])} \cap L \subseteq W_{M(t[j])} \cap L$.

Definition 18. A learner M is said to be *set-driven* iff for all $\sigma, \tau \in (\mathcal{D} \cup \{\sharp\})^*$, if $\operatorname{cnt}(\sigma)$ is equal to $\operatorname{cnt}(\tau)$ then $M(\sigma) = M(\tau)$. We write $M(D)$ for $M(\sigma)$, for any member σ of $(\mathcal{D} \cup \{\sharp\})^*$ with $\operatorname{cnt}(\sigma) = D$.

Property 19. *A set-driven learner M Ex-identifies $\mathcal{L}$ iff there is a recursive function f mapping (canonical indices of) finite sets to r.e. indices such that for all $L \in \mathcal{L}$, there exists a finite subset D of L such that for all finite subsets E of L, if $D \subseteq E$ then $f(E) = f(D)$ and $f(D)$ is an r.e. index of L.*

Monotonicity and strong monotonicity cannot be enforced by bounds on the data consumption complexity beyond the trivial bounds 0 for strong monotonicity and 1 for monotonicity (the trivial bounds are obtained from the fact that mind change complexity 1 enforces strong monotonicity and 2 enforces monotonicity):

Example 20. If $\mathcal{L}$ consists of $2\mathbb{N}$ and, for all $x \in \mathbb{N}$, the finite sets
$$\{0, 2, \ldots, 2x\} \cup \{2x + 1\} \text{ and } \{0, 2, \ldots, 2x\} \cup \{2x + 1, 2x + 2, 2x + 3\},$$
then some learner whose DC complexity is 2 Ex-identified $\mathcal{L}$, but no monotonic learner Ex-identifies $\mathcal{L}$.

Consistency, strong-monotonicity, and frugality guarantee that DC complexity is defined:

Proposition 21. *If some consistent, strong-monotonic and confident learner Ex-identifies $\mathcal{L}$ then some frugal learner Ex-identifies $\mathcal{L}$.*

Proof. Let N be a consistent, strong-monotonic and confident learner that Ex-identifies $\mathcal{L}$. We define a memory function h and a learner M having h-memory as follows. Put $M(()) = N(())$. Let $\sigma \in (\mathcal{D} \cup \{\sharp\})^*$ and $x \in \mathcal{D} \cup \{\sharp\}$ be given. The definition of $h(\sigma \star x)$ and $M(\sigma \star x)$ is by cases.
    Case 1: $N(\tau)$ is defined for all initial segments τ of $h(\sigma) \star x$ and $N(h(\sigma) \star x)$ is equal to $N(h(\sigma))$. Then $h(\sigma \star x) = h(\sigma)$.
    Case 2: $N(\tau)$ is defined for all initial segments τ of $h(\sigma) \star x$ but $N(h(\sigma) \star x)$ is distinct from $N(h(\sigma))$. Then $h(\sigma \star x) = h(\sigma) \star x$ and $M(\sigma \star x) = N(h(\sigma \star x))$.
    Case 3: Otherwise, both $h(\sigma \star x)$ and $M(\sigma \star x)$ are undefined.
    Note that Case 3 happens if and only if $\sigma \star x$ is not consistent in $\mathcal{L}$. Let t be an infinite enumeration of members of $\mathcal{D} \cup \{\sharp\}$ such that for all $i \in \mathbb{N}$, $t[i]$ is consistent in $\mathcal{L}$ and assume that $N(t[i])$ is defined. Then $M(t[i])$ is defined for all $i \in \mathbb{N}$, and since the mind change complexity of N is defined, $\{h(t[i]) : i \in \mathbb{N}\}$ is finite. Hence the mind change complexity of M is also defined.
    Using the facts that N is consistent and strong-monotonic, and Ex-identifies $\mathcal{L}$, it is easily verified that:

 – M itself is consistent and strong-monotonic;
 – for all $L \in \mathcal{L}$, texts t for L and $i \in \mathbb{N}$, $M(t[i]) \subseteq L$.

We infer that M converges on any text for L, for any member L of $\mathcal{L}$. $\square$

If the strong-monotonicity requirement is lifted, then there is no longer any guarantee that the data consumption complexity is defined:

Proposition 22. *It is possible to choose $\mathcal{L}$ such that:*

- *some learner whose MC complexity is equal to 1 Ex-identifies $\mathcal{L}$;*
- *some confident, consistent, monotonic learner Ex-identifies $\mathcal{L}$;*
- *some confident, consistent, conservative learner Ex-identifies $\mathcal{L}$;*
- *no frugal learner Ex-identifies $\mathcal{L}$.*

Proof. Let $\mathcal{L}$ consist of the set $2\mathbb{N}$ of even numbers and all sets of the form $D \cup \{2x+1\}$ where $D \subseteq \{2, 4, \ldots\}$ and $|D| = x$. A learner that waits until either 0 or a number of the form $2x + 1$ together with x members of $\{2, 4, \ldots\}$ have appeared can obviously Ex-identify $\mathcal{L}$ with no mind change.

Define a learner M as follows. Let $\sigma \in (\mathcal{D} \cup \{\sharp\})^*$ be given and choose the appropriate case.

Case 1: If all members of $\mathrm{cnt}(\sigma)$ are even then $M(\sigma) = \{0, 2, 4, \ldots\}$.

Case 2: If $\mathrm{cnt}(\sigma)$ contains a unique number of the form $2x+1$ and less than x even numbers then $M(\sigma) = \{2x + 1, 0, 2, 4, \ldots\}$.

Case 3: If $\mathrm{cnt}(\sigma)$ contains a unique number of the form $2x + 1$ and precisely x even numbers then $M(\sigma) = \mathrm{cnt}(\sigma)$.

Case 4: Otherwise $M(\sigma)$ is undefined.

Note that:

- for all texts t for $\{0, 2, 4, \ldots\}$ and $i \in \mathbb{N}$, $M(t[i]) = \{0, 2, 4, \ldots\}$;
- for all members L of $\mathcal{L}$ of the form $L = \{2x + 1, y_1, y_2, \ldots, y_x\}$ and for all texts t for L, M will output in response the longer and longer initial segments of t only the hypotheses $\{0, 2, 4, \ldots\}$, $\{2x + 1, 0, 2, 4, \ldots\}$ and L (maybe not all of them), in that order, and $L \cap \{0, 2, 4, \ldots\} \subseteq L \cap \{2x+1, 0, 2, 4, \ldots\} \subseteq L$.

Hence M is monotonic, and it is easily verified that M is consistent, has a defined mind change complexity, and Ex-identifies $\mathcal{L}$.

Define a learner N as follows. Let $\sigma \in (\mathcal{D} \cup \{\sharp\})^*$ be given. The definition of $N(\sigma)$ is by cases.

Case 1: If all members of $\mathrm{cnt}(\sigma)$ are even then $N(\sigma) = \{0, 2, 4, \ldots\}$.

Case 2: If $\mathrm{cnt}(\sigma)$ contains a unique number of the form $2x + 1$ and at most x even numbers then $N(\sigma) = \mathrm{cnt}(\sigma)$.

Case 3: Otherwise $N(\sigma)$ is undefined.

It is immediately verified that N is a consistent and conservative learner that Ex-identifies $\mathcal{L}$, and whose mind change complexity is defined and equal to $\omega + 1$.

Let P be a learner that has h memory, for some memory function h whose ordinal complexity is defined. Let a sequence $(\sigma)_{n \in \mathbb{N}}$ of finite sequences be defined as follows. Put $\sigma_0 = ()$. Let a nonnull $n \in \mathbb{N}$ be given, and assume that σ_m has been defined for all $m < n$, but σ_n has not been defined yet. If there exists a sequence τ consisting of two members of $\{6n, 6n+2, 6n+4\}$ such that $h(\sigma_{n-1} \star \tau)$ is distinct from $h(\sigma_{n-1})$ then $\sigma_n = \sigma_{n-1} \star \tau$ for such a sequence τ. Otherwise $\sigma_m = \sigma_n$ for all $m \geq n$. Since the ordinal complexity of h is defined, there exists a least $p \in \mathbb{N}$ with $\sigma_{p-1} = \sigma_p$. Note that σ_p contains precisely $2p$ even numbers. Then $e_1 = \sigma_p \star (6p, 4p + 1, \sharp, \sharp, \ldots)$ and $e_2 = \sigma_p \star (6p + 2, 4p + 1, \sharp, \sharp, \ldots)$ are two texts for two distinct members of $\mathcal{L}$ but for all $m \geq 2p$, $P(e_1[m]) = P(e_2[m])$, hence P fails to Ex-identify $\mathcal{L}$. $\qquad\square$

5   Relationships with Some Learning Criteria

Frugality turns out to be related to learnability from good examples. There are two main notions of learnability from good examples [5,9,15]:

Definition 23. $\mathcal{L}$ is said to be *class-comprisingly learnable from good examples* iff there is a numbering $(H_i)_{i \in \mathbb{N}}$ of uniformly recursively enumerable sets containing all members of $\mathcal{L}$, a recursive function g mapping r.e. indices to canonical indices of finite sets and a set-driven learner M mapping canonical indices of finite sets to r.e. indices such that for all $e \in \mathbb{N}$:

  - if $H_e \in \mathcal{L}$ then $D_{g(e)} \subseteq H_e$;
  - if $H_e \in \mathcal{L}$, $D_{g(e)} \subseteq E \subseteq H_e$ and E is finite then $H_{M(E)} = H_e$.

Moreover, if $\mathcal{L} = \{H_0, H_1, \ldots\}$ then $\mathcal{L}$ is said to be *class-preservingly learnable from good examples*.

Example 24. [9, Theorem 1(b)] It is possible to choose $\mathcal{L}$ such that $\mathcal{L}$ is confidently learnable, but not learnable from good examples. An example of such a class consists of the following subsets of $\mathbb{N} \times \mathbb{N}$: $\{(i,0), (i,1), \ldots\}$ for all i and, for a given recursive repetition-free enumeration $j_0, j_1, \ldots$ of the halting-problem, each set $\{(j_i, 0), (j_i, 1), \ldots, (j_i, k)\}$ with $k \leq i$.

So confidently learnable classes may fail to be learnable from good examples, but this result does not carry over to frugally learnable classes:

Proposition 25. *Suppose that some frugal learner Ex-identifies $\mathcal{L}$. Then $\mathcal{L}$ is class-comprisingly learnable from good examples. More precisely, there is a superclass of $\mathcal{L}$ which is class-preservingly learnable from good examples with respect to a repetition-free enumeration of this class.*

Proof. Let a memory function h and a frugal learner M be such that M has h-memory and M Ex-identifies $\mathcal{L}$. First one introduces some useful concepts. Let t be any recursive sequence over $\mathbb{N} \cup \{\sharp\}$ that contains infinitely many occurrences of each member of $\mathbb{N} \cup \{\sharp\}$. Given $F \subseteq \mathbb{N}$, let t_F be such that for all $i \in \mathbb{N}$, $t_F(i) = t(i)$ if $t(i) \in F$ and $t_F(i) = \sharp$ otherwise. Given $F \subseteq \mathbb{N}$, define σ_F to be the shortest initial segment of t_F such that $h(\sigma_F)$ is defined and for all initial segments τ of t_F that extend $t_F(i)$, $h(\tau)$ is defined and equal to $h(\sigma_F)$; if such an initial segment does not exist then σ_F is undefined. Intuitively, this means that whenever σ_F exists, M does not remember any member of t_F that occurs in t_F beyond σ_F, and therefore there is no $x \in F \cup \{\#\}$ such that M remembers the last occurrence of x in $\sigma_F \star x$. Note that the partial function that maps a finite subset D of $\mathbb{N}$ such that σ_D exists, to σ_D itself, is partial recursive.

We now define the enumeration of the superclass which is class-preservingly learnable from good examples. We let $(\eta_i)_{i \in \mathbb{N}}$ be a recursive repetition-free enumeration of all defined sequences σ_D for finite sets D; Since M is a frugal learner, σ_D is defined at least for all those D which are consistent with $\mathcal{L}$. Having this, we define H_i to be the union of $\text{cnt}(\eta_i)$ with

$$\{x \in W_{M(\eta_i)} - \text{cnt}(\eta_i) : \sigma_D \text{ exists and } \sigma_D = \eta_i \text{ where } D = \text{cnt}(\eta_i) \cup \{x\}\}$$

and we verify the following: (a) $\mathcal{L} \subseteq \{H_i : i \in \mathbb{N}\}$; (b) the enumeration $(H_i)_{i \in \mathbb{N}}$ is repetition-free; (c) $\{H_i : i \in \mathbb{N}\}$ is class-preservingly learnable from good examples via the function G mapping the set i to the set $G(i) = \text{cnt}(\eta_i)$ of good examples of H_i and the learner N mapping each finite set E to the index i of the string η_i equal to σ_E whenever σ_E exists; N is undefined if σ_E does not exist.

For (a), consider any $L \in \mathcal{L}$ and the sequence σ_L. Note that $\sigma_L = \sigma_D$ for the finite set $D = \text{cnt}(\sigma_L)$. Therefore there is an index i with $\sigma_L = \eta_i$. Since M converges on t_L to an index of L it holds that $W_{M(\sigma_L)} = L$. Every $x \in L$ satisfies that $E = D \cup \{x\}$ is consistent with $\mathcal{L}$ and thus there σ_E exists. Furthermore, $\sigma_E = \sigma_D$ since $D = \text{cnt}(\sigma_L) \subseteq E \subseteq L$. Thus $H_i = L$.

For (b), consider any i, j with $H_i = H_j$. Then η_i and η_j are both prefixes of t_{H_i}, say $\eta_i \preceq \eta_j$. It follows that $h(\eta_j) = h(\eta_i)$ since otherwise there is a $x \in \text{cnt}(\eta_j) - \text{cnt}(\eta_i)$ which would then be in $H_j - H_i$ in contradiction to $H_i = H_j$. Since the enumeration $(\eta_k)_{k \in \mathbb{N}}$ is repetition-free, $i = j$ and the enumeration $(H_k)_{k \in \mathbb{N}}$ is also repetition-free.

For (c), consider any $i \in \mathbb{N}$ and H_i. It follows directly from the definition of H_i that $G(i) \subseteq H_i$. Furthermore, every finite $D \subseteq H_i$ with $G(i) \subseteq D \subseteq H_i$ satisfies that η_i is a prefix of t_D and that $h(\eta_i x) = h(\eta_i)$ for all $x \in D \cup \{\sharp\}$. Thus $\sigma_D = \eta_i$ and $N(D)$ is defined and equal to i. So N is a learner which infers $\{H_i : i \in \mathbb{N}\}$ class-comprisingly from good examples with respect to the repetition-free enumeration $(H_i)_{i \in \mathbb{N}}$. $\qquad\square$

Note that one can replace every iterative learner for $\mathcal{L}$ by an equivalent learner M that converges on every text for a finite set. Then M satisfies the property that σ_D exists for every σ consistent in $\mathcal{L}$. This property was the only essential condition used in the proof which follows from the definition of a frugal learner but not from the definition of an iterative learner. Thus one obtains:

Corollary 26. *If $\mathcal{L}$ is iteratively learnable then $\mathcal{L}$ is class-comprisingly learnable from good examples.*

By [9, Theorem 2] that there are classes which are iteratively learnable as they consist of finite sets only, but which are not class-preservingly learnable from good examples. For an example of such a class, consider the class consisting of all $\{x\}$ with $x \in K'$ and $\{x, y\}$ with $x < y$; K' is the halting problem for computations relative to K. Still, this class does not have a class-preserving iterative learner. The next example shows that there is also a class-comprisingly frugally learnable class which is not class-preservingly learnable from good examples.

Proposition 27. *There is a class which can be learned with data consumption complexity 3, but which is not class-preservingly learnable from good examples.*

Proof. If a class $\mathcal{L}$ can be learned class-preservingly from good examples then there is a total function φ_i such that $W_{\varphi_i(0)}, W_{\varphi_i(1)}, \ldots$ is an enumeration of $\mathcal{L}$ (not containing any nonmember of $\mathcal{L}$) and there is a recursive function φ_j mapping every e to the finite subset $D_{\varphi_j(e)}$ of $W_{\varphi_i(e)}$ such that no $L \in \mathcal{L}$ satisfies $D_{\varphi_j(e)} \subseteq L \subset W_{\varphi_i(e)}$.

The goal is to construct a class $\mathcal{L}$ which violates this constraint. The class $\mathcal{L}$ is given by an indexed family which consists of $\emptyset$ and the following sets:

- $L_{i,j} = \{(i,j,0),(i,j,1),\ldots\}$ for all $i,j \in \mathbb{N}$;
- $F_{i,j} = D_{\varphi_j(e_{i,j})} \cup \{(i,j,s_{i,j}+1)\}$ whenever there is a least pair $(e_{i,j}, s_{i,j}) \in \mathbb{N}^2$ such that $\varphi_j(e_{i,j})$ is defined,

$$\emptyset \subset D_{\varphi_j(e_{i,j})} \subset \{(i,j,0),(i,j,1),\ldots,(i,j,s_{i,j})\} \cap W_{\varphi_i(e_{i,j})},$$

$e_{i,j} \leq s_{i,j}$, and all these facts can be verified in time $s_{i,j}$. If such a pair $(e_{i,j}, s_{i,j})$ does not exist then no set $F_{i,j}$ is added to $\mathcal{L}$.

Note that whenever $W_{\varphi_i(0)}, W_{\varphi_i(1)}, \ldots$ is a class-preserving enumeration of $\mathcal{L}$ and φ_j maps every $e \in \mathbb{N}$ to the canonical index of a strict finite subset of $W_{\varphi_i(e)}$, then $e_{i,j}$ must exist and $W_{\varphi_i(e_{i,j})} = L_{i,j}$. Indeed, $W_{\varphi_i(e_{i,j})}$, belonging to $\mathcal{L}$, is equal either to $L_{i,j}$ or to $F_{i,j}$. But if $W_{\varphi_i(e_{i,j})}$ were equal to $F_{i,j}$ then one would derive

$$W_{\varphi_i(e_{i,j})} = D_{\varphi_j(e_{i,j})} \cup \{(i,j,s_{i,j}+1)\} \subset W_{\varphi_i(e_{i,j})} \cup \{(i,j,s_{i,j}+1)\} = W_{\varphi_i(e_{i,j})},$$

which is impossible. Hence $W_{\varphi_i(e_{i,j})} = L_{i,j}$. Furthermore,

$$D_{\varphi_j(e_{i,j})} \subseteq F_{i,j} \subset L_{i,j}.$$

Then $\mathcal{L}$ has no class-preserving learner from good examples which uses the numbering $(W_{\varphi_i(k)})_{k \in \mathbb{N}}$ and the function φ_j to compute the set of good examples from the index since such a learner would have to map $F_{i,j}$ to $F_{i,j}$ and to $L_{i,j}$ at the same time. So $\mathcal{L}$ is not class-preservingly learnable from good examples.

A class-preserving learner for $\mathcal{L}$ has data consumption complexity 3. It is initialized with $\emptyset$ and it memorizes a new datum (i,j,k) iff:

- all previously memorized data (i',j',k') satisfy $i' = i$, $j' = j$ and $k' < k$;
- either (i,j,k) is the first datum to be memorized,
  or the set $F_{i,j}$ exists and $k = s_{i,j}+1$,
  or the set $F_{i,j}$ exists and the previous hypothesis is $F_{i,j}$ and $k > s_{i,j}+1$.

Although it is impossible to check whether $F_{i,j}$ exists one can check whether $F_{i,j}$ exists and $s_{i,j} < k$.

When the leaner memorizes a new datum (i,j,k), either $F_{i,j}$ exists and $s_{i,j}+1$ is equal to k, in which case the learner outputs $F_{i,j}$, or the learner outputs $L_{i,j}$.

It is easy to see that the learner is correct and memorizes a maximum amount of data when the hypotheses $L_{i,j}, F_{i,j}, L_{i,j}$ are output; a new datum is then memorized for each hypothesis. □

6   Conclusion

Traditional models of computation and learning have looked at intrinsic uncertainty (for example, conditions under which a class of languages is learnable with no less than a given number of mind changes), but do not conceive of 'self-imposed' uncertainty as a desirable feature. These models do not capture the behaviour of human beings in most real-life decisions: even when he knows that the degree of uncertainty will eventually decrease, a decision maker accepts the extra uncertainty of the moment and takes action. In this paper we have proposed a preliminary attempt to formally justify why uncertainty might be desirable. The model is crude, in particular because the notion of data consumption complexity is very restrictive; it will be generalized in future work. We also intend to extend our work from the numerical setting to the logical setting, expecting to benefit from the expressive power of the latter.

Acknowledgments. The authors would like to thank Steffen Lange as well as the anonymous referees for their very helpful comments.

References

[1] Ambainis, A., Jain, S., Sharma, A.: *Ordinal Mind Change Complexity of Language Identification.* In Ben-David, S.: Proc. of the 3rd Europ. Conf. on Comput. Learning Theory. Springer-Verlag, LNCS 1208 pp. 301-315 (1997)

[2] Dana Angluin. *Inductive inference of formal languages from positive data.* Information and Control, 45(2): 117–135 (1980)

[3] Case, J., Jain, S., Sharma, A.: *Vacillatory Learning of Nearly Minimal Size Grammars.* Journal of Computer and System Sciences 49: 189-207 (1994)

[4] Case, J., Jain, S., Lange, S., Zeugmann, T.: *Incremental Concept Learning for Bounded Data Mining.* Information and Computation 152(1): 74-110 (1999)

[5] Freivalds, R. Kinber, E. B., Wiehagen, R.: *On the Power of Inductive Inference from Good Examples.* Theoretical Computer Science 110(1): 131-144 (1993)

[6] Freivalds, R., Kinber, E. B., Smith, C. H.: *On the Impact of Forgetting on Learning Machines.* In Pitt, L.: Proc. of the 6th Annual Conf. of Comput. Learning Theory. ACM Press pp. 165-174 (1993)

[7] Freivalds, R., Smith, C. H.: *On the role of procrastination for machine learning.* Information and Computation 107(2): 237-271 (1993)

[8] Gold, E. M.: *Language identification in the limit.* Inform. and Control 10 (1967)

[9] Jain, S., Lange, S., Nessel, J.: *On the learnability of recursively enumerable languages from good examples.* Theoretical Computer Science 261(1): 3-29 (2001)

[10] S. Jain, D. N. Osherson. J. S. Royer and A. Sharma. *Systems that learn: An Introduction to Learning Theory, Second Edition.* The MIT Press (1999)

[11] Jain, S., Sharma, A.: *On monotonic strategies for learning r.e. languages.* In Jantke, K., Arikawa, S.: Proc. of the 5th Intern. Workshop on Alg. Learning Theory. Springer-Verlag, LNAI 872 pp. 349-364 (1994)

[12] Jain, S., Sharma, A.: *Mind change complexity of learning logic programs.* Theoretical Computer Science 284(1): 143-160 (2002)

[13] Kinber, E. B., Stephan, F.: *Language learning from texts: mind changes, limited memory and monotonicity.* Information and Computation 123(2): 224-241 (1995)

[14] Lange, S., Grieser, G.: *On the power of incremental learning.* Theoretical Computer Science 288(2): 277-307 (2002)

[15] Lange, S., Nessel, J., Wiehagen, R.: *Learning Recursive Languages from Good Examples.* Annals of Mathematics and Artificial Intelligence 23(1-2): 27-52 (1998)

[16] Lange, S., Zeugmann, T., Kapur, S: *Monotonic and Dual Monotonic Language Learning.* Theoretical Computer Science 155(2): 365-410 (1996)

[17] Martin, E., Sharma, A., Stephan, F.: *Logic, Learning, and Topology in a Common Framework*. In Cesa-Bianchi, N., Numao, M., Reischuk, R.: Proc. of the 13th Intern. Conf. on Alg. Learning Theory. Springer-Verlag, LNAI 2533 pp. 248-262 (2002)

[18] Martin, E., Sharma, A, Stephan, F.: *On Ordinal VC-Dimension and Some Notions of Complexity*. In Gavalda, R., Jantke, P., Takimoto, E.: Proc. of the 14th Intern. Conf. on Alg. Learning Theory. Springer-Verlag, LNAI 2842 pp. 54-68 (2003)

[19] Osherson, D., Stob, M., Weinstein, S. *Systems that learn*. The MIT Press (1986)

[20] Sharma, A., Stephan, F., Ventsov, Y.: *Generalized Notions of Mind Change Complexity*. In Freund, Y., Shapire, R.: Proc. of the 10th Annual Conf. of Comput. Learning Theory. ACM Press pp. 96-108 (1997)

[21] Zeugmann, T., Lange, S., Kapur, S.: *Characterizations of Monotonic and Dual Monotonic Language Learning*. Inform, and Comput. 120(2): 155-173 (1995)

Comparison of Query Learning and Gold-Style Learning in Dependence of the Hypothesis Space

Steffen Lange[1] and Sandra Zilles[2]

[1] Fachhochschule Darmstadt,
FB Informatik, Haardtring 100, 64295 Darmstadt, Germany,
`s.lange@fbi.fh-darmstadt.de`
[2] Technische Universität Kaiserslautern,
FB Informatik, Postfach 3049, 67653 Kaiserslautern, Germany,
`zilles@informatik.uni-kl.de`

Abstract. Different formal learning models address different aspects of learning. Below we compare *learning via queries*—interpreting learning as a *one-shot process* in which the learner is required to identify the target concept with just one hypothesis—to *Gold-style learning*—interpreting learning as a *limiting process* in which the learner may change its mind arbitrarily often before converging to a correct hypothesis.

Although these two approaches seem rather unrelated, a previous study has provided characterisations of different models of Gold-style learning (learning in the limit, conservative inference, and behaviourally correct learning) in terms of query learning. Thus under certain circumstances it is possible to replace limit learners by equally powerful one-shot learners. Both this previous and the current analysis are valid in the general context of learning indexable classes of recursive languages.

The main purpose of this paper is to solve a challenging open problem from the previous study. The solution of this problem leads to an important observation, namely that there is a natural query learning type hierarchically in-between Gold-style learning in the limit and behaviourally correct learning. Astonishingly, this query learning type can then again be characterised in terms of Gold-style inference.

In connection with this new in-between inference type we have gained new insights into the basic model of conservative learning and the way conservative learners work. In addition to these results, we compare several further natural inference types in both models to one another.

1 Introduction

Undeniably, there is no formal scheme spanning all aspects of human learning. Thus each learning model analysed within the scope of learning theory addresses only special facets of our understanding of learning. For example, Angluin's [2,3] model of *learning with queries* focusses learning as a finite process of interaction between a learner and a teacher. The learner asks questions of a specified type about the target concept and the teacher answers these questions truthfully. After finitely many steps of interaction the learner is supposed to return its sole

S. Ben-David, J. Case, A. Maruoka (Eds.): ALT 2004, LNAI 3244, pp. 99–113, 2004.
© Springer-Verlag Berlin Heidelberg 2004

hypothesis—correctly describing the target concept. Here the crucial features of the learner are its ability to demand special information on the target concept and its restrictiveness in terms of mind changes. Since a query learner is required to identify the target concept with just a single hypothesis, we refer to this phenomenon as *one-shot learning*.[1]

In contrast to that, Gold's [7] model of *identification in the limit* is concerned with learning as a limiting process of creating, modifying, and improving hypotheses about a target concept. These hypotheses are based upon instances of the target concept offered as information. In the limit, the learner is supposed to stabilize on a correct guess, but during the learning process one will never know whether or not the current hypothesis is already correct. Here the ability to change its mind is a crucial feature of the learner.

[11] is concerned with a first systematic analysis of common features of these two seemingly unrelated approaches, thereby focussing on the identification of formal languages, ranging over indexable classes of recursive languages, as target concepts, see [1,9,14]. Characterising different types of Gold-style language learning in terms of query learning has pointed out interesting correspondences between the two models. In particular, the results in [11] demonstrate how learners identifying languages in the limit can be replaced by one-shot learners without loss of learning power. That means, under certain circumstances the capabilities of limit learners are equal to those of one-shot learners using queries.

The analysis summarized in this paper has initially been motivated by an open problem in [11], namely whether or not the capabilities of query learners using superset queries in Gödel numberings are equal to those of behaviourally correct Gold-style learners using Gödel numberings as their hypothesis spaces. Below we will answer this question to the negative, which will lead to the following astonishing observation: there is a natural inference type (learning via superset queries in Gödel numberings) which lies *in-between* Gold-style learning in the limit from text and behaviourally correct Gold-style learning from text in Gödel numberings.[2] Up to now, no such inference type has been known.

This observation immediately raises a second question, namely whether there is an analogue of this query learning type in terms of Gold-style learning and thus whether there is also a *Gold-style* inference type between learning in the limit and behaviourally correct learning. Indeed such a relation can be observed with conservative inference in Gödel numberings by learners using an oracle for the halting problem; see [13] for further results on learning with oracles.

Studying such relations between two different approaches to language learning allows for transferring theoretically approved insights from one model to the other. In particular, our characterisations may serve as 'interfaces' between an analysis of query learning and an analysis of Gold-style learning through which proofs on either model can be simplified using properties of the other.

---

[1] Most studies on query learning mainly deal with the efficiency of query learners, whereas below we are only interested in qualitative learnability results in this context.

[2] That means that the capabilities of the corresponding learners lie in-between. Concerning the notions of inference, see [7,1,14] and the preliminaries below.

Most of our proofs provided below make use of recursion-theoretic conceptions, thus in particular providing a second quite accessible example—after the one in [11]—for a class identifiable by a behaviourally correct learner in Gödel numberings but not identifiable in the limit. The interesting feature of these classes is that they are defined without any diagonal construction—very unlike the corresponding classes known before, see for instance [1].

Comparing our results to a result from [13] points out a related open problem in Gold-style lea...ing: Note that, by [13], an indexable class is learnable conservatively using an oracle for the halting problem and a *uniformly recursive hypothesis space* if and only if it is learnable in the limit. In contrast to that, we show that conservative learners using an oracle for the halting problem and a *Gödel numbering as a hypothesis space* are more capable than limit learners. This implies that, in the context of conservative inference, oracle learners may benefit from using a Gödel numbering instead of uniformly recursive numbering as a hypothesis space. Now the related open problem is: do conservative learners (without the help of oracles) also benefit from Gödel numberings instead of uniformly recursive numberings? Though this question is quite natural, it has not been discussed in the literature so far. Unfortunately, we can provide an answer only for a special case: if a learner is required to work both conservatively and consistently on the relevant data, Gödel numberings do not increase the capabilities when compared to uniformly recursive hypothesis spaces. Additional results below relate several further natural inference types in both models to each other.

2   Preliminaries

Familiarity with standard recursion theoretic and language theoretic notions is assumed, see [12,8]. Subsequently, let Σ be a finite alphabet with $\{a, b\} \subseteq \Sigma$. A *word* is any element from Σ^* and a *language* any subset of Σ^*. The *complement* $\overline{L}$ of a language L is the set $\Sigma^* \setminus L$. Any infinite sequence $t = (w_i)_{i \in \mathbb{N}}$ with $\{w_i \mid i \in \mathbb{N}\} = L$ is called a *text* for L. Then, for any $n \in \mathbb{N}$, t_n denotes the initial segment $(w_0, \dots, w_n)$ and $content(t_n)$ denotes the set $\{w_0, \dots, w_n\}$.

A family $(A_i)_{i \in \mathbb{N}}$ of languages is *uniformly recursive* (*uniformly r. e.*) if there is a recursive (partial recursive) function f with $A_i = \{w \in \Sigma^* \mid f(i, w) = 1\}$ for all $i \in \mathbb{N}$. A family $(A_i)_{i \in \mathbb{N}}$ is *uniformly 2-r. e.*, if there is a recursive function g with $A_i = \{w \in \Sigma^* \mid g(i, w, n) = 1$ for all but finitely many $n\}$ for all $i \in \mathbb{N}$. Note that for uniformly recursive families membership is uniformly decidable.

Let $\mathcal{C}$ be a class of recursive languages. $\mathcal{C}$ is said to be an *indexable class of recursive languages* (in the sequel we will write *indexable class* for short), if there is a uniformly recursive family $(L_i)_{i \in \mathbb{N}}$ of all and only the languages in $\mathcal{C}$. Such a family will subsequently be called an *indexing* of $\mathcal{C}$.

A family $(T_i)_{i \in \mathbb{N}}$ of *finite* languages is *recursively generable*, if there is a recursive function that, given $i \in \mathbb{N}$, enumerates all elements of T_i and stops.

In the sequel, let φ be a Gödel numbering of all partial recursive functions and Φ the associated Blum complexity measure, see [5] for a definition. For $i, n \in \mathbb{N}$ we will write $\varphi_i[n]$ for the initial segment $(\varphi_i(0), \dots, \varphi_i(n))$ and say that $\varphi_i[n]$ is defined if all the values $\varphi_i(0), \ldots, \varphi_i(n)$ are defined. For convenience, $\varphi_i[-1]$ is always considered defined. Moreover, let $Tot = \{i \in \mathbb{N} \mid \varphi_i \text{ is a total function}\}$ and $K = \{i \in \mathbb{N} \mid \varphi_i(i) \text{ is defined}\}$. The family $(W_i)_{i \in \mathbb{N}}$ of languages is given by $W_i = \{w_j^* \mid \varphi_i(j) \text{ is defined}\}$ for all $i \in \mathbb{N}$, where $(w_j^*)_{j \in \mathbb{N}}$ is some fixed effective enumeration of Σ^* without repetitions. Moreover, we use a bijective recursive function coding a pair (x, y) with $x, y \in \mathbb{N}$ into a number $\langle x, y \rangle \in \mathbb{N}$.

2.1 Language Learning via Queries

In the query learning model, a learner has access to a teacher that truthfully answers queries of a specified kind. A *query learner* M is an algorithmic device that, depending on the reply on the previous queries, either computes a new query or returns a hypothesis and halts, see [2]. Its queries and hypotheses are coded as natural numbers; both will be interpreted with respect to an underlying *hypothesis space*. When learning an indexable class $\mathcal{C}$, any indexing $\mathcal{H} = (L_i)_{i \in \mathbb{N}}$ of $\mathcal{C}$ may form a hypothesis space. So, as in the original definition, see [2], when learning $\mathcal{C}$, M is only allowed to query languages belonging to $\mathcal{C}$.

More formally, let $\mathcal{C}$ be an indexable class, let $L \in \mathcal{C}$, let $\mathcal{H} = (L_i)_{i \in \mathbb{N}}$ be an indexing of $\mathcal{C}$, and let M be a query learner. *M learns L with respect to $\mathcal{H}$ using some type of queries* if it eventually halts and its only hypothesis, say i, correctly describes L, i.e., $L_i = L$. So M returns its unique and correct guess i after only finitely many queries. Moreover, *M learns $\mathcal{C}$ with respect to $\mathcal{H}$ using some type of queries*, if it learns every $L' \in \mathcal{C}$ with respect to $\mathcal{H}$ using queries of the specified type. In order to learn a language L, a query learner M may ask:

Membership queries. The input is a string w and the answer is 'yes' or 'no', depending on whether or not w belongs to L.
Restricted superset queries. The input is an index of a language $L' \in \mathcal{C}$. The answer is 'yes' or 'no', depending on whether or not L' is a superset of L.
Restricted disjointness queries. The input is an index of a language $L' \in \mathcal{C}$. The answer is 'yes' or 'no', depending on whether or not L' and L are disjoint.

MemQ, *rSupQ*, and *rDisQ* denote the collections of all indexable classes $\mathcal{C}'$ for which there are a query learner M' and a hypothesis space $\mathcal{H}'$ such that M' learns $\mathcal{C}'$ with respect to $\mathcal{H}'$ using membership, restricted superset, and restricted disjointness queries, respectively. In the sequel we will omit the term 'restricted' for convenience and also neglect other types of queries analysed in the literature, see [2,3]. Obviously, superset and disjointness queries are in general not decidable, i.e. the teacher may be non-computable.

Note that learning via queries focusses the aspect of one-shot learning, i.e., it is concerned with scenarios in which learning eventuates without mind changes.

Having a closer look at the different models of query learning, one easily finds negative learnability results. Some examples in [11] point to a drawback of Angluin's query model, namely the demand that a query learner is restricted to pose queries concerning languages contained in the class of possible target languages. That means there are very simple classes of languages, for which any learner must fail just because it is barred from asking the 'appropriate' queries.

To overcome this drawback, it seems reasonable to allow the query learner to formulate its queries with respect to any uniformly recursive family comprising the target class $\mathcal{C}$. An *extra query learner* (see also [10,11]) for an indexable class $\mathcal{C}$ is permitted to query languages in any uniformly recursive family $(L'_i)_{i\in\mathbb{N}}$ comprising $\mathcal{C}$. We say that $\mathcal{C}$ is learnable with extra superset (disjointness) queries respecting $(L'_i)_{i\in\mathbb{N}}$ iff there is an extra query learner M learning $\mathcal{C}$ with respect to $(L'_i)_{i\in\mathbb{N}}$ using superset (disjointness) queries concerning $(L'_i)_{i\in\mathbb{N}}$. Then $rSupQ_{\mathrm{rec}}$ ($rDisQ_{\mathrm{rec}}$) denotes the collection of all indexable classes $\mathcal{C}$ learnable with extra superset (disjointness) queries respecting a uniformly recursive family.

It is conceivable to permit even more general hypothesis spaces, i.e., to demand a more potent teacher. Thus, let $rSupQ_{\mathrm{r.e.}}$ ($rDisQ_{\mathrm{r.e.}}$) denote the collection of all indexable classes which are learnable with superset (disjointness) queries respecting a uniformly r.e. family. Obviously, each class in $rSupQ_{\mathrm{r.e.}}$ ($rDisQ_{\mathrm{r.e.}}$) can be identified respecting our fixed numbering $(W_i)_{i\in\mathbb{N}}$. Similarly, replacing the subscript 'r.e.' by '2-r.e.', we consider learning in a uniformly 2-r.e. family.

Note that the capabilities of $rSupQ$-learners ($rDisQ$-learners) already increase with the additional permission to ask membership queries. Yet, as has been shown in [11], combining superset or disjointness queries with membership queries does not yield the same capability as extra queries do. For convenience, we denote the family of classes which are learnable with a combination of superset (disjointness) and membership queries by $rSupMemQ$ ($rDisMemQ$).

2.2   Gold-Style Language Learning

Let $\mathcal{C}$ be an indexable class, $\mathcal{H} = (L_i)_{i\in\mathbb{N}}$ any uniformly recursive family (called *hypothesis space*), and $L \in \mathcal{C}$. An *inductive inference machine* (*IIM*) M is an algorithmic device that reads longer and longer initial segments t_n of a text and outputs numbers $M(t_n)$ as its hypotheses. An IIM M returning some i is construed to hypothesize the language L_i. Given a text t for L, M *identifies L from t with respect to $\mathcal{H}$ in the limit*, if the sequence of hypotheses output by M, when fed t, stabilizes on a number i (i.e., past some point M always outputs the hypothesis i) with $L_i = L$. M *identifies $\mathcal{C}$ in the limit from text* with respect to $\mathcal{H}$, if it identifies every $L' \in \mathcal{C}$ from every corresponding text. $Lim\,Txt_{\mathrm{rec}}$ denotes the collection of all indexable classes $\mathcal{C}'$ for which there are an IIM M' and a uniformly recursive family $\mathcal{H}'$ such that M' identifies $\mathcal{C}'$ in the limit from text with respect to $\mathcal{H}'$. A quite natural and often studied modification of $Lim\,Txt_{\mathrm{rec}}$ is defined by the model of *conservative inference*, see [1]. M is a *conservative* IIM for $\mathcal{C}$ with respect to $\mathcal{H}$, if M performs only justified mind changes, i.e., if M, on some text t for some $L \in \mathcal{C}$, outputs hypotheses i and later j, then M must have seen some element $w \notin L_i$ before returning j. An important property of conservative learners is that they never hypothesize proper supersets of the language currently to be learned. The collection of all indexable classes identifiable from text by a conservative IIM is denoted by $Consv\,Txt_{\mathrm{rec}}$. Note that $Consv\,Txt_{\mathrm{rec}} \subset Lim\,Txt_{\mathrm{rec}}$ [14]. Since we consider learning from text only, we will assume in the sequel that all languages to be learned are *non-empty*. One main aspect of human learning modelled in the approach of learning in the limit is the ability to change one's mind during learning. Thus learning is a process in which the learner may change its hypothesis arbitrarily often before stabilizing on its final correct guess. In particular, it is undecidable whether or not the final hypothesis has been reached, i. e., whether or not a success in learning has already eventuated.

If only uniformly recursive families are used as hypothesis spaces, $Lim\,Txt_{rec}$ coincides with the collection of indexable classes identifiable in a behaviourally correct manner, see [6]: If $\mathcal{C}$ is an indexable class, $\mathcal{H} = (L_i)_{i \in \mathbb{N}}$ a uniformly recursive family, M an IIM, then M is a *behaviourally correct* learner for $\mathcal{C}$ from text with respect to $\mathcal{H}$, if for each $L \in \mathcal{C}$ and each text t for $\mathcal{C}$, all but finitely many outputs i of M on t fulfil $L_i = L$. Here M may alternate different correct hypotheses instead of converging to a single hypothesis. Defining $Bc\,Txt_{rec}$ correspondingly as usual yields $Bc\,Txt_{rec} = Lim\,Txt_{rec}$ (a folklore result).

This relation no longer holds, if more general types of hypothesis spaces are considered. Assume $\mathcal{C}$ is an indexable class and $\mathcal{H}^+ = (A_i)_{i \in \mathbb{N}}$ is any uniformly r. e. family of languages comprising $\mathcal{C}$. Then it is also conceivable to use $\mathcal{H}^+$ as a hypothesis space. For $I \in \{Lim, Consv, Bc\}$, $I\,Txt_{r.e.}$ denotes the collection of all indexable classes learnable as in the definition of $I\,Txt_{rec}$, if the demand for a uniformly recursive family $\mathcal{H}$ as a hypothesis space is loosened to demanding a uniformly r. e. family $\mathcal{H}^+$ as a hypothesis space. Note that each class in $I\,Txt_{r.e.}$ can also be $I\,Txt$-identified in the hypothesis space $(W_i)_{i \in \mathbb{N}}$. Interestingly, $Lim\,Txt_{rec} = Lim\,Txt_{r.e.}$ (a folklore result), i. e., in learning in the limit, the capabilities of IIMs do not increase, if the constraints concerning the hypothesis space are weakened by allowing for arbitrary uniformly r. e. families. In contrast to that, for $Bc\,Txt$-identification, weakening these constraints yields an add-on in learning power, i. e., $Bc\,Txt_{rec} \subset Bc\,Txt_{r.e.}$. In particular, $Lim\,Txt_{rec} \subset Bc\,Txt_{r.e.}$ and so $Lim\,Txt$- and $Bc\,Txt$-learning no longer coincide for identification with respect to arbitrary uniformly r. e. families, see also [4,1].

The main results of our analysis will be comparisons of these inference types with different query learning types. For that purpose we will make use of well-known characterizations based on so-called families of *telltales*, see [1].

Definition 1. *Let $(L_i)_{i \in \mathbb{N}}$ be a uniformly recursive family and $(T_i)_{i \in \mathbb{N}}$ a family of finite non-empty sets. $(T_i)_{i \in \mathbb{N}}$ is a telltale family for $(L_i)_{i \in \mathbb{N}}$ iff for all $i, j \in \mathbb{N}$:*

1. $T_i \subseteq L_i$.
2. *If $T_i \subseteq L_j \subseteq L_i$, then $L_j = L_i$.*

Telltale families are the best known concept to illustrate the specific differences between indexable classes in $Lim\,Txt_{rec}$, $Consv\,Txt_{rec}$, and $Bc\,Txt_{r.e.}$. Their algorithmic structure has turned out to be crucial for learning, see [1,9,4]:

Theorem 1. *Let $\mathcal{C}$ be an indexable class of languages.*

1. *$\mathcal{C} \in Lim\,Txt_{rec}$ iff there is an indexing of $\mathcal{C}$ possessing a uniformly r. e. family of telltales.*
2. *$\mathcal{C} \in Consv\,Txt_{rec}$ iff there is a uniformly recursive family comprising $\mathcal{C}$ and possessing a recursively generable family of telltales.*
3. *$\mathcal{C} \in Bc\,Txt_{r.e.}$ iff there is an indexing of $\mathcal{C}$ possessing a family of telltales.*

3   Hypothesis Spaces in Query Learning

Concerning the influence of the query and hypothesis spaces in query learning, various interesting results have been established in [11]. These reveal a hierarchy of capabilities of query learners resulting from a growing generality of the hypothesis spaces. Interestingly, in some but not in all cases, the capabilities of superset query learners and disjointness query learners coincide:

Theorem 2. *[11]*
$$rSupQ_{\text{rec}} = rDisQ_{\text{rec}} \subset rDisQ_{\text{r.e.}} \subset rSupQ_{\text{r.e.}} \subseteq rSupQ_{\text{2-r.e.}} = rDisQ_{\text{2-r.e.}} \; .$$

In [11] it has remained open, whether or not there is an indexable class in $rSupQ_{\text{2-r.e.}} \setminus rSupQ_{\text{r.e.}}$—a problem which will be solved below. Moreover, [11] studies original superset (disjointness) query learners which are additionally permitted to ask membership queries. Their capabilities are in-between those of the original learners and extra query learners.

Theorem 3. *[11]* (a) $rSupQ \subset rSupMemQ \subset rSupQ_{\text{rec}}$.
(b) $rDisQ \subset rDisMemQ \subset rDisQ_{\text{rec}}$.

Comparing these results, notice that Theorem 2 analyses the relationship between superset and disjointness query learning, whereas Theorem 3 avoids corresponding statements. That means, it has remained open, how the inference types $rSupQ$ and $rSupMemQ$ relate to $rDisQ$ and $rDisMemQ$.

As an answer to this question, we can state that $rSupQ$ and $rSupMemQ$ are incomparable to both $rDisQ$ and $rDisMemQ$, an immediate consequence of the following theorem.

Theorem 4. (a) $rSupQ \not\subseteq rDisMemQ$.   (b) $rDisQ \not\subseteq rSupMemQ$.

Proof. We provide the separating indexable classes without a proof.
(a) The class $\mathcal{C}_a$ containing $L = \{b\}$ and $L_k = \{a^k, b\}$ for $k \geq 0$ belongs to $rSupQ \setminus rDisMemQ$.
(b) A class $\mathcal{C}_b \in rDisQ \setminus rSupMemQ$ is defined as follows: for $k \in \mathbb{N}$, let $\mathcal{C}_b$ contain the languages $L_k = \{a^k b^z \mid z \geq 0\}$ and $L'_k = \{ba^{\langle k,j \rangle} \mid j \geq 0\}$. Additionally, if $k \notin K$, then $\mathcal{C}_b$ contains $L^1_{k,j} = \{ba^{\langle k,j \rangle}\}$ for all $j \in \mathbb{N}$; whereas, if $k \in K$, then $\mathcal{C}_b$ contains $L^2_{k,j} = \{a^k b^z \mid z \leq \Phi_k(k) \text{ or } z > \Phi_k(k) + j\}$ as well as $L^3_{k,j} = \{ba^{\langle k,j \rangle}\} \cup \{a^k b^{\Phi_k(k)+j}\}$ for all $j \in \mathbb{N}$. □

The more challenging open question is whether or not the inference types $rSupQ_{\text{r.e.}}$ and $rSupQ_{\text{2-r.e.}}$ coincide. Interestingly, this is not the case, that means, 2-r. e. numberings provide a further benefit for learning with superset queries.

Theorem 5. $rSupQ_{\text{r.e.}} \subset rSupQ_{\text{2-r.e.}}$.

Though our current tools allow for a verification of this theorem, the proof would be rather lengthy. Since a characterisation of $rSupQ_{\text{r.e.}}$ in terms of Gold-style learning simplifies the proof considerably, we postpone the proof for now.

4   Query Learning and Gold-Style Learning — Relations

In [11], a couple of relations between query learning and Gold-style learning have been elaborated. The following theorem summarizes the corresponding results.

Theorem 6. *[11] (a)* $rSupQ_{rec} = rDisQ_{rec} = Consv\,Txt_{rec}$.
(b) $rDisQ_{r.e.} = Lim\,Txt_{rec} = Bc\,Txt_{rec}$.
(c) $rSupQ_{2\text{-}r.e.} = rDisQ_{2\text{-}r.e.} = Bc\,Txt_{r.e.}$.

By Theorems 2 and 5 this implies $Lim\,Txt_{rec} \subset rSupQ_{r.e.} \subset Bc\,Txt_{r.e.}$, i.e., we have found a natural type of learners the capabilities of which are strictly between those of $Lim\,Txt$-learners and those of $Bc\,Txt$-learners. This raises the question whether the learning type $rSupQ_{r.e.}$ can also be characterised in terms of Gold-style learning. This is indeed possible if we consider learners which have access to some oracle. In the sequel the notion $Consv\,Txt_{r.e.}[K]$ refers to the collection of indexable classes which are learnable in the sense of $Consv\,Txt_{r.e.}$, if also K-recursive learners are admitted, see [13].

Theorem 7. $rSupQ_{r.e.} = Consv\,Txt_{r.e.}[K]$.

Proof. First, we prove $rSupQ_{r.e.} \subseteq Consv\,Txt_{r.e.}[K]$. For that purpose assume $\mathcal{C}$ is an indexable class in $rSupQ_{r.e.}$. Let M be a query learner identifying $\mathcal{C}$ in $(W_i)_{i\in\mathbb{N}}$ and assume wlog that each hypothesis ever returned by M corresponds to the intersection of all queries answered with 'yes' in the preceding scenario.[3]

Let $L \in \mathcal{C}$, t a text for L. Let $M'(t_0)$ be an index of the language $content(t_0)$. Given $n \geq 1$, a learner M' works on input t_n as follows: M' simulates M for n steps of computation. Whenever M asks a superset query i, M' transmits the answer 'yes' to M, if $content(t_n) \subseteq W_i$, the answer 'no', otherwise (* this test is K-recursive *). If M returns a hypothesis i within n steps of computation, let M' return i on t_n; otherwise let $M'(t_n) = M'(t_{n-1})$.

Note that there must be some n, such that M' answers all queries of M truthfully respecting L. Thus it is not hard to verify that the K-recursive IIM M' learns L in the limit from text. Moreover, $W_{M'(t_n)} \not\supseteq L$ for all n: assuming $W_{M'(t_n)} \supset L$ implies, by normalisation of M, that all queries M' has answered with 'yes' in the simulation of M indeed represent supersets of L. Since all 'no'-answers are truthful respecting L by definition, this yields a truthful query-scenario for L. As M learns L from superset queries, the hypothesis i must correctly describe L—a contradiction. So M' learns $\mathcal{C}$ without ever returning an index of a proper superset of a language currently to be identified. Now it is not hard to modify M' into a K-recursive IIM which works conservatively for the class $\mathcal{C}$ (a hypothesis will only be changed if its inconsistency is verified with the help of a K-oracle). Thus $\mathcal{C} \in Consv\,Txt_{r.e.}[K]$ and $rSupQ_{r.e.} \subseteq Consv\,Txt_{r.e.}[K]$.

---

[3] Think of M as a normalisation of a superset query learner M^-: M copies M^- until M^- returns the hypothesis i. Now M asks a query for the language W_i instead of returning a hypothesis. Then let M return a hypothesis j representing the intersection of all queries answered with 'yes' in its preceding scenario. Given a fair scenario for W_i and a successful learner M^-, this implies $W_i = W_j$ and thus M is successful.

Second, we show $Consv\,Txt_{r.e.}[K] \subseteq rSupQ_{r.e.}$. For that purpose assume $\mathcal{C}$ is an indexable class in $Consv\,Txt_{r.e.}[K]$. Let M be a K-recursive IIM identifying $\mathcal{C}$ with respect to $(W_i)_{i\in\mathbb{N}}$. Suppose $L \in \mathcal{C}$ is the target language. An $rSupQ$-learner M' for L with respect to $(W_i)_{i\in\mathbb{N}}$ is defined by steps, starting in step 0. Note that representations in $(W_i)_{i\in\mathbb{N}}$ can be computed for all queries to be asked. In step 0, M' finds the minimal m, such that the query for $\Sigma^* \setminus \{w_m^*\}$ is answered 'no'. M' sets $t(0) = w_m^*$ and goes to step 1. In general, step $n{+}1$ reads as follows:

– Ask a superset query for $\Sigma^* \setminus \{w_{n+1}^*\}$. If the answer is 'no', let $t(n{+}1) = w_{n+1}^*$; if the answer is 'yes', let $t(n + 1) = t(n)$.
(* Note that $content(t_{n+1}) = L \cap \{w_x^* \mid x \leq n + 1\}$. *)
– Simulate M on input t_{n+1}. Whenever M wants to access a K-oracle for the question whether $j \in K$, formulate a superset query for the language

$$W_j' = \begin{cases} \Sigma^*, & \text{if } \varphi_j(j) \text{ is defined}, \\ \emptyset, & \text{otherwise}. \end{cases}$$

and transmit the received answer to M.
(* Note that W_j' is uniformly r.e. in j and $W_j' \supseteq L$ iff $\varphi_j(j)$ is defined. *)
As soon as M returns $i = M(t_{n+1})$, pose a superset query for W_i. If the answer is 'yes', then return the hypothesis i and stop (* since M learns L conservatively, we have $W_i \not\supseteq L$ and thus $W_i = L$ *). If the answer is 'no', then go to step $n + 2$.

Now it is not hard to verify that M' learns $\mathcal{C}$ with superset queries in $(W_i)_{i\in\mathbb{N}}$. Details are omitted. Thus $\mathcal{C} \in rSupQ_{r.e.}$ and $Consv\,Txt_{r.e.}[K] \subseteq rSupQ_{r.e.}$.   □

Using this characterisation, Theorem 5 translates as follows:

Theorem 5' $Consv\,Txt_{r.e.}[K] \subset Bc\,Txt_{r.e.}$.

Proof. By Theorems 6 and 7 it suffices to prove $Bc\,Txt_{r.e.} \setminus Consv\,Txt_{r.e.}[K] \neq \emptyset$. For that purpose we provide an indexable class $\mathcal{C}_{bc} \in Bc\,Txt_{r.e.} \setminus Consv\,Txt_{r.e.}[K]$. For all $k \in \mathbb{N}$, $\mathcal{C}_{bc}$ contains the language $L_k = \{a^k b^z \mid z \geq 0\}$. Moreover, for all $k, i, j \in \mathbb{N}$ for which $\varphi_k[i - 1]$ is defined and $j \leq i$, let $\mathcal{C}_{bc}$ contain the language

$$L_{k,i,j} = \begin{cases} \{a^k b^z \mid z \leq j\}, & \text{if } \varphi_k(i) \text{ is undefined}, \\ \{a^k b^z \mid z \leq j\} \cup \{ba^{\Phi_k(i)}\}, & \text{if } \varphi_k(i) \text{ is defined}. \end{cases}$$

To show that $\mathcal{C}_{bc} \in Bc\,Txt$, it suffices by Theorem 1 to prove the existence of telltales corresponding to some indexing of $\mathcal{C}_{bc}$. This is quite simple: as each language $L_{k,i,j} \in \mathcal{C}_{bc}$ is finite, it forms a telltale for itself. Moreover, as for all k there are only finitely many subsets of L_k in $\mathcal{C}_{bc}$, telltales for L_k must exist, too.

Finally, it remains to prove that $\mathcal{C}_{bc} \notin Consv\,Txt_{r.e.}[K]$. Assume the opposite, i.e., there is some K-recursive IIM M which $Consv\,Txt$-identifies $\mathcal{C}_{bc}$ in $(W_i)_{i\in\mathbb{N}}$. The idea is to deduce a contradiction by concluding that Tot is K-recursive. For that purpose, define a K-recursive procedure on input k as follows:

– Let $t = a^k, a^k b, a^k b^2, \ldots$ be the 'canonical' text for L_k.
– Simulate M on input $t_0, t_1, t_2, \ldots$ until some n is found with $content(t_n) \subset W_{M(t_n)} \subseteq L_k$. (* n exists, as M learns L_k. Determining n is K-recursive. *)
– If $\varphi_k(i)$ is defined for all $i \leq n$, then return '1'; otherwise return '0'.

Obviously, this procedure is K-recursive. Note that it returns '0' only in case φ_k is not total. So assume it returns '1'. Then there is some n such that $content(t_n) \subset W_{M(t_n)} \subseteq L_k$. If φ_k was not total, the minimal i for which $\varphi_k(i)$ is undefined would be greater than n. Thus $L = \{a^k b^z \mid z \leq n\} \in \mathcal{C}_{bc}$. Now t_n is also a text segment for L, but $L = content(t_n) \subset W_{M(t_n)}$. Thus M hypothesizes a proper superset of L on input t_n and hence M fails to learn L conservatively. This contradicts the choice of M, so φ_k is total.

Consequently, our procedure decides Tot, i.e., Tot is K-recursive. As this is impossible, we have $\mathcal{C}_{bc} \notin Consv\,Txt_{r.e.}[K]$.   □

In particular, the class $\mathcal{C}_{bc}$ defined in this proof constitutes a second quite accessible example—after the one in [11]—for a class identifiable by a behaviourally correct learner in Gödel numberings but not identifiable in the limit. An interesting feature is that these classes are defined without any diagonal construction—very unlike the corresponding classes known before, see for instance [1].

Finally, thus Theorem 5 is proven, too. This is an example for the advantages of our characterisations; verifying Theorem 5 without Theorems 6 and 7 would have been possible, but more complicated. So features of Gold-style learning can be exploited in the context of query learning. Note that, with Theorems 6 and 7, we have characterised all types of extra query learning in terms of Gold-style learning. In order to better describe and understand the capabilities of the original query learners (the types $rSupQ$, $rSupMemQ$, $rDisQ$, $rDisMemQ$), let us have a closer look at the results established up to now.

We know that $rSupQ_{rec} = rDisQ_{rec} = Consv\,Txt_{rec}$. Note that, according to [9], for successful conservative learning, it is decisive, whether or not the learner is allowed to hypothesize languages not belonging to the target class. That means, if we denote by $PConsv\,Txt$ the family of all indexable classes $\mathcal{C}$, for which there is an indexing $(L_i)_{i \in \mathbb{N}}$ exactly describing $\mathcal{C}$ and an IIM $Consv\,Txt$-learning $\mathcal{C}$ in $(L_i)_{i \in \mathbb{N}}$, then we obtain $PConsv\,Txt \subset Consv\,Txt_{rec}$.

Similarly, the decisive difference between extra query learners and the original query learners is the ability to pose queries representing languages not belonging to the target class.

This raises the question how the original types of query learning can be compared to class-preserving conservative inference. As it turns out, $PConsv\,Txt$-learners have much in common with $rSupMemQ$-learners. In contrast, significant discrepancies between $PConsv\,Txt$ and the query learning types $rSupQ$, $rDisQ$, and $rDisMemQ$ can be observed.

Theorem 8. (a) $PConsv\,Txt \subset rSupMemQ$.
(b) $\mathcal{T} \# PConsv\,Txt$ for all $\mathcal{T} \in \{rSupQ, rDisQ, rDisMemQ\}$.

Proof. (a) The proof of $PConsv\,Txt \subseteq rSupMemQ$ results from a slight modification of the proof of $Consv\,Txt_{rec} \subseteq rSupQ$ in [10]:

Fix $\mathcal{C} \in PConsv\,Txt$. Then there is an indexing $(L_i)_{i \in \mathbb{N}}$ of $\mathcal{C}$ and an IIM M, such that M is a $PConsv\,Txt$-learner for $\mathcal{C}$ in $(L_i)_{i \in \mathbb{N}}$. Note that, as in the general case of conservative inference, if $L \in \mathcal{C}$ and t is a text for L, then M never returns an index i with $L \subset L_i$ on any initial segment of t.

An $rSupMemQ$-learner M' identifying any $L \in \mathcal{C}$ may use membership queries to construct a text for L and then simulate M on this text until M returns an index of a superset of L. This index is then returned by M':

First, to effectively enumerate a text t for L, M' determines the set T of all words in Σ^*, for which a membership query is answered with 'yes'. Any recursive enumeration of T yields a text for L.

Second, to compute its hypothesis, M' executes steps 0, 1, 2, ... until it receives a stop signal. In general, step n, $n \in \mathbb{N}$, reads as follows:

– Determine $i := M(t_n)$, where t is a recursive enumeration of the set T. Pose a query referring to L_i. If the answer is 'yes', hypothesize the language L_i and stop. (* As M never hypothesizes a proper superset of L, L_i equals L. *) If the answer is 'no', then go to step $n + 1$.

It is not hard to verify that M' is a successful $rSupMemQ$-learner for $\mathcal{C}$. Further details are omitted. So $P\,Consv\,Txt \subseteq rSupMemQ$.

To prove $rSupMemQ \setminus P\,Consv\,Txt \neq \emptyset$, we provide a separating class $\mathcal{C}_{\sup}$: for all $k \in \mathbb{N}$, let $\mathcal{C}_{\sup}$ contain the language $L_k = \{a^k b^z \mid z \geq 0\}$ and, if $k \in K$, additionally the languages $L_{k,j}^1 = \{a^k b^z \mid z \leq \Phi_k(k) \text{ or } [z > \Phi_k(k) + j \text{ and } z \text{ is odd}]\}$ and $L_{k,j}^2 = \{a^k b^z \mid z \leq \Phi_k(k) \text{ or } [z > \Phi_k(k) + j \text{ and } z \text{ is even}]\}$.

Using the indexing $(L'_{\langle k,j \rangle})_{k,j \in \mathbb{N}}$, given by $L'_{\langle k,0 \rangle} = L_k$, $L'_{\langle k,2j+y \rangle} = L^y_{\langle k,j \rangle}$ if $k \in K$, and $L'_{\langle k,2j+y \rangle} = L_k$ if $k \notin K$, one easily verifies $\mathcal{C}_{\sup} \in rSupQ$ and thus $\mathcal{C}_{\sup} \in rSupMemQ$. In contrast to that, $\mathcal{C}_{\sup} \notin P\,Consv\,Txt$, because otherwise K would be recursive. Details are omitted.

(b) $rDisQ \setminus P\,Consv\,Txt \neq \emptyset$ and $rDisMemQ \setminus P\,Consv\,Txt \neq \emptyset$ follow from Theorems 8(a), 3(b), and 4(b). For the other claims we just provide the separating classes: $P\,Consv\,Txt \setminus rDisMemQ \neq \emptyset$ is witnessed by the class $\mathcal{C}_a$ from the proof of Theorem 4(a). The class $\mathcal{C}_{\sup}$ (see above) belongs to $rSupQ \setminus P\,Consv\,Txt$, whereas the class consisting of the language $L = \{a\}^* \cup \{b\}$ and all the languages $L_k = \{a, \dots, a^k\}$, $k \geq 0$, belongs to $P\,Consv\,Txt \setminus rSupQ$. $\qquad\square$

5   Discussion

New relations have been established between learning via queries and Gold-style language learning—depending on the hypothesis space. In particular, learning with superset queries in uniformly r. e. numberings has revealed a natural inference type in-between $Lim\,Txt_{r.e.}$ and $Bc\,Txt_{r.e.}$. In correspondence to other characterisations this inference type has an analogue in Gold-style learning.

As we have seen, the learning capabilities of query learners depend on the choice of the query and hypothesis space. A similar phenomenon may be observed also in the context of Gold-style language learning, where for instance $Bc\,Txt_{r.e.} \supset Bc\,Txt_{rec} = Lim\,Txt_{rec}$. In contrast to that, for some models of Gold-style learning, the choice of the hypothesis space is ineffectual: Recall that $Lim\,Txt_{r.e.} = Lim\,Txt_{rec}$. Now assume $(A_i)_{i \in \mathbb{N}}$ is any family (not necessarily uniformly r. e.) and $\mathcal{C}$ is any indexable class of recursive languages. It is not hard to prove that

- If $\mathcal{C}$ is $Lim\,Txt$-learnable wrt $(A_i)_{i\in\mathbb{N}}$, then $\mathcal{C} \in Lim\,Txt_{\text{rec}}$.
- If $\mathcal{C}$ is $Bc\,Txt$-learnable wrt $(A_i)_{i\in\mathbb{N}}$, then $\mathcal{C} \in Bc\,Txt_{\text{r.e.}}$.

But to what extent is the choice of the hypothesis space relevant in conservative learning in the limit? Whereas each class $\mathcal{C} \in Lim\,Txt_{\text{rec}}$ can even be identified with respect to a uniformly recursive indexing exactly enumerating $\mathcal{C}$ (a folklore result), class-preserving conservative learners may be poor compared to unrestricted $Consv\,Txt_{\text{rec}}$-learners, i.e., $P\,Consv\,Txt \subset Consv\,Txt_{\text{rec}}$, see [9]. So it remains to analyse the relevance of uniformly r.e. hypothesis spaces in the context of conservative learning. It turns out that uniformly r.e. numberings are not sufficient for conservative IIMs to achieve the capabilities of $Lim\,Txt$-learners.

Theorem 9. $Consv\,Txt_{\text{r.e.}} \subset Lim\,Txt_{\text{rec}}$.

Proof. $Consv\,Txt_{\text{r.e.}} \subseteq Lim\,Txt_{\text{rec}}$ follows from $Lim\,Txt_{\text{r.e.}} \subseteq Lim\,Txt_{\text{rec}}$.

$Lim\,Txt_{\text{rec}} \setminus Consv\,Txt_{\text{r.e.}} \neq \emptyset$ is witnessed by an indexable class $\mathcal{C}$ from [9]: For each k, $\mathcal{C}$ contains the language $L_k = \{a^k b^z \mid z \geq 0\}$ and, if $k \in K$, additionally the languages $L_{k,j} = \{a^k b^z \mid z \leq j\}$ for all $j \leq \Phi_k(k)$. [9] shows that $\mathcal{C} \in Lim\,Txt_{\text{rec}} \setminus Consv\,Txt_{\text{rec}}$. Adopting the corresponding proof one can verify $\mathcal{C} \notin Consv\,Txt_{\text{r.e.}}$ and thus $Consv\,Txt_{\text{r.e.}} \subset Lim\,Txt_{\text{rec}}$. □

Whether or not each class in $Consv\,Txt_{\text{r.e.}}$ can also be identified conservatively in some uniformly *recursive* numbering, remains unanswered. Interestingly, if a class $\mathcal{C} \in Consv\,Txt_{\text{r.e.}}$ can be identified by a learner which is conservative *and consistent* for $\mathcal{C}$, then $\mathcal{C} \in Consv\,Txt_{\text{rec}}$—see Theorem 10. If $(A_i)_{i\in\mathbb{N}}$ is any family of languages, M an IIM, and $\mathcal{C}$ some indexable class, then we say that M learns $\mathcal{C}$ consistently in $(A_i)_{i\in\mathbb{N}}$, if $content(t_n) \subseteq A_{M(t_n)}$ for all text segments t_n of languages in $\mathcal{C}$. For convenience, we denote by $Cons\text{-}ConsvTxt_{\text{r.e.}}$ the family of all indexable classes $\mathcal{C}$, for which there is a uniformly r.e. family $(A_i)_{i\in\mathbb{N}}$ and an IIM M, such that M learns $\mathcal{C}$ both consistently and conservatively in $(A_i)_{i\in\mathbb{N}}$.

The proof of Theorem 10 will make use of the fact that $Consv\,Txt_{\text{rec}} = Cons\text{-}ConsvTxt_{\text{rec}}$ according to [9], where $Cons\text{-}ConsvTxt_{\text{rec}}$ is defined as usual.

Theorem 10. $Consv\,Txt_{\text{rec}} = Cons\text{-}ConsvTxt_{\text{r.e.}}$.

Proof. By $Consv\,Txt_{\text{rec}} \subseteq Cons\text{-}ConsvTxt_{\text{rec}} \subseteq Cons\text{-}ConsvTxt_{\text{r.e.}}$ it remains to prove $Cons\text{-}ConsvTxt_{\text{r.e.}} \subseteq Consv\,Txt_{\text{rec}}$. For that purpose suppose $\mathcal{C}$ is an indexable class in $Cons\text{-}ConsvTxt_{\text{r.e.}}$. If $\mathcal{C}$ is finite, then $\mathcal{C}$ trivially belongs to $Consv\,Txt_{\text{rec}}$. So suppose $\mathcal{C}$ is an infinite class.

By definition, there is an IIM M which learns $\mathcal{C}$ consistently and conservatively in the limit in $(W_i)_{i\in\mathbb{N}}$. Moreover, let $(L_i)_{i\in\mathbb{N}}$ be an indexing for $\mathcal{C}$.

Given $k \in \mathbb{N}$, define the *canonical text* t^k for L_k as follows: $t^k(0) = w_m^*$, where $m = \min\{i \mid w_i^* \in L_k\}$. For $n > 0$ let $t^k(n) = w_{m+n}^*$, if $w_{m+n}^* \in L_k$; $t^k(n) = t^k(n-1)$, if $w_{m+n}^* \notin L_k$. Now let $(k_i, n_i)_{i\in\mathbb{N}}$ be an effective enumeration of all pairs (k, n) of indices such that $n = 0$ or $M(t_n^k) \neq M(t_{n-1}^k)$.

The aim is to define an indexing $(L_i')_{i\in\mathbb{N}}$ comprising $\mathcal{C}$ and a recursively generable family $(T_i')_{i\in\mathbb{N}}$ of telltales for $(L_i')_{i\in\mathbb{N}}$. Using Theorem 1 this implies $\mathcal{C} \in Consv\,Txt_{\text{rec}}$. For that purpose we will define several auxiliary indexings.

Define an indexing $(A_i)_{i \in \mathbb{N}}$ as follows: for $j \in \mathbb{N}$ let

$$A'_j = \begin{cases} L_{k_j} & \text{if } M(t^{k_j}_{n_j+x}) = M(t^{k_j}_{n_j}) \text{ for all } x \geq 0\,, \\ content(t^{k_j}_{n_j+x-1}) & \text{if } x \text{ is minimal with } M(t^{k_j}_{n_j+x}) \neq M(t^{k_j}_{n_j})\,. \end{cases}$$

Claim 1. For each $L \in \mathcal{C}$ there is some $i \in \mathbb{N}$ with $A'_i = L_{k_i} = L$.
The proof of Claim 1 is omitted.

Fix an indexing $(A_i)_{i \in \mathbb{N}}$ enumerating all the languages A'_j without repetitions. This is possible, since, by Claim 1, $(A'_i)_{i \in \mathbb{N}}$ comprises the infinite class $\mathcal{C}$. Accordingly, let $(y_i, z_i)_{i \in \mathbb{N}}$ be an effective enumeration with $t^{y_i}_{z_i} = t^{k_j}_{n_j}$ if $A_i = A'_j$.

Claim 2. For each $L \in \mathcal{C}$ there is some $i \in \mathbb{N}$ with $A_i = L_{y_i} = L$.

Claim 3. Let $i \in \mathbb{N}$. Then $A_i \subseteq W_h$ for $h = M(t^{y_i}_{z_i})$.

Claim 4. Let $i \in \mathbb{N}$. $A_i = L_{y_i}$ iff $W_h = L_{y_i}$ for $h = M(t^{y_i}_{z_i})$.

The proof of Claims 2–4 is left to the reader. Now we define indexings $(B_i)_{i \in \mathbb{N}}$, $(T_i)_{i \in \mathbb{N}}$: for $i \in \mathbb{N}$, construct B_i and T_i according to the following procedure:
(* The construction will yield $B_i = A_i$ or $B_i = \emptyset$. Finally, it will be uniformly decidable whether or not $B_i = \emptyset$. *)
– If $t^{y_j}_{z_j} \neq t^{y_i}_{z_i}$ for all $j < i$, then let $B_i = A_i$ and $T_i = content(t^{y_i}_{z_i})$.
– If some $j < i$ fulfils $t^{y_j}_{z_j} = t^{y_i}_{z_i}$, then act according to the following instructions:

- Let $h = M(t^{y_i}_{z_i})$ and $\{j_1, \ldots, j_s\} = \{j < i \mid t^{y_j}_{z_j} = t^{y_i}_{z_i}\}$.
- Execute Searches (a) and (b) until one of them terminates:

  (a) Search for some x with $M(t^{y_i}_{z_i+x}) \neq h$.
  (b) Search for $x_{j_1}, \ldots, x_{j_s}$ with $M(t^{y_j}_{z_j+x_j}) \neq h$ for all $j \in \{j_1, \ldots, j_s\}$.

  (* Note that, for all $j \in \{j_1, \ldots, j_s\}$, there must be some x with $M(t^{y_i}_{z_i+x}) \neq h$ or $M(t^{y_j}_{z_j+x}) \neq h$ $(= M(t^{y_j}_{z_j}))$. Otherwise one would obtain $A_i = L_{y_i}$ and $A_j = L_{y_j}$. Since $h = M(t^{y_i}_{z_i}) = M(t^{y_j}_{z_j})$, Claim 4 would imply $W_h = L_{y_i} = L_{y_j}$ and thus $A_i = A_j$. This is impossible since $(A_i)_{i \in \mathbb{N}}$ avoids repetitions. *)
- If Search (a) terminates first, let $B_i = T_i = \emptyset$. If Search (b) terminates first, then execute Searches (b.1) and (b.2) until one of them terminates:

  (b.1) Search for some x with $M(t^{y_i}_{z_i+x}) \neq h$.
  (b.2) Search for $w_{j_1}, \ldots, w_{j_s}$ with $w_j \in A_i \setminus B_j$ for all $j \in \{j_1, \ldots, j_s\}$.

  (* Suppose $j \in \{j_1, \ldots, j_s\}$. Note that there is some x with $M(t^{y_i}_{z_i+x}) \neq h$ or some $w \in A_i \setminus B_j$. Otherwise we would have $A_i \subseteq B_j$ and $M(t^{y_i}_{z_i+x}) = h$ for all $x \in \mathbb{N}$. This yields $A_i = L_{y_i}$ and, with Claim 4, $A_i = W_h$. Therefore $W_h \subseteq B_j$. Claim 3 then implies $B_j \subseteq W_h$ and hence $A_i = W_h = B_j = A_j$, which is a contradiction to the injectivity of the indexing $(A_i)_{i \in \mathbb{N}}$. *)
- If Search (b.1) terminates first, let $B_i = T_i = \emptyset$. If Search (b.2) terminates first, then let $B_i = A_i$ and $T_i = content(t^{y_i}_{z_i}) \cup \{w_{j_1}, \ldots, w_{j_s}\}$.

This procedure yields a uniformly recursive indexing $(B_i)_{i \in \mathbb{N}}$ and a recursively generable family $(T_i)_{i \in \mathbb{N}}$ of (possibly empty) finite sets with $T_i \subseteq B_i$ for all i. The proof is left to the reader. Note that $T_i = \emptyset$ iff $B_i = \emptyset$. Moreover, $B_i = A_i$ iff $B_i \neq \emptyset$. In particular, it is uniformly decidable whether or not $B_i = \emptyset$.

Claim 5. $(B_i)_{i \in \mathbb{N}}$ comprises $\mathcal{C}$.

Proof of Claim 5. Let $L \in \mathcal{C}$. By Claim 2 there is some $i \in \mathbb{N}$ with $A_i = L_{y_i} = L$. So, by definition, $M(t^{y_i}_{z_i + x}) = M(t^{y_i}_{z_i}) = h$ for all $x \in \mathbb{N}$. Thus either $t^{y_j}_{z_j} \neq t^{y_i}_{z_i}$ for all $j < i$ or Searches (b) and (b.2) terminate first in the construction of B_i. This yields $B_i = A_i = L$. Hence $(B_i)_{i \in \mathbb{N}}$ comprises $\mathcal{C}$.   qed Claim 5.

Finally, define an indexing $(L'_i)_{i \in \mathbb{N}}$ by removing the empty language from $(B_i)_{i \in \mathbb{N}}$. For i and j with $L'_i = B_j$ let $T'_i = T_j$. Thus $(T'_i)_{i \in \mathbb{N}}$ is a recursively generable family of non-empty finite sets with $T'_i \subseteq L'_i$ for all i. It remains to show that $\mathcal{C}$, $(L'_i)_{i \in \mathbb{N}}$, and $(T'_i)_{i \in \mathbb{N}}$ fulfil the conditions of Theorem 1.2, i.e.,

(i) $(L'_i)_{i \in \mathbb{N}}$ comprises $\mathcal{C}$,

(ii) $(T'_i)_{i \in \mathbb{N}}$ is a telltale family for $(L'_i)_{i \in \mathbb{N}}$.

ad (i). This is an immediate consequence of Claim 5 and the definition of $(L'_i)_{i \in \mathbb{N}}$.

ad (ii). To show that $T'_i \subseteq L'_j \subseteq L'_i$ implies $L'_j = L'_i$, suppose $T'_{i'} \subseteq L'_{j'} \subset L'_{i'}$ holds for some $i', j' \in \mathbb{N}$. Let $i, j \in \mathbb{N}$ with $L'_{i'} = B_i$ and $L'_{j'} = B_j$. This yields $L'_{i'} = A_i$ and $L'_{j'} = A_j$. By the properties of canonical texts, $t^{y_i}_{z_i}$ is an initial segment of t^{y_j}. Therefore one of the segments $t^{y_j}_{z_j}$, $t^{y_i}_{z_i}$ is an initial segment of the other. Let $h_i = M(t^{y_i}_{z_i})$, $h_j = M(t^{y_j}_{z_j})$ and consider three cases.

Case 1. $z_j < z_i$. Then $t^{y_j}_{z_j}$ is a proper initial segment of $t^{y_i}_{z_i}$. In particular, $t^{y_i}_{z_j} = t^{y_j}_{z_j}$ and $M(t^{y_i}_{z_j}) = h_j$. Note that $content(t^{y_i}_{z_i}) \subseteq T'_{i'} \subseteq L'_{j'} = A_j$. Moreover, by Claim 3, $A_j \subseteq W_{h_j}$ and thus $content(t^{y_i}_{z_i}) \subseteq W_{h_j}$. Since M is conservative on any text for $L_{y_i} \supseteq A_i$, this yields $h_j = M(t^{y_i}_{z_j}) = M(t^{y_i}_{z_j + 1}) = \cdots = M(t^{y_i}_{z_i})$. By definition of the family $(k_i, n_i)_{i \in \mathbb{N}}$, we have $M(t^{y_i}_{z_i}) \neq M(t^{y_i}_{z_i - 1})$. This results in $z_i = z_j$ and thus in a contradiction.

Case 2. $z_i < z_j$. Then $t^{y_i}_{z_i}$ is a proper initial segment of $t^{y_j}_{z_j}$. In particular, $t^{y_j}_{z_i} = t^{y_i}_{z_i}$ and $M(t^{y_j}_{z_i}) = h_i$. Note that $content(t^{y_j}_{z_j}) \subseteq L'_{j'} \subseteq L'_{i'} = A_i$. Moreover, by Claim 3, $A_i \subseteq W_{h_i}$ and thus $content(t^{y_j}_{z_j}) \subseteq W_{h_i}$. Similarly as above, this results in $z_i = z_j$ and thus in a contradiction.

Case 3. $z_i = z_j$. Then $t^{y_i}_{z_i} = t^{y_j}_{z_j}$. First, assume $i > j$. Since $B_i \neq \emptyset$, in the construction of B_i some $w \in A_i \setminus B_j$ is included in T_i. This yields $w \in T'_{i'} \subseteq L'_{j'}$. So $w \in L'_{j'} \setminus B_j$ in contradiction to $L'_{j'} = B_j$. Second, assume $i < j$. Since $B_j \neq \emptyset$, during the construction of B_j some $w \in A_j \setminus B_i$ is found. This yields $w \in L'_{j'} \setminus L'_{i'}$ in contradiction to $L'_{j'} \subseteq L'_{i'}$.

Since each case yields a contradiction, our assumption has been wrong, i.e., there are no indices $i', j' \in \mathbb{N}$ such that $T'_{i'} \subseteq L'_{j'} \subset L'_{i'}$. This finally proves (ii).

By Theorem 1.2, the families $(L'_i)_{i \in \mathbb{N}}$ and $(T'_i)_{i \in \mathbb{N}}$ witness $\mathcal{C} \in Consv\,Txt_{rec}$. Since $\mathcal{C} \in Cons\text{-}ConsvTxt_{r.e.}$ was chosen arbitrarily, our argument directly proves $Cons\text{-}ConsvTxt_{r.e.} \subseteq Consv\,Txt_{rec}$ and so $Consv\,Txt_{rec} = Cons\text{-}ConsvTxt_{r.e.}$. □

As it turns out, throughout the whole proof we never use the fact that the hypothesis space for *Cons-ConsvTxt*-identification is uniformly r.e. This implies the following corollary: Assume $(A_i)_{i \in \mathbb{N}}$ is any family of languages (not necessarily uniformly r.e.) and $\mathcal{C}$ is any indexable class of recursive languages.

- If $\mathcal{C}$ is *Cons-ConsvTxt*-learnable wrt $(A_i)_{i \in \mathbb{N}}$, then $\mathcal{C} \in Consv\,Txt_{rec}$.

The following figure summarizes our main results.

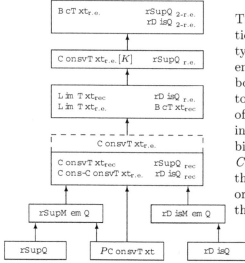

This graph illustrates the relations between different inference types studied above. If two inference types are contained in one box, they are equal. Each vector indicates a proper inclusion of inference types, whereas missing links symbolize incomparability. The dashed box around $Consv\,Txt_{r.e.}$ is used to indicate that it is not yet known, whether or not $Consv\,Txt_{r.e.}$ belongs to the adjacent box below.

References

[1] D. Angluin. Inductive inference of formal languages from positive data. *Information and Control*, 45:117–135, 1980.

[2] D. Angluin. Queries and concept learning. *Machine Learning*, 2:319–342, 1988.

[3] D. Angluin. Queries revisited. *Theoretical Computer Science*, 313:175–194, 2004.

[4] G. Baliga, J. Case, S. Jain. The synthesis of language learners. *Information and Computation*, 152:16–43, 1999.

[5] M. Blum. A machine-independent theory of the complexity of recursive functions. *Journal of the ACM*, 14:322–336, 1967.

[6] J. Case, C. Lynes. Machine inductive inference and language identification. In: *Proc. ICALP 1982*, LNCS 140, 107–115, Springer, 1982.

[7] E. M. Gold. Language identification in the limit. *Information and Control*, 10:447–474, 1967.

[8] J. E. Hopcroft, J. D. Ullman. *Introduction to Automata Theory, Languages, and Computation*. Addison-Wesley Publishing Company, 1979.

[9] S. Lange, T. Zeugmann. Language learning in dependence on the space of hypotheses. In: *Proc. COLT 1993*, 127–136, ACM Press, 1993.

[10] S. Lange, S. Zilles. On the learnability of erasing pattern languages in the query model. In: *Proc. ALT 2003*, LNAI 2842, 129–143, Springer, 2003.

[11] S. Lange, S. Zilles. Replacing limit learners with equally powerful one-shot query learners. In: *Proc. COLT 2004*, LNAI 3120, 155–169, Springer, 2004.

[12] H. Rogers. *Theory of Recursive Functions and Effective Computability*, MIT Press, 1987.

[13] F. Stephan. *Degrees of Computing and Learning*. Habilitationsschrift, Ruprecht-Karls-Universität, Heidelberg, 1999.

[14] T. Zeugmann, S. Lange. A guided tour across the boundaries of learning recursive languages. In: *Algorithmic Learning for Knowledge-Based Systems*, LNAI 961, 190–258, Springer, 1995.

Learning r-of-k Functions by Boosting[*]

Kohei Hatano and Osamu Watanabe

Dept. of Mathematical and Computing Sciences, Tokyo Institute of Technology
{hatano, watanabe}@is.titech.ac.jp

Abstract. We investigate further improvement of boosting in the case
that the target concept belongs to the class of r-of-k threshold Boolean
functions, which answer "+1" if at least r of k relevant variables are positive, and answer "−1" otherwise. Given m examples of a r-of-k function
and literals as base hypotheses, popular boosting algorithms (e.g., AdaBoost) construct a consistent final hypothesis by using $O(k^2 \log m)$ base
hypotheses. While this convergence speed is tight in general, we show
that a modification of AdaBoost (confidence-rated AdaBoost [SS99] or
InfoBoost [Asl00]) can make use of the property of r-of-k functions that
make less error on one-side to find a consistent final hypothesis by using $O(kr \log m)$ hypotheses. Our result extends the previous investigation by Hatano and Warmuth [HW04] and gives more general examples
where confidence-rated AdaBoost or InfoBoost has an advantage over
AdaBoost.

1 Introduction

Boosting is a method of constructing strongly accurate classifiers by combining
weakly accurate base classifiers, and it is now one of the most fundamental techniques in machine learning. A typical boosting algorithm proceeds in rounds as
follows: At each round, it assigns a distribution on the given data, and finds
a moderately accurate base classifier with respect to the distribution. Then it
updates the distribution so that the last chosen classifier is insignificant for it.
It has been shown that this algorithm converges relatively quickly under the assumption that a base hypothesis with error less than $1/2 - \gamma$ can be found at each
iteration. For example, under this assumption, Freund showed [Fre95] a boosting
algorithm and proved that it yields a ε-approximation of the correct hypothesis
by using $O((1/\gamma^2) \log(1/\varepsilon))$ base hypotheses. Freund also proved that the result
is in a sense tight; that is, if the final hypothesis is of a majority of weak hypotheses (like his boosting algorithm does), then any boosting algorithm needs, in the
worst case, $\Omega((1/\gamma^2) \log(1/\varepsilon))$ weak hypotheses to obtain an ε-approximation.
While Freund's result is tight in general, it is still possible to improve boosting
for some particular cases. For example, Dasgupta and Long [DL03] showed that
the above boosting algorithm by Freund works more efficiently when the set
of base classifiers contains the subset of good "diverse" classifiers. This paper

---

[*] This work is supported in part by a Grant-in-Aid for Scientific Research on Priority
Areas "Statistical-Mechanical Approach to Probabilistic Information Processing".

S. Ben-David, J. Case, A. Maruoka (Eds.): ALT 2004, LNAI 3244, pp. 114–126, 2004.

studies one of such cases; here we consider the situation where error occurs less often in one side.

Let us see the following illustrative example. Consider learning k-disjunctions. That is, given m labeled examples for a target k-disjunction f over n Boolean variables, our task is to find a hypothesis consistent with f on these examples. Let $\mathcal{H}$ be the set of very simple Boolean functions that are either a function defined by one literal or a constant $+1$ or -1, and let $\mathcal{H}_+$ be the subset of $\mathcal{H}$ consisting of functions defined by one Boolean variable, i.e., a positive literal. By using functions in $\mathcal{H}$ as base classifiers, a popular boosting algorithm (e.g., AdaBoost) can find a consistent hypotheses using $O(k^2 \log m)$ base hypotheses. In contrast, a use of the greedy set-covering algorithm can accomplish the same task with $O(k \log m)$ hypotheses, as learning of k-disjunctions can be reduced to the set-covering problem [Nat91,KV94]. Note that for the set-covering problem this bound cannot be improved by a constant factor efficiently under a realistic complexity-theoretic assumption [Fei98]. Now it is natural to ask whether boosting algorithms can beat the greedy set-covering algorithm in this learning problem. Hatano and Warmuth [HW04] showed that a modification of AdaBoost, called confidence-rated AdaBoost [SS99] or InfoBoost [Asl00] (in the following, we simply call it InfoBoost), can achieve $O(k \log m)$ bound. Moreover, they showed that AdaBoost does need $\Omega(k^2 \log m)$ hypotheses under some technical conditions[1].

In the above case, we may assume that all base hypotheses in $\mathcal{H}_+$ have one-sided error property; that is, their positive predictions are always correct, in other words, all these base hypotheses have 0 false positive error. InfoBoost is designed so that it can make use of this situation, and this is why it performs better than AdaBoost. In general, when this one-sided error property can be assumed for good base hypotheses, InfoBoost can reduce the number of boosting iterations from $O((1/\gamma^2) \log m)$ to $O((1/\gamma) \log m)$. Besides this extreme case, we may naturally expect that InfoBoost can also make use of "partially" one-sided error property. This is the question we discuss in this paper. As a concrete example of "partially" one-sided error situations, we consider here the problem of learning r-of-k threshold functions. For any r and k, a r-of-k function (over n Boolean variables) consists of k relevant variables, and it answers $+1$ if at least r of the k variables are positive, and otherwise answers -1. We learn these functions by using again $\mathcal{H}$ as the set of base classifiers. Note that k-disjunctions are nothing but 1-of-k functions; hence, our learning task is a generalization of learning k-disjunctions. Also for small r, we may expect that hypotheses in $\mathcal{H}_+$ have *on average* small (but may not be 0) false positive error. We show that InfoBoost can still make use of this one-sided error property and find a consistent hypothesis by using $O(kr \log m)$ base hypotheses. Thus, the running

---

[1] A typical setting is that a boosting algorithm has a pool of base hypotheses and it can choose hypotheses greedily from the pool. But in the setting of [HW04] it has only access to a weak learner oracle, which is just guaranteed to return a hypotheses with its error below a fixed threshold j.

time of InfoBoost is from $O(k \log m)$ (when $r = O(1)$, e.g., k-disjunctions) to $O(k^2 \log m)$ (when $r = \Omega(k)$, e.g., k-variable majority functions).

Unfortunately, we know few related results on learning of r-of-k functions. The online learning algorithm WINNOW [Lit88] (more precisely, WINNOW2) can be used to learn r-of-k functions. With its fixed parameters $\alpha = 1 + 1/2r$, and $\theta = n$, WINNOW has a mistake bound of $O(kr \log n)$ for r-of-k functions. (Note that n is the number of Boolean variables in the domain, not the number of the examples m.) However, unlike confidence-rated AdaBoost or InfoBoost, it needs the knowledge of r in advance.

Other related optimization problems might be covering integer programs [Sri99,Sri01] and mixed covering integer programs [L01]. The former can be viewed as a general form of the set-covering problem, and the latter is a further generalization the former, motivated by the problem of learning the minimum majority of base hypotheses. Both problems can be approximately solved by randomized polynomial time algorithms, whose solutions have size $O(dopt \log opt)$ and $O(dopt^2)$, respectively (here, opt denotes the size of the optimal solution and d is called pseudo-dimension. See [L01] for the details). Learning of r-of-k functions may be characterized by an "intermediate" problem of the both.

Technically our contribution is to develop a way to show a base hypothesis with reasonable advantage *and* small error probability on one side from the fact that $\mathcal{H}$ has *on average* reasonable advantage and small false positive error.

2   Preliminaries

In this section, we give basic definitions. Throughout this paper, the domain of interest is $\mathcal{X} = \{-1, +1\}^n$. By a "Boolean function" we will mean a function from $\mathcal{X}$ to $\{-1, +1\}$. We use X_i, $i = 1 \ldots$, to denote Boolean variables, which naturally define functions from $\mathcal{X}$ to $\{-1, +1\}$. Let F_k^r be the set of r-of-k functions, i.e., Boolean functions on k Boolean variables that return $+1$ if at least r of these k variables are assigned $+1$. For any $f \in F_k^r$, $\mathrm{Rel}(f)$ is the set of the relevant Boolean variables of f.

For any $f \in F_k^r$, a pair $(x, f(x))$ is called an *example* of f. A set of such pairs is called a *sample*. We will use $\mathcal{H} = \{X_1, \ldots, X_n, +1, -1\}$ as the set of base hypotheses (or weak hypotheses). For any distribution D, any Boolean function f, and any hypothesis $h \in \mathcal{H}$, we define

$$\mathrm{err}|_D^+(f, h) = \Pr_D[\, f(x) = +1 \,|\, h(x) = -1 \,],$$

$$\mathrm{err}_D^+(f, h) = \Pr_D[\, f(x) = +1, h(x) = -1 \,],$$

$$\mathrm{err}|_D^-(f, h) = \Pr_D[\, f(x) = -1 \,|\, h(x) = +1 \,],$$

$$\mathrm{err}_D^-(f, h) = \Pr_D[\, f(x) = -1, h(x) = +1 \,], \text{ and}$$

$$\mathrm{error}_D(f, h) = \mathrm{err}_D^+(f, h) + \mathrm{err}_D^-(f, h).$$

We will omit D and f in the notation when it is clear from the context.

Given: A set S of m examples $\{(x, y) \mid x \in \mathcal{X}, y = f(x)\}$.
We denote elements of S as (x_1, y_1), ..., (x_m, y_m).

begin

1. Let $D_1(i) = 1/m$, for $i = 1, ..., m$. (I.e., $D_1(i) = D_0(x_i)$.)
2. For $t = 1$ to T, repeat the following procedures:
   a) Select $h_t \in \mathcal{H}$ that minimizes Z_t defined below (see (1)).
   b) Let $\alpha_t(+1) = \frac{1}{2} \ln \frac{1 - \mathrm{err}|^-(h_t)}{\mathrm{err}|^-(h_t)}$ and $\alpha_t(-1) = \frac{1}{2} \ln \frac{1 - \mathrm{err}|^+(h_t)}{\mathrm{err}|^+(h_t)}$.
   c) Define the next distribution D_{t+1} as follows for each $i = 1, ..., m$,
   $$D_{t+1}(i) = \frac{D_t(i) \exp\{-y_i \cdot \alpha_t(h_t(x_i)) \cdot h_t(x_i)\}}{Z_t},$$
   (Z_t defined by (1) is the normalization factor.)
3. Output the final hypothesis f_{out} defined by
$$f_{\mathrm{out}}(x) = sign\left(\sum_{t=1}^{T} \alpha_t(h_t(x_i)) \cdot h_t(x_i)\right).$$

Fig. 1. A Boosting Algorithm

For our learning algorithm, we will consider InfoBoost [Asl00] (or confidence-rated AdaBoost [SS99]) with $\mathcal{H}$ as the set of weak hypothesis; Figure 2 shows the description of this boosting algorithm on a given sample $S = \{(x, y) \mid x \in \mathcal{X}, y = f(x)\}$ of m examples for some target concept f. Recall that the goal of this algorithm is to obtain a (combined) hypothesis f_{out} that is consistent with f on S, which we will simply call a *consistent hypothesis*. More precisely, for any $x \in \mathcal{X}$, define $D_0(x) = 1/m$ if x appears in S and $D_0(x) = 0$ otherwise. Then the consistent hypothesis, which we want to get, is f_{out} such that $\mathrm{error}_{D_0}(f, f_{\mathrm{out}}) = 0$. For this goal, the following boosting property is known [SS99,Asl00].

Theorem 1. *For any $T \geq 1$, let f_{out} be the hypothesis that the boosting algorithm yields after T iterations. Then the following bound holds for the training error of this hypothesis.*

$$\mathrm{error}_{D_0}(f, f_{\mathrm{out}}) \leq \prod_{t=1}^{T} Z_t.$$

Here Z_t is the normalization factor of the t-th iteration, which is defined as follows.

$$Z_t = \sum_{1 \leq i \leq m} D_t(i) \exp\{-y_i \alpha(h_t(x_i)) h_t(x_i)\}. \tag{1}$$

3   Main Result

Theorem 1 gives the convergence speed of the boosting algorithm of Figure 2. In our setting, it is easy to bound Z_t by $\sqrt{1 - 1/O(k^2)}$ for any r-of-k target function, from which it is shown that the algorithm yields a consistent hypothesis in $O(k^2 \log m)$ steps. Our technical contribution is to improve this bound to $\sqrt{1 - 1/O(rk)}$, thereby improving the upper bound for the boosting steps to $O(kr \log m)$.

In the following, for any $r \geq 1$ and $k \geq 1$, consider any r-of-k function f for our target concept, let it be fixed, and we will estimate the normalization factor Z_t of each step $t \geq 1$. Our goal is to prove the following bound. (For Z_1, by definition we have $Z_1 \leq 1$.)

Theorem 2. *For any $t \geq 2$, we have*

$$ Z_t \leq \sqrt{1 - \frac{1}{512rk}}. $$

We first show some key properties used to derive this bound. In the following, let any $t \geq 2$ be fixed, and let us simply denote Z_t as Z. Also let D be the distribution D_t defined in our algorithm at the t-th iteration. Precisely speaking, D_t is defined on $i = 1, ..., m$; but we may regard this as a distribution D_t on $\mathcal{X}$ such that $D_t(x) = D_t(i)$ if $x = x_i$ for some $i = 1, ..., m$, and $D_t(x) = 0$ otherwise. Let D denote this distribution. Then the following fact is checked easily.

Fact 1. *For our distribution D, we have $\Pr_D[f(x) = +1] = \Pr_D[f(x) = -1] = 1/2$.*

We say that such a distribution D is *balanced* (with respect to f).

Using this property and the assumption that f is a r-of-k function, the following weak hypothesis can be guaranteed. In the following, let $\mathcal{H}'$ be the non-constant hypotheses of $\mathcal{H}$; that is, $\mathcal{H}' = \{X_1, ..., X_n\}$. Also when $h = X_i$, we simply write $\mathrm{err}|_i^+$ and $\mathrm{err}|_i^-$ for $\mathrm{err}|_D^+(f, h)$ and $\mathrm{err}|_D^-(f, h)$ respectively.

Lemma 1. *There exists a hypothesis $h \in \mathcal{H}'$ (in fact, some $h \in \mathrm{Rel}(f)$) with*
$$ \mathrm{error}(h) \leq \frac{1}{2} - \frac{1}{2k}. $$

Proof. Consider the total number of mistakes made by hypotheses X_i in $\mathrm{Rel}(f)$. For any positive instance, the total number of mistakes is at most $k - r$. Hence, we have $\sum_{X_i \in \mathrm{Rel}(f)} \mathrm{err}_i^+ = \sum_{X_i \in \mathrm{Rel}(f)} \Pr_D\{X_i(x) = -1, f(x) = 1\} \leq (k - r) \cdot \Pr_D\{f(x) = 1\} = (k - r)/2$, because D is balanced. By a similar argument for negative instances, we have $\sum_{X_i \in \mathrm{Rel}(f)} \mathrm{err}_i^- \leq (r - 1)/2$. In total, we have

$$ \sum_{X_i \in \mathrm{Rel}(f)} \mathrm{error}(X_i) \leq \frac{k - r}{2} + \frac{r - 1}{2} = \frac{k - 1}{2}. $$

On the other hand, $\mathrm{Rel}(f)$ has k variables; therefore, by the averaging argument, there should be at least one X_i satisfying the lemma.   □

This bound is somewhat standard. In fact, using this bound, one can bound Z by $\sqrt{1 - 1/(2k)^2}$. While this bound cannot be improved in general, we may be able to have better bounds if the error is estimated separately for positive and negative instances, which is the advantage of using InfoBoost. For example, if the target function f is the disjunction of some k variables (i.e., $r = 1$), then any $h \in \text{Rel}(f)$ does not make a mistake on negative instances; thus, it follows above that there exists $h \in \mathcal{H}'$ whose general error probability is bounded by $1/2 - 1/2k$ and whose error probability on negative instances (i.e., $\text{err}^-(h)$) is 0. The bound $O(k \log m)$ [HW04] is derived from this observation. Here we would like to generalize this argument. In the case of k-disjunctions (or 1-of-k functions), it is guaranteed that base classifiers in $\mathcal{H}'$ have good advantage on average and *all* of them have 0 false positive error. But now the assumption we can use is that they have good advantage and small false positive error both *on average*. Our technical contribution is to derive a similar consequence from this assumption.

Lemma 2. *There exists a hypothesis $h \in \mathcal{H}'$ (in fact, $h \in \text{Rel}(f)$) such that the following holds for some integer a, $1 \le a \le 4k$ with constant $c_0 = 2$.*

$$\text{error}(h) \le \frac{1}{2} - \frac{a}{8k}, \quad \text{and} \tag{2}$$

$$\text{err}^-(h) \le \frac{c_0(r-1)a^2}{k}. \tag{3}$$

Proof. Consider k hypotheses $h_1, ..., h_k$ in $\text{Rel}(f)$; that is, each h_i is a Boolean variables relevant to the target function f. Consider first the case that there are more than $k/2$ "relatively good" h_i in $\text{Rel}(f)$ that satisfies $\text{error}(h_i) \le 1/2 - 1/4k$. As discussed in the proof of Lemma 1, we have $\sum_{h_i \in \text{Rel}(f)} \text{err}_i^- \le (r-1)/2$. Thus, among such relatively good h_i, there must be some h_i such that $\text{err}_i^- \le ((r-1)/2) \div (k/2) = (r-1)/k$. This clearly satisfies the lemma with $a = 1$.

Consider next the case that we do not have so many relatively good hypotheses. For each h_i, let $w_i = (1/2 - 1/(2k)) - \text{error}(h_i) < 1/2$. Here note that some h_i may have negative w_i; for example, a hypothesis h_i that is not "relatively good" has weight $w_i < -1/(4k)$. Also note that the total, i.e., $\sum_{i=1}^{k} w_i$ must be at least 0, because $\text{error}(h_i)$ is at most $1/2 - 1/(2k)$ on average (see the proof of Lemma 1).

Consider the set H of hypotheses h_i that have nonnegative weights, and let s be the number of such hypotheses. Since more than $k/2$ hypotheses are not "relatively good", the total weights of all negative w_i's is less than $-(1/(4k))(k/2) = -1/8$. Thus, letting $\sigma = \sum_{h_i \in H} w_i$, we have $\sigma \ge 1/8$. Now we use Lemma A in Appendix with these w_i's, s, σ, and $t = 8k$. Then from the lemma, we have either (i) $s \ge k/2$, or (ii) there exists some $a \le 4k$ for which the following holds.

$$\left| \left\{ i : w_i \ge \frac{a}{8k} \right\} \right| \ge \frac{k}{4a^2}.$$

Note, however, that the case (i) cannot happen because we assume that there are not such many good hypotheses. Hence consider the case (ii). For the parameter

a for which the above bound holds, consider hypotheses h_i's such that $w_i \geq a/8k$. Let H' be the set of such hypotheses. Clearly, any h_i in H' satisfies (2). Again since H' has $s \geq k/(4a^2)$ hypotheses and the sum of their err_i^-'s, i.e., $\sum_{h_i \in H'} \mathrm{err}_i^-$, is still at most $(r-1)/2$, there must be some hypothesis in H' such that $\mathrm{err}_i^- \leq 2a^2(r-1)/k$, satisfying the lemma.   □

Now we are ready to prove our theorem.

Proof of Theorem 2. Let err^-, $\mathrm{err}|^-$, err^+, $\mathrm{err}|^+$, and err denote respectively $\mathrm{err}_D^-(h)$, $\mathrm{err}|_D^-(h)$, $\mathrm{err}_D^+(h)$, $\mathrm{err}|_D^+(h)$ and $\mathrm{error}_D(h)$ for the hypothesis h selected at the t-th iteration under the distribution D $(= D_t)$. First we restate (1) as follows (see, e.g., [Asl00]).

$$
Z = 2 \left\{ \sum_{i:h(x_i)=+1} D(i)\sqrt{(1-\mathrm{err}|^-)\mathrm{err}|^-} + \sum_{i:h(x_i)=-1} D(i)\sqrt{(1-\mathrm{err}|^+)\mathrm{err}|^+} \right\}.
$$

By using the fact that D is balanced, it is easy to restate it further as

$$
Z = 2\sqrt{\left(\frac{1}{2}-\mathrm{err}^+\right)\mathrm{err}^-} + 2\sqrt{\left(\frac{1}{2}-\mathrm{err}^-\right)\mathrm{err}^+}.
$$

We consider two cases.

(Case 1: $\mathcal{H}$ has a quite good hypothesis)
Suppose that $\mathcal{H}$ has a good hypothesis so that we have $\mathrm{err} < 1/2 - 1/(16\sqrt{rk})$ for the selected h. Recall that $\mathrm{err} = \mathrm{err}^+ + \mathrm{err}^+$; then it is easy to see that, for any fixed value of err, Z takes the maximum when $\mathrm{err}^- = \mathrm{err}^+ = \mathrm{err}/2$. Thus, considering this situation, we have

$$
Z \leq 2\sqrt{\mathrm{err}\,(1-\mathrm{err})} \leq \sqrt{1 - \frac{1}{64rk}}.
$$

(Case 2: $\mathcal{H}$ does not have such good hypothesis)
That is, suppose that $\mathcal{H}$ has no hypothesis whose error is less than $1/2 - 1/(16\sqrt{rk})$. Together with this assumption, it follows from Lemma 2 we have some hypothesis $h \in \mathcal{H}$ satisfying the conditions (2) and (3) for some integer a, $1 \leq a \leq (1/2)\sqrt{(k/r)}$. Then by Lemma B given in Appendix, an upper bound of Z is obtained by assuming the equalities in the conditions (2) and (3). Note that the constraints of Lemma B are satisfied for our choice of a. Thus, for any

$r > 1$, we have[2]

$$Z = 2\sqrt{\left(\frac{1}{2} - \text{err}^-\right)\text{err}^+ + 2\sqrt{\text{err}^-\left(\frac{1}{2} - \text{err}^+\right)}}$$

$$= 2\sqrt{\left(\sqrt{\left(\frac{1}{2} - \text{err}^-\right)\text{err}^+} + \sqrt{\text{err}^-\left(\frac{1}{2} - \text{err}^+\right)}\right)^2}$$

$$= 2\sqrt{\frac{\text{err}^- + \text{err}^+}{2} - 2\text{err}^-\text{err}^+ + 2\sqrt{\text{err}^-\text{err}^+\left(\frac{1}{2} - \text{err}^-\right)\left(\frac{1}{2} - \text{err}^+\right)}}$$

$$= 2\sqrt{\frac{\text{error}}{2} - 2\text{err}^-\text{err}^+ + 2\sqrt{\text{err}^-\text{err}^+\left(\frac{1}{4} - \frac{\text{err}^- + \text{err}^+}{2} + \text{err}^-\text{err}^+\right)}}$$

$$\leq \sqrt{1 - \frac{a}{4k} - 8\text{err}^-\text{err}^+ + 8\sqrt{\text{err}^-\text{err}^+\left(\frac{a}{16k} + \text{err}^-\text{err}^+\right)}}$$

$$= \sqrt{1 - \frac{a}{4k} - 8\text{err}^-\text{err}^+ + 8\text{err}^-\text{err}^+\sqrt{\left(\frac{a}{16k\text{err}^-\text{err}^+} + 1\right)}}$$

Since it holds by using the Tayler series that $\sqrt{1+x} \leq 1 + \frac{x}{2} - \frac{x^2}{16}$ for x ($0 \leq x < 1$), the quantity Z is bounded by the square root of

$$1 - \frac{a}{4k} - 8\text{err}^-\text{err}^+ + 8\text{err}^-\text{err}^+\left(1 + \frac{1}{2} \cdot \frac{a}{16k\text{err}^-\text{err}^+} - \frac{1}{16}\frac{a^2}{(16k\text{err}^-\text{err}^+)^2}\right).$$

By simplifying this, we have

$$Z \leq \sqrt{1 - \frac{a^2}{512k^2\text{err}^-\text{err}^+}}.$$

Then by substituting $\text{err}^- = \frac{1}{2} - \frac{a}{8k} - \frac{2a^2(r-1)}{k} = \frac{4k - a - 16a^2(r-1)}{8k}$ and $\text{err}^+ = \frac{2a^2(r-1)}{k}$, we obtain

$$Z \leq \sqrt{1 - \frac{4}{512(r-1)(4k - a - 16(r-1)a^2)}}$$

$$< \sqrt{1 - \frac{1}{512kr}}.$$

$\square$

Finally we state the following corollary that is derived from Theorem 1 and Theorem 2 by a standard analysis.

Corollary 1. *For any r and k, $1 \leq r \leq k/2$ and $2 \leq k \leq n$, and for any target r-of-k function f, the boosting algorithm given in Figure 2 yields a hypothesis that is consistent with f if $T \geq (1024kr \log m + 1)$.*

---

[2] Here we explain the case $r > 1$. The case $r = 1$ can be treated by much simpler analysis, which can be found in [HW04].

4   Concluding Remarks

We proved that for r-of-k functions, InfoBoost can find consistent hypotheses in $O(rk \log m)$ iterations (where m is the number of examples). On the other hand, AdaBoost seems to need $O(k^2 \log m)$ iterations (which has been indeed proved conditionally in [HW04]); thus, our result indicates that InfoBoost performs better than AdaBoost when we may assume less error on one classification side. A problem of theoretical interest is to show the tightness of our analysis. (We conjecture that our upper bound is tight except for the constant factor.)

Another interesting open problem on InfoBoost, which is also important in practice, is its generalization error. We are still unaware of the way to bound the generalization error of InfoBoost. Recall that Schapire et al. [SFBL98] showed that "margin" can be used to estimate the generalization error of a hypothesis defined as a linear combination of hypotheses. While this analysis is applicable for hypotheses produced by InfoBoost, it may be the case that InfoBoost produces a hypothesis with "small margin", which is not enough to guarantee a small generalization error (see [SS99] for the detail). One way to avoid arguments on generalization error is to introduce the boosting by filtering framework [Sch91, Fre95]. In this framework, instead of being given a set of examples in advance, the learner can directly draw examples randomly according to a fixed unknown distribution. Several researchers pointed out that AdaBoost does not fit this scheme because it constructs too "skew" distributions from which it is hard to sample examples [DW00,BG01,Ser01,Gav03]. This also accounts for InfoBoost. They proposed variants of AdaBoost that create "smooth" distributions enabling us to sample efficiently. One of the interesting problems is to extend some of these ideas to InfoBoost.

Acknowledgements. We thank Manfred Warmuth and Phil Long for helpful discussions and leading us to study the problem discussed in this paper. We also thank anonymous referees for their suggestions.

References

[Asl00]   J.A. Aslam, Improving algorithms for boosting, in *Proc. 13th Annu. Conference on Comput. Learning Theory*, ACM, 200–207, 2000.

[BG01]   N.H. Bshouty and D. Gavinsky, On boosting with optimal poly-bounded distributions, in *Proc. 14th Annual Conference on Computational Learning Theory and 5th European Conference on Computational Learning Theory*, Lecture Notes in Artificial Intelligence 2111, 490–506, 2001.

[DL03]   S. Dasgupta and P.M. Long, Boosting with diverse base classifiers, in *Learning Theory and Kernel Machines, 16th Annual Conference on Learning Theory and 7th Kernel Workshop*, Lecture Notes in Artificial Intelligence 2777, Springer, 273–287, 2003.

[DW00]   C. Domingo and O. Watanabe, MadaBoost: a modification of AdaBoost, in *Proc. 13th Annu. Conference on Computational Learning Theory*, ACM, 180–189, 2000.

[Fei98]   U. Feige, A threshold of ln n for approximating set cover, *Journal of the ACM (JACM)*, 45(4), 634–652, 1998.

[Fre95]   Y. Freund, Boosting a weak learning algorithm by majority, *Inform. Comput.*, 121(2), 256–285, 1995.

[Gav03]   D. Gavinsky, Optimally-smooth adaptive boosting and application to agnostic learning, *Journal of Machine Learning Research* 4, 101-117, 2003.

[HW04]   K. Hatano and M.K. Warmuth. Boosting versus covering, in *Advances in Neural Information Processing Systems 16* (S. Thrun, L. Saul, and B. Schölkopf eds.), MIT Press, 2004.

[KV94]   M.J. Kearns and U.V. Vazirani, *An Introduction to Computational Learning Theory*, MIT Press, 1994.

[Lit88]   N. Littlestone, Learning Quickly When Irrelevant Attributes Abound: A New Linear-Threshold Algorithm, *Machine Learning* 2(4), 285–318, 1988.

[L01]   P. M. Long, Using the Pseudo-Dimension to Analyze Approximation Algorithms for Integer Programming, in *Proc. of the Seventh International Workshop on Algorithms and Data Structures*, 26–37, 2001.

[Nat91]   B.K. Natarajan. *Machine Learning: A Theoretical Approach*, Morgan Kaufmann, 1991.

[Sch91]   R.E. Schapire, The strength of weak learnability, *Machine Learning* 5(2), 197–227, 1990.

[Ser01]   R. A. Servedio, Smooth Boosting and Learning with Malicious Noise, in *14th Annual Conference on Computational Learning Theory, COLT 2001 and 5th European Conference on Computational Learning Theory, EuroCOLT 2001*, Lecture Notes in Artificial Intelligence 2111, 473–489, 2001.

[SFBL98]   R.E. Schapire, Y. Freund, P. Bartlett, and W.S. Lee, Boosting the margin: A new explanation for the effectiveness of voting methods, *The Annals of Statistics* 26(5), 1651-1686, 1998.

[Sri99]   A. Srinivasan, Improved approximation guarantees for packing and covering integer programs. *SIAM Journal on Computing*, 29, 648–670, 1999.

[Sri01]   A. Srinivasan, New approaches to covering and packing problems, in *Proc. ACM-SIAM Symposium on Discrete Algorithms (SODA)*, 567-576, 2001.

[SS99]   R.E. Schapire and Y. Singer, Improved boosting algorithms using confidence-rated predictions, *Machine Learning* 37(3), 297–336, 1999.

Appendix

Lemma A. *Let $\{w_1, ..., w_s\}$ be a set of weights such that $0 \le w_i \le 1/2$ for all i, $1 \le i \le s$, and $\sum_{i=1}^{s} w_i = \sigma$. Then for any $t > 0$, either $s \ge \sigma t/2$, or there exists some a $(1 \le a \le t/2)$, such that the following holds.*

$$\left| \left\{ i : w_i \ge \frac{a}{t} \right\} \right| \ge \frac{d_0 \sigma t}{a^2},$$

where we may set $d_0 = 1/4$.

Remark. Note that the average weight $(\sum w_i)/s = \sigma/s$. Then the Markov inequality claims that $|\{w_i \ge a/t\}|$ $(= |\{w_i \ge \alpha(\sigma/s)\}| \le s(1/\alpha) =) \sigma t/a$ for all $a > 0$, where $\alpha = sa/(\sigma t)$. Thus, the lemma is regarded as a lower bound version of the Markov inequality. We can improve this bound by replacing the denominator a^2 with smaller one, e.g., $a(\log a)^2$; but on the other hand, it is also easy to see that we cannot use the denominator a like the Markov inequality.

Proof. Assume that the lemma does not hold (i.e., neither $s \geq \sigma t/2$ nor some a exists satisfying the lemma), and we will lead a contradiction. For any integer $j \geq 0$, define $n(j) = d_0\sigma t/(2^{2j})$. We may assume that $w_1 \leq w_2 \leq \cdots \leq w_s$. Then we have $w_i < 1/t$ for the first $s_0 \geq s - n(0)$ weights, because otherwise, we would have more than $n(0)$ weights that are larger than $1/t$, contradicting our assumption. Similarly, we have $w_i < 2/t$ for the next $s_1 \geq s - s_0 - n(1)$ weights, $w_i < 2^2/t$ for the next $s_2 \geq s - s_0 - s_1 - n(2)$ weights, and so on. It is easy to see that $\sum w_i$ becomes largest if $s_0 = n(0)$, $s_1 = s - s_0 - n(1)$, ... Thus, estimate $\sum w_i$ with $s_0 = n(0)$, $s_1 = s - s_0 - n(1) = s - (s - n(0)) - n(1) = n(0) - n(1)$, $s_2 = s - s_0 - s_1 - n(2) = n(1) - n(2)$, ... Then we have

$$
\sum_{i=1}^{s} w_i < \frac{1}{t} \cdot (s - n(0)) + \frac{2}{t} \cdot (n(0) - n(1))
$$
$$
+ \frac{2^2}{t} \cdot (n(1) - n(2)) + \frac{2^3}{t} \cdot (n(2) - n(3)) + \cdots
$$
$$
= \frac{1}{t} \left(s + n(0) + 2n(1) + 2^2 n(2) + 2^3 n(3) \cdots \right)
$$
$$
= \frac{s}{t} + (d_0\sigma) \left(\frac{1}{1} + \frac{2}{2^2} + \frac{2^2}{2^4} + \frac{2^3}{2^6} + \cdots \right)
$$
$$
= \frac{s}{t} + (d_0\sigma) \left(1 + \frac{1}{2} + \frac{1}{4} + \frac{1}{8} + \cdots \right),
$$

which is, from our assumption on s and the choice of d_0, less than σ. A contradiction. □

Lemma B. *Consider the following optimization problem.*

$$
Maximize \quad V(b,c) = \sqrt{b\left(\frac{1}{2} - c\right)} + \sqrt{\left(\frac{1}{2} - b\right)c}
$$

subject to

$$
\begin{cases}
b + c \leq \dfrac{1}{2} - \gamma, \\
c \leq \dfrac{1}{4} - \dfrac{\gamma}{2} - \delta, \\
b, c \geq 0,
\end{cases}
$$

for given γ and δ such that $\gamma > 0$ and $0 < \delta \leq (1/2 - \gamma)/2 = 1/4 - \gamma/2$. Then the maximum is obtained if $b + c = 1/2 - \gamma$ and $c = 1/4 - \gamma/2 - \delta$.

Proof. For any β, $0 < \beta \leq 1/2 - \gamma$, define $Z(\beta)$ by

$$
Z(\beta) = \max_{b,c} V(b,c) = \max_{b,c} \sqrt{b\left(\frac{1}{2} - c\right)} + \sqrt{\left(\frac{1}{2} - b\right)c},
$$

where $b, c \geq 0$ are chosen so that $b + c = \beta$, and $c \leq 1/4 - \gamma/2 - \delta$. We consider the following two cases.

(Case 1: $\beta \le 1/2 - \gamma - 2\delta$)

In this case, since $\beta/2 \le 1/4 - \gamma/2 - \delta$, it is possible to choose $b = c = \beta/2$, which maximize $V(b, c) = \sqrt{(1-\beta)\beta}$. Hence, $Z(\beta) = \sqrt{(1-\beta)\beta}$. Since this $Z(\beta)$ is monotone increasing, its maximum Z_1 is obtained with $\beta = 1/2 - \gamma - 2\delta$, and we have

$$Z_1 = \sqrt{\frac{1}{4} - (\gamma + 2\delta)^2}.$$

(Case 2: $\beta > 1/2 - \gamma - 2\delta$)

Since $V(\beta - c, c)$ is monotone increasing for $c \le 1/4 - \gamma/2 - \delta$, it is maximized when $c = 1/4 - \gamma/2 - \delta$; hence, we have

$$Z(\beta) = \sqrt{\left(\beta - \frac{1}{4} + \frac{\gamma}{2} + \delta\right)\left(\frac{1}{4} + \frac{\gamma}{2} + \delta\right)}$$
$$+ \sqrt{\left(\frac{3}{4} - \beta - \frac{\gamma}{2} - \delta\right)\left(\frac{1}{4} - \frac{\gamma}{2} - \delta\right)}.$$

Again this $Z(\beta)$ is monotone increasing, we have the maximum

$$Z_2 = \sqrt{\left(\frac{1}{4} + \delta\right)^2 - \frac{\gamma^2}{4}} + \sqrt{\left(\frac{1}{4} - \delta\right)^2 - \frac{\gamma^2}{4}},$$

when $\beta = 1/2 - \gamma$ (i.e., $b + c = 1/2 - \gamma$ and $c = 1/4 - \gamma/2 - \delta$).

Now we show that $Z_1 \le Z_2$ for any δ such that $0 < \delta < 1/4 - \gamma/2$. Let $g(x) = \sqrt{x}$ and $\Delta = 1/16 - (\delta + \gamma/2)^2$. Then we have

$$Z_2 - Z_1 = g(\Delta + p) + g(\Delta - q) - 2g(\Delta), \tag{4}$$

where we let $p = 2\delta^2 + \delta\gamma + \delta/2$, and $q = -2\delta^2 - \delta\gamma + \delta/2$. Note that $p, q > 0$ by the definition of δ and γ. Since the function $g(x)$ is concave and monotone increasing, it follows that $g(\Delta + p) \ge g(\Delta) + g'(\Delta + p)p$ and $g(\Delta - q) \ge g(\Delta) - g'(\Delta - q)q$. Therefore the quantity (4) is bounded from below by

$$g'(\Delta + p)p - g'(\Delta - q)q = \frac{2\delta^2 + \delta\gamma + \frac{\delta}{2}}{2\sqrt{\left(\frac{1}{4} + \delta\right)^2 - \frac{\gamma^2}{4}}} - \frac{-2\delta^2 - \delta\gamma + \frac{\delta}{2}}{2\sqrt{\left(\frac{1}{4} - \delta\right)^2 - \frac{\gamma^2}{4}}}$$

$$= \frac{\delta\left(2\delta + \gamma + \frac{1}{2}\right)\sqrt{\left(\frac{1}{4} - \delta\right)^2 - \frac{\gamma^2}{4}}}{2\sqrt{\left(\frac{1}{4} + \delta\right)^2 - \frac{\gamma^2}{4}}\sqrt{\left(\frac{1}{4} - \delta\right)^2 - \frac{\gamma^2}{4}}}$$

$$- \frac{\delta(-2\delta - \gamma + \frac{1}{2})\sqrt{\left(\frac{1}{4} + \delta\right)^2 - \frac{\gamma^2}{4}}}{2\sqrt{\left(\frac{1}{4} + \delta\right)^2 - \frac{\gamma^2}{4}}\sqrt{\left(\frac{1}{4} - \delta\right)^2 - \frac{\gamma^2}{4}}}.$$

In order to show that $Z_2 - Z_1 \geq 0$, it is sufficient to prove that

$$\left(2\delta + \gamma + \frac{1}{2}\right)^2 \left\{\left(\frac{1}{4} - \delta\right)^2 - \frac{\gamma^2}{4}\right\} - \left(-2\delta - \gamma + \frac{1}{2}\right)^2 \left\{\left(\frac{1}{4} + \delta\right)^2 - \frac{\gamma^2}{4}\right\}$$

is positive. Let us denote the quantity above as $\tilde{\Delta}$. Then we get

$$
\begin{aligned}
\tilde{\Delta} &= \left\{(2\delta + \gamma)^2 + (2\delta + \gamma) + \frac{1}{4}\right\} \left\{\left(\frac{1}{16} + \delta^2 - \frac{\gamma^2}{4}\right) - \frac{\delta}{2}\right\} \\
&\quad - \left\{(2\delta + \gamma)^2 - (2\delta + \gamma) + \frac{1}{4}\right\} \left\{\left(\frac{1}{16} + \delta^2 - \frac{\gamma^2}{4}\right) + \frac{\delta}{2}\right\} \\
&= 2(2\delta + \gamma)\left(\frac{1}{16} + \delta^2 - \frac{\gamma^2}{4}\right) - 2 \cdot \frac{\delta}{2}\left\{(2\delta + \gamma)^2 + \frac{1}{4}\right\} \\
&= \frac{\gamma}{8} - 2\delta^2\gamma - 2\delta\gamma^2 - \frac{\gamma^3}{2} \\
&= \frac{\gamma}{2}\left\{\left(\frac{1}{2}\right)^2 - (2\delta + \gamma)^2\right\} > 0,
\end{aligned}
$$

as desired.   □

Boosting Based on Divide and Merge

Eiji Takimoto, Syuhei Koya, and Akira Maruoka

Graduate School of Information Sciences
Tohoku University, Sendai 980-8579, Japan.
{t2,s_koya,maruoka}@ecei.tohoku.ac.jp

Abstract. InfoBoost is a boosting algorithm that improves the performance of the master hypothesis whenever each weak hypothesis brings non-zero mutual information about the target. We give a somewhat surprising observation that InfoBoost can be viewed as an algorithm for growing a branching program that divides and merges the domain repeatedly. We generalize the merging process and propose a new class of boosting algorithms called BP.InfoBoost with various merging schema. BP.InfoBoost assigns to each node a weight as well as a weak hypothesis and the master hypothesis is a threshold function of the sum of the weights over the path induced by a given instance. InfoBoost is a BP.InfoBoost with an extreme scheme that merges all nodes in each round. The other extreme that merges no nodes yields an algorithm for growing a decision tree. We call this particular version DT.InfoBoost. We give an evidence that DT.InfoBoost improves the master hypothesis very efficiently, but it has a risk of overfitting because the size of the master hypothesis may grow exponentially. We propose a merging scheme between these extremes that improves the master hypothesis nearly as fast as the one without merge while keeping the branching program in a moderate size.

1 Introduction

Since the stage-wise process of AdaBoost was explained in terms of a Newton-like method for minimizing an exponential cost function [2,5], designing and analyzing boosting algorithms by using results from the optimization theory has been a mainstream of this research area [9,3,4,11]. In the most common scheme of boosting, the booster iteratively makes probability weightings over the sample and receives weak hypotheses that slightly correlate with the sample with respect to the current weightings. The booster then produces a linear combination of the weak hypotheses as a master hypothesis with a good performance guarantee expressed in terms of the margin [6,12]. Here, the correlation between a weak hypothesis and the sample is defined as the expected margin, which intuitively mean how well the hypothesis classifies the sample.

As oppose to the margin based criterion, there is an information-theoretic approach where the correlation is defined by the mutual information, i.e., how much amount of information the hypotheses bring on the sample. In this scheme, the requirement for weak hypotheses can be relaxed to have non-zero mutual

S. Ben-David, J. Case, A. Maruoka (Eds.): ALT 2004, LNAI 3244, pp. 127–141, 2004.
© Springer-Verlag Berlin Heidelberg 2004

information, rather than non-zero margin, to obtain a good master hypothesis. The first theoretical result on information-based boosting is due to Kearns and Mansour [8] who give theoretical justification to empirically successful heuristics in top-down decision tree learning. The result is naturally generalized for learning multiclass classification problems [14] and is improved to avoid overfitting by merging some sets of nodes [10]. A modification of the latter algorithm is applied to the problem of boosting in the presence of noise [7]. These algorithms are quite different from AdaBoost-like algorithms in that they grow a decision tree or a branching program as a master hypothesis that is far from the form of linear combinations. Moreover, the probability weightings they make are not based on the principle of minimizing any cost function. Later we give an evidence that these algorithms are inefficient in the sense that they make the complexity of the master hypothesis unnecessarily large. Aslam proposed a promising method of information-based boosting called InfoBoost [1]. InfoBoost is interesting because the weight update is obtained by minimizing the same cost function as AdaBoost and the master hypothesis has an "quasi-linear" form (the coefficients are not constants but depend on the values of weak hypotheses).

In this paper, we generalize InfoBoost and propose a new class of information-based boosting algorithms. We first give a somewhat surprising observation that InfoBoost can be viewed as a process of growing a branching program that divides and merges the domain repeatedly. We show that the merging process used in InfoBoost can be replaced by *any* merging scheme with the boosting property preserved. So we have a class of boosting algorithms with various merging schema. We call any of them a BP.InfoBoost. BP.InfoBoost assigns to each node a weight as well as a weak hypothesis, and the master hypothesis is a threshold function of the sum of the weights over the path induced by a given instance. Note that this is different from the previous BP based boosting algorithms [10, 7] where the master hypothesis is just a branching program. InfoBoost is a BP.InfoBoost using an extreme scheme that merges all nodes in each round. The other extreme that merges no nodes yields an algorithm for growing a decision tree. We particularly call this version DT.InfoBoost. DT.InfoBoost has a *totally corrective* update property. (The notion of totally corrective updates was originally proposed for a better booster in the margin based criterion [9].) Specifically, a totally corrective update makes the weight D_{t+1} for the next round so that *all* weak hypotheses $h_1, \ldots, h_t$ obtained so far are uncorrelated with the sample with respect to D_{t+1}. This implies that any weak hypothesis h_{t+1} that correlates with the sample must contain novel information that $h_1, \ldots, h_t$ do not have. Note that AdaBoost and InfoBoost make D_{t+1} so that only h_t is uncorrelated. So we can expect that DT.InfoBoost improves the master hypothesis much faster than InfoBoost. On the other hand, since the size of the decision tree may grow exponentially in t, DT.InfoBoost has more risk of overfitting than InfoBoost[1].

---

[1] The decision tree produced by DT.InfoBoost uses the same weak hypothesis h_t as the decision rule at all nodes of depth $t - 1$. So we can expect that DT.InfoBoost

There must be an appropriate merging scheme between the two extremes that takes advantages of the two extremes. In this paper, we propose a merging scheme that reduces the training error of the master hypothesis nearly as fast as the one we would have without merge while keeping the master hypothesis (branching program) in a moderate size.

2   Preliminaries

Let X denote an instance space and $Y = \{-1, +1\}$ the set of labels. We fix a sample $S = \{(x_1, y_1), \ldots, (x_m, y_m)\} \subseteq X \times Y$ on which we discuss the performance of boosting algorithms. The procedure of boosting is described as in the following general protocol with two parties, the booster and the weak learner. On each round t, the booster makes a probability distribution D_t on the index set $\{1, \ldots, m\}$ of the sample S and gives S with D_t to the weak learner; The weak learner returns a weak hypothesis $h_t : X \to Y$ to the booster (denoted $h_t = \mathrm{WL}(S, D_t)$); The booster updates the distribution to D_{t+1}. Repeating the above procedure for T rounds for some T, the booster combines the weak hypotheses $h_1, \ldots, h_T$ obtained so far and makes a master hypothesis.

In this paper we measure the performance of a weak hypothesis h_t in terms of the information that h_t brings. For the entropy function, we use $G(p) = 2\sqrt{p(1-p)}$ defined for $p \in [0, 1]$ so that we can interpret the progress of boosting as the product of conditional entropies. This function is used to describe the performance of various boosting algorithms [1,8,10,14]. Note that since the function G upper bounds Shannon entropy, small entropy in terms of G implies small Shannon entropy. For a probability distribution D over $\{1, \ldots, m\}$, we sometimes consider X and Y as random variables that take values x_i and y_i (resp.) with probability $D(i)$. Especially we call Y the target random variable. Let the probability that the target Y takes value 1 under D be denoted by

$$p = \Pr_D(y_i = 1) = \sum_{i=1}^{m} D(i)[\![y_i = 1]\!],$$

where $[\![C]\!]$ is the indicator function that is 1 if the condition C holds and 0 otherwise. Then $the\ entropy\ of\ the\ target\ Y\ with\ respect\ to\ D$ is defined as

$$H_D(Y) = G(p) = 2\sqrt{p(1-p)}.$$

Furthermore, for any function $g : X \to Z$ for some countable set Z, $the\ conditional\ entropy\ of\ Y\ given\ g\ with\ respect\ to\ D$ is defined as

$$H_D(Y|g) = \sum_{z \in Z} \Pr_D(g(x_i) = z)H_D(Y|g(x_i) = z) = \sum_{z \in Z} \Pr_D(g(x_i) = z)G(p_z)$$

where $p_z = \Pr_D(y_i = 1 \mid g(x_i) = z)$. The entropies $H_D(Y)$ and $H_D(Y|g)$ are interpreted as uncertainty of the target before and after seeing the value

---

has less risk of overfitting than the classical top-down algorithms that produce trees with exponentially many different decision rules.

of g, respectively. So the mutual information $H_D(Y) - H_D(Y|g)$ represents the amount of information that g brings. In particular, since the distribution D_t we consider in this paper always satisfies $H_{D_t}(Y) = 1$, we measure the performance of the weak hypothesis h_t by the conditional entropy $H_{D_t}(Y|h_t)$. The inequality $H_{D_t}(Y|h_t) < 1$ implies that the weak hypothesis h_t brings non-zero information about the target.

Here we give some basic properties of the entropies. Let D be a distribution over $\{1, \ldots, m\}$ and g' be another function defined on X. Then, we have

$$H_D(Y|g) = 2 \sum_{z \in Z} \sqrt{\Pr_D(g(x_i) = z, y_i = 1)\Pr_D(g(x_i) = z, y_i = -1)}, \quad (1)$$

$$H_D(Y|g, g') \leq H_D(Y|g). \quad (2)$$

3   InfoBoost Growing a Branching Program

In this section, we show that InfoBoost can be viewed as a top-down algorithm for growing a branching program.

First we briefly review how InfoBoost works. In each round t, when given a weak hypothesis h_t, InfoBoost updates the distribution to

$$D_{t+1}(i) = \frac{D_t(i) \exp\left(-\alpha_t[h_t(x_i)]h_t(x_i)y_i\right)}{Z_t}$$

for appropriately chosen real numbers $\alpha_t[-1]$ and $\alpha[1]$, where Z_t is for normalization. The two parameters $\alpha_t[-1]$ and $\alpha_t[1]$ are chosen so that the normalization factor Z_t is minimized. Interestingly, for these choices of parameters we have $Z_t = H_{D_t}(Y|h_t)$. The master hypothesis that InfoBoost produces is given by $\text{sign}(F_T(x))$, where

$$F_T(x) = \sum_{t=1}^{T} \alpha_t[h_t(x)]h_t(x). \quad (3)$$

The detail of the algorithm is given in Fig. 3. The performance of InfoBoost is summarized as in the following inequality [1]:

$$\Pr_U\left(\text{sign}(F_T(x_i)) \neq y_i\right) \leq \prod_{t=1}^{T} H_{D_t}(Y|h_t), \quad (4)$$

where U is the uniform distribution over $\{1, \ldots, m\}$. This implies that the training error of the master hypothesis decreases rapidly as T becomes large, as long as the weak hypotheses h_t bring non-zero information with respect to D_t, i.e., $H_{D_t}(Y|h_t) < 1$. In particular, if all hypotheses h_t satisfy $H_{D_t}(Y|h_t) \leq 1 - \gamma$ for some $\gamma > 0$, then $\Pr_U\left(\text{sign}(F_T(x_i)) \neq y_i\right) \leq \epsilon$ with $T = (1/\gamma)\ln(1/\epsilon)$.

Now we interpret InfoBoost as a process of growing a branching program. At the beginning of round t (except $t = 1$), we have the set L_{t-1} of two leaves. When given h_t, each leaf $l \in L_{t-1}$ becomes an internal node with two child leaves

Input: $S = \{(x_1, y_1), \ldots, (x_m, y_m)\}$

Initialize $D_1(i) = 1/m$;

for $t = 1$ to T do

$\quad h_t = \mathrm{WL}(S, D_t)$;

$\quad$ Choose real numbers $\alpha_t[-1]$ and $\alpha_t[1]$ so that for any $a \in \{-1, 1\}$,

$$\alpha_t[a] = \frac{a}{2} \ln \frac{\mathrm{Pr}_D(h_t(x_i) = a, y_i = 1)}{\mathrm{Pr}_D(h_t(x_i) = a, y_i = -1)}$$

$\quad$ Update D_t to D_{t+1} so that

$$D_{t+1}(i) = D_t(i) \exp\bigl(-\alpha_t[h_t(x_i)]h_t(x_i)y_i\bigr)/Z_t$$

$\quad$ holds for $1 \le i \le m$, where Z_t is for normalization;

Let $F_T : x \mapsto \sum_{t=1}^{T} \alpha_t[h_t(x)]h_t(x)$;

Output $\mathrm{sign}(F_T(x))$

Fig. 1. The algorithm of InfoBoost.

l_{-1} and l_1, just as in a decision tree growing algorithm. Note that the same hypothesis h_t is used for the decision done at any $l \in L_{t-1}$ and the outcomes -1 and 1 correspond to the edges (l, l_{-1}) and (l, l_1), respectively. Here we have four leaves. Then for each $a \in \{-1, 1\}$, the set $\{l_a \mid l \in L_{t-1}\}$ of two leaves are merged into a single leaf and it is labeled with weight $a \cdot \alpha_t[a]$. The new leaves corresponding to $a = -1$ and $a = 1$ are called a (-1)-node and a 1-node, respectively. Thus, in the end of round t, we have the set L_t of two leaves again. So each round consists of two phases, dividing and merging the subset of the instance space. See Fig. 2.

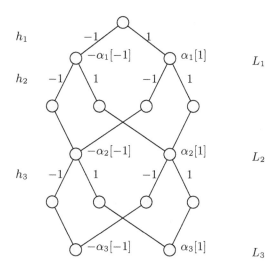

Fig. 2. A branching program that InfoBoost grows.

By virtue of the branching program representation, we give natural interpretations of how the distribution D_{t+1} and the combined hypothesis F_T are determined. An instance $x \in X$ induces a path of the branching program based on the outcome sequence $h_1(x), \ldots, h_T(x)$ in the obvious way. Let $\ell_t : X \to L_t$ denote the function that maps an instance x to the node in L_t on the path that x induces. Note that for the branching program generated by InfoBoost, $\ell_t(x)$ depends only on $h_t(x)$ and so $H_D(Y|\ell_t) = H_D(Y|h_t)$ for any D. Intuitively, the distribution D_{t+1} is determined so that ℓ_t (and thus h_t) is uncorrelated with Y and the total weight of leaf $l \in L_t$ is proportional to the uncertainty of Y at the leaf l. More precisely, (as we will see later for a general branching program), the distribution D_{t+1} satisfies that

$$H_{D_{t+1}}(Y|\ell_t) = H_{D_{t+1}}(Y|h_t) = 1. \tag{5}$$

and for any $l \in L_t$,

$$\Pr_{D_{t+1}}\big(\ell_t(x_i) = l\big) = \frac{\Pr_{D_t}\big(\ell_t(x_i) = l\big) H_{D_t}\big(Y|\ell_t(x_i) = l\big)}{H_{D_t}\big(Y|\ell_t\big)}. \tag{6}$$

The property of (5) is essential because otherwise the next hypothesis h_{t+1} would be the same as h_t for which $H_{D_{t+1}}(Y|h_{t+1}) < 1$ but no additional information is obtained. The property of (6) is reasonable since this means that the leaf with larger entropy will be more focused with the hope that the next hypothesis h_{t+1} would reduce the whole entropy efficiently.

The combined hypothesis F_T given by (3) is also represented in terms of the branching program. For each node $l \in L_t$, let $w[l]$ denote the weight labeled at l. That is, $w[l] = -\alpha_t[-1]$ if l is a (-1)-node and $w[l] = \alpha_t[1]$ if l is a 1-node. It is easy to see that for a given instance x, $F_T(x)$ is represented as the sum of the weights of the nodes on the path induced by x. That is,

$$F_T(x) = \sum_{t=1}^{T} w[\ell_t(x)]. \tag{7}$$

4   BP.InfoBoost

In this section, we generalize the merging scheme used by InfoBoost and propose a class of boosting algorithms called BP.InfoBoost with various merging schema. Curiously, we show that the bound (4) on the training error remains to hold for BP.InfoBoost with *any* merging scheme.

First we describe how BP.InfoBoost works. For convenience, we represent the set of leaves L_t as a partition of $\{-1, 1\}^t$. That is, a leaf $l \in L_t$ is a subset of $\{-1, 1\}^t$. For a given partition L_t, the function $\ell_t : X \to L_t$ is defined as

$$\ell_t(x) = l \Leftrightarrow (h_1(x), \ldots, h_t(x)) \in l.$$

At the beginning of round t, we have the set L_{t-1} of leaves. Now L_{t-1} may contain more than two leaves. When given h_t, each leaf $l \in L_{t-1}$ becomes an internal node with two child leaves l_{-1} and l_1. Formally, the leaf l_a with $a \in \{-1, 1\}$ is a subset of $\{-1, 1\}^t$ and given by $l_a = \{(v, a) \mid v \in l\}$. So, an instance x that reaches a leaf $l \in L_{t-1}$ (i.e., $\ell_{t-1}(x) = l$) goes to l_a if $h_t(x) = a$. Here we have twice as many leaves as in L_{t-1}. Then for any $a \in \{-1, 1\}$ the set $\{l_a \mid l \in L_{t-1}\}$ is partitioned *somehow* into $L'_{a,1}, \ldots, L'_{a,k_a}$ for some k_a and the leaves in each $L'_{a,i}$ are merged into a single leaf, which is formally given by $\bigcup_{l_a \in L'_{a,i}} l_a$. Thus we have the set L_t of leaves of size $k_{-1} + k_1$. Fig. 3 illustrates how the branching program grows. A merging scheme is a procedure of deciding how the sets $\{l_a \mid l \in L_{t-1}\}$ are partitioned. For example, InfoBoost is a BP.InfoBoost with a particular merging scheme that lets each set $\{l_a \mid l \in L_{t-1}\}$ be a partition of itself.

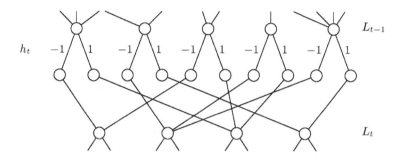

Fig. 3. A branching program that a BP.InfoBoost grows. Note that any leaf in L_t is determined by a leaf in L_{t-1} and the outcome of h_t.

Each leaf $l \in L_t$ is labeled with the weight given by

$$w[l] = \frac{1}{2} \ln \frac{\Pr_{D_t} (\ell_t(x_i) = l, y_i = 1)}{\Pr_{D_t} (\ell_t(x_i) = l, y_i = -1)}. \tag{8}$$

With the notations w and ℓ_t, we can write the update rule and the master hypothesis as in the same way as for the case of InfoBoost. That is, the distribution is updated to

$$D_{t+1}(i) = \frac{D_t(i) \exp(-w[\ell_t(x_i)]y_i)}{Z_t} \tag{9}$$

where Z_t is for normalization, and the master hypothesis is $\mathrm{sign}(F_T(x))$, where F_T is given by (7). The details of the algorithm is given in Fig. 4. Note that ℓ_t can be viewed as a domain-partitioning weak hypothesis and the weights $w[l]$ derived in (8) are identical to the confidences assigned by Schapire and Singer [13].

Now we show that a BP.InfoBoost with any merging scheme has the same form of upper bound on the training error. We need some technical lemmas. The first one is immediately obtained by recursively applying the update rule (9).

Input: $S = \{(x_1, y_1), \ldots, (x_m, y_m)\}$
Initialize $D_1(i) = 1/m$, $L_0 = \{\epsilon\}$, $\ell_0 : x \mapsto \epsilon$;
for $t = 1$ to T do
    $h_t = \mathrm{WL}(S, D_t)$;
    Let $l_a = \{(v, a) \mid v \in l\}$ for $l \in L_{t-1}$ and $a \in \{-1, 1\}$;
    for $a \in \{-1, 1\}$ do
        Partition $\{l_a \mid l \in L_{t-1}\}$ into $L'_{a,1}, \ldots, L'_{a,k_a}$;
    $L_t = \left\{ \bigcup_{l_a \in L'_{a,i}} l_a \mid 1 \leq i \leq k_a, a \in \{-1, 1\} \right\}$;
    Let $\ell_t : x \mapsto l \in L_t$ where $(h_1(x), \ldots, h_t(x)) \in l$;
    for $l \in L_t$ do
        Let $w[l] = \dfrac{1}{2} \ln \dfrac{\mathrm{Pr}_{D_t}\left(\ell_t(x_i) = l, y_i = 1\right)}{\mathrm{Pr}_{D_t}\left(\ell_t(x_i) = l, y_i = -1\right)}$;
    Update D_t to
        $D_{t+1}(i) = D_t(i) \exp\left(-w[\ell_t(x_i)]y_i\right)/Z_t$
    for $1 \leq i \leq m$, where Z_t is for normalization;
Let $F_T : x \mapsto \sum_{t=1}^{T} w[\ell_t(x)]$;
Output $\mathrm{sign}(F_T(x))$

Fig. 4. The algorithm of a BP.InfoBoost.

Lemma 1. *Let Z_t be the normalization factor in (9) and D_{T+1} be the distribution obtained in the final round. Then,*

$$D_{T+1}(i) = \frac{D_1(i)}{Z_1 \cdots Z_T} \exp\left(-\sum_{t=1}^{T} w[\ell_t(x_i)]y_i\right) = \frac{D_1(i)}{Z_1 \cdots Z_T} \exp\left(-F_T(x_i)y_i\right).$$

The next lemma shows that the normalization factor Z_t can be rewritten as the conditional entropy.

Lemma 2. $Z_t = H_{D_t}(Y \mid \ell_t) \leq H_{D_t}(Y \mid h_t)$.

Proof. First we show the equality part. By (8) we have

$$Z_t = \sum_{i=1}^{m} D_t(i) \exp\left(-w[\ell_t(x_i)]y_i\right)$$

$$= \sum_{l \in L_t} \sum_{a \in \{-1,1\}} \sum_{i=1}^{m} D_t(i) [\![\ell_t(x_i) = l, y_i = a]\!] \exp(-w[l]a)$$

$$= \sum_{l \in L_t} \sum_{a \in \{-1,1\}} \mathrm{Pr}_{D_t}\left(\ell_t(x_i) = l, y_i = a\right) \left(\frac{\mathrm{Pr}_{D_t}\left(\ell_t(x_i) = l, y_i \neq a\right)}{\mathrm{Pr}_{D_t}\left(\ell_t(x_i) = l, y_i = a\right)}\right)^{1/2}$$

$$= 2 \sum_{l \in L_t} \sqrt{\mathrm{Pr}_{D_t}\left(\ell_t(x_i) = l, y_i = 1\right) \mathrm{Pr}_{D_t}\left(\ell_t(x_i) = l, y_i = -1\right)}$$

$$= H_{D_t}(Y \mid \ell_t).$$

The last line is derived from (1).

For the inequality part, since the last component of any vector in the set $\ell_t(x)$ is $h_t(x)$, we have $H_{D_t}(Y|\ell_t) = H_{D_t}(Y|\ell_t, h_t)$, which is at most $H_{D_t}(Y|h_t)$ by (2). $\qquad\square$

Now we are ready to give an upper bound on the training error.

Theorem 1. *Let F_T be the combined hypothesis of a BP.InfoBoost. Then*

$$\mathrm{Pr}_U\left(\mathrm{sign}(F_T(x_i)) \neq y_i\right) \leq \prod_{t=1}^{T} H_{D_t}(Y|\ell_t) \leq \prod_{t=1}^{T} H_{D_t}(Y|h_t).$$

Proof. By Lemma 2, it suffices to show that $\mathrm{Pr}_U\left(\mathrm{sign}(F_T(x_i)) \neq y_i\right) \leq \prod_{t=1}^{T} Z_t$. Since the initial distribution D_1 is uniform, we have

$$\mathrm{Pr}_U\left(\mathrm{sign}(F_T(x_i)) \neq y_i\right) = \sum_{i=1}^{m} D_1(i)[\![\mathrm{sign}(F_T(x_i)) \neq y_i]\!].$$

Using $[\![\mathrm{sign}(F_T(x_i)) \neq y_i]\!] \leq \exp\left(-F_T(x_i)y_i\right)$ and Lemma 1, we have

$$\mathrm{Pr}_U\left(\mathrm{sign}(F_T(x_i)) \neq y_i\right) \leq \sum_{i=1}^{m} D_1(i)\exp\left(-F_T(x_i)y_i\right)$$

$$= Z_1 \cdots Z_T \sum_{i=1}^{m} D_{T+1}(i)$$

$$= Z_1 \cdots Z_T.$$

$\qquad\square$

Theorem 1 means that the upper bound on the training error for a BP.InfoBoost is not larger than that for InfoBoost provided that the same distributions D_t and weak hypotheses h_t are used. Moreover, when there is a large gap between $H_{D_t}(Y|\ell_t)$ and $H_{D_t}(Y|h_t)$, then the BP.InfoBoost would improve the master hypothesis faster than InfoBoost.

Next we consider any possible construction of the master hypothesis. Since any master hypothesis $f : X \rightarrow \{-1, 1\}$ should be constructed from the weak hypotheses $h_1, \ldots, h_T$, it must hold that $H_U(Y|h_1, \ldots, h_T) \leq H_U(Y|f)$ and so the l.h.s. gives an information-theoretic limitation of the performance of f. The next theorem shows how much the entropy $H_U(Y|h_1, \ldots, h_T)$ is reduced as T grows. For an instance x, $\ell_{1..T}(x)$ is short for the path $(\ell_1(x), \ldots, \ell_T(x)) \in L_{1..T} \equiv L_1 \times \cdots \times L_T$.

Theorem 2.

$$H_U(Y|h_1, \ldots, h_T) = H_U(Y|\ell_{1..T}) = \left(\prod_{t=1}^{T} H_{D_t}(Y|\ell_t)\right) H_{D_{T+1}}(Y|\ell_{1..T}).$$

Proof. The first equality holds since there is one-to-one correspondence between the set of paths $\ell_{1..T}(x)$ of the branching program and the set of outcome sequences $(h_1(x), \ldots, h_T(x))$.

By (1) we have

$$
\begin{aligned}
&H_{D_{T+1}}(Y|\ell_{1..T}) \\
&= 2 \sum_{l \in L_{1..T}} \sqrt{\Pr_{D_{T+1}}(\ell_{1..T}(x_i) = l, y_i = 1) \Pr_{D_{T+1}}(\ell_{1..T}(x_i) = l, y_i = -1)}.
\end{aligned}
$$

Lemma 1 says that the distribution $D_{T+1}(i)$ depends on the path $\ell_{1..T}(x_i)$ on which an instance x_i goes through. So for a particular path $l = (l_1, \ldots, l_T) \in L_{1..T}$ and for any $a \in \{-1, 1\}$, we have

$$
\begin{aligned}
\Pr_{D_{T+1}}(\ell_{1..T}(x_i) = l, y_i = a) &= \sum_i D_{T+1}(i)[\![\ell_{1..T}(x_i) = l, y_i = a]\!] \\
&= \frac{\exp\left(-a \sum_{t=1}^{T} w[l_t]\right)}{Z_1 \cdots Z_T} \sum_i D_1(i)[\![\ell_{1..T}(x_i) = l, y_i = a]\!] \\
&= \frac{\exp\left(-a \sum_{t=1}^{T} w[l_t]\right)}{Z_1 \cdots Z_T} \Pr_U(\ell_{1..T}(x_i) = l, y_i = a).
\end{aligned}
$$

By multiplying the above probabilities with $a = 1$ and $a = -1$ the exponential terms are canceled and we get

$$
H_{D_{T+1}}(Y|\ell_{1..T}) = \frac{H_U(Y|\ell_{1..t})}{Z_1 \cdots Z_T},
$$

which completes the theorem. □

Theorem 1 and Theorem 2 imply that our master hypothesis $\operatorname{sign}(F(x))$ would be nearly optimal if $H_{D_{T+1}}(Y|\ell_{1..T})$ is not too small. Although we do not know a lower bound on $H_{D_{T+1}}(Y|\ell_{1..T})$ in general, the distribution satisfies $H_{D_{T+1}}(Y|\ell_T) = 1$ as shown in (5) for the case of InfoBoost. That is, BP.InfoBoost updates the distribution so that ℓ_T is uncorrelated with Y. The next lemma shows that a BP.InfoBoost makes D_{t+1} so that ℓ_t is uncorrelated with the sample. This implies that the weak hypothesis h_{t+1} (and ℓ_{t+1} as well) with non-zero correlation must have some information that the function ℓ_t does not have. This gives an intuitive justification why the improvement of the master hypothesis for a BP.InfoBoost is upper bounded by the product of $H_{D_t}(Y|\ell_t)$.

Lemma 3. *For any $1 \le t \le T$, a BP.InfoBoost updates the distribution to D_{t+1} so that $H_{D_{t+1}}(Y|\ell_t) = 1$ holds.*

Proof. It suffices to show that for any leaf $l \in L_t$, $\Pr_{D_{t+1}}(y_i = 1 \mid \ell_t(x_i) = l) = 1/2$, or equivalently

$$
\Pr_{D_{t+1}}(\ell_t(x_i) = l, y_i = 1) = \Pr_{D_{t+1}}(\ell_t(x_i) = l, y_i = -1). \tag{10}
$$

By (9) and (8), it is straightforward to see that the both sides of (10) are equal to

$$\frac{\sqrt{\mathrm{Pr}_{D_t}\left(\ell_t(x_i) = l, y_i = 1\right)\mathrm{Pr}_{D_t}\left(\ell_t(x_i) = l, y_i = -1\right)}}{Z_t}$$

□

Note that [7] also suggests to make D_{t+1} be uncorrelated with ℓ_t but in a trivial way: D_{t+1} is restricted to a single leaf l and set so that $\mathrm{Pr}_{D_{t+1}}(y_i = 1 \mid l) = 1/2$. This means that the weak leaner must be invoked for all leaves in L_t with different distributions. On the other hand, our distribution (9) assigns positive weights to all nodes l unless $H_{D_t}(Y \mid \ell_t(x_i) = l) = 0$, and the weak leaner is invoked only once for each depth t.

5 DT.InfoBoost

As we stated, InfoBoost is a BP.InfoBoost with a particular merging scheme that merges all nodes l_1 into one leaf and all nodes l_{-1} into the other leaf. Since $H_{D_t}(Y|\ell_t) = H_{D_t}(Y|h_t)$, InfoBoost takes no advantage of the branching program representation.

Next we consider the BP.InfoBoost with no merging phase, i.e., DT.InfoBoost. In this case, since a path of the decision tree is uniquely determined by the leaf of the path, we have $H_{D_t}(Y|\ell_t) = H_{D_t}(Y|h_1, \ldots, h_t)$. Since $H_{D_t}(Y|h_1, \ldots, h_t)$ is likely to be much smaller than $H_{D_t}(Y|h_t)$, DT.InfoBoost would improve the master hypothesis more efficiently than InfoBoost. Lemma 3 implies

$$H_{D_t1}(Y|h_1, \ldots, h_t) = H_{D_{t+1}}(Y|\ell_t) = 1.$$

So, DT.InfoBoost has a totally corrective update. This means that all the hypotheses $h_1, \ldots, h_t$ obtained so far are uncórrelated with Y. So the next hypothesis h_{t+1} will bring truly new information that $h_1, \ldots, h_t$ do not have, provided $H_{D_{t+1}}(Y|h_{t+1}) < 1$. This contrasts with the case of InfoBoost, where h_{t+1} is only guaranteed to bring information that h_t does not have. Moreover, with the fact that $H_{D_{T+1}}(Y|\ell_T) = 1$, Theorem 1 and Theorem 2 gives the performance of DT.InfoBoost nicely as

$$\mathrm{Pr}_U\left(\mathrm{sign}(F_T(x_i)) \neq y_i\right) \leq H_U(Y|h_1, \ldots, h_T) = \prod_{t=1}^{T} H_{D_t}(Y|h_t).$$

This implies that DT.InfoBoost extracts information very effectively from the weak learner. Actually, we observe in experiments that DT.InfoBoost reduces the generalization error as well as the training error very rapidly in early rounds. Unfortunately, however, the generalization error sometimes turns to be increasing in later rounds. This is because the complexity of the master hypothesis grows exponentially in the number of rounds.

Generally, there is a tradeoff between the size of L_t and $H_{D_t}(Y|\ell_t)$. More precisely, the larger the size of L_t is (i.e, the less nodes we merge), the smaller

$H_{D_t}(Y|\ell_t)$ becomes (i.e., the more rapidly the training error decreases). In the next section, we propose a merging scheme that makes $H_{D_t}(Y|\ell_t)$ nearly as small as the one we would have without merge, while keeping L_t in a moderate size.

6   A Merging Scheme

Assume we are given a weak hypothesis h_t in the tth round and each node $l \in L_{t-1}$ grows two child leaves l_1 and l_{-1}. Now we have twice as many leaves as L_{t-1}. Let the set of leaves be denoted by

$$\tilde{L}_t = \{l_1 \mid l \in L_{t-1}\} \cup \{l_{-1} \mid l \in L_{t-1}\}$$

and let $\tilde{\ell}_t : X \to \tilde{L}_t$ be defined analogously, that is, $\tilde{\ell}_t(x)$ is the leaf in $\tilde{L}_t$ that instance x reaches. If we merge no nodes in $\tilde{L}_t$, then we would have $L_t = \tilde{L}_t$ and $\tilde{\ell}_t = \ell_t$. So, $H_{D_t}(Y|\tilde{\ell}_t)$ gives a lower bound on $H_{D_t}(Y|\ell_t)$ for ℓ_t induced by any merging for $\tilde{L}_t$. Let $H_{D_t}(Y|\tilde{\ell}_t) = 1 - \gamma_t$. The merging scheme we give guarantees that $H_{D_t}(Y|\ell_t) \leq 1 - c\gamma_t$ for some constant $0 < c < 1$. For this purpose, we could use the merging method developed by Mansour and McAllester [10].

Lemma 4 ([10]). *For any function $f : X \to Z$, any distribution D over $X \times Y$, and for any $0 < \lambda, \delta < 1$, there exists a function $g : Z \to M$ such that*

$$H_D(Y|g \circ f) \leq (1 + \lambda)H_D(Y|f) + \delta \quad and \quad |M| = O((1/\lambda)\log(1/\delta)).$$

Clearly, letting $\tilde{\ell}_t$, $\tilde{L}_t$ and L_t correspond to f, Z and M, respectively, we have a merging scheme induced by g so that $g \circ f = \ell_t$. So by choosing $\lambda = (1 - c)\gamma_t/2(1 - \gamma_t)$ and $\delta = (1 - c)\gamma_t/2$, we have $H_{D_t}(Y|\ell_t) \leq 1 - c\gamma_t$. Unfortunately, however, the size of L_t is too big, i.e., $|L_t| = O((1/\gamma_t)\ln(1/\gamma_t))$. In the following, we give a new merging method that guarantees the same bound on $H_{D_t}(Y|\ell_t)$ with significantly small L_t, i.e., $|L_t| = O(\ln(1/\gamma_t))$.

Theorem 3. *Let $f : X \to Z$ with $H_D(Y|f) = 1 - \gamma$ for some $0 < \gamma < 1$. Then, for any $0 < c < 1$, there exists a function $g : Z \to M$ such that*

$$H_D(Y|g \circ f) \leq 1 - c\gamma \quad and \quad |M| = O\left(\frac{\log(1/((1-c)\gamma))}{\log(1 + 1/c)}\right).$$

Proof. For each $z \in Z$, let

$$p_z = \Pr_D(f(x_i) = z) \quad and \quad q_z = \Pr_D(y_i = 1 \mid f(x_i) = z).$$

Note that

$$H_D(Y|f) = \sum_{z \in Z} p_z G(q_z) = 1 - \gamma, \tag{11}$$

where $G(q) = 2\sqrt{q(1 - q)}$ is our entropy function. Let $a = 2c/(1 - c)$, $\epsilon_0 = 0$ and for each $j \geq 1$, let

$$\epsilon_j = \left(\frac{1 + a}{a}\right)^{j-1} \frac{c\gamma}{a}.$$

Let k be the smallest integer such that $\epsilon_k \geq 1$. Now we define the function g. For each $1 \leq j \leq k$, let

$$S_{-j} = \{z \in Z \mid p_z < 1/2, \epsilon_{j-1} \leq 1 - G(q_z) < \epsilon_j\}$$

and

$$S_j = \{z \in Z \mid p_z \geq 1/2, \epsilon_{j-1} \leq 1 - G(q_z) < \epsilon_j\}.$$

That is, Z is partitioned into $S_{-k} \cup \cdots \cup S_k$. Let $M = \{j, -j \mid 1 \leq j \leq k\}$ and for any $z \in Z$, let $g(z) = j$ such that $z \in S_j$. It is easy to see that $|M| = O\left(\frac{\log(1/((1-c)\gamma))}{\log(1+1/c)}\right)$. So it suffices to show that $H_D(Y|g \circ f) \leq 1 - c\gamma$.

For each j, let

$$p(S_j) = \sum_{z \in S_j} p_z \quad \text{and} \quad \mu_j = \sum_{z \in S_j} \tilde{p}_z q_z,$$

where $\tilde{p}_z = p_z/p(S_j)$ with $z \in S_j$. Then,

$$H_D(Y|g \circ f) = \sum_{j \in M} p(S_j) G(\mu_j).$$

Since $G(\mu_j) \leq 1 - \epsilon_{j-1}$, we have

$$\sum_{j \in M} p(S_j) G(\mu_j) \leq 1 - \sum_{j \in M} p(S_j) \epsilon_{j-1}.$$

If $\sum_{j \in M} p(S_j) \epsilon_{j-1} \geq c\gamma$, then we are done. So in what follows, we assume

$$\sum_{j \in M} p(S_j) \epsilon_{j-1} < c\gamma. \tag{12}$$

Since both $G(\mu_j)$ and $\sum_{z \in S_j} \tilde{p}_z G(q_z)$ are in the range $(1 - \epsilon_j, 1 - \epsilon_{j-1}]$, we have

$$G(\mu_j) \leq \sum_{z \in S_j} \tilde{p}_z G(q_z) + \epsilon_j - \epsilon_{j-1}$$

and this with (11) gives

$$H_D(Y|g \circ f) \leq 1 - \gamma + \sum_{j \in M} p(S_j)(\epsilon_j - \epsilon_{j-1}). \tag{13}$$

By our choices of ϵ_j,

$$\epsilon_{j-1} = a(\epsilon_j - \epsilon_{j-1})$$

holds for $j \geq 2$. Plugging this into (13) and using (12), we get

$$H_D(Y|g \circ f) \leq 1 - \gamma + \frac{c\gamma}{a} + \epsilon_1(p(S_{-1}) + p(S_1)) \leq 1 - c\gamma.$$

$\square$

Again, letting $\tilde{\ell}_t$ and ℓ_t correspond to f and $g \circ f$, respectively, we have a merging scheme as desired. Intuitively, the parameter c controls the tradeoff between $H_{D_t}(Y|\ell_t)$ and $|L_t|$. That is, if we let c close to 1, then $H_{D_t}(Y|\ell_t)$ is as small as $H_{D_t}(Y|\tilde{\ell}_t)$ while $|L_t|$ is unbounded. This implies that the BP.InfoBoost behaves like DT.InfoBoost. On the other hand, if we let c close to 0, then $H_{D_t}(Y|\ell_t)$ is unbounded (naturally bounded by $H_{D_t}(Y|h_t)$) while $|L_t|$ is as small as a constant. Thus, the BP.InfoBoost behaves like InfoBoost. So, we can expect that BP.InfoBoost with appropriate choice of parameter c outperforms both InfoBoost and DT.InfoBoost.

Finally, we remark that we develop the merging method in a different philosophy from the one of Mansour and McAllester [10] in the following two points.

- Our merging scheme is based on the current distribution D_t while that of [10] is based on the uniform distribution over the sample.
- Our merging scheme aims to make the function ℓ_t perform not much worse than $\tilde{\ell}_t$ as a *weak* hypothesis. On the other hand, [10] aims to make ℓ_t perform getting better as a *master* hypothesis, so that $H_U(Y|\ell_t)$ converges to 0. So their method needs much more leaves and the complexity of the branching program becomes unnecessarily large.

7   Remarks and Future Works

1. Our analysis suggests that the weak learner should produce h_t so that $H_{D_t}(Y|\ell_t)$, rather than $H_{D_t}(Y|h_t)$, is as small as possible.
2. Our algorithm uses the same cost function $\sum_i e^{-F_T(x_i)y_i}$ as AdaBoost and InfoBoost. This seems to nicely mesh with our entropy function $G(q) = 2\sqrt{q(1-q)}$. What is the relation between the choices of cost functions and corresponding entropy functions?
3. The combined hypothesis $F_T(x) = \sum_{t=1}^T w[\ell_t(x)]$ can be rewritten as the dot product $F_T(x) = W \cdot H(x)$ where W and $H(x)$ are vectors indexed by paths $\sigma \in L_1 \times \cdots \times L_T$ and its $\sigma = (\sigma_1, \ldots, \sigma_T)$th components are $W_\sigma = \sum_{t=1}^T w[\sigma_t]$ and $H_\sigma(x) = \prod_{t=1}^T [\![\ell_t(x) = \sigma_t]\!]$, respectively. This defines feature maps from the node space to the path space. Can we analyze BP.InfoBoost in terms of the path space?
4. We need to give a criterion of choosing the tradeoff parameter c (that may depend on round t).
5. We need to analyze the complexity of the master hypothesis, say, in terms of VC dimension.
6. We are evaluating the performance of BP.InfoBoost on data sets from the UCI Machine Learning Repository. Preliminary experiments show that the BP.InfoBoost with the merging scheme developed in Section 6 performs well as compared to InfoBoost and DT.InfoBoost.

Acknowledgments. The authors are grateful to Tatsuya Watanabe for showing a preliminary version of merging method for Theorem 3.

References

[1] J. A. Aslam. Improving algorithms for boosting. In *Proc. 13th Annu. Conference on Comput. Learning Theory*, pages 200–207. Morgan Kaufmann, San Francisco, 2000.

[2] L. Breiman. Prediction games and arcing algorithms. *Neural Computation*, 11(7):1493–1518, 1999.

[3] C. Domingo and O. Watanabe. MadaBoost: A modification of AdaBoost. In *Proc. 13th Annu. Conference on Comput. Learning Theory*, pages 180–189. Morgan Kaufmann, San Francisco, 2000.

[4] N. Duffy and D. Helmbold. A geometric approach to leveraging weak learners. *Theoret. Comput. Sci.*, 284(1):67–108, 2002.

[5] J. Friedman, T. Hastie, and R. Tibshirani. Additive logistic regression: a statistical view of boosting. *Annals of Statistics*, 2:337–374, 2000.

[6] A. J. Grove and D. Schuurmans. Boosting in the limit: Maximizing the margin of learned ensembles. In *15th AAAI*, pages 692–699, 1998.

[7] A. Kalai and R. A. Servedio. Boosting in the presence of noise. In *Proceedings of the 35th Annual ACM Symposium on Theory of Computing, San Diego, California, USA, June 9-11, 2003*, pages 196–205. ACM Press, 2003.

[8] M. Kearns and Y. Mansour. On the boosting ability of top-down decision tree learning algorithms. *J. of Comput. Syst. Sci.*, 58(1):109–128, 1999.

[9] J. Kivinen and M. K. Warmuth. Boosting as entropy projection. In *Proc. 12th Annu. Conf. on Comput. Learning Theory*, pages 134–144. ACM Press, New York, NY, 1999.

[10] Y. Mansour and D. A. McAllester. Boosting using branching programs. *J. of Comput. Syst. Sci.*, 64(1):103–112, 2002. Special Issue for COLT 2000.

[11] G. Rätsch and M. K. Warmuth. Maximizing the margin with boosting. In *15th Annual Conference on Computational Learning Theory, COLT 2002, Sydney, Australia, July 2002, Proceedings*, volume 2375 of *Lecture Notes in Artificial Intelligence*, pages 334–350. Springer, 2002.

[12] R. E. Schapire, Y. Freund, P. Bartlett, and W. S. Lee. Boosting the margin: a new explanation for the effectiveness of voting methods. *Annals of Statistics*, 26(5):1651–1686, 1998.

[13] R. E. Schapire and Y. Singer. Improved boosting algorithms using confidence-rated predictions. *Machine Learning*, 37(3):297–336, 1999.

[14] E. Takimoto and A. Maruoka. Top-down decision tree learning as information based boosting. *Theoret. Comput. Sci.*, 292(2):447–464, 2003.

Learning Boolean Functions in AC^0 on Attribute and Classification Noise[*]

Akinobu Miyata[**], Jun Tarui, and Etsuji Tomita

Department of Information and Communication Engineering,
The University of Electro-Communications
Chofugaoka 1-5-1, Chofu, Tokyo 182-8585, Japan.
{miyacchi,tarui,tomita}@ice.uec.ac.jp

Abstract. Linial, Mansour and Nisan introduced a learning algorithm of Boolean functions in AC^0 under the *uniform* distribution. Following their work, Bshouty, Jackson and Tamon, also Ohtsuki and Tomita extended the algorithm to one that is robust for noisy data. The noise process we are concerned here is as follows: for an *example* $\langle x, f(x) \rangle$ $(x \in \{0,1\}^n$, $f(x) \in \{-1, 1\})$, each bit of the vector x and the $f(x)$ are obliged to change independently with probability η during a learning process. Before our present paper, we were on the assumption that the correct noise rate η or its upper bound is known in advance. In this paper, we eliminate the assumption. We estimate an upper bound of the noise rate by evaluating noisy power spectrum on the frequency domain by using a sampling trick. Thereby, by combining this procedure with Ohtsuki *et al.*'s algorithm, we obtain a quasipolynomial time learning algorithm that can cope with noise without knowing any information about noise in advance.

1 Introduction

Linial *et al.* [5] proposed a learning algorithm of Boolean functions in AC^0 under the *uniform* distribution. Following their work, even when we are suffered from classification and attribute noise with the noise rate $\eta < 1/2$, Bshouty *et al.* [1] showed a learning algorithm with exact value of η. Ohtsuki *et al.*[7], [8] presented an algorithm which required only its upper bound η_0 on η. Bshouty *et al.* [2] also showed how to eliminate their previous assumption, provided that the upper bound of the noise rate is known.

The noise rate η exists certainly in $0 \leq \eta < 1/2$. Thus it could be possible to get rid of such a requirement for an upper bound η_0 on the noise rate η.

Until now a lot of learning problems under noise have been investigated. Laird [4] showed that we can estimate such an upper bound in the presence of classification

---

[*] This work has been supported in part by Grants-in-Aid for Scientific Research Nos. 13680435 and 16300001 from the Ministry of Education, Culture, Sports, Science and Technology, Japan.

[**] Presently with Nomura Research Institute, Tower S, Kiba 1-5-25, Koto-ku, Tokyo 130-4452, Japan.

noise. Then what happened in the case where the noise process contains not only classification errors but also attribute errors in an example? For estimating noise rate η and biased Fourier coefficients, Bshouty et al.[2] needed some sort of noise oracles on the assumption that a learner knows the number of necessary examples in advance. On the other hand, Ohtsuki et al. [7], [8] showed that a learner can estimate noise rate η from only examples containing noise.

In this paper, we eliminate the assumption that an upper bound η_0 on the noise rate is known. We propose an estimating method that compares values between prediction and experiment on the frequency domain. Note that we can apply this estimating method to other classes, in which the power spectrum of the Boolean function is concentrated enough in low degrees. By combining this procedure with Ohtsuki et al.'s learning algorithm, we can obtain an algorithm which assumes only $\eta < 1/2$ with respect to unknown noise rate η. If we do not need to know exact η or an upper bound η_0 on η in advance, it is more reasonable that we only require that examples may be changed with an unknown probability η. A preliminary version of this paper appeared in [6].

2   Preliminaries

A Boolean function f on n variables is a mapping : $\{0,1\}^n \to \{-1,1\}$. For $x \in \{0,1\}^n$, let $|x|$ be the hamming weight of x , i.e. the number of 1 contained in x, and $x[i]$ be an i-th bit of x. The bitwise exclusive-or of two n-bit vectors x^1 and x^2 is denoted $x^1 \oplus x^2$. In this paper, we have changed the range from $\{0,1\}$ to $\{-1,1\}$.

Let F_n be a concept class over $\{0,1\}^n$ and let $f,h \in F_n$. We consider the following learning model. A learning algorithm receives examples selected uniformly at random, and then outputs hypothesis h and halts. An example $\langle x, f(x) \rangle$ is a pair of input $x \in \{0,1\}^n$ and output $f(x) \in \{1,-1\}$. $\Pr[f(x) \neq h(x)]$ is the probability that h differs from the target f under the uniform distribution and we denote $\Pr[f(x) \neq h(x)] = error(h)$. The success of the learning is evaluated by two parameters, error parameter ϵ and confidence parameter δ. For any $f \in F_n$, $0 < \epsilon < 1, 0 < \delta < 1$, a learning algorithm L outputs a hypothesis h within ϵ errors with probability at least $1 - \delta$.

Also, the hypothesis h is called ϵ-good if and only if $error(h) \leq \epsilon$, otherwise ϵ-bad. A concept class F_n is said to be learnable if and only if there exists some learning algorithm for F_n.

3   A Learning Algorithm via the Fourier Transform

Let f be a real valued function from $\{0,1\}^n$ to $[-1,1]$. For $\alpha \in \{0,1\}^n$, define the orthonomial basis $\chi_\alpha(x) = (-1)^{\alpha \cdot x}$ $(\alpha \cdot x = \sum_i \alpha[i]x[i])$ over $\{0,1\}^n$. Then by using Fourier methods, any Boolean function f can be represented by $f(x) = \sum_\alpha \hat{f}(\alpha)\chi_\alpha(x)$, where $\hat{f}(\alpha)$ is the Fourier coefficient of f at α. We call $|\alpha|$ the frequency of α.

3.1 Learning Constant Depth Circuits [5]

Let f be a Boolean function that can be computed by a constant depth, poly-nomial size circuit (AC^0 circuit). The learning algorithm by Linial et al.[5] is based on the following ideas. First, let a hypothesis h be of a form $h(x) = \sum_\alpha \hat{h}(\alpha)\chi_\alpha(x)$ over $\{0,1\}^n$ for $\alpha \in \{0,1\}^n$, if we can approximate $\hat{f}(\alpha)$ well, then the hypothesis h can be an ϵ-good hypothesis. Secondly, we can compose h by estimating only $O(n^k)$ coefficients for $k = O(\log^d n/\epsilon)$ since the Fourier coefficients of AC^0 are concentrated enough in low degrees ($\sum_\alpha \hat{f}(\alpha)^2 \leq \epsilon/2$ for any α s.th. $|\alpha| \leq k$). Thirdly, since $\hat{f}(\alpha) = E[f(x)\chi_\alpha(x)]$, we estimate $a_\alpha = (\sum_{j=1}^m f(x^j)\chi_\alpha(x^j))/m$ from m examples $\{\langle x^j, f(x^j)\rangle\}_{j=1}^m$, where a_α is an estimated value of $\hat{f}(\alpha)$ and used as $\hat{h}(\alpha)$. Also, from **Chernoff bounds [3]**, we need $m = (4n^k/\epsilon)\ln(2n^k/\delta)$ examples to guarantee that

$$\Pr\left[|\hat{f}(\alpha) - a_\alpha| \leq \sqrt{\frac{\epsilon}{2n^k}} \text{ for each } \alpha \text{ s.th. } |\alpha| \leq k\right] \geq 1 - \delta \ .$$

4 Noise Rate and Its Upper Bound

In literatures [7], [8], a part of [1], [2], and here, we are concerned with both attribute and classification noise model. A learning algorithm makes a call to oracle EX() and receives an *example* $\langle x, f(x)\rangle$ from EX() under the *uniform* distribution. However, the noise process changes an *example* $\langle x, f(x)\rangle$ to a noisy *example* $\langle x \oplus x_N, f(x)y_N\rangle$ ($x_N \in \{0,1\}^n, y_N \in \{1,-1\}$) with probability

$$\prod_{x_N[i]=1} \eta \prod_{x_N[i]=0} (1-\eta) \prod_{y_N=-1} \eta \prod_{y_N=1} (1-\eta),$$

where we call η the noise rate with $0 \leq \eta < 1/2$.

Laird [4] showed that in some learning problems from noisy examples, its sample size increases inversely proportional to $1 - 2\eta$, and thus we need to know noise rate η exactly or its upper bound η_0 on η to determine a proper sample size in advance.

An upper bound η_0 is a "looser" estimate of unknown noise rate η. Could not we estimate such an upper bound by observing only noisy sample ?

Laird also showed that we can estimate such an upper bound under the clas-sification noise model. The classification noise process is that for an *example* $\langle x, f(x)\rangle$, only $f(x)$ is changed with probability η. The process of estimating such an upper bound makes a learning algorithm try for successively larger val-ues of η_0. If one value of such successively larger values is close enough to real noise rate η, the best hypothesis among the outputs of the learning algorithm should be ϵ-good under the classification noise model.

In the case where examples are suffered from not only classification errors but also attribute errors, sometimes unacceptable examples are generated. There are examples seemed to be generated from the target function on the one hand, but at the same time there are considerable examples that negate the target function. Although we can ignore such examples by requesting proper amounts of examples even if the noise rate η is close to $1/2$ under the classification noise model, it may happen that the number of examples that negate the target function exceeds the number of examples correspond to the target function depending on the target function and noise rate under the both classification and attribute noise model. Because of this, we need to restrict target functions and noise rate, to acquire the hypothesis with desired accuracy, or we can't distinguish whether an example from noisy oracle is contained originally in correct target function or not. Hence, it is difficult to use an error check on such unacceptable examples, since the hypothesis that accounts noisy sample best is not necessarily the desired hypothesis. For further details of this, see *Chapter 5: Identification from Noisy Examples* in Laird [4].

Instead of using the above estimating process, we develop a procedure that estimates an upper bound of η by using a sampling trick on frequency domain and combine a robust k-lowdegree algorithm [7], [8] that learns AC^0 under noise to be shown in **4.1**. As a result, we can obtain a learning algorithm that performs well without any noise information in advance.

4.1　An Algorithm with an Upper Bound η_0 as an Input

We show robust k-lowdegree algorithm [7], [8](rkl) that works under the condition that an upper noise bound η_0 is given to a learner. The rkl algorithm searches a natural number t by increasing it by Δt step by step.

Robust k-Lowdegree Algorithm [7], [8] (ϵ, δ, η_0):

Define $m = 1568n^{k+2} \left(1/(1 - 2\eta_0)\right)^{2k+4} (1/\epsilon) \ln\left((2n^k)/\delta\right)$,
$\gamma_u = \ln\left(1 + \sqrt{\epsilon}/2\right)/(k+1)$,
$\Delta t = \ln\left[(1 - (1 - 2\eta_0)\gamma_u)^2 + ((1 - 2\eta_0)\sqrt{\epsilon})/(4n)\right]^{-1}/(4k + 4)$.

Step1. Request noisy examples $\{\langle x^j \oplus x_N^j, f(x^j)y_N^j \rangle\}_{j=1}^m$. For each α s.th. $|\alpha| \leq k$, calculate $c_\alpha = \frac{1}{m}\sum_{j=1}^m f(x^j)y_N^j\chi_\alpha(x^j \oplus x_N^j)$.

Step2. Initialize $t = 1$, then increase t by Δt until t satisfies the following inequality or $t \geq \frac{1}{1-2\eta_0}$. Regard such t as an estimated value of $\frac{1}{1-2\eta}$.

$$\sum_{i=0}^k (\sum_{|\alpha|=i} c_\alpha^2)t^{2i+2} \geq (1 - (1 - 2\eta_0)\gamma_u)^2 + \frac{3(1 - 2\eta_0)\sqrt{\epsilon}}{28n} .$$

Step3. Output the hypothesis $h(x) = \text{sign}(\sum_{|\alpha|\leq k} c_\alpha t^{|\alpha|+1}\chi_\alpha(x))$, and halt.

For a learning from noisy sample, a learning algorithm is permitted to run in the time quasipolynomial in n, $1/\epsilon$, $1/\delta$ and $1/(1-2\eta)$. The running time of the robust k-lowdegree algorithm [7], [8](rkl) is shown as follows.

Theorem 1. [Ohtsuki et al.[7], [8]] Let f be a Boolean function and assume that $0 < \epsilon, \delta < 1$, and an upper bound η_0 s.th. $0 \leq \eta \leq \eta_0 < 1/2$ is given. Request the following m examples, then the rkl algorithm runs in $O(mn^k)$ time and then outputs hypothesis h within ϵ errors with probability at least $1 - \delta$, where $k = O(\log^d(n)/((1-2\eta_0)\epsilon))$.

$$m = 1568n^{k+2}\left(\frac{1}{1-2\eta_0}\right)^{2k+4}\left(\frac{1}{\epsilon}\right)\ln\left(\frac{2n^k}{\delta}\right) .$$

Sketch of the Proof. First, consider the influence of noise.

Lemma 2 [Ohtsuki et al.[7], [8]]. Let f be a Boolean function and assume that $0 \leq \eta < 1/2$. If $x_N \in \{0,1\}^n$ and $y_N \in \{-1,+1\}$ are produced with probability $\prod_{x_N[i]=1}\eta\prod_{x_N[i]=0}(1-\eta)$, $\prod_{y_N=-1}\eta\prod_{y_N=1}(1-\eta)$ respectively, then from noisy examples $\{\langle x^j \oplus x_N^j, f(x^j)y_N^j\rangle\}_{j=1}^m$ we get: $E[f(x)y_N\chi_\alpha(x \oplus x_N)] = (1-2\eta)^{|\alpha|+1}\hat{f}(\alpha)$.

Proof of Lemma 2. Since x, x_N and y_N are independent each other, we have the above Lemma 2 immediately.   □

Thus, we have true coefficients $\hat{f}(\alpha)$ by estimating $1/(1-2\eta)$. Let c_α be an estimated value of the biased Fourier coefficient $(1-2\eta)^{|\alpha|+1}\hat{f}(\alpha)$ and t be an estimate of $1/(1-2\eta)$. Note that $t > 1$. Assuming $\sum_\alpha \hat{f}(\alpha)^2 \simeq 0$ for α s.th. $|\alpha| > k$, we estimate t that satisfies $\sum_{i=0}^k\left(\sum_{|\alpha|=i}c_\alpha^2\right)t^{2i+2} \simeq 1$. Such t should be a good approximator of $1/(1-2\eta)$ since for any α s.th. $|\alpha| \leq k$ $\sum_\alpha \hat{f}(\alpha)^2 \simeq 1$.

Lemma 3 [Ohtsuki et al.[7], [8]]. Let f be a Boolean function. Assume that a known upper bound such that $0 \leq \eta \leq \eta_0 < 1/2$ is given and $k = O(\log^d(n)/((1-2\eta_0)\epsilon))$. If we have t such that $|t - 1/(1-2\eta)| \leq \gamma_u$ and c_α such that $|c_\alpha - (1-2\eta)^{|\alpha|+1}\hat{f}(\alpha)| \leq \gamma_c$, where $\gamma_u = \ln(1 + \sqrt{\epsilon}/2)/(k+1)$ and $\gamma_c = ((1-2\eta)^{k+2}\sqrt{\epsilon})/(28n\sqrt{n^k})$, then we obtain a hypothesis $h = \text{sign}\left(\sum_{|\alpha|\leq k}c_\alpha t^{|\alpha|+1}\chi_\alpha(x)\right)$ such that error(h)$\leq \epsilon$.

Proof of Lemma 3. Since the value η_0 ($\eta_0 \geq \eta$) is given, we determine the value of k and γ_c. Thus we have $\sum_\alpha \hat{f}(\alpha)^2 \leq ((1-2\eta_0)\epsilon)/(28n)$ for any α s.th. $|\alpha| > k$. Consequently, by evaluating errors between such esitmated values c_α and true values $\hat{f}(\alpha)$, and considering the fact that $\sum_\alpha \hat{f}(\alpha)^2 \leq ((1-2\eta_0)\epsilon)/(28n)$ for any α s.th. $|\alpha| > k$, we have the above Lemma 3.

□

Lemma 4 [Ohtsuki *et al.*[7], [8]]. Let f be a Boolean function. Assume that an upper bound η_0 is given, $k = O(\log^d(n)/((1 - 2\eta_0)\epsilon))$. Also assume that we have c_α such that $|c_\alpha - (1 - 2\eta)^{|\alpha|+1}\hat{f}(\alpha)| \leq \gamma_c$, where $\gamma_c = ((1 - 2\eta_0)^{k+2}\sqrt{\epsilon})/(28n\sqrt{n^k})$. If t satisfies the following inequality, then $|t - 1/(1 - 2\eta)| \leq \gamma_u$, where $\gamma_u = \ln(1 + \sqrt{\epsilon}/2)/(k + 1)$.

$$\sum_{i=0}^{k}(\sum_{|\alpha|=i} c_\alpha^2)t^{2i+2} \geq (1 - (1 - 2\eta_0)\gamma_u)^2 + \frac{3(1 - 2\eta_0)\sqrt{\epsilon}}{28n}.$$

Proof of Lemma 4. Consider the contraposition of the above Lemma 4. After pluging such t ($t < 1/(1 - 2\eta) - \gamma_u$) into $\sum_{i=0}^{k}(\sum_{|\alpha|=i} c_\alpha^2)t^{2i+2}$, we have the following inequality.

$$\sum_{i=0}^{k}(\sum_{|\alpha|=i} c_\alpha^2)t^{2i+2} < (1 - (1 - 2\eta_0)\gamma_u)^2 + \frac{3(1 - 2\eta_0)\sqrt{\epsilon}}{28n}.$$

Hence we have the above **Lemma 4**. Note that we do not consider the case where $1/(1 - 2\eta) + \gamma_u < t$, since we start searching t from $t = 1$ ($1/(1 - 2\eta) \geq 1$).
□

Consequently, the problem of estimating $1/(1 - 2\eta)$ can be regarded as the problem of searching a real value t that satisfies the condition in Lemma 4. In order to avoid estimating t s.th. considerably deviates from real $1/(1 - 2\eta)$, Ohtsuki et al.[7], [8] estimated such t by increasing it by Δt step by step, where

$$\Delta t = \frac{1}{4k + 4} \ln \left[(1 - (1 - 2\eta_0)\gamma_u)^2 + \frac{(1 - 2\eta_0)\sqrt{\epsilon}}{4n}\right]^{-1}.$$

Lastly, from **Chernoff Bound [3]**, if we have the following m examples given below, then we have $|c_\alpha - (1 - 2\eta)^{|\alpha|+1}\hat{f}(\alpha)| \leq \gamma_c$, where $\gamma_c = ((1 - 2\eta_0)^{k+2}\sqrt{\epsilon})/(28n\sqrt{n^k})$.

$$m = 1568n^{k+2}\left(\frac{1}{1 - 2\eta_0}\right)^{2k+4}\left(\frac{1}{\epsilon}\right)\ln\left(\frac{2n^k}{\delta}\right).$$

As a whole, Lemma 3 holds from the above sample size m and Lemma 4, and thus we can complete the proof of **Theorem 1**.

Q.E.D.

5   Estimating an Upper Bound η_0

The rkl algorithm needs to know an upper bound η_0 on η in advance (which should be given as an input).
In this chapter, provided that $\eta < 1/2$, we present a method which estimates such an upper bound η_0.

5.1 How Do We Guess an Unknown η?

On the assumption that the noise rate η is unknown for a learner, we will begin with a simple observation. Could not we get any information with respect to noise from only noisy sample? It is the point to be observed that for α s.th. $|\alpha| \leq k$ a noisy power spectrum $\sum_\alpha c_\alpha^2$ estimated from noisy sample is an experimental value of $\sum_\alpha (1 - 2\eta)^{2|\alpha|+2} \hat{f}(\alpha)^2$, namely

$$\sum_\alpha c_\alpha^2 \simeq \sum_\alpha (1 - 2\eta)^{2|\alpha|+2} \hat{f}(\alpha)^2 = (1 - 2\eta)^{2|\alpha|+2} \sum_\alpha \hat{f}(\alpha)^2 \ .$$

This implies that $\sum_\alpha c_\alpha^2$ for α s.th. $|\alpha| \leq k$ offers a key to estimate η. We can guess how those Fourier coefficients are reduced by the effect of the noise.

Let us now look into estimating an upper bound η_0 in detail. First, we analyze why the rkl algorithm needs such an upper bound η_0. Secondly, we implement η' $(0 \leq \eta' < 1/2)$ as an estimate of an upper bound η_0. Then we claim that if such η' satisfies a certain condition in the frequency domain then the estimate η' is larger than or equal to η. Thirdly, we present a procedure for estimating such an upper bound.

5.2 Why the rkl Algorithm Needs an Upper Bound η_0?

The rkl algorithm needs the following two conditions with respect to a known upper bound η_0.

i For a target Boolean function f, the rkl algorithm sets $k = O(\log^d(n)/((1 - 2\eta_0)\epsilon))$ so that for α s.th. $|\alpha| > k$ $\sum_\alpha \hat{f}(\alpha)^2 \leq ((1 - 2\eta_0)\epsilon)/(28n)$.

ii The rkl algorithm requests the size m examples to guarantee that $|c_\alpha - (1 - 2\eta)^{|\alpha|+1} \hat{f}(\alpha)| \leq \gamma_c$ $(\gamma_c = ((1 - 2\eta_0)^{k+2}\sqrt{\epsilon})/(28n\sqrt{n^k}))$ with high probability.

Namely, the rkl algorithm needs η_0 to decide proper values of k and m.

Instead of using a known η_0, we shall determine the values of k and m by introducing a predicted value η' $(0 \leq \eta' < 1/2)$ aiming at η_0.

Since we have no information how close η is to $1/2$, we will use an iterative search with $\eta' = 0, 1/4, 3/8, 7/16, \ldots$, and in each step we determine k and m step by step. As a result, we get predicted η' such that $\eta' \geq \eta$ and satisfy the above two conditions before **Step 2**.

Here, the main property we want to establish is the following Theorem 5.

Theorem 5. Let η' $(0 \leq \eta' < 1/2)$ be a predicted value of η. We request the following $m(\eta', k)$ examples

$$m(\eta', k) = 1568n^{2k+2} \left(\frac{1}{1 - 2\eta'} \right)^{4k+4} \left(\frac{1}{\epsilon} \right) \ln \left(\frac{2n^{2k}}{\delta} \right) ,$$

then by estimating biased Fourier coefficient c_α for α s.th. $|\alpha| \le k$, we have that $\eta' \ge \eta$ if and only if $(1 - 2\eta')^{2|\alpha|+2} \le \sum_\alpha c_\alpha^2 - s(\eta', k)$, where $s(\eta', k) = ((1 - 2\eta')^{2k+2}\sqrt{\epsilon})/(14n)$ is some error bound between an estimate $\sum_\alpha c_\alpha^2$ and an expected value $(1 - 2\eta')^{2|\alpha|+2} \sum_\alpha \hat{f}(\alpha)^2$.

Proof. There are the following two claims to prove Theorem 5.

  i In any frequency $|\alpha|$ for any α s.th. $|\alpha| \le k$, an error between an estimate $\sum_\alpha c_\alpha^2$ from noisy sample and an expected value $\sum_\alpha (1 - 2\eta)^{2|\alpha|+2} \hat{f}(\alpha)^2$ is within $s(\eta', k)$. Namely, for any α s.th. $|\alpha| \le k$

$$\sum_\alpha c_\alpha^2 - s(\eta', k) \le (1 - 2\eta)^{2|\alpha|+2} \sum_\alpha \hat{f}(\alpha)^2 .$$

  ii For a predicted value η', η' is larger than or equal to η if and only if

$$(1 - 2\eta')^{2|\alpha|+2} \le \sum_\alpha \{c_\alpha^2|\ \alpha \text{ s.th. } |\alpha| \le k\} - s(\eta', k) .$$

Proof of i) Consider now the first claim. Let η' be a predicted value of an upper bound η_0, if we request the above $m(\eta', k)$ examples, then we have an estimate c_α within $\gamma_c' = ((1 - 2\eta')^{2k+2}\sqrt{\epsilon})/(28n^{k+1})$ error to its expected value $(1 - 2\eta)^{|\alpha|+1} \hat{f}(\alpha)$ with probability at least $1 - \delta$. For each α s.th. $|\alpha| \le k$, we can guarantee $|(1 - 2\eta)^{|\alpha|+1} \hat{f}(\alpha) - c_\alpha| \le \gamma_c'$ from **Chernoff bound [3]**. Since $0 \le |(1 - 2\eta)^{|\alpha|+1} \hat{f}(\alpha)|$, $|c_\alpha| \le 1$ for any α s.th. $|\alpha| \le k$, we get:

$$|(1 - 2\eta)^{2|\alpha|+2} \hat{f}(\alpha)^2 - c_\alpha^2|$$
$$= |(1 - 2\eta)^{|\alpha|+1} \hat{f}(\alpha) + c_\alpha||(1 - 2\eta)^{|\alpha|+1} \hat{f}(\alpha) - c_\alpha| \le 2\gamma_c'$$

$$\Rightarrow \sum_\alpha |(1 - 2\eta)^{2|\alpha|+2} \hat{f}(\alpha)^2 - c_\alpha^2| \le 2\gamma_c' \times n^k = \frac{(1 - 2\eta')^{2k+2}}{14n}\sqrt{\epsilon} .$$

From these for any α s.th. $|\alpha| \le k$, we get the estimate $\sum_\alpha c_\alpha^2$ within $s(\eta', k) = \frac{(1-2\eta')^{2k+2}}{14n}\sqrt{\epsilon}$ error bounds to its expectation $\sum_\alpha (1 - 2\eta)^{2|\alpha|+2} \hat{f}(\alpha)^2$.

Consequently, the above sample size $m(\eta', k)$ is large enough to guarantee for any α s.th. $|\alpha| \le k$:

$$\sum_\alpha |(1 - 2\eta)^{2|\alpha|+2} \hat{f}(\alpha)^2 - c_\alpha^2| \le s(\eta', k) .$$

Hence we get the following inequality for any α s.th. $|\alpha| \le k$.

$$\sum_\alpha c_\alpha^2 - s(\eta', k) \le (1 - 2\eta)^{2|\alpha|+2} \sum_\alpha \hat{f}(\alpha)^2 .$$

Proof of ii)   Then consider now the second claim. We assume that a real value p $(0 \le p \le 1)$ satisfies for any α s.th. $|\alpha| \le k$:

$$p \le \sum_{\alpha} c_{\alpha}^2 - s(\eta', k) .$$

Since for any α s.th. $|\alpha| \le k$ $\sum_{\alpha} c_{\alpha}^2$ is an estimate to its expected value $(1 - 2\eta)^{2|\alpha|+2} \sum_{\alpha} \hat{f}(\alpha)^2$ and $\sum_{\alpha} \hat{f}(\alpha)^2$ is fixed for each f, for a real value p $(0 \le p \le 1)$, we define $p = (1 - 2\eta')^{2|\alpha|+2}$ and get

$$(1 - 2\eta')^{2|\alpha|+2} \le \sum_{\alpha} c_{\alpha}^2 - s(\eta', k) \le (1 - 2\eta)^{2|\alpha|+2} \sum_{\alpha} \hat{f}(\alpha)^2$$

$$\Rightarrow (1 - 2\eta')^{2|\alpha|+2} \le (1 - 2\eta)^{2|\alpha|+2} \sum_{\alpha} \hat{f}(\alpha)^2$$

$$\Rightarrow \left(\frac{1 - 2\eta'}{1 - 2\eta} \right)^{2|\alpha|+2} \le \sum_{\alpha} \hat{f}(\alpha)^2 \quad (\text{since } 0 \le \sum_{\alpha} \hat{f}(\alpha)^2 \le 1)$$

$$\Rightarrow \eta' \ge \eta .$$

We can now give a proof of Theorem 5 by using the above two claims.

Q.E.D

In the following subsection, we shall present a procedure that halts satisfying conditions in the above Theorem 5.

5.3   A Procedure for Estimating an Upper Bound

To put it plainly, the procedure compares the predicted power spectrum from η' with the observed power spectrum from noisy sample, and then judges whether such η' is larger than or equal to noise rate η or not.

A Procedure for Estimating $\eta'(\epsilon, \delta)$:
Define $m_r(\eta', k)$ and $s(\eta', k)$ as follows,

$$m_r(\eta', k) = 1568 \left(\frac{1}{1 - 2\eta'} \right)^{4k+4} \left(\frac{n^{2k+2}}{\epsilon} \right) \ln \left(\frac{2^{r+1} n^{2k}}{\delta} \right) ,$$

$$s(\eta', k) = (1 - 2\eta')^{2k+2} \frac{\sqrt{\epsilon}}{14n} .$$

Input: δ $(0 < \delta < 1)$, ϵ $(0 < \epsilon < 1)$
Output: η' such that $\eta' \ge \eta$
Procedure

1 $r := 1$, $\eta' := 0$, $k = O \left(\log^d \frac{n}{\epsilon} \right)$
2 (round r) Repeat until the halt condition is satisfied.
    2.1 Request $m(\eta', k)$ examples.

2.2 For each α s.th. $|\alpha| \leq k$, obtain

$$c_\alpha = \frac{1}{m} \sum_{j=1}^{m} f(x^j) y_N^j \chi_\alpha(x^j \oplus x_N^j) .$$

2.3 $p := (1 - 2\eta')$, $s := s(\eta', k)$

2.4 If the following inequality is satisfied in some frequency i $(0 \leq i \leq k)$, then halt and output η'.

$$p^{2i+2} < \sum_{\alpha \text{ s.th. } |\alpha|=i} c_\alpha^2 - s$$

2.5 Else, execute the followings and go to the next round.

$$r := r+1, \ \eta' := \frac{1}{2} - \frac{1}{2^{r+1}}, \ k = O\left(\log^d \frac{n}{(1-2\eta')\epsilon}\right)$$

Theorem 6. Define $m_r(\eta', k)$ as follows.

$$m_r(\eta', k) = 1568 \left(\frac{1}{1-2\eta'}\right)^{4k+4} \left(\frac{n^{2k+2}}{\epsilon}\right) \ln\left(\frac{2^{r+1}n^{2k}}{\delta}\right) .$$

Then with probability at least $1 - \delta$, the above procedure halts in or before round $r_0 = 2 + \lceil \log_2(1 - 2\eta)^{-1} \rceil$ and outputs η' such that $\eta' \geq \eta$.

Proof. To begin with, we will examine the probability that for any α in any round r,

$$|(1 - 2\eta)^{|\alpha|+1} \hat{f}(\alpha) - c_\alpha| \geq \gamma_c' . \tag{1}$$

After r round independent trials, there are 2^r possible rounds. So by dividing the probability that formula (1) occurs, we can bound the probability within $\delta/2$ for any round. Namely, the sample size $m_r(\eta', k)$ is defined to guarantee for any α s.th. $|\alpha| \leq k$ in any round r that

$$\Pr[\sum_\alpha |(1 - 2\eta)^{|\alpha|+1} \hat{f}(\alpha) - c_\alpha| \geq \gamma_c'] \leq \frac{\delta/2}{2^r \times n^k} \times 2^r \times n^k = \frac{\delta}{2} .$$

We now turn to discuss the procedure for estimating an upper bound. Therefore we show that the procedure satisfies the followings with probability at least $1-\delta$.

First, we show that if the procedure halts satisfying the halt condition in Step 2, then its output η' is larger than or equal to η.
Assume that the procedure halts in round r_0. By using $m_r(\eta', k)$ examples, the procedure guarantees $\sum_\alpha c_\alpha^2 \leq (1 - 2\eta)^{2|\alpha|+2} + s(\eta', k)$ with probability at least $1-\delta/2$. Also the halt of the procedure implies $(1-2\eta')^{2|\alpha|+2}+s(\eta', k) \leq \sum_\alpha c_\alpha^2$ for any α s.th. $|\alpha| \leq k$. Thus, from these inequalities together, we get the following inequality and hence $\eta' \geq \eta$.

$$(1 - 2\eta')^{2|\alpha|+2} + s(\eta', k) \leq (1 - 2\eta)^{2|\alpha|+2} + s(\eta', k) .$$

Secondly, we show that procedure halts in or before round $r_0 = 2 + \lceil \log_2(1 - 2\eta)^{-1} \rceil$.
Now assume that $\eta'_r = \frac{1}{2} - \frac{1}{2^{r+1}}$ in round r and satisfy

$$(1 - 2\eta'_r)^{2|\alpha|+2} \cdot 1 = (1 - 2\eta)^{2|\alpha|+2} \cdot 1 . \tag{2}$$

Namely, $\eta'_r = \eta$ in round r.
In $r + 1$ round, since $\eta'_{r+1} = \frac{1}{2} - \frac{1}{2^{r+2}}$, we get $(1 - 2\eta'_{r+1})^{2|\alpha|+2} = \left(\frac{1}{2}\right)^{2|\alpha|+2}(1 - 2\eta'_r)^{2|\alpha|+2}$. Compared with the equality (2), the lefthand side is reduced by $\left(\frac{1}{2}\right)^{2|\alpha|+2}$ times. Therefore, in $r + 1$ round, we show that the following inequality (3) holds in some frequency $|\alpha| = i$ for any α s.th. $|\alpha| \leq k$.

$$(1 - 2\eta'_r)^{2|\alpha|+2} \left(\frac{1}{2}\right)^{2|\alpha|+2} < (1 - 2\eta)^{2|\alpha|+2} \sum_\alpha \hat{f}(\alpha)^2 . \tag{3}$$

At that time, the procedure satisfies this and then halts. Since we assume that $\eta'_r = \eta$, the above inequality (3) can be regarded as the following inequality

$$\left(\frac{1}{2}\right)^{2|\alpha|+2} < \sum_\alpha \{\hat{f}(\alpha)^2| \ \alpha \text{ s.th. } |\alpha| = i\} .$$

To show that the inequality (3) holds in at least one frequency $|\alpha|$ for α s.th. $|\alpha| \leq k$, for both sides by summing over $0 \leq |\alpha| \leq k$ we get

$$\sum_{|\alpha|=0}^{k} \left(\frac{1}{2}\right)^{2|\alpha|+2} = \frac{1}{3}\left(1 - \left(\frac{1}{4}\right)^{k+1}\right) < \frac{1}{3} \text{ and } \sum_\alpha \hat{f}(\alpha)^2 \geq 1 - \frac{\epsilon}{4} \geq \frac{3}{4} \tag{4}$$

since for any α s.th. $|\alpha| > k$ $\sum_\alpha \hat{f}(\alpha)^2 \leq \epsilon/4$.
Thus we have

$$\sum_{|\alpha|=0}^{k} \left(\frac{1}{2}\right)^{2|\alpha|+2} < \sum_{\alpha \text{ s.th. } |\alpha|\leq k} \hat{f}(\alpha)^2 . \tag{5}$$

As a result, by using formulas (2) and (4) we can show that the inequality (4) holds. This implies that the procedure halts in or before $r + 1$ round. Since η' is updated $1 + \lceil \log_2(1 - 2\eta)^{-1} \rceil$ times by r round, hence the procedure halts in or before $r_0 = r + 1 = 2 + \lceil \log_2(1 - 2\eta)^{-1} \rceil$.
Finally, since both of the above two points only fail with probability at most $\delta/2$ respectively, hence the procedure fails with probability at most δ. Hence Theorem 6 holds.   **Q.E.D**

By combining the above procedure with the rkl algorithm, we get a learning algorithm without knowing any information about noise rate η in advance. It is obvious that the learning algorithm outputs hypothesis h within ϵ errors with probability at least $1 - \delta$. Also, since the procedure requests $O(rm)$ examples, its time complexity is

$$O(rmn^k) = O\left(n^{2k+2}\left(\frac{1}{1-2\eta}\right)^{4k+4}\left(\frac{1}{\epsilon}\right)\ln\left(\frac{2n^{2k}}{\delta(1-2\eta)}\right)\right).$$

6 Conclusion

In this paper we have presented a procedure that estimates an upper bound η_0 on the frequency domain. By combining it with Ohtsuki et $al.$'s algorithm, we get a more powerful learning algorithm that works without knowing η in advance.

Acknowledgement. We deeply thank Kazuhiro Ohtsuki for his great contribution on the basis of our present work. We would like to thank Tomonori Nakamura and referees whose comments helped to improve the presentation.

References

[1] N. H. Bshouty, J. C. Jackson, and C. Tamon: "Uniform-distribution attribute noise learnability," COLT1999, pp.75-80 (1999).
[2] N. H. Bshouty, J. C. Jackson, and C. Tamon: "Uniform-distribution attribute noise learnability," Information and Computation, Vol.187(2), pp.277-290 (2003).
[3] T. Hagerup and C. Rub: "A guided tour of the Chernoff bounds," Information Processing Letters, Vol.33, pp.305-308 (1989).
[4] P. D. Laird: "Learning from Good and Bad Data," Kluwer Academic (1988).
[5] L. Linial, Y. Mansour, and N. Nisan: "Constant depth circuits, Fourier transform, and learnability," Journal of the ACM, Vol.40, pp.607-620 (1993).
[6] A. Miyata, J. Tarui, and E. Tomita: "Learning AC^0 Boolean functions on attribute and label noise," Technical Report of IEICE, COMP2003-70, pp.9-16 (2004).
[7] K. Ohtsuki and E. Tomita: "An algorithm for learning a certain Boolean function from noisy data," Technical Report of the Department of Communications and Systems Engineering, UEC-CAS20-2, The University of Electro-Communications (2000).
[8] K. Ohtsuki: "On learning a certain Boolean function from noisy data," Master's dissertation at the Department of Communications and Systems Engineering in the Graduate School of Electro-Communications, The University of Electro-Communications (2001).

Appendix

Supplement to the Proof of Theorem 1

Proof of Lemma 3 ([7], [8]).

$$\text{error}\left(\text{sign}\left(\sum_\alpha c_\alpha t^{|\alpha|+1}\chi_\alpha(x)\right)\right) = \Pr\left[f(x) \neq h(x)\right]$$

$$\leq \sum_{\alpha \text{ s.th. } |\alpha|\leq k} (\hat{f}(\alpha) - c_\alpha t^{|\alpha|+1}\chi_\alpha(x))^2 + \sum_{\alpha \text{ s.th. } |\alpha|>k} \hat{f}(\alpha)^2$$

$$\leq (e^{\gamma_u(k+1)} - 1)^2 \sum_{i=0}^{k}\sum_{|\alpha|=i} \hat{f}(\alpha)^2 + 2\gamma_c(e^{\gamma_u(k+1)} - 1)\sum_{i=0}^{k}\sum_{|\alpha|=i} |\hat{f}(\alpha)|t^{i+1}$$

$$+\gamma_c^2 \sum_{i=0}^{k}\sum_{|\alpha|=i} t^{2i+2} + \sum_{\alpha \text{ s.th. } |\alpha|>k} \hat{f}(\alpha)^2$$

$$\leq (e^{\gamma_u(k+1)} - 1)^2 + 2\gamma_c(e^{\gamma_u(k+1)} - 1)e^{\gamma_u(k+1)}\left(\frac{1}{1-2\eta}\right)^{k+1}\sqrt{n^k}$$

$$+\gamma_c^2\left(\frac{1}{1-2\eta}\right)^{2k+2} e^{\gamma_u(2k+2)}n^k + \sum_{\alpha \text{ s.th. } |\alpha|>k} \hat{f}(\alpha)^2$$

Thus we get error $\left(\text{sign}\left(\sum_{\alpha \text{ s.th. } |\alpha|\leq k} c_\alpha t^{|\alpha|+1}\chi_\alpha(x)\right)\right) < \epsilon$ for any α s.th. $|\alpha| \leq k$, since $\gamma_u = \ln(1 + \sqrt{\epsilon}/2)/(k+1)$, $\gamma_c = ((1 - 2\eta)^{k+2}\sqrt{\epsilon})/(28n\sqrt{n^k})$ and $\sum_\alpha \hat{f}(\alpha)^2 \leq ((1 - 2\eta_0)\epsilon)/(28n)$ for any α s.th. $|\alpha| > k$. $\square$

Proof of Lemma 4 ([7], [8]). Consider the contraposition. If we assume that $\frac{1}{1-2\eta} - \gamma_u > t$, then

$$\sum_{i=0}^{k}\left(\sum_{|\alpha|=i} c_\alpha^2\right)t^{2i+2}$$

$$< \sum_{i=0}^{k}\sum_{|\alpha|=i}(1-2\eta)^{2i+2}\hat{f}(\alpha)^2 t^{2i+2} + 2\gamma_c\sum_{i=0}^{k}\sum_{|\alpha|=i}(1-2\eta)^{i+1}|\hat{f}(\alpha)|t^{2i+2}$$

$$+\gamma_c^2\sum_{i=0}^{k}\sum_{|\alpha|=i} t^{2i+2}$$

$$< (1-(1-2\eta_0)\gamma_u)^2\sum_{|\alpha|\leq k} \hat{f}(\alpha)^2$$

$$+2\gamma_c\left(\frac{1}{1-2\eta_0}\right)^{k+1}\sum_{i=0}^{k}\sum_{|\alpha|=i}|\hat{f}(\alpha)| + \gamma_c^2\left(\frac{1}{1-2\eta_0}\right)^{2k+2}$$

$$\leq (1 - (1 - 2\eta_0)\gamma_u)^2 + 2\gamma_c \left(\frac{1}{1 - 2\eta_0}\right)^{k+1} \sqrt{n^k} + \gamma_c^2 \left(\frac{1}{1 - 2\eta_0}\right)^{2k+2} n^k$$

$$\leq (1 - (1 - 2\eta_0)\gamma_u)^2 + \frac{3(1 - 2\eta_0)\sqrt{\epsilon}}{28n} \ .$$

$\square$

Decision Trees: More Theoretical Justification for Practical Algorithms

Amos Fiat[1] and Dmitry Pechyony[2][*][**]

[1] School of Computer Science, Tel Aviv University, Tel Aviv, Israel. fiat@tau.ac.il
[2] Department of Computer Science, Technion - Israel Institute of Technology, Haifa, Israel. pechyony@tx.technion.ac.il

Abstract. We study impurity-based decision tree algorithms such as CART, C4.5, *etc.*, so as to better understand their theoretical underpinnings. We consider such algorithms on special forms of functions and distributions. We deal with the uniform distribution and functions that can be described as a boolean linear threshold functions or a read-once DNF.

We show that for boolean linear threshold functions and read-once DNF, maximal purity gain and maximal influence are logically equivalent. This leads us to the exact identification of these classes of functions by impurity-based algorithms given sufficiently many noise-free examples. We show that the decision tree resulting from these algorithms has minimal size and height amongst all decision trees representing the function. Based on the statistical query learning model, we introduce the noise-tolerant version of practical decision tree algorithms. We show that if the input examples have small classification noise and are uniformly distributed, then all our results for practical noise-free impurity-based algorithms also hold for their noise-tolerant version.

1 Introduction

Introduced in 1983 by Breiman *et al.* [4], decision trees are one of the few knowledge representation schemes which are easily interpreted and may be inferred by very simple learning algorithms. The practical usage of decision trees is enormous (see [24] for a detailed survey). The most popular practical decision tree algorithms are CART [4], C4.5 [25] and their various modifications. The heart of these algorithms is the choice of splitting variables according to maximal purity gain value. To compute this value these algorithms use various impurity functions. For example, CART employs the Gini index impurity function and C4.5 uses an impurity function based on entropy. We refer to this family of algorithms as "impurity-based".

Despite practical success, most commonly used algorithms and systems for building decision trees lack strong theoretical basis. It would be interesting to

---

[*] The work was done while the author was M.Sc. student at Tel Aviv University.
[**] *Supported by the Deutsch Institute.*

obtain the bounds on the generalization errors and on the size of decision trees resulting from these algorithms given some predefined number of examples.

There have been several theoretical results justifying practical decision tree building algorithms. Kearns and Mansour showed in [19] that if the function, used for labelling nodes of tree, is a weak approximator of the target function then the impurity-based algorithms for building decision tree using Gini index, entropy or the new index are boosting algorithms. This property ensures distribution-free PAC learning and arbitrary small generalization error given sufficiently input examples. This work was recently extended by Takimoto and Maruoka [26] for functions having more than two values and by Kalai and Servedio [17] for noisy examples.

We restrict ourselves to the input of uniformly distributed examples. We provide new insight into practical impurity-based decision tree algorithms by showing that for unate boolean functions, the choice of splitting variable according to maximal exact purity gain is equivalent to the choice of variable according to the maximal influence. Then we introduce the algorithm **DTExactPG**, which is a modification of impurity-based algorithms that uses exact probabilities and purity gain rather that estimates. Let $f(x)$ be a read-once DNF or a boolean linear threshold function (LTF) and let h be the minimal depth of decision tree representing $f(x)$. The main results of our work are:

Theorem 1. *The algorithm **DTExactPG** builds a decision tree representing $f(x)$ and having minimal size amongst all decision trees representing $f(x)$. The resulting tree has also minimal height amongst all decision trees representing $f(x)$.*

Theorem 2. *For any $\delta > 0$, given $O\big(2^{9h} \ln^2 \frac{1}{\delta}\big) = poly(2^h, \ln \frac{1}{\delta})$ uniformly distributed noise-free random examples of $f(x)$, with probability at least $1-\delta$, CART and C4.5 build a decision tree computing $f(x)$ exactly. The resulting tree has minimal size and minimal height amongst all decision trees representing $f(x)$.*

Theorem 3. *For any $\delta > 0$, given $O\big(2^{9h} \ln^2 \frac{1}{\delta}\big) = poly(2^h, \ln \frac{1}{\delta})$ uniformly distributed random examples of $f(x)$ corrupted by classification noise with constant rate $\eta < 0.5$, with probability at least $1 - \delta$, a noise-tolerant version of impurity-based algorithms builds a decision tree representing $f(x)$. The resulting tree has minimal size and minimal height amongst all decision trees representing $f(x)$.*

Figure 1 summarizes the bounds on the size and height of decision trees, obtained in our work.

We stress that our primary concern is theoretical justification of practical algorithms. Thus our the results of learnability of read-once DNF and boolean LTF are not necessary optimal. This non-optimality stems mainly from inherent redundancy of decision tree representation of boolean functions.

1.1   Previous Work

Building in polynomial time a decision tree of minimal height or with a minimal number of nodes, consistent with all examples given, is NP-hard [15].

Function	Exact Influence	Exact Purity Gain	CART, C4.5, etc. $poly(2^h)$ uniform noise-free examples	Modification of CART, C4.5, etc., $poly(2^h)$ uniform examples with small classification noise
Boolean LTF	min size min height	min size min height	min size min height	min size min height
Read-once DNF	min size min height	min size min height	min size min height	min size min height

Fig. 1. Summary of bounds on decision trees, obtained in our work.

The single polynomial-time deterministic approximation algorithm, known today, for approximating the height of decision trees is the simple greedy algorithm [23], achieving the factor $O(\ln(m))$ (m is the number of input examples). Combining the results of [13] and [10], it can be shown that the depth of decision tree cannot be approximated within a factor $(1 - \epsilon)\ln(m)$ unless $NP \subseteq DTIME(n^{O(\log \log(n))})$. Hancock et al. showed in [12] that the problem of building a decision tree with a minimal number of nodes cannot be approximated within a factor $2^{\log^\delta \text{OPT}}$ for any $\delta < 1$, unless NP $\subset$ RTIME$[2^{poly \log n}]$. Blum et al. showed at [3] that decision trees cannot even be weakly learned in polynomial time from statistical queries dealing with uniformly distributed examples. This result is an evidence for the difficulty of PAC learning of decision trees of arbitrary functions in the noise-free and noisy settings.

Figure 2 summarizes the best results obtained by known theoretical algorithms for learning decision trees from noise-free examples. Many of them may be modified, to obtain corresponding noise-tolerant versions.

Kearns and Valiant [20] proved that distribution-free weak learning of read-once DNF using any representation is equivalent to several cryptographic problems widely believed to be hard. Mansour and Schain give in [22] the algorithm for proper PAC-learning of read-once DNF in polynomial time from random examples taken from any maximum entropy distribution. This algorithm may be easily modified to obtain polynomial-time probably correct learning in case the underlying function has a decision tree of logarithmic depth and input examples are uniformly distributed, matching the performance of our algorithm in this case. Using both membership and equivalence queries Angluin et al. showed in [1] a polynomial-time algorithm for exact identification of read-once DNF by read-once DNF using examples taken from any distribution.

Boolean linear threshold functions are polynomially properly PAC learnable from both noise-free examples (folk result) and examples with small classification noise [9]. In both cases the examples may be taken from any distribution.

1.2   Structure of the Paper

In Section 2 we give relevant definitions. In Section 3 we introduce a new algorithm for building decision trees using an oracle for influence and prove several properties of the resulting decision trees. In Section 4 we prove Theorem 1. In

Algorithm	Model, Distribution	Running Time	Hypothesis	Bounds on the Size of DT	Function Learned
Jackson and Servedio [16]	PAC, uniform	$poly(2^h)$	Decision Tree	none	almost any DNF
Impurity-Based Algorithms (Kearns and Mansour [19])	PAC, any	$poly((\frac{1}{\epsilon})^{\frac{c}{\gamma^2}})$	Decision Tree	none	any function satisfying Weak Hypothesis Assumption
Bshouty and Burroughs [5]	PAC, any	$poly(2^n)$	Decision Tree	at most min-sized DT representing the function	any
Kushilevitz and Mansour [21], Bshouty and Feldman [6], Bshouty et al. [7]	PAC, examples from uniform random walk	$poly(2^h)$	Fourier Series	N/A	any
Impurity-Based Algorithms (our work)	PC (exact, identification), uniform	$poly(2^h)$	Decision Tree	minimal size, minimal height	read-once DNF, boolean LTF

Fig. 2. Summary of decision tree noise-free learning algorithms.

Section 5 we prove Theorem 2. In Section 6 we introduce the noise-tolerant version of impurity-based algorithms and prove Theorem 3. In Section 7 we outline directions for further research.

2   Background

In this paper we use standard definitions of PAC [27] and statistical query [18] learning models. All our results are in the PAC model with zero generalization error. We denote this model by PC (Probably Correct).

A boolean function (*concept*) is defined as $f : \{0,1\}^n \to \{0,1\}$ (for boolean formulas, e.g. read-once DNF) or as $f : \{-1,1\}^n \to \{0,1\}$ (for arithmetic formulas, e.g. boolean linear threshold functions). Let x_i be the i-th variable or *attribute*. Let $x = (x_1, \ldots, x_n)$, and $f(x)$ be the *target* or *classification* of x. The vector $(x_1, x_2, \ldots, x_n, f(x))$, is called an *example*. Let $f_{x_i=a}(x)$, $a \in \{0,1\}$ be the function $f(x)$ restricted to $x_i = a$. We refer to the assignment $x_i = a$ as a *restriction*. Given the set of restrictions $R = \{x_{i_1} = a_1, \ldots, x_{i_k} = a_k\}$, the restricted function $f_R(x)$ is defined similarly. $x_i \in R$ iff there exists a restriction $x_i = a \in R$, where a is any value.

A *literal* $\tilde{x}_i$ is a boolean variable x_i itself or its negation $\bar{x}_i$. A *term* is a conjunction of literals and a *DNF (Disjunctive Normal Form) formula* is a dis-

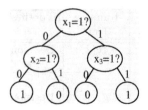

Fig. 3. Example of the decision tree representing $f(x) = x_1 x_3 \vee \overline{x_1} \overline{x_2}$

junction of terms. Let $|F|$ be the number of terms in the DNF formula F and $|t_i|$ be the number of literals in the term t_i. Essentially F is a set of terms $F = \{t_1, \ldots, t_{|F|}\}$ and t_i is a set of literals, $t_i = \{\tilde{x}_{i_1}, \ldots, \tilde{x}_{i_{|t_i|}}\}$. The term t_i is *satisfied* iff $\tilde{x}_{i_1} = \ldots = \tilde{x}_{i_{|t_i|}} = 1$.

If for all $1 \leq i \leq n$, $f(x)$ is monotone w.r.t. x_i or $\overline{x}_i$ then $f(x)$ is a *unate function*. A DNF is *read-once* if each variable appears at most once. Given a weight vector $\overrightarrow{a} = (a_1, \ldots, a_n)$, such that for all $1 \leq i \leq n$, $a_i \in \Re$, and a threshold $t \in \Re$, the boolean linear threshold function $f_{a,t}$ is $f_{a,t}(x) = \sum_{i=1}^{n} a_i x_i > t$. Both read-once DNF and boolean linear threshold function are unate functions.

Let e_i be the vector of n components, containing 1 in the i-th component and 0 in all other components. The *influence* of x_i on $f(x)$ under distribution $\mathcal{D}$ is $I_f(i) = \Pr_{x \sim \mathcal{D}}[f(x) \neq f(x \oplus e_i)]$. We use the notion of *influence oracle* as an auxiliary tool. The influence oracle runs in time $O(1)$ and returns the exact value of $I_f(i)$ for any f and i.

In our work we restrict ourselves to binary univariate decision trees for boolean functions. We use the standard definitions of *inner nodes*, *leaves* and *splitting variables* (see [25]). The left (right) son of inner node s is also called the 0-son (1-son) and is referred to as s_0 (s_1). Let $c(l)$ be the label of the leaf l. Upon arriving to the node s, we pass the input x to the $(x_i = 1?)$-son of s. The classification given to the input x by the T is denoted by $c_T(x)$. The path from the root to the node s corresponds to the set of restrictions of values of variables leading to s. Thus the node s corresponds to the restricted function $f_R(x)$. In the sequel we use the identifier s of the node and its corresponding restricted function interchangeably.

The *height* of T, $h(T)$, is the maximal length of path from the root to any node. The *size* of T, $|T|$, is the number of nodes in T. A decision tree T *represents* $f(x)$ iff $f(x) = c_T(x)$ for all x. An example of a decision tree is shown in Fig. 3. The function $\phi(x) : [0,1] \to \Re$ is an *impurity function* if it is concave, $\phi(x) = \phi(1-x)$ for any $x \in [0,1]$ and $\phi(0) = \phi(1) = 0$. Examples of impurity functions are the Gini index $\phi(x) = 4x(1-x)$ ([4]), the entropy function $\phi(x) = -x \log x - (1-x) \log(1-x)$ ([25]) and the new index $\phi(x) = 2\sqrt{x(1-x)}$ ([19]).

Let $s_a(i)$, $a \in \{0,1\}$, denote the a-son of s that would be created if x_i is placed at s as a splitting variable. For each node s let $\Pr[s_a(i)]$, $a \in \{0,1\}$, denote the probability that a random example from the uniform distribution arrives at $s_a(i)$ given that it has already arrived at s. Let $p(s)$ be the probability that an example arriving at s is positive. The *impurity sum* (IS) of x_i at s using impurity function $\phi(x)$ is $\text{IS}(s, x_i, \phi) = \Pr[s_0(i)]\phi(p(s_0(i))) + \Pr[s_1(i)]\phi(p(s_1(i)))$. The *purity gain*

DTApproxPG(s, X, R, ϕ)
1: **if** all examples arriving at s have the same classification **then**
2:    Set s as a leaf with that value.
3: **else**
4:    Choose $x_i = \arg\max_{x_i \in X}\{\widehat{PG}(f_R, x_i, \phi)\}$ to be a splitting variable.
5:    Run **DTApproxPG**$(s_1, X - \{x_i\}, R \cup \{x_i = 1\}, \phi)$.
6:    Run **DTApproxPG**$(s_0, X - \{x_i\}, R \cup \{x_i = 0\}, \phi)$.
7: **end if**

Fig. 4. DTApproxPG algorithm - generic structure of all impurity-based algorithms.

DTInfluence(s, X, R)
1: **if** $\forall x_i \in X, I_{f_R}(i) = 0$ **then**
2:    Set classification of s as a classification of any example arriving to it.
3: **else**
4:    Choose $x_i = \arg\max_{x_i \in X}\{I_{f_R}(i)\}$ to be a splitting variable.
5:    Run **DTInfluence**$(s_1, X - \{x_i\}, R \cup \{x_i = 1\})$.
6:    Run **DTInfluence**$(s_0, X = \{x_i\}, R \cup \{x_i = 0\})$.
7: **end if**

Fig. 5. DTInfluence algorithm.

(PG) of x_i at s is: $PG(s, x_i, \phi) = \phi(p(s)) - IS(s, x_i, \phi)$. The estimated values of all these quantities are $\widehat{PG}, \widehat{IS}$, etc. We say that the quantity A is estimated within accuracy $\alpha \geq 0$ if $A - \alpha < \hat{A} < A + \alpha$.

Since the value of $\phi(p(s))$ is attribute-independent, the choice of maximal $PG(s, x_i, \phi)$ is equivalent to the choice of minimal $IS(s, x_i, \phi)$. For uniformly distributed examples $\Pr[s_0(i)] = \Pr[s_1(i)] = 0.5$. Thus if impurity sum is computed exactly, then $\phi(p(s_0(i)))$ and $\phi(p(s_1(i)))$ have equal weight.

Figure 4 gives the structure of all impurity-based algorithms. The algorithm takes four parameters: s, identifying current tree's node, X, standing for the set of attributes available for testing, R, which is a set of function's restrictions leading to s and ϕ, identifying the impurity function. Initially s is set to the root node, X contains all attribute variables and R is an empty set.

3   Building Decision Trees Using an Influence Oracle

In this section we introduce a new algorithm, named **DTInfluence** (see Fig. 5), for building decision trees using an influence oracle. This algorithm greedily chooses the splitting variable with maximal influence. Clearly, the resulting tree consists of only relevant variables. The parameters of the algorithm have the same meaning as those of **DTApproxPG**.

Lemma 1. *Let $f(x)$ be any boolean function. Then the decision tree T built by the algorithm **DTInfluence** represents $f(x)$ and has no inner node such that all examples arriving at it have the same classification.*

Proof. See online full version [11].   □

DTMinTerm(s, F)

1: **if** $\exists\, t_i \in F$ such that $t_i = \emptyset$ **then**
2:    Set s as a positive leaf.
3: **else**
4:    **if** $F = \emptyset$ **then**
5:       Set s as a negative leaf.
6:    **else**
7:       Let $t_{min} = \arg\min_{t_i \in F}\{|t_i|\}$. $t_{min} = \{\tilde{x}_{m_1}, \tilde{x}_{m_2}, \ldots, \tilde{x}_{m_{|t_{min}|}}\}$.
8:       Choose any $\tilde{x}_{m_i} \in t_{min}$. Let $t'_{min} = t_{min} \setminus \{\tilde{x}_{m_i}\}$.
9:       **if** $\tilde{x}_{m_i} = x_{m_i}$ **then**
10:          Run **DTMinTerm**$(s_1, F\setminus\{t_{min}\} \cup \{t'_{min}\})$, **DTMinTerm**$(s_0, F\setminus\{t_{min}\})$.
11:       **else**
12:          Run **DTMinTerm**$(s_0, F\setminus\{t_{min}\} \cup \{t'_{min}\})$, **DTMinTerm**$(s_1, F\setminus\{t_{min}\})$.
13:       **end if**
14:    **end if**
15: **end if**

Fig. 6. DTMinTerm algorithm.

3.1   Read-Once DNF

Lemma 2. *For any $f(x)$, which can be represented as a read-once DNF, the decision tree, built by the algorithm **DTInfluence**, has minimal size and minimal height amongst all decision trees representing $f(x)$.*

The proof of Lemma 2 consists of two parts. In the first part of the proof we introduce the algorithm **DTMinTerm** (see Fig. 6) and prove Lemma 2 for it. In the second part of the proof we show that the trees built by **DTMinTerm** and **DTInfluence** are the same.

Assume we are given read-once DNF formula F. We change the algorithm **DTInfluence** so that the splitting rule is to choose any variable x_i in the smallest term $t_j \in F$. The algorithm stops when the restricted function becomes constant (true or false). The new algorithm, denoted by **DTMinTerm**, is shown in Fig. 6. The initial value of the first parameter of the algorithm is the same as in **DTInfluence**, and the second parameter is initially set to function's DNF formula F. The next two lemmata are proved in the full online version of the paper [11].

Lemma 3. *For any $f(x)$ which can be represented as a read-once DNF, the decision tree T, built by the algorithm **DTMinTerm**,*

1. *Represents $f(x)$.*
2. *Has no node such that all inputs arriving at it have the same classification.*
3. *Has minimal size and height amongst all decision trees representing $f(x)$.*

Lemma 4. *Let $x_l \in t_i$ and $x_m \in t_j$. Then $|t_i| > |t_j| \leftrightarrow I_f(l) < I_f(m)$.*

DTCoeff(s, X, t_s)

1: **if** $\sum_{x_i \in X} |a_i| \le t_s$ or $-\sum_{x_i \in X} |a_i| > t_s$ **then**
2:     The function is constant. s is a leaf.
3: **else**
4:     Choose a variable x_i from X, having the largest $|a_i|$.
5:     Run **DTCoeff**$(s_1, X - \{x_i\}, t_s - a_i)$ and **DTCoeff**$(s_0, X - \{x_i\}, t_s + a_i)$.
6: **end if**

Fig. 7. DTCoeff algorithm.

Proof (Lemma 2). It follows from Lemmata 1, 3 and 4 that the trees produced by the algorithms **DTMinTerm** and **DTInfluence** have the same size and height. Moreover, due to part 3 of Lemma 3, this size and height is minimal amongst all decision trees representing $f(x)$.   □

3.2 Boolean Linear Threshold Functions

Lemma 5. *For any linear threshold function $f_{a,t}(x)$, the decision tree built by the algorithm **DTInfluence** has minimal size and minimal height amongst all decision trees representing $f_{a,t}(x)$.*

The proof of the Lemma 5 consists of two parts. In the first part of the proof we introduce the algorithm **DTCoeff** (see Fig. 7) and prove Lemma 5 for it. In the second part of the proof we show that the trees built by **DTCoeff** and **DTInfluence** have the same size.

The difference between **DTCoeff** and **DTinfuence** is in the choice of splitting variable. **DTCoeff** chooses the variable with the largest $|a_i|$ and stops when the restricted function becomes constant (true or false). The meaning and initial values of the first two parameters of the algorithm are the same as in **DTInfluence**, and the third parameter is initially set to the function's threshold t. The following lemma is proved in the full online version of the paper [11]:

Lemma 6. *For any boolean LTF $f_{a,t}(x)$ the decision tree T, built by the algorithm **DTCoeff**:*

1. *Represents $f_{a,t}(x)$.*
2. *Has no node such that all inputs arriving at it have the same classification.*
3. *Has minimal size and height amongst all decision trees representing $f_{a,t}(x)$.*

We now prove a sequence of lemmata connecting the influence and the coefficients of variables in the threshold formula. Let x_i and x_j be two different variables in $f(x)$. For each of the 2^{n-2} possible assignments to the remaining variables we get a 4 row truth table for different values of x_i and x_j. Let $G(i, j)$ be the multi set of 2^{n-2} truth tables, indexed by the assignment to the other variables. I.e., G_w is the truth table where the other variables are assigned values $w = w_1, w_2, \ldots, w_{n-2}$. The structure of a single truth table is shown in Fig. 8. In this figure, and generally from now on, v and v' are constants in $\{-1, 1\}$. Observe that $I_f(i)$ is proportional to the sum over the 2^{n-2} G_w's in $G(i, j)$ of the number of times

x_i	x_j	other variables	function value
v	v'	$w_1, w_2, w_3, \ldots, w_{n-2}$	t_1
$-v$	v'	$w_1, w_2, w_3, \ldots, w_{n-2}$	t_2
v	$-v'$	$w_1, w_2, w_3, \ldots, w_{n-2}$	t_3
$-v$	$-v'$	$w_1, w_2, w_3, \ldots, w_{n-2}$	t_4

Fig. 8. Structure of the truth table G_w from $G(i, j)$.

$t_1 \neq t_2$ plus the number of times $t_3 \neq t_4$. Similarly, $I_f(j)$ is proportional to the sum over the 2^{n-2} G_w's in $G(i,j)$ of the number of times $t_1 \neq t_3$ plus the number of times $t_2 \neq t_4$. We use these observations in the proof of the following lemma (see online full version [11]):

Lemma 7. *If $I_f(i) > I_f(j)$ then $|a_i| > |a_j|$.*

Note that if $I_f(i) = I_f(j)$ then there may be any relation between $|a_i|$ and $|a_j|$. The next lemma shows that choosing the variables with the same influence in any order does not change the size of the resulting decision tree. For any node s, let X_s be the set of all variables in X which are untested on the path from the root to s. Let $\hat{X}(s) = \{x_1, \ldots x_k\}$ be the variables having the same non-zero influence, which in turn is the largest influence amongst the influences of variables in X_s.

Lemma 8. *Let T_i (T_j) be the smallest decision tree one may get when choosing any $x_i \in \hat{X}_s$ ($x_j \in \hat{X}_s$) at s. Let $|T_{opt}|$ be the size of the smallest tree rooted at s. Then $|T_i| = |T_j| = |T_{opt}|$.*

Proof. Here we give the brief version of the proof. The full version of the proof appears in the online version of the paper [11].

The proof is by induction on k. For $k = 1$ the lemma trivially holds. Assume the lemma holds for all $\ell < k$. Next we prove the lemma for k. Consider two attributes x_i and x_j from $\hat{X}(s)$ and possible values of targets in any truth table $G_w \in G(i, j)$. Since the underlying function is a boolean linear threshold and $I_f(i) = I_f(j)$, targets may have 4 forms:

- Type A. All rows in G_w have target value 0.
- Type B. All rows in G_w have target value 1.
- Type C. Target value f in G_w is defined as $f = (a_i x_i > 0 \text{ and } a_j x_j > 0)$.
- Type D. Target value f in G_w is defined as $f = (a_i x_i > 0 \text{ or } a_j x_j > 0)$.

Consider the smallest tree T testing x_i at s. There are 3 cases to be considered:

1. Both sons of x_i are leaves. Since $I_f(i) > 0$ and $I_f(j) > 0$ there exists at least one $G_w \in G(i, j)$ having a target of type C or D. Thus no neither x_i nor x_j cannot determine the function and this case is impossible.
2. Both sons of x_i are non-leaves. By the inductive hypothesis there exist right and left smallest subtrees of x_i, each one rooted with x_j. Then x_i and x_j may be interchanged to produce an equivalent decision tree T' testing x_j at s and having the same size.

DTExactPG(s, X, R, φ)
1: **if** all examples arriving at s have the same classification **then**
2:    Set s as a leaf with that value.
3: **else**
4:    Choose $x_i = \arg\max_{x_i \in X}\{PG(f_R, x_i, \phi)\}$ to be a splitting variable.
5:    Run **DTExactPG**$(s_1, X - \{x_i\}, R \cup \{x_i = 1\}, \phi)$.
6:    Run **DTExactPG**$(s_0, X - \{x_i\}, R \cup \{x_i = 0\}, \phi)$.
7: **end if**

Fig. 9. DTExactPG algorithm.

3. Exactly one of the sons of x_i is a leaf.

Let us consider the third case. By the inductive hypothesis the non-leaf son of s tests x_j. It is not hard to see that in this case $G(i, j)$ contains either truth tables with targets of type A and C or truth tables with targets of type B and D (otherwise both sons of x_i are non-leaves). In both these cases some value of x_j determines the value of the function. Therefore if we place the test $x_j = 1$? at s, then exactly one of its sons is a leaf. Thus it can be easily verified that testing x_j and then x_i, or testing x_i, and then x_j results in a tree of the same size (see [11]).   □

Proof (Lemma 5). One can prove an analogous result for Lemma 8, dealing with the height rather than size. Combining this result with Lemmata 1, 6, 7 and 8 we obtain that the trees built by **DTInfluence** and **DTCoeff** have the same size and height. Moreover, due to part 3 of Lemma 6, these size and height are minimal amongst all decision trees representing $f_{a,t}(x)$.   □

4   Optimality of Exact Purity Gain

In this section we introduce a new algorithm for building decision trees, named **DTExactPG**, (see Fig. 9) using exact values of purity gain. The next lemma follows directly from the definition ofthe algorithm:

Lemma 9. *Let $f(x)$ be any boolean function. Then the decision tree T built by the algorithm **DTExactPG** represents $f(x)$ and there exists no inner node such that all inputs arriving at it have the same classification.*

Lemma 10. *For any boolean function $f(x)$, uniformly distributed x, and any node s, $p(s_0(i))$ and $p(s_1(i))$ are symmetric relative to $p(s)$: $|p(s_1(i)) - p(s)| = |p(s_0(i)) - p(s)|$ and $p(s_1(i)) \neq p(s_0(i))$.*

Proof. See online full version of the paper [11].   □

Lemma 11. *For any unate boolean function $f(x)$, uniformly distributed input x, and any impurity function ϕ, $I_f(i) > I_f(j) \leftrightarrow PG(f, x_i, \phi) > PG(f, x_j, \phi)$.*

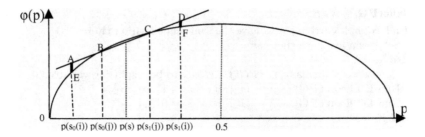

Fig. 10. Comparison of impurity sum of x_i and x_j

Proof. Since x is distributed uniformly, it is sufficient to prove $I_f(i) > I_f(j) \leftrightarrow$ $BIS(f, x_i, \phi) < BIS(f, x_j, \phi)$. Let d_i be number of pairs of examples differing only in x_i and having different target value. Since all examples have equal probability $I_f(i) = \frac{d_i}{2^n-1}$. Consider a split of node s according to x_i. All positive examples arriving at s may be divided into two categories:

1. Flipping the value of i-th attribute does not change the target value of example. Then the first half of such positive examples passes to s_1 and the second half passes to s_0. Consequently such positive examples contribute equally to the probabilities of positive examples in s_1 and s_0.
2. Flipping the value of i-th attribute changes the target value of example. Consider such pair of positive and negative examples, differing only in x_i. Since $f(x)$ is unate, either all positive example in such pairs have $x_i = 1$ and all negative examples in such pairs have $x_i = 0$, or vice versa. Consequently either all such positive examples pass either to s_1 or to s_0. Thus such examples increase the probability of positive examples in one of the nodes $\{s_1, s_0\}$ and decrease the probability of positive examples in the other.

The number of positive examples in the second category is d_i. Thus $I_f(i) > I_f(j) \leftrightarrow \max\{p(s_1(i)), p(s_0(i))\} > \max\{p(s_1(j)), p(s_0(j))\}$. By Lemma 10, if $\max\{p(s_1(i)), p(s_0(i))\} > \max\{p(s_1(j)), p(s_0(j))\}$ then the probabilities of x_i are more distant from $p(s)$ than those of x_j.

Figure 10 depicts one of the possible variants of reciprocal configuration of $p(s_1(i))$, $p(s_0(i))$, $p(s_1(j))$, $p(s_0(j))$ and $p(s)$, when all these probabilities are less than 0.5. Let $\phi(A)$ be the value of impurity function at point A. Then $BIS(f, x_j, \phi) = \phi(p(s_1(j))) + \phi(p(s_0(j))) = \phi(B) + \phi(C) = \phi(A) + \phi(D) > \phi(E) + \phi(F) = BIS(f, x_i, \phi)$. Note that the last inequality holds due to concavity of impurity function. The rest of the cases of reciprocal configurations of probabilities and 0.5 may be proved similarly. □

Proof (Theorem 1). Follows from combining Lemmata 1, 9, 11, 2 and 5. □

5   Optimality of Approximate Purity Gain

The purity gain computed by practical algorithms is not exact. However, under some conditions, approximate purity gain suffices. The proof of this result (which

DTStatQuery(s, X, R, ϕ, h)

1: **if** $\widehat{\Pr}[f_R = 1]\left(\frac{1}{2 \cdot 2^h}\right) > 1 - \frac{1}{2 \cdot 2^h}$ **then**
2:    Set s as a positive leaf.
3: **else**
4:    **if** $\widehat{\Pr}[f_R = 1]\left(\frac{1}{2 \cdot 2^h}\right) < \frac{1}{2 \cdot 2^h}$ **then**
5:       Set s as a negative leaf.
6:    **else**
7:       Choose $x_i = \arg\max_{x_i \in X}\{\widehat{PG}(f_R, x_i, \phi, \frac{1}{4 \cdot 2^{4h}})\}$ to be a splitting variable.
8:       Run **DTStatQuery**$(s_1, X - \{x_i\}, R \cup \{x_i = 1\}, \phi, h)$.
9:       Run **DTStatQuery**$(s_0, X - \{x_i\}, R \cup \{x_i = 0\}, \phi, h)$.
10:    **end if**
11: **end if**

Fig. 11. DTStatQuery algorithm. h is a minimal height of decision tree representing the function.

is essentially Theorem 2) is very technical and is based on the following lemmata (proved in the full online version of the paper [11]):

Lemma 12. *Let $f(x)$ be a boolean function, which can be represented by decision tree of depth h. Suppose x is distributed uniformly. Then* $\Pr(f(x) = 1) = \frac{r}{2^h}$, $r \in \mathbb{Z}$, $0 \le r \le 2^h$.

Lemma 13. *Let $\phi(x)$ be Gini index or the entropy or the new index impurity function. If for all $1 \le i \le n$ and all inner nodes s, the probabilities $\hat{p}(s_0(i))$, $\hat{p}(s_1(i))$, $\widehat{\Pr}[s_0(i)]$ and $\widehat{\Pr}[s_1(i)]$ are computed within accuracy $\epsilon = \frac{1}{4 \cdot 2^{4h}}$ then*

$$\widehat{IS}(s, x_i, \phi) > \widehat{IS}(s, x_j, \phi) \Leftrightarrow IS(s, x_i, \phi) > IS(s, x_j, \phi)$$

Proof (Theorem 2). Sketch. Follows from combining Lemma 13, Theorem 1, Hoeffding [14] and Chernoff [8] bounds. See [11] for the complete proof.   □

6   Noise-Tolerant Probably Correct Learning

In this section we assume that each input example is misclassified with probability $\eta < 0.5$. Since our noise-free algorithms learn probably correctly, we would like to obtain the same results of probable correctness with noisy examples. Our definition of PC learning with noise is that the examples are noisy yet, nonetheless, we insist upon zero generalization error. Previous learning algorithms with noise (e.g. [2] and [18]) require a non-zero generalization error.

   We introduce the algorithm **DTStatQuery**, which is a reformulation of the algorithm **DTApproxPG** in terms of statistical queries. [2] and [18] show how to simulate statistical queries from examples corrupted by small classification noise. We obtain our results by adapting this simulation to the case of PC learning and combining it with **DTStatQuery** algorithm.

Let $\widehat{\Pr}[f_R = 1](\alpha)$ be the estimation of probability $\Pr[f_R = 1](\alpha)$ within accuracy α. Thus $\widehat{\Pr}[f_R = 1](\alpha)$ is also a *statistical query* [18] of the predicate $f_R = 1$, computed within accuracy α. We refer to the computation of approximate purity gain, using the calls to statistical queries within accuracy α, as $\widehat{PG}(f_R, x_i, \phi, \alpha)$. The algorithm **DTStatQuery** is shown at Fig. 11.

Lemma 14. *Let $f(x)$ be a read-once DNF or a boolean linear threshold function. Then, for any impurity function, the decision tree, built by the algorithm **DTStatQuery**, represents $f(x)$ and has minimal size and minimal height amongst all decision trees representing $f(x)$.*

Proof. Sketch. Follows from Lemma 12 and Theorem 2. See [11] for the complete proof . $\square$

Kearns shows in [18] how to simulate statistical queries from examples corrupted by small classification noise. [1] This simulation involves the estimation of noise rate η. [18] shows that if statistical queries need to be computed within accuracy α then η should be estimated within accuracy $\Delta/2 = \Theta(\alpha)$. Such an estimation may be obtained by taking $\lceil \frac{1}{2\Delta} \rceil$ estimations of η of the form $i\Delta$, $i = 0, 1, \ldots, \lceil \frac{1}{2\Delta} \rceil$. Running the learning algorithm using each time different estimation we obtain $\lceil \frac{1}{2\Delta} \rceil + 1$ hypotheses $h_0, h_1, \ldots, h_{\lceil \frac{1}{2\Delta} \rceil}$. By the definition of Δ, amongst these hypotheses there exists at least one hypothesis h_j having the same generalization error as the statistical query algorithm. Then [18] describes a procedure how to recognize the hypothesis having generalization error of at most ϵ. The naïve approach to recognize the minimal sized decision tree having zero generalization error amongst $h_0, \ldots, h_{\lceil \frac{1}{2\Delta} \rceil}$ is to apply the procedure of [18] with $\epsilon = \frac{1}{2 \cdot 2^n}$. However in this case this procedure requires about 2^n noisy examples. Next we show how to recognize minimal size decision tree with zero generalization error using only $poly(2^h)$ uniformly distributed noisy examples.

Amongst $\lceil \frac{1}{2\Delta} \rceil$ estimations $\hat{\eta}_i = i\Delta$ of η there exists $i = j$ such that $|\eta - j\Delta| \leq \Delta/2$. Our current goal is to recognize such j.

Let $\gamma_i = \Pr_{EX^\eta(\mathcal{U})}[h_i(x) \neq f(x)]$ be the generalization error of h_i over the space of uniformly distributed noisy examples. Clearly, $\gamma_i \geq \eta$ for all i, and $\gamma_j = \eta$. Let $\hat{\gamma}_i$ be the estimation of γ within accuracy $\Delta/4$. Then $|\gamma_j - j\Delta| < \frac{3\Delta}{4}$. Let $H = \{i \mid |\hat{\gamma}_i - i\Delta| < \frac{3\Delta}{4}\}$. Clearly $j \in H$. Therefore if $|H| = 1$ then H contains only j. Consider the case of $|H| > 1$. Since for all i $\gamma_i \geq \eta$, if $i \in H$ then $i \geq j-1$. Therefore one of the two minimal values in H is j. Let i_1 and i_2 be two minimal values in H. If h_{i_1} and h_{i_2} are the same tree then clearly they are the one with smallest size representing the function. If $|i_1 - i_2| > 1$ then, using the argument $i \in H \to i \geq j-1$, we get that $j = \min\{i_1, i_2\}$. If $|i_1 - i_2| = 1$ and $|\hat{\gamma}_{i_1} - \hat{\gamma}_{i_2}| \geq \frac{\Delta}{2}$, then, since the accuracy of $\hat{\gamma}$ is $\Delta/4$, $j = \min\{i_1, i_2\}$. The final subcase to be

---

[1] Aslam and Decatur show in [2] more efficient procedure for simulation of statistical queries from noisy examples. However their procedure needs the same adaptation to PC learning model as that of Kearns [18]. For the sake of simplicity we show here the adaptation to PC model with the procedure of [18]. The procedure of [2] may be adapted to PC model in the similar manner.

considered is $|\hat{\gamma}_{i_1} - \hat{\gamma}_{i_2}| < \frac{\Delta}{2}$ and $|i_1 - i_2| = 1$. In this case $\hat{\eta} = (\hat{\gamma}_{i_1} + \hat{\gamma}_{i_2})/2$ estimates the true value of η within accuracy $\Delta/2$. Thus running the learning algorithm with the value $\hat{\eta}$ for noise rate produces the same tree as the one produced by statistical query algorithm.

It can be shown that to simulate statistical queries and recognize hypothesis with zero generalization error all estimations should be done within accuracy $poly(\frac{1}{2^h})$. Thus the sample complexity of the algorithm **DTNoiseTolerant** is the same as in **DTApproxPG**. Consequently, Theorem 3 follows.

7   Directions for Future Research

Basing on our results, the following open problems may be attacked:

1. **Extension to other types of functions.** In particular we conjecture that for all unate functions the algorithm **DTExactPG** builds minimal depth decision trees and the size of the resulting trees is not far from minimal.
2. **Extension to other distributions**. It may be verified that all our results hold for constant product distributions ($\forall i \; \Pr[x_i = 1] = c$) and does not hold for general product distributions ($\forall i \; \Pr[x_i = 1] = c_i$).
3. **Small number of examples.** The really interesting case is when number of examples is less than $poly(2^h)$. In this case nothing is known about the size and the depth of the resulting decision tree.

Moreover we would like to compare our noise-tolerant version of impurity-based algorithms *vs.* pruning methods. Finally, since influence and impurity gain are logically equivalent, it would be interesting to use the notion of purity gain in the field of analysis of boolean functions.

Acknowledgements. We thank Yishay Mansour for his great help with all aspects of this paper. We also thank Adam Smith who greatly simplified and generalized an earlier version of Theorem 1. We are grateful to Rocco Servedio for pointing us an error in the earlier version of the paper.

References

[1] D. Angluin, L. Hellerstein and M. Karpinski. Learning Read-Once Formulas with Queries. *Journal of the ACM*, 40(1):185-210, 1993.

[2] J.A. Aslam and S.E. Decatur. Specification and Simulation of Statistical Query Algorithms for Efficiency and Noice Tolerance. *Journal of Computer and System Sciences*, 56(2):191-208, 1998.

[3] A. Blum, M. Furst, J. Jackson, M. Kearns, Y. Mansour and S. Rudich. Weakly Learning DNF and Characterizing Statistical Query Learning Using Fourier Analysis. In *Proceedings of the 26th Annual ACM Symposium on the Theory of Computing*, pages 253-262, 1994.

[4] L. Breiman, J.H. Friedman, R.A. Olshen and C.J. Stone. *Classification and Regression Trees*. Wadsworth International Group, 1984.

[5] N.H. Bshouty and L. Burroughs. On the Proper Learning of Axis-Parallel Concepts. *Journal of Machine Learning Research*, 4:157-176, 2003.

[6] N.H. Bshouty and V. Feldman. On Using Extended Statistical Queries to Avoid Membership Queries. *Journal of Machine Learning Research*, 2:359-395, 2002.

[7] N.H. Bshouty, E. Mossel, R. O'Donnel and R.A. Servedio. Learning DNF from Random Walks. In *Proceedings of the 44th Annual Symposium on Foundations of Computer Science*, 2003.

[8] H. Chernoff. A Measure of Asymptotic Efficiency for Tests of a Hypothesis Based on the Sum of Observations. *Annals of Mathematical Statistics*, 23:493-509, 1952.

[9] E. Cohen. Learning Noisy Perceptron by a Perceptron in Polynomial Time. In *Proceedings of the 38th Annual Symposium on Foundations of Computer Science*, pages 514-523, 1997.

[10] U. Feige. A Threshold of $\ln n$ for Approximating Set Cover. *Journal of the ACM* 45(4):634-652, 1998.

[11] A. Fiat and D. Pechyony. Decision Trees: More Theoretical Justification for Practical Algorithms. Available at
http://www.cs.tau.ac.il/~fiat/cart_justification_full.ps

[12] T. Hancock, T. Jiang, M. Li and J. Tromp. Lower bounds on Learning Decision Trees and Lists. *Information and Computation*, 126(2):114-122, 1996.

[13] D. Haussler. Quantifying Inductive Bias: AI Learning Algorithms and Valiant's Learning Framework. *Artificial Intelligence*, 36(2): 177-221, 1988.

[14] W. Hoeffding. Probability Inequalities for Sums of Bounded Random Variables. *Journal of the American Statistical Association*, 58:13-30, 1963.

[15] L. Hyafil and R.L. Rivest. Constructing Optimal Binary Decision Trees is NP-Complete. *Information Processing Letters*, 5:15-17, 1976.

[16] J. Jackson, R.A. Servedio. Learning Random Log-Depth Decision Trees under the Uniform Distribution. In *Proceedings of the 16th Annual Conference on Computational Learning Theory*, pages 610-624, 2003.

[17] A. Kalai and R.A. Servedio. Boosting in the Presence of Noise. In *Proceedings of the 35th Annual Symposium on the Theory of Computing*, pages 195-205, 2003.

[18] M.J. Kearns. Efficient Noise-Tolerant Learning from Statistical Queries. *Journal of the ACM*, 45(6):983-1006, 1998.

[19] M.J. Kearns and Y. Mansour. On the Boosting Ability of Top-Down Decision Tree Learning Algorithms. *Journal of Computer and Systems Sciences*, 58(1):109-128, 1999.

[20] M.J. Kearns, L.G. Valiant. Cryptographic Limitations on Learning Boolean Formulae and Finite Automata. *Journal of the ACM*, 41(1):67-95, 1994.

[21] E. Kushilevitz and Y. Mansour. Learning Decision Trees using the Fourier Spectrum. *SIAM Journal on Computing*, 22(6):1331-1348, 1993.

[22] Y. Mansour and M. Schain. Learning with Maximum-Entropy Distributions. *Machine Learning*, 45(2):123-145, 2001.

[23] M. Moshkov. Approximate Algorithm for Minimization of Decision Tree Depth. In *Proceedings of 9th International Conference on Rough Sets, Fuzzy Sets, Data Mining and Granular Computing*, pages 611-614, 2003.

[24] S.K. Murthy. Automatic Construction of Decision Trees from Data: A Multi-Disciplinary Survey. *Data Mining and Knowledge Discovery*, 2(4): 345-389, 1998.

[25] J.R. Quinlan. *C4.5: Programs for Machine Learning*. Morgan Kaufmann, 1993.

[26] E. Takimoto and A. Maruoka. Top-Down Decision Tree Learning as Information Based Boosting. *Theoretical Computer Science*, 292:447-464, 2003.

[27] L.G. Valiant. A Theory of the Learnable. *Communications of the ACM*, 27(11):1134-1142, 1984.

Application of Classical Nonparametric Predictors to Learning Conditionally I.I.D. Data

Daniil Ryabko

Computer Learning Research Centre,
Royal Holloway, University of London,
Egham Hill, Egham, TW20 0EX
daniil@cs.rhul.ac.uk

Abstract. In this work we consider the task of pattern recognition under the assumption that examples are conditionally independent. Pattern recognition is predicting a sequence of labels based on objects given for each label and on examples (pairs of objects and labels) learned so far. Traditionally, this task is considered under the assumption that examples are independent and identically distributed (i.i.d). We show that some classical nonparametric predictors originally developed to work under the (strict) i.i.d. assumption, retain their consistency under a weaker assumption of conditional independence. By conditional independence we mean that objects are distributed identically and independently given their labels, while the only condition on the distribution of labels is that the rate of occurrence of each label does not tend to zero. The predictors we consider are partitioning and nearest neighbour estimates.

1   Introduction

Pattern recognition (or classification) is, informally, the following task. There is a finite number of classes of some complex objects. A predictor is learning to label objects according to the class they belong to (i.e. to classify), based only on some examples (labeled objects). One of the typical practical examples is recognition of a hand-written text. In this case, an object is a hand-written letter and a label is the letter of an alphabet it denotes. Another example is recognising some illness in a patient. An object here is the set of symptoms of a patient, and the classes are those of normal and ill.

The formal model of the task used most widely is described, for example, in [10], and can be briefly introduced as follows. The objects $x \in \mathbf{X}$ are drawn independently and identically distributed (i.i.d.) according to some unknown (but fixed) probability distribution P on $\mathbf{X}$. The labels $y \in \mathbf{Y}$ are given for each object according to some (also unknown but fixed) function $\eta(x)$[1]. The space

---

[1] Often (e.g. in [10]) a more general situation is considered, the labels are drawn according to some probability distribution $P(y|x)$, i.e. each object can have more than one possible label.

S. Ben-David, J. Case, A. Maruoka (Eds.): ALT 2004, LNAI 3244, pp. 171–180, 2004.
© Springer-Verlag Berlin Heidelberg 2004

Y of labels is assumed to be finite (often binary). The task is to construct the best predictor for the labels, based on the observed data, i.e. actually to "learn" $\eta(x)$.

This theoretical model fits many practical applications; however, the i.i.d. assumption is often violated in practice, although the object-label dependence is preserved, and so the pattern recognition methods seem to be applicable. Consider the following situation. Suppose we are trying to recognise a hand-written text. Obviously, letters in the text are dependent (for example, we strongly expect to meet "u" after "q"). Does it mean that we can not use pattern recognition methods developed within the i.i.d. model for the text recognition task? No, we can shuffle the letters of the text and then use those methods. But will the results of recognition change significantly if we do not shuffle the letters? It is intuitively clear that the answer is negative; it is intuitively clear if we are having in mind nearly any popular pattern recognition method. Moreover, in online tasks it is often not possible to permute the examples, and so the question is not idle.

In [9] another model for pattern recognition was proposed, which aims to overcome this obstacle. In this model, the i.i.d. assumption is replaced by the following.

The labels $y \in \mathbf{Y}$ are drawn according to some unknown (but fixed) distribution $\mathbf{P}(y)$, where $\mathbf{P}$ is a distribution over the set of all infinite sequences of labels. There can be any type of dependence between labels; moreover, we can assume that we are dealing with any (fixed) combinatorial sequence of labels. However, in this sequence the rate of occurrence of each label should keep above some positive threshold. For each label the corresponding object $x \in \mathbf{X}$ is generated according to some (unknown but fixed) probability distribution $P(x|y)$. The (deterministic) relation $y = \eta(x)$ for some function η is still required to hold. This model for pattern recognition is called *conditional (i.i.d.) model*.

In [9] some methods are developed to estimate the performance of pattern recognition methods in the conditional i.i.d. model.

In this paper we adapt these methods to the task of studying weak (universal) consistency, and prove that certain methods which are known to be consistent in the i.i.d. model, are consistent in the conditional model. More precisely, a predictor is called (universally) consistent if the probability of its error tends to zero for any i.i.d. distribution. In particular, partitioning and nearest neighbour estimates are universally consistent. We show that they are consistent in the conditional model, i.e. the probability of error tends to zero for any distribution satisfying the assumptions of the conditional model.

Various attempts to relaxing i.i.d. assumption in learning tasks have been proposed in the literature. Thus, in [6], [7] the authors study the nearest neighbour and kernel estimators for the task of regression estimation with continuous regression function, under the assumption that labels are conditionally independent of data given their objects. In [5] is presented a generalisation of PAC approach to Markov chains with finite or countable state space. In [1] and [8] the authors study the task of predicting a stationary and ergodic sequences, and construct a weakly consistent predictor.

The approach proposed in [9] and developed in the present paper differs from those mentioned above in that we do not construct a predictor for some particular model, but rather develop a framework to extend results about any predictor from the classical model to the proposed one. We then apply the results to different well-studied predictors.

2   Main Results

Consider a sequence of *examples* $(x_1, y_1), (x_2, y_2), \ldots$; each example $z_i := (x_i, y_i)$ consists of an *object* $x_i \in \mathbf{X}$ and a *label* $y_i := \eta(x_i) \in \mathbf{Y}$, where $\mathbf{X} = \mathbb{R}^d$ for some $d \in \mathbb{N}$ is called an *object space*, $\mathbf{Y} := \{0, 1\}$ is called a *label space* and $\eta : \mathbf{X} \to \mathbf{Y}$ is some deterministic function. For simplicity we made the assumption that the space $\mathbf{Y}$ is binary, but all results easily extend to the case of any finite space $\mathbf{Y}$. The notation $\mathbf{Z} := \mathbf{X} \times \mathbf{Y}$ is used for the measurable space of examples. Objects are drawn according to some probability distribution $\mathbf{P}$ on $\mathbf{X}^\infty$ (and labels are defined by η).

The notation $\mathbf{P}$ is used for distributions on $\mathbf{X}^\infty$ while the symbol P is reserved for distributions on $\mathbf{X}$. In the latter case P^∞ denotes the i.i.d. distribution on $\mathbf{X}^\infty$ generated by P.

Examples drawn according to a distribution $\mathbf{P}$ are called *conditionally i.i.d.* if $y_n = \eta(x_n)$ for some function η on $\mathbf{X}$ and each n, and if $\mathbf{P}$ satisfies the following two conditions.

First, for any $n \in \mathbb{N}$

$$\mathbf{P}(x_n \in A \mid y_n, z_1, \ldots, z_{n-1}) = \mathbf{P}(x_n \in A \mid y_n), \tag{1}$$

where A is any measurable set (an event) in $\mathbf{X}$. In other words, x_n is conditionally independent of $x_1, \ldots, x_{n-1}$ given y_n (on conditional independence see [2]).

Second, for any $y \in \mathbf{Y}$, for any $n_1, n_2 \in \mathbb{N}$ and for any event A in $\mathbf{X}$

$$\mathbf{P}(x_{n_1} \in A \mid y_{n_1} = y) = \mathbf{P}(x_{n_2} \in A \mid y_{n_2} = y). \tag{2}$$

Less formally, these conditions can be reformulated as follows. Assume that we have some sequence $(y_n)_{n \in \mathbb{N}}$ of labels and two probability distributions P_0 and P_1 on $\mathbf{X}$. Each example $x_n \in \mathbf{X}$ is drawn according to the distribution P_{y_n}; examples are drawn independently of each other.

Apart from the above two conditions we will need also a condition on the frequencies of labels. For any sequence of examples $z_1, z_2, \ldots$ denote $p(n) = \frac{1}{n} \#\{i \leq n : y_i = 1\}$. We say that the rates of occurrence of the labels are bounded from below if there exist such δ, $0 < \delta < 1/2$ that

$$\lim_{n \to \infty} \mathbf{P}(p(n) \in [\delta, 1 - \delta]) = 1. \tag{3}$$

A *predictor* is a measurable function $\Gamma(x_1, y_1, \ldots, x_{n-1}, y_{n-1}, x)$ taking values in $\mathbf{Y}$. Denote $\Gamma_n := \Gamma(x_1, y_1, \ldots, x_{n-1}, y_{n-1}, x)$.

The probability of an error of a predictor Γ on each step n is defined as

$$\mathrm{err}_n(\Gamma, \mathbf{P}, z_1, \ldots, z_{n-1}) := \mathbf{P}\{(x, y) \in \mathbf{Z} \mid y \neq \Gamma_n(z_1, \ldots, z_{n-1}, x)\}$$

(Here $\mathbf{P}$ in the list of arguments of err_n is understood as a distribution conditional on $z_1, \ldots, z_{n-1}$.) We will often use a shorter notation $\mathrm{err}_n(\Gamma, \mathbf{P})$ in place of $\mathrm{err}_n(\Gamma, \mathbf{P}, z_1, \ldots, z_{n-1})$.

In this paper we will consider two type of predictors: partitioning and nearest neighbour classifiers.

The nearest neighbour predictor assigns to a new object x the label of its nearest neighbour among $x_1, \ldots, x_n$:

$$\Gamma_n(x_1, y_1, \ldots, x_{n-1}, y_{n-1}, x) = y_j,$$

where $j = \mathrm{argmin}_{i=1,\ldots,n-1} \|x - x_i\|$.

For i.i.d. distributions this predictor is also consistent, i.e. $E(\mathrm{err}_n(\Gamma, P^\infty)) \to 0$, for any distribution P on $\mathbf{X}$, see [3].

We generalise this result as follows.

Theorem 1. *Let Γ be the nearest neighbour classifier. Let $\mathbf{P}$ be some distribution on $\mathbf{X}^\infty$ satisfying (1), (2) and (3). Then*

$$E(\mathrm{err}_n(\Gamma, \mathbf{P})) \to 0.$$

A partitioning predictor on each step n partitions the object space $\mathbb{R}^d$, $d \in \mathbb{N}$ into disjoint cells $A_1^n, A_2^n, \ldots$ and classifies in each cell according to the majority vote:

$$\Gamma_n(z_1, \ldots, z_{n-1}, x) = \begin{cases} 0 \text{ if } \sum_{i=1}^n I_{y_i=1} I_{x_i \in A(x)} \leq \sum_{i=1}^n I_{y_i=0} I_{x_i \in A(x)} \\ 1 \text{ otherwise,} \end{cases}$$

where $A(x)$ denotes the cell containing x. Denote $\mathrm{diam}(A) = \sup_{x,y \in A} \|x - y\|$ and $N(x) = \sum_{i=1}^n I_{x_i \in A(x)}$.

It is a well known result (see, e.g. [4]) that a partitioning predictor is weakly consistent, provided certain regulatory conditions on the size of cells. More precisely, let Γ be a partitioning predictor such that $\mathrm{diam}(A(X)) \to 0$ in probability and $N(X) \to \infty$ in probability. Then for any distribution P on $\mathbf{X}$

$$E(\mathrm{err}_n(\Gamma, P^\infty)) \to 0.$$

We generalise this result to the case of conditionally i.i.d. examples as follows.

Theorem 2. *Let Γ be a partitioning predictor such that $\mathrm{diam}(A(X)) \to 0$ in probability and $N(X) \to \infty$ in probability, for any distribution generating i.i.d. examples. Then*

$$E(\mathrm{err}_n(\Gamma, \mathbf{P})) \to 0.$$

for any distribution $\mathbf{P}$ on $\mathbf{X}^\infty$ satisfying (1), (2) and (3).

The proof of the two theorems above is based on the results of paper [9], which allow to construct estimates of the probability of an error in conditionally i.i.d. model based on the estimates in the i.i.d. model.

The details can be found in Section 4.

3   Discussion

In this work we have generalised certain consistency results to the model where the i.i.d. assumption is replaced by weaker conditions. It can be questioned whether these new assumptions are necessary, i.e. can our consistency results be generalised yet more in the same direction. In particular, the assumption (3) might appear redundant: if the rate of occurrence of some label tends to zero, can we just ignore this label without affecting the asymptotic?

It appears that this is not the case, as the following example illustrates. Let $\mathbf{X} = [0, 1]$, let $\eta(x) = 0$ if x is rational and $\eta(x) = 1$ otherwise. The distribution P_1 is uniform on the set of irrational numbers, while P_0 is any distribution such that $P(x) \neq 0$ for any rational x. The nearest neighbour predictor is consistent for any i.i.d. distribution which agrees with the definition, i.e. for any $p = P(y = 1) \in [0, 1]$. (This construction is due to T. Cover.) Next we construct a distribution $\mathbf{P}$ on $\mathbf{X}^\infty$ which satisfies assumptions (1) and (2) but for which the nearest neighbour predictor Γ is not consistent.

Fix some δ, $0 < \delta < 1$. Assume that according to $\mathbf{P}$ the first label is always 1, (i.e. $\mathbf{P}(y_1 = 1) = 1$; the object is an irrational number). Next k_1 labels are always 0 (rationals), then follows 1, then k_2 zeros, and so on. It easy to check that there exists such sequence $k_1, k_2, \ldots$ that with probability at least δ for each n and for each irrational $x \in x_1, \ldots, x_n$ each irrational is between two rationals and

$$\min_{i,j \leq n, \; x \text{ is between rational } x_i \text{ and } x_j} |x_i - x_j| \leq \frac{1 - \delta}{m(n)},$$

where $m(n)$ is the total number of rational objects up to the trial n. On each step n such that $n = t + \sum_{j=1}^{t-1} k_t$ for some $t \in \mathbb{N}$ (i.e. on each irrational object) we have

$$E(\mathrm{err}_n(\Gamma, \mathbf{P})) \geq \delta(1 - \sum_{j<n, \; x_j \text{ is irrational}} \mathbf{P}(x_j \text{ is the nearest neighbour of } x)) = \delta^2$$

As irrational objects are generated infinitely often (that is, with intervals k_i), the probability of error does not tend to zero.

4   Proofs

The *tolerance to data* $\Delta(\Gamma, P)$ of a predictor Γ is defined as follows

$$\Delta(\Gamma, P, z_1, \ldots, z_{n-1}) := \max_{j \leq \varkappa_n; \; \pi:\{1,\ldots,n\} \to \{1,\ldots,n\}} | \mathrm{err}_{n+1}(\Gamma, P^\infty, z_1, \ldots, z_n) -$$
$$\mathrm{err}_{n-j+1}(\Gamma, P^\infty, z_{\pi(1)}, \ldots, z_{\pi(n-j)})|,$$

where $\varkappa_n = \sqrt{n \log n}$. Tolerance to data reflects the response of a predictor to permutations and small changes in the training data: if small portion of the training data has been removed (and possibly the training set was permuted) then the probability of error should not change significantly.

We will also use another version of tolerance to data:

$$\bar{\Delta}(\Gamma, P, z_1, \ldots, z_{n-1}) := \max_{j \le \varkappa_n; \{i_1, \ldots, i_j\} \subset \{1, \ldots, n\}; z'_1, \ldots, z'_j}$$

$$| \operatorname{err}_{n+1}(\Gamma, P^\infty, z_1, \ldots, z_n) - \operatorname{err}_{n+1}(\Gamma, P^\infty, \zeta_1, \ldots, \zeta_n)|.$$

where $\zeta_i = z'_i$ if $i \in \{i_1, \ldots, i_j\}$ and $\zeta_i = z_i$ otherwise; the maximum is taken over all z'_i, $n - j < i \le n$ consistent with η.

It means that instead of removing (at most) $\varkappa_n$ examples from the training data $(z_1, \ldots, z_n)$ we replace them with an arbitrary sample.

Let $\mathbf{P}$ be some distribution on $\mathbf{X}^\infty$ satisfying (1) and (2). We say that a distribution P on $\mathbf{X}$ *agrees* with $\mathbf{P}$ if the conditional distribution $P(x|y)$ is equal to $\mathbf{P}_y$ and $P(y) \ne 0$ for each $y \in \mathbf{Y}$. Clearly, this defines the distribution P up to the parameter $p = P(y = 1) \in (0, 1)$. For a distribution $\mathbf{P}$ on $\mathbf{X}^\infty$ we denote the family of distributions which agree with $\mathbf{P}$ by $(P_p)_{p \in (0,1)}$ where $P_p(y = 1) = p$ for each p in $(0, 1)$.

The following fact is proved in [9].

Theorem 3 ([9]). *Suppose that a distribution $\mathbf{P}$ on $\mathbf{X}^\infty$ satisfies (1) and (2). Fix some $\delta \in (0, 1/2]$, denote $p(n) := \frac{1}{n}\#\{i \le n : y_i = 0\}$ and $C_n := \mathbf{P}(\delta \le |p(n)| \le 1 - \delta)$ for any $n \in \mathbb{N}$. For any predictor Γ*

$$\mathbf{P}(\operatorname{err}_n(\Gamma, \mathbf{P}) > \varepsilon) \le 2 \Big(\sup_{p \in [\delta, 1-\delta]} P_p(\operatorname{err}_n(\Gamma, P_p) > \delta\varepsilon/3)$$

$$+ 2 \sup_{p \in [\delta, 1-\delta]} P_p(\Delta_{n+\varkappa_n/2}(\Gamma, P_p) > \delta\varepsilon/6) \Big) + (1 - C_n).$$

for any $\varepsilon > 0$, any $n > e^{4\delta^{-2}}$.

It is easy to show after [9] that the theorem also holds if Δ is replaced by $\bar{\Delta}$. The condition (3) implies $(1 - C_n) \to 0$.

From these facts and Theorem 3 we can deduce the following supplementary result, which will help us to derive theorems 1 and 2.

Lemma 1. *Let Γ be such a predictor that*

$$\sup_{p \in [\delta, 1-\delta]} E(\operatorname{err}_n(\Gamma, P_p)) \to 0 \tag{4}$$

and either

$$\sup_{p \in [\delta, 1-\delta]} E(\Delta_n(\Gamma, P_p)) \to 0. \tag{5}$$

or

$$\sup_{p \in [\delta, 1-\delta]} E(\bar{\Delta}_n(\Gamma, P_p)) \to 0. \tag{6}$$

Then for any distribution $\mathbf{P}$ satisfying (1), (2), and (3) we have

$$E(\operatorname{err}_n(\Gamma, \mathbf{P})) \to 0$$

Observe that both nearest neighbour and partitioning predictors are symmetric, i.e. do not depend on the order of $z_1, \ldots, z_n$. Moreover,

$$\Delta(\Gamma, P, z_1, \ldots, z_{n-1})$$

$$= \max_{k > n - \varkappa_n; \{i_1, \ldots, i_k\} \subset \{1, \ldots, n\}} \left| \mathrm{err}_n(\Gamma, z_1, \ldots, z_n) - \mathrm{err}_k(\Gamma, z_{i_1}, \ldots, z_{i_k}) \right|$$

$$\leq \max_{k > n - \varkappa_n; \{i_1, \ldots, i_k\} \subset \{1, \ldots, n\}} \Big| P\{x, y : y = \Gamma(z_1, \ldots, z_n, x), y \neq \Gamma(z_{i_1}, \ldots, z_{i_k}, x)\}$$

$$- P\{x, y : y \neq \Gamma(z_1, \ldots, z_n, x), y = \Gamma(z_{i_1}, \ldots, z_{i_k}, x)\} \Big|$$

$$\leq 2 \max_{k > n - \varkappa_n; \{i_1, \ldots, i_k\} \subset \{1, \ldots, n\}} P\{x : \Gamma(z_1, \ldots, z_n, x) \neq \Gamma(z_{i_1}, \ldots, z_{i_k}, x)\}$$

$$\tag{7}$$

and

$$\bar{\Delta}(\Gamma, P, z_1, \ldots, z_{n-1}) \leq 2 \max_{j \leq \varkappa_n; \ \pi:\{1,\ldots,n\} \to \{1,\ldots,n\}, z'_{n-j+1}, \ldots, z'_n}$$

$$\tag{8}$$

$$P\{x : \Gamma(z_1, \ldots, z_n) \neq \Gamma(z_{\pi(1)}, \ldots, z_{\pi(n-j)}, z'_{n-j+1}, \ldots, z')\}\}.$$

Thus to obtain estimates on Δ ($\bar{\Delta}$) we need to estimate the expectation of the probability of a maximal area on which the decision of Γ changes if a portion of training examples is removed (replaced with an arbitrary sample).

Furthermore, we will show that for both predictors in question (6) and

$$E(\mathrm{err}(\Gamma, P)) \to 0 \tag{9}$$

for any distribution P on $\mathbf{X}$ (which we already have) imply (4). Than it will only remain to prove (6) for each predictor and apply Lemma 1.

We define the conditional probabilities of error of Γ as follows

$$\mathrm{err}_n^0(\Gamma) := \mathbf{P}(y_n \neq \Gamma_n \mid y_n = 0; x_1, y_1, \ldots, x_{n-1}, y_{n-1}),$$

$$\mathrm{err}_n^1(\Gamma) := \mathbf{P}(y_n \neq \Gamma_n \mid y_n = 1; x_1, y_1, \ldots, x_{n-1}, y_{n-1}),$$

(with the same notational convention as used with the definition of $\mathrm{err}_n(\Gamma)$).

In words, for each $y \in \mathbf{Y} = \{0, 1\}$ we define err_n^y as the probability of all $x \in \mathbf{X}$, such that Γ makes an error on n'th trial, given that $y_n = y$ and given (random variables) $x_1, y_1, \ldots, x_{n-1}, y_{n-1}$. We will also use more explicit notations for $\mathrm{err}_n^y(\Gamma)$ specifying the distribution or the input sequence of labels, when the context requires.

Obviously, $\mathrm{err}_n(\Gamma) \leq \mathrm{err}_n^0(\Gamma) + \mathrm{err}_n^1(\Gamma)$. Thus, we only need to show that (4) holds for, say, $\mathrm{err}_1(\Gamma)$, i.e. that

$$\sup_{p \in [\delta, 1-\delta]} E(\mathrm{err}_n^1(\Gamma, P_p)) \to 0. \tag{10}$$

Observe that for each of the predictors in question the probability of error given that the true label is 1 will not decrease if an arbitrary (possibly large) portion of training examples labeled with ones is changed to (arbitrary, but correct) portion of the same size of examples labeled with zeros. Thus, for any n and any $p \in [\delta, 1 - \delta]$ we can decrease the number of ones in our sample (by replacing the corresponding examples with examples from the other class) down to (say) $\delta/2$, not decreasing the probability of error on examples labeled with 1. So,

$$E(\mathrm{err}_n^1(\Gamma, P_p)) \le E(\mathrm{err}_n^1(\Gamma, P_{\delta/2}|p_n = n(\delta/2))) + P_p(p_n \le n(\delta/2)),$$

where $p_n = \#\{i \le n : y_i = 1\}$. Obviously, the last term (quickly) tends to zero. Moreover, it is easy to see that

$$E(\mathrm{err}_n^1(\Gamma, P_{\delta/2})|p_n = n(\delta/2))$$
$$\le E(\mathrm{err}_n^1(\Gamma, P_{\delta/2})|n(\delta/2) - \varkappa_n/2 \le p_n \le n(\delta/2) + \varkappa_n/2) + \bar{\Delta}_n(\Gamma, P_{\delta/2})$$
$$\le \frac{\sqrt{n} - 1}{\sqrt{n}} E(\mathrm{err}_n^1(\Gamma, P_{\delta/2})) + \bar{\Delta}_n(\Gamma, P_{\delta/2}),$$

which tends to zero if $\bar{\Delta}_n(\Gamma, P) \to 0$ (for any P). Thus, it remains to obtain (6). This we will establish for each of the predictors separately.

Nearest Neighbour predictor. We will derive the estimates on $\bar{\Delta}$ which do not depend on $p = P(y = 1)$ and tend to zero.

Fix some distribution P on $\mathbf{X}$ and some $\varepsilon > 0$. Fix also some $n \in \mathbb{N}$ and denote

$$B_n(x) := P\{t \in \mathbf{X} : t \text{ and } x \text{ have the same nearest neighbour among } x_1, \ldots, x_n\}$$

and $B_n := E(B_n(x))$ (we leave $x_1, \ldots, x_n$ implicit in these notations). Note that $E(B_n) = 1/n$, where the expectation is taken over $x_1, \ldots, x_n$. Denote $\mathcal{B} = \{(x_1, \ldots, x_n) \in \mathbf{X}^n : E(B_n) \le 1/n\varepsilon\}$ and $\mathcal{A}(x_1, \ldots, x_n) = \{x : B_n(x) \le 1/n\varepsilon^2\}$. Applying Markov's inequality twice, we obtain

$$E(\bar{\Delta}_n(\Gamma, P)) \le E(\bar{\Delta}_n(\Gamma, P)|(x_1, \ldots, x_n) \in \mathcal{B}) + \varepsilon$$
$$\le 2E\Big(\max_{k > n - \varkappa_n; \{i_1, \ldots, i_k\} \subset \{1, \ldots, n\}} P\{x : \Gamma(z_1, \ldots, z_n, x) \ne \Gamma(z_{i_1}, \ldots, z_{i_k}, x)|x \in \mathcal{A}\}$$
$$|(x_1, \ldots, x_n) \in \mathcal{B}\Big) + 2\varepsilon$$
$$\tag{11}$$

Observe that the same estimate holds true if P is replaced by either P_1 or P_0, the class-conditional versions of P. Thus (possibly increasing n) we can obtain (11) for all P_p, $p \in [\delta, 1 - \delta]$ simultaneously. Indeed, denoting for each $y \in \{0, 1\}$

$$B_n^y(x) := P\{t \in \eta^{-1}(y) : t \text{ and } x \text{ have the same nearest neighbour among } x_1, \ldots, x_n\}$$

we have

$$E(B_n) \le E(B_n^1) + E(B_n^0) \le E_{P_1}(B_{2n/\delta}^1) + E_{P_0}(B_{2n/\delta}^0) + P(p_n \notin [\delta/2, 1 - \delta/2]),$$

which is bounded uniformly in p.

Note that removing one point x_i from a sample $x_1, \ldots, x_n$ we can only change the value of Γ in the area

$$\{x \in \mathbf{X} : x_i \text{ is the nearest neighbour of x}\} = B_n(x_i),$$

while adding one point x_0 to the sample we can change the decision of Γ in the area

$$D_n(x_0) := \{x \in \mathbf{X} : x_0 \text{ is the nearest neighbour of x}\}.$$

It can be shown that the number of examples (among $x_1, \ldots, x_n$) for which a point x_0 is the nearest neighbour is not greater than a constant γ which depends only the space $\mathbf{X}$ (see [4], Corollary 11.1). Thus, $D_n(x_0) \subset \cup_{i=j_1, \ldots, j_\gamma} B_n(x_i)$ for some $j_1, \ldots, j_\gamma$, and so

$$E(\Delta_n(\Gamma, P)) \leq 2\varepsilon + 2(\gamma + 1)\varkappa_n E(\max_{x \in \mathbf{X}} B_n(x) | x \in \mathcal{A} | (x_1, \ldots, x_n) \in \mathcal{B})$$

$$\leq 2\varkappa_n \frac{\gamma + 1}{n\varepsilon^2} + 2\varepsilon,$$

which, increasing n, can be made less than 3ε.   ∎

Partitioning predictor. For any measurable sets $\mathcal{B} \in \mathbf{X}^n$ and $\mathcal{A} \in \mathbf{X}$ denote

$$D(\mathcal{A}, \mathcal{B}) := E\Big(\max_{j \leq \varkappa_n;\ \pi:\{1,\ldots,n\} \to \{1,\ldots,n\}, z'_{n-j+1}, \ldots, z'_n}$$

$$P\{x : \Gamma(z_1, \ldots, z_n) \neq \Gamma(z_{\pi(1)}, \ldots, z_{\pi(n-j)}, z'_{n-j+1}, \ldots, z') | x \in \mathcal{A}\}$$

$$\Big| (x_1, \ldots, x_n) \in \mathcal{B}\Big).$$

and $D := D(\mathbf{X}^n, \mathbf{X})$.

Fix some distribution P on $\mathbf{X}$ and some $\varepsilon > 0$. From the consistency results for i.i.d. model (see, e.g. [4], Chapter 5) we know that $E|\hat{\eta}_n(x) - \eta(x)| \to 0$. It can be also inferred from the proof (see [4], Theorem 6.1) that the convergence is uniform in $p = P(y = 1) \in [\delta, 1 - \delta]$. Hence, $E|\hat{\eta}_n(x) - \eta(x)| \leq \varepsilon^4$ from some n on for all $p \in [\delta, 1 - \delta]$. Fix any such n and denote $\mathcal{B} = \{(x_1, \ldots, x_n) : E|\hat{\eta}_n(x) - \eta(x)| \leq \varepsilon^2\}$. By Markov inequality we obtain $P(\mathcal{B}) \geq \varepsilon^2$. For any $(x_1, \ldots, x_n) \in \mathcal{B}$ denote $\mathcal{A}(x_1, \ldots, x_n)$ the union of all cells A_i^n for which $E(|\hat{\eta}_n - \eta||x \in A_i^n) \leq \varepsilon$. Clearly, with $x_1, \ldots, x_n$ fixed, $P(x \in \mathcal{A}(x_1, \ldots, x_n)) \geq \varepsilon$. Moreover, $D \leq D(\mathcal{B}, \mathcal{A}) + \varepsilon + \varepsilon^2$.

Since $\eta(x)$ is always either 0 or 1, to change a decision in any cell $A \subset \mathcal{A}$ we need to add or remove at least $(1 - \varepsilon)N(A)$ examples, where $N(A) = N(x)$ for any $x \in A$. Denote $N(k) = E(N(x))$ and $A(k) = E(P(A(x)))$. Clearly, $\frac{N(k)}{kA(k)} = 1$ for any n, as $E\frac{N(x)}{n} = A(n)$.

Thus, $\frac{\varepsilon^2 nA(n)}{N(n)} = \varepsilon^2$. As before, using Markov inequality and shrinking $\mathcal{A}$ if necessary we can have $P(\frac{\varepsilon^2 nA(x)}{N(n)} \leq \varepsilon | x \in \mathcal{A}) = 1$, $P(\frac{\varepsilon^2 nA(n)}{N(x)} \leq \varepsilon | x \in \mathcal{A}) = 1$, and $D \leq D(\mathcal{B}, \mathcal{A}) + 3\varepsilon + \varepsilon^2$. Thus, for all cells $A \in \mathcal{A}$ we have $N(x) \geq \varepsilon nA(n)$, so that the probability of error can be changed in at most $2\frac{\varkappa_n}{\varepsilon nA(n)}$ cells; but the probability of each cell is not greater than $\frac{N(n)}{\varepsilon n}$. Hence $E(\bar{\Delta}_n(\Gamma, P)) \leq 2\frac{\varkappa_n}{n\varepsilon^2} + 3\varepsilon + \varepsilon^2$.   ∎

Acknowledgements. The author would like to thank the anonymous reviewers for useful comments and relevant references. I am grateful to Royal Holloway, University of London for funding my Ph.D. studies. This research was partially supported by EPSRC (grant GR/R46670/01), BBSRC (grant 111/BIO14428) and Royal Society (grant ref: 15995).

References

[1] Paul Algoet, *Universal Schemas for Learning the Best Nonlinear Predictor Given the Infinite Past and Side Information* IEEE Transactions on Information Theory, Vol. 45, No. 4, 1999.

[2] A.P. Dawid *Conditional Independence in Statistical Theory.* Journal of the Royal Statistical Society, Series B (Methodological), Vol. 41 No 1, 1979, pp. 1–31

[3] Luc Devroye, *On asymptotic probability of error in nonparametric discrimination.* Annals of Statistics, vol 9, 1981, pp.1320-1327.

[4] Luc Devroye, László Györfi, Gábor Lugosi, *A probabilistic theory of pattern recognition.* New York: Springer, 1996.

[5] David Gamarnik, *Extension of the PAC Framework to Finite and Countable Markov Chains* IEEE Transactions on Information Theory, Vol. 49, No. 1, 2003.

[6] Sanjeev R. Kulkarni, Steven E. Posner, Sathyakama Sandilya. *Data-Dependent k_n-NN and Kernel Estimators Consistent for Arbitrary Processess.* IEEE Transactions on Information Theory, Vol. 48, No. 10, 2002, pp.2785-2788.

[7] Sanjeev R. Kulkarni, Steven E. Posner. *Rates of Convergence of Nearest Neighbour Estimation Under Arbitrary Sampling.* IEEE Transactions on Information Theory, Vol. 41, No. 10, 1995, pp.1028-1039.

[8] Gusztáv Morvai, Sidney J. Yakowitz, Paul Algoet, *Weakly Convergent Nonparametric Forecasting of Stationary Time Series* IEEE Transactions on Information Theory, Vol. 43, No. 2, 1997

[9] Daniil Ryabko, *Online Learning of Conditionally I.I.D. Data* Proceedings of the Twenty-First International Conference on Machine Learning, Banff, Canada, 2004, pp. 727-734. Edited by Russ Greiner and Dale Schuurmans

[10] Vladimir N. Vapnik, *Statistical Learning Theory*: New York etc.: John Wiley & Sons, Inc. 1998

Complexity of Pattern Classes and Lipschitz Property

Amiran Ambroladze and John Shawe-Taylor

University of Southampton, Southampton SO17 1BJ, UK,
{aa,jst}@ecs.soton.ac.uk

Abstract. Rademacher and Gaussian complexities are successfully used in learning theory for measuring the capacity of the class of functions to be learned. One of the most important properties for these complexities is their Lipschitz property: a composition of a class of functions with a fixed Lipschitz function may increase its complexity by at most twice the Lipschitz constant. The proof of this property is non-trivial (in contrast to the other properties) and it is believed that the proof in the Gaussian case is conceptually more difficult then the one for the Rademacher case. In this paper we give a detailed prove of the Lipschitz property for the general case (with the only assumption wich makes the complexity notion meaningful) including the Rademacher and Gaussian cases.

We also discuss a related topic about the Rademacher complexity of a class consisting of all the Lipschitz functions with a given Lipschitz constant. We show that the complexity is surprisingly low in the one-dimensional case.

1 Introduction

An important problem in learning theory is to choose a function from a given class of functions (pattern functions) which best imitates (fits) the underlying distribution (for example, has the smallest error for a classification problem). Usually we don't know the underlying distribution and we can only asess it via a finite sample generated by this distribution. For a success of this strategy we usually require that the difference between the sample and true performance is small for every function in the class (if the sample size is sufficiently large). This property is referred as *uniform convergence* over the class of functions.

If a set is so rich that it always contains a function that fits any given random dataset, then it is unlikely that the chosen function will fit a new dataset even if drawn from the same distribution. The ability of a function class to fit different data is known as its *capacity*. Clearly the higher the capacity of the class the greater the risk of overfitting the particular training date and identifying a spurious pattern. The critical question is how one should measure the capacity of a function class. One measure, successfully used in learning theory, is the Rademacher and Gaussian complexities. The definition rests on the intuition that we can evaluate the capacity of a class of functions by its ability to fit random data. We give first the definition for Rademacher complexity which can be then readily generalized for an arbitrary complexity.

S. Ben-David, J. Case, A. Maruoka (Eds.): ALT 2004, LNAI 3244, pp. 181–193, 2004.

Definition 1. (Rademacher complexity) *Let X be an input space, D be a distribution on X, and F be a real-valued function class defined on X. Let $S = \{x_1, \cdots, x_l\}$ be a random sample generated (independently) by D. The empirical Rademacher complexity of F for the given sample S is the following random variable:*

$$\hat{R}_l(F) = \mathbb{E}_r \left[\sup_{f \in F} \frac{2}{l} \left| \sum_{i=1}^{l} r_i f(x_i) \right| \right],$$

where $r = \{r_1, \cdots r_l\}$ are iid $\{\pm 1\}$-valued random variables with equal probabilities for $+1$ and -1 and the expectation is taken with respect to r.

The Rademacher complexity *of F is*

$$R_l(F) = \mathbb{E}_S \left[\hat{R}_l(F) \right] = \mathbb{E}_{Sr} \left[\sup_{f \in F} \frac{2}{l} \left| \sum_{i=1}^{l} r_i f(x_i) \right| \right].$$

Definition 2. (Gaussian complexity) *We get the definition of the Gaussian complexity if in Definition 1 we substitute the Rademacher ± 1-valued random variables $r_1, \cdots, r_l$ by the independent Gaussian $N(0, 1)$ random variables $g_1, \cdots, g_l$. The empirical Gaussian complexity and the Gaussian complexity are usually denoted by $\hat{G}_l(F)$ and $G_l(F)$ respectively.*

The relation between these complexities (Rademacher and Gaussian) is discussed in [2].

Definition 3. *In the same way as in Definition 1 we can define complexity for an arbitrary distribution μ on the real line (instead of the Rademacher distribution concentrated at the points ± 1). We just need to assume that the expectation integral is bounded for any choice of $f \in F$ and any choice of points $x_1, \cdots, x_l$). We can use the following general notations $\hat{C}_l(F)$ and $C_l(F)$ for the empirical μ-complexity and μ-complexity, respectively.*

Now we formulate a result which shows the importance of these notions. It bounds the error of pattern functions in terms of their empirical fit and the Rademacher complexity of the class. We formulate the result in the form more usual for applications: instead of the input space X we consider the sample space $Z := X \times Y$ (we can assume that $Y = \{1, -1\}$ as it is the case for the binary classification), and instead of the functions $F = \{f\}$ on X we consider (loss) functions $H = \{h\}$ defined on Z. A function $h(x, y)$ can be defined, for example, as some 'soft' thresholding at zero of a function $yf(x)$.

Theorem 1. *Fix $\delta \in (0, 1)$ and let H be a class of functions mapping from Z to $[0, 1]$. Let $z_1, \cdots, z_l$ be drawn independently according to a probability distribution D. Then with probability at least $1 - \delta$ over random draws of samples of size l, every $h \in H$ satisfies:*

$$\mathbb{E}_D[h(z)] \leq \hat{\mathbb{E}}[h(z)] + R_l(H) + \sqrt{\frac{\ln(2/\delta)}{2l}}$$

$$\leq \hat{\mathbb{E}}[h(z)] + \hat{R}_l(H) + 3\sqrt{\frac{\ln(2/\delta)}{2l}}, \tag{1}$$

where $\mathbb{E}_D[h(z)]$ is the true expectation of $h(z)$ and $\hat{\mathbb{E}}[h(z)]$ is the corresponding empirical one.

The idea with this result is that if we manage to find a function $h \in H$ with a small empirical expectation (the empirical loss is small) then the theorem guaranties (with a high probability) that the same h will provide a small value for the true loss (under the assumption that the Rademacher complexity of the pattern functions is small).

In complexity estimations (Rademacher or Gaussian) one uses different properties of the complexity function. In Section 2 we formulate the most important properties. Their proofs are relatively straightforward from the definition of complexity except for one: the Lipschitz property: a composition of a class of functions with a fixed Lipschitz function may increase its complexity by at most twice the Lipschitz constant. The proof of this property represented in the literature is quite non-trivial and uses different approaches for the Rademacher and Gaussian cases (see [5], Th.4.12 and Th.3.17). It is also believed (see [5], Th.4.12) that the proof in the Rademacher case is conceptually more simple. In Section 4 we give a detailed prove of the Lipschitz property for the general case. This general result we formulate in Section 2 and there also we discuss the importance of the Lipschitz property in complexity estimations for different function classes.

In Section 3 we discuss the following related question: Let $H = \{h\}$ be a set of Lipschitz functions defined on some space X. We assume that the corresponding Lipschitz constants are uniformly bounded by some quantity. We can assume that this quantity is 1 (this means that the functions $\{h\}$ are contractions); otherwise we could divide each function $h \in H$ by that quantity. Such function classes often arises in applications (see, for example, [3]). We ask the following question: what is the Rademacher complexity for the class H consisting of all contractions defined on the input space X? (To avoid unbounded function classes giving infinite Rademacher complexity, we need to normalize H in some way; one possible normalization in case $X = [0, 1]$ is to assume that $h(0) = 0$ for all $h \in H$. This makes H uniformly bounded on $[0, 1]$.) It turns out that in the one-dimensional case ($X = [0, 1]$) this complexity is surprisingly small and is at most twice as large as the Rademacher complexity of a single function $h(x) = x$. (See Theorem 7 for the details.)

This problem statement is somewhat opposite to that in Section 2: In that section we take a class of functions F and compose each function $f \in F$ with a fixed Lipschitz function ϕ (we can assume that ϕ is a contraction). Then the Rademacher complexity of the function class $\phi \circ F$ is at most twice the Rademacher complexity of the class F. Opposite to this, in Section 3 we take the class of all contractions H, say on $[0, 1]$, which can be considered as the compositions $h \circ I$ of the contractions $h \in H$ with a single function $I(x) = x$ (an identical mapping). It turns out that even in this case the Rademacher complexity of the composition class is at most twice the Rademacher complexity of the original function $I(x)$. Note that the function $I(x)$ is an element of the class H and the above result says that the Rademacher complexity of the whole class H is at most twice the Rademacher complexity of its single element.

2   Lipschitz Property for Rademacher and General Complexities

We start this section by giving an example about using the Lipschitz property for estimating the Rademacher complexity of the class H in Theorem 1.

Often in practice $h(x, y)$ ($h \in H$) is defined as some 'soft' thresholding at zero of a function $yf(x)$ ($f \in F$), say $h(x, y) = A(yf(x))$, where the function A is a 'smooth' version of the *Heaviside function*: one takes $A(t)$ to be a continuous function on $\mathbb{R}$ such that $A(t) > 0$ if $t > 0$, $A(t) = 0$ if $t < -\gamma$ (for some $\gamma > 0$) and $A(t)$ is linear on the interval $[-\gamma, 0]$. Evidently the function A is a Lipschitz function (with the Lipschitz constant $1/\gamma$), and here one has the use of the property that a composition of a class of functions with a fixed Lipschitz function increases the Rademacher complexity of the class by at most twice the Lipschitz constant. The Rademacher complexity of the class of functions $\{yf(x), \ f \in F\}$ (defined on $Z = X \times Y$) is the same (easy to see from the definition) as the Rademacher complexity of the class $\{f, \ f \in F\}$ (defined on X). It remains to estimate the Rademacher complexity of the class $\{f, \ f \in F\}$. In a particular but important case (for example when working with kernel methods) when $\{f\}$ are linear functions defined on the unit ball, the Rademacher complexity can be bounded by $2/\sqrt{l}$ (for more details see [4], Chapter 4).

Here we have described one application of the Lipschitz property to bounding the Rademacher complexity. For many other interesting applications of this property we recommend to see [2].

Now we formulate some useful properties for the Rademacher complexity. (Many of these properties are true even for the Gaussian complexity $\hat{G}_l$; the others hold for $\hat{G}_l$ with an additional factor $\ln l$. See [2] for the details):

Theorem 2. *Let* $F, F_1, \cdots, F_n$ *and* G *be classes of real functions. Then:*

(1) *If* $F \subseteq G$, *then* $\hat{R}_l(F) \leq \hat{R}_l(G)$.
(2) $\hat{R}_l(F) = \hat{R}_l(\text{conv}F)$.
(3) $\hat{R}_l(cF) = |c|\hat{R}_l(F)$ *for every* $c \in \mathbb{R}$.
(4) *If* $A : \mathbb{R} \longrightarrow \mathbb{R}$ *is a Lipschitz with constant* L *and satisfies* $A(0) = 0$, *then* $\hat{R}_l(A \circ F) \leq 2L\hat{R}_l(F)$.

(5) $\hat{R}_l(F + h) \leq \hat{R}_l(F) + 2\sqrt{\hat{\mathbb{E}}[h^2]/l}$ *for any function* h.
(6) *For any* $1 \leq q \leq \infty$, *let* $L_{F,h,q} = \{|f - h|^q, \ f \in F\}$. *If* $||f - h||_\infty \leq 1$ *for every* $f \in F$, *then* $\hat{R}_l(L_{F,h,q}) \leq 2q \left(\hat{R}_l(F) + 2\sqrt{\hat{\mathbb{E}}[h^2]/l.} \right)$

(7) $\hat{R}_l(\sum_{i=1}^n F_i) \leq \sum_{i=1}^n \hat{R}_l(F_i)$.

Here conv(F) means the convex hull of F and $A \circ F = \{A \circ f, \ f \in F\}$, where $A \circ f$ denotes the composition of A and f.

The proofs for these results, with the exception of (4), are all relatively straightforward applications of the definition of empirical Rademacher complexity. In Section 4 we prove the property (4) in the following general setting:

Theorem 3. *Let μ be an arbitrary distribution on $\mathbb{R}$ with zero mean. Let $\hat{C}_l$ denote the corresponding empirical complexity for this distribution (as defined in Definition 3). Let $A : \mathbb{R} \longrightarrow \mathbb{R}$ be a Lipschitz function with constant L and satisfy $A(0) = 0$. Then for any real-valued function class F we have:*

$$\hat{C}_l(A \circ F) \leq 2L\hat{C}_l(F).$$

If the function A is an odd function $(A(-t) = -A(t))$ then we can drop the factor 2 in the last theorem:

Theorem 4. *Let μ be an arbitrary distribution on $\mathbb{R}$ with zero mean. Let $\hat{C}_l$ denote the corresponding empirical complexity for this distribution (as defined in Definition 3). Let $A : \mathbb{R} \longrightarrow \mathbb{R}$ be an odd $(A(-t) = -A(t))$ Lipschitz function with constant L and satisfy $A(0) = 0$. Then for any real-valued function class F we have:*

$$\hat{C}_l(A \circ F) \leq L\hat{C}_l(F).$$

Note that the only condition on μ in the above theorems having zero mean is absolutely necessary to make the notion of complexity meaningfull. If the mean of μ is different from zero then even a single function which is an identical constant has a big complexity, which does not go to zero as the sample size goes to infinity; and this is unreasonable.

(In the above theorems we assume that the expectation integral of Definition 3 is bounded for any choice of $f \in F$ and any choice of points $x_1, \cdots, x_l$).

The assertions in the last two theorems trivially hold for the non-empirical complexity (C_l) as well.

Question: Is the factor 2 optimal in Theorem 3?

3   Rademacher Complexity of Lipschitz Functions

Let $X = [0, 1] \subset \mathbb{R}$. Our aim is to estimate the Rademacher complexity of the set of all Lipschitz functions on $[0, 1]$ with Lipschitz constant at most L. This set is of course not uniformly bounded (contains all the constant functions, for example), which makes its Rademacher complexity infinite. To make these functions uniformly bounded we request that each function vanishes at some point on $[0, 1]$. (This makes the function class uniformly bounded; one could demand this property instead.) It turns out that the Rademacher complexity of this class is very small and can be compared with the Rademacher complexity of a single function. We formulate Theorems 5 and 6 for the empirical Rademacher complexity $\hat{R}_l(H)$ and we estimate (the non-empirical complexity) $R_l(H)$ in Theorem 7.

Theorem 5. *Let H be the class of Lipschitz functions with Lipschitz constants at most L on the interval $\Delta = [0, 1]$ and vanishing at some point of this interval. Then for any set of points $\{x_1, \cdots, x_l\} \subset \Delta$ we have*

$$\hat{R}_l(H) \leq 2L\hat{R}_l(\mathbf{1}_\Delta),$$

where $\mathbf{1}_\Delta$ is the function identically equal to 1 on Δ.

If we consider the class of functions vanishing at the origin we gain factor 2:

Theorem 6. *Let H be the class of Lipschitz functions with Lipschitz constants at most L on the interval $\Delta = [0, 1]$ and vanishing at the point 0. Then for any set of points $\{x_1, \cdots, x_l\} \subset \Delta$ we have*

$$\hat{R}_l(H) \leq L\hat{R}_l(\mathbf{1}_\Delta),$$

where $\mathbf{1}_\Delta$ is the function identically equal to 1 on Δ.

In the above theorems we have compared the Rademacher complexity of the whole class H with the one of a single function $\mathbf{1}_\Delta$. In the next theorem we make comparison with the function which is the identical mapping $I(x) = x$:

Theorem 7. *Let H be the class of Lipschitz functions with Lipschitz constants at most L on the interval $\Delta = [0, 1]$ and vanishing at the point 0. Then for any symmetrical distribution D on $\Delta = [0, 1]$ (symmetrical with respect to the middle point $1/2$) we have*

$$R_l(H) \leq 2LR_l(I),$$

where I is the identical mapping $I(x) = x$.

Note that in Theorem 7 the function $I(x)$ is an element of the class H, and the theorem says that the Rademacher complexity of the whole class H is at most twice the Rademacher complexity of its single element. This result can be viewed also in another way: Composing all the functions $h \in H$ with a single function $I(x) = x$ (which does not change h) may increase the Rademacher complexity (compared with the Rademacher complexity of the single function $I(x)$) at most twice the Lipschitz constant L. It is interesting to compare this result with Theorem 3.

To estimate the Rademacher complexity in the right-hand sides of the last three theorems we can use property (5) of Theorem 2, where we take F containing only the identically zero function. This gives that $\hat{R}_l(F) = 0$ and consequently $\hat{R}_l(h) \leq 2/\sqrt{l}$ if $h \leq 1$ on $[0, 1]$.

The authors don't know the answers to the following questions:

Question. Is it possible to drop the factor 2 in Theorem 5?

4   Proofs

Proof of Theorem 3. Our proof is inspirated by the proof of Theorem 4.12 from [5], but we tried to simplify it and added some new components making it universal for arbitrary arbitrary distribution μ. Without loss of generality we can assume $L = 1$ for the Lipschitz constant. This means that the function A is a contraction: $|A(t) - A(s)| \leq |t - s|$. Fix $\{x_1, \cdots, x_l\}$. For simplicity of notations we denote $f(x_i) = f_i$. So now if $r = (r_1, \cdots, r_l)$ denote the i.i.d. random variables generated by μ, then we have to prove that

$$\mathbb{E}_r \left[\sup_{f \in F} \left| \sum_{i=1}^{l} r_i A(f_i) \right| \right] \leq 2\mathbb{E}_r \left[\sup_{f \in F} \left| \sum_{i=1}^{l} r_i f_i \right| \right] \tag{2}$$

Denote the left-hand side of the last inequality by L (don't mix with the Lipschitz constant, which, by our assumption, is now 1) and the right-hand side by R. We can assume that the function class F is closed with respect to the negation ($f \in F \implies -f \in F$), otherwise adding the set $\{-f\}$ to $F = \{f\}$ can only increase L and leaves R unchanged. We also assume that the identically zero function also belongs to F. This does not change R and does not change L (since $A(0) = 0$).

Denote $A^+(t) = A(t)$, $A^-(t) = -A(-t)$ and denote $A^\pm = \{A^+, A^-\}$. We introduce the following quantity:

$$M := \mathbb{E}_r \left[\sup_{f \in F, A \in A^\pm} \left| \sum_{i=1}^{l} r_i A(f_i) \right| \right]$$

It suffices to show that $L \le M$ and $M \le R$. The first inequality is evident. We need to prove that $M \le R$. Since F is closed with respect to negation, we can drop the absolute value sign in the expression for R. The same we can do in the expression for M (introducing A^- served this purpose). So, what we need to prove now is:

$$\mathbb{E}_r \left[\sup_{f \in F, A \in A^\pm} \sum_{i=1}^{l} r_i A(f_i) \right] \le 2 \mathbb{E}_r \left[\sup_{f \in F} \sum_{i=1}^{l} r_i A(f_i) \right] \tag{3}$$

Evidently, for each fixed $r = (r_1, \cdots, r_l)$ we have

$$\sup_{f \in F, A \in A^\pm} \sum_{i=1}^{l} r_i A(f_i) \le \sup_{f \in F} \sum_{i=1}^{l} r_i A^+(f_i) + \sup_{f \in F} \sum_{i=1}^{l} r_i A^-(f_i).$$

(Here we use the fact that the identically zero function belongs to F, which makes positive both terms in the right-hand side of the last inequality.)

It is this last inequality where the factor 2 comes from in Theorem 3.

Now in order to prove (3) it suffices to proof that

$$\mathbb{E}_r \left[\sup_{f \in F} \sum_{i=1}^{l} r_i A(f_i) \right] \le \mathbb{E}_r \left[\sup_{f \in F} \sum_{i=1}^{l} r_i f_i \right] \tag{4}$$

for arbitrary compression A with $A(0) = 0$.

The main idea now is the following : Instead for proving (4) immediately, we introduce an intermediate expression $\mathbb{E}_r \left[\sup_{f \in F} \sum_{i=1}^{l} r_i A_i(f_i) \right]$, where each A_i is either A or the identical mapping $I(t) = t$. If all the A_i are A, we get the left-hand side of (4), and if all the A_i are I we get the right-hand side. Now reducing the number of A_i's equal to A one-by-one (induction principle), we show that on each step we increase the value of $\mathbb{E}_r \left[\sup_{f \in F} \sum_{i=1}^{l} r_i A_i(f_i) \right]$.

It is enough to show the first step: Prove that

$$\mathbb{E}_r \left[\sup_{f \in F} (r_1 A_1(f_1) + r_2 A_2(f_2) + \cdots r_l A_l(f_l)) \right] \leq \tag{5}$$

$$\mathbb{E}_r \left[\sup_{f \in F} (r_1 f_1 + r_2 A_2(f_2) + \cdots r_l A_l(f_l)) \right].$$

A first naive attempt fails:

$$\left[\sup_{f \in F} (r_1 A_1(f_1) + r_2 A_2(f_2) + \cdots r_l A_l(f_l)) \right] \not\leq$$

$$\left[\sup_{f \in F} (r_1 f_1 + r_2 A_2(f_2) + \cdots r_l A_l(f_l)) \right].$$

Next attemt: Group $(r_1, r_2, \cdots, r_l)$, $r_1 \geq 0$, with $(-r_1, r_2, \cdots, r_l)$. Here, to start with, we make an extra assumption that the measure μ is symmetric. (For a technical simplicity you can even imagine that μ is a descrete measure.) Later we comment on the case when μ is not necessarily symmetric. So we have to prove that

$$\sup_{f \in F} (r_1 A_1(f_1) + r_2 A_2(f_2) + \cdots + r_l A_l(f_l)) + \tag{6}$$

$$\sup_{f \in F} (-r_1 A_1(f_1) + r_2 A_2(f_2) + \cdots + r_l A_l(f_l)) \leq$$

$$\sup_{f \in F} (r_1 \cdot f_1 + r_2 A_2(f_2) + \cdots + r_l A_l(f_l)) +$$

$$\sup_{f \in F} (-r_1 \cdot f_1 + r_2 A_2(f_2) + \cdots + r_l A_l(f_l)).$$

To prove the last inequality it suffices to show that for each couple of functions $\{f^+, f^-\} \subset F$ there is another couple of functions $\{g^+, g^-\} \subset F$ such that

$$(r_1 \cdot A(f_1^+) + r_2 A_2(f_2^+) + \cdots + r_l A_l(f_l^+)) +$$
$$(-r_1 \cdot A(f_1^-) + r_2 A_2(f_2^-) + \cdots + r_l A_l(f_l^-)) \leq$$

$$(r_1 \cdot g_1^+ + r_2 A_2(g_2^+) + \cdots + r_l A_l(g_l^+)) +$$
$$(-r_1 \cdot g_1^- + r_2 A_2(g_2^-) + \cdots + r_l A_l(g_l^-)).$$

The choice $g^+ = f^+$, $g^- = f^-$ gives

$$A(f_1^+) - A(f_1^-) \le f_1^+ - f_1^-.$$

The choice $g^+ = f^-$, $g^- = f^+$ gives

$$A(f_1^+) - A(f_1^-) \le f_1^- - f_1^+.$$

Due to the compression property of A, at least one of the last two inequalities is true, namely, the one for which the right-hand side is non-negative. This proves (6).

Now integrating both sides of (6) over the domain $[0, \infty) \times (-\infty, \infty)^{l-1}$ with respect to the measure $d\mu(r_1) \times \cdots \times d\mu(r_l)$ we get 5.

The proof above works in the case of symmetrical μ. If μ is not symmetrical we do as follows (a sketch of the proof): We appoximate μ by a smooth measure μ_1 which is in addition positive on the minimal interval containing the support of μ and which has zero mean. For a small ϵ devide the real line by points c_i, $i = 0, \pm 1, \pm 2, \cdots, \pm N$, so that $c_0 = 0$ and $\int_{c_{i-1}}^{c_i} r d\mu_1(r) = \epsilon$. Now from each interval $[c_{i-1}, c_i], i = 1, 2, \cdots N$ choose a point R_i so that $R_i \int_{c_{i-1}}^{c_i} d\mu_1(r) = \epsilon$. In the same way we choose points R_i from $[c_i, c_{i+1}], i = -1, -2, \cdots - N$. Consider a discrete measure μ_2 which puts masses $\int_{c_{i-1}}^{c_i} d\mu_1(r)$ at R_i and use this measure as an approximation for the initial measure μ. Now group together R_i and R_{-i}. This two points have different probabilities but they have equal expectations. This allows us to use arguments similar to those used in the symmetric case. Theorem 3 is proved.

Proof of Theorem 4. We need to prove that

$$\mathbb{E}_r \left[\sup_{f \in F} \left| \sum_{i=1}^{l} r_i A(f_i) \right| \right] \le \mathbb{E}_r \left[\sup_{f \in F} \left| \sum_{i=1}^{l} r_i f_i \right| \right]. \tag{7}$$

We assume again that F is closed with respect to negation (this does not change (7)). The expressions inside the absolute value signs in the both sides of (7) are odd functions in f. This means that we can drop the absolute value sings. The rest follows from (4).

Theorem 4 is proved.

Proof of Theorem 6. Without loss of generality we can assume that $L = 1$. Fix $\{x_1, \cdots, x_l\} \subset \Delta = [0, 1]$, $0 \le x_1 \le x_2 \le \cdots \le x_l \le 1$. Fix $r = (r_1, \cdots, r_l)$, $r_i = \pm 1$, $i = 1, \cdots, l$. It can be shown that the class H in the theorem is compact in the uniform (L^∞) metric. This means that the supremum in the definition of the Rademacher complexity is achieved for some function $h(x)$ (depending on $(r_1, \cdots, r_l)$ and $\{x_1, \cdots, x_l\}$). Then $-h(x)$ also provides the same supremum. So we can assume that

$$\sup_{f \in H} \left| \sum_{i=1}^{l} r_i f(x_i) \right| = \sum_{i=1}^{l} r_i h(x_i).$$

In particular, we have that

$$\sum_{i=1}^{l} r_i h(x_i) \geq \sum_{i=1}^{l} r_i f(x_i), \ \forall f \in H. \tag{8}$$

Denote $d_1 = x_1 - 0, \ d_2 = x_2 - x_1, \cdots, d_l = x_l - x_{l-1}$. We have

$$d_i \geq 0, \ \sum_{i=1}^{l} d_i \leq 1. \tag{9}$$

Due to the Lipschitz condition (with $L = 1$) we have $|h(x_1)| \leq d_1$. Consider the quantity $\mathrm{sgn}(r_1 + \cdots + r_l)$, where $\mathrm{sgn}(x) = 1$ if $x > 0$, $\mathrm{sgn}(x) = -1$ if $x < 0$ and $\mathrm{sgn}(0) = 0$. If $\mathrm{sgn}(r_1 + \cdots + r_l) > 0$, then we must have $h(x_1) = d_1$ in order to guarantee (8) (otherwise we could lift the function $h(x)$ on the interval $[x_1, 1]$; the new function still will be Lipschitz with constant 1, but this lift would increase the left-hand side in (8)). If $\mathrm{sgn}(r_1 + \cdots + r_l) < 0$, then we must have $h(x_1) = -d_1$. If $\mathrm{sgn}(r_1 + \cdots + r_l) = 0$, then the lifting of $h(x)$ up (or down) on the interval $[x_1, 1]$ does not effect the left-hand side in (8). So we can assume that

$$h(x_1) = d_1 \mathrm{sgn}(r_1 + \cdots + r_l).$$

Now having fixed $h(x_1)$ we can show in the same way that

$$h(x_2) = h(x_1) + d_2 \mathrm{sgn}(r_2 + \cdots + r_l) = d_1 \mathrm{sgn}(r_1 + \cdots + r_l) + d_2 \mathrm{sgn}(r_2 + \cdots + r_l).$$

In general for $i = 1, \cdots, l$ we have

$$h(x_i) = d_1 \mathrm{sgn}(r_1 + \cdots + r_l) + \cdots + d_i \mathrm{sgn}(r_i + \cdots + r_l).$$

The last equality gives an expression for the left-hand side in (8) only in terms of $r = (r_1, \cdots, r_l)$ (recall that $d_1, \cdots, d_l$ are fixed):

$$\sum_{i=1}^{l} r_i h(x_i) = r_1 [d_1 \mathrm{sgn}(r_1 + \cdots + r_l)] + \tag{10}$$

$$r_2 [d_1 \mathrm{sgn}(r_1 + \cdots + r_l) + d_2 \mathrm{sgn}(r_2 + \cdots + r_l)] + \cdots +$$

$$r_l [d_1 \mathrm{sgn}(r_1 + \cdots + r_l) + d_2 \mathrm{sgn}(r_2 + \cdots + r_l) + \cdots + d_l \mathrm{sgn}(r_l)].$$

The expectation of the last expression is exactly the empirical Rademacher complexity. In order to estimate this expectation we denote $m_{l-i+1} := \mathbb{E}_r[r_i(r_i + \cdots + r_l)]$. Evidently it depends only on the index $l-i+1$. Then for the Rademacher complexity we get from (10) that (now we write h_r instead of h to indicate the dependence of h on r):

$$\mathbb{E}_r\left[\sum_{i=1}^{l} r_i h_r(x_i)\right] = d_1 m_l + [d_1 m_l + d_2 m_{l-1}] + \cdots + \tag{11}$$

$$[d_1 m_l + d_2 m_{l-1} + \cdots + d_l m_1] =$$

$$d_1 [l \cdot m_l] + d_2 [(l-1) \cdot m_{l-1}] + \cdots + d_l [1 \cdot m_1].$$

Now we will show that $m_1, \cdots, m_l$ constitute the central (middle) elements in the Pascal triangle made of binomial coefficients (here each line should be divided 2 powered by the index of the line):

$$
\boxed{1}
$$
$$
\boxed{1}\ 1
$$
$$
1\ \boxed{2}\ 1
$$
$$
1\ \boxed{3}\ 3\ 1
$$
$$
1\ 4\ \boxed{6}\ 4\ 1
$$
$$
1\ 5\ \boxed{10}\ 10\ 5\ 1
$$

$$. \quad . \quad . \quad . \quad . \quad . \quad . \quad .$$

It is enough to calculate $\mathbb{E}_r[r_1 \cdot \mathrm{sgn}(r_1 + \cdots + r_l)]$ (since l is an arbitrary positive integer). The expression $r_1 \cdot \mathrm{sgn}(r_1 + \cdots + r_l)$ is an even function in $r = (r_1, \cdots, r_l)$, so we can assume $r_1 = 1$.

$$\mathbb{E}_r[r_1 \cdot \mathrm{sgn}(r_1 + \cdots + r_l)] = \mathbb{E}_r[1 \cdot \mathrm{sgn}(1 + r_2 + \cdots + r_l)] = \quad (12)$$
$$\mathbb{E}_r[\mathrm{sgn}(1 + r_2 + \cdots + r_l) \mid |r_2 + \cdots + r_l| > 1] \cdot \mathrm{Prob}\{|r_2 + \cdots + r_l| > 1\} +$$
$$\mathrm{sgn}(1 + 0) \cdot \mathrm{Prob}\{r_2 + \cdots + r_l = 0\} +$$
$$\mathrm{sgn}(1 + 1) \cdot \mathrm{Prob}\{r_2 + \cdots + r_l = 1\} +$$
$$\mathrm{sgn}(1 - 1) \cdot \mathrm{Prob}\{r_2 + \cdots + r_l = -1\}.$$

Note that if $|r_2 + \cdots + r_l| > 1$ then $\mathrm{sgn}(1 + r_2 + \cdots + r_l) = \mathrm{sgn}(r_2 + \cdots + r_l)$. Now taking into account that $\mathrm{sgn}(r_2 + \cdots + r_l)$ is an odd function in $r = (r_1, \cdots, r_l)$, we get that the first term in the right-hand side of (12) is zero. Note also that by our definition: $\mathrm{sgn}(1 - 1) = \mathrm{sgn}(0) = 0$, so even the last term in the right-hand side of (12) is zero. Consequently from (12) we get:

$$\mathbb{E}_r[r_1 \cdot \mathrm{sgn}(r_1 + \cdots + r_l)] = \quad (13)$$
$$1 \cdot \mathrm{Prob}\{r_2 + \cdots + r_l = 0\} + 1 \cdot \mathrm{Prob}\{r_2 + \cdots + r_l = 1\}.$$

To evaluate the last expression we consider two cases:

Case 1: l is even: $l = 2t$. In this case the equality $r_2 + \cdots + r_l = 0$ is impossible, so

$$\mathbb{E}_r[r_1 \cdot \mathrm{sgn}(r_1 + \cdots + r_l)] = \mathrm{Prob}\{r_2 + \cdots + r_l = 1\} = \quad (14)$$
$$\text{number of different } (t-1) - \text{tuples out of } 2t - 1 \text{ points} = \frac{1}{2^{2t-1}} \binom{2t-1}{t-1}.$$

Case 2: l is odd: $l = 2t + 1$. In this case the equality $r_2 + \cdots + r_l = 1$ is impossible, so

$$\mathbb{E}_r[r_1 \cdot \text{sgn}(r_1 + \cdots + r_l)] = \text{Prob}\{r_2 + \cdots + r_l = 0\} = \tag{15}$$

$$\text{number of different } t - \text{tuples out of } 2t \text{ points} = \frac{1}{2^{2t}}\binom{2t}{t}.$$

Now returning back to the equality (11) we we will prove that

$$lm_l \geq (l-1)m_{l-1} \geq \cdots \geq 1 \cdot m_1. \tag{16}$$

It suffices to prove that

$$\frac{(i+1)m_{i+1}}{im_i} \geq 1, \; i = 1, \cdots, l-1. \tag{17}$$

This is easy to do using (14) and (15). If $i = 2t$ (i is even) then using binomial formula we get

$$\frac{(i+1)m_{i+1}}{im_i} = \frac{2t+1}{2t} > 1. \tag{18}$$

In the case of odd i, $i = 2t + 1$, we get

$$\frac{(i+1)m_{i+1}}{im_i} = 1. \tag{19}$$

The last two equations give (17), so (16) is proved. Now (16) together with (9) show that the right-hand side of (11) will achieve its maximum if we take d_1 as big as possible, namely if we take $d_1 = 1$, which gives that $x_1 = x_2 = \cdots = x_l = 1$. And the Rademacher complexity in this case will be maximal if $|h(1)|$ is as big as possible. Due to the Lipschitz condition (with constant $L = 1$) the maximal value for $|h(1)|$ is 1. We can take $h(1) = 1$ for all $r = (r_1, \cdots, r_l)$. Evidently the Rademacher complexity in this case ($x_1 = x_2 = \cdots = x_l = 1$) is the same as the Rademacher complexity of the identical one function $1_{[0,1]}$ (for arbitrary choice of $\{x_1, \cdots, x_l\} \subset [0, 1]$).

Theorem 6 is proved.

Proof of Theorem 5. Evidently, Theorem 6 will stay true if instead of demanding that the functions vanish at $x = 0$ we demand that they vanish at $x = 1$. Now, any function $h(x)$ which vanishes at some point $x_0 \in [0, 1]$ can be written as $h(x) = h_1(x) + h_2(x)$, where $h_1(x)$ coincides with $h(x)$ on $[0, x_0]$ and is identically zero on $[x_0, 1]$, and $h_2(x)$ coincides with $h(x)$ on $[x_0, 1]$ and is identically zero on $[0, x_0]$. Evidently $h_1(x)$ vanishes at $x = 1$ and $h_2(x)$ vanishes at $x = 0$. If, in addition, $h(x)$ is a Lipschitz function with constant L, then both $h_1(x)$ and $h_2(x)$ are Lipschitz functions with the same constant. Finally, Theorem 5 follows from Theorem 6 and Theorem 2 (part (7)).

Proof of Theorem 7. We have $\mathbf{1}_{[0,1]}(x) = I(x) + (1 - I(x))$ on $[0, 1]$. Theorem 2 (part (7)) gives that

$$R_l(\mathbf{1}_{[0,1]}) \leq R_l(I) + R_l(1 - I).$$

Since the distribution D is symmetric and the two functions $I(x)$ and $1 - I(x)$ are reflections of each other in the vertical line $x = 1/2$, we get that $R_l(I) = R_l(1-I)$. This together with the last inequality proves Theorem 7.

References

[1] Cristianini N. and Shawe-Taylor J. *An Introduction to Support Vector Machines*, Cambridge University Press, 2000.

[2] Bartlett P.L. and Mendelson S. *Rademacher and Gaussian Complexities: Risk Bounds and Stuctural Results*, Journal of Machine Learning Research 3 (2002) 463-482.

[3] Shawe-Taylor J., Ambroladze A. and Wigelius O. Under preparation.

[4] Shawe-Taylor J. and Cristianini N. *Kernel Methods for Pattern Analysis*, Cambridge University Press, 2004.

[5] Ledoux M. and Talagrand M. *Probability in Banach Spaces*, Springer-Verlag, 1991.

On Kernels, Margins, and Low-Dimensional Mappings

Maria-Florina Balcan[1], Avrim Blum[1], and Santosh Vempala[2]

[1] Computer Science Department, Carnegie Mellon University
{ninamf,avrim}@cs.cmu.edu
[2] Department of Mathematics, MIT
vempala@math.mit.edu

Abstract. Kernel functions are typically viewed as providing an implicit mapping of points into a high-dimensional space, with the ability to gain much of the power of that space without incurring a high cost if data is separable in that space by a large margin γ. However, the Johnson-Lindenstrauss lemma suggests that in the presence of a large margin, a kernel function can also be viewed as a mapping to a *low-dimensional* space, one of dimension only $\tilde{O}(1/\gamma^2)$. In this paper, we explore the question of whether one can efficiently compute such implicit low-dimensional mappings, using only black-box access to a kernel function. We answer this question in the affirmative if our method is also allowed black-box access to the underlying distribution (i.e., unlabeled examples). We also give a lower bound, showing this is not possible for an arbitrary black-box kernel function, if we do not have access to the distribution. We leave open the question of whether such mappings can be found efficiently without access to the distribution for standard kernel functions such as the polynomial kernel.

Our positive result can be viewed as saying that designing a good kernel function is much like designing a good feature space. Given a kernel, by running it in a black-box manner on random unlabeled examples, we can generate an explicit set of $\tilde{O}(1/\gamma^2)$ features, such that if the data was linearly separable with margin γ under the kernel, then it is approximately separable in this new feature space.

1 Introduction

Kernels and margins have been a powerful combination in Machine Learning. A kernel function implicitly allows one to map data into a high-dimensional space and perform certain operations there without paying a high price computationally. Furthermore, if the data indeed has a large margin linear separator in that space, then one can avoid paying a high price in terms of sample size as well [6, 7,9,11,13,12,14,15].

The starting point for this paper is the observation that if a learning problem indeed has the large margin property under some kernel $K(x,y) = \phi(x) \cdot \phi(y)$, then by the Johnson-Lindenstrauss lemma, a *random* linear projection of the

S. Ben-David, J. Case, A. Maruoka (Eds.): ALT 2004, LNAI 3244, pp. 194–205, 2004.
© Springer-Verlag Berlin Heidelberg 2004

"ϕ-space" down to a *low* dimensional space approximately preserves linear separability [1,2,8,10]. Specifically, if a target function has margin γ in the ϕ-space, then a random linear projection of the ϕ-space down to a space of dimension $d = O\left(\frac{1}{\gamma^2} \log \frac{1}{\varepsilon\delta}\right)$ will, with probability at least $1 - \delta$, have a linear separator of error at most ε (see, e.g., Arriaga and Vempala [2] and also Theorem 3 of this paper). This means that for any kernel K and margin γ, we can, in principle, think of K as mapping the input space X into an $\tilde{O}(1/\gamma^2)$-dimensional space, in essence serving as a representation of the data in a new (and not too large) feature space.

The question we consider in this paper is whether, given kernel K, we can in fact produce such a mapping efficiently. The problem with the above observation is that it requires explicitly computing the function $\phi(x)$. In particular, the mapping of X into R^d is a function $F(x) = A\phi(x)$, where A is a random matrix. However, for a given kernel K, the dimensionality and description of $\phi(x)$ might be large or even unknown. Instead, what we would like is an efficient procedure that given $K(.,.)$ as a black-box program, produces a mapping with the desired properties but with running time that depends (polynomially) only on $1/\gamma$ and the time to compute the kernel function K, with no dependence on the dimensionality of the ϕ-space.

Our main result is a positive answer to this question, if our procedure for computing the mapping is also given black-box access to the distribution D (i.e., unlabeled data). Specifically, given black-box access to a kernel function $K(x,y)$, a margin value γ, access to unlabeled examples from distribution D, and parameters ε and δ, we can in polynomial time construct a mapping of the feature space $F : X \rightarrow R^d$ where $d = O\left(\frac{1}{\gamma^2} \log \frac{1}{\varepsilon\delta}\right)$, such that if the target concept indeed has margin γ in the ϕ-space, then with probability $1 - \delta$ (over randomization in our choice of mapping function), the induced distribution in R^d is separable with error $\leq \varepsilon$.

In particular, if we set $\varepsilon \ll \varepsilon'\gamma^2$, where ε' is our input error parameter, then the error rate of the induced target function in R^d is sufficiently small that a set S of $\tilde{O}(d/\varepsilon')$ labeled examples will, with high probability, be perfectly separable in the mapped space. This means that if the target function was truly separable with margin γ in the ϕ-space, we can apply an arbitrary zero-noise linear-separator learning algorithm in the mapped space (such as a highly-optimized linear-programming package). In fact, with high probability, not only will the data in R^d be separable, but it will be separable with margin $\gamma/2$. However, while the dimension d has a logarithmic dependence on $1/\varepsilon$, the number of (unlabeled) examples we use to produce the mapping is $\tilde{O}(1/(\gamma^2\varepsilon))$.

Given the above results, a natural question is whether it might be possible to perform mappings of this type without access to the underlying distribution. In Section 5 we show that this is in general *not* possible, given only black-box access (and polynomially-many queries) to an *arbitrary* kernel K. However, it may well be possible for specific standard kernels such as the polynomial kernel or the gaussian kernel.

Our goals are to some extent related to those of Ben-David et al [4,5]. They show negative results giving simple learning problems where one cannot construct mappings to low-dimensional spaces that preserve separability. We restrict ourselves to situations where we know that such mappings exist, but our goal is to produce them efficiently.

Outline of results: We begin in Section 3 by giving a simple mapping into a d-dimensional space for $d = O(\frac{1}{\varepsilon}[\frac{1}{\gamma^2} + \ln \frac{1}{\delta}])$ that approximately preserves both separability and margin. This mapping in fact is just the following: we draw a set S of d examples from D, run $K(x,y)$ over all pairs $x, y \in S$ to place S *exactly* into R^d, and then for general $x \in X$ define $F(x)$ to be the orthogonal projection of $\phi(x)$ down to this space (which can be computed using the kernel). That is, this mapping can be viewed as an orthogonal projection of the ϕ-space down to the space spanned by $\phi(S)$. In Section 4, we give a more sophisticated mapping to a space of dimension only $O(\frac{1}{\gamma^2} \log \frac{1}{\varepsilon\delta})$. This logarithmic dependence then means we can set ε small enough as a function of the dimension and our input error parameter that we can then plug in a generic zero-noise linear separator algorithm in the mapped space (assuming the target function was perfectly separable with margin γ in the ϕ-space). In Section 5 we argue that for a black-box kernel, one must have access to the underlying distribution D if one wishes to produce a good mapping into a low-dimensional space. Finally, we give a short discussion in Section 6.

An especially simple mapping: We also note that a corollary to one of our results (Lemma 1) is that if we are willing to use dimension $d = O(\frac{1}{\varepsilon}[\frac{1}{\gamma^2} + \ln \frac{1}{\delta}])$ and we are not concerned with preserving the margin and only want approximate separability, then the following especially simple procedure suffices. Just draw a random sample of d unlabeled points $x_1, \ldots, x_d$ and define $F(x) = (K(x, x_1), \ldots, K(x, x_d))$. That is, we define the ith "feature" of x to be $K(x, x_i)$. Then, with high probability, the data will be approximately separable in this d-dimensional space if the target function had margin γ in the ϕ space. Thus, this gives a particularly simple way of using the kernel and distribution for feature generation.

2   Notation and Definitions

We assume that data is drawn from some distribution D over an instance space X and labeled by some unknown target function $c : X \to \{-1, +1\}$. We use P to denote the combined distribution over labeled examples.

A *kernel* K is a pairwise function $K(x, y)$ that can be viewed as a "legal" definition of inner product. Specifically, there must exist a function ϕ mapping X into a possibly high-dimensional Euclidean space such that $K(x, y) = \phi(x) \cdot \phi(y)$. We call the range of ϕ the "ϕ-space", and use $\phi(D)$ to denote the induced distribution in the ϕ-space produced by choosing random x from D and then applying $\phi(x)$.

We say that for a set S of labeled examples, a vector w in the ϕ-space has margin γ if:

$$\min_{(x,\ell)\in S}\left[\ell\frac{w\cdot\phi(x)}{|w||\phi(x)|}\right]\geq\gamma.$$

That is, w has margin γ if any labeled example in S is correctly classified by the linear separator $w\cdot\phi(x)\geq 0$, and furthermore the cosine of the angle between w and $\phi(x)$ has magnitude at least γ. If such a vector w exists, then we say that S is linearly separable with margin γ under the kernel K. For simplicity, we are only considering separators that pass through the origin, though our results can be adapted to the general case as well.

We can similarly talk in terms of the distribution P rather than a sample S. We say that a vector w in the ϕ-space has margin γ with respect to P if:

$$\Pr_{(x,\ell)\in P}\left[\ell\frac{w\cdot\phi(x)}{|w||\phi(x)|}<\gamma\right]=0.$$

If such a vector w exists, then we say that P is (perfectly) linearly separable with margin γ under K. One can also weaken the notion of perfect separability. We say that a vector w in the ϕ-space has error α at margin γ if:

$$\Pr_{(x,\ell)\in P}\left[\ell\frac{w\cdot\phi(x)}{|w||\phi(x)|}<\gamma\right]\leq\alpha.$$

Our starting assumption in this paper will be that P is perfectly separable with margin γ under K, but we can also weaken the assumption to the existence of a vector w with error α at margin γ, with a corresponding weakening of the implications. Our goal is a mapping $F : X \to R^d$ where d is not too large that approximately preserves separability. We use $F(D)$ to denote the induced distribution in R^d produced by selecting points in X from D and then applying F, and use $F(P) = F(D,c)$ to denote the induced distribution on labeled examples.

For a set of vectors $v_1, v_2, \ldots, v_k$ in Euclidean space, let $\text{span}(v_1,\ldots,v_k)$ denote the span of these vectors: that is, the set of vectors v that can be written as a linear combination $a_1v_1 + \ldots + a_kv_k$. Also, for a vector v and a subspace Y, let $\text{proj}(v,Y)$ be the orthogonal projection of v down to Y. So, for instance, $\text{proj}(v,\text{span}(v_1,\ldots,v_k))$ is the orthogonal projection of v down to the space spanned by $v_1,\ldots,v_k$. We note that given a set of vectors $v_1,\ldots,v_k$ and the ability to compute dot-products, this projection can be computed efficiently by a solving a set of linear equalities.

3 A Simpler Mapping

Our goal is a procedure that given black-box access to a kernel function $K(.,.)$, unlabeled examples from distribution D, and a margin value γ, produces a (probability distribution over) mappings $F : X \to R^d$ such that if the target function indeed has margin γ in the ϕ-space, then with high probability our mapping will preserve approximate linear separability. In this section, we analyze a method that produces a space of dimension $O\left(\frac{1}{\varepsilon}\left[\frac{1}{\gamma^2} + \ln\frac{1}{\delta}\right]\right)$, where ε is our bound on the error rate of the best separator in the mapped space. We will, in fact, strengthen our goal somewhat to require that $F(P)$ be approximately separable at margin $\gamma/2$ (rather than just approximately separable) so that we can use this mapping as a first step in a better mapping in Section 4.

Informally, the method is just to draw a set S of d examples from D, and then (using the kernel K) to define $F(x)$ so that it is equivalent to an orthogonal projection of $\phi(x)$ down to the space spanned by $\phi(S)$.

The following lemma is key to our analysis.

Lemma 1. *Consider any distribution over labeled examples in Euclidean space such that there exists a vector w with margin γ. Then if we draw*

$$n \geq \frac{8}{\varepsilon}\left[\frac{1}{\gamma^2} + \ln\frac{1}{\delta}\right]$$

examples $z_1, \ldots, z_n$ iid from this distribution, with probability $\geq 1 - \delta$, there exists a vector w' in $\mathrm{span}(z_1, \ldots, z_n)$ that has error at most ε at margin $\gamma/2$.

Proof. We give here two proofs of this lemma. The first (which produces a somewhat worse bound on n) uses the machinery of margin bounds. Margin bounds [12,3] tell us that using $n = O(\frac{1}{\varepsilon}[\frac{1}{\gamma^2}\log^2(1/\gamma\varepsilon) + \log\frac{1}{\delta}])$ points, with high probability, *any* separator with margin $\geq \gamma$ over the observed data has a low true error rate. Thus, the projection of the target function w into this space will have a low error rate as well. (Projecting w into this space maintains the value of $w \cdot z_i$, while possibly shrinking the vector w, which can only increase the margin over the observed data.) The only technical issue is that we want as a conclusion for the separator not only to have a low error rate over the distribution, but also to have a large margin. However, we can easily get this from the standard double-sample argument. Specifically, rather than use a $\gamma/2$-cover as in the standard margin bound, one can use a $\gamma/4$-cover. When the double sample is randomly partitioned into (S_1, S_2), it is unlikely that any member of this cover will have zero error on S_1 at margin $3\gamma/4$, and yet substantial error on S_2 at the same margin, which then implies that (since this is a $\gamma/4$-cover) no separator has zero error on S_1 at margin γ and yet substantial error on S_2 at margin $\gamma/2$.

However, we also note that since we are only asking for an existential statement (the *existence* of w'), we do not need the full machinery of margin bounds, and give a second more direct proof (with better bounds on n) from first principles. For any set of points S, let $w_{in}(S)$ be the projection of w to $\mathrm{span}(S)$, and let $w_{out}(S)$ be the orthogonal portion of w, so that $w = w_{in}(S) + w_{out}(S)$ and $w_{in}(S) \perp w_{out}(S)$. Also, for convenience, assume w and all examples z are unit-length vectors (since we have defined margins in terms of angles, we can do this without loss of generality). Now, let us make the following definitions. Say that $w_{out}(S)$ is *large* if $\Pr_z(|w_{out}(S) \cdot z| > \gamma/2) \geq \varepsilon$, and otherwise say that $w_{out}(S)$ is *small*. Notice that if $w_{out}(S)$ is small, we are done, because $w \cdot z = (w_{in}(S) \cdot z) + (w_{out}(S) \cdot z)$, which means that $w_{in}(S)$ has the properties we want. On the other hand, if $w_{out}(S)$ is large, this means that a new random point z has at least an ε chance of improving the set S. Specifically, consider z such that $|w_{out}(S) \cdot z| > \gamma/2$. For $S' = S \bigcup \{z\}$, we have $w_{out}(S') = w_{out}(S) - \text{proj}(w_{out}(S), \text{span}(S')) = w_{out}(S) - (w_{out}(S) \cdot z')z'$, where $z' = (z - \text{proj}(z, \text{span}(S)))/|z - \text{proj}(z, \text{span}(S))|$ is the portion of z orthogonal to $\text{span}(S)$, stretched to be a unit vector. But since $|w_{out}(S) \cdot z'| \geq |w_{out}(S) \cdot z|$, this implies that $|w_{out}(S')|^2 < |w_{out}(S)|^2 - (\gamma/2)^2$. Now, since $|w|^2 = |w_{out}(\emptyset)|^2 = 1$ and $|w_{out}(S)|$ can never become negative, this can happen at most $4/\gamma^2$ times. So, we have a situation where so long as w_{out} is large, each example has at least an ε chance of reducing $|w_{out}|^2$ by at least $\gamma^2/4$. This can happen at most $4/\gamma^2$ times, so Chernoff bounds imply that with probability at least $1 - \delta$, $w_{out}(S)$ will be small for S a sample of size $\geq \frac{8}{\varepsilon}\left[\frac{1}{\gamma^2} + \ln\frac{1}{\delta}\right]$. $\qquad\square$

Lemma 1 implies that if P is linearly separable with margin γ under K, and we draw $n = \frac{8}{\varepsilon}[\frac{1}{\gamma^2} + \ln\frac{1}{\delta}]$ random unlabeled examples $x_1, \ldots, x_n$ from D, with probability at least $1 - \delta$ there is a separator w' in the ϕ-space with error rate at most ϵ that can be written as

$$w' = \alpha_1 \phi(x_1) + \ldots + \alpha_n \phi(x_n).$$

Notice that since $w' \cdot \phi(x) = \alpha_1 K(x, x_1) + \ldots + \alpha_n K(x, x_n)$, an immediate implication is that if we simply think of $K(x, x_i)$ as the ith "feature" of x — that is, if we define $\hat{F}(x) = (K(x, x_1), \ldots, K(x, x_n))$ — then with high probability $\hat{F}(P)$ will be approximately linearly separable as well. So, the kernel and distribution together give us a particularly simple way of performing feature generation that preserves (approximate) separability.

Unfortunately, the above mapping $\hat{F}$ may not preserve margins because we do not have a good bound on the length of the vector $(\alpha_1, \ldots, \alpha_n)$ defining the separator in the new space. Instead, to preserve margin we want to perform an orthogonal projection. Specifically, we draw a set $S = \{x_1, ..., x_n\}$ of $\frac{8}{\varepsilon}[\frac{1}{\gamma^2} + \ln\frac{1}{\delta}]$) unlabeled examples from D and run $K(x, y)$ for all pairs $x, y \in S$. Let $M(S) = (K(x_i, x_j))_{x_i, x_j \in S}$ be the resulting kernel matrix. We use $M(S)$ to define an embedding of S into R^n by Cholesky Factorization. More specifically, we decompose $M(S)$ into $M(S) = U'U$, where U is an upper triangular matrix, and we define our mapping $F(x_j)$ to be the j'th column of U.

We next extend the embedding to all of X by considering $F : X \to R^n$ to be a mapping defined as follows: for $x \in X$, let $F(x) \in R^n$ be the point such that $F(x) \cdot F(x_i) = K(x, x_i)$, for all $i \in \{1, ..., n\}$. In other words, this mapping is equivalent to orthogonally projecting $\phi(x)$ down to $\text{span}(\phi(x_1), \ldots, \phi(x_n))$. We can compute $F(x)$ by solving the system of linear equations $[F(x)]' U = (K(x, x_1), ..., K(x, x_n))$.

We now claim that by Lemma 1, this mapping F maintains approximate separability at margin $\gamma/2$.

Theorem 1. *Given $\varepsilon, \delta, \gamma < 1$, if P has margin γ in the ϕ-space, then with probability $\geq 1 - \delta$ our mapping F (into the space of dimension n) has the* *property that $F(P)$ is linearly separable with error at most ε at margin $\gamma/2$, given that we use $n \geq \frac{8}{\varepsilon}\left[\frac{1}{\gamma^2} + \ln\frac{1}{\delta}\right]$ unlabeled examples.*

Proof. Since $\phi(D)$ is separable at margin γ, it follows from Lemma 1 that, for $n \geq \frac{8}{\varepsilon}\left[\frac{1}{\gamma^2} + \ln\frac{1}{\delta}\right]$, with probability at least $1 - \delta$, there exists a vector w that can be written as $w = \alpha_1\phi(x_1)+...+\alpha_n\phi(x_n)$, that has error at most ε at margin $\gamma/2$ (with respect to $\phi(P)$), i.e.,

$$\Pr_{(x,\ell)\in P}\left[\frac{\ell(w \cdot \phi(x))}{|w||\phi(x)|} < \frac{\gamma}{2}\right] \leq \varepsilon.$$

Consider $\overline{w} \in R^n$, $\overline{w} = \alpha_1 F(x_1) + ... + \alpha_n F(x_n)$. Since $|\overline{w}| = |w|$ and since $w \cdot \phi(x) = \overline{w} \cdot F(x)$ and $|F(x)| \leq |\phi(x)|$ for every $x \in X$, we get that $\overline{w}$ has error at most ε at margin $\gamma/2$ (with respect to $F(P)$), i.e.,

$$\Pr_{(x,\ell)\in P}\left[\frac{\ell(\overline{w} \cdot F(x))}{|\overline{w}||F(x)|} < \frac{\gamma}{2}\right] \leq \varepsilon.$$

Therefore, for our choice of n, with probability at least $1-\delta$ (over randomization in our choice of F), there exists a vector $\overline{w} \in R^n$ that has error at most ε at margin $\gamma/2$ with respect to $F(P)$. □

Notice that the running time to compute $F(x)$ is polynomial in $1/\gamma, 1/\epsilon, 1/\delta$ and the time to compute the kernel function K.

4   An Improved Mapping

We now describe an improved mapping, in which the dimension d has only a logarithmic, rather than linear, dependence on $1/\varepsilon$. The idea is to perform a two-stage process, composing the mapping from the previous section with a random linear projection from the range of that mapping down to the desired space. Thus, this mapping can be thought of as combining two types of random projection: a projection based on points chosen at random from D, and a projection based on choosing points uniformly at random in the intermediate space.

We begin by stating a result from [2] that we will use. Here $N(0, 1)$ is the standard Normal distribution with mean 0 and variance 1 and $U(-1, 1)$ is the distribution that has probability $1/2$ on -1 and probability $1/2$ on 1.

Theorem 2 (Neuronal RP [2]). *Let $u, v \in R^n$. Let $u' = \frac{1}{\sqrt{k}}Au$ and $v' = \frac{1}{\sqrt{k}}Av$ where A is a random matrix whose entries are chosen independently from either $N(0, 1)$ or $U(-1, 1)$. Then,*

$$\Pr_{A}\left[(1 - \varepsilon)|u - v|^2 \leq |u' - v'|^2 \leq (1+\varepsilon)|u - v|^2\right] \geq 1 - 2e^{-(\varepsilon^2-\varepsilon^3)\frac{k}{4}}.$$

Let $F_1 : X \to R^n$ be the mapping from Section 3, with $\varepsilon/2$ and $\delta/2$ as its error and confidence parameters respectively. Let $F_2 : R^n \to R^d$ be a random projection as in Theorem 2. Specifically, we pick A to be a random $d \times n$ matrix whose entries are chosen i.i.d. $N(0,1)$ or $U(-1,1)$ (i.e., uniformly from $\{-1,1\}$). We then set $F_2(x) = \frac{1}{\sqrt{d}} Ax$. We finally consider our overall mapping $F : X \to R^d$ to be $F(x) = F_2(F_1(x))$.

We now claim that for $n = O\left(\frac{1}{\varepsilon}\left[\frac{1}{\gamma^2} + \ln\frac{1}{\delta}\right]\right)$ and $d = O\left(\frac{1}{\gamma^2}\log(\frac{1}{\varepsilon\delta})\right)$, with high probability, this mapping has the desired properties. The basic argument is that the initial mapping F_1 maintains approximate separability at margin $\gamma/2$ by Lemma 1, and then the second mapping approximately preserves this property by Theorem 2.

Theorem 3. *Given $\varepsilon, \delta, \gamma < 1$, if P has margin γ in the ϕ-space, then with probability at least $1-\delta$, our mapping into the space of dimension $d = O\left(\frac{1}{\gamma^2}\log(\frac{1}{\varepsilon\delta})\right)$ has the property that $F(P)$ is linearly separable with error at most ε at margin at most $\gamma/4$, given that we use $n = O\left(\frac{1}{\varepsilon}\left[\frac{1}{\gamma^2} + \ln\frac{1}{\delta}\right]\right)$ unlabeled examples.*

Proof. By Lemma 1, with probability at least $1 - \delta/2$ there exists a separator w in the intermediate space R^n with error at most $\varepsilon/2$ at margin $\gamma/2$. Let us assume this in fact occurs. Now, consider some point $x \in R^n$. Theorem 2 implies that under the random projection F_2, with high probability the lengths of w, x, and $w - x$ are all approximately preserved, which implies that the cosine of the angle between w and x (i.e., the margin of x with respect to w) is also approximately preserved. Specifically, for $d = O\left(\frac{1}{\gamma^2}\log(\frac{1}{\varepsilon\delta})\right)$, we have:

$$\text{For all } x, \quad \Pr_A\left[\left|\frac{w \cdot x}{|w||x|} - \frac{F_2(w) \cdot F_2(x)}{|F_2(w)||F_2(x)|}\right| \geq \gamma/4\right] \leq \varepsilon\delta/4.$$

This implies

$$\Pr_{x \in F_1(D), A}\left[\left|\frac{w \cdot x}{|w||x|} - \frac{F_2(w) \cdot F_2(x)}{|F_2(w)||F_2(x)|}\right| \geq \gamma/4\right] \leq \varepsilon\delta/4,$$

which implies that

$$\Pr_A\left[\Pr_{x \in F_1(D)}\left(\left|\frac{w \cdot x}{|w||x|} - \frac{F_2(w) \cdot F_2(x)}{|F_2(w)||F_2(x)|}\right| \geq \gamma/4\right) \geq \varepsilon/2\right] \leq \delta/2.$$

Since w has error $\leq \varepsilon/2$ at margin $\gamma/2$, this then implies that the probability that $F_2(w)$ has error more than ε over $F_2(F_1(D))$ at margin $\gamma/4$ is at most $\delta/2$. Combining this with the $\delta/2$ failure probability of F_1 completes the proof.   □

As before, the running time to compute our mappings is polynomial in $1/\gamma, 1/\varepsilon, 1/\delta$ and the time to compute the kernel function K.

Corollary 1. *Given $\varepsilon', \delta, \gamma < 1$, if P has margin γ in the ϕ-space then we can use $n = \tilde{O}(1/(\varepsilon'\gamma^4))$ unlabeled examples to produce a mapping into R^d for $d = O(\frac{1}{\gamma^2}\log\frac{1}{\varepsilon'\gamma\delta})$, that with probability $1 - \delta$ has the property that $F(P)$ is linearly separable with error $\ll \varepsilon'/d$.*

Proof. Just plug in the desired error rate into the bounds of Theorem 3.   □

Note that we can set the error rate in Corollary 1 so that with high probability a random labeled set of size $\tilde{O}(d/\epsilon')$ will be linearly separable, and therefore any linear separator will have low error by standard VC-dimension arguments. Thus, we can apply an arbitrary linear-separator learning algorithm in R^d to learn the target concept.

5   On the Necessity of Access to D

Our main algorithm constructs a mapping $F : X \to R^d$ using black-box access to the kernel function $K(x, y)$ together with unlabeled examples from the input distribution D. It is natural to ask whether it might be possible to remove the need for access to D. In particular, notice that the mapping resulting from the Johnson-Lindenstrauss lemma has nothing to do with the input distribution: if we have access to the ϕ-space, then no matter what the distribution is, a random projection down to R^d will approximately preserve the existence of a large-margin separator with high probability. So perhaps such a mapping F can be produced by just computing K on some polynomial number of cleverly-chosen (or uniform random) points in X.[1] In this section, we give an argument showing why this may not be possible for an arbitrary kernel. This leaves open, however, the case of specific natural kernels.

In particular, consider $X = \{0, 1\}^n$, let X' be a random subset of $2^{n/2}$ elements of X, and let D be the uniform distribution on X'. For a given target function c, we will define a special ϕ-function ϕ_c such that c is a large margin separator in the ϕ-space under distribution D, but that only the points in X' behave nicely, and points not in X' provide no useful information. Specifically, consider $\phi_c : X \to R^2$ defined as:

$$\phi_c(x) = \begin{cases} (1, 0) & \text{if } x \notin X' \\ (-1/2, \sqrt{3}/2) & \text{if } x \in X' \text{ and } c(x) = 1 \\ (-1/2, -\sqrt{3}/2) & \text{if } x \in X' \text{ and } c(x) = -1 \end{cases}$$

See figure 1. This then induces the kernel:

$$K_c(x, y) = \begin{cases} 1 & \text{if } x, y \notin X' \text{ or } [x, y \in X' \text{ and } c(x) = c(y)] \\ -1/2 & \text{otherwise} \end{cases}$$

Notice that the distribution $P = (D, c)$ over labeled examples has margin $\gamma = 1/2$ in the ϕ-space.

Now, consider any algorithm with black-box access to K attempting to create a mapping $F : X \to R^d$. Since X' is a random exponentially-small fraction of X, with high probability all calls made to K return the value 1. Furthermore, even though at "runtime" when x is chosen from D, the function $F(x)$ may itself call

---

[1] Let's assume X is a "nice" space such as the unit ball or $\{0, 1\}^n$.

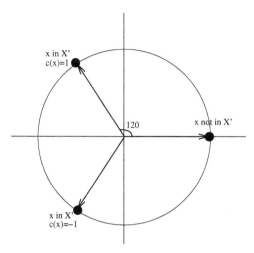

Fig. 1. Function ϕ_c used in lower bound.

$K(x, y)$ for different previously-computed points y, with high probability these will all give $K(x, y) = -1/2$. In particular, this means that the mapping F is with high probability independent of the target function c. Now, since X' has size $2^{n/2}$, there are exponentially many orthogonal functions c over D, which means that with high probability $F(D, c)$ will not even be weakly separable for a random function c over X' unless d is exponentially large in n.

Notice that the kernel in the above argument is positive semidefinite. If we wish to have a positive definite kernel, we can simply change "1" to "$1 - \alpha$" and "$-1/2$" to "$-\frac{1}{2}(1 - \alpha)$" in the definition of $K(x, y)$, except for $y = x$ in which case we keep $K(x, y) = 1$. This corresponds to a function ϕ in which rather that mapping points exactly into R^2, we map into R^{2+2^n} giving each example a $\sqrt{\alpha}$-component in its own dimension, and we scale the first two components by $\sqrt{1 - \alpha}$ to keep $\phi_c(x)$ a unit vector. The margin now becomes $\frac{1}{2}(1 - \alpha)$. Since the modifications provide no real change (an algorithm with access to the original kernel can simulate this one), the above arguments apply to this kernel as well.

Of course, these kernels are extremely unnatural, each with its own hidden target function built in. It seems quite conceivable that positive results independent of the distribution D can be achieved for standard, natural kernels.

6   Discussion and Open Problems

Our results show that given black-box access to a kernel function K and a distribution D (i.e., unlabeled examples) we can use K and D together to construct a new low-dimensional feature space in which to place our data that approximately preserves the desired properties of the kernel.

We note that if one has an unkernelized algorithm for learning linear separators with good margin-based sample-complexity bounds, then one does not necessarily need to perform a mapping first and instead can apply a more direct method. Specifically, draw a sufficiently large *labeled* set S as required by the algorithm's sample-complexity requirements, compute the kernel matrix $K(x, y)$ to place S into $R^{|S|}$, and use the learning algorithm to find a separator h in that space. New examples can be projected into that space using the kernel function (as in Section 3) and classified by h. Thus, our result is perhaps something more of interest from a conceptual point of view, or something we could apply if one had a generic (e.g., non-margin-dependent) linear separator algorithm.

One aspect that we find conceptually interesting is the relation of the two types of "random" mappings used in our approach. On the one hand, we have mappings based on random examples drawn from D, and on the other hand we have mappings based on uniform (or Gaussian) random vectors in the ϕ-space as in the Johnson-Lindenstrauss lemma.

Our main open question is whether, for natural standard kernel functions, one can produce mappings $F : X \to R^d$ in an oblivious manner, without using examples from the data distribution. The Johnson-Lindenstrauss lemma tells us that such mappings exist, but the goal is to produce them without explicitly computing the ϕ-function.

Acknowledgements. We would like to thank Adam Kalai and John Langford for helpful discussions. This work was supported in part by NSF grants CCR-0105488, NSF-ITR CCR-0122581, and NSF-ITR IIS-0312814.

References

[1] D. Achlioptas, "Database-friendly Random Projections", Symposium on Principles of Database Systems, 2001.

[2] R. I. Arriaga, S. Vempala, "An algorithmic theory of learning, Robust concepts and random projection", Proc. of the 40th Foundations of Computer Science, 616 - 623, 1999.

[3] P. Bartlett, J. Shawe-Taylor, "Generalization Performance of Support Vector Machines and Other Pattern Classifiers", Advances in Kernel Methods: Support Vector Learning, MIT Press, 1999.

[4] S. Ben-David, N. Eiron, H.U. Simon, "Limitations of Learning Via Embeddings in Euclidean Half-Spaces", Journal of Machine Learning Research 3: 441-461, 2002.

[5] S. Ben-David, "A Priori Generalization Bounds for Kernel Based Learning", NIPS 2001 Workshop on Kernel Based Learning.

[6] B. E. Boser, I. M. Guyon, V. N. Vapnik, "A Training Algorithm for Optimal Margin Classifiers", Proceedings of the Fifth Annual Workshop on Computational Learning Theory, 1992.

[7] C. Cortes, V. Vapnik, "Support-Vector Networks", Machine Learning, Volume 20(3): 273 - 297, 1995.

[8] S. Dasgupta, A. Gupta, "An elementary proof of the Johnson-Lindenstrauss Lemma", Tech Report, UC Berkeley, 1999.

[9] Y. Freund, R. E. Schapire, "Large Margin Classification Using the Perceptron Algorithm", Machine Learning, Volume 37, No. 3, 277-296, 1999.

[10] W. B. Johnson, J. Lindenstrauss, "Extensions of Lipschitz mappings into a Hilbert space", Conference in modern analysis and probability, 189–206, 1984.

[11] K. R. Muller, S. Mika, G. Ratsch, K. Tsuda, B. Scholkopf, "An Introduction to kernel-based learning algorithms", IEEE Transactions on Neural Networks, Vol. 12, pp. 181-201, 2001.

[12] J. Shawe-Taylor, P. L. Bartlett, R. C. Williamson, M. Anthony, "Structural Risk Minimization over Data-Dependent Hierarchies", IEEE Trans. on Information Theory, 44(5):1926-1940, 1998.

[13] A. J. Smola, P. Bartlett, B. Scholkopf, D. Schuurmans (Eds.), "Advances in Large Margin Classifiers", MIT Press, 2000.

[14] B. Scholkopf, A. J. Smola , "Learning with kernels. Support Vector Machines, Regularization, Optimization, and Beyond", MIT University Press, Cambridge, 2002.

[15] V. N. Vapnik, "Statistical Learning Theory", John Wiley and Sons Inc., New York, 1998.

Estimation of the Data Region Using Extreme-Value Distributions

Kazuho Watanabe[1] and Sumio Watanabe[2]

[1] Department of Computational Intelligence and Systems Science, Tokyo Institute of Technology, Mail Box:R2-5, 4259 Nagatsuta, Midori-ku, Yokohama, 226–8503 Japan
kazuho23@pi.titech.ac.jp
[2] P&I Lab, Tokyo Institute of Technology, Mail Box:R2-5, 4259 Nagatsuta, Midori-ku, Yokohama, 226–8503 Japan
swatanab@pi.titech.ac.jp

Abstract. In the field of pattern recognition or outlier detection, it is necessary to estimate the region where data of a particular class are generated. In other words, it is required to accurately estimate the support of the distribution that generates the data. Considering the 1-dimensional distribution whose support is a finite interval, the data region is estimated effectively by the maximum value and the minimum value in the samples. Limiting distributions of these values have been studied in the extreme-value theory in statistics. In this research, we propose a method to estimate the data region using the maximum value and the minimum value in the samples. We calculate the average loss of the estimator, and derive the optimally improved estimators for given loss functions.

1 Introduction

In the field of pattern recognition or outlier detection, it is often necessary to estimate the region where data of a particular class are generated. By setting a boundary that identifies the data region by learning from only examples of the target class, a new input is detected whether it is in the target class or it is, in fact, unknown.

Different methods have been developed to estimate the data region. Most often the probability density of the data is estimated using Parzen density estimation or Gaussian mixture model[3]. In these methods, the region over some probability threshold is estimated. However, setting the thresholds plagues these techniques. Assuming the data are generated from a probability distribution that has a compact support, the more precise prediction is realized by more accurately estimating the support of the distribution. For this purpose, some methods inspired by the support vector machines were proposed[4][5].

However, in a parametric model of distribution whose support is a finite interval and depends on a parameter, the log-likelihood of the model diverges. Hence, the regularity conditions of statistical estimation do not hold. The properties of such non-regular models have been clarified in some studies. It has been known that they have quite different properties from those of regular statistical

S. Ben-David, J. Case, A. Maruoka (Eds.): ALT 2004, LNAI 3244, pp. 206–220, 2004.
© Springer-Verlag Berlin Heidelberg 2004

models[2]. In estimating the support of the 1-dimensional distribution, the maximum and minimum values in the samples are used effectively. The properties of these values in the samples taken from a distribution have been studied in the theory of extreme-value statistics[1][6].

In this research, we propose a new method to estimate the data region using the maximum and minimum values in the samples. We derive the asymptotic distributions of the maximum and minimum values based on the theory of extreme-value statistics. By calculating the average loss of the estimator, the optimally improved estimators for given loss functions are derived.

In Section 2, the general theory of extreme-value statistics is introduced. In Section 3, we propose a method to estimate the data region and derive the average loss of the method. This method is derived by assuming some conditions on the distribution that generates the data. Therefore, we need to estimate some parameters of the distribution in order to use this method without any information of these parameters. In Section 4, a method to estimate these additional parameters is given. The efficiency of this method is demonstrated by simulation in Section 5.

The proposed method can also be applied to estimate a multi-dimensional data region by taking a 1-dimensional data set from multi-dimensional data. Using some mappings, some sets of 1-dimensional data are obtained. Then, a multi-dimensional data region is estimated by applying the proposed method to each 1-dimensional data set. In the latter half of Section 5, we present an experimental study on 2-dimensional data and demonstrate experimentally that the proposed method works effectively to estimate a 2-dimensional data region. Discussion and conclusions are given in Section 6. The proofs of theorems in Section 3 are in Appendix.

2 Extreme-Value Statistics

Suppose that $X^n = \{X_1, X_2, \cdots, X_n\}$ is a set of n samples independently and identically taken from a probability distribution with a density function $f(x)$ and a distribution function $F(x)$. Putting these samples in the order so that

$$X_{(1)} \leq X_{(2)} \leq \cdots \leq X_{(n)},$$

the random variable defined by the kth smallest value $X_{(k)}(1 \leq k \leq n)$ is called the order statistic. Especially, the extremely large or small variables such as $\max_{1 \leq i \leq n} X_i$, and $\min_{1 \leq i \leq n} X_i$ are called extreme-value statistics. In this section, we discuss the maximum value $M_n = \max_{1 \leq i \leq n} X_i$.

The distribution function of M_n is given by

$$P\{M_n \leq x\} = P\{X_1 \leq x, \cdots, X_n \leq x\}$$
$$= F(x)^n.$$

Differentiating this distribution function, we obtain the density function $f_{max}(x)$ of M_n as follows.

$$f_{max}(x) = nf(x)F(x)^{n-1}.$$

The following property of the maximum value $M_n = \max_{1 \le i \le n} X_i$ is well known on its asymptotic distribution function $F(x)^n$ as $n \to \infty$ [1][6].

If, for some sequences $a_n (> 0)$ and b_n, the distribution function of

$$a_n(M_n - b_n)$$

has an asymptotic distribution function $G(x)$, then $G(x)$ should have one of the following three forms.

1. $G(x) = \exp(-e^{-x}) \quad (-\infty < x < \infty),$

2. $G(x) = \begin{cases} 0 & (x \le 0), \\ \exp(-x^{-\alpha}) & (x > 0), \end{cases}$

3. $G(x) = \begin{cases} \exp(-(-x)^{\alpha}) & (x \le 0), \\ 1 & (x > 0), \end{cases}$

for some $\alpha > 0$.

The minimum value $\min_{1 \le i \le n} X_i$ also has the same property and corresponding three forms of distribution are known.

3   Estimation of the Data Region

We assume the following conditions on the density function $f(x)$.

(i) $\begin{cases} f(x) > 0 & (b < x < a), \\ f(x) = 0 & (\text{otherwise}). \end{cases}$

(ii) For $0 < \alpha, \beta < \infty$ and $0 < A, B < \infty$,

$$\lim_{x \to a-0} (a - x)^{1-\alpha} f(x) = A,$$

$$\lim_{x \to b+0} (x - b)^{1-\beta} f(x) = B.$$

The condition (i) means that the support of the distribution is a finite interval $[b, a]$. The condition (ii) means the behaviors of $f(x)$ around the endpoints a and b are determined by the parameters α, A and β, B respectively. We see that in the neighborhood of a, $f(x)$ diverges for $0 < \alpha < 1$ and converges to the positive number A for $\alpha = 1$ or to 0 for $\alpha > 1$, and the same holds for the parameter β around b. For example, when $f(x)$ is the Beta distribution on the interval $[0, 1]$, that is, $f(x) = \frac{1}{B(\phi_1, \phi_2)} x^{\phi_2 - 1}(1 - x)^{\phi_1 - 1}$ where $B(\phi_1, \phi_2) = \int_0^1 u^{\phi_1 - 1}(1 - u)^{\phi_2 - 1} du$, these conditions are satisfied with

$$a = 1, \quad b = 0, \quad \alpha = \phi_1, \quad \beta = \phi_2, \quad A = B = \frac{1}{B(\phi_1, \phi_2)}.$$

Under the above conditions, we estimate a and b, the endpoints of the density $f(x)$, by the estimators $\hat{a}, \hat{b}$. We define the estimators $\hat{a}, \hat{b}$ using the maximum and minimum values in the samples,

$$\hat{a} = \max_{1 \leq i \leq n} X_i + \frac{c_a}{n^{1/\alpha}}, \tag{1}$$

$$\hat{b} = \min_{1 \leq i \leq n} X_i - \frac{c_b}{n^{1/\beta}}, \tag{2}$$

where c_a and c_b are the coefficients that determine the correction from the maximum and minimum values respectively. The average loss of these estimators is defined later. Then we calculate the average loss and derive the optimal c_a and c_b that minimize the loss. Before defining the average loss of $\hat{a}$ and $\hat{b}$, let us consider the asymptotic distributions of the maximum and minimum values in the samples that determine the properties of the estimator $\hat{a}$ and $\hat{b}$. Following Theorem 1 and Theorem 2 are obtained.

Theorem 1. *For $M_n = \max_{1 \leq i \leq n} X_i$, $m_n = \min_{1 \leq i \leq n} X_i$, the asymptotic distributions of $(\frac{A}{\alpha}n)^{1/\alpha}(M_n - a)$ and $(\frac{B}{\beta}n)^{1/\beta}(m_n - b)$ have following distribution functions $G_{\max}(x)$ and $G_{\min}(x)$,*

$$G_{\max}(x) = \begin{cases} \exp(-(-x)^\alpha) & (x \leq 0), \\ 1 & (x > 0), \end{cases}$$

$$G_{\min}(x) = \begin{cases} 0 & (x < 0), \\ 1 - \exp(-x^\beta) & (x \geq 0). \end{cases}$$

Theorem 2. *Denoting by $G_n(s,t)$ the joint distribution function of $((\frac{A}{\alpha}n)^{1/\alpha}(M_n - a), (\frac{B}{\beta}n)^{1/\beta}(m_n - b))$,*

$$\lim_{n \to \infty} G_n(s,t) = G_{\max}(s)G_{\min}(t).$$

From Theorem 2 it is noted that the maximum M_n and minimum m_n are asymptotically independent of each other. Therefore we consider the estimation of each endpoints separately. More specifically, we put the left endpoint $b = 0$ and consider estimating only the right endpoint $a > 0$ hereafter. The estimator $\hat{b}$ of the left endpoint b and the coefficient c_b are determined by the estimator $\hat{a}$ and coefficient c_a derived from the set of samples $\{-X_1, \cdots, -X_n\}$.

We define the average loss of the estimator $\hat{a}$ eq.(1) as

$$E_{X^n}\left[U(|a - \hat{a}|)\right]. \tag{3}$$

where $E_{X^n}[\cdot]$ denotes the expectation value over all sets of samples and the function $U(x)$ is an arbitrary analytic function which satisfies $U(0) = 0$, and $U(x) \geq 0$.

In order to evaluate the average loss eq.(3), we prove the following Theorem 3 and Theorem 4.

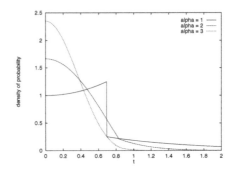

Fig. 1. Probability density of $T = n^{\frac{1}{\alpha}}|a - \hat{a}|$ $(\alpha = 1, 2, 3)$

Theorem 3. *Denoting by $H_n(t)$ the distribution function of $n^{k/\alpha}(\hat{a} - a)^k$ for any odd number $k > 0$ and by $\overline{H}_n(t)$ the distribution function of $n^{k/\alpha}|\hat{a} - a|^k$ for any natural number k,*

$$\lim_{n\to\infty} H_n(t) = \begin{cases} 1 & (t \geq c_a^k), \\ \exp(-\frac{A}{\alpha}(c_a - t^{1/k})^\alpha) & (0 < t < c_a^k), \end{cases} \tag{4}$$

and

$$\lim_{n\to\infty} \overline{H}_n(t) = \begin{cases} 1 - \exp(-\frac{A}{\alpha}(c_a + t^{1/k})^\alpha) & (t \geq c_a^k), \\ \exp(-\frac{A}{\alpha}(c_a - t^{1/k})^\alpha) - \exp(-\frac{A}{\alpha}(c_a + t^{1/k})^\alpha) & (0 < t < c_a^k). \end{cases} \tag{5}$$

If $c_a = 0$, the above asymptotic distribution functions are Weibull distribution functions.

By differentiating the above distribution functions eq.(5), we obtain the asymptotic density functions of $n^{k/\alpha}|\hat{a} - a|^k$. We illustrate them in Fig. 1 for $k = 1$, $\alpha = 1, 2, 3$, and in Fig. 2 for $k = 2$, $\alpha = 1, 2, 3$ In these figures the values of the coefficients c_a are set to be optimal described below.

Evaluating the expectation values of $n^{k/\alpha}(\hat{a} - a)^k$ and $n^{k/\alpha}|\hat{a} - a|^k$, we obtain the following theorem.

Theorem 4. *For an arbitrary natural number k,*

$$\lim_{n\to\infty} E_{X^n}\left[n^{k/\alpha}(\hat{a} - a)^k\right] = c_a^k + \sum_{i=1}^{k} c_a^{k-i}\binom{k}{i}\left(\frac{\alpha}{A}\right)^{\frac{i}{\alpha}}\frac{i}{\alpha}(-1)^i\Gamma\left(\frac{i}{\alpha}\right),$$

and if k is an odd number,

$$\lim_{n\to\infty} E_{X^n}\left[n^{k/\alpha}|\hat{a}-a|^k\right] = c_a^k + \sum_{i=1}^{k} c_a^{k-i}\binom{k}{i}\left(\frac{\alpha}{A}\right)^{\frac{i}{\alpha}}\frac{i}{\alpha}(-1)^i\{2\gamma\left(\frac{i}{\alpha}, \frac{A}{\alpha}c_a^\alpha\right) - \Gamma\left(\frac{i}{\alpha}\right)\},$$

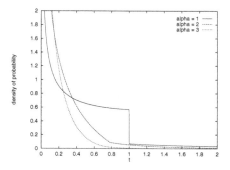

Fig. 2. Probability density of $T = n^{\frac{2}{\alpha}}|a - \hat{a}|^2$ ($\alpha = 1, 2, 3$)

where $\gamma(x, p)$ and $\Gamma(x)$ are respectively the incomplete gamma function and the gamma function. The definitions of these functions are

$$\gamma(x, p) = \int_0^p t^{x-1} e^{-t} dt, \quad \Gamma(x) = \int_0^\infty t^{x-1} e^{-t} dt.$$

From Theorem 4 we obtain the following two corollaries on the average loss eq.(3).

Corollary 1. If $a_1 = \frac{\partial U(0)}{\partial x} \neq 0$,

$$E_{X^n}\left[U(|a - \hat{a}|)\right] = \frac{a_1}{n^{1/\alpha}}\left[c_a - \left(\frac{\alpha}{A}\right)^{\frac{1}{\alpha}}\frac{1}{\alpha}\{2\gamma(\frac{1}{\alpha}, \frac{A}{\alpha}c_a^\alpha) - \Gamma(\frac{1}{\alpha})\}\right] + o\left(\frac{1}{n^{1/\alpha}}\right).$$

Denoting the optimal coefficient c_a that minimizes this average loss by c_a^*,

$$c_a^* = \left(\frac{\alpha}{A}\log 2\right)^{\frac{1}{\alpha}}.$$

Proof. Since

$$U(|a - \hat{a}|) = a_1|a - \hat{a}| + O(|a - \hat{a}|^2),$$

put $k = 1$ in Theorem 4. We obtain c_a^* by differentiating the average loss with respect to c_a using

$$\frac{\partial\gamma(x, p)}{\partial p} = p^{x-1}e^{-p}.$$

$\square$

Corollary 2. If $a_1 = \frac{\partial U(0)}{\partial x} = 0$ and $a_2 = \frac{1}{2}\frac{\partial^2 U(0)}{\partial x^2} \neq 0$,

$$E_{X^n}\left[U(|a - \hat{a}|)\right] = \frac{a_2}{n^{2/\alpha}}\left\{c_a^2 - 2\left(\frac{\alpha}{A}\right)^{\frac{1}{\alpha}}\frac{1}{\alpha}\Gamma(\frac{1}{\alpha})c_a + \left(\frac{\alpha}{A}\right)^{\frac{2}{\alpha}}\frac{2}{\alpha}\Gamma(\frac{2}{\alpha})\right\} + o\left(\frac{1}{n^{2/\alpha}}\right),$$

and

$$c_a^* = \left(\frac{\alpha}{A}\right)^{\frac{1}{\alpha}}\frac{1}{\alpha}\Gamma(\frac{1}{\alpha}).$$

Proof. Since
$$U(|a - \hat{a}|) = a_2|a - \hat{a}|^2 + O(|a - \hat{a}|^3),$$

put $k = 2$ in Theorem 4. □

4   Estimation of the Other Parameters

In the previous section, the optimal estimators were derived under the conditions
(i) and (ii) with parameters α, β, A, B. These parameters determine the behavior
of the density function $f(x)$ around the endpoints. If we estimate the data region
without any information on these parameters, we need to estimate them using
samples. In this section, we consider the case only the right endpoint is estimated
and propose a method to estimate the parameters α and A of condition (ii) in
the previous section.

The asymptotic distribution of the maximum value in the k samples is
uniquely specified if parameters α, A and endpoint a are given, and its density
function $p_k(x|\alpha, A, a)$ is given by

$$p_k(x|\alpha, A, a) = Ak(a - x)^{\alpha-1} \exp(-\frac{Ak}{\alpha}(a - x)^\alpha), \tag{6}$$

from Theorem 1 in the previous section.

Suppose that m samples $x_1, x_2, \cdots, x_m$ are independently and identically
taken from the above distribution. The log-likelihood function $L(\alpha, A, a)$ for the
m samples is given by

$$L(\alpha, A, a) = \sum_{i=1}^{m}\{\log Ak + (\alpha - 1)\log(a - x_i) - \frac{Ak}{\alpha}(a - x_i)^\alpha\}. \tag{7}$$

By dividing n samples taken from $f(x)$ into m groups and taking the maximum value in each group, the samples of maximum values are obtained. Assuming these are taken from the density eq.(6), we propose to estimate parameters
α and A by maximizing the log-likelihood eq.(7) in the case $k = n/m$. Parameters β, B and the left endpoint b is estimated in the same way using the set of
samples $\{-X_1, \cdots, -X_n\}$.

The log-likelihood eq.(7) can be maximized by an iterative algorithm. However, the maximization with respect to three variables α, A and a sometimes
makes the log-likelihood to diverge. For this reason, based on the result of the
previous section, we propose the more stable and reduced variate method where
only two variables α and A need to be estimated.

In the previous section, the endpoint a was estimated by the estimator

$$\hat{a} = \max_{1 \le i \le n} X_i + \frac{c_a}{n^{1/\alpha}}$$

with given α and A. From Corollary 1 and Corollary 2 in the previous section, c_a^*
that minimizes the average loss is represented by parameters α and A. Therefore,

the log-likelihood function eq.(7) becomes a function of two parameters α and A by replacing the parameter a with that of the form

$$a = \max_{1 \leq i \leq n} X_i + \frac{c_a^*}{n^{1/\alpha}}. \tag{8}$$

Denoting by $L(\alpha, A)$ this log-likelihood function with two variables, we propose to estimate parameters α and A by maximizing $L(\alpha, A)$ with an iterative algorithm. The gradient $(\frac{\partial L}{\partial \alpha}, \frac{\partial L}{\partial A})$ of $L(\alpha, A)$ used in the iterative algorithm is given by

$$\frac{\partial L}{\partial \alpha} = \sum_{i=1}^{m} \left[\{1 - \frac{Ak}{\alpha}(a - x_i)^\alpha\} \log(a - x_i) \right.$$

$$\left. + \frac{Ak}{\alpha^2}(a - x_i)^\alpha + \frac{1}{a - x_i}\{\alpha - 1 - Ak(a - x_i)^\alpha\} \frac{\partial a}{\partial \alpha} \right],$$

$$\frac{\partial L}{\partial A} = \sum_{i=1}^{m} \left[\frac{1}{A} - \frac{k}{\alpha}(a - x_i)^\alpha + \frac{1}{a - x_i}\{\alpha - 1 - Ak(a - x_i)^\alpha\} \frac{\partial a}{\partial A} \right],$$

where

$$\frac{\partial a}{\partial \alpha} = \frac{1}{\alpha^2}\{1 - \log \frac{\alpha \log 2}{An}\}\left(\frac{\alpha}{An} \log 2\right)^{\frac{1}{\alpha}},$$

$$\frac{\partial a}{\partial A} = -\frac{1}{\alpha A}\left(\frac{\alpha}{An} \log 2\right)^{\frac{1}{\alpha}},$$

using c_a^* of Corollary 1 in eq.(8), or

$$\frac{\partial a}{\partial \alpha} = \frac{1}{\alpha^2}\left\{(1 - \log \frac{\alpha}{An})\Gamma(1 + \frac{1}{\alpha}) - \Gamma'(1 + \frac{1}{\alpha})\right\}\left(\frac{\alpha}{An}\right)^{\frac{1}{\alpha}},$$

$$\frac{\partial a}{\partial A} = -\frac{1}{\alpha A}\left(\frac{\alpha}{An}\right)^{\frac{1}{\alpha}}\Gamma(1 + \frac{1}{\alpha}),$$

using c_a^* of Corollary 2.

5   Experiments

In this section, we demonstrate the efficiency of the proposed method by experimental results.

5.1   Estimation of the 1-Dimensional Data Region

First, taking n samples from the uniform distribution

$$f(x) = \begin{cases} 1 & (0 < x < 1), \\ 0 & (\text{otherwise}). \end{cases}$$

Table 1. The average loss (when $\alpha = A = 1.0$)

	Theoretical	α, A:known	α, A:unknown
$n(a - \hat{a})$	0.306	0.321(0.998)	0.322(1.060)
$n\lvert a - \hat{a}\rvert$	0.693	0.703(0.777)	0.760(0.806)

Table 2. The average loss (when $\alpha = A = 2.0$)

	Theoretical	α, A:known	α, A:unknown
$\sqrt{n}(a - \hat{a})$	0.053	0.061(0.463)	0.026(0.715)
$\sqrt{n}\lvert a - \hat{a}\rvert$	0.371	0.373(0.282)	0.572(0.430)

we estimated the right endpoint $a = 1.0$. This is the case when the parameters $\alpha = A = 1.0$. If α and A are known, the estimator $\hat{a}$ that minimizes $E_{X^n}\big[\lvert\hat{a} - a\rvert\big]$ is given by

$$\hat{a} = \max_{1 \le i \le n} X_i + \frac{\log 2}{n}$$

from Corollary 1 in Section 3. We set $n = 10000$ and estimated the endpoint $a = 1.0$ using the above estimator $\hat{a}$.

Then, on the assumption that α and A were unknown, we estimated the endpoint a, estimating α, A simultaneously by using the method described in Section 4. In this case, we divided 10000 samples into 100 groups and obtained 100 samples from the distribution of maximum value eq.(6).

We simulated this estimation 2000 times respectively and calculated the averages of $n(a - \hat{a})$ and $n\lvert a - \hat{a}\rvert$. The results are presented in Table 1. The standard deviations are in parentheses.

The other experiment was conducted in the case n samples were taken from the density

$$f(x) = \begin{cases} 2 - 2x & (0 < x < 1), \\ 0 & (\text{otherwise}). \end{cases}$$

In this case the endpoint $a = 1.0$ and the parameters $\alpha = A = 2.0$. If α and A are known, the estimator $\hat{a}$ that minimizes $E_{X^n}\big[\lvert\hat{a} - a\rvert\big]$ is given by

$$\hat{a} = \max_{1 \le i \le n} X_i + \sqrt{\frac{\log 2}{n}}.$$

We estimated the endpoint a again using the above $\hat{a}$ and the $\hat{a}$ that was constructed by estimating α and A simultaneously. The results of this case are given in Table 2.

We see that in the case where α, A are known, those results strongly support our theoretical results. If we estimate the parameters α, A simultaneously, the average loss becomes larger compared with the one of the case α, A are known. However, in the case when $\alpha = A = 1.0$, the results change little by estimating α and A simultaneously.

5.2   Estimation of the 2-Dimensional Data Region

A multi-dimensional data region can also be estimated by using the proposed method. For given multi-dimensional data generated in some region, we consider a mapping from multi-dimensional space to $\mathbb{R}$. The proposed method can be applied to 1-dimensional data obtained by applying this mapping to the given data. Using some mappings, some sets of 1-dimensional data are obtained. Then a multi-dimensional data region is estimated by applying the proposed method to each 1-dimensional data set.

In order to investigate the effectiveness of the proposed method when it is applied to estimate a multi-dimensional data region, we conducted an experiment where a 2-dimensional data region was estimated.

Given a set of d-dimensional data $\{\mathbf{x}_1, \cdots, \mathbf{x}_n\}$, we considered following two procedures, (P1) and (P2), in which we made k mappings $g_1(\mathbf{x}), \cdots, g_k(\mathbf{x})$ from a datum $\mathbf{x} \in \mathbb{R}^d$.

(P1): Generating vectors $\mathbf{a}_1, \cdots, \mathbf{a}_k \in \mathbb{R}^d$ randomly, define $g_i(\mathbf{x})$ by the inner product of the datum $\mathbf{x}$ and the vector $\mathbf{a}_i$, that is, $g_i(\mathbf{x}) = (\mathbf{a}_i, \mathbf{x})$.

(P2): Selecting k data $\mathbf{x}_{i_1}, \cdots, \mathbf{x}_{i_k}$ from $\{\mathbf{x}_1, \cdots, \mathbf{x}_n\}$, define $g_j(\mathbf{x})$ by the distance between $\mathbf{x}$ and $\mathbf{x}_{i_j}$ in the kernel-induced feature space. That is, $g_j(\mathbf{x}) = \|\phi(\mathbf{x}) - \phi(\mathbf{x}_{i_j})\| = \sqrt{K(\mathbf{x}, \mathbf{x}) - 2K(\mathbf{x}, \mathbf{x}_{i_j}) + K(\mathbf{x}_{i_j}, \mathbf{x}_{i_j})}$, where $\phi(\mathbf{x})$ is a mapping from the input space to the feature space, $\|\cdot\|$ is the norm in the feature space and $K(\mathbf{x}, \mathbf{y}) = (\phi(\mathbf{x}), \phi(\mathbf{y}))$ is a kernel function.

We fixed the number of samples $n = 200$ and generated 2-dimensional data uniformly in the region D^* defined by

$$D^* = \{(x_1\ x_2)^T \in \mathbb{R}^2 \mid x_1^4 + 2x_1^2 x_2^2 + x_2^4 - 2\sqrt{2}(x_1 x_2 + x_1 + x_2) + 4 \le 0\}. \quad (9)$$

Fig. 3 displays an example of this artificial data set.

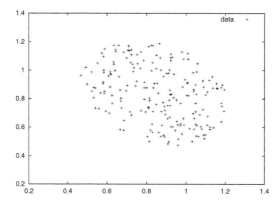

Fig. 3. An example of the 2-dimensional data set

Table 3. The error rate in the estimation of the 2-dimensional data region

	the average error rate(T_- O_+)(%)	
	$c_a = c_b = 0$	$c_a, c_b : optimal$
(P1)	3.54 (3.54 0.00)	2.40 (1.59 0.81)
(P2)	2.21 (2.20 0.01)	1.36 (1.06 0.30)

We made 40 sets of 1-dimensional data using each procedure described above respectively. More specifically, in the first procedure (P1), vectors $\mathbf{a}_1, \cdots, \mathbf{a}_{40}$ were generated uniformly on the unit circle, and in (P2), we used the polynomial kernel with degree 2, and picked out 40 data $\mathbf{x}_{i_1}, \cdots, \mathbf{x}_{i_{40}}$ that are closer to the average vector $\frac{1}{n} \sum_{i=1}^{n} \phi(\mathbf{x}_i)$ in the feature space[1].

To each 1-dimensional data set $\{g_i(\mathbf{x}_1), \cdots, g_i(\mathbf{x}_n)\}$, we applied the proposed method and estimated the right endpoint a. The coefficient c_a was set to be optimal c_a^* described in Corollary 1. And the left endpoint b was estimated by applying the proposed method to data set $\{-g_i(\mathbf{x}_1), \cdots, -g_i(\mathbf{x}_n)\}$ in the same way. For all data sets, 200 samples were divided into 40 groups and we obtained 40 samples from the distribution of the maximum value eq.(6) to estimate parameters α and A. Then we calculated the error rate on 10000 test samples. The test samples were generated on the lattice-shaped points in the region including the true data region D^* in it. By doing so, we evaluated the difference between the estimated region and the true region D^* by the square measure approximately.

The error rate is calculated by the sum of the two types of the error. One is the rate of the test data that are in the estimated region but out of the true region D^*. We denote this type of the error rate by O_+. And the other is the rate of the test data that are out of the estimated region but in D^*. We denote this by T_-.

In order to investigate the effectiveness of the proposed method where the coefficients c_a and c_b were set to be optimal, we also calculated the error rate in the case when the coefficients $c_a = c_b = 0$, that is, the maximum and minimum values were used directly to estimate the endpoints of the distribution of each 1-dimensional data set. Table 3 shows the average of the error rate over 5 data sets in the two cases when the procedures (P1) and (P2) were used in extracting 1-dimensional data sets. In parentheses, T_-(left) and O_+(right) are given.

We see that by setting c_a and c_b to be optimal, though O_+ increases, the accuracy of estimation was improved with respect to the total error rate.

---

[1] However, the explicit expression of the mapping $\phi(\mathbf{x})$ is not required since the mapping is implicitly carried out and the norm in the feature space is computed by using only the corresponding kernel function $K(\mathbf{x}, \mathbf{y}) = (1 + (\mathbf{x}, \mathbf{y}))^2$.

6   Discussion and Conclusions

In the previous sections, we evaluated $U(|\hat{a}-a|)$ as loss functions and derived the optimal estimators for the loss functions. These loss functions are symmetric with respect to $\hat{a}$ being greater(overestimation) or smaller(underestimation) than a. In some situations, it is more suitable to use loss functions that are not symmetric with respect to that. Let us consider the case that we use such asymmetric loss functions. Let l_1 and l_2 be positive constants and function $L(x)$ be

$$L(x) = \begin{cases} -l_1 x & (x < 0), \\ l_2 x & (x \geq 0). \end{cases}$$

Redefining the average loss by $E_{X^n}\left[L(\hat{a} - a)\right]$, we also obtain the following theorem in the same way.

Theorem 5. *Suppose $X_1, \cdots, X_n$ are independently and identically taken from density $f(x)$, and if the density function $f(x)$ satisfies the conditions (i),(ii) in Section 3, then*

$$E_{X^n}\left[L(\hat{a} - a)\right] = \frac{l_2}{n^{\frac{1}{\alpha}}}\left[c_a - \left(\frac{\alpha}{A}\right)^{\frac{1}{\alpha}}\frac{1}{\alpha}\left\{\left(1 + \frac{l_1}{l_2}\right)\gamma\left(\frac{1}{\alpha}, \frac{A}{\alpha}c_a^\alpha\right) - \frac{l_1}{l_2}\Gamma\left(\frac{1}{\alpha}\right)\right\}\right] + o\left(\frac{1}{n^{\frac{1}{\alpha}}}\right).$$

And denoting the optimal coefficient c_a that minimizes this average loss by c_a^*,

$$c_a^* = \left(\frac{\alpha}{A}\log\left(1 + \frac{l_1}{l_2}\right)\right)^{\frac{1}{\alpha}}.$$

In this paper, we proposed a method to estimate the data region using the maximum and minimum values in the samples. We calculated the asymptotic distributions of these values and derived the optimal estimators for given loss functions. By extracting 1-dimensional data, the proposed method has abundant practical applications. It can also be applied effectively to estimate a multi-dimensional data region by using some mappings to $\mathbb{R}^1$. We demonstrated this by the experimental study on 2-dimensional data in the latter half of Section 5. The shape of the estimated region and the accuracy of the estimation depend on the selection and the number of mappings to extract 1-dimensional data sets from the multi-dimensional data. To maximize the effectiveness of the proposed method, questions like the selection of those mappings and the optimization of the number of them have to be addressed.

Acknowledgement. This research was partially supported by the Ministry of Education, Science, Sports and Culture, Grant-in-Aid for Scientific Research 15500130 and for JSPS Fellows 4637, 2004.

References

[1] Leadbetter, M.R., Lindgren, G., Rootzen, H. : Extremes and Related Properties of Random Sequences and Processes. Springer-Verlag, New York Heidelberg Berlin. (1983)

[2] Akahira, M., Takeuchi, K.: Non-Regular Statistical Estimation. Springer-Verlag, New York. (1995)
[3] Markou, M., Singh, S.: Novelty Detection: A Review, Part I: Statistical Approaches. Signal Processing.**83** (2003) 2481–2497
[4] Scholkopf, B., Platt, J., Shawe-Taylor, J., Smola, A.J., Wiiliamson, R.C. : Estimating the support of a high-dimensional distribution. TR MSR 99-87, Microsoft Research, Redmond, WA (1999)
[5] Tax, D., Duin, R.: Support vector domain description. Pattern Recognition Letters. **20** (1999) 1191–1199
[6] Gumbel, E.J.: Statistics of Extremes. Columbia University Press (1958)
[7] Watanabe, K., Watanabe, S.: Estimating the Data Region Using the Asymptotic Distributions of Extreme-value Statistics. Proc. of Sixth Workshop on Information-Based Induction Sciences, IBIS2003 (2003) 59–64 (in Japanese)
[8] Watanabe, K., Watanabe, S.: Learning Method of the Data Region Based on Extreme-value Theory. Proc. of International Symposium on Information Theory and its Applications, ISITA2004 to appear

Appendix

Proof of Theorem 1

Proof. From assumptions (i) and (ii), in a neighborhood of a we have

$$f(x) = A(a - x)^{\alpha-1} + o((a - x)^{\alpha-1}),$$

and

$$1 - F(x) = \frac{A}{\alpha}(a - x)^{\alpha} + o((a - x)^{\alpha}).$$

Putting

$$u_n = \left(\frac{A}{\alpha}n\right)^{-1/\alpha} x + a,$$

for $x \leq 0$,

$$\begin{aligned}
\Pr\{(\frac{A}{\alpha}n)^{1/\alpha}(M_n - a) \leq x\} &= F(u_n)^n \\
&= \{1 - (1 - F(u_n))\}^n \\
&= \{1 - \frac{(-x)^{\alpha}}{n} + o(\frac{1}{n})\}^n \\
&\to \exp(-(-x)^{\alpha}) \quad (n \to \infty).
\end{aligned}$$

Since $1 - F(u_n) = 0$ for $x > 0$, we obtain $G_{\max}(x)$. By a similar argument, we also obtain $G_{\min}(x)$. □

Proof of Theorem 2

Proof. Putting

$$u_n = \left(\frac{A}{\alpha}n\right)^{-1/\alpha} s + a, \quad v_n = \left(\frac{B}{\beta}n\right)^{-1/\beta} t + b,$$

we have

$$\Pr\{((\frac{A}{\alpha}n)^{1/\alpha}(M_n - a) \leq s, \ (\frac{B}{\beta}n)^{1/\beta}(m_n - b)) \leq t\}$$
$$= F(u_n)^n - \{F(u_n) - F(v_n)\}^n. \tag{10}$$

It follows from Theorem 1 that

$$F(u_n)^n \to \exp(-(-s)^\alpha) \quad (n \to \infty),$$

and that

$$\{F(u_n) - F(v_n)\}^n = \{1 - (1 - F(u_n)) - F(v_n)\}^n$$
$$= \{1 - \frac{(-s)^\alpha}{n} - \frac{t^\beta}{n} + o(\frac{1}{n})\}^n$$
$$\to \exp(-(-s)^\alpha - t^\beta) \quad (n \to \infty).$$

Then we have

$$G_n(s, t) \to \exp(-(-s)^\alpha)(1 - \exp(-t^\beta)) \quad (n \to \infty).$$

$\square$

Proof of Theorem 3

Proof. We define

$$\underline{t} = a - n^{-\frac{1}{\alpha}}(t^{\frac{1}{k}} + c_a),$$
$$\overline{t} = a - n^{-\frac{1}{\alpha}}(-t^{\frac{1}{k}} + c_a),$$

then $n^{k/\alpha}(\hat{a} - a)^k \leq t$ is equivalent to

$$\max_{1 \leq i \leq n} X_i \leq \overline{t}$$

for any odd number $k > 0$, and $n^{k/\alpha}|\hat{a} - a|^k \leq t$ is equivalent to

$$\underline{t} \leq \max_{1 \leq i \leq n} X_i \leq \overline{t}$$

for any natural number k.
    Hence

$$H_n(t) = \begin{cases} 1 & (t \geq c_a^k), \\ F(\overline{t})^n & (t < c_a^k), \end{cases}$$

and

$$\overline{H}_n(t) = \begin{cases} 1 - F(\underline{t})^n & (t \geq c_a^k), \\ F(\overline{t})^n - F(\underline{t})^n & (t < c_a^k). \end{cases}$$

Since, in a neighborhood of a, we have

$$1 - F(x) = \frac{A}{\alpha}(a - x)^\alpha + o((a - x)^\alpha),$$

we obtain

$$F(\underline{t})^n = \{1 - \frac{1}{n}\frac{A}{\alpha}(t^{1/k} + c_a)^\alpha + o(\frac{1}{n})\}^n$$
$$\to \exp(-\frac{A}{\alpha}(c_a + t^{1/k})^\alpha) \quad (n \to \infty)$$

and

$$F(\overline{t})^n = \{1 - \frac{1}{n}\frac{A}{\alpha}(-t^{1/k} + c_a)^\alpha + o(\frac{1}{n})\}^n$$
$$\to \exp(-\frac{A}{\alpha}(c_a - t^{1/k})^\alpha) \quad (n \to \infty).$$

Thus we have eq.(4) and eq.(5). □

Proof of Theorem 4

Proof. If k is an odd number,

$$E_{X^n}\left[n^{k/\alpha}(\hat{a} - a)^k\right] \to c_a^k - \int_{-\infty}^{c_a^k} \exp(-\frac{A}{\alpha}(c_a - t^{1/k})^\alpha)dt \quad (n \to \infty)$$
$$= c_a^k - \frac{k}{A}\int_0^\infty \{c_a - (\frac{\alpha}{A}t)^{\frac{1}{\alpha}}\}^{k-1}(\frac{\alpha}{A}t)^{\frac{1}{\alpha}-1}e^{-t}dt.$$

For natural number k

$$E_{X^n}\left[n^{k/\alpha}|\hat{a} - a|^k\right] \to c_a^k - \int_0^{c_a^k} \exp(-\frac{A}{\alpha}(c_a - t^{1/k})^\alpha)dt$$
$$+ \int_0^\infty \exp(-\frac{A}{\alpha}(c_a + t^{1/k})^\alpha)dt \quad (n \to \infty)$$
$$= c_a^k - \frac{k}{A}\int_0^{\frac{A}{\alpha}c_a^\alpha} \{c_a - (\frac{\alpha}{A}t)^{\frac{1}{\alpha}}\}^{k-1}(\frac{\alpha}{A}t)^{\frac{1}{\alpha}-1}e^{-t}dt$$
$$+ \frac{k}{A}\int_{\frac{A}{\alpha}c_a^\alpha}^\infty \{(\frac{\alpha}{A}t)^{\frac{1}{\alpha}} - c_a\}^{k-1}(\frac{\alpha}{A}t)^{\frac{1}{\alpha}-1}e^{-t}dt$$

Expanding $(c_a - (\frac{\alpha}{A}t)^{\frac{1}{\alpha}})^{k-1}$ completes the proof. □

Maximum Entropy Principle in Non-ordered Setting

Victor Maslov[1] and Vladimir V'yugin[2]

[1] Moscow State University, Vorob'evy gory, Moscow 119992, Russia
[2] Institute for Information Transmission Problems, Russian Academy of Sciences,
Bol'shoi Karetnyi per. 19, Moscow GSP-4, 127994, Russia. `vyugin@iitp.ru`

Abstract. We consider the Maximum Entropy principle for non-ordered data in a non-probabilistic setting. The main goal of this paper is to deduce asymptotic relations for the frequencies of the energy levels in a non-ordered sequence $\omega^N = [\omega_1, \ldots, \omega_N]$ from the assumption of maximality of the Kolmogorov complexity $K(\omega^N)$ given a constraint $\sum_{i=1}^{N} f(\omega_i) = NE$, where E is a number and f is a numerical function.

1   Introduction

Jaynes' Maximum Entropy Principle is the well-known method for inductive inference and probabilistic forecasting in the case when some a priori constrains for the mathematical expectation and other moments are given (Jaynes [3], Cover and Thomas [1], Section 11). Extremal relations between the cost of the information transmission and the capacity of the channel were considered in [11] (Chapter 3). This principle was originated in statistical physics for computation the numerical characteristics of the ideal gases in the equilibrium state (Landau and Lifshits [8]).

Let $f(a)$ be a function taking numerical values at all letters of an alphabet $B = \{a_1, \ldots a_M\}$. For each collection of letters $\omega_1, \ldots, \omega_N$ from the alphabet B we consider the sum $\sum_{i=1}^{N} f(\omega_i)$. The value $f(\omega_i)$ can have various physical or economic meanings. It may describe the cost of the element ω_i of a message or a loss (fine) under the occurrence of the event ω_i. In thermodynamics, $f(\omega_i)$ is the energy of a particle or volume element in the state ω_i.

In contrast to [1], [3], [11], we consider non-ordered sequences, or bags, to be more concise, we consider the well known in statistical physics Bose – Einstein model [8], [10] for a system of N indistinguishable particles of n types. This type of data is typical for finance, where non-ordered and indistinguishable collections of items (like banknots or stocks) are considered.

In this work, we do not assume the existence of any probabilistic mechanism generating elements of the collection $\omega_1, \ldots, \omega_N$. Instead of this, we consider combinatorial models for describing possible collections of outcomes $\omega_1, \ldots, \omega_N$ typical for statistical mechanics; more precise, we assume that the collection of outcomes under consideration are "chaotic" or "generic" elements in some

S. Ben-David, J. Case, A. Maruoka (Eds.): ALT 2004, LNAI 3244, pp. 221–233, 2004.

simple sets. We refer to this collection as to a *microstate* (the correct definition see below). The notions of chaoticity and simplicity are introduced with the use of the algorithmic complexity (algorithmic entropy) introduced by Kolmogorov in [4].

The main goal of this paper is to deduce asymptotic relations for the frequencies of the energy levels in a microstate $\omega^N = [\omega_1, \ldots, \omega_N]$ from the assumption of maximality of the Kolmogorov complexity $K(\omega^N)$ given the cost

$$f(\omega^N) = \sum_{i=1}^{N} f(\omega_i) \text{ of the message (microstate) } \omega^N.$$

2   Preliminaries

We refer readers for details of the theory of Kolmogorov complexity and algorithmic randomness to [9]. In this section we briefly introduce some definitions used in the following.

Kolmogorov complexity is defined for any constructive (finite) object. Any set of all words in a finite alphabet is the typical example of the set of constructive objects. The definition of Kolmogorov complexity is based on the theory of algorithms. Algorithms define computable functions transforming constructive objects. Let $B(p, y)$ be an arbitrary computable function from two arguments, where p is a finite binary word, and y is a word (possibly) in a different alphabet. We suppose also that the method of decoding is prefix: if $B(p, y)$ and $B(p', y)$ are defined then none of the words p and p' is an extension of the other[1] . The measure of complexity (with respect to B) of a constructive object x given a constructive object y is defined

$$K_B(x|y) = \min\{l(p) \mid B(p, y) = x\},$$

where $l(p)$ is the length of the binary word p (we set $\min \emptyset = \infty$). We consider the function $B(p, y)$ as a method of decoding of constructive objects, where p is a code of an object under a condition y. An optimal method of decoding exists. A decoding method $B(p, y)$ is called optimal if for any other method of decoding $B'(p, y)$ the inequality $K_B(x|y) \leq K_{B'}(x|y) + O(1)$ holds, where the constant $O(1)$ does not depend on x and y (but does depend on the function B')[2] . Any two optimal decoding methods determine measures of complexity different by a constant. We fix one such optimal decoding method, denote the corresponding measure of complexity by $K(x|y)$, and call it the (conditional) Kolmogorov complexity of x with respect to y. The unconditional complexity of the word x is defined as $K(x) = K(x|\Lambda)$, where Λ is the empty sequence.

---

[1] The original Kolmogorov's definition did not used the prefix property.

[2] The expression $f(x_1, \ldots, x_n) \leq g(x_1, \ldots, x_n) + O(1)$ means that there exists a constant c such that the inequality $f(x_1, \ldots, x_n) \leq g(x_1, \ldots, x_n) + c$ holds for all $x_1, \ldots, x_n$. The expression $f(x_1, \ldots, x_n) = g(x_1, \ldots, x_n) + O(1)$ means that $f(x_1, \ldots, x_n) \leq g(x_1, \ldots, x_n) + O(1)$ and $g(x_1, \ldots, x_n) \leq f(x_1, \ldots, x_n) + O(1)$. In the following the expression $F(N) = O(G(N))$ means that a constant c exists (not depending on N) such that $|F(N)| \leq cG(N)$ for all N.

We will use the following relations that hold for the prefix complexity of positive integer numbers n (see [9]). For any $\epsilon > 0$

$$K(n) \leq \log n + (1 + \epsilon) \log \log n + O(1). \tag{1}$$

Besides,

$$K(n) \geq \log n + \log \log n \tag{2}$$

for infinitely many n.

Given the list of all elements of a finite set D we can encode any specific element of it by a a binary sequence of length[3] $\lceil \log |D| \rceil$. This encoding is prefix-free. Then we have

$$K(x|D) \leq \log |D| + O(1).$$

Moreover, for any $c > 0$, the number of all $x \in D$ for which

$$K(x|D) < \log |D| - c, \tag{3}$$

does not exceed $2^{-c}|D|$, i.e. the majority of elements of the set D have conditional Kolmogorov complexity close to its maximal value. Kolmogorov [6], [7], defined the notion of *the deficiency of algorithmic randomness* of an element x of a finite set D of constructing objects

$$d(x|D) = \log |D| - K(x|D).$$

Let $\mathrm{Rand}_m(D) = \{x \in D : d(x|D) \leq m\}$ be the set of all *m-random (chaotic)* elements of D. It holds $|\mathrm{Rand}_m(D)| \geq (1 - 2^{-m})|D|$.

Let $\mathcal{X}$ be a finite set of constructive objects and $\Xi(\alpha)$ be a computable function from $\mathcal{X}$ to some set of constructive objects. We refer to $\mathcal{X}$ as to a *sufficient statistics* (similar ideas can be found in [2], [9]). We will identify the value $\Xi(\alpha)$ of sufficient statistics and its whole prototype $\Xi[\alpha] = \Xi^{-1}(\Xi(\alpha))$. So, we identify the sufficient statistics Ξ and the corresponding *partition* of the set $\mathcal{X}$. We refer to the set $\Xi[\alpha]$ as to a *macrostate* correspondent to a *microstate* α.

We will use the following important relation which is valid for prefix Kolmogorov complexity.

$$K(x, y) = K(y) + K(x|y, K(y)) + O(1), \tag{4}$$

where x and y are arbitrary constructive objects [9].

Since $K(\alpha, \Xi(\alpha)) = K(\alpha) + O(1)$, we obtain from (4) a natural representation of the complexity of a microstate through its conditional complexity with respect to its macrostate and the complexity of the macrostate itself

$$K(\alpha) = K(\alpha|\Xi(\alpha), K(\Xi(\alpha))) + K(\Xi(\alpha)) + O(1). \tag{5}$$

---

[3] In the following $\log r$ denote the logarithm of r on the base 2, $\lceil r \rceil$ is the minimal integer number $\geq r$, $|D|$ is the cardinality of the set D.

The deficiency of randomness of a microstate α with respect to a sufficient statistics $\Xi(\alpha)$ (or to the corresponding partition) is defined

$$d_\Xi(\alpha) = \log|\Xi[\alpha]| - K(\alpha|\Xi(\alpha), K(\Xi(\alpha))) + O(1). \tag{6}$$

By definition for any $\alpha \in \Xi$ it holds $K(\alpha|\Xi, K(\Xi)) \leq \log|\Xi| + O(1)$, where Ξ is an arbitrary element of the partition. We have $d_\Xi(\alpha) \geq -c$ for all $\alpha \in \mathcal{X}$, where $c \geq 0$ is a constant. Besides, for any $m \geq 0$ the number of all $\alpha \in \mathcal{X}$ such that $d_\Xi(\alpha) > m$ does not exceed $2^{-m}|\mathcal{X}|$.

By (6) the following representation of the complexity of an element $\alpha \in \mathcal{X}$ is valid

$$K(\alpha) = \log|\Xi[\alpha]| + K(\Xi(\alpha)) - d_\Xi(\alpha) + O(1). \tag{7}$$

Let $B = \{a_1, \ldots, a_M\}$ be some finite alphabet, $f(a)$ be a function on B, and let $\epsilon_1, \ldots, \epsilon_n$ be all its different values (energy levels); we suppose that these values are computable real numbers. We also suppose that $3 \leq n \leq M$. Define $G_j = \{a : f(a) = \epsilon_j\}$, $g_j = |G_j|$, $j = 1, \ldots n$. It holds $\sum_{j=1}^n g_j = M$.

Let us consider the set $\mathcal{B}^N$ of all non-ordered sequences (bags or multi-sets) $\omega^N = [\omega_1, \ldots, \omega_N]$, which can be obtained from the set B^N by factorization with respect to the group of all permutations of the elements $\omega_1, \ldots, \omega_N$. Any multi-set ω^N can be identified with the constructive object – M-tuple

$$< (a_1, k_1), \ldots, (a_M, k_M) >, \tag{8}$$

where each letter a_i is supplied by its multiplicity $k_i = |\{j : \omega_j = a_i\}|$, $i = 1, \ldots, M$. The size of this multi-set ω^N is equal to the sum of all multiplicities $N = \sum_{i=1}^M k_i$.

Let Π_N^n a set (a simplex) of all n-tuples of nonnegative integer numbers $(N_1, \ldots, N_n)$ such that $\sum_{i=1}^n N_i = N$. A sufficient statistics $\Xi(\omega^N)$ on $\mathcal{B}^N$ with the range in Π_N^n is defined as follows. Put $\Xi(\omega^N) = (N_1, \ldots, N_n)$, where

$$N_i = N_i(\omega^N) = |\{j : 1 \leq j \leq N, f(\omega_j) = \epsilon_i\}| \tag{9}$$

for $i = 1, \ldots n$. This means that the element $\Xi_N^{N_1, \ldots, N_n}$ of the corresponding partition of the set $\mathcal{B}^N$ consists of all non-ordered sequences $\omega^N = [\omega_1, \ldots, \omega_N]$ satisfying (9). In other words, it consists of M-tuples $< (a_1, k_1), \ldots (a_M, k_M) >$ such that

$$\sum_{a_j \in G_i} k_j = N_i$$

for $i = 1, \ldots, n$. By definition

$$\Xi_N^{N_1, \ldots N_n} = \Pi_{N_1}^{g_1} \otimes \ldots \otimes \Pi_{N_n}^{g_n}.$$

Therefore, we have

$$|\Xi_N^{N_1, \ldots N_n}| = \binom{g_1 + N_1 - 1}{g_1} \ldots \binom{g_n + N_n - 1}{g_n}. \tag{10}$$

The number $\rho = N/M$ is called *density*. Let $p_i = (g_i - 1)/M$, $i = 1, \ldots, n$. We will consider asymptotic relations for $N \to \infty$, $M \to \infty$ such that $N/M \to \rho > 0$; the numbers ρ and $p_1, \ldots, p_n$ are supposed to be arbitrary positive constants.

Let $\omega^N \in \Xi_N^{N_1, \ldots N_n}$, $\nu_i = \nu_i(\omega^N) = N_i/N$, $i = 1, \ldots, n$. By Stirling formula and by (6), (7) we obtain

$$K(\omega^N) = NH(\nu_1, \ldots, \nu_n) -$$

$$-\sum_{i=1}^n \frac{1}{2} \log \frac{N_i(g_i - 1)}{N_i + g_i - 1} + K(\Xi(\omega^N)) - d_\Xi(\omega^N) + O(1), \tag{11}$$

where the leading (linear by N) member of this representation

$$H(\nu_1, \ldots, \nu_n) = \tag{12}$$

$$= \sum_{i=1}^n ((\nu_i + p_i \rho^{-1}) \log(\nu_i + p_i \rho^{-1}) - \nu_i \log \nu_i - p_i \rho^{-1} \log(p_i \rho^{-1}))$$

is called the *Bose entropy* of the frequency distribution $(\nu_1, \ldots, \nu_n)$. Notice that (12) tends to Shannon entropy of this frequency distribution when $\rho \to 0$.

The definition of the Bose entropy on the basis of Kolmogorov complexity gives us some justification of this notion.

Let the mean cost E of the transmission of a letter is given (we suppose that E is a computable real number). Denote by $\mathcal{L}^N$ the set of all microstates ω^N of size N satisfying

$$|\sum_{i=1}^n \epsilon_i N_i(\omega^N) - EN| \leq C, \tag{13}$$

where C is a constant. For C sufficiently large the number of all n-tuples $(N_1, \ldots, N_n) \in \Pi_N^n$, satisfying (13), is of order $O(N^{n-2})$.

The maximum H_{max} of the Bose entropy (12) given constrains

$$\sum_{i=1}^n \nu_i \epsilon_i = E, \quad \sum_{i=1}^n \nu_i = 1 \tag{14}$$

is computed using the method of Lagrange multipliers and reached at

$$\tilde{\nu}_i = \frac{p_i}{2^{\lambda \epsilon_i + \mu} - \rho}, \tag{15}$$

where λ and μ are defined by equations (14) (see also [8]).

Outside the field of thermododynamics the Bose - Einstein model can be applied to financial problems. For example, we can consider n groups G_i of stocks, where $i = 1, \ldots, n$. Each stock of the group G_i is of one of g_i types and brings the same income ϵ_i. We would like to predict the market equilibrium distribution of N stocks by values of income to receive the mean income E. This distribution is given by (15).

Jaynes' [3] "entropy concentration theorem" says that for any $\epsilon > 0$ the portion of all (ordered) sequences or words $\omega^N = \omega_1 \ldots \omega_N$ of the alphabet B^N

of the length N satisfying (14) and such that $|\nu_i(\omega^N) - \tilde{\nu}_i| \geq \epsilon$ for some $1 \leq i \leq n$, does not exceed e^{-cN}, where $(\tilde{\nu}_1, \ldots, \tilde{\nu}_n)$ is the point at which the maximum of the Shannon entropy $H = \sum_{i=1}^{n} -\nu_i \log \nu_i$ given constrains (14) is attained, and c is a constant depending of ϵ.

An analogue of the Jaynes' theorem holds for the set of all non-ordered sequences $\mathcal{B}^N$.

Theorem 1. *For any $\epsilon > 0$ the portion of all microstates from $\mathcal{L}^N$ such that*

$$\sum_{i=1}^{n}(\nu_i - \tilde{\nu}_i)^2 \geq \epsilon \tag{16}$$

does not exceed e^{-cN}, where $\nu_i = \nu_i(\omega^N)$ and the numbers $\tilde{\nu}_i$ are defined by (15), $i = 1, \ldots, n$. Here the constant c depends on ϵ.

Proof. Let $(N_1, \ldots, N_n) \in \Pi_N^n$ satisfies (13). Put $\delta\tilde{\nu}_i = \nu_i - \tilde{\nu}_i$. It is easy to calculate the variation of the Bose entropy inside the layer $\mathcal{L}^N$ at the point of its maximum

$$\delta H(\tilde{\nu}_1, \ldots, \tilde{\nu}_n) = H(\nu_1, \ldots, \nu_n) - H(\tilde{\nu}_1, \ldots, \tilde{\nu}_n) =$$
$$= -\sum_{i=1}^{n} \frac{(\delta\tilde{\nu}_i)^2}{\tilde{\nu}_i(1 + \rho\tilde{\nu}_i/p_i)} + o((\delta\tilde{\nu}_i)^2). \tag{17}$$

Let us suppose that (16) holds for all sufficiently large N. Then by (17) we have

$$H \leq H_{max} - c\epsilon,$$

where H is the Bose entropy (12) of the frequency distribution ν_i of the microstate ω^N, $i = 1, \ldots, n$, and c is a positive constant. Analogously to the Bernoulli case it is easy to see that the number of all microstates of size N with the entropy H is equal to $2^{NH+O(\log N)}$. The total number of all macrostates satisfying (13) is of order $O(N^{n-2})$. Hence, the number of all microstates of size N with entropy $H < H_{max} - c\epsilon$ decreases exponentially. $\square$

3   Asymptotic Relations for Frequencies of Energy Levels

The Jaynes' concentration theorem can be generalized to an asymptotic form.

Theorem 2. *There exists a sequence of sets $\mathcal{A}_N \subseteq \mathcal{L}^N$, $N = 1, 2 \ldots$, such that*

$$\lim_{N \to \infty} (|\mathcal{A}_N|/|\mathcal{L}^N|) = 1$$

and such that for any sequence of microstates $\omega^N \in \mathcal{A}^N$ the following asymptotic relation holds

$$\lim_{N \to \infty} \sum_{i=1}^{n}(\nu_i(\omega^N) - \tilde{\nu}_i)^2 = 0, \tag{18}$$

where the numbers $\tilde{\nu}_i$ are defined by (15) for $i = 1, \ldots, n$.

A pointwise version of this theorem can be formulated in terms of Kolmogorov complexity. Let $\sigma(N)$ be a nondecreasing numerical function such that $\sigma(N) = o(N)$, and ω^N, $N = 1, 2 \ldots$, be a sequence of microstates such that $\omega^N \in \mathcal{L}^N$ and

$$K(\omega^N) \geq NH_{max} - \sigma(N)$$

for all sufficiently large N. Then the asymptotic relation (18) holds.

Proof. To prove the first part of the theorem define $\mathcal{A}_N$ be equal to the set of all ω^N such that $|\nu_i - \tilde{\nu}_i| \leq N^{-1/4}$ for all $i = 1, \ldots N$.

Let us consider the pointwise version of the theorem. By (11) and (17) we have

$$K(\omega^N) = NH_{max} - \sum_{i=1}^{n} \frac{(N_i - N\tilde{\nu}_i)^2}{N\tilde{\nu}_i(1 + \rho\tilde{\nu}_i/p_i)} - \frac{1}{2}n \log N -$$
$$-d_{\equiv}(\omega^N) + K(N_1, \ldots, N_n|N, K(N)) + K(N) + o(N(\delta\tilde{\nu}_i)^2). \qquad (19)$$

By (19) and by condition this theorem we obtain

$$\sum_{i=1}^{n}(\nu_i(\omega^N) - \tilde{\nu}_i)^2 = O((\log N)/N) + o(1) = o(1).$$

We also take into account that nearby the maximum point (15) the second member in (11) can be approximated by $\frac{1}{2}n \log N + O(1)$. The theorem is proved. $\square$

The following theorem is the starting point for several following theorems presenting more tight asymptotic bounds for the frequencies. These bounds are presented in the "worst" case.

Theorem 3. *It holds*

$$\max_{\omega^N \in \mathcal{L}^N} K(\omega^N) = NH_{max} - \log N + K(N) + O(1). \qquad (20)$$

The proof of this theorem is given in Section 4.

The bound (20) is noncomputable. Two computable lower bounds, the first one holds for "most" N, the second one, trivial, holds for all N, are presented in Corollary 1; they also will be used in the definitions (22) and (24) below.

We will consider limits by the *base*

$$B_L^m = \{N : N \geq L, \quad K(N) \geq \log N - m\},$$

where $m, L = 0, 1, \ldots$. It is easy to see that $B_{L+1}^m \subseteq B_L^m$ and

$$\lim_{m \to \infty} \liminf_{N \to \infty} \frac{|B_L^m \cap \{L, \ldots, L + N - 1\}|}{N} = 1$$

for all m and L.

Indeed, taking into account that the number of all programs of length $<$ $\log N' - m$, where $N' \leq L + N - 1$, does not exceed $2^{-m}(L + N - 1)$, we obtain

$$\frac{|B_L^m \cap \{L, \ldots, L+N-1\}|}{N} \geq 1 - 2^{-m+1}$$

for all sufficiently large N.

Corollary 1. *For any $\epsilon > 0$, $m > 0$ and $N \in B_0^m$*

$$NH_{max} - m - O(1) \leq \max_{w^N \in \mathcal{L}^N} K(w^N) \leq NH_{max} +$$
$$+(1 + \epsilon) \log \log N + O(1). \qquad (21)$$

The upper bound in (21) is valid for all N. A trivial lower estimate which is valid for all N is

$$\max_{w^N \in \mathcal{L}^N} K(w^N) \geq NH_{max} - \log N - O(1).$$

The bound (21) can be obtained by applying (1) to (20).

Let σ be a nonnegative number. Let us define the set of all σ-*random microstates* in the layer (13)

$$\text{Rand}(E, \sigma, N) = \{w^N : w^N \in \mathcal{L}^N, K(w^N) \geq NH_{max} - \sigma\}. \qquad (22)$$

By Corollary 1 for all m and $N \in B_0^m$ the set $\text{Rand}(E, \sigma, N)$ is nonempty when $\sigma \geq m + O(1)$ and contains all microstates $w^N \in \mathcal{L}^N$ at which the maximum of the complexity given constrains (14) is attained. In the following we suppose that $\sigma = \sigma(N) = o(\log \log N)$.

Theorem 4. *For any m and for any nondecreasing numerical function $\sigma(N)$, such that $\sigma(N) \geq m + O(1)$ for all N and $\sigma(N) = o(\log \log N)$, the following asymptotic relation holds*

$$\limsup_{B_N^m} \sup_{w^N \in \text{Rand}(E, \sigma(N), N)} \sum_{i=1}^{n} \left(\frac{N_i - N\tilde{\nu}_i}{\sqrt{N\tilde{\nu}_i(1 + \rho\tilde{\nu}_i/p_i) \log \log N}} \right)^2 = 1, \qquad (23)$$

where the numbers $N_i = N_i(w^N)$ are defined by (9), and the values $\tilde{\nu}_i$ are defined by (15) for $i = 1, \ldots, n$.

The proof of this theorem is given in Section 4.

Let us consider the second computable lower estimate for the maximum of the complexity given constrains (14). Let us define

$$\text{Rand}'(E, \sigma, N) = \{w^N : w^N \in \mathcal{L}^N, K(w^N) \geq NH_{max} - \log N - \sigma\}. \qquad (24)$$

The following theorem holds.

Theorem 5. *For any nonnegative number σ*

$$\limsup_{N\to\infty} \sup_{\omega^N \in \mathrm{Rand}'(E,\sigma,N)} \sum_{i=1}^{n} \left(\frac{N_i - N\tilde{\nu}_i}{\sqrt{N\tilde{\nu}_i(1 + \rho\tilde{\nu}_i/p_i)}\mathrm{K}(N)} \right)^2 = 1.$$

where the notations are the same as in Theorem 4.

See the sketch of the proof of this theorem in Section 4.

The following corollary asserts that the maximum of the complexity is attained on a "random" microstate with respect to a "random" macrostate. For any $m > 0$ and N define

$$\mathrm{Max}(E, m, N) = \{\omega^N : \mathrm{K}(\omega^N) \geq \max_{\alpha^N \in \mathcal{L}^N} \mathrm{K}(\alpha^N) - m\}.$$

Corollary 2. *(from Theorem 3). For any $m > 0$ and $\omega^N \in \mathrm{Max}(E, m, N)$ relations $d_{\Xi}(\omega^N) = O(1)$ and $\mathrm{K}(N_1, \ldots, N_n | N, \mathrm{K}(N)) = \frac{1}{2}(n-2)\log N + O(1)$ hold for all N, where $\Xi = \Xi(\omega^N)$.*

Also, the following relation holds

$$\limsup_{N\to\infty} \sup_{\omega^N \in \mathrm{Max}(E,m,N)} \sum_{i=1}^{n} \left(\frac{N_i - N\tilde{\nu}_i}{\sqrt{N\tilde{\nu}_i(1 + \rho\tilde{\nu}_i/p_i)}} \right)^2 = 1,$$

where we use the same notations as in Theorem 4.

The proof of this corollary see in Section 4.

References

[1] Cover T.M., Thomas J.A. Elements of Information Theory. Wiley. 1991.
[2] Gács P., Tromp J., Vitanyi P. Algorithmic Statistics. IEEE Trans. Inform. Theory. 2001. V. 20. N5. P.1-21.
[3] Jaynes E.T. Papers on Probability, Statistics and Statistical Physics. Kluwer Academic Publisher. 2nd edition. 1989.
[4] Kolmogorov A.N. Three Approaches to the Quantitative Definition of Information. Problems Inform. Transmission. 1965. V.1 N1. P.4–7.
[5] Kolmogorov A.N. The Logical Basis for Information Theory and Probability Theory. IEEE Trans. Inf. Theory. 1968. IT. V.14. P.662–664.
[6] Kolmogorov A.N. Combinatorial Basis of Information Theory and Probability Theory. Russ. Math. Surveys. 1983. V.38 P.29–40.
[7] Kolmogorov A.N., Uspensky V.A. Algorithms and Randomness. Theory Probab. Applic. 1987. V.32. P.389–412.
[8] Landau L.D., Lifshits E.M. Statisticheskaia phisika. Chast' 1. (Statistical Physics. Part 1) Moscow: Nauka. 1984.
[9] Li M., Vitányi P. An Introduction to Kolmogorov Complexity and Its Applications, 2nd ed. New York: Springer–Verlag. 1997.
[10] Shiryaev A.N. Probability. Berlin: Springer. 1984.
[11] Stratonovich R.L. Teoriya informatsii (Information Theory). Moscow.: Sovetskoe radio. 1975.

4   Appendix: Proofs

Proof of Theorem 4. Let ω^N be a sequence of microstates such that $\omega^N \in \mathcal{L}^N$ for all N and

$$\mathrm{K}(\omega^N) \geq NH_{max} - o(\log \log N).$$

Denote $\Xi = \Xi(\omega^N)$. Let $\epsilon > 0$ be a sufficiently small number. By (1)

$$\mathrm{K}(N) \leq \log N + (1 + \frac{1}{4}\epsilon) \log \log N + O(1).$$

By this inequality and by (19) we obtain

$$(1 - \frac{1}{4}\epsilon) \sum_{i=1}^{n} \frac{(N_i - N\tilde{\nu}_i)^2}{N\tilde{\nu}_i(1 + \rho\tilde{\nu}_i/p_i)} \leq \mathrm{K}(N_1, \ldots, N_n | N, \mathrm{K}(N)) -$$

$$-\frac{1}{2}(n - 2) \log N + (1 + \frac{1}{4}\epsilon) \log \log N + o(\log \log N). \tag{25}$$

Suppose that for some positive integer number L the following inequality holds

$$\sum_{i=1}^{n} \frac{(N_i - N\tilde{\nu}_i)^2}{N\tilde{\nu}_i(1 + \rho\tilde{\nu}_i/p_i)} \leq (1 - \frac{1}{4}\epsilon)^{-1}L + o(\log \log N). \tag{26}$$

Since each number $\tilde{\nu}_i$, $i = 1, \ldots, n$, is computable, using relation (26) we can effectively find the corresponding interval of integer numbers with center in $N\tilde{\nu}_i$ containing the number N_i. The program for N_i is bounded by the length of this interval and by the number $i \leq n$. So, we have

$$\mathrm{K}(N_i | L, N) \leq \frac{1}{2} \log N + \frac{1}{2} \log L + o(\log \log N). \tag{27}$$

Hence, taking into account constrains (14) on $(N_1, \ldots, N_n)$, we obtain the inequality

$$\mathrm{K}(N_1, \ldots, N_n | L, N) - \frac{1}{2}(n - 2) \log N \leq$$

$$\leq \frac{1}{2}(n - 2) \log L + o(\log \log N).$$

Using the standard inequality $\mathrm{K}(x | L) \geq \mathrm{K}(x) - K(L) - O(1)$, we obtain

$$\mathrm{K}(N_1, \ldots, N_n | N, \mathrm{K}(N)) - \frac{1}{2}(n - 2) \log N \leq$$

$$\leq \frac{1}{2}n \log L + o(\log \log N). \tag{28}$$

Since (26) holds for L equal to the maximum of the integer part of the number

$$\mathrm{K}(N_1, \ldots, N_n | N, \mathrm{K}(N)) - \frac{1}{2}(n - 2) \log N + (1 + \frac{1}{4}\epsilon) \log \log N$$

and the number one, we obtain by (28)

$$L \le \frac{1}{2} n \log L + (1 + \frac{1}{4}\epsilon) \log \log N + o(\log \log N). \tag{29}$$

Then we have

$$K(N_1, \ldots, N_n | N, K(N)) - \frac{1}{2}(n - 2) \log N + (1 + \frac{1}{4}\epsilon) \log \log N) \le$$

$$\le (1 + \frac{1}{2}\epsilon) \log \log N + o(\log \log N). \tag{30}$$

By (25) we have for any $\epsilon > 0$

$$\sum_{i=1}^{n} \frac{(N_i - N\tilde{\nu}_i)^2}{N\tilde{\nu}_i(1 + \rho\tilde{\nu}_i/p_i)} \le (1 + \epsilon) \log \log N + o(\log \log N). \tag{31}$$

Hence,

$$\limsup_{B_N^m} \sup_{\omega^N \in \mathrm{Rand}(E, \sigma(N), N)} \sum_{i=1}^{n} \frac{(N_i - N\tilde{\nu}_i)^2}{N\tilde{\nu}_i(1 + \rho\tilde{\nu}_i/p_i) \log \log N} \le (1 + \epsilon) \tag{32}$$

for any $\epsilon > 0$. Since ϵ is an arbitrary positive real number, we can replace $1 + \epsilon$ in (32) on 1.

Now, let us prove that the lower bound in (23) is also valid. The simplex Π_N^n and the layer $\mathcal{L}^N$ contain the center of the ellipsoid

$$\sum_{i=1}^{n} \frac{(N_i - N\tilde{\nu}_i)^2}{N\tilde{\nu}_i(1 + \rho\tilde{\nu}_i/p_i) \log \log N} \le 1, \tag{33}$$

considered in the n-dimensional space $\mathcal{R}^n$. Let ϵ be a sufficiently small positive real number. The volume of the layer

$$1 - \epsilon \le \sum_{i=1}^{n} \frac{(N_i - N\tilde{\nu}_i)^2}{N\tilde{\nu}_i(1 + \rho\tilde{\nu}_i/p_i) \log \log N} \le 1 - \frac{\epsilon}{2}, \tag{34}$$

is equal to $c(\epsilon)V$, where V is the volume of the whole ellipsoid (33), and the constant $c(\epsilon)$ depends on ϵ, but does not depend on N. An analogous relation holds for the volume of intersection of the simplex Π_N^n and the layer $\mathcal{L}^N$ with the ellipsoid (33) and for the volume of analogous intersection of these two sets with the layer (34), correspondingly. Since the volume of any ellipsoid is proportional to the product of lengths of its semi-axes, the total number of all n-tuples $(N_1, \ldots, N_n)$ locating in the intersection of the layer (34) with the simplex Π_N^n and the layer $\mathcal{L}^N$ is proportional to $(N \log \log N)^{\frac{1}{2}(n-2)}$. Choose an n-tuple $(N_1, \ldots, N_n)$ of the general position locating in this intersection. We have

$$K(N_1, \ldots, N_n | N, K(N)) = \frac{1}{2}(n - 2) \log N + \log c(\epsilon) + o(\log \log N)$$

for this n-tuple. Let $\Xi = \Xi_N^{N_1,\ldots,N_n}$ be the corresponding macrostate. Then for any $\omega^N \in \Xi$ such that $d_\Xi(\omega^N) = O(1)$ the following inequality holds

$$
\begin{aligned}
K(\omega^N) \geq{} & NH_{max} - (1 - \tfrac{1}{2}\epsilon)\log\log N - \tfrac{1}{2}n\log N + \\
& + K(N_1,\ldots,N_n|N,K(N)) + K(N) + O(\log\log N) = \\
={} & NH_{max} + K(N) - \log N - \log\log N + \tfrac{1}{2}\epsilon\log\log N + \\
& + \log c(\epsilon) + o(\log\log N).
\end{aligned}
\tag{35}
$$

We have for this n-tuple $(N_1,\ldots,N_n)$ of general position

$$
\sum_{i=1}^n \frac{(N_i - N\tilde\nu_i)^2}{N\tilde\nu_i(1 + \rho\tilde\nu_i/p_i)\log\log N} \geq 1 - \epsilon.
\tag{36}
$$

By (2) the inequality $K(N) \geq \log N + \log\log N$ holds for infinitely many N. By this property and by (35) for any $\epsilon > 0$ and for any microstate ω^N of sufficiently large size N chosen as above inequalities (36) and $K(\omega^N) \geq NH_{max}$ hold. The needed lower bound follows from these inequalities. $\square$

Sketch of the proof of Theorem 5. The proof of this theorem is similar to the proof of Theorem 4, where in the second part for any $\epsilon > 0$ we can take an n-tuple $(N_1,\ldots,N_n)$ of the general position which is located in the intersection of the layer

$$
1 - \epsilon \leq \sum_{i=1}^n \frac{(N_i - N\tilde\nu_i)^2}{N\tilde\nu_i(1 + \rho\tilde\nu_i/p_i)K(N)} \leq 1 - \frac{\epsilon}{2}
\tag{37}
$$

with the simplex P_N^n and the layer $\mathcal{L}^N$, i.e. such that

$$
K(N_1,\ldots,N_n|N,K(N)) \geq \frac{1}{2}(n-2)\log N + O(1).
$$

$\square$

Proof of Theorem 3. Let us consider an n-tuple $(N_1,\ldots,N_n)$ of the general position located in the intersection of the layer

$$
1 - \epsilon \leq \sum_{i=1}^n \frac{(N_i - N\tilde\nu_i)^2}{N\tilde\nu_i(1 + \rho\tilde\nu_i/p_i)} \leq 1 - \frac{\epsilon}{2}
\tag{38}
$$

with the simplex P_N^n and the layer $\mathcal{L}^N$, i.e. such that

$$
K(N_1,\ldots,N_n|N,K(N)) \geq \frac{1}{2}(n-2)\log N + O(1),
$$

where Ξ is the corresponding macrostate. In this case, we have by (19) that for any microstate $\omega^N \in \Xi$ such that $d_\Xi(\omega^N) = O(1)$ the following inequality holds

$$
\max_{\omega^N \in \mathcal{L}^N} K(\omega^N) \geq NH_{max} - \log N + K(N) - O(1).
\tag{39}
$$

The left - hand part of the relation (20) follows from this inequality for all $N \in B_0^m$.

Assume that the maximum of the Kolmogorov complexity given constrains (14) is attained on a microstate ω^N. As was proved above, in this case the inequality

$$K(\omega^N) \geq NH_{max} - \log N + K(N) + O(1)$$

holds. By the proof of the first part of Theorem 4 we obtain

$$K(N_1, \ldots, N_n | N, K(N)) - \frac{1}{2}(n-2)\log N = O(1). \tag{40}$$

Applying (19) and taking into account (40) we obtain

$$K(\omega^N) \leq NH_{max} - \log N + K(N) + O(1).$$

The right - hand inequality of (20) follows from this relation. Theorem is proved. $\square$

Proof of Corollary 2. By

$$K(\omega^N) = NH_{max} - \log N + K(N) + O(1)$$

and representation (11) it is easy to obtain

$$\sum_{i=1}^{n}(N_i - N\tilde{\nu}_i)^2/(N\tilde{\nu}_i(1 + \rho\tilde{\nu}_i/p_i)) = O(1),$$

and also (40). Then by (11) we obtain the assertion of the corollary. $\square$

Universal Convergence of Semimeasures on Individual Random Sequences[*]

Marcus Hutter[1] and Andrej Muchnik[2]

[1] IDSIA, Galleria 2, CH-6928 Manno-Lugano, Switzerland
marcus@idsia.ch, http://www.idsia.ch/~marcus
[2] Institute of New Technologies, 10 Nizhnyaya Radischewskaya
Moscow 109004, Russia, muchnik@lpcs.math.msu.ru

Abstract. Solomonoff's central result on induction is that the posterior of a universal semimeasure M converges rapidly and with probability 1 to the true sequence generating posterior μ, if the latter is computable. Hence, M is eligible as a universal sequence predictor in case of unknown μ. Despite some nearby results and proofs in the literature, the stronger result of convergence for all (Martin-Löf) random sequences remained open. Such a convergence result would be particularly interesting and natural, since randomness can be defined in terms of M itself. We show that there are universal semimeasures M which do not converge for all random sequences, i.e. we give a partial negative answer to the open problem. We also provide a positive answer for some non-universal semimeasures. We define the incomputable measure D as a mixture over all computable measures and the enumerable semimeasure W as a mixture over all enumerable nearly-measures. We show that W converges to D and D to μ on all random sequences. The Hellinger distance measuring closeness of two distributions plays a central role.

1 Introduction

A sequence prediction task is defined as to predict the next symbol x_n from an observed sequence $x = x_1...x_{n-1}$. The key concept to attack general prediction problems is Occam's razor, and to a less extent Epicurus' principle of multiple explanations. The former/latter may be interpreted as to keep the simplest/all theories consistent with the observations $x_1...x_{n-1}$ and to use these theories to predict x_n. Solomonoff [Sol64,Sol78] formalized and combined both principles in his universal prior M which assigns high/low probability to simple/complex environments x, hence implementing Occam and Epicurus. Formally it is a mixture of all enumerable semimeasures. An abstract characterization of M by Levin [ZL70] is that M is a universal enumerable semimeasure in the sense that it multiplicatively dominates all enumerable semimeasures.

[*] This work was partially supported by the Swiss National Science Foundation (SNF grant 2100-67712.02) and the Russian Foundation for Basic Research (RFBR grants N04-01-00427 and N02-01-22001).

S. Ben-David, J. Case, A. Maruoka (Eds.): ALT 2004, LNAI 3244, pp. 234–248, 2004.

Solomonoff's [Sol78] central result is that if the probability $\mu(x_n|x_1...x_{n-1})$ of observing x_n at time n, given past observations $x_1...x_{n-1}$ is a computable function, then the universal posterior $M_n := M(x_n|x_1...x_{n-1})$ converges (rapidly!) *with μ-probability 1* (w.p.1) for $n \to \infty$ to the true posterior $\mu_n := \mu(x_n|x_1...x_{n-1})$, hence M represents a universal predictor in case of unknown "true" distribution μ. Convergence of M_n to μ_n w.p.1 tells us that M_n is close to μ_n for sufficiently large n for almost all sequences $x_1x_2....$ It says nothing about whether convergence is true for any *particular* sequence (of measure 0).

Martin-Löf (M.L.) randomness is the standard notion for randomness of individual sequences [ML66,LV97]. A M.L.-random sequence passes *all* thinkable effective randomness tests, e.g. the law of large numbers, the law of the iterated logarithm, etc. In particular, the set of all μ-random sequences has μ-measure 1. It is natural to ask whether M_n converges to μ_n (in difference or ratio) individually for all M.L.-random sequences. Clearly, Solomonoff's result shows that convergence may at most fail for a set of sequences with μ-measure zero. A convergence result for M.L.-random sequences would be particularly interesting and natural in this context, since M.L.-randomness can be defined in terms of M itself [Lev73]. Despite several attempts to solve this problem [Vov87,VL00, Hut03b], it remained open [Hut03c].

In this paper we construct an M.L.-random sequence and show the existence of a universal semimeasure which does not converge on this sequence, hence answering the open question negatively for some M. It remains open whether there exist (other) universal semimeasures, probably with particularly interesting additional structure and properties, for which M.L.-convergence holds. The main positive contribution of this work is the construction of a non-universal enumerable semimeasure W which M.L.-converges to μ as desired. As an intermediate step we consider the incomputable measure $\hat{D}$, defined as a mixture over all computable measures. We show posterior M.L.-convergence of W to $\hat{D}$ and of $\hat{D}$ to μ. The Hellinger distance measuring closeness of two posterior distributions plays a central role in this work.

The paper is organized as follows: In Section 2 we give basic notation and results (for strings, numbers, sets, functions, asymptotics, computability concepts, prefix Kolmogorov complexity), and define and discuss the concepts of (universal) (enumerable) (semi)measures. Section 3 summarizes Solomonoff's and Gács' results on posterior convergence of M to μ with probability 1. Both results can be derived from a bound on the expected Hellinger sum. We present an improved bound on the expected exponentiated Hellinger sum, which implies very strong assertions on the convergence rate. In Section 4 we investigate whether convergence for all Martin-Löf random sequences hold. We construct a universal semimeasure M and an μ-M.L.-random sequence on which M does not converge to μ for some computable μ. In Section 5 we present our main positive result. We derive a finite bound on the Hellinger sum between μ and $\hat{D}$, which is exponential in the randomness deficiency of the sequence and double exponential in the complexity of μ. This implies that the posterior of $\hat{D}$ M.L.-converges to

μ. Finally, in Section 6 we show that W is non-universal and asymptotically M.L.-converges to $\hat{D}$. Section 7 contains discussion and outlook.

2 Notation and Universal Semimeasures M

Strings. Let $i,k,n,t \in \mathbb{N} = \{1,2,3,...\}$ be natural numbers, $x,y,z \in \mathcal{X}^* = \bigcup_{n=0}^{\infty} \mathcal{X}^n$ be finite strings of symbols over finite alphabet $\mathcal{X} \ni a,b$. We denote strings x of length $\ell(x) = n$ by $x = x_1 x_2 ... x_n \in \mathcal{X}^n$ with $x_t \in \mathcal{X}$ and further abbreviate $x_{k:n} := x_k x_{k+1} ... x_{n-1} x_n$ for $k \le n$, and $x_{<n} := x_1 ... x_{n-1}$, and $\epsilon = x_{<1} = x_{n+1:n} \in \mathcal{X}^0 = \{\epsilon\}$ for the empty string. Let $\omega = x_{1:\infty} \in \mathcal{X}^\infty$ be a generic and $\alpha \in \mathcal{X}^\infty$ a specific infinite sequence. For a given sequence $x_{1:\infty}$ we say that x_t is on-sequence and $\bar{x}_t \ne x_t$ is off-sequence. x_t' may be on- or off-sequence. We identify strings with natural numbers (including zero, $\mathcal{X}^* \cong \mathbb{N} \cup \{0\}$).

Sets and functions. $\mathbb{Q}$, $\mathbb{R}$, $\mathbb{R}_+ := [0,\infty)$ are the sets of fractional, real, and non-negative real numbers, respectively. $\#\mathcal{S}$ denotes the number of elements in set $\mathcal{S}$, $\ln()$ the natural and $\log()$ the binary logarithm.

Asymptotics. We abbreviate $\lim_{n\to\infty}[f(n) - g(n)] = 0$ by $f(n) \overset{n\to\infty}{\longrightarrow} g(n)$ and say f converges to g, without implying that $\lim_{n\to\infty} g(n)$ itself exists. We write $f(x) \overset{\times}{\le} g(x)$ for $f(x) = O(g(x))$ and $f(x) \overset{+}{\le} g(x)$ for $f(x) \le g(x) + O(1)$.

Computability. A function $f: \mathcal{S} \to \mathbb{R} \cup \{\infty\}$ is said to be enumerable (or lower semi-computable) if the set $\{(x,y) : y < f(x), x \in \mathcal{S}, y \in \mathbb{Q}\}$ is recursively enumerable. f is co-enumerable (or upper semi-computable) if $[-f]$ is enumerable. f is computable (or estimable or recursive) if f and $[-f]$ are enumerable. f is approximable (or limit-computable) if there is a computable function $g: \mathcal{S} \times \mathbb{N} \to \mathbb{R}$ with $\lim_{n\to\infty} g(x,n) = f(x)$. The set of enumerable functions is recursively enumerable.

Complexity. The conditional prefix (Kolmogorov) complexity $K(x|y) := \min\{\ell(p) : U(y,p) = x \text{ halts}\}$ is the length of the shortest binary program $p \in \{0,1\}^*$ on a universal prefix Turing machine U with output $x \in \mathcal{X}^*$ and input $y \in \mathcal{X}^*$ [LV97]. $K(x) := K(x|\epsilon)$. For non-string objects o we define $K(o) := K(\langle o \rangle)$, where $\langle o \rangle \in \mathcal{X}^*$ is some standard code for o. In particular, if $(f_i)_{i=1}^n$ is an enumeration of all enumerable functions, we define $K(f_i) = K(i)$. We only need the following elementary properties: The co-enumerability of K, the upper bounds $K(x|\ell(x)) \overset{+}{\le} \ell(x)\log|\mathcal{X}|$ and $K(n) \overset{+}{\le} 2\log n$, and $K(x|y) \overset{+}{\le} K(x)$, subadditivity $K(x) \overset{+}{\le} K(x,y) \overset{+}{\le} K(y) + K(x|y)$, and information non-increase $K(f(x)) \overset{+}{\le} K(x) + K(f)$ for recursive $f: \mathcal{X}^* \to \mathcal{X}^*$.

We need the concepts of (universal) (semi)measures for strings [ZL70].

Definition 1 ((Semi)measures). *We call $\nu : \mathcal{X}^* \to [0,1]$ a semimeasure if $\nu(x) \ge \sum_{a \in \mathcal{X}} \nu(xa) \, \forall x \in \mathcal{X}^*$, and a (probability) measure if equality holds and $\nu(\epsilon) = 1$. $\nu(x)$ denotes the ν-probability that a sequence starts with string x. Further, $\nu(a|x) := \frac{\nu(xa)}{\nu(x)}$ is the posterior ν-probability that the next symbol is $a \in \mathcal{X}$, given sequence $x \in \mathcal{X}^*$.*

Definition 2 (Universal semimeasures M). *A semimeasure M is called a universal element of a class of semimeasures $\mathcal{M}$, if*

$$M \in \mathcal{M} \text{ and } \forall \nu \in \mathcal{M} \ \exists w_\nu > 0 : M(x) \geq w_\nu \cdot \nu(x) \ \forall x \in \mathcal{X}^*.$$

From now on we consider the (in a sense) largest class $\mathcal{M}$ which is relevant from a constructive point of view (but see [Sch02,Hut03b] for even larger constructive classes), namely the class of *all* semimeasures, which can be enumerated (=effectively be approximated) from below:

$$\mathcal{M} := \text{ class of all enumerable semimeasures.} \tag{1}$$

Solomonoff [Sol64, Eq.(7)] defined the universal posterior $M(x|y) = M(xy)/M(y)$ with $M(x)$ defined as the probability that the output of a universal monotone Turing machine starts with x when provided with fair coin flips on the input tape. Levin [ZL70] has shown that this M is a universal enumerable semimeasure. Another possible definition of M is as a (Bayes) mixture [Sol64,ZL70,Sol78,LV97, Hut03b]: $\tilde{M}(x) = \sum_{\nu \in \mathcal{M}} 2^{-K(\nu)} \nu(x)$, where $K(\nu)$ is the length of the shortest program computing function ν. Levin [ZL70] has shown that the class of *all* enumerable semimeasures is enumerable (with repetitions), hence $\tilde{M}$ is enumerable, since K is co-enumerable. Hence $\tilde{M} \in \mathcal{M}$, which implies

$$M(x) \geq w_{\tilde{M}} \tilde{M}(x) \geq w_{\tilde{M}} 2^{-K(\nu)} \nu(x) = w'_\nu \nu(x), \quad \text{where} \quad w'_\nu \stackrel{\times}{=} 2^{-K(\nu)}. \tag{2}$$

Up to a multiplicative constant, M assigns higher probability to all x than any other enumerable semimeasure. All M have the same very slowly decreasing (in ν) domination constants w'_ν, essentially because $\tilde{M} \in \mathcal{M}$. We drop the prime from w'_ν in the following. The mixture definition $\tilde{M}$ immediately generalizes to arbitrary weighted sums of (semi)measures over other countable classes than $\mathcal{M}$, but the class may not contain the mixture, and the domination constants may be rapidly decreasing. We will exploit this for the construction of the non-universal semimeasure W in Sections 5 and 6.

3   Posterior Convergence with Probability 1

The following convergence results for M are well-known [Sol78,LV97,Hut03a].

Theorem 3 (Convergence of M to μ w.p.1). *For any universal semimeasure M and any computable measure μ it holds:*

$$M(x'_n|x_{<n}) \to \mu(x'_n|x_{<n}) \text{ for any } x'_n \text{ and } \frac{M(x_n|x_{<n})}{\mu(x_n|x_{<n})} \to 1, \text{ both w.p.1 for } n \to \infty$$

The first convergence in difference is Solomonoff's [Sol78] celebrated convergence result. The second convergence in ratio has first been derived by Gács [LV97]. Note the subtle difference between the two convergence results. For *any* sequence $x'_{1:\infty}$ (possibly constant and not necessarily random), $M(x'_n|x_{<n}) - \mu(x'_n|x_{<n})$ converges to zero w.p.1 (referring to $x_{1:\infty}$), but no statement is possible for $M(x'_n|x_{<n})/\mu(x'_n|x_{<n})$, since $\liminf \mu(x'_n|x_{<n})$ could be zero. On the other hand, if we stay *on*-sequence ($x'_{1:\infty} = x_{1:\infty}$), we have

$M(x_n|x_{<n})/\mu(x_n|x_{<n})\to 1$ (whether $\inf\mu(x_n|x_{<n})$ tends to zero or not does not matter). Indeed, it is easy to give an example where $M(x'_n|x_{<n})/\mu(x'_n|x_{<n})$ diverges. For $\mu(1|x_{<n})=1-\mu(0|x_{<n})=\frac{1}{2}n^{-3}$ we get $\mu(0_{1:n})=\prod_{t=1}^{n}(1-\frac{1}{2}t^{-3})\overset{n\to\infty}{\longrightarrow}c=0.450...>0$, i.e. $0_{1:\infty}$ is μ-random. On the other hand, one can show that $M(0_{<n})=O(1)$ and $M(0_{<n}1)\overset{\times}{=}2^{-K(n)}$, which implies $\frac{M(1|0_{<n})}{\mu(1|0_{<n})}\overset{\times}{=}n^3$. $2^{-K(n)}\overset{\times}{\not<} n\to\infty$ for $n\to\infty$ ($K(n)\overset{+}{\not<}2\log n$).

Theorem 3 follows from (the discussion after) Lemma 4 due to $M(x)\geq w_\mu\mu(x)$. Actually the Lemma strengthens and generalizes Theorem 3. In the following we denote expectations w.r.t. measure ρ by $\mathbf{E}_\rho$, i.e. for a function $f:\mathcal{X}^n\to\mathbb{R}$, $\mathbf{E}_\rho[f]=\sum'_{x_{1:n}}\rho(x_{1:n})f(x_{1:n})$, where $\sum'$ sums over all $x_{1:n}$ for which $\rho(x_{1:n})\neq 0$. Using $\sum'$ instead $\sum$ is important for partial functions f undefined on a set of ρ-measure zero. Similarly $\mathbf{P}_\rho$ denotes the ρ-probability.

Lemma 4 (Expected Bounds on Hellinger Sum). *Let μ be a measure and ν be a semimeasure with $\nu(x)\geq w\cdot\mu(x)\ \forall x$. Then the following bounds on the Hellinger distance $h_t(\nu,\mu|\omega_{<t}):=\sum_{a\in\mathcal{X}}(\sqrt{\nu(a|\omega_{<t})}-\sqrt{\mu(a|\omega_{<t})})^2$ hold:*

$$\sum_{t=1}^{\infty}\mathbf{E}\left[\left(\sqrt{\frac{\nu(\omega_t|\omega_{<t})}{\mu(\omega_t|\omega_{<t})}}-1\right)^2\right]\overset{(i)}{\leq}\sum_{t=1}^{\infty}\mathbf{E}[h_t]\overset{(ii)}{\leq}2\ln\{\mathbf{E}[\exp(\tfrac{1}{2}\sum_{t=1}^{\infty}h_t)]\}\overset{(iii)}{\leq}\ln w^{-1}$$

where $\mathbf{E}$ means expectation w.r.t. μ.

The $\ln w^{-1}$-bounds on the first and second expression have first been derived in [Hut03a], the second being a variation of Solomonoff's bound $\sum_n\mathbf{E}[(\nu(0|x_{<n})-\mu(0|x_{<n}))^2]\leq\frac{1}{2}\ln w^{-1}$. If sequence $x_1x_2...$ is sampled from the probability measure μ, these bounds imply

$$\nu(x'_n|x_{<n})\to\mu(x'_n|x_{<n})\text{ for any }x'_n\text{ and }\frac{\nu(x_n|x_{<n})}{\mu(x_n|x_{<n})}\to 1,\text{ both w.p.1 for }n\to\infty,$$

where w.p.1 stands here and in the following for 'with μ-probability 1'.

Convergence is "fast" in the following sense: The second bound ($\sum_t\mathbf{E}[h_t]\leq\ln w^{-1}$) implies that the expected number of times t in which $h_t\geq\varepsilon$ is finite and bounded by $\frac{1}{\varepsilon}\ln w^{-1}$. The new third bound represents a significant improvement. It implies by means of a Markov inequality that the probability of even only marginally exceeding this number is extremely small, and that $\sum_t h_t$ is very unlikely to exceed $\ln w^{-1}$ by much. More precisely:

$$\mathbf{P}[\#\{t:h_t\geq\varepsilon\}\geq\tfrac{1}{\varepsilon}(\ln w^{-1}+c)]\ \leq\ \mathbf{P}[\sum_t h_t\geq\ln w^{-1}+c]$$

$$=\ \mathbf{P}[\exp(\tfrac{1}{2}\sum_t h_t)\geq e^{c/2}w^{-1/2}]\ \leq\ \sqrt{w}\mathbf{E}[\exp(\tfrac{1}{2}\sum_t h_t)]e^{-c/2}\ \leq\ e^{-c/2}.$$

Proof. We use the abbreviations $\rho_t=\rho(x_t|x_{<t})$ and $\rho_{1:n}=\rho_1\cdot...\cdot\rho_n=\rho(x_{1:n})$ for $\rho\in\{\mu,\nu,R,N,...\}$ and $h_t=\sum_{x_t}(\sqrt{\nu_t}-\sqrt{\mu_t})^2$.

(i) follows from

$$\mathbf{E}[(\sqrt{\tfrac{\nu_t}{\mu_t}}-1)^2|x_{<t}]\equiv\sum_{x_t:\mu_t\neq 0}\mu_t(\sqrt{\tfrac{\nu_t}{\mu_t}}-1)^2=\sum_{x_t:\mu_t\neq 0}(\sqrt{\nu_t}-\sqrt{\mu_t})^2\leq h_t$$

by taking the expectation $\mathbf{E}[]$ and sum $\sum_{t=1}^{\infty}$.

(ii) follows from Jensen's inequality $\exp(\mathbf{E}[f]) \le \mathbf{E}[\exp(f)]$ for $f = \frac{1}{2}\sum_t h_t$.

(iii) We exploit a construction used in [Vov87, Thm.1]. For discrete (semi)measures p and q with $\sum_i p_i = 1$ and $\sum_i q_i \le 1$ it holds:

$$\sum_i \sqrt{p_i q_i} \;\le\; 1 - \tfrac{1}{2}\sum_i (\sqrt{p_i} - \sqrt{q_i})^2 \;\le\; \exp[-\tfrac{1}{2}\sum_i (\sqrt{p_i} - \sqrt{q_i})^2]. \qquad (3)$$

The first inequality is obvious after multiplying out the second expression. The second inequality follows from $1 - x \le e^{-x}$. Vovk [Vov87] defined a measure $R_t := \sqrt{\mu_t \nu_t}/N_t$ with normalization $N_t := \sum_{x_t}\sqrt{\mu_t \nu_t}$. Applying (3) for measure μ and semimeasure ν we get $N_t \le \exp(-\frac{1}{2}h_t)$. Together with $\nu(x) \ge w \cdot \mu(x)\ \forall x$ this implies

$$\prod_{t=1}^{n} R_t \;=\; \prod_{t=1}^{n} \frac{\sqrt{\mu_t \nu_t}}{N_t} \;=\; \frac{\sqrt{\mu_{1:n}\nu_{1:n}}}{N_{1:n}} \;=\; \mu_{1:n}\sqrt{\frac{\nu_{1:n}}{\mu_{1:n}}}\,N_{1:n}^{-1} \;\ge\; \mu_{1:n}\sqrt{w}\exp(\tfrac{1}{2}\sum_{t=1}^{n} h_t).$$

Summing over $x_{1:n}$ and exploiting $\sum_{x_t} R_t = 1$ we get $1 \ge \sqrt{w}\mathbf{E}[\exp(\frac{1}{2}\sum_t h_t)]$, which proves ($iii$).

The bound and proof may be generalized to $1 \ge w^\kappa \mathbf{E}[\exp(\frac{1}{2}\sum_t\sum_{x_t}(\nu_t^\kappa - \mu_t^\kappa)^{1/\kappa})]$ with $0 \le \kappa \le \frac{1}{2}$ by defining $R_t = \mu_t^{1-\kappa}\nu_t^\kappa/N_t$ with $N_t = \sum_{x_t}\mu_t^{1-\kappa}\nu_t^\kappa$ and exploiting $\sum_i p_i^{1-\kappa}q_i^\kappa \le \exp(-\frac{1}{2}\sum_i (p_i - q_i)^{1/\kappa})$. □

One can show that the constant $\frac{1}{2}$ in Lemma 4 can essentially not been improved. Increasing it to a constant $\alpha > 1$ makes the expression infinite for some (Bernoulli) distribution μ (however we choose ν). For $\nu = M$ the expression can become already infinite for $\alpha > \frac{1}{2}$ and some computable measure μ.

4   Non-convergence in Martin-Löf Sense

Convergence of $M(x_n|x_{<n})$ to $\mu(x_n|x_{<n})$ with μ-probability 1 tells us that $M(x_n|x_{<n})$ is close to $\mu(x_n|x_{<n})$ for sufficiently large n on "most" sequences $x_{1:\infty}$. It says nothing whether convergence is true for any *particular* sequence (of measure 0). Martin-Löf randomness can be used to capture convergence properties for individual sequences. Martin-Löf randomness is a very important concept of randomness of individual sequences, which is closely related to Kolmogorov complexity and Solomonoff's universal semimeasure M. Levin gave a characterization equivalent to Martin-Löf's original definition [Lev73]:

Definition 5 (Martin-Löf random sequences). *A sequence $\omega = \omega_{1:\infty}$ is μ-Martin-Löf random (μ.M.L.) iff there is a constant $c < \infty$ such that $M(\omega_{1:n}) \le c \cdot \mu(\omega_{1:n})$ for all n. Moreover, $d_\mu(\omega) := \sup_n \{\log \frac{M(\omega_{1:n})}{\mu(\omega_{1:n})}\} \le \log c$ is called the randomness deficiency of ω.*

One can show that an M.L.-random sequence $x_{1:\infty}$ passes *all* thinkable effective randomness tests, e.g. the law of large numbers, the law of the iterated logarithm, etc. In particular, the set of all μ.M.L.-random sequences has μ-measure 1.

The open question we study in this section is whether M converges to μ (in difference or ratio) individually for all Martin-Löf random sequences. Clearly, Theorem 3 implies that convergence μ.M.L. may at most fail for a set of sequences with μ-measure zero. A convergence M.L. result would be particularly interesting and natural for M, since M.L.-randomness can be defined in terms of M itself (Definition 5).

The state of the art regarding this problem may be summarized as follows: [Vov87] contains a (non-improvable?) result which is slightly too weak to imply M.L.-convergence, [LV97, Thm.5.2.2] and [VL00, Thm.10] contain an erroneous proof for M.L.-convergence, and [Hut03b] proves a theorem indicating that the answer may be hard and subtle (see [Hut03b] for details).

The main contribution of this section is a partial answer to this question. We show that M.L.-convergence fails at least for some universal semimeasures:

Theorem 6 (Universal semimeasure non-convergence). *There exists a universal semimeasure M and a computable measure μ and a μ.M.L.-random sequence α, such that*
$$M(\alpha_n|\alpha_{<n}) \not\to \mu(\alpha_n|\alpha_{<n}) \quad \text{for} \quad n \to \infty.$$

This implies that also M_n/μ_n does not converge (since $\mu_n \leq 1$ is bounded). We do not know whether Theorem 6 holds for *all* universal semimeasures. The proof idea is to construct an enumerable (semi)measure ν such that ν dominates M on some μ-random sequence α, but $\nu(\alpha_n|\alpha_{<n}) \not\to \mu(\alpha_n|\alpha_{<n})$. Then we mix M to ν to make ν universal, but with larger contribution from ν, in order to preserve non-convergence. There is also non-constructive proof showing that an arbitrary small contamination with ν can lead to non-convergence. We only present the constructive proof.

Proof. We consider binary alphabet $\mathcal{X} = \{0,1\}$ only. Let $\mu(x) = \lambda(x) := 2^{-\ell(x)}$ be the uniform measure. We define the sequence α as the (in a sense) lexicographically first (or equivalently left-most in the tree of sequences) λ.M.L.-random sequence. Formally we define α, inductively in $n = 1,2,3,...$ by

$$\alpha_n = 0 \text{ if } M(\alpha_{<n}0) \leq 2^{-n}, \text{ and } \alpha_n = 1 \text{ else.} \tag{4}$$

We know that $M(\epsilon) \leq 1$ and $M(\alpha_{<n}0) \leq 2^{-n}$ if $\alpha_n = 0$. Inductively, assuming $M(\alpha_{<n}) \leq 2^{-n+1}$ for $\alpha_n = 1$ we have $2^{-n+1} \geq M(\alpha_{<n}) \geq M(\alpha_{<n}0) + M(\alpha_{<n}1) \geq 2^{-n} + M(\alpha_{<n}1)$ since M is a semimeasure, hence $M(\alpha_{<n}1) \leq 2^{-n}$. Hence

$$M(\alpha_{1:n}) \leq 2^{-n} \equiv \lambda(\alpha_{1:n}) \, \forall n, \text{ i.e. } \alpha \text{ is } \lambda.\text{M.L.-random.} \tag{5}$$

Let M^t with $t = 1,2,3,...$ be computable approximations of M, which enumerate M, i.e. $M^t(x) \nearrow M(x)$ for $t \to \infty$. W define α^t like α but with M replaced by M^t in the definition. $M^t \nearrow M$ implies $\alpha^t \nearrow \alpha$ (lexicographically increasing). We define an enumerable semimeasure ν as follows:

$$\nu^t(x) := \begin{cases} 2^{-t} & \text{if } \ell(x) = t \quad \text{and} \quad x < \alpha^t_{1:t} \\ 0 & \text{if } \ell(x) = t \quad \text{and} \quad x \geq \alpha^t_{1:t} \\ 0 & \text{if } \ell(x) > t \\ \nu^t(x0) + \nu^t(x1) & \text{if } \ell(x) < t \end{cases} \tag{6}$$

where $<$ is the lexicographical ordering on sequences. ν^t is a semimeasure, and with α^t also ν^t is computable and monotone increasing in t, hence $\nu := \lim_{t\to\infty} \nu^t$ is an enumerable semimeasure (indeed, $\frac{\nu(x)}{\nu(\epsilon)}$ is a measure). We could have defined a ν_{tn} by replacing $\alpha^t_{1:t}$ with $\alpha^n_{1:t}$ in (6). Since ν_{tn} is monotone increasing in t and n, any order of $t, n \to \infty$ leads to ν, so we have chosen arbitrarily $t = n$. By induction (starting from $\ell(x) = t$) it follows that

$$\nu^t(x) = 2^{-\ell(x)} \quad \text{if} \quad x < \alpha^t_{1:\ell(x)} \quad \text{and} \quad \ell(x) \le t, \qquad \nu^t(x) = 0 \quad \text{if} \quad x > \alpha^t_{1:\ell(x)}$$

On-sequence, i.e. for $x = \alpha_{1:n}$, ν^t is somewhere in-between 0 and $2^{-\ell(x)}$. Since sequence $\alpha := \lim_t \alpha^t$ is λ.M.L.-random it contains 01 infinitely often, actually $\alpha_n \alpha_{n+1} = 01$ for a non-vanishing fraction of n. In the following we fix such an n. For $t \ge n$ we get

$$\nu^t(\alpha_{<n}) = \nu^t(\alpha_{<n}0) + \nu^t(\underbrace{\alpha_{<n}1}_{>\alpha_{1:n} \ge \alpha^t_{1:n}, \text{ since } \alpha_n = 0}) = \nu^t(\alpha_{<n}0) = \nu^t(\alpha_{1:n}) \quad \Rightarrow \quad \nu(\alpha_{<n}) = \nu(\alpha_{1:n})$$

This ensures $\nu(\alpha_n | \alpha_{<n}) = 1 \ne \frac{1}{2} = \lambda_n$. For $t > n$ large enough such that $\alpha^t_{1:n+1} = \alpha_{1:n+1}$ we get:

$$\nu^t(\alpha_{1:n}) = \nu^t(\alpha^t_{1:n}) \ge \nu^t(\underbrace{\alpha^t_{1:n}0}_{<\alpha^t_{1:n+1}, \text{ since } \alpha_{n+1}=1}) = 2^{-n-1} \quad \Rightarrow \quad \nu(\alpha_{1:n}) \ge 2^{-n-1}$$

This ensures $\nu(\alpha_{1:n}) \ge 2^{-n-1} \ge \frac{1}{2}M(\alpha_{1:n})$ by (5). Let M be any universal semimeasure and $0 < \gamma < \frac{1}{5}$. Then $M'(x) := (1-\gamma)\nu(x) + \gamma M(x) \, \forall x$ is also a universal semimeasure with

$$M(\alpha_{<n}) \le 2^{-n+1} \text{ and } M(\alpha_{1:n}) \ge 0$$

$$
M'(\alpha_n|\alpha_{<n}) = \frac{(1-\gamma)\nu(\alpha_{1:n}) + \gamma M(\alpha_{1:n})}{(1-\gamma)\nu(\alpha_{<n}) + \gamma M(\alpha_{<n})} \overset{\downarrow}{\ge} \frac{(1-\gamma)\nu(\alpha_{1:n})}{(1-\gamma)\nu(\alpha_{<n}) + \gamma 2^{-n+1}}
$$

$$
\underset{\overset{\uparrow}{\nu(\alpha_{<n}) = \nu(\alpha_{1:n})}}{=} \frac{1-\gamma}{1-\gamma+\gamma 2^{-n+1}/\nu(\alpha_{1:n})} \underset{\overset{\uparrow}{\nu(\alpha_{1:n}) \ge 2^{-n-1}}}{\ge} \frac{1-\gamma}{1+3\gamma} > \frac{1}{2}.
$$

For instance for $\gamma = \frac{1}{9}$ we have $M'(\alpha_n|\alpha_{<n}) \ge \frac{2}{3} \ne \frac{1}{2} = \lambda(\alpha_n|\alpha_{<n})$ for a non-vanishing fraction of n's.   □

A converse of Theorem 6 can also be shown:

Theorem 7 (Convergence on non-random sequences). *For every universal semimeasure M there exist computable measures μ and non-μ.M.L.-random sequences α for which $M(\alpha_n|\alpha_{<n})/\mu(\alpha_n|\alpha_{<n}) \to 1$.*

5   Convergence in Martin-Löf Sense

In this and the next section we give a positive answer to the question of posterior M.L.-convergence to μ. We consider general finite alphabet $\mathcal{X}$.

Theorem 8 (Universal predictor for M.L.-random sequences). *There exists an enumerable semimeasure W such that for every computable measure μ and every μ.M.L.-random sequence ω, the posteriors converge to each other:*

$$W(a|\omega_{<t}) \overset{t\to\infty}{\longrightarrow} \mu(a|\omega_{<t}) \quad \text{for all} \quad a \in \mathcal{X} \quad \text{if} \quad d_\mu(\omega) < \infty.$$

The semimeasure W we will construct is not universal in the sense of dominating all enumerable semimeasures, unlike M. Normalizing W shows that there is also a measure whose posterior converges to μ, but this measure is not enumerable, only approximable. For proving Theorem 8 we first define an intermediate measure D as a mixture over all computable measures, which is not even approximable. Based on Lemmas 4,9,10, Proposition 11 shows that D M.L.-converges to μ. We then define the concept of quasimeasures and an enumerable semimeasure W as a mixture over all enumerable quasimeasures. Proposition 12 shows that W M.L.-converges to D. Theorem 8 immediately follows from Propositions 11 and 12.

Lemma 9 (Hellinger Chain). *Let $h(p,q) := \sum_{i=1}^{N}(\sqrt{p_i} - \sqrt{q_i})^2$ be the Hellinger distance between $p = (p_i)_{i=1}^{N} \in \mathbb{R}_+^N$ and $q = (q_i)_{i=1}^{N} \in \mathbb{R}_+^N$. Then*

i) for $p,q,r \in \mathbb{R}_+^N$ $h(p,q) \leq (1+\beta)\, h(p,r) + (1+\beta^{-1})\, h(r,q),\ $ any $\beta > 0$

ii) for $p^1,...,p^m \in \mathbb{R}_+^N$ $h(p^1,p^m) \leq 3 \sum_{k=2}^{m} k^2\, h(p^{k-1},p^k)$

Proof. (i) For any $x,y \in \mathbb{R}$ and $\beta > 0$ we have $(x+y)^2 \leq (1+\beta)x^2 + (1+\beta^{-1})y^2$. Inserting $x = \sqrt{p_i} - \sqrt{r_i}$ and $y = \sqrt{r_i} - \sqrt{q_i}$ and summing over i proves (i).

(ii) Apply (i) for the triples (p^k, p^{k+1}, p^m) for and in order of $k = 1,2,...,m-2$ with $\beta = \beta_k = k(k+1)$ and finally use $\prod_{j=1}^{k-2}(1+\beta_j^{-1}) \leq e \leq 3$. $\square$

We need a way to convert expected bounds to bounds on individual M.L. random sequences, sort of a converse of "M.L. implies w.p.1". Consider for instance the Hellinger sum $H(\omega) := \sum_{t=1}^{\infty} h_t(\mu,\rho)/\ln w^{-1}$ between two computable measures $\rho \geq w{\cdot}\mu$. Then H is an enumerable function and Lemma 4 implies $\mathbf{E}[H] \leq 1$, hence H is an integral μ-test. H can be increased to an enumerable μ-submartingale $\bar{H}$. The universal μ-submartingale M/μ multiplicatively dominates all enumerable submartingales (and hence $\bar{H}$). Since $M/\mu \leq 2^{d_\mu(\omega)}$, this implies the desired bound $H(\omega) \overset{\times}{\leq} 2^{d_\mu(\omega)}$ for individual ω. We give a self-contained direct proof, explicating all important constants.

Lemma 10 (Expected to Individual Bound). *Let $F(\omega) \geq 0$ be an enumerable function and μ be an enumerable measure and $\varepsilon > 0$ be co-enumerable. Then:*

If $\mathbf{E}_\mu[F] \leq \varepsilon$ then $F(\omega) \stackrel{\times}{\leq} \varepsilon \cdot 2^{K(\mu,F,\,1/\varepsilon)+d_\mu(\omega)}$ $\forall\omega$

where $d_\mu(\omega)$ is the μ-randomness deficiency of ω and $K(\mu,F,\,1/\varepsilon)$ is the length of the shortest program for μ, F, and $1/\varepsilon$.

Lemma 10 roughly says that for μ, F, and $\varepsilon \stackrel{\times}{=} \mathbf{E}_\mu[F]$ with short program ($K(\mu,F,1/\varepsilon)=O(1)$) and μ-random ω ($d_\mu(\omega)=O(1)$) we have $F(\omega) \stackrel{\times}{\leq} \mathbf{E}_\mu[F]$.

Proof. Let $F(\omega)=\lim_{n\to\infty}F_n(\omega)=\sup_n F_n(\omega)$ be enumerated by an increasing sequence of computable functions $F_n(\omega)$. $F_n(\omega)$ can be chosen to depend on $\omega_{1:n}$ only, i.e. $F_n(\omega)=F_n(\omega_{1:n})$ is independent of $\omega_{n+1:\infty}$. Let $\varepsilon_n \searrow \varepsilon$ co-enumerate ε. We define

$$\bar\mu_n(\omega_{1:k}) := \varepsilon_n^{-1} \sum_{\omega_{k+1:n}\in\mathcal{X}^{n-k}} \mu(\omega_{1:n})F_n(\omega_{1:n}) \text{ for } k\leq n, \text{ and } \bar\mu_n(\omega_{1:k})=0 \text{ for } k>n.$$

$\bar\mu_n$ is a computable semimeasure for each n (due to $\mathbf{E}_\mu[F_n]\leq\varepsilon$) and increasing in n, since

$$\bar\mu_n(\omega_{1:k}) \geq 0 = \bar\mu_{n-1}(\omega_{1:k}) \quad \text{for} \quad k \geq n \quad \text{and}$$

$$\bar\mu_n(\omega_{<n}) \geq \underset{\uparrow\,\omega_n\in\mathcal{X}}{\sum} \varepsilon_n^{-1}\mu(\omega_{1:n})F_{n-1}(\omega_{<n}) = \underset{\uparrow}{\varepsilon_n^{-1}\mu(\omega_{<n})F_{n-1}(\omega_{<n})} \geq \underset{\uparrow}{\bar\mu_{n-1}(\omega_{<n})}$$

$$F_n \geq F_{n-1} \qquad\qquad \mu \text{ measure} \qquad\qquad \varepsilon_n \leq \varepsilon_{n-1}$$

and similarly for $k<n-1$. Hence $\bar\mu:=\bar\mu_\infty$ is an enumerable semimeasure (indeed $\bar\mu$ is proportional to a measure). From dominance (2) we get

$$M(\omega_{1:n}) \stackrel{\times}{\geq} 2^{-K(\bar\mu)}\bar\mu(\omega_{1:n}) \geq 2^{-K(\bar\mu)}\bar\mu_n(\omega_{1:n}) = 2^{-K(\bar\mu)}\varepsilon_n^{-1}\mu(\omega_{1:n})F_n(\omega_{1:n}). \tag{7}$$

In order to enumerate $\bar\mu$, we need to enumerate μ, F, and ε^{-1}, hence $K(\bar\mu) \stackrel{+}{\leq} K(\mu,F,1/\varepsilon)$, so we get

$$F_n(\omega) \equiv F_n(\omega_{1:n}) \stackrel{\times}{\leq} \varepsilon_n \cdot 2^{K(\mu,F,1/\varepsilon)} \cdot \frac{M(\omega_{1:n})}{\mu(\omega_{1:n})} \leq \varepsilon_n \cdot 2^{K(\mu,F,1/\varepsilon)+d_\mu(\omega)}.$$

Taking the limit $F_n \nearrow F$ and $\varepsilon_n \searrow \varepsilon$ completes the proof. $\qquad\square$

Let $\mathcal{M}=\{\nu_1,\nu_2,...\}$ be an enumeration of all enumerable semimeasures, $J_k:=\{i\leq k : \nu_i \text{ is measure}\}$, and $\delta_k(x):=\sum_{i\in J_k}\varepsilon_i\nu_i(x)$. The weights ε_i need to be computable and exponentially decreasing in i and $\sum_{i=1}^\infty \varepsilon_i \leq 1$. We choose $\varepsilon_i = i^{-6}2^{-i}$. Note the subtle and important fact that although the definition of J_k is non-constructive, as a finite set of finite objects, J_k is decidable (the program is unknowable for large k). Hence, δ_k is computable, since enumerable measures are computable.

$$D(x) = \delta_\infty(x) = \sum_{i\in J_\infty}\varepsilon_i\nu_i(x) = \text{mixture of all computable measures}.$$

In contrast to J_k and δ_k, the set J_∞ and hence D are neither enumerable nor co-enumerable. We also define the measures $\hat\delta_k(x):=\delta_k(x)/\delta_k(\epsilon)$ and $\hat D(x):=D(x)/D(\epsilon)$. The following Proposition implies posterior convergence of D to μ on μ-random sequences.

Proposition 11 (Convergence of incomputable measure $\hat{D}$). *Let μ be a computable measure with index k_0, i.e. $\mu = \nu_{k_0}$. Then for the incomputable measure $\hat{D}$ and the computable but non-constructive measures $\hat{\delta}_{k_0}$ defined above, the following holds:*

$$i) \; \sum_{t=1}^{\infty} h_t(\hat{\delta}_{k_0},\mu) \; \stackrel{+}{\leq} \; 2\ln 2 \cdot d_\mu(\omega) + 3k_0$$

$$ii) \; \sum_{t=1}^{\infty} h_t(\hat{\delta}_{k_0},\hat{D}) \; \stackrel{\times}{\leq} \; k_0^7 2^{k_0 + d_\mu(\omega)}$$

Combining (i) and (ii), using Lemma $9(i)$, we get $\sum_{t=1}^{\infty} h_t(\mu,\hat{D}) \leq c_\omega f(k_0) < \infty$ for μ-random ω, which implies $D(b|\omega_{<t}) \equiv \hat{D}(b|\omega_{<t}) \to \mu(b|\omega_{<t})$. We do not know whether on-sequence convergence of the ratio holds. Similar bounds hold for $\hat{\delta}_{k_1}$ instead $\hat{\delta}_{k_0}$, $k_1 \geq k_0$. The principle proof idea is to convert the expected bounds of Lemma 4 to individual bounds, using Lemma 10. The problem is that $\hat{D}$ is not computable, which we circumvent by joining with Lemma 9, bounds on $\sum_t h_t(\hat{\delta}_{k-1},\hat{\delta}_k)$ for $k = k_0, k_0 + 1, \ldots$.

Proof. (i) Let $H(\omega) := \sum_{t=1}^{\infty} h_t(\hat{\delta}_{k_0},\mu)$. μ and $\hat{\delta}_{k_0}$ are measures with $\hat{\delta}_{k_0} \geq \delta_{k_0} \geq \varepsilon_{k_0}\mu$, since $\delta_k(\epsilon) \leq 1$, $\mu = \nu_{k_0}$ and $k_0 \in J_{k_0}$. Hence, Lemma 4 applies and shows $\mathbf{E}_\mu[\exp(\frac{1}{2}H)] \leq \varepsilon_{k_0}^{-1/2}$. H is well-defined and enumerable for $d_\mu(\omega) < \infty$, since $d_\mu(\omega) < \infty$ implies $\mu(\omega_{1:t}) \neq 0$ implies $\hat{\delta}_{k_0}(\omega_{1:t}) \neq 0$. So $\mu(b|\omega_{1:t})$ and $\hat{\delta}_{k_0}(b|\omega_{1:t})$ are well defined and computable (given J_{k_0}). Hence $h_t(\hat{\delta}_{k_0},\mu)$ is computable, hence $H(\omega)$ is enumerable. Lemma 10 then implies $\exp(\frac{1}{2}H(\omega)) \stackrel{\times}{\leq} \varepsilon_{k_0}^{-1/2} \cdot 2^{K(\mu,H,\sqrt{\varepsilon}_{k_0}) + d_\mu(\omega)}$. We bound

$$K(\mu, H, \sqrt{\varepsilon}_{k_0}) \stackrel{+}{\leq} K(H|\mu,k_0) + K(k_0) \stackrel{+}{\leq} K(J_{k_0}|k_0) + K(k_0) \stackrel{+}{\leq} k_0 + 2\log k_0.$$

The first inequality holds, since k_0 is the index and hence a description of μ, and ε_* is a simple computable function. H can be computed from μ, k_0 and J_{k_0}, which implies the second inequality. The last inequality follows from $K(k_0) \stackrel{+}{\leq} 2\log k_0$ and the fact that for each $i \leq k_0$ one bit suffices to specify (non)membership to J_{k_0}, i.e. $K(J_{k_0}|k_0) \stackrel{+}{\leq} k_0$. Putting everything together we get

$$H(\omega) \stackrel{+}{\leq} \ln \varepsilon_{k_0}^{-1} + [k_0 + 2\log k_0 + d_\mu(\omega)]2\ln 2 \stackrel{+}{\leq} (2\ln 2)d_\mu(\omega) + 3k_0.$$

(ii) Let $H^k(\omega) := \sum_{t=1}^{\infty} h_t(\hat{\delta}_k,\hat{\delta}_{k-1})$ and $k > k_0$. $\hat{\delta}_{k-1} \leq \hat{\delta}_k$ implies

$$\frac{\hat{\delta}_{k-1}(x)}{\hat{\delta}_k(x)} \leq \frac{\delta_k(\epsilon)}{\delta_{k-1}(\epsilon)} \leq \frac{\delta_{k-1}(\epsilon) + \varepsilon_k}{\delta_{k-1}(\epsilon)} = 1 + \frac{\varepsilon_k}{\delta_{k-1}(\epsilon)} \leq 1 + \frac{\varepsilon_k}{\varepsilon_O},$$

where $O := \min\{i \in J_{k-1}\} = O(1)$. Note that $J_{k-1} \ni k_0$ is not empty. Since $\hat{\delta}_{k-1}$ and $\hat{\delta}_k$ are measures, Lemma 4 applies and shows $\mathbf{E}_{\hat{\delta}_{k-1}}[H^k] \leq \ln(1 + \frac{\varepsilon_k}{\varepsilon_O}) \leq \frac{\varepsilon_k}{\varepsilon_O}$. Exploiting $\varepsilon_{k_0}\mu \leq \hat{\delta}_{k-1}$, this implies $\mathbf{E}_\mu[H^k] \leq \frac{\varepsilon_k}{\varepsilon_O \varepsilon_{k_0}}$. Lemma 10 then implies $H^k(\omega) \stackrel{\times}{\leq} \frac{\varepsilon_k}{\varepsilon_O \varepsilon_{k_0}} \cdot 2^{K(\mu,H^k,\varepsilon_O \varepsilon_{k_0}/\varepsilon_k) + d_\mu(\omega)}$. Similarly as in (i) we can bound

$$K(\mu,H^k,\varepsilon_{k_0}/\varepsilon_O\varepsilon_k) \stackrel{+}{\leq} K(J_k|k) + K(k) + K(k_0) \stackrel{+}{\leq} k + 2\log k + 2\log k_0, \quad \text{hence}$$

$$H^k(\omega) \;\overset{\times}{\leq}\; \frac{\varepsilon_k}{\varepsilon_O \varepsilon_{k_0}} \cdot k_0^2 k^2 2^k c_\omega \;\overset{\times}{=}\; k_0^8 2^{k_0} k^{-4} c_\omega, \quad \text{where} \quad c_\omega := 2^{d_\mu(\omega)}.$$

Chaining this bound via Lemma 9(*ii*) we get for $k_1 > k_0$:

$$\sum_{t=1}^{n} h_t(\hat{\delta}_{k_0}, \hat{\delta}_{k_1}) \leq \sum_{t=1}^{n} 3 \sum_{k=k_0+1}^{k_1} (k - k_0 + 1)^2 h_t(\hat{\delta}_{k-1}, \hat{\delta}_k)$$

$$\leq 3 \sum_{k=k_0+1}^{k_1} k^2 H^k(\omega) \;\overset{\times}{\leq}\; 3k_0^8 2^{k_0} c_\omega \sum_{k=k_0+1}^{k_1} k^{-2} \;\leq\; 3k_0^7 2^{k_0} c_\omega$$

If we now take $k_1 \to \infty$ we get $\sum_{t=1}^{n} h_t(\hat{\delta}_{k_0}, \hat{D}) \;\overset{\times}{\leq}\; 3k_0^7 2^{k_0 + d_\mu(\omega)}$. Finally let $n \to \infty$.

$\square$

The main properties allowing for proving $\hat{D} \to \mu$ were that $\hat{D}$ is a measure with approximations $\hat{\delta}_k$, which are computable in a certain sense. $\hat{D}$ is a mixture over all enumerable/computable measures and hence incomputable.

6   M.L.-Converging Enumerable Semimeasure W

The next step is to enlarge the class of computable measures to an enumerable class of semimeasures, which are still sufficiently close to measures in order not to spoil the convergence result. For convergence w.p.1. we could include *all* semimeasures (Theorem 3). M.L.-convergence seems to require a more restricted class. Included non-measures need to be zero on long strings. We convert semimeasures ν to "quasimeasures" $\tilde{\nu}$ as follows:

$$\tilde{\nu}(x_{1:n}) := \nu(x_{1:n}) \quad \text{if} \quad \sum_{y_{1:n}} \nu(y_{1:n}) > 1 - \frac{1}{n} \quad \text{and} \quad \nu(x_{1:n}) := 0 \quad \text{else.}$$

If the condition is violated for some n it is also violated for all larger n, hence with ν also $\tilde{\nu}$ is a semimeasure. $\tilde{\nu}$ is enumerable if ν is enumerable. So if $\nu_1, \nu_2, \dots$ is an enumeration of all enumerable semimeasures, then $\tilde{\nu}_1, \tilde{\nu}_2, \dots$ is an enumeration of all enumerable quasimeasures. The for us important properties are that $\tilde{\nu}_i \leq \nu_i$ -and- if ν_i is a measure, then $\tilde{\nu}_i \equiv \nu_i$, else $\nu_i(x) = 0$ for sufficiently long x. We define the enumerable semimeasure

$$W(x) := \sum_{i=1}^{\infty} \varepsilon_i \tilde{\nu}_i(x), \quad \text{and} \quad D(x) = \sum_{i \in J} \varepsilon_i \tilde{\nu}_i(x) \text{ with } J := \{i : \tilde{\nu}_i \text{ is measure}\}$$

with $\varepsilon_i = i^{-6} 2^{-i}$ as before.

Proposition 12 (Convergence of enumerable W to incomputable D).
For every computable measure μ and for ω being μ-random, the following holds for $t \to \infty$:

(i) $\dfrac{W(\omega_{1:t})}{D(\omega_{1:t})} \to 1$,   (ii) $\dfrac{W(\omega_t | \omega_{<t})}{D(\omega_t | \omega_{<t})} \to 1$,   (iii) $W(a | \omega_{<t}) \to D(a | \omega_{<t}) \ \forall a \in \mathcal{X}$.

The intuitive reason for the convergence is that the additional contributions of non-measures to W absent in D are zero for long sequences.

Proof. (i)

$$D(x) \leq W(x) = D(x) + \sum_{i \notin J} \varepsilon_i \tilde{\nu}_i(x) \leq D(x) + \sum_{i=k_x}^{\infty} \varepsilon_i \tilde{\nu}_i(x), \qquad (8)$$

where $k_x := \min_i \{i \notin J : \tilde{\nu}_i(x) \neq 0\}$. For $i \notin J$, $\tilde{\nu}_i$ is not a measure. Hence $\tilde{\nu}_i(x) = 0$ for sufficiently long x. This implies $k_x \to \infty$ for $\ell(x) \to \infty$, hence $W(x) \to D(x)$ $\forall x$. To get convergence in ratio we have to assume that $x = \omega_{1:n}$ with ω being μ-random, i.e. $c_\omega := \sup_n \frac{M(\omega_{1:n})}{\mu(\omega_{1:n})} = 2^{d_\mu(\omega)} < \infty$.

$$\Rightarrow \tilde{\nu}_i(x) \leq \nu_i(x) \leq \frac{1}{w_{\nu_i}} M(x) \leq \frac{c_\omega}{w_{\nu_i}} \mu(x) \leq \frac{c_\omega}{w_{\nu_i} \varepsilon_{k_0}} D(x),$$

The last inequality holds, since μ is a computable measure of index k_0, i.e. $\mu = \nu_{k_0} = \tilde{\nu}_{k_0}$. Inserting $1/w_{\nu_i} \leq c' \cdot i^2$ for some $c = O(1)$ and ε_i we get $\varepsilon_i \tilde{\nu}_i(x) \leq \frac{c' c_\omega}{\varepsilon_{k_0}} i^{-4} 2^{-i} D(x)$, which implies $\sum_{i=k_x}^{\infty} \varepsilon_i \tilde{\nu}_i(x) \leq \varepsilon'_x D(x)$ with $\varepsilon'_x := \frac{2c' c_\omega}{\varepsilon_{k_0}} k_x^{-4} 2^{-k_x} \to 0$ for $\ell(x) \to \infty$. Inserting this into (8) we get

$$1 \leq \frac{W(x)}{D(x)} \leq 1 + \varepsilon'_x \overset{\ell(x) \to \infty}{\longrightarrow} 1 \quad \text{for } \mu\text{-random } x.$$

(ii) Obvious from (i) by taking a double ratio.

(iii) Let $a \in \mathcal{X}$. From $W(xa) \geq D(xa)$ $(W \geq D)$ and $W(x) \leq (1 + \varepsilon'_x) D(x)$ (i) we get

$$W(a|x) \geq (1 + \varepsilon'_x)^{-1} D(a|x) \geq (1 - \varepsilon'_x) D(a|x) \qquad \forall a \in \mathcal{X}, \quad \text{and}$$

$$1 - W(a|x) \geq \sum_{b \neq a} W(b|x) \geq (1 - \varepsilon'_x) \sum_{b \neq a} D(b|x) = (1 - \varepsilon'_x)(1 - D(a|x)),$$

where we used in the second line that W is a semimeasure and D proportional to a measure. Together this implies $|W(a|x) - D(a|x)| \leq \varepsilon'_x$. Since $\varepsilon'_x \to 0$ for μ-random x, this shows (iii). $h_x(W, D) \leq \varepsilon'_x$ can also be shown. $\square$

Speed of convergence. The main convergence Theorem 8 now immediately follows from Propositions 11 and 12. We briefly remark on the convergence rate. Lemma 4 shows that $\mathbf{E}[\sum_t h_t(X, \mu)]$ is logarithmic in the index k_0 of μ for $X = M$ $(\ln w_{k_0}^{-1} \overset{\times}{=} \ln k_0)$, but linear for $X = [W, D, \delta_{k_0}]$ $(\ln \varepsilon_{k_0} \overset{\times}{=} k_0)$. The individual bounds for $\sum_t h_t(\hat{\delta}_{k_0}, \mu)$ and $\sum_t h_t(\hat{\delta}_{k_0}, \hat{D})$ in Proposition 11 are linear and exponential in k_0, respectively. For $W \overset{M.L.}{\longrightarrow} D$ we could not establish any convergence speed.

Finally we show that W does not dominate all enumerable semimeasures, as the definition of W suggests. We summarize all computability, measure, and dominance properties of M, D, $\hat{D}$, and W in the following theorem:

Theorem 13 (Properties of M, W, D, and $\hat{D}$).
(i) M is an enumerable semimeasure, which dominates all enumerable semimeasures. M is not computable and not a measure.

(ii) $\hat{D}$ is a measure, D is proportional to a measure, both dominating all enumerable quasimeasures. D and $\hat{D}$ are not computable and do not dominate all enumerable semimeasures.

(iii) W is an enumerable semimeasure, which dominates all enumerable quasimeasures. W is not itself a quasimeasure, is not computable, and does not dominate all enumerable semimeasures.

We conjecture that D and $\hat{D}$ are not even approximable (limit-computable), but lie somewhere higher in the arithmetic hierarchy. Since W can be normalized to an approximable measure M.L.-converging to μ, and D was only an intermediate quantity, the question of approximability of D seems not too interesting.

7   Conclusions

We investigated a natural strengthening of Solomonoff's famous convergence theorem, the latter stating that with probability 1 (w.p.1) the posterior of a universal semimeasure M converges to the true computable distribution μ ($M \xrightarrow{w.p.1} \mu$). We answered partially negative the question of whether convergence also holds individually for all Martin-Löf (M.L.) random sequences ($\exists M : M \xrightarrow{M.L.} \mu$). We constructed random sequences α for which there exist universal semimeasures on which convergence fails. Multiplicative dominance of M is the key property to show convergence w.p.1. Dominance over all measures is also satisfied by the restricted mixture W over all quasimeasures. We showed that W converges to μ on all M.L.-random sequences by exploiting the incomputable mixture D over all measures. For $D \xrightarrow{M.L.} \mu$ we achieved a (weak) convergence rate; for $W \xrightarrow{M.L.} D$ and $W/D \xrightarrow{M.L.} 1$ only an asymptotic result. The convergence rate properties w.p.1. of D and W are as excellent as for M.

We do not know whether $D/\mu \xrightarrow{M.L.} 1$ holds. We also don't know the convergence rate for $W \xrightarrow{M.L.} D$, and the current bound for $D \xrightarrow{M.L.} \mu$ is double exponentially worse than for $M \xrightarrow{w.p.1} \mu$. A minor question is whether D is approximable (which is unlikely). Finally there could still exist *universal* semimeasures M (dominating all enumerable semimeasures) for which M.L.-convergence holds ($\exists M : M \xrightarrow{M.L.} \mu$?). In case they exist, we expect them to have particularly interesting additional structure and properties. While most results in algorithmic information theory are independent of the choice of the underlying universal Turing machine (UTM) or universal semimeasure (USM), there are also results which depend on this choice. For instance, one can show that $\{(x,n) : K_U(x) \leq n\}$ is tt-complete for some U, but not tt-complete for others [MP02]. A potential U dependence also occurs for predictions based on monotone complexity [Hut03d]. It could lead to interesting insights to identify a class of "natural" UTMs/USMs which have a variety of favorable properties. A more moderate approach may be to consider classes $\mathcal{C}_i$ of UTMs/USMs satisfying certain properties $\mathcal{P}_i$ and showing that the intersection $\cap_i \mathcal{C}_i$ is not empty.

Another interesting and potentially fruitful approach to the convergence problem at hand is to consider other classes of semimeasures $\mathcal{M}$, define mixtures M over $\mathcal{M}$, and (possibly) generalized randomness concepts by using this M in Definition 5. Using this approach, in [Hut03b] it has been shown that convergence holds for a subclass of Bernoulli distributions if the class is dense, but fails if the class is gappy, showing that a denseness characterization of $\mathcal{M}$ could be promising in general.

Acknowledgements. We want to thank Alexey Chernov for his invaluable help.

References

[Hut03a] M. Hutter. Convergence and loss bounds for Bayesian sequence prediction. *IEEE Transactions on Information Theory*, 49(8):2061–2067, 2003.

[Hut03b] M. Hutter. On the existence and convergence of computable universal priors. In *Proc. 14th International Conf. on Algorithmic Learning Theory (ALT-2003)*, volume 2842 of *LNAI*, pages 298–312, Berlin, 2003. Springer.

[Hut03c] M. Hutter. An open problem regarding the convergence of universal a priori probability. In *Proc. 16th Annual Conf. on Learning Theory (COLT-2003)*, volume 2777 of *LNAI*, pages 738–740, Berlin, 2003. Springer.

[Hut03d] M. Hutter. Sequence prediction based on monotone complexity. In *Proc. 16th Annual Conf. on Learning Theory (COLT-2003)*, Lecture Notes in Artificial Intelligence, pages 506–521, Berlin, 2003. Springer.

[Lev73] L. A. Levin. On the notion of a random sequence. *Soviet Mathematics Doklady*, 14(5):1413–1416, 1973.

[LV97] M. Li and P. M. B. Vitányi. *An introduction to Kolmogorov complexity and its applications*. Springer, 2nd edition, 1997.

[ML66] P. Martin-Löf. The definition of random sequences. *Information and Control*, 9(6):602–619, 1966.

[MP02] An. A. Muchnik and S. Y. Positselsky. Kolmogorov entropy in the context of computability theory. *Theoretical Computer Science*, 271(1–2):15–35, 2002.

[Sch02] J. Schmidhuber. Hierarchies of generalized Kolmogorov complexities and nonenumerable universal measures computable in the limit. *International Journal of Foundations of Computer Science*, 13(4):587–612, 2002.

[Sol64] R. J. Solomonoff. A formal theory of inductive inference: Part 1 and 2. *Information and Control*, 7:1–22 and 224–254, 1964.

[Sol78] R. J. Solomonoff. Complexity-based induction systems: comparisons and convergence theorems. *IEEE Transaction on Information Theory*, IT-24:422–432, 1978.

[VL00] P. M. B. Vitányi and M. Li. Minimum description length induction, Bayesianism, and Kolmogorov complexity. *IEEE Transactions on Information Theory*, 46(2):446–464, 2000.

[Vov87] V. G. Vovk. On a randomness criterion. *Soviet Mathematics Doklady*, 35(3):656–660, 1987.

[ZL70] A. K. Zvonkin and L. A. Levin. The complexity of finite objects and the development of the concepts of information and randomness by means of the theory of algorithms. *Russian Mathematical Surveys*, 25(6):83–124, 1970.

A Criterion for the Existence of Predictive Complexity for Binary Games*

Yuri Kalnishkan, Vladimir Vovk, and Michael V. Vyugin

Department of Computer Science, Royal Holloway, University of London, Egham, Surrey, TW20 0EX, UK {yura,vovk,misha}@cs.rhul.ac.uk

Abstract. It is well known that there exists a universal (i.e., optimal to within an additive constant if allowed to work infinitely long) algorithm for lossless data compression (Kolmogorov, Levin). The game of lossless compression is an example of an on-line prediction game; for some other on-line prediction games (such as the simple prediction game) a universal algorithm is known not to exist. In this paper we give an analytic characterisation of those binary on-line prediction games for which a universal prediction algorithm exists.

1 Introduction

We consider the following on-line prediction protocol: the prediction algorithm is fed with a sequence of bits $\omega_1, \omega_2, \ldots$, and its goal is to predict each ω_t, $t = 1, 2, \ldots$, given the previous bits $\omega_1, \ldots, \omega_{t-1}$. The loss suffered by the algorithm at each trial is measured by a loss function λ. We are interested in universal prediction algorithms for this problem.

The first universal algorithm was found back in 1965 by Kolmogorov for a batch version of this problem. Kolmogorov found a universal method of compression: for each string one can generate shorter and shorter compressed strings so that optimal compression is achieved in the limit; the original string can be restored from each of these compressed string by a computable function. The length of the shortest compressed string is known as the (plain) *Kolmogorov complexity* of the original string.

Slightly later Levin (in [1]) put Kolmogorov's ideas in an on-line framework constructing a universal algorithm for on-line data compression; the version of Kolmogorov complexity given by Levin's construction is denoted KM (the log of the *a priori* semimeasure). There are also several 'semi-on-line' versions of Kolmogorov complexity (such as prefix and monotone complexity).

Much later (see [2]) it was shown that a universal algorithm exists for a wide class of on-line prediction games including, besides some traditional games of prediction, the data compression game and games of playing the market; the loss suffered by the universal algorithm on a string is called the *predictive*

---

* A version of this paper with more details is available as Technical Report CLRC-TR-04-04 (revised), Computer Learning Research Centre, Royal Holloway, University of London; see http://www.clrc.rhul.ac.uk/publications/techrep.htm

S. Ben-David, J. Case, A. Maruoka (Eds.): ALT 2004, LNAI 3244, pp. 249–263, 2004.

complexity of that string. The technical basis for this result is provided by the theory of prediction with expert advice (see [3,4,5]).

The first on-line prediction games for which a universal prediction algorithm (equivalently, predictive complexity) does not exist appear in [6,7]. They include such important games as the simple prediction game and the absolute-loss game. The main result of this paper, Theor. 1, is an analytic characterisation of those on-line prediction games for which a universal prediction algorithm exists. The theorem states that a universal algorithm exists if and only if the game is mixable.

The proof relies on an analytical characterisation of mixable games provided in Sect. 4. It generalises the criterion from [8] and may be used for checking whether a game is mixable.

2   Preliminaries

2.1   Games and Superpredictions

An *(on-line prediction) game* $\mathfrak{G}$ is a triple $\langle \mathbb{B}, \Gamma, \lambda \rangle$, where $\mathbb{B} = \{0,1\}$ is the *outcome space*[1], Γ is the *prediction space*, and $\lambda : \mathbb{B} \times \Gamma \to \mathbb{R} \cup \{+\infty\}$ is the *loss function*.

It is essential to allow λ to take the value $+\infty$; however we do not allow $-\infty$ since the sum $+\infty + (-\infty)$ is undefined. We also prohibit the values of λ to approach $-\infty$: we require that there is some $a \in \mathbb{R}$ such that $\lambda(\omega, \gamma) \geq a$ for all $\omega \in \mathbb{B}$ and $\gamma \in \Gamma$. Having permitted $+\infty$, we need to ensure that at least some values of λ are finite, otherwise the game is degenerate. We require that there is $\gamma_0 \in \Gamma$ such that both $\lambda(0, \gamma_0)$ and $\lambda(1, \gamma_0)$ are finite numbers. In fact, our main result remains true for the games that do not satisfy these requirements, but we do not cover such games in this paper.

We need to impose computability requirements on the games. Assume that with every game there comes an oracle that is able to answer natural questions about the game. All computations involving the game can include calls to the oracle. The exact requirements to the oracle are given in Sect. 5.

We will denote elements of $\mathbb{B}^*$ (i.e., finite strings of elements of $\mathbb{B}$) by bold letters, e.g., $\boldsymbol{x}, \boldsymbol{y}$. The length (i.e., the number of elements) of a string $\boldsymbol{x}$ is denoted by $|\boldsymbol{x}|$; the number of ones in $\boldsymbol{x}$ and the number of zeroes in $\boldsymbol{x}$ are denoted by $\sharp_1 \boldsymbol{x}$ and $\sharp_0 \boldsymbol{x}$, respectively.

Let us describe the intuition behind the concept of a game. Consider a prediction algorithm $\mathfrak{A}$ working according to the following protocol:

for $t = 1, 2, \ldots$
   (1) $\mathfrak{A}$ chooses a prediction $\gamma_t \in \Gamma$
   (2) $\mathfrak{A}$ observes the actual outcome $\omega_t \in \mathbb{B}$

---

[1] In this paper we restrict ourselves to games with the outcome space $\mathbb{B}$. These games are sometimes called 'binary'. A more general definition is possible.

(3) $\mathfrak{A}$ suffers loss $\lambda(\omega_t, \gamma_t)$
end for

The algorithm $\mathfrak{A}$ suffers the total loss $\mathrm{Loss}_{\mathfrak{A}}(\omega_1, \omega_2, \ldots, \omega_T) = \sum_{t=1}^{T} \lambda(\omega_t, \gamma_t)$ over the first T trials. By definition, put $\mathrm{Loss}_{\mathfrak{A}}(\Lambda) = 0$, where Λ denotes the empty string.

The function $\mathrm{Loss}_{\mathfrak{A}}(x)$ can be treated as the predictive complexity of x in the game $\mathfrak{G}$ w.r.t. $\mathfrak{A}$. We will call these functions *loss processes*. Unfortunately, the set of all loss processes for a given game has no minimal elements except in some degenerate cases. The set of loss processes should be extended to the set of superloss processes.

2.2 Superloss Processes and Predictive Complexity

Take a game $\mathfrak{G} = \langle \mathbb{B}, \Gamma, \lambda \rangle$. We say that a pair $(s_0, s_1) \in (-\infty, +\infty]^2$ is a superprediction if there is $\gamma \in \Gamma$ such that the inequalities $\lambda(0, \gamma) \leq s_0$ and $\lambda(1, \gamma) \leq s_1$ hold. The set of superpredictions is denoted by S and is an important object characterising the game.

The requirements we have imposed on functions λ can be reformulated in terms of S as follows. The set $S \cap \mathbb{R}^2$, the finite part of S, is not empty and there is $a \in \mathbb{R}$ such that $S \subseteq [a, +\infty]^2$.

A function $L : \mathbb{B}^* \to \mathbb{R} \cup \{+\infty\}$ is called a *superloss process* w.r.t. $\mathfrak{G}$ (see [2]) if the following conditions hold:(1) $L(\Lambda) = 0$, (2) for every $x \in \mathbb{B}^*$, the pair $(L(x0) - L(x), L(x1) - L(x))$ is a superprediction w.r.t. $\mathfrak{G}$, and (3) L is semi-computable from above (w.r.t. the oracle of the game).

We will say that a superloss process K is *universal* if for any superloss process L there exists a constant C such that $K(x) \leq L(x) + C$ for all $x \in \mathbb{B}^*$. The difference between two universal superloss processes w.r.t. $\mathfrak{G}$ is bounded by a constant. If universal superloss processes w.r.t. $\mathfrak{G}$ exist, we may pick one and denote it by $\mathcal{K}^{\mathfrak{G}}$. It follows from the definition that, for every prediction algorithm $\mathfrak{A}$, there is a constant C such that for every x we have $\mathcal{K}^{\mathfrak{G}}(x) \leq \mathrm{Loss}_{\mathfrak{A}}^{\mathfrak{G}}(x) + C$. We call $\mathcal{K}^{\mathfrak{G}}$ *(predictive) complexity* w.r.t. $\mathfrak{G}$. We will usually omit the superscript and write just $\mathcal{K}$.

2.3 Mixability

Mixability was introduced in [5,2]. Take a parameter $\beta \in (0, 1)$ and consider the homeomorphism $\mathfrak{B}_\beta : (-\infty, +\infty]^2 \to [0, +\infty)^2$ specified by the formula $\mathfrak{B}_\beta(x, y) = (\beta^x, \beta^y)$. A game $\mathfrak{G}$ with the set of superpredictions S is called β-*mixable* if the set $\mathfrak{B}_\beta(S)$ is convex. A game $\mathfrak{G}$ is *mixable* if it is β-mixable for some $\beta \in (0, 1)$.

Examples of mixable games are the logarithmic game with $\Gamma = [0, 1]$ and λ given by the formulae $\lambda(0, \gamma) = -\log_2(1 - \gamma)$ and $\lambda(1, \gamma) = -\log_2(\gamma)$ and also the square-loss game with $\Gamma = [0, 1]$ and $\lambda(\omega, \gamma) = (\omega - \gamma)^2$. They specify the logarithmic complexity $\mathcal{K}^{\log}$ and the square-loss complexity $\mathcal{K}^{\mathrm{sq}}$, respectively (see [2]). Logarithmic complexity coincides with the negative logarithm of Levin's a

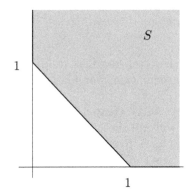

Fig. 1. The set of superpredictions S for the absolute-loss game.

priori semimeasure (see [9] for a definition). The negative logarithm of Levin's a priori semimeasure is a variant of Kolmogorov complexity. Thus we may say that Kolmogorov complexity is a special case of predictive complexity.

Natural examples of games that are not mixable (*non-mixable*) are provided by the absolute-loss game with $\Gamma = [0,1]$ and $\lambda(\omega, \gamma) = |\omega - \gamma|$ (the set of superpredictions for the absolute-loss game is shown in Fig. 1) and the simple prediction game with $\Gamma = \mathbb{B}$ and $\lambda(\omega, \gamma) = 0$ if and only if $\omega = \gamma$.

It is easy to prove the mixability or non-mixability of the above games using Theor. 2 below.

3   The Main Result and the Idea of the Proof

Theorem 1. *Predictive complexity w.r.t. a game $\mathfrak{G}$ exists if and only if $\mathfrak{G}$ is mixable.*

It is assumed in the theorem that the oracle for the game $\mathfrak{G}$ satisfies the requirements from Sect. 5. We include those to make the statement of the theorem precise.

The 'if' part of the theorem is proved in [2]. The 'only if' part is proved in Appendix A.

In order to illustrate the idea of the proof, we consider a special case. Let us show that there is no predictive complexity for the absolute-loss game defined in Subsect. 2.3. The set of superpredictions for the absolute-loss game is shown in Fig. 1. The proof is by *reductio ad absurdum*. Suppose that $\mathcal{K}$ is predictive complexity w.r.t. the absolute-loss game.

The set S of superpredictions for the absolute-loss game lies above the straight line $x/2 + y/2 = 1/2$. It is easy to see that

$$\mathbf{E}\mathcal{K}\left(\xi_1^{(1/2)}, \xi_2^{(1/2)}, \dots, \xi_n^{(1/2)}\right) \geq n/2 \qquad (1)$$

for all positive integers n, where $\xi_1^{(1/2)}, \xi_2^{(1/2)}, \ldots, \xi_n^{(1/2)}$ are results of n independent Bernoulli trials with the probability of success equal to $1/2$. Indeed, the mean 'loss' of L on each 'trial' is at least $1/2$ (see Lemma 1).

Consider the prediction strategy that outputs 0 no matter what outcomes actually occur. It suffers loss $L(\boldsymbol{x}) = \sharp_1 \boldsymbol{x}$ for all strings $\boldsymbol{x}$. It follows from the definition of predictive complexity that there is a constant C such that $\mathcal{K}(\boldsymbol{x}) \leq L(\boldsymbol{x}) + C_1 = \sharp_1 \boldsymbol{x} + C_1$ for all strings $\boldsymbol{x}$. Similar considerations imply that $\mathcal{K}(\boldsymbol{x}) \leq \sharp_0 \boldsymbol{x} + C_0$ for some $C_0 > 0$. Letting $C = \max(C_0, C_1) > 0$ yields

$$\mathcal{K}(\boldsymbol{x}) \leq \min(\sharp_0 \boldsymbol{x}, \sharp_1 \boldsymbol{x}) + C \leq \frac{|\boldsymbol{x}|}{2} + C \ . \tag{2}$$

Let $\Xi \subseteq \mathbb{B}^n$ be the set of strings having $n/2 + \sqrt{n}$ or more 0s. We will use the upper bound $\mathcal{K}(\boldsymbol{x}) \leq L(\boldsymbol{x}) + C \leq n/2 - \sqrt{n} + C$ on $\mathcal{K}$ for $\boldsymbol{x} \in \Xi$ and the upper bound (2) for all other values of $\boldsymbol{x}$. It follows from the DeMoivre-Laplace limit theorem (see, e.g., [10]) that $\Pr(\Xi)$ tends to a positive constant δ as n tends to ∞, where $\Pr(\Xi)$ is the probability of the event $(\xi_1^{(1/2)}, \xi_2^{(1/2)}, \ldots, \xi_n^{(1/2)}) \in \Xi$. Thus

$$\mathbf{E}\mathcal{K}\left(\xi_1^{(1/2)}, \xi_2^{(1/2)}, \ldots, \xi_n^{(1/2)}\right) \leq \left(\frac{n}{2} - \sqrt{n}\right)\Pr(\Xi) + \frac{n}{2}(1 - \Pr(\Xi)) + C$$
$$= \frac{n}{2} - \sqrt{n}(\delta + o(1)) + C$$

as $n \to +\infty$. This contradicts (1).

In the general case we approximate the boundary of the set of superpredictions S with line segments and perform a similar trick. The approximation takes place near a point where mixability gets violated. In order to find such a point, we need the concept of a canonical specification and a criterion of mixability formulated in Sect. 4.

4   Canonical Specifications

The proof of the main theorem is based on the concept of canonical specification. In this section we introduce canonical specifications and establish a criterion of mixability in terms of canonical specifications. The criterion is of independent interest because it reduces the question of whether a game is mixable to a simple analytical problem.

4.1   Definitions

Let $\mathfrak{G}$ be a game with the set of superpredictions S. Consider the function $\tilde{f} : \mathbb{R} \to (-\infty, +\infty]$ defined by $\tilde{f}(x) = \inf\{y \in \mathbb{R} \mid (x, y) \in S\}$ for each $x \in \mathbb{R}$ (here we assume that $\inf \varnothing = +\infty$).

Let $a = \sup\{x \in \mathbb{R} \mid \tilde{f}(x) = +\infty\}$; since by our assumption S has a non-empty finite part, $a < +\infty$. Let $b = \inf\{x \in \mathbb{R} \mid \tilde{f}$ is constant on $[x, +\infty)\}$, where we again assume that $\inf \varnothing = +\infty$. It is possible that $b = +\infty$. Clearly,

$b \geq a$. If $b > a$, let f be the restriction of $\tilde{f}$ to (a, b). We will call such $f : (a, b) \rightarrow \mathbb{R}$ the *canonical specification* of the game $\mathfrak{G}$.

If $a = b$, then the closure of $S \cap \mathbb{R}^2$ coincides with the set $[a, +\infty] \times [c, +\infty]$ for some $c \in \mathbb{R}$. It is easy to see that a game with the set of superpredictions $S = [a, +\infty] \times [c, +\infty]$ is mixable and if the requirements to the oracle from Sect. 5 hold, then there is predictive complexity w.r.t. this game.

Note that if S is the closure of its finite part, then the canonical specification $f : (a, b) \rightarrow \mathbb{R}$ uniquely determines S. Indeed, in this case S is the closure w.r.t. the extended[2] topology of the set $\{(x, y) \in [-\infty, +\infty]^2 \mid \exists u \in (a, b) : x \geq u \text{ and } y \geq f(x)\}$.

For example, the canonical specification for the absolute-loss game defined in Subsect. 2.3 is $f(x) = 1 - x$, $x \in (0, 1)$.

Corollary 1 from [8] provides a criterion of mixability for the case of twice differentiable canonical specifications. Namely, it states that the game is mixable if and only if the fraction $f''/(f'(f' - 1))$ is positive and separated from 0. We are going to generalise this criterion to a more general case where the existence of f' and f'' is not assumed.

4.2   Derivatives

Let $f : (a, b) \rightarrow \mathbb{R}$ be the canonical specification of a game $\mathfrak{G}$ with the set of superpredictions S.

We need to define the following derivatives that make sense even if f is not smooth. First let us define the left and right derivatives:

$$f_l'(x) = \lim_{\Delta x \to 0-} \frac{f(x + \Delta x) - f(x)}{\Delta x} \quad , \quad f_r'(x) = \lim_{\Delta x \to 0+} \frac{f(x + \Delta x) - f(x)}{\Delta x} \ .$$

If $f_l'(x) = f_r'(x)$ at some point x, we say that the derivative $f'(x) = f_l'(x) = f_r'(x)$ exists.

Suppose the derivative $f'(x)$ exists at $x \in (a, b)$. Let

$$\underline{f_l''} = \liminf_{\Delta x \to 0-} \frac{f(x + \Delta x) - (f(x) + f'(x)\Delta x)}{\frac{1}{2}(\Delta x)^2} \ , \tag{3}$$

$$\underline{f_r''} = \liminf_{\Delta x \to 0+} \frac{f(x + \Delta x) - (f(x) + f'(x)\Delta x)}{\frac{1}{2}(\Delta x)^2} \ . \tag{4}$$

By definition, lower limits always exist though their values may reach $-\infty$. Let $\underline{f''}(x) = \min(\underline{f_l''}(x), \underline{f_r''}(x))$.

If $S \cap \mathbb{R}^2$, the finite part of S, is convex, then f is convex. Since convex functions always have one-sided derivatives, $f_l'(x)$ and $f_r'(x)$ exist for each $x \in (a, b)$. Moreover they coincide everywhere except on a countable subset of the interval (a, b) (see, e.g., [11], Theor. 11.C). The derivatives $\underline{f_l''}$ and $\underline{f_r''}$ are nonnegative for convex functions f.

---

[2] The extended topology on the set $[-\infty, +\infty]$ is generated by the Euclidean topology of $\mathbb{R}$ and all sets $(a, +\infty]$ and $[-\infty, a)$, $a \in \mathbb{R}$. The extended topology on the set $[-\infty, +\infty]^2$ is generated by the Cartesian product of extended topologies.

4.3 An Analytical Characterisation of Mixable Games

In this subsection we formulate some results characterising mixability in terms of canonical specifications.

Theorem 2. *Let $\mathfrak{G}$ be a game with the set of superpredictions S and a canonical specification $f : (a, b) \to \mathbb{R}$. Then $\mathfrak{G}$ is mixable if and only if the following conditions hold: $S = \overline{S} \cap \mathbb{R}^2$ w.r.t. the extended topology, f is convex, and*

$$\inf_{x \in (a,b) \setminus D} \frac{\underline{f''}(x)}{f'(x)(f'(x) - 1)} > 0 \; , \tag{5}$$

where D is the set of points $y \in (a, b)$ such that $f'_l(y) \neq f'_r(y)$.

This theorem follows from the next theorem:

Theorem 3. *Let $\mathfrak{G}$ be a game with the set of superpredictions S and the canonical specification $f : (a, b) \to \mathbb{R}$; let $\beta \in (0, 1)$. Let $\overline{S}$ be the closure of its finite part, $S = \overline{S} \cap \mathbb{R}^2$. Then $\mathfrak{G}$ is β-mixable if and only if the following conditions hold: f is convex and*

$$\underline{f''}(x) \geq -f'(x)(f'(x) - 1) \ln \beta \tag{6}$$

for all $x \in (a, b) \setminus D$, where D is the set of points $y \in (a, b)$ such that $f'_l(y) \neq f'_r(y)$.

The theorem can be proved similarly to Corollary 1 from [8]. Note that the computability requirements from Sect. 5 are not used in the proofs of the two theorems from this subsection.

5 Computability

In this section we discuss the requirements the oracle for a game $\mathfrak{G}$ with the set of superpredictions S should satisfy. The general principle is that the oracle should be able to answer all 'reasonable' questions about the game; we do not want, however, to formalise the notion of 'reasonable' and just present a rather long list of questions that the oracle should be able to answer for our proofs to work. All those questions can be easily answered for games specified in a natural analytical form, e.g., for all games defined in Subsect. 2.3. Thus the requirements are not particularly restrictive as far as applications are concerned.

A *rational interval* is either an interval (p, q), where p and q are rational numbers or $+\infty$ or $-\infty$, one of the intervals $[-\infty, p)$, $(p, +\infty]$, where p is a rational number, or $[-\infty, +\infty]$. A rational interval is open w.r.t. the extended topology of $[-\infty, +\infty]$. We say that a sequence of nested intervals specifies some number $x \in [-\infty, +\infty]$ if it shrinks to x, i.e., the intersection of all intervals from the sequence is the one-point set $\{x\}$.

In order to prove the existence of complexity for mixable games, we require that the interior of the set of superpredictions S is constructively open w.r.t. the oracle in the sense of the following definition. Suppose that the oracle is (simultaneously) getting two sequences of rational intervals shrinking to x and y. If the point (x, y) belongs to the interior of S, the oracle should be able to tell it eventually. This requirement is used in the proof of the 'if' part of the main theorem.

Now suppose that the game has a canonical specification $f : (a, b) \to \mathbb{R}$. The oracle should be able to tell whether

$$\inf_{x \in (a,b)} \frac{\underline{f''}(x)}{f'(x)(f'(x) - 1)} = 0 \ , \tag{7}$$

and if so it must produce a sequence of points $x_m \in \mathbb{R}$, $m = 1, 2, \ldots$ (by saying that the oracle produces the sequence we mean that given m and l the oracle produces a rational interval with endpoints $p_{m,l}$ and $q_{m,l}$ so that for each m the intervals with endpoints $p_{m,l}$ and $q_{m,l}$, $l = 1, 2, \ldots$, shrink to x_m) with the following properties: the values $f'(x_m)$ exist for all positive integers m;

$$\lim_{m \to +\infty} \frac{\underline{f''}(x_m)}{f'(x_m)(f'(x_m) - 1)} = 0 \ ; \tag{8}$$

x_m converges to $x_0 \in [a, b]$; the sequence x_m is monotone; the values $f(x_m)$, $f'(x_m)$, $\underline{f'_l}(x_m)$, and $\underline{f''}(x_m)$ can be produced by the oracle; for each m the oracle can produce a sequence $\Delta x_{m,k}$, $k = 1, 2, \ldots$, such that: $\Delta x_{m,k} \to 0$ as $k \to +\infty$ for all positive integers m; for each positive integer m the values $\Delta x_{m,k}$ are of the same sign; the values $f(x_m + \Delta x_{m,k})$ can be produced by the oracle for all positive integers m and k; for every positive integer m the value of $\underline{f''}(x_m)$ is achieved on the sequence $\Delta x_{m,k}$, $k = 1, 2, \ldots$, i.e.,

$$\underline{f''}(x_m) = \lim_{k \to +\infty} \frac{f(x_m + \Delta x_{m,k}) - (f(x_m) + f'(x_m)\Delta x_{m,k})}{\frac{1}{2}(\Delta x_{m,k})^2} \ .$$

Acknowledgements. The authors have been supported by EPSRC through the grant GR/R46670 "Complexity Approximation Principle and Predictive Complexity: Analysis and Applications". The authors would also like to thank the reviewers of this paper for their detailed comments.

References

[1] Zvonkin, A.K., Levin, L.A.: The complexity of finite objects and the development of the concepts of information and randomness by means of the theory of algorithms. Russian Math. Surveys **25** (1970) 83–124

[2] Vovk, V., Watkins, C.J.H.C.: Universal portfolio selection. In: Proceedings of the 11th Annual Conference on Computational Learning Theory. (1998) 12–23

[3] Cesa-Bianchi, N., Freund, Y., Haussler, D., Helmbold, D.P., Schapire, R.E., Warmuth, M.K.: How to use expert advice. Journal of the ACM **44** (1997) 427–485

[4] Haussler, D., Kivinen, J., Warmuth, M.K.: Sequential prediction of individual sequences under general loss functions. IEEE Transactions on Information Theory **44** (1998) 1906–1925

[5] Vovk, V.: A game of prediction with expert advice. Journal of Computer and System Sciences **56** (1998) 153–173

[6] Kalnishkan, Y., Vovk, V., Vyugin, M.V.: Loss functions, complexities, and the Legendre transformation. Theoretical Computer Science **313** (2004) 195–207

[7] Kalnishkan, Y., Vyugin, M.V.: On the absence of predictive complexity for some games. In: Algorithmic Learning Theory, 13th International Conference, Proceedings. Volume 2533 of Lecture Notes in Artificial Intelligence., Springer (2002) 164–172

[8] Kalnishkan, Y., Vyugin, M.V.: Mixability and the existence of weak complexities. In: Computational Learning Theory, 15th Annual Conference, Proceedings. Volume 2375 of Lecture Notes in Artificial Intelligence., Springer (2002) 105–120

[9] Li, M., Vitányi, P.: An Introduction to Kolmogorov Complexity and Its Applications. Springer, New York (1997)

[10] Feller, W.: An Introduction to Probability Theory and Its Applications. 3rd edn. Volume I. John Wiley & Sons, Inc (1968)

[11] Roberts, A.W., Varberg, D.E.: Convex Functions. Academic Press (1973)

[12] Petrov, V.V.: Sums of Independent Random Variables. Springer (1975)

[13] Kalnishkan, Y.: General linear relations among different types of predictive complexity. Theoretical Computer Science **271** (2002) 181–200

Appendix A: Proof of the Main Result

In this section we prove the 'only if' part of Theor. 1, which is the main result of this paper. The proof is divided into several stages.

Assume the converse. Let $\mathfrak{G}$ be a non-mixable game with the set of superpredictions S and $\mathcal{K}$ be predictive complexity w.r.t. $\mathfrak{G}$.

Let $\mathfrak{G}_1$ and $\mathfrak{G}_2$ be two games with sets of superpredictions S_1 and S_2. If S_1 is the closure of S_2 w.r.t. the extended topology, then $\mathfrak{G}_1$ and $\mathfrak{G}_2$ are mixable simultaneously and predictive complexity w.r.t. $\mathfrak{G}_1$ exists if and only if predictive complexity w.r.t. $\mathfrak{G}_2$ exists. It is easy to check that if S is not a subset of the closure of its finite part $S \cap \mathbb{R}^2$, the game is not mixable and does not specify predictive complexity. It is readily seen that a game with the set of superpredictions S is mixable if and only if a game with the set of superpredictions $S + (a, b) = \{(x+a, y+b) \in (-\infty, +\infty] \mid (x, y) \in S\}$ is mixable and the same applies to the existence of predictive complexity. Finally, Lemma 7 from [6] states that if $S \cap \mathbb{R}^2$ is not convex, the game does not specify predictive complexity. Therefore we assume for the rest of the proof that S is the closure of the convex set $S \cap \mathbb{R}^2$ and $S \subseteq [0, +\infty]^2$.

Introductory stage. The case $S = [a, +\infty] \times [c, +\infty]$ is trivial (see Subsect. 4.1). Let $f : (a, b) \to \mathbb{R}$ be the canonical specification of $\mathfrak{G}$. The function f is convex. It follows from Theor. 2 that

$$\inf_{x \in (a,b) \setminus D} \frac{f''(x_m)}{f'(x_m)(f'(x_m) - 1)} = 0 \ , \tag{9}$$

where $D \subseteq (a, b)$ is the set of points where $f'(x)$ does not exist. The requirements from Sect. 5 state that the oracle can produce a sequence $x_n \in (a, b)$, $n = 1, 2, \ldots$, such that the derivative $f'(x_n)$ exists for each n and

$$\lim_{n \to +\infty} \frac{f''(x_n)}{f'(x_n)(f'(x_n) - 1)} = 0 \ . \tag{10}$$

It can be assumed that this sequence is monotone and converges to $x_0 \in [a, b]$ (it is possible that $x_0 = b = +\infty$).

For each $m = 1, 2, \ldots$ there is a sequence $\Delta x_{m,k}$, $k = 1, 2, \ldots$, such that $\Delta x_{m,k} \to 0$ as $k \to +\infty$ and

$$f(x_m + \Delta x_{m,k}) = f(x_m) + f'(x_m)\Delta x_{m,k} + \underline{f''}(x_m)\frac{\Delta x_{m,k}^2}{2} + \nu_m(\Delta x_{m,k})\Delta x_{m,k}^2, \tag{11}$$

where for each $m = 1, 2, \ldots$ we have $\nu_m(t) \to 0$ as $t \to 0$.

For each positive integer m let

$$p_m = 1/(1 - f'(x_m)) \ . \tag{12}$$

Since $f'(x_m) < 0$, we have $p_m \in (0, 1)$. It is easy to check that the line $(1 - p_m)x + p_m y = (1 - p_m)x_m + p_m f(x_m)$ is a tangent line to S at $(x_m, f(x_m))$. A simple calculation yields $f'(x_m) = -(1 - p_m)/p_m$.

Single point processes. We need to construct some superloss processes. To make the descriptions more intuitive, we will use the term 'strategy' in the following general sense. Take a superloss process L. We say that L is the loss of a strategy $\mathfrak{A}$ that outputs the prediction $(L(x0) - L(x), L(x1) - L(x))$ on input x for all sequences $x \in \mathbb{B}^*$.

Let $\mathfrak{A}_m$ be the strategy that always predicts $(x_m, f(x_m))$, $m = 1, 2, \ldots$. We denote the loss of $\mathfrak{A}_m$ on a string $x \in \mathbb{B}^*$ by $L_m(x)$. Now we are going to construct sequences of positive numbers $\varepsilon_{m,k}$, $m, k = 1, 2, \ldots$ such that for every m we have $\varepsilon_{m,k} \to 0$ as $k \to 0$ and strategies $\mathfrak{A}_m^{\varepsilon_{m,k}}$.

The requirements from Sect. 5 imply that we can assume that all $\Delta x_{m,k}$ are of the same sign. There are two possibilities for the sign. If they are all negative, we let $\varepsilon_{m,k} = -\Delta x_{m,k}$ and if they are all positive, we let $\varepsilon_{m,k} = \Delta x_{m,k}$ for all positive integers m and k. These two possibilities are illustrated by Figures 2 and 3, where $E_m = (1 - p_m)x_m + p_m f(x_m)$ so that $(1 - p_m)x + p_m y = E_m$ is the tangent line to S at $(x_m, f(x_m))$.

Let $\xi_1^{(p)}, \xi_2^{(p)}, \ldots, \xi_n^{(p)}$ be the outcomes of Bernoulli trials with the probability of success equal to p and let

$$\Phi(x) = \frac{1}{\sqrt{2\pi}} \int_{-\infty}^{x} e^{-x^2} dx \ . \tag{13}$$

We will now show that there are functions $\alpha_m(t)$ such that for every positive integer m we have $\alpha_m(t) \to 0$ as $t \to 0$ and the inequality

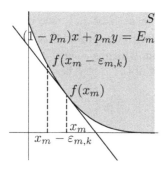

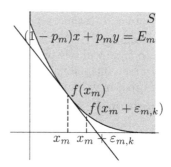

Fig. 2. The case $\varepsilon_{m,k} = -\Delta x_{m,k}$ **Fig. 3.** The case $\varepsilon_{m,k} = \Delta x_{m,k}$

$$
L_m(\xi_1^{(p_m)}, \xi_2^{(p_m)}, \ldots, \xi_n^{(p_m)}) - L_m^{\varepsilon_{m,k}}(\xi_1^{(p_m)}, \xi_2^{(p_m)}, \ldots, \xi_n^{(p_m)}) \geq
$$
$$
-\underline{f}''(x_m) \frac{\varepsilon_{m,k}^2}{2} n p_m + \varepsilon_{m,k} \sqrt{n \frac{1-p_m}{p_m}} - \underline{f}''(x_m) \frac{\varepsilon_{m,k}^2}{2} \sqrt{n p_m(1-p_m)}
$$
$$
+ \alpha_m(\varepsilon_{m,k}) \varepsilon_{m,k}^2 \left(\sqrt{n p_m(1-p_m)} + n p_m \right) , \quad (14)
$$

holds with probability at least $\Phi(-1) - 1/\sqrt{n p_m(1-p_m)}$. Let us consider the two possibilities mentioned above separately.

The case of negative increments. First suppose that $\Delta x_{m,k}$ are all negative and $\varepsilon_{m,k} = -\Delta x_{m,k}$. Let $\mathfrak{A}_m^\varepsilon$ be the strategy that always outputs the prediction $(x_m - \varepsilon, f(x_m - \varepsilon))$, $\varepsilon \in (0, x_m)$. We denote the loss of $\mathfrak{A}_m^\varepsilon$ on $x \in \mathbb{B}^*$ by $L_m^\varepsilon(x)$. See Fig. 2 for an illustration of this case.

Take a positive integer m, a string x of length n and $\varepsilon \in (0, x_m - a)$. It is easy to see that if x contains $l^{(0)}$ zeroes or more, then $L_m^\varepsilon(x) - L_m(x) \geq \varepsilon l^{(0)} - (f(x_m - \varepsilon) - f(x_m))(n - l^{(0)})$. Let $l^{(0)} = l_{n,m}^{(0)} = n(1 - p_m) + \sqrt{n p_m(1 - p_m)}$. Taking into account (11), for each x having $l_{n,m}^{(0)}$ zeroes or more, we get

$$
L_m(x) - L_m^{\varepsilon_{m,k}}(x) \geq \varepsilon_{m,k} \left(n(1 - p_m) + \sqrt{n p_m(1 - p_m)} \right)
$$
$$
- \left(-f'(x_m)\varepsilon_{m,k} + \underline{f}''(x_m) \frac{\varepsilon_{m,k}^2}{2} + \nu_m(-\varepsilon_{m,k}) \varepsilon_{m,k}^2 \right)
$$
$$
\times \left(n p_m - \sqrt{n p_m(1 - p_m)} \right)
$$

$$(15)$$

$$
= -\underline{f}''(x_m) \frac{\varepsilon_{m,k}^2}{2} n p_m + \varepsilon_{m,k} \sqrt{n \frac{1-p_m}{p_m}}
$$
$$
+ \underline{f}''(x_m) \frac{\varepsilon_{m,k}^2}{2} \sqrt{n p_m(1 - p_m)}
$$

$$(16)$$

$$
+ \nu_m(-\varepsilon_{m,k}) \varepsilon_{m,k}^2 \left(\sqrt{n p_m(1 - p_m)} - n p_m \right) .
$$

In order to estimate the probability of getting at least $l_{n,m}^{(0)}$ zeroes among the outcomes $\xi_1^{(p)}, \xi_2^{(p)}, \ldots, \xi_n^{(p)}$ of Bernoulli trials with the probability of success equal to p, we will rely on the following proposition, which is a special case of the Berry-Essen inequality. A more general statement of the Berry-Essen Inequality and a proof may be found in [12], Sect. V.2.

Proposition 1. *Let* $p \in (0, 1)$. *If* $S_n = \xi_1^{(p)} + \xi_2^{(p)} + \ldots + \xi_n^{(p)}$ *and*

$$F_n^{(p)}(x) = \Pr\left\{ \frac{S_n - np}{\sqrt{np(1-p)}} \leq x \right\} , \tag{17}$$

then

$$\sup_{-\infty \leq x \leq +\infty} |F_n^{(p)}(x) - \Phi(x)| \leq \frac{p^2 + (1-p)^2}{\sqrt{np(1-p)}} \tag{18}$$

for all $n = 1, 2, \ldots$.

It is easy to see that

$$\Pr\{S_n \leq np - \sqrt{np(1-p)}\} = \Pr\left\{ \frac{S_n - np}{\sqrt{np(1-p)}} \leq -1 \right\} = F_n^{(p)}(-1) \tag{19}$$

and $p^2 + (1-p)^2 \leq 1$ for all $p \in (0,1)$. Thus the probability to get $l_{n,m}^{(0)}$ or more zeroes among $\xi_1^{(p)}, \xi_2^{(p)}, \ldots, \xi_n^{(p)}$ is at least $\Phi(-1) - 1/\sqrt{np(1-p)}$.

The case of positive increments can be considered in a similar way.

Approaching the contradiction. The following lemma is required (see [13], Lemma 3):

Lemma 1. *Let* $\mathfrak{G}$ *be a game with the set of superpredictions* S *and* $p \in (0,1)$. *If for every* $(u, v) \in S$ *the inequality* $(1-p)u + pv \geq m$ *holds, then for each superloss process* L *w.r.t.* $\mathfrak{G}$ *we get* $\mathbf{E}L(\xi_1^{(p)} \ldots \xi_n^{(p)}) \geq mn$, *where* $\xi_1^{(p)}, \xi_2^{(p)}, \ldots, \xi_n^{(p)}$ *are results of independent Bernoulli trials with the probability of 1 being equal to* p.

It follows from the lemma that

$$\mathbf{E}\mathcal{K}\left(\xi_1^{(p_m)}, \xi_2^{(p_m)}, \ldots, \xi_n^{(p_m)}\right) \geq \mathbf{E}L_m\left(\xi_1^{(p_m)}, \xi_2^{(p_m)}, \ldots, \xi_n^{(p_m)}\right) \tag{20}$$

$$= ((1 - p_m)x_m + p_m f(x_m))n , \tag{21}$$

where $\xi_1^{(p_m)}, \xi_2^{(p_m)}, \ldots, \xi_n^{(p_m)}$ are results of n independent Bernoulli trials with the probability of success equal to p_m. We are going to obtain a contradiction by beating this estimate through the use of (14). In order to do this, we will construct two strategies, $\mathfrak{A}_0$ and $\mathfrak{A}_0'$ that work as follows. There is a strictly increasing sequence of positive integers $n_1 < n_2 < \ldots$ and for each x of length n such that $n_{i-1} < n \leq n_i$ the strategy $\mathfrak{A}_0$ simulates $\mathfrak{A}_{m_i}$ while $\mathfrak{A}_0'$ simulates $\mathfrak{A}_{m_i}^{\varepsilon_{m_i}, k_i}$ for some m_i and k_i. Figure 4 presents a diagram of how the strategies work. We denote the loss of $\mathfrak{A}_0$ by L_0 and the loss of $\mathfrak{A}_0'$ by L_0'.

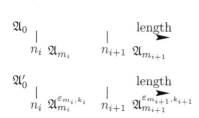

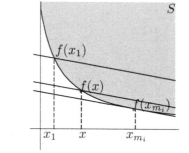

Fig. 4. The operation of the strategies $\mathfrak{A}_0$ and $\mathfrak{A}_0'$

Fig. 5. The estimate on expectations

There is a number of possibilities for the location of the limit point $x_0 \in [a, b]$. One of the following statements is true: (1) $x_0 = a$, (2) $x_0 \in (a, b)$, or (3) $x_0 = b$ (note that b may be equal to $+\infty$).

The first case can be reduced to the others by mirroring S w.r.t. the straight line $x = y$ (recall the remark about mirroring at the end of Sect. 5). In the second case $\underline{f}''(x_n) \to 0$ since $f'(x)$ is separated from 0 in a vicinity of x_0. In the third case there are two possibilities, either $f'(x_n)$ is separated from zero and, respectively, $\underline{f}''(x_n) \to 0$, or $f'(x_n) \to 0$ and thus $\underline{f}''(x_n)/f'(x_n) \to 0$ as $n \to +\infty$. The first possibility is not essentially different from the second case above, while the other one requires a separate treatment.

We obtain two essentially different situations to consider:

1. $x_m \to x_0 \in (a, b]$, there is $c > 0$ such that $f'(x_m) \le -c < 0$ for all $m = 1, 2, \ldots$, and $\underline{f}''(x_m) \to 0$ as $m \to +\infty$
2. $x_m \to b$, $f'(x_m) \to 0$, and $\underline{f}''(x_m)/f'(x_m) \to 0$ as $m \to +\infty$.

In the first case, we can assume that all predictions made by $\mathfrak{A}_m$ and $\mathfrak{A}_m^{\varepsilon_{m,k}}$, where m and k are positive integers, belong to some finite square $[0, M]^2 \subseteq \mathbb{R}^2$, where $0 < M < +\infty$. On the other hand, it follows from the definition (12) that p_m converges to $p_0 \in (0, 1)$ as $m \to +\infty$.

In the second case we cannot guarantee that all predictions are taken from some bounded area. It is possible that $x_0 = +\infty$. We will rely on monotonicity of x_m. As far as the probabilities are concerned, (12) implies that $p_m \to 1$ as $m \to +\infty$.

The case $f'(x_m) \to 0$. We are going to rely on the convergence

$$\frac{\underline{f}''(x_m)p_m}{1 - p_m} = -\frac{\underline{f}''(x_m)}{f'(x_m)} \to 0+ \tag{22}$$

as $m \to +\infty$.

Let $\theta = x_1 + |x_1 - f(x_1)|$. Suppose that $\mathfrak{A}_0$ and $\mathfrak{A}_0'$ have already been constructed for all x of length less than or equal to n_{i-1}. Consider the inequalities:

$$1 \le \underline{f}''(x_m)\varepsilon_{m,k}^2 n \le 2 , \tag{23}$$

$$n_{i-1} < n \;, \tag{24}$$

$$\frac{1}{\sqrt{np_m(1-p_m)}} \leq \frac{\Phi(-1)}{2} \;, \tag{25}$$

$$2n_{i-1}(\theta+1) \leq \frac{\Phi(-1)}{4} \sqrt{\frac{1-p_m}{\underline{f}''(x_m)p_m}} \;, \tag{26}$$

$$\varepsilon_{m,k} \leq 1 \;, \tag{27}$$

$$|\alpha_m(\varepsilon_{m,k})| \leq \underline{f}''(x_m) \;. \tag{28}$$

They are consistent, i.e., there are positive integers n, m, and k that satisfy these inequalities. For example, first let m to be sufficiently large to satisfy (25) and (26) and then tune k and n.

Now take n_i, m_i, and k_i equal to some n, m, and k satisfying the inequalities (recall that the way $\mathfrak{A}_0$ and $\mathfrak{A}_0'$ operate is illustrated by Fig. 4). It follows from (14) that

$$L_{m_i}\left(\xi_1^{(p_{m_i})}, \xi_2^{(p_{m_i})}, \ldots, \xi_{n_i}^{(p_{m_i})}\right) - L_{m_i}^{\varepsilon_{m_i},k_i}\left(\xi_1^{(p_{m_i})}, \xi_2^{(p_{m_i})}, \ldots, \xi_{n_i}^{(p_{m_i})}\right) \geq$$

$$\sqrt{\frac{1-p_{m_i}}{\underline{f}''(x_{m_i})p_{m_i}}} - 3\left(p_{m_i} + \sqrt{\frac{p_{m_i}(1-p_{m_i})}{n_i}}\right) \tag{29}$$

holds with probability at least $\Phi(-1)/2$. Let $\Xi_{n_i} \subseteq \mathbb{B}^{n_i}$ be the set of all strings x of length n_i such that (29) holds on x, i.e., inequality (29) holds if and only if $\xi_1^{(p_{m_i})}\xi_2^{(p_{m_i})}\ldots\xi_{n_i}^{(p_{m_i})} \in \Xi_{n_i}$, where $i = 1, 2, \ldots$.

We use L_0' to estimate the value $\mathcal{K}(x)$ on $x \in \Xi_{n_i}$ and L_0 on $x \in \mathbb{B}^{n_i} \setminus \Xi_{n_i}$. There is a constant C such that

$$\mathbf{E}\mathcal{K}\left(\xi_1^{(p_{m_i})}, \xi_2^{(p_{m_i})}, \ldots, \xi_{n_i}^{(p_{m_i})}\right) \leq$$

$$\sum_{x \in \Xi_{n_i}} L_0'(x)\Pr{}_{p_{m_i}}(x) + \sum_{x \in \mathbb{B}^{n_i} \setminus \Xi_{n_i}} L_0(x)\Pr{}_{p_{m_i}}(x) + C \tag{30}$$

for all positive integers i, where $\Pr_p(x)$ denotes the probability of the event $\xi_1^{(p)}\xi_2^{(p)}\ldots\xi_n^{(p)} = x$.

In order to obtain an estimate in terms of L_{m_i} and $L_{m_i}^{\varepsilon_{m_i},k_i}$, consider the equality

$$\sum_{x \in \Xi_{n_i}} L_0'(x)\Pr{}_{p_{m_i}}(x) + \sum_{x \in \mathbb{B}^{n_i} \setminus \Xi_{n_i}} L_0(x)\Pr{}_{p_{m_i}}(x) =$$

$$\sum{}' (L_0'(\tilde{x}\bar{x}) - L_0'(\tilde{x}))\Pr{}_{p_{m_i}}(\tilde{x}\bar{x}) + \sum{}'' (L_0(\tilde{x}\bar{x}) - L_0(\tilde{x}))\Pr{}_{p_{m_i}}(\tilde{x}\bar{x}) +$$

$$\sum{}' L_0'(\tilde{x})\Pr{}_{p_{m_i}}(\tilde{x}\bar{x}) + \sum{}'' L_0(\tilde{x})\Pr{}_{p_{m_i}}(\tilde{x}\bar{x}) \;, \tag{31}$$

where the sum $\sum'$ is taken over all $\tilde{x}$ of length n_{i-1} and $\bar{x}$ of length $n_i - n_{i-1}$ such that $\tilde{x}\bar{x} \in \Xi_{n_i}$ while the sum $\sum''$ is taken over all $\tilde{x}$ of length n_{i-1} and $\bar{x}$

of length $n_i - n_{i-1}$ such that $\tilde{x}\bar{x} \in \mathbb{B}^{n_i} \setminus \Xi_{n_i}$. The formula will hold if we replace L_0 by L_{m_i} and L'_0 by $L_{m_i}^{\varepsilon_{m_i,k_i}}$. Since by construction we have

$$L_0(\tilde{x}\bar{x}) - L_0(\tilde{x}) = L_{m_i}(\tilde{x}\bar{x}) - L_{m_i}(\tilde{x}) , \tag{32}$$

$$L'_0(\tilde{x}\bar{x}) - L'_0(\tilde{x}) = L_{m_i}^{\varepsilon_{m_i,k_i}}(\tilde{x}\bar{x}) - L_{m_i}^{\varepsilon_{m_i,k_i}}(\tilde{x}) \tag{33}$$

for all $\tilde{x}$ of length n_{i-1} and $\bar{x}$ of length $n_i - n_{i-1}$, we get

$$\left| \left(\sum_{x \in \Xi_{n_i}} L'_0(x)\Pr_{p_{m_i}}(x) + \sum_{x \in \mathbb{B}^{n_i} \setminus \Xi_{n_i}} L_0(x)\Pr_{p_{m_i}}(x) \right) - \right.$$

$$\left. \left(\sum_{x \in \Xi_{n_i}} L_{m_i}^{\varepsilon_{m_i,k_i}}(x)\Pr_{p_{m_i}}(x) + \sum_{x \in \mathbb{B}^{n_i} \setminus \Xi_{n_i}} L_{m_i}(x)\Pr_{p_{m_i}}(x) \right) \right| \le$$

$$\mathbf{E}\max\left(L_0\left(\xi_1^{p_{m_i}}, \xi_2^{p_{m_i}}, \ldots, \xi_{n_{i-1}}^{p_{m_i}}\right), L'_0\left(\xi_1^{p_{m_i}}, \xi_2^{p_{m_i}}, \ldots, \xi_{n_{i-1}}^{p_{m_i}}\right)\right)$$

$$+ \mathbf{E}\max\left(L_{m_i}\left(\xi_1^{p_{m_i}}, \xi_2^{p_{m_i}}, \ldots, \xi_{n_{i-1}}^{p_{m_i}}\right), L_{m_i}^{\varepsilon_{m_i,k_i}}\left(\xi_1^{p_{m_i}}, \xi_2^{p_{m_i}}, \ldots, \xi_{n_{i-1}}^{p_{m_i}}\right)\right) \le$$

$$\mathbf{E}L_0\left(\xi_1^{p_{m_i}}, \xi_2^{p_{m_i}}, \ldots, \xi_{n_{i-1}}^{p_{m_i}}\right) + \mathbf{E}L_{m_i}\left(\xi_1^{p_{m_i}}, \xi_2^{p_{m_i}}, \ldots, \xi_{n_{i-1}}^{p_{m_i}}\right) + 2n_{i-1} . \tag{34}$$

The last inequality follows from (27) and the following observation: for all $x \in \mathbb{B}^*$ and positive integers m and k, we have $|L_m(x) - L_m^{\varepsilon_{m,k}}(x)| \le \varepsilon_{m,k}|x|$.

We will now prove the inequalities $\mathbf{E}L_0\left(\xi_1^{p_{m_i}}, \xi_2^{p_{m_i}}, \ldots, \xi_{n_{i-1}}^{p_{m_i}}\right) \le \theta n_{i-1}$ and $\mathbf{E}L_{m_i}\left(\xi_1^{p_{m_i}}, \xi_2^{p_{m_i}}, \ldots, \xi_{n_{i-1}}^{p_{m_i}}\right) \le \theta n_{i-1}$. Indeed, while the length is less than n_{i-1}, the strategies $\mathfrak{A}_0$ and $\mathfrak{A}_{m_i}$ output predictions $(x, f(x))$, where $x \in [x_1, x_{m_i}]$. Since S is convex, all such points $(x, f(x))$ lie above the tangent line $(1-p_{m_i})x + p_{m_i}y = (1 - p_{m_i})x_{m_i} + p_{m_i}f(x_{m_i})$ but below the parallel line $(1 - p_{m_i})x + p_{m_i}y = (1-p_{m_i})x_1 + p_{m_i}f(x_1)$ (see Fig. 5). Hence $(1-p_{m_i})x + p_{m_i}f(x) \le (1-p_{m_i})x_1 + p_{m_i}f(x_1) \le \theta$. This provides us with the desired inequalities.

Taking into account (26), we get

$$\mathbf{E}\mathcal{K}\left(\xi_1^{(p_{m_i})}, \xi_2^{(p_{m_i})}, \ldots, \xi_{n_i}^{(p_{m_i})}\right) \le \sum_{x \in \Xi_{n_i}} L_{m_i}^{\varepsilon_{m_i,k_i}}(x)\Pr_{p_{m_i}}(x)$$

$$+ \sum_{x \in \mathbb{B}^{n_i} \setminus \Xi_{n_i}} L_{m_i}(x)\Pr_{p_{m_i}}(x) + \frac{\Phi(-1)}{4}\sqrt{\frac{1-p_m}{\underline{f''}(x_m)p_m}} + C . \tag{35}$$

Comparison with (20) and (29) yields

$$\left(\frac{1}{2}\sqrt{\frac{1-p_{m_i}}{\underline{f''}(x_{m_i})p_{m_i}}} - 3\left(p_{m_i} + \sqrt{\frac{p_{m_i}(1-p_{m_i})}{n_i}}\right)\right)\frac{\Phi(-1)}{2} \le C . \tag{36}$$

The left-hand side tends to infinity as i tends to $+\infty$ and this is a contradiction.

The case $f'(x_m) \not\to 0$. The proof in this case can be carried out in essentially the same way. It can even be significantly simplified since all predictions made by $\mathfrak{A}_m$ and $\mathfrak{A}_m^{\varepsilon_{m,k}}$ can be taken from a bounded set.

Full Information Game with Gains and Losses

Chamy Allenberg-Neeman[1] and Benny Neeman[2]

[1] School of Computer Science, Tel Aviv University, Tel Aviv 69978, Israel.
chamy_a@netvision.net.il
[2] School of Computer Science, The Interdisciplinary Center, Herzliya, Israel.
neeman.benny@idc.ac.il

Abstract. In the Full Information Game the player sequentially selects one out of K actions. After the player has made his choice, the K payoffs of the actions become known and the player receives the payoff of the action he selected. The *Gain-Loss game* is the variant of this game, where both gains from $[0,1]$ and losses from $[0,1]$ are possible payoffs. This game has two well studied special cases: the Full Loss game where only losses are allowed, and the Full Gain game where only gains are allowed. For each of these cases the appropriate variant of Freund and Schapire's algorithm Hedge [7,3] can be used to obtain nearly optimal regrets. Both of these variants have an immediate adaptations to the Full Gain-Loss game. However these solutions are not always optimal.
The first result of this paper is a new variant of algorithm Hedge that achieves a regret of $O(\sqrt{\ln K}\sqrt{G_j + L_j})$ for the Full Gain-Loss game, where j is the index of one of the actions in the game, G_j, the total gain of j, is the sum of all the positive payoffs that the jth action had in the game, and L_j is the absolute value of the sum of all its negative payoffs. In addition, the new algorithm achieves matches the performance of the known Hedge algorithms in the special cases of gains only and losses only.
The second result is an application of the new algorithm that achieves new upper bounds on the regrets of the original Full Gain game and Full Loss game. The new upper bounds are a function of a new parameter.
The third result is a method for combining online learning algorithms online. This method yields an $O\big(\min\big(\sqrt{L_{opt}\ln K}, \sqrt{(T-L_{opt})\ln K}\big)\big)$ upper bound on the regret of the the Full Loss game, and an $O\big(\min\big(\sqrt{G_{opt}\ln K}, \sqrt{(T-G_{opt})\ln K}\big)\big)$ upper bound on the regret of the the Full Gain game.

1 Introduction

The *Full Information Game* was defined by Freund and Schapire in [8]. On each day (or other time step), an adversary assigns K payoffs to K given actions. Then, without knowing which payoffs the adversary has chosen, the player has to select one of the K actions. After the player has made his (possibly randomized) choice, the payoffs of all the actions become known, and the player receives the payoff of the action he had chosen. After T days, the expected total payoff of the player is the sum of his expected payoffs over all the days of the game.

S. Ben-David, J. Case, A. Maruoka (Eds.): ALT 2004, LNAI 3244, pp. 264–278, 2004.

We compare the performance of the player - the online algorithm, with the performance of an adversary who has the advantage of being able to make his choice *after* seeing all the future T payoff vectors. However, our adversary is limited to choosing only *one* action, and then this *same* action becomes his choice for the entire game. The goal of the player is, therefore, to minimize the *regret* which is the difference between his total expected payoff and the total payoff of the best action in the game (over all the days in the game). The adversary's goal is to maximize the regret.

We consider three variants of this game. The *Full Loss Game* is the variant of the Full Information game in which the adversary is limited to assigning losses from $[0,1]$ only, i.e., payoffs from $[-1,0]$ only. The *Full Gain Game* is the variant of the full information game where the adversary is limited to assigning only zero or positive payoffs from $[0,1]$ (i.e., gains). For the first result of this paper we consider the *Full Gain-Loss Game*, which is a variant of the Full Information game where any payoff from $[-1,1]$ is possible. In addition to being theoretically interesting, allowing both gains and losses is necessary for modelling many practical scenarios including financial investments and the stock market.

Algorithm **Hedge** and its proof technique by Freund and Schapire in [8] presents a generalized version of the online prediction methods. These methods were developed in steps, starting from Littlestone and Warmuth's [11] **Weighted Majority** algorithm and Vovk's [12] **Aggregating Strategies**. The Weighted Majority algorithm left a parameter to be tuned. A similar but more restricted game than the Full Information game was considered by Cesa-Bianchi, et al. in [5]. They took a major step and showed that the Weighted Majority technique's parameter can be tuned yielding an upper bound on the regret that is of the order of the square root of the total payoff of the best action.

1.1   Upper Bound for the Full Gain-Loss Game

The first result of this paper focuses on finding and investigating the update rules that are best for the case of the Full Information Game where both gains and losses are allowed.

Freund and Schapire's [8] algorithm **Hedge**(β) has an upper bound of $O(\sqrt{\ln K}\sqrt{L_{min}})$ on the regret of the Full Loss game, where L_{min} is the total loss of the action that has a minimal total loss (maximal total payoff) in the game. Algorithm **Hedge**(α) that appeared in Auer et al. [3] is the variant of Hedge for the Full Gain game. By a trivial transformation of the range of the losses or the gains, both Hedge(β) and Hedge(α) can be applied to the Full Gain-Loss game, yielding analogous upper bounds on the regret. Let us consider using Hedge(α) via the transformation where any $x_i(t)$, a payoff of action i in iteration t, is substituted by $\frac{1}{2}(1 + x_i(t))$. The Hedge technique's upper bound on the regret of the Gain-Loss game is $O\big(\min_{i \in \{1,2,...,K\}} \sqrt{\ln K} \sqrt{T + \sum_{t=1}^{T} x_i(t)} \,\big)$, where T is the number of days in the game. Using Hedge(β) with the analogous transformation yields an upper bound of $O\big(\min_{i \in \{1,2,...,K\}} \sqrt{\ln K} \sqrt{T - \sum_{t=1}^{T} x_i(t)} \,\big)$

on the regret of the Gain-Loss game. This result means an $O(\sqrt{\ln K}\sqrt{T})$ upper bound in the case where we used Hedge(α) but $\min_{i\in\{1,2,...,K\}}\sum_{t=1}^{T} x_i(t)$ was positive, or if we used Hedge(β) but $\min_{i\in\{1,2,...,K\}}\sum_{t=1}^{T} x_i(t)$ turned out to be negative, or in any case where $\min_{i\in\{1,2,...,K\}}\sum_{t=1}^{T} x_i(t)$ was small.

In this work we present algorithm **GL**. This algorithm, is a variant of Hedge that has a new generalized update rule.

If we are given in advance $\overline{G_{\mathrm{OPT}}+L_{\mathrm{OPT}}}$, an upper bound on $G_{\mathrm{OPT}}+L_{\mathrm{OPT}}$, where OPT is an action that achieves the maximal total payoff, then **GL**(α), the parameterized version of GL, can be tuned to achieve a regret of $O(\sqrt{\ln K}\sqrt{\overline{G_{\mathrm{OPT}}+L_{\mathrm{OPT}}}})$ (Corollary 2 section 3.3). Let G_j be the sum of all the positive intakes (gains) of the j'th action in the game, and let L_j be the sum of all the negative intakes (losses) of the j'th action in the game. The more general version of the last result states that for any action a_j, if an upper bound $\overline{G_j+L_j} \geq G_j+L_j$ is given in advance, then GL(α) can be tuned to achieve a regret of $O(\sqrt{\ln K}\sqrt{\overline{G_j+L_j}})$ (Corollary 1 section 3.3).

For the case where no prior knowledge is assumed, **GL.1**, the variant of the new algorithm that uses the known doubling technique (used in [3], [4] and [5]) guarantees that there exists an action a_j such that the regret is $O(\sqrt{\ln K}\sqrt{G_j+L_j})$. This upper bound matches the lower bound, that is mentioned later, up to the choice of actions in the regret expression.

The parameter T of the known results can be substantially larger than the parameter G_j+L_j, that the results of this paper depend on. For each day, 1 is the theoretical upper bound on the gain or loss of an action per day, and therefore may be far apart from the common actual gain and loss value. For G_j+L_j to be equal to T, this maximal gain or loss of 1 per day has to be the payoff of action a_j every day. The constants of the new result are slightly better than those of the known results as the above transformations add a $\sqrt{2}$ multiplicative factor to the upper bound.

The lower bound of $\Omega(\sqrt{T\ln K})$ in Cesa-Bianchi, et al. [5] implies an $\Omega(\sqrt{L_{\min}\ln K})$ lower bound on the Full Loss game, where $L_{\min}$ is the total loss of the action that achieves the minimal total loss. It also implies an $\Omega(\sqrt{G_{\max}\ln K})$ lower bound on the Full Gain game, where $G_{\max}$ is the total gain of the action that achieves the maximal total gain. These lower bounds can be combined to show that the regret of the Full Gain-Loss game has an $\Omega(\sqrt{\ln K}\sqrt{G_{\max}+L_{\min}})$ lower bound. The significance of this lower bound is that it shows that the regret of the Gain-Loss game cannot be a function of the optimal (maximal) net payoff of the best action in the game (i.e., cannot be $G_{\mathrm{OPT}}-L_{\mathrm{OPT}}$). In fact, the proportion between the regret and the optimal net payoff is unbounded. For example, the optimal net payoff may be zero, while the minimal G_j+L_j for any action a_j, can be as large as T.

In the Full Gain-Loss game, the a priori range of payoffs is $[-1,1]$. Both the Full Gain game and the Full Loss game are special cases of the Full Gain-Loss game. In both cases if it is known in advance that a special case is about to take place, the appropriate Hedge algorithms can be applied yielding nearly optimal regrets for these special cases. In particular, if we know in advance that all the payoffs will be gains, Hedge(α) can be applied yielding the upper bound of $O(\sqrt{G_{\max} \ln K})$ on the regret. If we know in advance that all the payoffs will be losses, Hedge(β) can be used to achieve an upper bound of $O(\sqrt{L_{\min} \ln K})$ on the regret.

The new algorithm GL does not require prior knowledge of whether the coming game would be a special case or not, and yet if a special case takes place, GL achieves the known regret of the special case. That is, in the special case where all the payoffs turn out to be from [0,1], GL.1, the doubling version of GL, achieves an upper bound of $O(\sqrt{G_{\max} \ln K})$ on the regret, and in the special case where all the payoffs turn out to be from [-1,0], GL.1 achieves an upper bound of $O(\sqrt{L_{\min} \ln K})$ on the regret. The constants in these cases match those of Hedge. If it turns out that the game is not a special case, the same algorithm GL.1 still achieves the new and improved general-case result and guarantees that there exists an action a_j such that the $O(\sqrt{\ln K} \sqrt{G_j + L_j})$ upper bound on the regret holds.

1.2   New Upper Bounds for the Full Information Game

The second result of this paper is an application of algorithm GL that achieves new upper bounds on the regrets of the Full Gain game and Full Loss game. While the new algorithms and results are based on the GL technique which in turn is based on the Hedge technique of Freund and Schapire [8], they require the addition of a new technique. The new upper bounds are a function of a new parameter. Only in its worst case does this parameter become equal to the parameters of the original upper bounds - the optimal total gain and optimal total loss. Given an online algorithm A, for any arm a_i, we define D_i^A, the *exceeding value of a_i with respect to A*, as $\sum_{t \text{ s.t. } g_i(t) > g_A(t)} \left(g_i(t) - g_A(t) \right)$ where $g_A(t)$ is the expected gain of the online algorithm A in iteration t, and $g_i(t)$ is the gain of action a_i in iteration t. For the Full Gain game, algorithm GGL (from section 4) achieves a regret of $O(\sqrt{\ln K} \sqrt{D_j^A})$, where a_j is one of the actions $j \in \{1, 2, ..., K\}$ (Theorem 2 and Theorem 3 from section 4). According to this new update rule, we judge an action not by its absolute accumulative payoff, but by the offsets it has from the payoff of the mixture of actions that we expected to be best, that is, by the "surprises" this action gave us from what we believed to be a good choice. It is interesting to see that such a rule is enough to ensure the ability to compete with the optimum.

We can show that in the Full Gain game for all actions $j \in \{1, 2, ..., K\}$, $D_j^A \leq G_{\text{OPT}}$ and therefore depending on this new parameter could be better than depending on the original G_{OPT} parameter However, our constants are slightly weaker than those of the known Hedge upper bounds on the regrets from [8] - we have an additional $\sqrt{2}$ multiplicative factor on our upper bounds that the known results do not have.

Theoretically, the interesting point about these new results is that they show the first relation between the ability to approach the performance of the best action and how different the good actions are from the performance of the mixture of actions that we expected to be best. Intuitively, it seems that the new results are more explicit in showing that the less adversarial the input (of payoffs) is, the better the new algorithm can perform. Our hope is that this can lead to upper bounds that guarantee a good regret in the worst case, but in addition, know how to capitalize on the good fortune of better behaved sources of payoffs, and have an improved performance in those cases. Our preliminary experiments support this hope.

One can conduct similar discussions about the Full Loss game and the Full Gain-Loss game, and show that they have the same type of $O(\sqrt{\ln K}\sqrt{D_j^A})$ upper bound on the regret.

1.3   Combining Online Learning Algorithms Online

In [8] Freund and Schapire generalized the **Weighted Majority** technique of N. Littlestone and M. K. Warmuth from [11], and presented algorithm **Hedge**(β) for the Full Loss game Let H_I denote the doubling variant of algorithm Hedge(β), i.e., the variant of Hedge(β) that tunes β using the standard doubling technique that was used in [3], [4] and [5]

Algorithm **Hedge**(α) of Auer, Cesa-Bianchi, Freund and Schapire's [2] is designed for the Full Gain game (discussed in section 4), however via an immediate transformation from losses to gains it can be applied to the Full Loss game. In this transformation we "translate" any loss $l \in [0,1]$ from the real input of the Full Loss game to a "simulated gain" $g = 1 - l$. Hedge(α) can then run on these simulated gains. Let H_{II} be the variant of Hedge(α) that uses this transformation and tunes α using the standard doubling technique.

By the Freund and Schapire's generalized Weighted Majority technique of [8], H_I achieves an upper bound of $O(\sqrt{L_{opt} \ln K})$ on the regret of the Full Loss game. An upper bound of $O(\sqrt{(T - L_{opt}) \ln K})$ on the regret of H_{II} follows from the analysis of Hedge(α) that appears in Auer, Cesa-Bianchi, Freund and Schapire's [2].

In this work we construct an algorithm that guarantees a regret that is upper bounded simultaneously by both of the above upper bounds, that is, a regret that is upper bound by $O(\min(\sqrt{L_{opt}}, \sqrt{T - L_{opt}}) \cdot \sqrt{\ln K})$. The motivation for such a result is the basic online and online learning fields competitive approach where once certain performances are possible, we want an online algorithm with a performance that is not much worse than any of them.

When considering the goal of an $O(\min(\sqrt{L_{opt}}, \sqrt{T - L_{opt}}) \cdot \sqrt{\ln K})$ upper bound on the regret of the Full Loss game, the first, but yet wrong, impression is that this goal can be met by the immediate following construction. Let us consider combining algorithms H_I and H_{II} in the obvious way - using a master Hedge algorithm that has a set of two actions, which are algorithms H_I and H_{II}. This master algorithm would achieve, up to the regret, the performance of the one out of the two that turns out to be the best in hindsight. This bootstrapping idea doesn't work, since we have to choose what type of master Hedge algorithm to use, the options are a Hedge algorithm that is a H_I type or one that is a H_{II} type. This a priori choice dictates the upper bound on the regret of the master algorithm. If we chose the first option of a H_I type of master algorithm, we get an upper bound that depends on $\sqrt{L_{opt}}$. Otherwise (if we chose the second option) we obtain an upper bound that depends on $\sqrt{T - L_{opt}}$.

In this work a new technique for combining online learning algorithms is presented. With this technique algorithms H_I and H_{II} are combined into a new algorithm. This new algorithm is called algorithm **Zapping**, and it achieves an upper bound of $O\left(\min\left(\sqrt{L_{opt}}, \sqrt{T - L_{opt}}\right) \cdot \sqrt{\ln K}\right)$ on the regret of the Full Loss game (Theorem 4 section 5). The new technique also yields an analogous result for the Full Gain game.

2   Notation and Terminology

The *Full Information Game* was defined by Freund and Schapire [8]. All three versions of the Full Information game are carried out in T iterations. Each iteration is done as follows:

1. The adversary chooses $x(t) \in [-1, 1]^K$, a vector of K payoffs, for the current iteration t. The i'th component $x_i(t)$ is the payoff that is associated with action i. This is the payoff that we will receive if we choose the i'th action in this iteration.
2. Without knowing the adversary's choice, we are asked to choose one action $a_{i_t} \in \{a_1, a_2, \dots, a_K\}$.
3. The payoff vector $x(t)$ becomes known.

When making our choice in step 2, we, the online algorithm, are allowed to use randomization. We can also use the information we have accumulated in former iterations.

There are three variants of the Full Information game. For any choice of payoffs from $[-1, 1]$ that is made by the adversary, if $x_i(t)$, the payoff of action a_i at time t, is positive it is called a gain, and it has an additional notation $g_i(t)$. If $x_i(t)$ is negative we denote the absolute value of it by $l_i(t)$, and call it a loss. X_i denotes the total payoff of action i throughout the game.

G_i, the total gain of action i throughout the game, is the summation of $g_i(t)$ over all the iterations where $x_i(t)$ is positive.

L_i, the total loss of action a_i, is the summation of $l_i(t)$ over all the iterations where $x_i(t)$ was negative. Trivially, $X_i = G_i - L_i$, and may be positive, negative, or zero.

No stochastic assumptions are made as to how the adversary generates the payoffs. We compare our performance to X_{OPT} the *optimal payoff* which is the performance of the best action OPT. X_{OPT} is defined as X_i maximized over all the actions $i \in \{1, 2, ..., K\}$. In other words, we compete against X_{OPT}, the maximal total payoff of any consistent choice of action in this game. Our performance measurement, the *regret of an online algorithm A*, is the expected total payoff of A minus the optimal payoff, maximized (sup) over all possible assignments of payoffs in the game. The regret of the game is the regret of an online algorithm A, minimized (inf) over all online algorithms A.

3   Full Gain-Loss Game with Prior Knowledge

3.1   The New Update Rule

Let us consider Hedge(β) for the Full Loss game. In algorithm Hedge(β), initially equal weights are given to the K actions. At each iteration Hedge chooses an action according to a probability distribution that is obtained by normalizing the weight vector. At the end of each iteration after $l(t)$ the loss vector of the actions, becomes known. Hedge(β) updates the weight of each action by multiplying it with a multiplicative factor. The most discussed multiplicative factor for Hedge(β) is, for arm a_i : $\beta^{l_i(t)}$.

When looking for a variant of Hedge for the Gain-Loss game, the immediate choice of a multiplicative update factor for the weights is β^l for the case where the payoff is a loss l, and $(\frac{1}{\beta})^g$ for the case where the payoff is a gain g. This choice satisfies the naive intuition that a gain of 1 plus a loss of 1 should have the same effect as a net profit of 0 that comes from no loss and no gain. In other words this intuitive update rule has the quality that all actions with identical net profit are given the same weight. However, it turns out that in the case of the Full Gain game, the Hedge proof technique cannot be successfully applied to this choice of update rule. Moreover, the above naive intuition had to be abandoned before the new update rule could be found.

In this paper a new generalized update rule is suggested for the Gain-Loss game. In this rule the multiplicative factor for the weights is $(1 + \alpha)^g$ when the payoff is a gain g, and $(1 - \alpha)^l$ when the payoff is a loss l. In the general case, the new rule does not necessarily give equal weights to actions that have identical cumulative payoffs. Rather, between two actions that have an identical net profit, there would be a higher weight for the action a_i that has the smaller $G_i(t) + L_i(t)$, which is intuitively the one with the "smaller circulation", or the one that is "more stable". This quality corresponds to the conclusion of the worst case risk analysis that says that if two investments have the same net profit the one with the smaller $G_i(t) + L_i(t)$, is less risky, and is therefore preferable. We call the algorithm that uses the new update rule GL. For this update rule a variant of the Hedge proof technique by Freund and Schapire [8] can be applied, yielding the new upper bounds of algorithm GL.

3.2   Algorithm GL(α) and Its Analysis

Algorithm GL(α), the parameterized version of GL, is described in Figure 1. If the parameter α is tuned using a given in advance upper bound $\overline{G_{\text{OPT}} + L_{\text{OPT}}}$ on $G_{\text{OPT}} + L_{\text{OPT}}$, GL($\alpha$) achieves an upper bound of $O\left(\sqrt{(\overline{G_{\text{OPT}} + L_{\text{OPT}})} \ln K}\right)$ on the regret.

Algorithm GL(α)
Parameters: A real number $0 < \alpha < 1$.
Initialization:
For $i = 1, 2, ..., K$ set the initial weight of action a_i, $w_i 1 := \frac{1}{K}$.

Repeat for $t = 1, 2, ...$ until game ends:

1. Choose action i_t according to distribution $P(t)$,
   where $P_i(t) = \frac{w_i^t}{\sum_{j=1}^{K} w_j^t}$, and where w_i^t is the
   weight of action i at the beginning of iteration t.
2. Observe the reward vector $x(t)$ and receive payoff $x_{i_t}(t)$.
3. Update the weights:

   For any action that received a positive or zero payoff
   (a gain $g_i(t)$) in the current iteration:

$$w_i^{t+1} = w_i^t \cdot (1 + \alpha)^{g_i(t)}$$

   For any action that received a negative payoff
   (a loss $l_i(t)$) in the current iteration:

$$w_i^{t+1} = w_i^t \cdot (1 - \alpha)^{l_i(t)}$$

Fig. 1. Parameterized version of algorithm GL

Algorithm GL, like algorithm Hedge, is actually a family of algorithms, as the proof technique allow some freedom in the choice of the update rule. In GL the multiplicative update for a loss l can be any function $U_\alpha(l)$ s.t. $(1 - \alpha)^l \le U_\alpha(l) \le 1 - \alpha l$, and the multiplicative update for a gain g can be any function $U_\alpha(l)$ s.t. $(1 + \alpha)^g \le U_\alpha(g) \le 1 + \alpha g$. The linear rule $1 + \alpha x$ is also a member of the Hedge family of update rules. However for the rest of the Hedge family of update rules, we can't show the performance of the GL family of update rules.

Theorem 1. *For all $0 < \alpha < 1$, any action a_j s.t. $j \in \{1, 2, ...K\}$ and any choice of payoffs from $[-1, 1]$ that is made by the adversary, the expected total payoff of algorithm $GL(\alpha)$ is at least,*

$$X_{GL(\alpha)} \ge \frac{G_j \cdot \ln(1 + \alpha) + L_j \cdot \ln(1 - \alpha) - \ln K}{\alpha} .$$

The proof of Theorem 1 is a variant of Freund and Schapire's proof of the performance of algorithm Hedge from [8], that includes an adaptation to our case.

3.3   Tuning the Parameter Using Prior Knowledge

Corollary 1. *For any choice of payoffs from $[-1,1]$ that is made by the adversary, and any action a_j s.t. $j \in \{1, 2, ..., K\}$, given an upper bound $\overline{G_j + L_j} \geq G_j + L_j$, if the parameter α is set to be $\dfrac{\sqrt{2 \ln K}}{\sqrt{\overline{G_j + L_j}} + \sqrt{2 \ln K}}$, then the expected total payoff of algorithm $GL(\alpha)$ is at least,*

$$X_{\mathrm{GL}(\alpha)} \geq G_j - L_j - \left(\sqrt{2 \ln K} \cdot \sqrt{\overline{G_j + L_j}} + \ln K\right) .$$

In particular, this inequality is valid when action a_j is OPT, the action that achieves the maximal total payoff over all actions in the game.

4   New Upper Bound for the Full Gain Game

In the Full Gain game, in any iteration t the adversary chooses a vector of "input" gains $g(t) \in [0,1]^K$. In algorithm $GGL(\alpha)$ we apply a new transformation on these "input" gains. Then we feed the transformed values to $GL(\alpha)$. For this transformation we refer to the expected payoff of our online algorithm $GGL(\alpha)$ in iteration t, which is $X_{\mathrm{on}}(t) = P(t) \cdot g(t)$.

Theorem 2. *In the Full Gain game, for any choice of payoffs from $[0,1]$ that is made by the adversary, If algorithm $GGL(\alpha)$ is given in advance $D_{\mathrm{OPT}}^{GGL(\alpha)} \geq D_{\mathrm{OPT}}^{GGL(\alpha)}$, an upper bound on the exceeding value of OPT, where OPT is the action that achieves a maximal total gain over all the other actions in the game, then if the parameter α is set to be $\dfrac{\sqrt{\ln K}}{\sqrt{D_{\mathrm{OPT}}^{GGL(\alpha)}} + \sqrt{\ln K}}$, then algorithm $GGL(\alpha)$ achieves,*

$$X_{GGL(\alpha)} \geq G_{\mathrm{OPT}} - 2\sqrt{\ln K} \cdot \sqrt{D_{\mathrm{OPT}}^{GGL(\alpha)}} - \ln K .$$

The proof of Theorem 2 is in Appendix A . It is based on the proof of Theorem 1 and Corollary 1 (the analysis of algorithm $GL(\alpha)$) which are based on the technique of Freund and Schapire's proof in [8]. However this analysis requires the addition of a new technique.

Let us define algorithm GGL.1 as the doubling variant of GGL that is constructed using the known doubling technique (used in [3], [4] and [5]).

Theorem 3. *In the Full Gain game, for any choice of payoffs from $[0,1]$ that is made by the adversary, there exists an action a_j s.t. algorithm GGL.1 the doubling variant of algorithm GGL achieves, $X_{GGL.1} \geq$ $G_{\mathrm{OPT}} - 5.7\sqrt{2 \ln K} \cdot \sqrt{D_j^{GGL(\alpha)}} - 1.3 \ln K \log_2(D_j^{GGL.1}) - 7.3 \ln K$.*

Lemma 1. *In the Full Gain game, for any choice of gains that the adversary makes, for any action a_j s.t. $j \in \{1, 2, ..., K\}$, $D_j^{GGL(\alpha)} < G_{\mathrm{OPT}}$.*

Proof of Lemma 1

For any action a_i: By definition
$$D_j^{\text{GGL}(\alpha)} = \sum_{t \text{ s.t. } g_i(t) \geq X_{\text{GGL}(\alpha)}} \left(g_i(t) - X_{\text{GGL}(\alpha)}(t)\right).$$
Since in the Full Gain game $X_{\text{GGL}(\alpha)}(t)$ is always positive or zero,
$$D_{\text{OPT}}^{\text{GGL}(\alpha)} \leq \sum_{t \text{ s.t. } g_i(t) \geq X_{\text{GGL}(\alpha)}} g_i(t) \leq \sum_{t=1}^{T} g_i(t) = G_j \leq G_{\text{OPT}} .$$

Algorithm GGL(α):

Parameters: A real number $0 < \alpha < 1$.
Initialization: Initialize algorithm GL(α).

Repeat for $t = 1, 2, \ldots$ until game ends:
Apply algorithm GL(α) to iteration t in the following way:

1. Let GL(α) produce a probability vector $P(t)$,
   and choose an action for iteration t according to $P(t)$.
2. Calculate the expected payoff of iteration t, $X_{\text{on}}(t) = P(t) \cdot g(t)$.
3. For any action i, calculate $y_i(t) := g_i(t) - X_{\text{on}}(t)$.
   /* Note that for all iteration t and action i, $y_i(t) \in [-1, 1]$. */
4. Let GL(α) receive the vector $y(t)$ as the vector of payoffs
   for iteration t.
5. Let GL(α) update its weights according to $y(t)$.

Fig. 2. Parameterized version of algorithm GGL

5   Combining Online Learning Algorithms

Let H_I denote The doubling version of algorithm **Hedge**(β) from Freund and Schapire's [8]. Let H_{II} denote The doubling version of algorithm **Hedge**(α) from Auer et al.'s [3]. algorithm **Zapping** is described in figure 3. This algorithm can be viewed as a master algorithm that in each iteration let one out of the two algorithms, H_I or H_{II}, handle the current iteration. In any run of algorithm Zapping the two algorithms H_I and H_{II} split the sequence of iterations between them such that each algorithm handles only a (not necessarily continuous) subsequence of the iterations, and completely ignores the rest of the iterations.

In each iteration t, one and only one of these two algorithms is the *active algorithm*, i.e., is the algorithm that is used for choosing the action, and has its weights and variables updated at the end of the iteration. The algorithm that did not become the active algorithm in iteration t is not considered when choosing the action in iteration t, and its weights and variables remain unchanged as if iteration t never took place.

Let S_I and S_{II} denote the two subsequences that are handled by algorithms H_I and H_{II} respectively. These subsequence of S are not necessarily continuous, rather, each of them is consisted of a subset of the iterations of S such that the original order between the iterations is preserved. The subset of the iterations that are in S_I and the one of S_{II} are disjoined and together they cover all the iterations of S.

The decision of how to split S into the two subsequences S_I and S_{II} is made online. A simple deterministic rule is used for deciding to which of the two subsequences the current iteration belongs, that is, which algorithm should be the active algorithm in the current iteration. This rule is not the greedy one - not necessarily the algorithm that had the best performance (or the best regret) up to this iteration will be the active algorithm in the current iteration. Rather the algorithm (H_I or H_{II}) that had the smallest "Hedge technique upper bound on the local regret" so far will be the active algorithm in the coming iteration.

5.1 Definitions

The sequence of iterations 1 through t from $S = 1, 2, \ldots, T$ is denoted $S(t)$. $S_I(t)$ denotes the subsequence of $S(t)$ that contains only the iterations where algorithm H_I is active, and $S_{II}(t)$ is analogous.

Let us consider any given choice of losses that is made by the adversary. For S', a subsequence of iterations, $opt(S')$ denotes the action that is optimal when only the iterations of S' are considered, i.e., the action a_i that achieves,

$$\sum_{t \in S'} l_i(t) = \min_{j \in \{1,2,\ldots,K\}} \left(\sum_{t \in S'} l_j(t) \right) .$$

$L_{opt(S')}(S^*)$ the *cumulative loss of action* $opt(S')$ *over the subsequence* S^* is,
$$L_{opt(S')}(S^*) \doteq \sum_{t \in S^*} l_{opt(S')}(t) .$$

For a subsequence of the iterations S', $L_{opt(S')}(S')$ is the *optimal loss with respect to S'*.

Let A_t denotes the active algorithm of iteration t.

$l(A_t, t)$ is the loss of the action that A_t chooses in iteration t, i.e., the loss that is incurred in iteration t. Since H_I and H_{II} are randomized algorithms $l(A_t, t)$ is a random variable.

The *local loss of algorithm A over the subsequence of iterations S'* is, $L_A(S') \doteq E[\sum_{t' \in S'} l(A, t')]$.

The *local regret of algorithm H_I at the beginning of iteration t* is the difference between the local loss of algorithm H_I over $S_I(t-1)$ and the optimal loss with respect to $S_I(t-1)$.

Analogously, the *local regret of algorithm H_{II} at the beginning of iteration t* is the difference between the local loss of algorithm H_{II} over $S_{II}(t-1)$ and the optimal loss with respect to $S_{II}(t-1)$.

5.2 The Rule That Algorithm Zapping Uses

We will use the following function for the description of the upper bounds on the regret: $Q(X) \doteq 5.7 \cdot \sqrt{\ln K} \cdot X + \ln K \cdot log_2(X+1) + 6.9 \ln K$.

The following upper bounds follow from Freund and Schapire [8]. *The local regret of H_I at the beginning of iteration t* is upper bounded by $Q(\sqrt{L_{opt(S_I(t-1))}(S_I(t-1))}\,)$. *The local regret of H_{II} at the beginning of iteration t* is upper bounded by $Q(\sqrt{|S_{II}(t-1)| - L_{opt(S_{II}(t-1))}(S_{II}(t-1))}\,)$.

At each iteration, the Zapping algorithm chooses the current active algorithm. The goal behind this choice is to get the above upper bounds on the local regrets that H_I and H_{II} will have at the end of the game to be very close. As can be seen in the analysis in the next section, achieving this goal is enough to obtain this paper's new upper bound.

The rule that the Zapping algorithm uses in order to select the active algorithm for the current iteration is: The Zapping algorithm lets the algorithm that had the smaller upper bound on the local regret so far, be the active algorithm in the current iteration. Our analysis shows that this local rule achieves the above global goal of close local regrets at the end of the game. This is not immediate since that the locally optimal action can change from one iteration to the next.

Theorem 4. *In the Full Loss game, for any $K \geq 2$ number of actions, any T number of iterations, and any possible assignment of losses that is made by the adversary, the regret of algorithm Zapping is upper bounded by*

$$2 \cdot \min\left(Q(\sqrt{L_{opt}}), Q(\sqrt{T - L_{opt}}\,)\right) + 1,$$

where $Q(X) \doteq 5.7 \cdot \sqrt{\ln K} \cdot X + \ln K \cdot log_2(X+1) + 6.9 \ln K$.

Algorithm Zapping

Initialization: Initialize algorithms H_I and H_{II}.

For $t = 1, 2, \ldots$ until game ends do steps 1 to 3 :

1. Calculate the local optimal losses :

$$optimal\_loss(H_I, t-1) := \min_{j \in \{1,2,\ldots,K\}} \sum_{t' \in S_I(t-1)} l_j(t')$$

$$optimal\_loss(H_{II}, t-1) := \min_{j \in \{1,2,\ldots,K\}} \sum_{t' \in S_{II}(t-1)} l_j(t')$$

2. If $optimal\_loss(H_I, t-1)$
   $\leq |S_{II}(t-1)| - optimal\_loss(H_{II}, t-1)$,   Then let algorithm H_I be A_t - the active algorithm in iteration t.

   Otherwise, let algorithm H_{II} be A_t.
3. Apply algorithm A_t to the current iteration t, i.e., let A_t choose the action for the current iteration t, and then feed back the loss vector $l(t)$ to A_t. Let A_t update its weight accordingly.

Fig. 3.

6 Open Questions

The Partial Information Game (the adversarial multi-armed bandit problem) was defined in Auer, Cesa-Bianchi, Freund and Schapire's [3]. This game is similar to the Full Information game except that in this case at the end of the iteration (step 3) only the payoff that was associated with the action that the online algorithm had chosen becomes known.

In Auer et al.'s [3] an upper bound of $O(\sqrt{K \ln K G_{opt}})$ is shown on the regret of the gain variant of the Partial Information game. In Allenberg-Neeman, Auer and Cesa-Bianchi's [2] an upper bound of $O(K \ln K \sqrt{L_{opt}})$ is shown for the loss variant. It remain an open question whether the results of this paper, can be extended to the Partial Information Game.

Acknowledgement. We would like to thank Amos Fiat for advising to work on the gain-loss question, and for constructive suggestions. We would also like to thank Nicolò Cesa-Bianchi, Yishay Mansour and Leah Epstein for helpful discussions.

References

[1] Chamy Allenberg. Individual sequence prediction - upper bounds and applications to complexity. *Proceedings of the 12th Annual Conference on Computer Learning Theory*, 1999.

[2] Chamy Allenberg, Peter Auer and Nicolò Cesa-Bianchi. On the loss version of the adversarial multi-armed bandit problem. To appear.

[3] Peter Auer, Nicolò Cesa-Bianchi, Yoav Freund and Robert E. Schapire. Gambling in a rigged casino: The adversarial multi-armed bandit problem . In *Proceedings of the 36th Annual Symposium on Foundation of Computer Science*, 1995.

[4] Peter Auer, Nicolò Cesa-Bianchi and C. Gentile Adaptive and Self-Confidence On-line Learning Algorithms. In *JCSS* 64(1):48-75, 2002.

[5] Nicolò Cesa-Bianchi, Yoav Freund, David P. Helmbold, David Haussler, Robert E. Schapire and Manfred K. Warmuth. How to use expert advice. In *Proceedings of the Twenty-Fifth Annual ACM Symposium on the Theory of Computing*, pages 382–391, 1993.

[6] Thomas M. Cover and Joy A. Thomas. *Elements of Information Theory*. Wiley, 1991.

[7] Amos Fiat, Dean P. Foster, Howard Karloff, Yuval Rabani and Yiftach Ravid Competitive algorithms for Layered Graph Traversal. In *Proceedings of the 32th Annual Symposium on Foundation of Computer Science*, page 288, 1991.

[8] Yoav Freund and Robert E. Schapire. A decision-theoretic generalization of online learning and an application to boosting. In *Computational Learning Theory: Second European Conference, EuroCOLT '95*, pages 23–37. Springer-Verlag, 1995.

[9] J. C. Gittins. *Multi- armed Bandit Allocation Indices*. John Wiley and Sons, 1989.

[10] T. L. Lai and Herbert Robbins. Asymptotically efficient adaptive allocation rules. *Advances in Applied Mathematics*, 6:4–22, 1985.

[11] Nick Littlestone and Manfred K. Warmuth. The weighted majority algorithm. *Information and Computation*, 108:212–261, 1994.

[12] Volodimir G. Vovk. Aggregating strategies. In *Proceedings of the Third Annual Workshop on Computational Learning Theory*, pages 371–383, 1990.

Appendix A

Proof of Theorem 2

Let w_i^t denote the weight of action i at the beginning of iteration t.

Like in the original Weighted Majority[11] and Hedge[8] technique, we define $W(t)$ as $\sum_{i=1}^{K} w_i^t$, and conduct the analysis by showing an upper and a lower bound on $ln \frac{W(T+1)}{W(1)}$.

An Upper Bound on $ln \frac{W(T+1)}{W(1)}$:

GL(α) receives $y_i(t)$ as the payoff of actions a_i in iteration t. The upper bound is developed in the same way as in the proof of Theorem 1:

$$\ln \frac{W(t+1)}{W(t)} \le \alpha \cdot \sum_{i=1}^{k} p_i(t) \cdot y_i(t)$$

$X_{GL(\alpha)}(t)$ is the payoff of algorithm $GL(\alpha)$ in iteration t. It is always a gain since unlike the simulated values that GL(α) receives ($y_i(t)$), the real values of the actions in this game are in [0,1]. Let us substitute the simulated values with the real ones:

$$\ln \frac{W(t+1)}{W(t)} \le \alpha \cdot \sum_{i=1}^{k} p_i(t) \cdot (x_i(t) - X_{GGL(\alpha)}(t))$$

where $p_i(t)$ is the probability by which algorithm GL(α) chooses action a_i on iteration t.

$$\ln \frac{W(t+1)}{W(t)} \le \alpha \cdot (X_{GGL(\alpha)}(t) - X_{GGL(\alpha)}(t)) = 0$$

$$\ln \frac{W(T+1)}{W(1)} = \sum_{t=1}^{T} \ln \frac{W(t+1)}{W(t)} \le 0$$

A Lower Bound on $ln \frac{W(T+1)}{W(1)}$:

For any action $j \in 1, 2, ...K$,

$$W(T+1) \ge (1+\alpha)^{\sum_{t \in M} y_j(t)} \cdot (1-\alpha)^{\sum_{t \in L} |y_j(t)|} \cdot \frac{1}{K}$$

where M is the set of iterations where $g_i(t) \ge X_{on}(t)$ and therefore $y_j(t) \ge 0$ ("More").

L is the set of iterations where $g_i(t) \le X_{on}(t)$ and therefore $y_j(t) \le 0$ ("Less"),

and by the GL algorithm the loss in these iterations is $|y_j(t)|$.

Taking ln and noticing that $W(1) = 1$, gives us:

$\ln W(T + 1) \geq \sum_{t \in M} y_j(t) \cdot \ln(1 + \alpha) + \sum_{t \in L} |y_j(t)| \cdot \ln(1 - \alpha) - \ln K$.

Combining the above two bounds yields:

$0 \geq \sum_{t \in M} y_j(t) \cdot \ln(1 + \alpha) + \sum_{t \in L} |y_j(t)| \cdot \ln(1 - \alpha) - \ln K$.

Dividing by α, and applying the approximation from claim 1 yields:

$0 \geq \sum_{t \in M} y_j(t) \cdot \frac{\ln(1+\alpha)}{\alpha} + \sum_{t \in L} |y_j(t)| \cdot \frac{\ln(1-\alpha)}{\alpha} - \ln K$

$0 \geq \sum_{t \in M} y_j(t) \cdot \left(1 - \frac{\alpha}{2}\right) - \sum_{t \in L} |y_j(t)| \cdot \left(1 + \frac{\alpha}{2(1-\alpha)}\right) - \frac{\ln K}{\alpha}$

$\geq \sum_{t \in M} y_j(t) - \sum_{t \in L} |y_j(t)| - \frac{\alpha}{2(1-\alpha)} \left(\sum_{t \in M} y_j(t) + \sum_{t \in L} |y_j(t)| \right) - \frac{\ln K}{\alpha}$.

Let us substitute the simulated values with the real ones,

$y_j(t) = g_j(t) - X_{GGL(\alpha)}(t)$.

Note that $\sum_{t \in M} g_j(t) + \sum_{j \in L} g_j(t) = G_j$ (where G_j is the total gain of action j), and $\sum_{t \in M} X_{GGL(\alpha)}(t) + \sum_{t \in L} X_{GGL(\alpha)}(t) = X_{GGL(\alpha)}$.

Hence, $\sum_{j \in M} y_j(t) - \sum_{t \in L} |y_j(t)| = G_j - X_{GGL(\alpha)}$

We obtain that for any action a_j,

$X_{GGL(\alpha)} \geq G_j - \frac{\alpha}{2(1-\alpha)} \left(\sum_{t \in M} y_j(t) + \sum_{t \in L} |y_j(t)| \right) - \frac{\ln K}{\alpha}$.

Let us consider the case where action a_j is OPT:

If $X_{GGL(\alpha)} \geq G_{\text{OPT}}$ then Theorem 7 holds. Otherwise, $X_{GGL(\alpha)} < G_{\text{OPT}}$ and therefore the summation of $y_{\text{OPT}}(t) = g_{\text{OPT}}(t) - X_{GGL(\alpha)}(t)$ over all the iterations where $X_{GGL(\alpha)} < G_{\text{OPT}}$ is larger than the summation of $y_{\text{OPT}}(t) = g_{\text{OPT}}(t) - X_{\text{on}}(t)$ over all the iterations where $X_{GGL(\alpha)} \geq G_{\text{OPT}}$.

We obtain,

$$X_{GGL(\alpha)} \geq G_{\text{OPT}} - \frac{\alpha}{2(1 - \alpha)} \cdot 2 \sum_{t \in M} y_{\text{OPT}}(t) - \frac{\ln K}{\alpha} .$$

$\sum_{t \in M} y_{\text{OPT}}(t)$ is the summation of the difference $y_{\text{OPT}}(t) = g_{\text{OPT}}(t) - X_{GGL(\alpha)}(t)$ over all the iterations t where $g_{\text{OPT}}(t) \geq X_{GGL(\alpha)}(t)$. By definition it is the measurement $D_{\text{OPT}}^{GGL(\alpha)}$, the exceeding value of i with respect to $GGL(\alpha)$. Hence,

$$X_{GGL(\alpha)} \geq G_{\text{OPT}} - \frac{2\alpha}{2(1 - \alpha)} D_{\text{OPT}}^{GGL(\alpha)} - \frac{\ln K}{\alpha} .$$

Substituting α according to the theorem completes the proof.

Prediction with Expert Advice by Following the Perturbed Leader for General Weights*

Marcus Hutter and Jan Poland

IDSIA, Galleria 2, CH-6928 Manno-Lugano, Switzerland
{marcus,jan}@idsia.ch, http://www.idsia.ch/~{marcus,jan}

Abstract. When applying aggregating strategies to Prediction with Expert Advice, the learning rate must be adaptively tuned. The natural choice of $\sqrt{\text{complexity/current loss}}$ renders the analysis of Weighted Majority derivatives quite complicated. In particular, for arbitrary weights there have been no results proven so far. The analysis of the alternative "Follow the Perturbed Leader" (FPL) algorithm from [KV03] (based on Hannan's algorithm) is easier. We derive loss bounds for adaptive learning rate and both finite expert classes with uniform weights and countable expert classes with arbitrary weights. For the former setup, our loss bounds match the best known results so far, while for the latter our results are new.

1 Introduction

The theory of Prediction with Expert Advice (PEA) has rapidly developed in the recent past. Starting with the Weighted Majority (WM) algorithm of Littlestone and Warmuth [LW89,LW94] and the aggregating strategy of Vovk [Vov90], a vast variety of different algorithms and variants have been published. A key parameter in all these algorithms is the *learning rate*. While this parameter had to be fixed in the early algorithms such as WM, [CB97] established the so-called doubling trick to make the learning rate coarsely adaptive. A little later, incrementally adaptive algorithms were developed [AG00,ACBG02,YEYS04,Gen03]. Unfortunately, the loss bound proofs for the incrementally adaptive WM variants are quite complex and technical, despite the typically simple and elegant proofs for a static learning rate.

The complex growing proof techniques also had another consequence: While for the original WM algorithm, assertions are proven for countable classes of experts with arbitrary weights, the modern variants usually restrict to finite classes with uniform weights (an exception being [Gen03], see the discussion section). This might be sufficient for many practical purposes but it prevents the application to more general classes of predictors. Examples are extrapolating (=predicting) data points with the help of a polynomial (=expert) of degree $d=1,2,3,...$ –or– the (from a computational point of view largest) class of all computable predictors. Furthermore, most authors have concentrated on predicting

---

* This work was supported by SNF grant 2100-67712.02.

S. Ben-David, J. Case, A. Maruoka (Eds.): ALT 2004, LNAI 3244, pp. 279–293, 2004.
© Springer-Verlag Berlin Heidelberg 2004

binary sequences, often with the 0/1 loss for {0,1}-valued and the absolute loss for [0,1]-valued predictions. Arbitrary losses are less common. Nevertheless, it is easy to abstract completely from the predictions and consider the resulting losses only. Instead of predicting according to a "weighted majority" in each time step, one chooses one *single* expert with a probability depending on his past cumulated loss. This is done e.g. in [FS97], where an elegant WM variant, the Hedge algorithm, is analyzed.

A different, general approach to achieve similar results is "Follow the Perturbed Leader" (FPL). The principle dates back to as early as 1957, now called Hannan's algorithm [Han57]. In 2003, Kalai and Vempala published a simpler proof of the main result of Hannan and also succeeded to improve the bound by modifying the distribution of the perturbation [KV03]. The resulting algorithm (which they call FPL*) has the same performance guarantees as the WM-type algorithms for fixed learning rate, save for a factor of $\sqrt{2}$. A major advantage we will discover in this work is that its analysis remains easy for an adaptive learning rate, in contrast to the WM derivatives. Moreover, it generalizes to online decision problems other than PEA.

In this work we study the FPL algorithm for PEA. The problems of WM algorithms mentioned above are addressed: We consider countable expert classes with arbitrary weights, adaptive learning rate, and arbitrary losses. Regarding the adaptive learning rate, we obtain proofs that are simpler and more elegant than for the corresponding WM algorithms. (In particular the proof for a self-confident choice of the learning rate, Theorem 7, is less than half a page). Further, we prove the first loss bounds for *arbitrary weights* and adaptive learning rate. Our result even seems to be the first for *equal weights* and *arbitrary losses*, however the proof technique from [ACBG02] is likely to carry over to this case.

This paper is structured as follows. In Section 2 we give the basic definitions. Sections 3 and 4 derive the main analysis tools, following the lines of [KV03], but with some important extensions. They are applied in order to prove various upper bounds in Section 5. Section 6 proposes a hierarchical procedure to improve the bounds for non-uniform weights. Section 7 treats some additional issues. Finally, in Section 8 we discuss our results, compare them to references, and state some open problems.

2   Setup and Notation

Setup. Prediction with Expert Advice proceeds as follows. We are asked to perform sequential predictions $y_t \in \mathcal{Y}$ at times $t = 1, 2, \ldots$. At each time step t, we have access to the predictions $(y_t^i)_{1 \leq i \leq n}$ of n experts $\{e_1, \ldots, e_n\}$. After having made a prediction, we make some observation $x_t \in \mathcal{X}$, and a Loss is revealed for our and each expert's prediction. (E.g. the loss might be 1 if the expert made an erroneous prediction and 0 otherwise. This is the 0/1-loss.) Our goal is to achieve a total loss "not much worse" than the best expert, after t time steps.

We admit $n \in I\!N \cup \{\infty\}$ experts, each of which is assigned a known complexity $k^i \geq 0$. Usually we require $\sum_i e^{-k^i} \leq 1$, for instance $k^i = \ln n$ if $n < \infty$ or $k^i = \frac{1}{2} + 2\ln i$

if $n=\infty$. Each complexity defines a weight by means of e^{-k^i} and vice versa. In the following we will talk rather of complexities than of weights. If n is finite, then usually one sets $k^i=\ln n$ for all i, this is the case of *uniform complexities/weights*. If the set of experts is countably infinite $(n=\infty)$, uniform complexities are not possible. The vector of all complexities is denoted by $k=(k^i)_{1\leq i\leq n}$. At each time t, each expert i suffers a loss[1] $s^i_t=\mathrm{Loss}(x_t,y^i_t)\in[0,1]$, and $s_t=(s^i_t)_{1\leq i\leq n}$ is the vector of all losses at time t. Let $s_{<t}=s_1+...+s_{t-1}$ (respectively $s_{1:t}=s_1+...+s_t$) be the total past loss vector (including current loss s_t) and $s^{min}_{1:t}=\min_i\{s^i_{1:t}\}$ be the loss of the *best expert in hindsight (BEH)*. Usually we do not know in advance the time $t\geq 0$ at which the performance of our predictions are evaluated.

General decision spaces. The setup can be generalized as follows. Let $\mathcal{S}\subset I\!\!R^n$ be the *state space* and $\mathcal{D}\subset I\!\!R^n$ the *decision space*. At time t the state is $s_t\in\mathcal{S}$, and a decision $d_t\in\mathcal{D}$ (which is made before the state is revealed) incurs a loss $d_t\circ s_t$, where "$\circ$" denotes the inner product. This implies that the loss function is *linear* in the states. Conversely, each linear loss function can be represented in this way. The decision which minimizes the loss in state $s\in\mathcal{S}$ is

$$M(s) := \arg\min_{d\in\mathcal{D}}\{d\circ s\} \tag{1}$$

if the minimum exists. The application of this general framework to PEA is straightforward: $\mathcal{D}$ is identified with the space of all unit vectors $\mathcal{E}=\{e_i:1\leq i\leq n\}$, since a decision consists of selecting a single expert, and $s_t\in[0,1]^n$, so states are identified with losses. Only Theorem 2 will be stated in terms of general decision space, where we require that all minima are attained.[2] Our main focus is $\mathcal{D}=\mathcal{E}$. However, all our results generalize to the simplex $\mathcal{D}=\Delta=\{v\in[0,1]^n:\sum_i v^i=1\}$, since the minimum of a linear function on Δ is always attained on $\mathcal{E}$.

Follow the Perturbed Leader. Given $s_{<t}$ at time t, an immediate idea to solve the expert problem is to "Follow the Leader" (FL), i.e. selecting the expert e_i which performed best in the past (minimizes $s^i_{<t}$), that is predict according to expert $M(s_{<t})$. This approach fails for two reasons. First, for $n=\infty$ the minimum in (1) may not exist. Second, for $n=2$ and $s=\begin{pmatrix}0\,1\,0\,1\,0\,1...\\ \frac{1}{2}\,0\,1\,0\,1\,0...\end{pmatrix}$, FL always chooses the wrong prediction [KV03]. We solve the first problem by penalizing each expert by its complexity, i.e. predicting according to expert $M(s_{<t}+k)$. The *FPL (Follow the Perturbed Leader)* approach solves the second problem by adding to each expert's loss $s^i_{<t}$ a random perturbation. We choose this perturbation to be negative *exponentially distributed*, either independent in each time step or once and for all at the very beginning at time $t=0$. The former choice is preferable in order to protect against an adaptive adversary who generates the s_t, and in order to get bounds with high probability (Section 7). For the main analysis however, the latter is more convenient. Due to linearity of expectations, these two possibilities are equivalent when dealing with *expected losses*, so we can henceforth assume without loss of generality one initial perturbation q.

---

[1] The setup, analysis and results easily scale to $s^i_t\in[0,S]$ for $S>0$ other than 1.

[2] Apparently, there is no natural condition on $\mathcal{D}$ and/or $\mathcal{S}$ which guarantees the existence of all minima for $n=\infty$.

The FPL algorithm is defined as follows:

Choose random vector $q \overset{d.}{\sim} \exp$, i.e. $P[q^1...q^n] = e^{-q^1} \cdot ... \cdot e^{-q^n}$ for $q \geq 0$.

For $t = 1,...,T$

- Choose learning rate ε_t.
- Output prediction of expert i which minimizes $s^i_{<t} + (k^i - q^i)/\varepsilon_t$.
- Receive loss s^i_t for all experts i.

Other than $s_{<t}$, k and q, FPL depends on the *learning rate* ε_t. We will give choices for ε_t in Section 5, after having established the main tools for the analysis. The expected loss at time t of FPL is $\ell_t := E[M(s_{<t} + \frac{k-q}{\varepsilon_t}) \circ s_t]$. The key idea in the FPL analysis is the use of an intermediate predictor *IFPL* (for *Implicit or Infeasible FPL*). IFPL predicts according to $M(s_{1:t} + \frac{k-q}{\varepsilon_t})$, thus under the knowledge of s_t (which is of course not available in reality). By $r_t := E[M(s_{1:t} + \frac{k-q}{\varepsilon_t}) \circ s_t]$ we denote the expected loss of IFPL at time t. The losses of IFPL will be upper bounded by BEH in Section 3 and lower bounded by FPL in Section 4.

Notes. Observe that we have stated the FPL algorithm regardless of the actual *predictions* of the experts and possible *observations*, only the *losses* are relevant. Note also that an expert can implement a highly complicated strategy depending on past outcomes, despite its trivializing identification with a constant unit vector. The complex expert's (and environment's) behavior is summarized and hidden in the state vector $s_t = \text{Loss}(x_t, y^i_t)_{1 \leq i \leq n}$. Our results therefore apply to *arbitrary prediction and observation spaces* $\mathcal{Y}$ and $\mathcal{X}$ and *arbitrary bounded loss functions*. This is in contrast to the major part of PEA work developed for binary alphabet and 0/1 or absolute loss only. Finally note that the setup allows for losses generated by an adversary who tries to maximize the regret of FPL and knows the FPL algorithm and all experts' past predictions/losses. If the adversary also has access to FPL's past decisions, then FPL must use independent randomization at each time step in order to achieve good regret bounds.

3   IFPL Bounded by Best Expert in Hindsight

In this section we provide tools for comparing the loss of IFPL to the loss of the best expert in hindsight. The first result bounds the expected error induced by the exponentially distributed perturbation.

Lemma 1 (Maximum of Shifted Exponential Distributions). *Let* $q^1,...,q^n$ *be exponentially distributed random variables, i.e.* $P[q^i] = e^{-q^i}$ *for* $q^i \geq 0$ *and* $1 \leq i \leq n \leq \infty$, *and* $k^i \in \mathbb{R}$ *be real numbers with* $u := \sum_{i=1}^n e^{-k^i}$. *Then*

$$E[\max_i \{q^i - k^i\}] \leq 1 + \ln u.$$

Proof. Using $P[q^i \geq b] \leq e^{-b}$ for $b \in \mathbb{R}$ we get

$$P[\max_i \{q^i - k^i\} \geq a] = P[\exists i : q^i - k^i \geq a] \leq \sum_{i=1}^n P[q^i - k^i \geq a] \leq \sum_{i=1}^n e^{-a-k^i} = u \cdot e^{-a}$$

where the first inequality is the union bound. Using $E[z] \leq E[\max\{0,z\}] = \int_0^\infty P[\max\{0,z\} \geq y]dy = \int_0^\infty P[z \geq y]dy$ (valid for any real-valued random variable z) for $z = \max_i\{q^i - k^i\} - \ln u$, this implies

$$E[\max_i\{q^i - k^i\} - \ln u] \leq \int_0^\infty P\big[\max_i\{q^i - k^i\} \geq y + \ln u\big]dy \leq \int_0^\infty e^{-y}dy = 1,$$

which proves the assertion.   □

If n is finite, a lower bound $E[\max_i q^i] \geq 0.57721 + \ln n$ can be derived, showing that the upper bound on $E[\max]$ is quite tight (at least) for $k^i = 0 \ \forall i$. The following bound generalizes [KV03, Lem.3] to arbitrary weights.

Theorem 2 (IFPL bounded by BEH). *Let $\mathcal{D} \subseteq \mathbb{R}^n$, $s_t \in \mathbb{R}^n$ for $1 \leq t \leq T$ (both $\mathcal{D}$ and s may even have negative components, but we assume that all required extrema are attained), and $q,k \in \mathbb{R}^n$. If $\varepsilon_t > 0$ is decreasing in t, then the loss of the infeasible FPL knowing s_t at time t in advance (l.h.s.) can be bounded in terms of the best predictor in hindsight (first term on r.h.s.) plus additive corrections:*

$$\sum_{t=1}^T M(s_{1:t} + \frac{k-q}{\varepsilon_t}) \circ s_t \leq \min_{d \in \mathcal{D}}\{d \circ (s_{1:T} + \frac{k}{\varepsilon_T})\} + \frac{1}{\varepsilon_T}\max_{d \in \mathcal{D}}\{d \circ (q-k)\} - \frac{1}{\varepsilon_T}M(s_{1:T} + \frac{k}{\varepsilon_T}) \circ q$$

Proof. For notational convenience, let $\varepsilon_0 = \infty$ and $\tilde{s}_{1:t} = s_{1:t} + \frac{k-q}{\varepsilon_t}$. Consider the losses $\tilde{s}_t = s_t + (k-q)(\frac{1}{\varepsilon_t} - \frac{1}{\varepsilon_{t-1}})$ for the moment. We first show by induction on T that the infeasible predictor $M(\tilde{s}_{1:t})$ has zero regret, i.e.

$$\sum_{t=1}^T M(\tilde{s}_{1:t}) \circ \tilde{s}_t \leq M(\tilde{s}_{1:T}) \circ \tilde{s}_{1:T}. \tag{2}$$

For $T=1$ this is obvious. For the induction step from $T-1$ to T we need to show

$$M(\tilde{s}_{1:T}) \circ \tilde{s}_T \leq M(\tilde{s}_{1:T}) \circ \tilde{s}_{1:T} - M(\tilde{s}_{<T}) \circ \tilde{s}_{<T}.$$

This follows from $\tilde{s}_{1:T} = \tilde{s}_{<T} + \tilde{s}_T$ and $M(\tilde{s}_{1:T}) \circ \tilde{s}_{<T} \geq M(\tilde{s}_{<T}) \circ \tilde{s}_{<T}$ by minimality of M. Rearranging terms in (2), we obtain

$$\sum_{t=1}^T M(\tilde{s}_{1:t}) \circ s_t \leq M(\tilde{s}_{1:T}) \circ \tilde{s}_{1:T} - \sum_{t=1}^T M(\tilde{s}_{1:t}) \circ (k-q)\left(\frac{1}{\varepsilon_t} - \frac{1}{\varepsilon_{t-1}}\right) \tag{3}$$

Moreover, by minimality of M,

$$M(\tilde{s}_{1:T}) \circ \tilde{s}_{1:T} \leq M\left(s_{1:T} + \frac{k}{\varepsilon_T}\right) \circ \left(s_{1:T} + \frac{k-q}{\varepsilon_T}\right) \tag{4}$$

$$= \min_{d \in \mathcal{D}}\left\{d \circ (s_{1:T} + \frac{k}{\varepsilon_T})\right\} - M\left(s_{1:T} + \frac{k}{\varepsilon_T}\right) \circ \frac{q}{\varepsilon_T}$$

holds. Using $\frac{1}{\varepsilon_t} - \frac{1}{\varepsilon_{t-1}} \geq 0$ and again minimality of M, we have

$$\sum_{t=1}^{T}(\frac{1}{\varepsilon_t} - \frac{1}{\varepsilon_{t-1}})M(\tilde{s}_{1:t}) \circ (q-k) \leq \sum_{t=1}^{T}(\frac{1}{\varepsilon_t} - \frac{1}{\varepsilon_{t-1}})M(k-q) \circ (q-k) \qquad (5)$$

$$= \frac{1}{\varepsilon_T}M(k-q) \circ (q-k) = \frac{1}{\varepsilon_T}\max_{d \in \mathcal{D}}\{d \circ (q-k)\}$$

Inserting (4) and (5) back into (3) we obtain the assertion. □

Assuming q random with $E[q^i] = 1$ and taking the expectation in Theorem 2, the last term reduces to $-\frac{1}{\varepsilon_T}\sum_{i=1}^{n}M(s_{1:T} + \frac{k}{\varepsilon_T})^i$. If $\mathcal{D} \geq 0$, the term is negative and may be dropped. In case of $\mathcal{D} = \mathcal{E}$ or Δ, the last term is identical to $-\frac{1}{\varepsilon_T}$ (since $\sum_i d^i = 1$) and keeping it improves the bound. Furthermore, we need to evaluate the expectation of the second to last term in Theorem 2, namely $E[\max_{d \in \mathcal{D}}\{d \circ (q-k)\}]$. For $\mathcal{D} = \mathcal{E}$ and q being exponentially distributed, using Lemma 1, the expectation is bounded by $1 + \ln u$. We hence get the following bound:

Corollary 3 (IFPL bounded by BEH). *For* $\mathcal{D} = \mathcal{E}$ *and* $\sum_i e^{-k^i} \leq 1$ *and* $P[q^i] = e^{-q^i}$ *for* $q \geq 0$ *and decreasing* $\varepsilon_t > 0$*, the expected loss of the infeasible FPL exceeds the loss of expert* i *by at most* k^i/ε_T*:*

$$r_{1:T} \leq s^i_{1:T} + \frac{1}{\varepsilon_T}k^i \quad \forall i.$$

Theorem 2 can be generalized to expert dependent factorizable $\varepsilon_t \rightsquigarrow \varepsilon^i_t = \varepsilon_t \cdot \varepsilon^i$ by scaling $k^i \rightsquigarrow k^i/\varepsilon^i$ and $q^i \rightsquigarrow q^i/\varepsilon^i$. Using $E[\max_i\{\frac{q^i-k^i}{\varepsilon^i}\}] \leq E[\max_i\{q^i - k^i\}]/\min_i\{\varepsilon^i\}$, Corollary 3, generalizes to

$$E[\sum_{t=1}^{T}M(s_{1:t} + \frac{k-q}{\varepsilon^i_t}) \circ s_t] \leq s^i_{1:T} + \frac{1}{\varepsilon^i_T}k^i + \frac{1}{\varepsilon^{min}_T} \quad \forall i,$$

where $\varepsilon^{min}_T := \min_i\{\varepsilon^i_T\}$. For example, for $\varepsilon^i_t = \sqrt{k^i/t}$, additionally assuming $k^i \geq 1 \; \forall i$, we get the desired bound $s^i_{1:T} + \sqrt{T \cdot (k^i+1)}$. Unfortunately we were not able to generalize Theorem 4 to expert-dependent ε, necessary for the final bound on FPL. In Section 6 we solve this problem by a hierarchy of experts.

4   Feasible FPL Bounded by Infeasible FPL

This section establishes the relation between the FPL and IFPL losses. Recall that $\ell_t = E[M(s_{<t} + \frac{k-q}{\varepsilon_t}) \circ s_t]$ is the expected loss of FPL at time t and $r_t = E[M(s_{1:t} + \frac{k-q}{\varepsilon_t}) \circ s_t]$ is the expected loss of IFPL at time t.

Theorem 4 (FPL bounded by IFPL). *For $\mathcal{D}=\mathcal{E}$ and $0\leq s_t^i\leq 1$ $\forall i$ and arbitrary $s_{<t}$ and $P[q]=\mathrm{e}^{-\sum_i q^i}$ for $q\geq 0$, the expected loss of the feasible FPL is at most a factor $\mathrm{e}^{\varepsilon_t}>1$ larger than for the infeasible FPL:*

$$\ell_t\leq \mathrm{e}^{\varepsilon_t}r_t, \quad \text{which implies} \quad \ell_{1:T}-r_{1:T}\leq \sum_{t=1}^{T}\varepsilon_t\ell_t.$$

Furthermore, if $\varepsilon_t\leq 1$, then also $\ell_t\leq(1+\varepsilon_t+\varepsilon_t^2)r_t\leq(1+2\varepsilon_t)r_t$.

Proof. Let $s=s_{<t}+\frac{1}{\varepsilon}k$ be the past cumulative penalized state vector, q be a vector of independent exponential distributions, i.e. $P[q^i]=\mathrm{e}^{-q^i}$, and $\varepsilon=\varepsilon_t$. We now define the random variables $I:=\mathrm{argmin}_i\{s^i-\frac{1}{\varepsilon}q^i\}$ and $J:=\mathrm{argmin}_i\{s^i+s_t^i-\frac{1}{\varepsilon}q^i\}$, where $0\leq s_t^i\leq 1$ $\forall i$. Furthermore, for fixed vector $x\in \mathbb{R}^n$ and fixed j we define $m:=\min_{i\neq j}\{s^i-\frac{1}{\varepsilon}x^i\}\leq \min_{i\neq j}\{s^i+s_t^i-\frac{1}{\varepsilon}x^i\}=:m'$. With this notation and using the independence of q^j from q^i for all $i\neq j$, we get

$$P[I=j|q^i=x^i\,\forall i\neq j] \;=\; P[s^j-\tfrac{1}{\varepsilon}q^j\leq m|q^i=x^i\,\forall i\neq j] \;=\; P[q^j\geq\varepsilon(s^j-m)]$$

$$\leq\; \mathrm{e}^{\varepsilon}P[q^j\geq\varepsilon(s^j-m+1)] \;\leq\; \mathrm{e}^{\varepsilon}P[q^j\geq\varepsilon(s^j+s_t^j-m')]$$

$$=\; \mathrm{e}^{\varepsilon}P[s^j+s_t^j-\tfrac{1}{\varepsilon}q^j\leq m'|q^i=x^i\,\forall i\neq j] \;=\; \mathrm{e}^{\varepsilon}P[J=j|q^i=x^i\,\forall i\neq j],$$

where we have used $P[q^j\geq a]\leq \mathrm{e}^{\varepsilon}P[q^j\geq a+\varepsilon]$. Since this bound holds under any condition x, it also holds unconditionally, i.e. $P[I=j]\leq \mathrm{e}^{\varepsilon}P[J=j]$. For $\mathcal{D}=\mathcal{E}$ we have $s_t^I=M(s_{<t}+\frac{k-q}{\varepsilon})\circ s_t$ and $s_t^J=M(s_{1:t}+\frac{k-q}{\varepsilon})\circ s_t$, which implies

$$\ell_t \;=\; E[s_t^I] \;=\; \sum_{j=1}^{n}s_t^j\cdot P[I=j] \;\leq\; \mathrm{e}^{\varepsilon}\sum_{j=1}^{n}s_t^j\cdot P[J=j] \;=\; \mathrm{e}^{\varepsilon}E[s_t^J] \;=\; \mathrm{e}^{\varepsilon}r_t.$$

Finally, $\ell_t-r_t\leq\varepsilon_t\ell_t$ follows from $r_t\geq \mathrm{e}^{-\varepsilon_t}\ell_t\geq(1-\varepsilon_t)\ell_t$, and $\ell_t\leq \mathrm{e}^{\varepsilon_t}r_t\leq(1+\varepsilon_t+\varepsilon_t^2)r_t\leq(1+2\varepsilon_t)r_t$ for $\varepsilon_t\leq 1$ is elementary.   □

Remark. As in [KV03], one can prove a similar statement for general decision space $\mathcal{D}$ as long as $\sum_i|s_t^i|\leq A$ is guaranteed for some $A>0$: In this case, we have $\ell_t\leq \mathrm{e}^{\varepsilon_t A}r_t$. If n is finite, then the bound holds for $A=n$. For $n=\infty$, the assertion holds under the somewhat unnatural assumption that $\mathcal{S}$ is l^1-bounded.

5   Combination of Bounds and Choices for ε_t

Throughout this section, we assume

$$\mathcal{D}=\mathcal{E}, \quad s_t\in[0,1]^n\ \forall t, \quad P[q]=\mathrm{e}^{-\sum_i q^i}\text{ for }q\geq 0, \quad \text{and}\quad \sum_i \mathrm{e}^{-k^i}\leq 1. \quad (6)$$

We distinguish *static* and *dynamic* bounds. Static bounds refer to a constant $\varepsilon_t\equiv\varepsilon$. Since this value has to be chosen in advance, a static choice of ε_t requires certain prior information and therefore is not practical in many cases. However, the static bounds are very easy to derive, and they provide a good means to compare different PEA algorithms. If on the other hand the algorithm shall be applied without appropriate prior knowledge, a dynamic choice of ε_t depending only on t and/or past observations, is necessary.

Theorem 5 (FPL bound for static $\varepsilon_t = \varepsilon \propto 1/\sqrt{L}$). *Assume (6) holds, then the expected loss ℓ_t of feasible FPL, which employs the prediction of the expert i minimizing $s^i_{<t} + \frac{k^i - q^i}{\varepsilon_t}$, is bounded by the loss of the best expert in hindsight in the following way:*

i) For $\varepsilon_t = \varepsilon = 1/\sqrt{L}$ with $L \geq \ell_{1:T}$ we have

$$\ell_{1:T} \leq s^i_{1:T} + \sqrt{L}(k^i + 1) \quad \forall i$$

ii) For $\varepsilon_t = \sqrt{K/L}$ with $L \geq \ell_{1:T}$ and $k^i \leq K \; \forall i$ we have

$$\ell_{1:T} \leq s^i_{1:T} + 2\sqrt{LK} \quad \forall i$$

iii) For $\varepsilon_t = \sqrt{k^i/L}$ with $L \geq \max\{s^i_{1:T}, k^i\}$ we have

$$\ell_{1:T} \leq s^i_{1:T} + 2\sqrt{Lk^i} + 3k^i$$

Note that according to assertion (iii), knowledge of only the *ratio* of the complexity and the loss of the best expert is sufficient in order to obtain good static bounds, even for non-uniform complexities.

Proof. (i,ii) For $\varepsilon_t = \sqrt{K/L}$ and $L \geq \ell_{1:T}$, from Theorem 4 and Corollary 3, we get

$$\ell_{1:T} - r_{1:T} \leq \sum_{t=1}^{T} \varepsilon_t \ell_t = \ell_{1:T}\sqrt{K/L} \leq \sqrt{LK} \quad \text{and} \quad r_{1:T} - s^i_{1:T} \leq k^i/\varepsilon_T = k^i\sqrt{L/K}$$

Combining both, we get $\ell_{1:T} - s^i_{1:T} \leq \sqrt{L}(\sqrt{K} + k^i/\sqrt{K})$. (i) follows from $K = 1$ and (ii) from $k^i \leq K$.

(iii) For $\varepsilon = \sqrt{k^i/L} \leq 1$ we get

$$\ell_{1:T} \leq e^\varepsilon r_{1:T} \leq (1 + \varepsilon + \varepsilon^2) r_{1:T} \leq (1 + \sqrt{\frac{k^i}{L}} + \frac{k^i}{L})(s^i_{1:T} + \sqrt{\frac{L}{k^i}}k^i)$$

$$\leq s^i_{1:T} + \sqrt{Lk^i} + (\sqrt{\frac{k^i}{L}} + \frac{k^i}{L})(L + \sqrt{Lk^i}) = s^i_{1:T} + 2\sqrt{Lk^i} + (2 + \sqrt{\frac{k^i}{L}})k^i$$

$\square$

The static bounds require knowledge of an upper bound L on the loss (or the ratio of the complexity of the best expert and its loss). Since the instantaneous loss is bounded by 1, one may set $L = T$ if T is known in advance. For finite n and $k^i = K = \ln n$, bound (ii) gives the classic regret $\propto \sqrt{T \ln n}$. If neither T nor L is known, a dynamic choice of ε_t is necessary. We first present bounds with regret $\propto \sqrt{T}$, thereafter with regret $\propto \sqrt{s^i_{1:T}}$.

Theorem 6 (FPL bound for dynamic $\varepsilon_t \propto 1/\sqrt{t}$). *Assume (6) holds.*

i) For $\varepsilon_t = 1/\sqrt{t}$ we have $\ell_{1:T} \leq s^i_{1:T} + \sqrt{T}(k^i + 2) \quad \forall i$

ii) For $\varepsilon_t = \sqrt{K/2t}$ and $k^i \leq K \; \forall i$ we have $\ell_{1:T} \leq s^i_{1:T} + 2\sqrt{2TK} \quad \forall i$

Proof. For $\varepsilon_t = \sqrt{K/2t}$, using $\sum_{t=1}^{T} \frac{1}{\sqrt{t}} \leq \int_0^T \frac{dt}{\sqrt{t}} = 2\sqrt{T}$ and $\ell_t \leq 1$ we get

$$\ell_{1:T} - r_{1:T} \leq \sum_{t=1}^{T} \varepsilon_t \leq \sqrt{2TK} \quad \text{and} \quad r_{1:T} - s_{1:T}^i \leq k^i/\varepsilon_T = k^i\sqrt{\frac{2T}{K}}$$

Combining both, we get $\ell_{1:T} - s_{1:T}^i \leq \sqrt{2T}(\sqrt{K} + k^i/\sqrt{K})$. (i) follows from $K = 2$ and (ii) from $k^i \leq K$. $\square$

In Theorem 5 we assumed knowledge of an upper bound L on $\ell_{1:T}$. In an adaptive form, $L_t := \ell_{<t} + 1$, known at the beginning of time t, could be used as an upper bound on $\ell_{1:t}$ with corresponding adaptive $\varepsilon_t \propto 1/\sqrt{L_t}$. Such choice of ε_t is also called *self-confident* [ACBG02].

Theorem 7 (FPL bound for self-confident $\varepsilon_t \propto 1/\sqrt{\ell_{<t}}$). *Assume (6) holds.*

> $i)$ *For* $\varepsilon_t = 1/\sqrt{2(\ell_{<t} + 1)}$ *we have*
>
> $$\ell_{1:T} \leq s_{1:T}^i + (k^i + 1)\sqrt{2(s_{1:T}^i + 1)} + 2(k^i + 1)^2 \quad \forall i$$
>
> $ii)$ *For* $\varepsilon_t = \sqrt{K/2(\ell_{<t} + 1)}$ *and* $k^i \leq K \ \forall i$ *we have*
>
> $$\ell_{1:T} \leq s_{1:T}^i + 2\sqrt{2(s_{1:T}^i + 1)K} + 8K \quad \forall i$$

Proof. Using $\varepsilon_t = \sqrt{K/2(\ell_{<t} + 1)} \leq \sqrt{K/2\ell_{1:t}}$ and $\frac{b-a}{\sqrt{b}} = (\sqrt{b} - \sqrt{a})(\sqrt{b} + \sqrt{a})\frac{1}{\sqrt{b}} \leq 2(\sqrt{b} - \sqrt{a})$ for $a \leq b$ and $t_0 := \min\{t : \ell_{1:t} > 0\}$ we get

$$\ell_{1:T} - r_{1:T} \leq \sum_{t=t_0}^{T} \varepsilon_t \ell_t \leq \sqrt{\frac{K}{2}} \sum_{t=t_0}^{T} \frac{\ell_{1:t} - \ell_{<t}}{\sqrt{\ell_{1:t}}} \leq \sqrt{2K} \sum_{t=t_0}^{T} [\sqrt{\ell_{1:t}} - \sqrt{\ell_{<t}}] = \sqrt{2K}\sqrt{\ell_{1:T}}$$

Adding $r_{1:T} - s_{1:T}^i \leq \frac{k^i}{\varepsilon_T} \leq k^i\sqrt{2(\ell_{1:T} + 1)/K}$ we get

$$\ell_{1:T} - s_{1:T}^i \leq \sqrt{2\bar{\kappa}^i(\ell_{1:T} + 1)}, \quad \text{where} \quad \sqrt{\bar{\kappa}^i} := \sqrt{K} + k^i/\sqrt{K}.$$

Taking the square and solving the resulting quadratic inequality w.r.t. $\ell_{1:T}$ we get

$$\ell_{1:T} \leq s_{1:T}^i + \bar{\kappa}^i + \sqrt{2(s_{1:T}^i + 1)\bar{\kappa}^i + (\bar{\kappa}^i)^2} \leq s_{1:T}^i + \sqrt{2(s_{1:T}^i + 1)\bar{\kappa}^i} + 2\bar{\kappa}^i$$

For $K = 1$ we get $\sqrt{\bar{\kappa}^i} = k^i + 1$ which yields (i). For $k^i \leq K$ we get $\bar{\kappa}^i \leq 4K$ which yields (ii). $\square$

The proofs of results similar to (ii) for WM for 0/1 loss all fill several pages [ACBG02,YEYS04]. The next result establishes a similar bound, but instead of using the *expected* value $\ell_{<t}$, the *best loss so far* $s_{<t}^{min}$ is used. This may have computational advantages, since $s_{<t}^{min}$ is immediately available, while $\ell_{<t}$ needs to be evaluated (see discussion in Section 7).

Theorem 8 (FPL bound for adaptive $\varepsilon_t \propto 1/\sqrt{s_{<t}^{min}}$). *Assume (6) holds.*

> *i) For* $\varepsilon_t = 1/\min_i\{k^i + \sqrt{(k^i)^2 + 2s_{<t}^i + 2}\}$ *we have*
>
> $$\ell_{1:T} \leq s_{1:T}^i + (k^i + 2)\sqrt{2s_{1:T}^i} + 2(k^i + 2)^2 \quad \forall i$$
>
> *ii) For* $\varepsilon_t = \sqrt{\frac{1}{2}} \cdot \min\{1, \sqrt{K/s_{<t}^{min}}\}$ *and* $k^i \leq K \; \forall i$ *we have*
>
> $$\ell_{1:T} \leq s_{1:T}^i + 2\sqrt{2Ks_{1:T}^i} + 5K\ln(s_{1:T}^i) + 3K + 6 \quad \forall i$$

We briefly motivate the strangely looking choice for ε_t in (i). The first naive candidate, $\varepsilon_t \propto 1/\sqrt{s_{<t}^{min}}$, turns out too large. The next natural trial is requesting $\varepsilon_t = 1/\sqrt{2\min\{s_{<t}^i + \frac{k^i}{\varepsilon_t}\}}$. Solving this equation results in $\varepsilon_t = 1/(k^i + \sqrt{(k^i)^2 + 2s_{<t}^i})$, where i be the index for which $s_{<t}^i + \frac{k^i}{\varepsilon_t}$ is minimal.

Proof. Similar to the proof of the previous theorem, but more technical. $\square$

The bound (i) is a complete square, and also the bounds of Theorem 7 when adding 1 to them. Hence the bounds can be written as $\sqrt{\ell_{1:T}} \leq \sqrt{s_{1:T}^i} + \sqrt{2}(k^i + 2)$ and $\sqrt{\ell_{1:T}} \leq \sqrt{s_{1:T}^i + 1} + \sqrt{8K}$ and $\sqrt{\ell_{1:T}} \leq \sqrt{s_{1:T}^i + 1} + \sqrt{2}(k^i + 1)$, respectively, hence the $\sqrt{\text{Loss}}$-regrets are bounded for $T \to \infty$.

Remark. The same analysis as for Theorems [5-8](ii) applies to general $\mathcal{D}$, using $\ell_t \leq e^{\varepsilon_t n} r_t$ instead of $\ell_t \leq e^{\varepsilon_t} r_t$, and leading to an additional factor $\sqrt{n}$ in the regret. Compare the remark at the end of Section 4.

6   Hierarchy of Experts

We derived bounds which do not need prior knowledge of L with regret $\propto \sqrt{TK}$ and $\propto \sqrt{s_{1:T}^i K}$ for a finite number of experts with equal penalty $K = k^i = \ln n$. For an infinite number of experts, unbounded expert-dependent complexity penalties k^i are necessary (due to constraint $\sum_i e^{-k^i} \leq 1$). Bounds for this case (without prior knowledge of T) with regret $\propto k^i\sqrt{T}$ and $\propto k^i\sqrt{s_{1:T}^i}$ have been derived. In this case, the complexity k^i is no longer under the square root. It is likely that improved regret bounds $\propto \sqrt{Tk^i}$ and $\propto \sqrt{s_{1:T}^i k^i}$ as in the finite case hold. We were not able to derive such improved bounds for FPL, but for a (slight) modification. We consider a two-level hierarchy of experts. First consider an FPL for the subclass of experts of complexity K, for each $K \in I\!N$. Regard these FPL^K as (meta) experts and use them to form a (meta) FPL. The class of meta experts now contains for each complexity only one (meta) expert, which allows us to derive good bounds. In the following, quantities referring to complexity class K are superscripted by K, and meta quantities are superscripted by $\tilde{}$.

Consider the class of experts $\mathcal{E}^K := \{i : K - 1 < k^i \leq K\}$ of complexity K, for each $K \in I\!N$. FPL^K makes randomized prediction $I_t^K := \text{argmin}_{i \in \mathcal{E}^K}\{s_{<t}^i + \frac{k^i - q^i}{\varepsilon_t^K}\}$

with $\varepsilon_t^K := \sqrt{K/2t}$ and suffers loss $u_t^K := s_t^{I_t^K}$ at time t. Since $k^i \leq K \ \forall i \in \mathcal{E}^k$ we can apply Theorem 6(ii) to FPL^K:

$$E[u_{1:T}^K] \ = \ \ell_{1:T}^K \ \leq \ s_{1:T}^i + 2\sqrt{2TK} \quad \forall i \in \mathcal{E}^K \quad \forall K \in I\!N. \tag{7}$$

We now define a meta state $\tilde{s}_t^K = u_t^K$ and regard FPL^K for $K \in I\!N$ as meta experts, so meta expert K suffers loss $\tilde{s}_t^K$. (Assigning expected loss $\tilde{s}_t^K = E[u_t^K] = \ell_t^K$ to FPL^K would also work.) Hence the setting is again an expert setting and we define the meta $\widetilde{\text{FPL}}$ to predict $\tilde{I}_t := \mathrm{argmin}_{K \in I\!N} \{ \tilde{s}_{<t}^K + \frac{\tilde{k}^K - \tilde{q}^K}{\tilde{\varepsilon}_t} \}$ with $\tilde{\varepsilon}_t = 1/\sqrt{t}$ and $\tilde{k}^K = \frac{1}{2} + 2\ln K$ (implying $\sum_{K=1}^{\infty} e^{-\tilde{k}^K} \leq 1$). Note that $\tilde{s}_{1:t}^K = \tilde{s}_1^K + ... + \tilde{s}_t^K = s_1^{I_1^K} + ... + s_t^{I_t^K}$ sums over the same meta state components K, but over different components I_t^K in normal state representation.

By Theorem 6(i) the $\tilde{q}$-expected loss of $\widetilde{\text{FPL}}$ is bounded by $\tilde{s}_{1:T}^K + \sqrt{T}(\tilde{k}^K + 2)$. As this bound holds for all q it also holds in q-expectation. So if we define $\tilde{\ell}_{1:T}$ to be the q and $\tilde{q}$ expected loss of $\widetilde{\text{FPL}}$, and chain this bound with (7) for $i \in \mathcal{E}^K$ we get:

$$\tilde{\ell}_{1:T} \leq E[\tilde{s}_{1:T}^K + \sqrt{T}(\tilde{k}^K + 2)] \ = \ \ell_{1:T}^K + \sqrt{T}(\tilde{k}^K + 2)$$
$$\leq s_{1:T}^i + \sqrt{T}[2\sqrt{2(k^i + 1)} + \tfrac{1}{2} + 2\ln(k^i + 1) + 2],$$

where we have used $K \leq k^i + 1$. This bound is valid for all i and has the desired regret $\propto \sqrt{Tk^i}$. Similarly we can derive regret bounds $\propto \sqrt{s_{1:T}^i k^i}$ by exploiting that the bounds in Theorems 7 and 8 are concave in $s_{1:T}^i$ and using Jensen's inequality.

Theorem 9 (Hierarchical FPL bound for dynamic ε_t). *The hierarchical $\widetilde{\text{FPL}}$ employs at time t the prediction of expert $i_t := I_t^{\tilde{I}_t}$, where*

$$I_t^K := \mathrm{arg}\min_{i:\lceil k^i \rceil = K} \{ s_{<t}^i + \frac{k^i - q^i}{\varepsilon_t^K} \} \quad and \quad \tilde{I}_t := \mathrm{arg}\min_{K \in I\!N} \Big\{ s_1^{I_1^K} + ... + s_{t-1}^{I_{t-1}^K} + \frac{\frac{1}{2} + 2\ln K - \tilde{q}^K}{\tilde{\varepsilon}_t} \Big\}$$

Under assumptions (6) and $P[\tilde{q}] = e^{-\sum_K \tilde{q}^K}$, the expected loss $\tilde{\ell}_{1:T} = E[s_1^{i_1} + ... + s_T^{i_T}]$ of $\widetilde{\text{FPL}}$ is bounded as follows:

a) *For $\varepsilon_t^K = \sqrt{K/2t}$ and $\tilde{\varepsilon}_t = 1/\sqrt{t}$ we have*
$$\tilde{\ell}_{1:T} \leq s_{1:T}^i + 2\sqrt{2Tk^i} \cdot (1 + O(\tfrac{\ln k^i}{\sqrt{k^i}})) \quad \forall i.$$

b) *For $\tilde{\varepsilon}_t$ as in (i) and ε_t^K as in (ii) of Theorem $\{ \substack{7 \\ 8} \}$ we have*
$$\tilde{\ell}_{1:T} \leq s_{1:T}^i + 2\sqrt{2s_{1:T}^i k^i} \cdot (1 + O(\tfrac{\ln k^i}{\sqrt{k^i}})) + \{ \substack{O(k^i) \\ O(k^i \ln s_{1:T}^i)} \} \quad \forall i.$$

The hierarchical $\widetilde{\text{FPL}}$ differs from a direct FPL over all experts $\mathcal{E}$. One potential way to prove a bound on direct FPL may be to show (if it holds) that FPL performs better than $\widetilde{\text{FPL}}$, i.e. $\ell_{1:T} \leq \tilde{\ell}_{1:T}$. Another way may be to suitably generalize Theorem 4 to expert dependent ε.

7 Miscellaneous

Lower Bound on FPL. For finite n, a lower bound on FPL similar to the upper bound in Theorem 2 can also be proven. For any $\mathcal{D} \subseteq \mathbb{R}^n$ and $s_t \in \mathbb{R}$ such that the required extrema exist, $q \in \mathbb{R}^n$, and $\varepsilon_t > 0$ decreasing, the loss of FPL for uniform complexities can be lower bounded in terms of the best predictor in hindsight plus/minus additive corrections:

$$\sum_{t=1}^{T} M(s_{<t} - \frac{q}{\varepsilon_t}) \circ s_t \geq \min_{d \in \mathcal{D}} \{d \circ s_{1:T}\} - \frac{1}{\varepsilon_T} \max_{d \in \mathcal{D}} \{d \circ q\} + \sum_{t=1}^{T} (\frac{1}{\varepsilon_t} - \frac{1}{\varepsilon_{t-1}}) M(s_{<t}) \circ q \tag{8}$$

For $\mathcal{D} = \mathcal{E}$ and any $\mathcal{S}$ and all k^i equal and $P[q^i] = e^{-q^i}$ for $q \geq 0$ and decreasing $\varepsilon_t > 0$, this reduces to

$$\ell_{1:T} \geq s_{1:T}^{min} - \frac{\ln n}{\varepsilon_T} \tag{9}$$

The upper and lower bounds on $\ell_{1:T}$ (Theorem 4 and Corollary 3 and (9)) together show that

$$\frac{\ell_{1:t}}{s_{1:t}^{min}} \to 1 \quad \text{if} \quad \varepsilon_t \to 0 \quad \text{and} \quad \varepsilon_t \cdot s_{1:t}^{min} \to \infty \quad \text{and} \quad k^i = K \; \forall i. \tag{10}$$

For instance, $\varepsilon_t = \sqrt{K/2s_{<t}^{min}}$. For $\varepsilon_t = \sqrt{K/2(\ell_{<t}+1)}$ we proved the bound in Theorem 7(ii). Knowing that $\sqrt{K/2(\ell_{<t}+1)}$ converges to $\sqrt{K/2s_{<t}^{min}}$ due to (10), we can derive a bound similar to Theorem 7(ii) for $\varepsilon_t = \sqrt{K/2s_{<t}^{min}}$. This choice for ε_t has the advantage that we do not have to compute $\ell_{<t}$ (see below), as also achieved by Theorem 8(ii). We do not know whether (8) can be generalized to expert dependent complexities k^i.

Initial versus independent randomization. So far we assumed that the perturbations are sampled only once at time $t=0$. As already indicated, under the expectation this is equivalent to generating a new perturbation q_t at each time step t, i.e. Theorems 4–9 remain valid for this case. While the former choice was favorable for the analysis, the latter has two advantages. First, if the losses are generated by an adaptive adversary, then he may after some time figure out the initial random perturbation and use it to force FPL to have a large loss. On the other hand, for independent randomization, one can show that our bounds remain valid, even if the environment has access to FPL's past predictions. Second, repeated sampling of the perturbations guarantees better bounds with high probability.

Bounds with high probability. We have derived several bounds for the expected loss $\ell_{1:T}$ of FPL. The *actual* loss at time t is $u_t = M(s_{<t} + \frac{k-q}{\varepsilon_t}) \circ s_t$. A simple Markov inequality shows that the total actual loss $u_{1:T}$ exceeds the total expected loss $\ell_{1:T} = E[u_{1:T}]$ by a factor of $c > 1$ with probability at most $1/c$:

$$P[u_{1:T} \geq c \cdot \ell_{1:T}] \leq 1/c.$$

Randomizing independently for each t as described in the previous paragraph, the actual loss is $u_t = M(s_{<t} + \frac{k-q_t}{\varepsilon_t}) \circ s_t$ with the same expected loss $\ell_{1:T} = E[u_{1:T}]$ as before. The advantage of independent randomization is that we can get a much better high-probability bound. We can exploit a Chernoff-Hoeffding bound [McD89, Cor.5.2b], valid for arbitrary independent random variables $0 \leq u_t \leq 1$ for $t = 1,...,T$:

$$P\left[|u_{1:T} - E[u_{1:T}]| \geq \delta E[u_{1:T}]\right] \leq 2\exp(-\tfrac{1}{3}\delta^2 E[u_{1:T}]), \qquad 0 \leq \delta \leq 1.$$

For $\delta = \sqrt{3c/\ell_{1:T}}$ we get

$$P[|u_{1:T} - \ell_{1:T}| \geq \sqrt{3c\ell_{1:T}}] \leq 2e^{-c} \quad \text{as soon as} \quad \ell_{1:T} \geq 3c. \tag{11}$$

Using (11), the bounds for $\ell_{1:T}$ of Theorems 5-8 can be rewritten to yield similar bounds with high probability $(1 - 2e^{-c})$ for $u_{1:T}$ with small extra regret $\propto \sqrt{c \cdot L}$ or $\propto \sqrt{c \cdot s_{1:T}^i}$. Furthermore, (11) shows that with high probability, $u_{1:T}/\ell_{1:T}$ converges rapidly to 1 for $\ell_{1:T} \to \infty$. Hence we may use the easier to compute $\varepsilon_t = \sqrt{K/2u_{<t}}$ instead of $\varepsilon_t = \sqrt{K/2(\ell_{<t}+1)}$, with similar bounds on the regret.

Computational Aspects. It is easy to generate the randomized decision of FPL. Indeed, only a single initial exponentially distributed vector $q \in \mathbb{R}^n$ is needed. Only for adaptive $\varepsilon_t \propto 1/\sqrt{\ell_{<t}}$ (see Theorem 7) we need to compute expectations explicitly. Given ε_t, from $t \rightsquigarrow t+1$ we need to compute ℓ_t in order to update ε_t. Note that $\ell_t = w_t \circ s_t$, where $w_t^i = P[I_t=i]$ and $I_t := \operatorname{argmin}_{i \in \mathcal{E}}\{s_{<t}^i + \frac{k^i - q^i}{\varepsilon_t}\}$ is the actual (randomized) prediction of FPL. With $s := s_{<t} + k/\varepsilon_t$, $P[I_t=i]$ has the following representation:

$$P[I_t=i] = \int_{-\infty}^{s^{min}} \varepsilon_t e^{-\varepsilon_t(s^i - m)} \prod_{j \neq i} (1 - e^{-\varepsilon_t(s^j - m)})dm = \sum_{\mathcal{M}:\{i\} \subseteq \mathcal{M} \subseteq \mathcal{N}} \frac{(-1)^{|\mathcal{M}|-1}}{|\mathcal{M}|} e^{-\varepsilon_t \sum_{j \in \mathcal{M}}(s^j - s^{min})}$$

In the last equality we expanded the product and performed the resulting exponential integrals. For finite n, the one-dimensional integral should be numerically feasible. Once the product $\prod_{j=1}^n (1 - e^{-\varepsilon_t(s^j - m)})$ has been computed in time $O(n)$, the argument of the integral can be computed for each i in time $O(1)$, hence the overall time to compute ℓ_t is $O(c \cdot n)$, where c is the time to numerically compute one integral. For infinite[3] n, the last sum may be approximated by the dominant contributions. The expectation may also be approximated by (monte carlo) sampling I_t several times. Recall that approximating $\ell_{<t}$ can be avoided by using $s_{<t}^{min}$ (Theorem 8) or $u_{<t}$ (bounds with high probability) instead.

Deterministic prediction and absolute loss. Another use of w_t from the last paragraph is the following: If the decision space is $\mathcal{D} = \Delta$, then FPL may make a deterministic decision $d = w_t \in \Delta$ at time t with bounds now holding for sure, instead of selecting e_i with probability w_t^i. For example for the absolute loss $s_t^i = |x_t - y_t^i|$ with observation $x_t \in [0,1]$ and predictions $y_t^i \in [0,1]$, a master

---

[3] For practical realizations in case of infinite n, one must use finite subclasses of increasing size, compare [LW94].

algorithm predicting deterministically $w_t \circ y_t \in [0,1]$ suffers absolute loss $|x_t - w_t \circ y_t| \le \sum_i w_t^i |x_t - y_t^i| = \ell_t$, and hence has the same (or better) performance guarantees as FPL. In general, masters can be chosen deterministic if prediction space $\mathcal{Y}$ and loss-function $\mathrm{Loss}(x,y)$ are convex.

8   Discussion and Open Problems

How does FPL compare with other expert advice algorithms? We briefly discuss four issues.

Static bounds. Here the coefficient of the regret term $\sqrt{KL}$, referred to as the *leading constant* in the sequel, is 2 for FPL (Theorem 5). It is thus a factor of $\sqrt{2}$ worse than the Hedge bound for arbitrary loss [FS97], which is sharp in some sense [Vov95]. For special loss functions, the bounds can sometimes be improved, e.g. to a leading constant of 1 in the static WM case with 0/1 loss [CB97].

Dynamic bounds. Not knowing the right learning rate in advance usually costs a factor of $\sqrt{2}$. This is true for Hannan's algorithm [KV03] as well as in all our cases. Also for binary prediction with uniform complexities and 0/1 loss, this result has been established recently – [YEYS04] show a dynamic regret bound with leading constant $\sqrt{2}(1+\varepsilon)$. Remarkably, the best dynamic bound for a WM variant proven in [ACBG02] has a leading constant $2\sqrt{2}$, which matches ours. Considering the difference in the static case, we therefore conjecture that a bound with leading constant of 2 holds for a dynamic Hedge algorithm.

General weights. While there are several dynamic bounds for uniform weights, the only result for non-uniform weights we know of is [Gen03, Cor.16], which gives a dynamic bound for a p-norm algorithm for the absolute loss if the weights are rapidly decaying. Our hierarchical FPL bound in Theorem 9 (*b*) generalizes it to arbitrary weights and losses and strengthens it, since both, asymptotic order and leading constant, are smaller. Also the FPL analysis gets more complicated for general weights. We conjecture that the bounds $\propto \sqrt{Tk^i}$ and $\propto \sqrt{s_{1:T}^i k^i}$ also hold without the hierarchy trick, probably by using expert dependent learning rate ε_t^i.

Comparison to Bayesian sequence prediction. We can also compare the *worst-case* bounds for FPL obtained in this work to similar bounds for *Bayesian sequence prediction*. Let $\{\nu_i\}$ be a class of probability distributions over sequences and assume that the true sequence is sampled from $\mu \in \{\nu_i\}$ with complexity k^μ ($\sum_i 2^{-k^{\nu_i}} \le 1$). Then it is known that the Bayes-optimal predictor based on the $2^{-k^{\nu_i}}$-weighted mixture of ν_i's has an expected total loss of at most $L^\mu + 2\sqrt{L^\mu k^\mu} + 2k^\mu$, where L^μ is the expected total loss of the Bayes-optimal predictor based on μ [Hut03a, Thm.2]. Using FPL, we obtained the same bound except for the leading order constant, but for any sequence independently of the assumption that it is generated by μ. This is another indication that a PEA bound with leading constant 2 could hold. See [Hut03b, Sec.6.3] for a more detailed comparison of Bayes bounds with PEA bounds.

References

[ACBG02] P. Auer, N. Cesa-Bianchi, and C. Gentile. Adaptive and self-confident on-line learning algorithms. *Journal of Computer and System Sciences*, 64(1):48–75, 2002.

[AG00] P. Auer and C. Gentile. Adaptive and self-confident on-line learning algorithms. In *Proceedings of the 13th Conference on Computational Learning Theory*, pages 107–117. Morgan Kaufmann, San Francisco, 2000.

[CB97] N. Cesa-Bianchi et al. How to use expert advice. *Journal of the ACM*, 44(3):427–485, 1997.

[FS97] Y. Freund and R. E. Schapire. A decision-theoretic generalization of on-line learning and an application to boosting. *Journal of Computer and System Sciences*, 55(1):119–139, 1997.

[Gen03] C. Gentile. The robustness of the p-norm algorithm. *Machine Learning*, 53(3):265–299, 2003.

[Han57] J. Hannan. Approximation to Bayes risk in repeated plays. In M. Dresher, A. W. Tucker, and P. Wolfe, editors, *Contributions to the Theory of Games 3*, pages 97–139. Princeton University Press, 1957.

[Hut03a] M. Hutter. Convergence and loss bounds for Bayesian sequence prediction. *IEEE Transactions on Information Theory*, 49(8):2061–2067, 2003.

[Hut03b] M. Hutter. Optimality of universal Bayesian prediction for general loss and alphabet. *Journal of Machine Learning Research*, 4:971–1000, 2003.

[KV03] A. Kalai and S. Vempala. Efficient algorithms for online decision. In *Proceedings of the 16th Annual Conference on Learning Theory (COLT-2003)*, Lecture Notes in Artificial Intelligence, pages 506–521, Berlin, 2003. Springer.

[LW89] N. Littlestone and M. K. Warmuth. The weighted majority algorithm. In *30th Annual Symposium on Foundations of Computer Science*, pages 256–261, Research Triangle Park, North Carolina, 1989. IEEE.

[LW94] N. Littlestone and M. K. Warmuth. The weighted majority algorithm. *Information and Computation*, 108(2):212–261, 1994.

[McD89] C. McDiarmid. On the method of bounded differences. *Surveys in Combinatorics*, 141, London Mathematical Society Lecture Notes Series:148–188, 1989.

[Vov90] V. G. Vovk. Aggregating strategies. In *Proceedings of the Third Annual Workshop on Computational Learning Theory*, pages 371–383, Rochester, New York, 1990. ACM Press.

[Vov95] V. G. Vovk. A game of prediction with expert advice. In *Proceedings of the 8th Annual Conference on Computational Learning Theory*, pages 51–60. ACM Press, New York, NY, 1995.

[YEYS04] R. Yaroshinsky, R. El-Yaniv, and S. Seiden. How to better use expert advice. *Machine Learning*, 2004.

On the Convergence Speed of MDL Predictions for Bernoulli Sequences[*]

Jan Poland and Marcus Hutter

IDSIA, Galleria 2 CH-6928 Manno (Lugano), Switzerland
{jan,marcus}@idsia.ch

Abstract. We consider the Minimum Description Length principle for online sequence prediction. If the underlying model class is discrete, then the total expected square loss is a particularly interesting performance measure: (a) this quantity is bounded, implying convergence with probability one, and (b) it additionally specifies a *rate of convergence*. Generally, for MDL only exponential loss bounds hold, as opposed to the linear bounds for a Bayes mixture. We show that this is even the case if the model class contains only Bernoulli distributions. We derive a new upper bound on the prediction error for countable Bernoulli classes. This implies a small bound (comparable to the one for Bayes mixtures) for certain important model classes. The results apply to many Machine Learning tasks including classification and hypothesis testing. We provide arguments that our theorems generalize to countable classes of i.i.d. models.

1 Introduction

"Bayes mixture", "Solomonoff induction", "marginalization", all these terms refer to a central induction principle: Obtain a predictive distribution by integrating the product of prior and evidence over the model class. In many cases however, the Bayes mixture cannot be computed, and even a sophisticated approximation is expensive. The MDL or MAP (maximum a posteriori) estimator is both a common approximation for the Bayes mixture and interesting for its own sake: Use the model with the largest product of prior and evidence. (In practice, the MDL estimator is usually being approximated too, in particular when only a local maximum is determined.)

How good are the predictions by Bayes mixtures and MDL? This question has attracted much attention. In the context of prediction, arguably the most important quality measure is the *total* or cumulative *expected loss* of a predictor. A very common choice of loss function is the square loss. Throughout this paper, we will study this quantity in an *online setup*.

Assume that the outcome space is finite, and the model class is continuously parameterized. Then for Bayes mixture prediction, the cumulative expected square loss is usually small but unbounded, growing with $\log n$, where

---

[*] This work was supported by SNF grant 2100-67712.02.

n is the sample size [1]. This corresponds to an *instantaneous* loss bound of $\frac{1}{n}$. For the MDL predictor, the losses behave similarly [2,3] under appropriate conditions, in particular with a specific prior. (Note that in order to do MDL for continuous model classes, one needs to *discretize* the parameter space, e.g. [4].)

On the other hand, if the model class is discrete, then Solomonoff's theorem [5,6] bounds the cumulative expected square loss for the Bayes mixture predictions finitely, namely by $\ln w_\mu^{-1}$, where w_μ is the prior weight of the "true" model μ. The only necessary assumption is that the true distribution μ is contained in the model class. For the corresponding MDL predictions, we have shown [7] that a bound of w_μ^{-1} holds. This is exponentially larger than the Solomonoff bound, and it is sharp in general. A finite bound on the total expected square loss is particularly interesting:

1. It implies convergence of the predictive to the true probabilities with probability one. In contrast, an instantaneous loss bound which tends to zero implies only convergence in probability.
2. Additionally, it gives a *convergence speed*, in the sense that errors of a certain magnitude cannot occur too often.

So for both, Bayes mixtures and MDL, convergence with probability one holds, while the convergence rate is exponentially worse for MDL compared to the Bayes mixture.

It is therefore natural to ask if there are model classes where the cumulative loss of MDL is comparable to that of Bayes mixture predictions. Here we will concentrate on the simplest possible stochastic case, namely discrete Bernoulli classes (compare also [8]). It might be surprising to discover that in general the cumulative loss is still exponential. On the other hand, we will give mild conditions on the prior guaranteeing a small bound. We will provide arguments that these results generalize to arbitrary i.i.d. classes. Moreover, we will see that the instantaneous (as opposed to the cumulative) bounds are always small ($\approx \frac{1}{n}$). This corresponds to the well-known fact that the instantaneous square loss of the Maximum Likelihood estimator decays as $\frac{1}{n}$ in the Bernoulli case.

A particular motivation to consider discrete model classes arises in Algorithmic Information Theory. From a computational point of view, the largest relevant model class is the countable class of all computable models (isomorphic to programs) on some fixed universal Turing machine. We may study the corresponding Bernoulli case and consider the countable set of computable reals in $[0,1]$. We call this the *universal setup*. The description length $K(\vartheta)$ of a parameter $\vartheta \in [0,1]$ is then given by the length of the shortest program that outputs ϑ, and a prior weight may be defined by $2^{K(\vartheta)}$.

Many Machine Learning tasks are or can be reduced to sequence prediction tasks. An important example is classification. The task of classifying a new instance z_n after having seen (instance,class) pairs $(z_1, c_1), ..., (z_{n-1}, c_{n-1})$ can be phrased as to predict the continuation of the sequence $z_1 c_1...z_{n-1} c_{n-1} z_n$. Typically the (instance,class) pairs are i.i.d.

Our main tool for obtaining results is the Kullback-Leibler divergence. Lemmata for this quantity are stated in Section 2. Section 3 shows that the exponential error bound obtained in [7] is sharp in general. In Section 4, we give an upper bound on the instantaneous and the cumulative losses. The latter bound is small e.g. under certain conditions on the distribution of the weights, this is the subject of Section 5. Section 6 treats the universal setup. Finally, in Section 7 we discuss the results and give conclusions.

2   Kullback-Leibler Divergence

Let $\mathbb{B} = \{0,1\}$ and consider finite strings $x \in \mathbb{B}^*$ as well as infinite sequences $x_{<\infty} \in \mathbb{B}^\infty$, with the first n bits denoted by $x_{1:n}$. If we know that x is generated by an i.i.d random variable, then $P(x_i = 1) = \vartheta_0$ for all $1 \leq i \leq \ell(x)$ where $\ell(x)$ is the length of x. Then x is called a Bernoulli sequence, and $\vartheta_0 \in \Theta \subset [0,1]$ the *true parameter*. In the following we will consider only countable Θ, e.g. the set of all computable numbers in $[0,1]$.

Associated with each $\vartheta \in \Theta$, there is a *complexity* or description length $Kw(\vartheta)$ and a *weight* or (semi)probability $w_\vartheta = 2^{-Kw(\vartheta)}$. The complexity will often but need not be a natural number. Typically, one assumes that the weights sum up to at most one, $\sum_{\vartheta \in \Theta} w_\vartheta \leq 1$. Then, by the Kraft inequality, for all $\vartheta \in \Theta$ there exists a prefix-code of length $Kw(\vartheta)$. Because of this correspondence, it is only a matter of convenience if results are developed in terms of description lengths or probabilities. We will choose the former way. We won't even need the condition $\sum_\vartheta w_\vartheta \leq 1$ for most of the following results. This only means that Kw cannot be interpreted as a prefix code length, but does not cause other problems.

Given a set of distributions $\Theta \subset [0,1]$, complexities $\big(Kw(\vartheta)\big)_{\vartheta \in \Theta}$, a true distribution $\vartheta_0 \in \Theta$, and some observed string $x \in \mathbb{B}^*$, we define an *MDL estimator*[1]:

$$\vartheta^x = \arg\max_{\vartheta \in \Theta}\{w_\vartheta P(x|\vartheta_0 = \vartheta)\}.$$

Here, $P(x|\vartheta_0 = \vartheta)$ is the probability of observing x if ϑ is the true parameter. Clearly, $P(x|\vartheta_0 = \vartheta) = \vartheta^{\mathbb{I}(x)}(1-\vartheta)^{\ell(x)-\mathbb{I}(x)}$, where $\mathbb{I}(x)$ is the number of ones in x. Hence $P(x|\vartheta_0 = \vartheta)$ depends only on $\ell(x)$ and $\mathbb{I}(x)$. We therefore see

$$\vartheta^x = \vartheta^{(\alpha,n)} = \arg\max_{\vartheta \in \Theta}\{w_\vartheta \left(\vartheta^\alpha(1-\vartheta)^{1-\alpha}\right)^n\} \qquad (1)$$
$$= \arg\min_{\vartheta \in \Theta}\{n \cdot D(\alpha\|\vartheta) + Kw(\vartheta) \cdot \ln 2\},$$

where $n = \ell(x)$ and $\alpha := \frac{\mathbb{I}(x)}{\ell(x)}$ is the *observed fraction* of ones and

$$D(\alpha\|\vartheta) = \alpha \ln \frac{\alpha}{\vartheta} + (1-\alpha)\ln\frac{1-\alpha}{1-\vartheta}$$

---

[1] Precisely, we define a MAP (maximum a posteriori) estimator. For two reasons, our definition might not be considered as MDL in the strict sense. First, MDL is often associated with a specific prior, while we admit arbitrary priors. Second and more importantly, when coding some data x, one can exploit the fact that once the parameter ϑ^x is specified, only data which leads to this ϑ^x needs to be considered. This allows for a description shorter than $Kw(\vartheta^x)$. Nevertheless, the *construction principle* is commonly termed MDL, compare e.g. the "ideal MDL" in [9].

is the Kullback-Leibler divergence. Let $\vartheta, \tilde{\vartheta} \in \Theta$ be two parameters, then it follows from (1) that in the process of choosing the MDL estimator, ϑ is being preferred to $\tilde{\vartheta}$ iff

$$n\big(D(\alpha\|\tilde{\vartheta}) - D(\alpha\|\vartheta)\big) \geq \ln 2 \cdot \big(Kw(\vartheta) - Kw(\tilde{\vartheta})\big). \tag{2}$$

In this case, we say that ϑ *beats* $\tilde{\vartheta}$. It is immediate that for increasing n the influence of the complexities on the selection of the maximizing element decreases. We are now interested in the *total expected square prediction error* (or cumulative square loss) of the MDL estimator $\sum_{n=1}^{\infty} \mathbf{E}(\vartheta^{x_{1:n}} - \vartheta_0)^2$. In terms of [7], this is the *static MDL prediction* loss, which means that a predictor/estimator ϑ^x is chosen according to the current observation x. The *dynamic* method on the other hand would consider both possible continuations $x0$ and $x1$ and predict according to ϑ^{x0} and ϑ^{x1}. In the following, we concentrate on static predictions. They are also preferred in practice, since computing only one model is more efficient.

Let $A_n = \{\frac{k}{n} : 0 \leq k \leq n\}$. Given the true parameter ϑ_0 and some $n \in \mathbb{N}$, the *expectation* of a function $f^{(n)} : \{0, \ldots, n\} \to \mathbb{R}$ is given by

$$\mathbf{E}f^{(n)} = \sum_{\alpha \in A_n} p(\alpha|n)f(\alpha n), \text{ where } p(\alpha|n) = \binom{n}{k}\Big(\vartheta_0^{\alpha}(1-\vartheta_0)^{1-\alpha}\Big)^n. \tag{3}$$

(Note that the probability $p(\alpha|n)$ depends on ϑ_0, which we do not make explicit in our notation.) Therefore,

$$\sum_{n=1}^{\infty} \mathbf{E}(\vartheta^{x_{1:n}} - \vartheta_0)^2 = \sum_{n=1}^{\infty} \sum_{\alpha \in A_n} p(\alpha|n)(\vartheta^{(\alpha,n)} - \vartheta_0)^2. \tag{4}$$

Denote the relation $f = O(g)$ by $f \overset{\times}{\leq} g$. Analogously define "$\overset{\times}{>}$" and "$\overset{\times}{=}$". From [7, Corollary 12], we immediately obtain the following result.

Theorem 1. *The cumulative loss bound* $\sum_n \mathbf{E}(\vartheta^{x_{1:n}} - \vartheta_0)^2 \overset{\times}{\leq} 2^{Kw(\vartheta_0)}$ *holds.*

This is the "slow" convergence result mentioned in the introduction. In contrast, for a Bayes mixture, the total expected error is bounded by $Kw(\vartheta_0)$ rather than $2^{Kw(\vartheta_0)}$ (see [5] or [6, Th.1]). An upper bound on $\sum_n \mathbf{E}(\vartheta^{x_{1:n}} - \vartheta_0)^2$ is termed as *convergence in mean sum* and implies convergence $\vartheta^{x_{1:n}} \to \vartheta_0$ with probability 1 (since otherwise the sum would be infinite).

We now establish relations between the Kullback-Leibler divergence and the quadratic distance. We call bounds of this type *entropy inequalities*.

Lemma 2. *Let* $\vartheta, \tilde{\vartheta} \in (0,1)$ *and* $\vartheta^* = \arg\min\{|\vartheta - \frac{1}{2}|, |\tilde{\vartheta} - \frac{1}{2}|\}$, *i.e.* ϑ^* *is the element from* $\{\vartheta, \tilde{\vartheta}\}$ *which is closer to* $\frac{1}{2}$. *Then*

$$2 \cdot (\vartheta - \tilde{\vartheta})^2 \overset{(i)}{\leq} D(\vartheta\|\tilde{\vartheta}) \overset{(ii)}{\leq} \tfrac{8}{3}(\vartheta - \tilde{\vartheta})^2 \text{ and}$$

$$\frac{(\vartheta - \tilde{\vartheta})^2}{2\vartheta^*(1 - \vartheta^*)} \overset{(iii)}{\leq} D(\vartheta\|\tilde{\vartheta}) \overset{(iv)}{\leq} \frac{3(\vartheta - \tilde{\vartheta})^2}{2\vartheta^*(1 - \vartheta^*)}.$$

Thereby, (ii) requires $\vartheta, \tilde{\vartheta} \in [\frac{1}{4}, \frac{3}{4}]$, (iii) requires $\vartheta, \tilde{\vartheta} \le \frac{1}{2}$, and (iv) requires $\vartheta \le \frac{1}{4}$ and $\tilde{\vartheta} \in [\frac{\vartheta}{3}, 3\vartheta]$. Statements (iii) and (iv) have symmetric counterparts for $\vartheta \ge \frac{1}{2}$.

Proof. The lower bound (i), is standard, see e.g. [10, p. 329]. In order to verify the upper bound (ii), let $f(\eta) = D(\vartheta\|\eta) - \frac{8}{3}(\eta - \vartheta)^2$. Then (ii) follows from $f(\eta) \le 0$ for $\eta \in [\frac{1}{4}, \frac{3}{4}]$. We have that $f(\vartheta) = 0$ and $f'(\eta) = \frac{\eta - \vartheta}{\eta(1-\eta)} - \frac{16}{3}(\eta - \vartheta)$. This difference is nonnegative if and only if $\eta - \vartheta \le 0$ since $\eta(1 - \eta) \ge \frac{3}{16}$. This implies $f(\eta) \le 0$. Statements (iii) and (iv) giving bounds if ϑ is close to the boundary are proven similarly. $\qquad\square$

Lemma 2 (ii) is sufficient to prove the lower bound on the error in Proposition 5. The bounds (iii) and (iv) are only needed in the technical proof of the upper bound in Theorem 8, which will be omitted. It requires also similar upper and lower bounds for the absolute distance, and if the second argument of $D(\cdot\|\cdot)$ tends to the boundary. The lemma remains valid for the extreme cases $\vartheta, \tilde{\vartheta} \in \{0, 1\}$ if the fraction $\frac{0}{0}$ is properly defined. It is likely to generalize to arbitrary alphabet, for (i) this is shown in [6].

It is a well-known fact that the binomial distribution may be approximated by a Gaussian. Our next goal is to establish upper and lower bounds for the binomial distribution. Again we leave out the extreme cases.

Lemma 3. *Let $\vartheta_0 \in (0, 1)$ be the true parameter, $n \ge 2$ and $1 \le k \le n - 1$, and $\alpha = \frac{k}{n}$. Then the following assertions hold.*

$$(i) \ \ p(\alpha|n) \le \frac{1}{\sqrt{2\pi\alpha(1 - \alpha)n}} \exp\left(-nD(\alpha\|\vartheta_0)\right),$$

$$(ii) \ \ p(\alpha|n) \ge \frac{1}{\sqrt{8\alpha(1 - \alpha)n}} \exp\left(-nD(\alpha\|\vartheta_0)\right).$$

The lemma is verified using Stirling's formula. The upper bound is sharp for $n \to \infty$ and fixed α. Lemma 3 can be easily combined with Lemma 2, yielding Gaussian estimates for the Binomial distribution. The following lemma is proved by simply estimating the sums by appropriate integrals.

Lemma 4. *Let $z \in \mathbb{R}^+$, then*

$$(i) \ \ \frac{\sqrt{\pi}}{2z^3} - \frac{1}{z\sqrt{2e}} \le \sum_{n=1}^{\infty} \sqrt{n} \cdot \exp(-z^2 n) \le \frac{\sqrt{\pi}}{2z^3} + \frac{1}{z\sqrt{2e}} \ \ and$$

$$(ii) \ \ \sum_{n=1}^{\infty} n^{-\frac{1}{2}} \exp(-z^2 n) \le \sqrt{\pi}/z.$$

3 Lower Bound

We are now in the position to prove that even for Bernoulli classes the upper bound from Theorem 1 is sharp in general.

Proposition 5. *Let $\vartheta_0 = \frac{1}{2}$ be the true parameter generating sequences of fair coin flips. Assume there are $2^N - 1$ other parameters $\vartheta_1, \ldots, \vartheta_{2^N-1}$ with $\vartheta_k = \frac{1}{2} + 2^{-k-1}$. Let all complexities be equal, i.e. $Kw(\vartheta_0) = Kw(\vartheta_1) = \ldots = Kw(\vartheta_{2^N-1}) = N$. Then*

$$\sum_{n=1}^{\infty} \mathbf{E}(\vartheta_0 - \vartheta^x)^2 \geq \tfrac{1}{84}(2^N - 5) \stackrel{\times}{=} 2^{Kw(\vartheta_0)}.$$

Proof. Recall that $\vartheta^x = \vartheta^{(\alpha,n)}$ the maximizing element for some observed sequence x only depends on the length n and the observed fraction of ones α. In order to obtain an estimate for the total prediction error $\sum_n \mathbf{E}(\vartheta_0 - \vartheta^x)^2$, partition the interval $[0,1]$ into 2^N disjoint intervals I_k, such that $\bigcup_{k=0}^{2^N-1} I_k = [0,1]$. Then consider the contributions for the observed fraction α falling in I_k separately:

$$C(k) = \sum_{n=1}^{\infty} \sum_{\alpha \in A_n \cap I_k} p(\alpha|n)(\vartheta^{(\alpha,n)} - \vartheta_0)^2 \qquad (5)$$

(compare (3)). Clearly, $\sum_n \mathbf{E}(\vartheta_0 - \vartheta^x)^2 = \sum_k C(k)$ holds. We define the partitioning (I_k) as $I_0 = [0, \frac{1}{2} + 2^{-2^N}) = [0, \vartheta_{2^N-1})$, $I_1 = [\frac{3}{4}, 1] = [\vartheta_1, 1]$, and

$$I_k = [\vartheta_k, \vartheta_{k-1}) \text{ for all } 2 \leq k \leq 2^N - 1.$$

Fix $k \in \{2, \ldots, 2^N - 1\}$ and assume $\alpha \in I_k$. Then

$$\vartheta^{(\alpha,n)} = \arg\min_{\vartheta}\{nD(\alpha\|\vartheta) + Kw(\vartheta)\ln 2\} = \arg\min_{\vartheta}\{nD(\alpha\|\vartheta)\} \in \{\vartheta_k, \vartheta_{k-1}\}$$

according to (1). So clearly $(\vartheta^{(\alpha,n)} - \vartheta_0)^2 \geq (\vartheta_k - \vartheta_0)^2 = 2^{-2k-2}$ holds. Since $p(\alpha|n)$ decreases for increasing $|\alpha - \vartheta_0|$, we have $p(\alpha|n) \geq p(\vartheta_{k-1}|n)$. The interval I_k has length 2^{-k-1}, so there are at least $\lfloor n2^{-k-1} \rfloor \geq n2^{-k-1} - 1$ observed fractions α falling in the interval. From (5), the total contribution of $\alpha \in I_k$ can be estimated by

$$C(k) \geq \sum_{n=1}^{\infty} 2^{-2k-2}(n2^{-k-1} - 1)p(\vartheta_{k-1}|n).$$

Note that the terms in the sum even become negative for small n, which does not cause any problems. We proceed with

$$p(\vartheta_{k-1}|n) \geq \frac{1}{\sqrt{8 \cdot 2^{-2n}}} \exp\left[-nD(\tfrac{1}{2} + 2^{-k}\|\tfrac{1}{2})\right] \geq \frac{1}{\sqrt{2n}} \exp\left[-n\tfrac{8}{3}2^{-2k}\right]$$

according to Lemma 3 and Lemma 2 (ii). By Lemma 4 (i) and (ii), we have

$$\sum_{n=1}^{\infty} \sqrt{n} \exp\left[-n\tfrac{8}{3}2^{-2k}\right] \geq \frac{\sqrt{\pi}}{2}\left(\frac{3}{8}\right)^{\frac{3}{2}} 2^{3k} - \frac{1}{\sqrt{2e}}\sqrt{\frac{3}{8}}2^k \text{ and}$$

$$-\sum_{n=1}^{\infty} n^{-\frac{1}{2}} \exp\left[-n\tfrac{8}{3}2^{-2k}\right] \geq -\sqrt{\pi}\sqrt{\frac{3}{8}}2^k.$$

Considering only $k \geq 5$, we thus obtain

$$C(k) \geq \frac{1}{\sqrt{2}}\sqrt{\frac{3}{8}}2^{-2k-2}\left[\frac{3\sqrt{\pi}}{16}2^{2k-1} - \frac{1}{\sqrt{2e}}2^{-1} - \sqrt{\pi}2^k\right]$$

$$\geq \frac{\sqrt{3}}{16}\left[3\sqrt{\pi}2^{-5} - \frac{1}{\sqrt{2e}}2^{-2k-1} - \sqrt{\pi}2^{-k}\right] \geq \frac{\sqrt{3\pi}}{8}2^{-5} - \frac{\sqrt{3}}{16\sqrt{2e}}2^{-11} > \frac{1}{84}.$$

Ignoring the contributions for $k \leq 4$, this implies the assertion.   □

This result shows that if the parameters and their weights are chosen in an appropriate way, then the total expected error is of order w_0^{-1} instead of $\ln w_0^{-1}$. Interestingly, this outcome seems to depend on the arrangement and the weights of the *false* parameters rather than on the weight of the *true* one. One can check with moderate effort that the proposition still remains valid if e.g. w_0 is twice as large as the other weights. Actually, the proof of Proposition 5 shows even a slightly more general result, namely the same bound holds when there are additional arbitrary parameters with larger complexities. This will be used for Example 14. Other and more general assertions can be proven similarly.

4   Upper Bounds

Although the cumulative error may be large, as seen in the previous section, the instantaneous error is always small.

Proposition 6. *For $n \geq 3$, the expected instantaneous square loss is bounded:*

$$\mathbf{E}(\vartheta_0 - \hat{\vartheta}^{x_{1:n}})^2 \leq \frac{(\ln 2)Kw(\vartheta_0)}{2n} + \frac{\sqrt{2(\ln 2)Kw(\vartheta_0)\ln n}}{n} + \frac{6\ln n}{n}.$$

Proof. We give an elementary proof for the case $\vartheta_0 \in (\frac{1}{4}, \frac{3}{4})$ only. Like in the proof of Proposition 5, we consider the contributions of different α separately. By Hoeffding's inequality, $\mathbf{P}(|\alpha - \vartheta_0| \geq \frac{c}{\sqrt{n}}) \leq 2e^{-2c^2}$ for any $c > 0$. Letting $c = \sqrt{\ln n}$, the contributions by these α are thus bounded by $\frac{2}{n^2} \leq \frac{\ln n}{n}$.

On the other hand, for $|\alpha - \vartheta_0| \leq \frac{c}{\sqrt{n}}$, recall that ϑ_0 *beats* any ϑ iff (2) holds. According to $Kw(\vartheta) \leq 1$, $|\alpha - \vartheta_0| \leq \frac{c}{\sqrt{n}}$, and Lemma 2 (*i*) and (*ii*), (2) is already implied by $|\alpha - \vartheta| \geq \sqrt{\frac{\frac{1}{2}(\ln 2)Kw(\vartheta_0) + \frac{4}{3}c^2}{n}}$. Clearly, a contribution only occurs if ϑ beats ϑ_0, therefore if the opposite inequality holds. Using $|\alpha - \vartheta_0| \leq \frac{c}{\sqrt{n}}$ again and the triangle inequality, we obtain that

$$(\vartheta - \vartheta_0)^2 \leq \frac{5c^2 + \frac{1}{2}(\ln 2)Kw(\vartheta_0) + \sqrt{2(\ln 2)Kw(\vartheta_0)c^2}}{n}$$

in this case. Since we have chosen $c = \sqrt{\ln n}$, this implies the assertion.   □

One can improve the bound in Proposition 6 to $\mathbf{E}(\vartheta_0 - \hat{\vartheta}^{x_{1:n}})^2 \overset{\times}{\leq} \frac{Kw(\vartheta_0)}{n}$ by a refined argument, compare [4]. But the high-level assertion is the same: Even if the cumulative upper bound may tend to infinity, the instantaneous error converges rapidly to 0. Moreover, the convergence speed depends on $Kw(\vartheta_0)$ as opposed to $2^{Kw(\vartheta_0)}$. Thus $\hat{\vartheta}$ tends to ϑ_0 rapidly in probability (recall that the assertion is not strong enough to conclude almost sure convergence). The proof does not exploit $\sum w_\vartheta \leq 1$, but only $w_\vartheta \leq 1$, hence the assertion even holds for a maximum likelihood estimator (i.e. $w_\vartheta = 1$ for all $\vartheta \in \Theta$). The theorem generalizes to i.i.d. classes. For the example in Proposition 5, the instantaneous bound implies that the bulk of losses occurs very late. This does *not* hold for general (non-i.i.d.) model classes: The losses in [7, Example 9] grow linearly in the first n steps.

We will now state our main positive result that upper bounds the cumulative loss in terms of the negative logarithm of the true weight and the *arrangement* of the false parameters. We will only give the proof idea – which is similar to that of Proposition 5 – and omit the lengthy and tedious technical details.

Consider the cumulated sum square error $\sum_n \mathbf{E}(\vartheta^{(\alpha,n)} - \vartheta_0)^2$. In order to upper bound this quantity, we will partition the open unit interval $(0,1)$ into a sequence of intervals $(I_k)_{k=1}^\infty$, each of measure 2^{-k}. (More precisely: Each I_k is either an interval or a union of two intervals.) Then we will estimate the contribution of each interval to the cumulated square error,

$$C(k) = \sum_{n=1}^\infty \sum_{\alpha \in A_n, \vartheta^{(\alpha,n)} \in I_k} p(\alpha|n)(\vartheta^{(\alpha,n)} - \vartheta_0)^2$$

(compare (3) and (5)). Note that $\vartheta^{(\alpha,n)} \in I_k$ precisely reads $\vartheta^{(\alpha,n)} \in I_k \cap \Theta$, but for convenience we generally assume $\vartheta \in \Theta$ for all ϑ being considered. This partitioning is also used for α, i.e. define the contribution $C(k,j)$ of $\vartheta \in I_k$ where $\alpha \in I_j$ as

$$C(k,j) = \sum_{n=1}^\infty \sum_{\alpha \in A_n \cap I_j, \vartheta^{(\alpha,n)} \in I_k} p(\alpha|n)(\vartheta^{(\alpha,n)} - \vartheta_0)^2.$$

We need to distinguish between α that are located close to ϑ_0 and α that are located far from ϑ_0. "Close" will be roughly equivalent to $j > k$, "far" will be approximately $j \leq k$. So we get $\sum_n \mathbf{E}(\vartheta^{(\alpha,n)} - \vartheta_0)^2 = \sum_k^\infty C(k) = \sum_k \sum_j C(k,j)$. In the proof,

$$p(\alpha|n) \overset{\times}{\leq} [n\alpha(1-\alpha)]^{-\frac{1}{2}} \exp\left[-nD(\alpha\|\vartheta_0)\right]$$

is often applied, which holds by Lemma 3 (recall that $f \overset{\times}{\leq} g$ stands for $f = O(g)$). Terms like $D(\alpha\|\vartheta_0)$, arising in this context and others, can be further estimated using Lemma 2. We now give the constructions of intervals I_k and complementary intervals J_k.

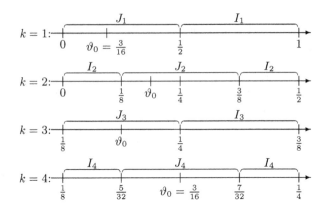

Fig. 1. Example of the first four intervals for $\vartheta_0 = \frac{3}{16}$. We have an l-step, a c-step, an l-step and another c-step. All following steps will be also c-steps.

Definition 7. Let $\vartheta_0 \in \Theta$ be given. Start with $J_0 = [0,1)$. Let $J_{k-1} = [\vartheta_k^l, \vartheta_k^r)$ and define $d_k = \vartheta_k^r - \vartheta_k^l = 2^{-k+1}$. Then $I_k, J_k \subset J_{k-1}$ are constructed from J_{k-1} according to the following rules.

$$\vartheta_0 \in [\vartheta_k^l, \vartheta_k^l + \tfrac{3}{8}d_k) \Rightarrow J_k = [\vartheta_k^l, \vartheta_k^l + \tfrac{1}{2}d_k), \; I_k = [\vartheta_k^l + \tfrac{1}{2}d_k, \vartheta_k^r), \quad (6)$$

$$\vartheta_0 \in [\vartheta_k^l + \tfrac{3}{8}d_k, \vartheta_k^l + \tfrac{5}{8}d_k) \Rightarrow J_k = [\vartheta_k^l + \tfrac{1}{4}d_k, \vartheta_k^l + \tfrac{3}{4}d_k), \quad (7)$$

$$I_k = [\vartheta_k^l, \vartheta_k^l + \tfrac{1}{4}d_k) \cup [\vartheta_k^l + \tfrac{3}{4}d_k, \vartheta_k^r),$$

$$\vartheta_0 \in [\vartheta_k^l + \tfrac{5}{8}d_k, \vartheta_k^r) \Rightarrow J_k = [\vartheta_k^l + \tfrac{1}{2}d_k, \vartheta_k^r), \; I_k = [\vartheta_k^l, \vartheta_k^l + \tfrac{1}{2}d_k). \quad (8)$$

We call the kth step of the interval construction an *l-step* if (6) applies, a *c-step* if (7) applies, and an *r-step* if (8) applies, respectively. Fig. 1 shows an example for the interval construction.

Clearly, this is not the only possible way to define an interval construction. Maybe the reader wonders why we did not center the intervals around ϑ_0. In fact, this construction would equally work for the proof. However, its definition would not be easier, since one still has to treat the case where ϑ_0 is located close to the boundary. Moreover, our construction has the nice property that the interval bounds are finite binary fractions. Given the interval construction, we can identify the $\vartheta \in I_k$ with lowest complexity:

$$\vartheta_k^I = \arg\min\{Kw(\vartheta) : \vartheta \in I_k \cap \Theta\},$$
$$\vartheta_k^J = \arg\min\{Kw(\vartheta) : \vartheta \in J_k \cap \Theta\}, \text{ and}$$
$$\Delta(k) = \max\{Kw(\vartheta_k^I) - Kw(\vartheta_k^J), 0\}.$$

If there is no $\vartheta \in I_k \cap \Theta$, we set $\Delta(k) = Kw(\vartheta_k^I) = \infty$.

Theorem 8. Let $\Theta \subset [0,1]$ be countable, $\vartheta_0 \in \Theta$, and $w_\vartheta = 2^{-Kw(\vartheta)}$, where $Kw(\vartheta)$ is some complexity measure on Θ. Let $\Delta(k)$ be as introduced in the last paragraph, then

$$\sum_{n=0}^{\infty} \mathbf{E}(\vartheta_0 - \vartheta^x)^2 \overset{\times}{\le} Kw(\vartheta_0) + \sum_{k=1}^{\infty} 2^{-\Delta(k)}\sqrt{\Delta(k)}.$$

The proof is omitted. But we briefly discuss the assertion of this theorem. It states an error bound in terms of the arrangement of the false parameters which directly depends on the interval construction. As already indicated, a different interval construction would do as well, provided that it exponentially contracts to the true parameter. For a reasonable distribution of parameters, we might expect that $\Delta(k)$ increases linearly for k large enough, and thus $\sum 2^{-\Delta(k)}\sqrt{\Delta(k)}$ remains bounded. In the next section, we identify cases where this holds.

5   Uniformly Distributed Weights

We are now able to state some positive results following from Theorem 8.

Theorem 9. *Let* $\Theta \subset [0,1]$ *be a countable class of parameters and* $\vartheta_0 \in \Theta$ *the true parameter. Assume that there are constants* $a \geq 1$ *and* $b \geq 0$ *such that*

$$\min\left\{Kw(\vartheta) : \vartheta \in [\vartheta_0 - 2^{-k}, \vartheta_0 + 2^{-k}] \cap \Theta, \vartheta \neq \vartheta_0\right\} \geq \frac{k - b}{a} \qquad (9)$$

holds for all $k > aKw(\vartheta_0) + b$. *Then we have*

$$\sum_{n=0}^{\infty} \mathbf{E}(\vartheta_0 - \vartheta^x)^2 \overset{\times}{\leq} aKw(\vartheta_0) + b \overset{\times}{\leq} Kw(\vartheta_0).$$

Proof. We have to show that

$$\sum_{k=1}^{\infty} 2^{-\Delta(k)}\sqrt{\Delta(k)} \overset{\times}{\leq} aKw(\vartheta_0) + b,$$

then the assertion follows from Theorem 8. Let $k_1 = \lceil aKw(\vartheta_0) + b + 1 \rceil$ and $k' = k - k_1$. It is not hard to see that $\max_{\vartheta \in I_k} |\vartheta - \vartheta_0| \leq 2^{-k+1}$ holds. Together with (9), this implies

$$\sum_{k=1}^{\infty} 2^{-\Delta(k)}\sqrt{\Delta(k)} \leq \sum_{k=1}^{k_1} 1 + \sum_{k=k_1+1}^{\infty} 2^{-Kw(\vartheta_k^I) + Kw(\vartheta_0)}\sqrt{Kw(\vartheta_k^I) - Kw(\vartheta_0)}$$

$$\leq k_1 + 2^{Kw(\vartheta_0)} \sum_{k=k_1+1}^{\infty} 2^{-\frac{k-b}{a}}\sqrt{\frac{k-b}{a}}$$

$$\leq k_1 + 2^{Kw(\vartheta_0)} \sum_{k'=1}^{\infty} 2^{-\frac{k'+k_1-b}{a}}\sqrt{\frac{k'+k_1-b}{a}}$$

$$\leq aKw(\vartheta_0) + b + 2 + \sum_{k'=1}^{\infty} 2^{-\frac{k'}{a}}\sqrt{\frac{k'}{a} + Kw(\vartheta_0)}.$$

Observe $\sqrt{\frac{k'}{a} + Kw(\vartheta_0)} \leq \sqrt{\frac{k'}{a}} + \sqrt{Kw(\vartheta_0)}$, $\sum_{k'} 2^{-\frac{k'}{a}} \overset{\times}{\leq} a$, and by Lemma 4 (i), $\sum_{k'} 2^{-\frac{k'}{a}}\sqrt{\frac{k'}{a}} \overset{\times}{\leq} a$. Then the assertion follows. $\qquad\square$

Letting $j = \frac{k-b}{a}$, (9) asserts that parameters ϑ with complexity $Kw(\vartheta) = j$ must have a minimum distance of 2^{-ja-b} from ϑ_0. That is, if parameters with equal weights are (approximately) uniformly distributed in the neighborhood of ϑ_0, in the sense that they are not too close to each other, then fast convergence holds. The next two results are special cases based on the set of all finite binary fractions,

$$\mathbb{Q}_{\mathbb{B}^*} = \{\vartheta = 0.\beta_1\beta_2\ldots\beta_{n-1}1 : n \in \mathbb{N}, \beta_i \in \mathbb{B}\} \cup \{0,1\}.$$

If $\vartheta = 0.\beta_1\beta_2\ldots\beta_{n-1}1 \in \mathbb{Q}_{\mathbb{B}^*}$, its length is $\ell(\vartheta) = n$. Moreover, there is a binary code $\beta_1'\ldots\beta_{n'}'$ for n, having at most $n' \leq \lfloor\log_2(n+1)\rfloor$ bits. Then $0\beta_1'0\beta_2'\ldots0\beta_{n'}'1\beta_1\ldots\beta_{n-1}$ is a prefix-code for ϑ. For completeness, we can define the codes for $\vartheta = 0,1$ to be 10 and 11, respectively. So we may define a complexity measure on $\mathbb{Q}_{\mathbb{B}^*}$ by

$$Kw(0) = 2, \ Kw(1) = 2, \text{ and } Kw(\vartheta) = \ell(\vartheta) + 2\lfloor\log_2(\ell(\vartheta)+1)\rfloor \text{ for } \vartheta \neq 0,1. \tag{10}$$

There are other similar simple prefix codes on $\mathbb{Q}_{\mathbb{B}^*}$ such that $Kw(\vartheta) \geq \ell(\vartheta)$.

Corollary 10. *Let* $\Theta = \mathbb{Q}_{\mathbb{B}^*}$, $\vartheta_0 \in \Theta$ *and* $Kw(\vartheta) \geq \ell(\vartheta)$, *then* $\sum_n \mathbf{E}(\vartheta_0 - \vartheta^x)^2 \overset{\times}{\leq} Kw(\vartheta_0)$ *holds.*

The proof is trivial, since Condition (9) holds with $a = 1$ and $b = 0$. This is a special case of a uniform distribution of parameters with equal complexities. The next corollary is more general, it proves fast convergence if the uniform distribution is distorted by some function φ.

Corollary 11. *Let* $\varphi : [0,1] \to [0,1]$ *be an injective, N times continuously differentiable function. Let* $\Theta = \varphi(\mathbb{Q}_{\mathbb{B}^*})$, $Kw(\varphi(t)) \geq \ell(t)$ *for all* $t \in \mathbb{Q}_{\mathbb{B}^*}$, *and* $\vartheta_0 = \varphi(t_0)$ *for a* $t_0 \in \mathbb{Q}_{\mathbb{B}^*}$. *Assume that there is $n \leq N$ and $\varepsilon > 0$ such that*

$$\left|\frac{d^n\varphi}{dt^n}(t)\right| \geq c > 0 \text{ for all } t \in [t_0 - \varepsilon, t_0 + \varepsilon] \text{ and}$$

$$\frac{d^m\varphi}{dt^m}(t_0) = 0 \text{ for all } 1 \leq m < n.$$

Then we have

$$\sum \mathbf{E}(\vartheta_0 - \vartheta^x)^2 \overset{\times}{\leq} nKw(\vartheta_0) + 2\log_2(n!) - 2\log_2 c + n\log_2\varepsilon \overset{\times}{\leq} nKw(\vartheta_0).$$

Proof. Fix $j > Kw(\vartheta_0)$, then

$$Kw(\varphi(t)) \geq j \text{ for all } t \in [t_0 - 2^{-j}, t_0 + 2^{-j}] \cap \mathbb{Q}_{\mathbb{B}^*}. \tag{11}$$

Moreover, for all $t \in [t_0 - 2^{-j}, t_0 + 2^{-j}]$, Taylor's theorem asserts that

$$\varphi(t) = \varphi(t_0) + \frac{\frac{d^n\varphi}{dt^n}(\tilde{t})}{n!}(t - t_0)^n \tag{12}$$

for some $\tilde{t}$ in (t_0, t) (or (t, t_0) if $t < t_0$). We request in addition $2^{-j} \leq \varepsilon$, then $\left|\frac{d^n \varphi}{dt^n}\right| \geq c$ by assumption. Apply (12) to $t = t_0 + 2^{-j}$ and $t = t_0 - 2^{-j}$ and define $k = \lceil jn + \log_2(n!) - \log_2 c \rceil$ in order to obtain $|\varphi(t_0 + 2^{-j}) - \vartheta_0| \geq 2^{-k}$ and $|\varphi(t_0 - 2^{-j}) - \vartheta_0| \geq 2^{-k}$. By injectivity of φ, we see that $\varphi(t) \notin [\vartheta_0 - 2^{-k}, \vartheta_0 + 2^{-k}]$ if $t \notin [t_0 - 2^{-j}, t_0 + 2^{-j}]$. Together with (11), this implies

$$Kw(\vartheta) \geq j \geq \frac{k - \log_2(n!) + \log_2 c - 1}{n} \quad \text{for all } \vartheta \in [\vartheta_0 - 2^{-k}, \vartheta_0 + 2^{-k}] \cap \Theta.$$

This is condition (9) with $a = n$ and $b = \log_2(n!) - \log_2 c + 1$. Finally, the assumption $2^{-j} \leq \varepsilon$ holds if $k \geq k_1 = n \log_2 \varepsilon + \log_2(n!) - \log_2 c + 1$. This gives an additional contribution to the error of at most k_1. □

Corollary 11 shows an implication of Theorem 8 for *parameter identification*: A class of models is given by a set of parameters $\mathbb{Q}_{\mathbb{B}*}$ and a mapping $\varphi : \mathbb{Q}_{\mathbb{B}*} \to \Theta$. The task is to identify the true parameter t_0 or its image $\vartheta_0 = \varphi(t_0)$. The injectivity of φ is not necessary for fast convergence, but it facilitates the proof. The assumptions of Corollary 11 are satisfied if φ is for example a polynomial. In fact, it should be possible to prove fast convergence of MDL for many common parameter identification problems. For sets of parameters other than $\mathbb{Q}_{\mathbb{B}*}$, e.g. the set of all rational numbers $\mathbb{Q}$, similar corollaries can easily be proven.

How large is the constant hidden in "$\overset{\times}{\leq}$"? When examining carefully the proof of Theorem 8, the resulting constant is quite large. This is mainly due to the frequent "wasting" of small constants. Supposably a smaller bound holds as well, perhaps 16. On the other hand, for the actual *true* expectation (as opposed to its upper bound) and complexities as in (10), numerical simulations indicate that $\sum_n \mathbf{E}(\vartheta_0 - \vartheta^x)^2 \leq \frac{1}{2} Kw(\vartheta_0)$.

Finally, we state an implication which almost trivially follows from Theorem 8, since there $\sum_k 2^{-\Delta(k)} \sqrt{\Delta(k)} \leq N$ is obvious. However, it may be very useful for practical purposes, e.g. for hypothesis testing.

Corollary 12. *Let Θ contain N elements, $Kw(\cdot)$ be any complexity function on Θ, and $\vartheta_0 \in \Theta$. Then we have*

$$\sum_{n=1}^{\infty} \mathbf{E}(\vartheta_0 - \vartheta^x)^2 \overset{\times}{\leq} N + Kw(\vartheta_0).$$

6   The Universal Case

We briefly discuss the important universal setup, where $Kw(\cdot)$ is (up to an additive constant) equal to the prefix Kolmogorov complexity K (that is the length of the shortest self-delimiting program printing ϑ on some universal Turing machine). Since $\sum_k 2^{-K(k)} \sqrt{K(k)} = \infty$ no matter how late the sum starts (otherwise there would be a shorter code for large k), we cannot apply Theorem 8. This means in particular that we do not even obtain our previous result, Theorem 1. But probably the following strengthening of the theorem holds under the same conditions, which then easily implies Theorem 1 up to a constant.

Conjecture 13. $\sum_n \mathbf{E}(\vartheta_0 - \vartheta^x)^2 \overset{\times}{\leq} K(\vartheta_0) + \sum_k 2^{-\Delta(k)}$.

Then, take an incompressible finite binary fraction $\vartheta_0 \in \mathbb{Q}_{\mathbb{B}^*}$, i.e. $K(\vartheta_0) \overset{\pm}{=} \ell(\vartheta_0) + K(\ell(\vartheta_0))$. For $k > \ell(\vartheta_0)$, we can reconstruct ϑ_0 and k from ϑ_k^I and $\ell(\vartheta_0)$ by just truncating ϑ_k^I after $\ell(\vartheta_0)$ bits. Thus $K(\vartheta_k^I) + K(\ell(\vartheta_0)) \overset{\times}{\geq} K(\vartheta_0) + K(k|\vartheta_0, K(\vartheta_0))$ holds. Using Conjecture 13, we obtain

$$\sum_n \mathbf{E}(\vartheta_0 - \vartheta^x)^2 \overset{\times}{\leq} K(\vartheta_0) + 2^{K(\ell(\vartheta_0))} \overset{\times}{\leq} \ell(\vartheta_0)\big(\log_2 \ell(\vartheta_0)\big)^2, \tag{13}$$

where the last inequality follows from the example coding given in (10). So, under Conjecture 13, we obtain a bound which slightly exceeds the complexity $K(\vartheta_0)$ if ϑ_0 has a certain structure. It is not obvious if the same holds for all computable ϑ_0. In order to answer this question positive, one could try to use something like [11, Eq.(2.1)]. This statement implies that as soon as $K(k) \geq K_1$ for all $k \geq k_1$, we have $\sum_{k \geq k_1} 2^{-K(k)} \overset{\times}{\leq} 2^{-K_1} K_1 (\log_2 K_1)^2$. It is possible to prove an analogous result for ϑ_k^I instead of k, however we have not found an appropriate coding that does without knowing ϑ_0. Since the resulting bound is exponential in the code length, we therefore have not gained anything.

Another problem concerns the size of the multiplicative constant that is hidden in the upper bound. Unlike in the case of uniformly distributed weights, it is now of exponential size, i.e. $2^{O(1)}$. This is no artifact of the proof, as the following example shows.

Example 14. Let U be some universal Turing machine. We construct a second universal Turing machine U' from U as follows: Let $N \geq 1$. If the input of U' is $1^N p$, where 1^N is the string consisting of N ones and p is some program, then U will be executed on p. If the input of U' is 0^N, then U' outputs $\frac{1}{2}$. Otherwise, if the input of U' is x with $x \in \mathbb{B}^N \setminus \{0^N, 1^N\}$, then U' outputs $\frac{1}{2} + 2^{-x-1}$. For $\vartheta_0 = \frac{1}{2}$, the conditions of a slight generalization of Proposition 5 are satisfied (where the complexity is relative to U'), thus $\sum_n \mathbf{E}(\vartheta^x - \vartheta_0)^2 \overset{\times}{\geq} 2^N$.

Can this also happen if the underlying universal Turing machine is not "strange" in some sense, like U', but "natural"? Again this is not obvious. One would have to define first a "natural" universal Turing machine which rules out cases like U'. If N is not too large, then one can even argue that U' *is* natural in the sense that its compiler constant relative to U is small.

There is a relation to the class of all *deterministic* (generally non-i.i.d.) measures. For this setup, MDL predicts the next symbol just according to the *monotone complexity Km*, see [12]. According to [12, Theorem 5], 2^{-Km} is very close to the universal semimeasure M (this is due to [13]). Then the total prediction error (which is defined slightly differently in this case) can be shown to be bounded by $2^{O(1)} Km(x_{<\infty})^3$ [14]. The similarity to the (unproven) bound (13) "huge constant $\times$ polynomial" for the universal Bernoulli case is evident.

7   Discussion and Conclusions

We have discovered the fact that the instantaneous and the cumulative loss bounds can be *incompatible*. On the one hand, the cumulative loss for MDL predictions may be exponential, i.e. $2^{Kw(\vartheta_0)}$. Thus it implies almost sure convergence at a slow rate, even for arbitrary discrete model classes [7]. On the other hand, the instantaneous loss is always of order $\frac{1}{n}Kw(\vartheta_0)$, implying fast convergence in probability and a cumulative loss bound of $Kw(\vartheta_0)\ln n$. Similar logarithmic loss bounds can be found in the literature for continuous model classes [2].

A different approach to assess convergence speed is presented in [4]. There in index of resolvability is introduced, which can be interpreted as the difference of the expected MDL code length and the expected code length under the true model. For discrete model classes, they show that the index of resolvability converges to zero as $\frac{1}{n}Kw(\vartheta_0)$ [4, Equation (6.2)]. Moreover, they give a convergence of the predictive distributions in terms of the Hellinger distance [4, Theorem 4]. This implies a cumulative (Hellinger) loss bound of $Kw(\vartheta_0)\ln n$ and therefore fast convergence in probability.

If the prior weights are arranged nicely, we have proven a small finite loss bound $Kw(\vartheta_0)$ for MDL (Theorem 8). If parameters of equal complexity are uniformly distributed or not too strongly distorted (Theorem 9 and Corollaries), then the error is within a small multiplicative constant of the complexity $Kw(\vartheta_0)$. This may be applied e.g. for the case of parameter identification (Corollary 11). A similar result holds if Θ is finite and contains only few parameters (Corollary 12), which may be e.g. satisfied for hypothesis testing. In these cases and many others, one can interpret the conditions for fast convergence as the presence of prior knowledge. One can show that if a predictor converges to the correct model, then it performs also well under arbitrarily chosen bounded loss-functions [15, Theorem 4]. Moreover, we can then conclude good properties for other machine learning tasks such as classification, as discussed in the introduction. From an information theoretic viewpoint one may interpret the conditions for a small bound in Theorem 8 as "good codes".

The main restriction of our positive result is the fact that we have proved it only for the Bernoulli case. We therefore argue that it generalizes to arbitrary i.i.d settings. Let $\vartheta_0 \in [0,1]^N$, $\sum_i \vartheta_0^{(i)} = 1$ be a probability vector that generates sequences of i.i.d. samples in $\{1,\ldots,N\}^\infty$. Assume that ϑ_0 stays away from the boundary (the other case is treated similarly). Then we can define a sequence of nested sets in dimension $N-1$ in analogy to the interval construction. The main points of the proof are now the following two: First, for an observed parameter α far from ϑ_0, the probability of α decays exponentially, and second, for α close to ϑ_0, some ϑ far from ϑ_0 can contribute at most for short time. These facts hold in the general i.i.d case like in the Bernoulli case. However, the rigorous proof of it is yet more complicated and technical than for the Bernoulli case. (Compare the proof of the main result in [2].)

We conclude with an open question. In abstract terms, we have proven a convergence result for the Bernoulli (or i.i.d) case by mainly exploiting the *geometry* of the space of distributions. This is in principle very easy, since for Bernoulli this space is just the unit interval, for i.i.d it is the space of probability vectors. It is not obvious how (or if at all) this approach can be transferred to general (computable) measures.

References

[1] Clarke, B.S., Barron, A.R.: Information-theoretic asymptotics of Bayes methods. IEEE Trans. on Information Theory **36** (1990) 453–471

[2] Rissanen, J.J.: Fisher Information and Stochastic Complexity. IEEE Trans. on Information Theory **42** (1996) 40–47

[3] Barron, A.R., Rissanen, J.J., Yu, B.: The minimum description length principle in coding and modeling. IEEE Trans. on Information Theory **44** (1998) 2743–2760

[4] Barron, A.R., Cover, T.M.: Minimum complexity density estimation. IEEE Trans. on Information Theory **37** (1991) 1034–1054

[5] Solomonoff, R.J.: Complexity-based induction systems: comparisons and convergence theorems. IEEE Trans. Information Theory **IT-24** (1978) 422–432

[6] Hutter, M.: Convergence and error bounds for universal prediction of nonbinary sequences. Proc. 12th Eurpean Conference on Machine Learning (ECML-2001) (2001) 239–250

[7] Poland, J., Hutter, M.: Convergence of discrete MDL for sequential prediction. In: 17th Annual Conference on Learning Theory (COLT). (2004) 300–314

[8] Vovk, V.G.: Learning about the parameter of the bernoulli model. Journal of Computer and System Sciences **55** (1997) 96–104

[9] Vitányi, P.M., Li, M.: Minimum description length induction, Bayesianism, and Kolmogorov complexity. IEEE Trans. on Information Theory **46** (2000) 446–464

[10] Li, M., Vitányi, P.M.B.: An introduction to Kolmogorov complexity and its applications. 2nd edn. Springer (1997)

[11] Gács, P.: On the relation between descriptional complexity and algorithmic probability. Theoretical Computer Science **22** (1983) 71–93

[12] Hutter, M.: Sequence prediction based on monotone complexity. In: Proc. 16th Annual Conference on Learning Theory (COLT-2003). Lecture Notes in Artificial Intelligence, Berlin, Springer (2003) 506–521

[13] Zvonkin, A.K., Levin, L.A.: The complexity of finite objects and the development of the concepts of information and randomness by means of the theory of algorithms. Russian Mathematical Surveys **25** (1970) 83–124

[14] Hutter, M.: Sequential predictions based on algorithmic complexity. Technical report (2004) IDSIA-16-04.

[15] Hutter, M.: Convergence and loss bounds for Bayesian sequence prediction. IEEE Trans. on Information Theory **49** (2003) 2061–2067

Relative Loss Bounds and Polynomial-Time Predictions for the K-LMS-NET Algorithm

Mark Herbster[*]

Department of Computer Science
University College London
Gower Street, London WC1E 6BT, UK
M.Herbster@cs.ucl.ac.uk

Abstract. We consider a two-layer network algorithm. The first layer consists of an uncountable number of linear units. Each linear unit is an *LMS* algorithm whose inputs are first "kernelized." Each unit is indexed by the value of a parameter corresponding to a parameterized reproducing kernel. The first-layer outputs are then connected to an *exponential weights* algorithm which combines them to produce the final output. We give loss bounds for this algorithm; and for specific applications to prediction relative to the best convex combination of kernels, and the best width of a Gaussian kernel. The algorithm's predictions require the computation of an expectation which is a quotient of integrals as seen in a variety of Bayesian inference problems. Typically this computational problem is tackled by MCMC, importance sampling, and other sampling techniques for which there are few polynomial time guarantees of the quality of the approximation in general and none for our problem specifically. We develop a novel deterministic polynomial time approximation scheme for the computations of expectations considered in this paper.

1 Introduction

We give performance guarantees and a tractable method of computation for the two-layer network algorithm K-LMS-NET. The performance guarantees measure online performance in a non-statistical learning framework introduced by Littlestone [13,14]. Here, learning proceeds in trials $t = 1, 2, \ldots, \ell$. In each trial t the algorithm receives a *pattern* x_t. It then gives a prediction denoted $\hat{y}_t \in \mathbb{R}$. The algorithm then receives an *outcome* $y_t \in \mathbb{R}$, and incurs a loss $L(y_t, \hat{y}_t)$ measuring the discrepancy between y_t and $\hat{y}_t$; in this paper $L(y_t, \hat{y}_t) = (y_t - \hat{y}_t)^2$. A *relative loss bound* performance guarantee bounds the cumulative loss of the algorithm with the cumulative loss of any member $c : \mathcal{X} \to \mathbb{R}$ of a comparison class $\mathcal{C}$ of predictors plus an additional term. These bounds are of the following form, for all data sequences $S = \langle (x_1, y_1), (x_2, y_2), \ldots, (x_\ell, y_\ell) \rangle$,

$$\sum_{t=1}^{\ell} L(y_t, \hat{y}_t) \le \sum_{t=1}^{\ell} L(y_t, c(x_t)) + O(r(S, \mathcal{C}, c)) \quad \forall c \in \mathcal{C}$$

_____

[*] This work was supported in part by the IST Programme of the European Community, under the PASCAL Network of Excellence, IST-2002-506778.

S. Ben-David, J. Case, A. Maruoka (Eds.): ALT 2004, LNAI 3244, pp. 309–323, 2004.

where $r(S, C, c)$ is known as the *regret*, since it measures our "regret" at using our algorithm versus the "best" predictor c in the comparison class. In the ideal case the regret is a slowly growing function of the data sequence, the comparison class, and the particular predictor. Surprisingly, such bounds are possible without probabilistic assumptions on the sequence of examples.

The architecture of the K-LMS-NET algorithm is a simple chaining of two well-known online algorithms. The first layer consists of an uncountable number of linear units. Each unit is an LMS algorithm [4] whose inputs are first "kernelized." Each unit is indexed by the value of a parameter ($\alpha \in [0, 1]$) corresponding to a parameterized reproducing kernel [2], for example a Gaussian kernel and its width $k_\alpha(\mathbf{v}, \mathbf{w}) = e^{-\alpha \|\mathbf{v} - \mathbf{w}\|^2}$. The first-layer outputs are then directed to an *exponential weights* algorithm [20,14,12] which combines them to produce the final output (prediction). This topology gives an algorithm whose comparison class (hypothesis space) is a union of linear spaces of functions.

The results of this research are twofold. First, we give a general bound for the K-LMS-NET algorithm. This general bound is then applied to the problem of predicting almost as well as any function i) from the space defined by the "best" convex combination of two kernels and ii) from the space defined by the "best" width of an isotropic Gaussian kernel. Second, though the second layer combines an uncountable number of outputs from the first layer we show that the final prediction may be well-approximated in polynomial time. This prediction is an expectation (5) whose form is a quotient of integrals which does not have an analytic closed form; thus we resort to a novel sampling scheme. The significance of our sampler is that it produces a provably polynomial time approximation to our predictions. The sampler is deterministic, and relies on finding the critical points of the functions to be integrated; this leads to a limitation on the types of parameterized kernels for which we can give predictions in polynomial time. The applications for which we give bounds are among those whose predictions may be approximated in polynomial time by our sampling scheme.

1.1 Related Work

In [7] Freund applied the *exponential weights* algorithm to predicting as well as the best "biased coin" that modeled a data sequence, with an uncountable set of predictors each corresponding to a probability of "heads." In [21] an algorithm similar to ridge regression was given, where the set of predictors corresponded to each linear function on $\mathbb{R}^n$; these were then combined with an *exponential weights* algorithm. For those algorithms exact computation of the prediction was possible; exact computation, however, is not possible for the K-LMS-NET algorithm.

In [4], relative loss bounds are proven for the classical LMS algorithm; the bounds naturally apply to kernel LMS. Some recent relative-loss bounds for variants of kernel LMS have appeared in [11,9]. In contrast, our kernel function has a free parameter; hence our comparison class (hypothesis space) is not a single kernel space, but a union of kernel spaces.

The problem of learning the best parameters of a kernel function has been modeled as a regularized optimization problem in [16,15,23]. Methods based on

Gaussian process regression have proven to be practical for learning or predicting with a mixture of kernel parameterizations, for which we cite only a few of the many offline [22,8] and online algorithms [6,19] developed. The parameterized kernel function now corresponds to a parameterized covariance function. A key difference in focus is that our free parameter is a one-dimensional scalar, whereas in Gaussian process regression the free parameter vector is often in the hundreds of dimensions. The one-dimensional case we consider is certainly much simpler than the multidimensional case. However, we make no statistical assumptions on the data generation process, we give non-asymptotic relative loss bounds and we observe that even in the "simple" one-dimensional case it is not obvious how to sample so that predictions of *guaranteed* accuracy are produced in polynomial time.

The predictions (5) of K-LMS-NET algorithm are of the following (simplified) form,

$$\hat{y}_t = \frac{\int_0^1 \hat{\mathbf{y}}_t^i(\alpha) \exp(-L_{[1,t]}(\alpha)) d\alpha}{\int_0^1 \exp(-L_{[1,t]}(\alpha)) d\alpha} \quad ; \tag{1}$$

here $\hat{\mathbf{y}}_t^i(\alpha)$ and $L_{[1,t]}(\alpha)$ are the outputs and cumulative losses, respectively, of each of the kernel LMS algorithms at time t. In the applications to be discussed $\hat{\mathbf{y}}_t^i(\alpha)$ and $L_{[1,t]}(\alpha)$ reduce to either polynomials or to polynomials after a change in variables. The problem of estimating such expectations is common in Bayesian statistics. Since we cannot expect to compute $\hat{y}_t$ exactly, we consider that a good polynomial time approximation scheme for $\hat{y}_t$ should have the following property: for every $\epsilon \in (0,1)$, an *absolute* error approximation $\bar{y}_t$, should satisfy $|\bar{y}_t - \hat{y}_t| \le \epsilon$ and be computable in time polynomial in $O(\frac{1}{\epsilon})$. It is also natural to extend the previous to a randomized approximations schemes; however the scheme we produce is fully deterministic. Hoeffding bounds [10] allow one to produce an absolute error approximation for the Monte-Carlo integration of $\int f \, d\mu$, with $\bar{y} = \frac{1}{n}\sum_{i=1}^n f(x_i)$ and where x_i is sampled from the probability measure μ and $\epsilon = O(\frac{1}{\sqrt{n}})$. Hoeffding bounds are not applicable to the approximation of (1) as it is a nontrivial problem in itself to produce samples from the distribution $\frac{\exp(-L_{[1,t]}(\alpha))}{\int_0^1 \exp(-L_{[1,t]}(\alpha)) d\alpha}$ in polynomial time; nor can we can we apply Hoeffding bounds individually to the integrals in the numerator and the denominator, as absolute error bounds do not "divide" naturally. A variety of other bounds have been proven for numeric integration within the *information-based complexity* framework [18]; however, as these are absolute error bounds they are likewise not applicable. Another approach to the approximation of equations of the form (1) which has proven useful in practice for similar applications is to use one of the many variants of MCMC sampling [1]. We are not aware of any bounds for MCMC sampling methods which give a polynomial time guarantee for randomized approximation to $\hat{y}_t$ which are applicable to this research. Our sampling methodology is discussed in Sect. 3; the key to our method is to produce a sampler for 1-d integrals with a provable *relative* error approximation, which unlike the absolute error approximation, is, loosely speaking, closed under division.

1.2   Preliminaries

The symbol $\mathcal{X}$ denotes an abstract space, for example $\mathcal{X}$ could be a set of strings. Given a vector space $\langle V; +\rangle$, the sum of two subsets F and G of V is defined by $F + G = \{f + g : f \in F, g \in G\}$. A Hilbert space $\mathcal{H}$ denotes a complete inner product space. The inner product between vectors $\mathbf{v}$ and $\mathbf{w}$ in $\mathcal{H}$ is denoted by $\langle \mathbf{v}, \mathbf{w}\rangle$ and the norm by $\|\mathbf{v}\|$. In this paper, we will consider Hilbert spaces determined by a reproducing kernel $k : \mathcal{X} \times \mathcal{X} \to \mathbb{R}$. The prehilbert space induced by kernel k is the set $H_k = \text{span}(\{k(x, \cdot)\}_{\forall x \in \mathcal{X}})$ and the inner product of $f = \sum_{i=1}^m \beta_i k(x_i, \cdot)$ and $g = \sum_{j=1}^n \beta'_i k(x'_j, \cdot)$ is $\langle f, g\rangle = \sum_{i=1}^m \sum_{j=1}^n \beta_i \beta'_j k(x_i, x'_j)$. The completion of H_k is denoted $\mathcal{H}_k$. Two kernels $k_0 : \mathcal{X} \times \mathcal{X} \to \mathbb{R}$ and $k_1 : \mathcal{X}' \times \mathcal{X}' \to \mathbb{R}$ are termed *domain compatible* if $\mathcal{X} = \mathcal{X}'$. The *reproducing* property of the kernel is that given any $f \in \mathcal{H}_k$ and any $x \in \mathcal{X}$ then $f(x) = \langle f(\cdot), k(x, \cdot)\rangle$; other useful properties of reproducing kernels, and introductory material may be found in [5]. In this paper we are particularly interested in parameterized kernels k_α with an associated Hilbert Space $\mathcal{H}_\alpha$, inner product $\langle \cdot, \cdot\rangle_\alpha$, and norm $\|\cdot\|_\alpha$, for every $\alpha \in [0, 1]$. We denote the Lebesque measure of a set A by $\mu(A)$.

An *absolute ϵ-approximation* of $y \in \mathbb{R}$ by $\hat{y} \in \mathbb{R}$ satisfies

$$|y - \hat{y}| \le \epsilon \tag{2}$$

denoted by $\hat{y} \overset{a}{\approx}_\epsilon y$. A *relative ϵ-approximation* of $y \in \mathbb{R}^+$ by $\hat{y} \in \mathbb{R}^+$ satisfies

$$(1 - \epsilon)y \le \hat{y} \le (1 + \epsilon)y, \tag{3}$$

which is denoted by $\hat{y} \overset{r}{\approx}_\epsilon y$. A polynomial ϵ-approximation scheme requires for each $\epsilon \in (0, 1)$ that we can compute $\hat{y}$ s.t. $\hat{y} \approx_\epsilon y$ in time $O(\frac{1}{\epsilon})$. For simplicity, we describe the time complexity of our algorithms in terms of a naive real-valued model of computation, where arithmetic operations on real numbers, e.g., addition, exponentiation, kernel evaluation, etc., all require $O(1)$ "steps."

2   The K-LMS-NET Algorithm

The following general bound for the K-LMS-NET algorithm is applied to predicting as well as the convex combination of two kernels and predicting as well as the best width of a Gaussian kernel over a discretized domain.

Theorem 1. *The* K-LMS-NET *algorithm with parameterized kernel function* k_α *($\alpha \in [0, 1]$) with any data sequence* $\langle (x_1, y_1), (x_2, y_2), \dots, (x_\ell, y_\ell)\rangle \in (\mathcal{X}, [r_1, r_2])^\ell$ *when the algorithm is tuned with constants* $r_1, r_2,$ *and* $\eta,$ *the total square loss of the algorithm will satisfy*

$$\sum_{t=1}^\ell L(y_t, \hat{y}_t) \le \sup_{\alpha \in \mathcal{A}} \left[\sum_{t=1}^\ell L(y_t, h_\alpha(x_t))\right] + 2\sqrt{\hat{L}_\mathcal{A}\hat{H}_\mathcal{A}\hat{X}_\mathcal{A}} + \hat{H}_\mathcal{A}^2\hat{X}_\mathcal{A}^2 + 2(r_2 - r_1)^2 \ln\frac{1}{\mu(\mathcal{A})} \tag{8}$$

for all measurable sets $\mathcal{A} \subseteq [0, 1]$ *for all tuples of functions* $(h_\alpha)_{\alpha \in \mathcal{A}} \in \prod_{\alpha \in \mathcal{A}} \mathcal{H}_\alpha$ *and for all constants* $\hat{L}_\mathcal{A}, \hat{H}_\mathcal{A},$ *and,* $\hat{X}_\mathcal{A},$ *where for all* $\alpha \in \mathcal{A}$ *the following four conditions must hold:* $\sum_{t=1}^\ell L(y_t, h_\alpha(x_t)) \le \hat{L}_\mathcal{A}, \|h_\alpha\|_\alpha^2 \le \hat{H}_\mathcal{A}^2, \forall t : k_\alpha(x_t, x_t) \le \hat{X}_\mathcal{A}^2,$ *and* $\eta = [1 + \frac{\sqrt{\hat{L}_\mathcal{A}}}{\hat{H}_\mathcal{A}\hat{X}_\mathcal{A}})\hat{X}_\mathcal{A}^2]^{-1}.$

Parameters: $\mathcal{X}$: a pattern space;
$\quad k_\alpha : \mathcal{X} \times \mathcal{X} \rightarrow \mathbb{R}$: a parameterized kernel function ($\alpha \in [0,1]$);
$\quad \{\mathcal{H}_\alpha\}$: a set of Hilbert spaces induced by k_α;
$\quad \eta$: a learning rate; $[r_1, r_2]$: an outcome range.

Data: An online sequence $\langle (x_1, y_1), (x_2, y_2), \ldots, (x_\ell, y_\ell) \rangle \in (\mathcal{X}, [r_1, r_2])^\ell$.

Initialization: $r = (r_2 - r_1)$, $\mathbf{w}^i_{\alpha,1}(x) = \mathbf{0}$, $\mathbf{w}^{ii}_1(\alpha) = 1$,
$\quad \Phi^i(x) = \max(r_1, \min(r_2, x))$; $\Phi^{ii}_t(w) = \max(\exp(-\frac{t}{2}), w)$.

for $t = 1, \ldots, \ell$ **do**
$\quad$ **Predict**: receive x_t,

$$\hat{\mathbf{y}}^i_t(\alpha) = \mathbf{w}^i_{\alpha,t}(x_t) = \eta \sum_{j=1}^{t-1} (y_j - \hat{\mathbf{y}}^i_j(\alpha)) k_\alpha(x_j, x_t) \qquad (4)$$

$$\hat{y}_t = \frac{\int_0^1 \mathbf{w}^{ii}_t(\alpha) \Phi^i(\hat{\mathbf{y}}^i_t(\alpha)) d\alpha}{\int_0^1 \mathbf{w}^{ii}_t(\alpha) d\alpha} \qquad (5)$$

$\quad$ **Update**: receive y_t,

$$\mathbf{w}^i_{\alpha, t+1}(x) = \mathbf{w}^i_{\alpha, t}(x) + \eta(y_t - \hat{\mathbf{y}}^i_t(\alpha)) k_\alpha(x_t, x) \qquad (6)$$

$$L_{[1,t]}(\alpha) = L_{[1,t-1]}(\alpha) + (y_t - \hat{\mathbf{y}}^i_t(\alpha))^2$$

$$\mathbf{w}^{ii}_{t+1}(\alpha) = \Phi^{ii}_t(\exp(\frac{1}{2r^2} L_{[1,t]}(\alpha))) \qquad (7)$$

end

Algorithm 1: K-LMS-NET algorithm

The bound is a straightforward chaining of the well known loss bounds [4] of the LMS (GD) algorithm and a variant of the *exponential weights* algorithm [20,14, 12] that implements direct clipping of the inputs to guarantee a loss bound and an amortized clipping of the cumulative loss to enable efficient sampling.

The generic bound given is neither a pure relative loss bound nor does it give an indication of whether the K-LMS-NET is polynomially tractable for a particular parameterized kernel. The bound is not a "pure" relative loss bound insofar as the regret (the final term of (8)) for any particular predictor is infinite (since $\mathcal{A}$ is then a point set thus $\frac{1}{\mu(\mathcal{A})} = \infty$). A pure relative loss bound may be given if we can determine how the loss and the norm of a particular predictor in $\mathcal{H}_{\alpha'}$ is related to near comparable predictors in $\mathcal{H}_{\alpha''}$ when $|\alpha' - \alpha''|$ is small. In the following we "flesh out" the generic bound of Theorem 1 by giving pure relative loss bounds for two particular parameterized kernels; then in Sect. 3 we sketch how the prediction with these kernels is computable by a polynomial-time approximation scheme.

2.1 Applications to Specific Parameterized Kernels

Relative loss bounds are given in Theorems 4 and 5 for a parameterized kernel which is a parameterized convex combination of kernels and for a Gaussian kernel with a parameterized width, respectively. Each of these bounds given are in terms of adjunct norms $\mathcal{C}(\cdot)$ and $\mathcal{S}(\cdot)$ on the kernel spaces rather than the norms inherited from the underlying kernel space. The norms $\mathcal{C}(\cdot)$ and $\mathcal{S}(\cdot)$ are tighter and weaker, respectively, than their inherited norm $\|\cdot\|_\alpha$. The proofs of the theorems follow directly from Theorem 1 in conjunction with Lemmas 5 and 6 which appear in Appendix A.

Predicting Almost as Well as the Best Convex Combination of Two Kernels. We consider the convex combination of two domain-compatible kernels. Hence our parameterized kernel function $k_\alpha = (1-\alpha)k_0 + \alpha k_1$ where k_0 and k_1 are two distinct kernel functions. We further require in this abstract that the corresponding Hilbert spaces $\mathcal{H}_0$ and $\mathcal{H}_1$ be disjoint except for the zero function, i.e., $\mathcal{H}_0 \bigcap \mathcal{H}_1 = \{\mathbf{0}\}$. Typical kernel spaces that are disjoint except for the zero, include spaces derived from polynomial kernels of differing degree and wavelet kernels at two distinct levels of resolution. The following useful theorem from Aronszajn [2] gives a basis for our following observations.

Theorem 2 ([2]). *If k_i are the domain-compatible kernels of Hilbert spaces $\mathcal{H}_i$ with the norms $\|\cdot\|_i$, then $k = k_0 + k_1$ is the kernel of Hilbert space $\mathcal{H} = \mathcal{H}_0 + \mathcal{H}_1$ of all functions $f = f_0 + f_1$ with $f_i \in \mathcal{H}_i$, and with the norm defined by*

$$\|f\|^2 = \inf \left[\|f_0\|_0^2 + \|f_1\|_1^2 \right] ,$$

which is the infimum taken for all decompositions $f = f_0 + f_1$ with $f_i \in \mathcal{H}_i$.

Therefore given $\alpha', \alpha'' \in (0,1)$ the three sets $\mathcal{H}_{\alpha'}$, $\mathcal{H}_{\alpha''}$, and $\bigcup_{\alpha \in [0,1]} \mathcal{H}_\alpha$ contain exactly the same functions; however in general $\|f\|_{\alpha'} \neq \|f\|_{\alpha''}$. Observe that with the assumption $\mathcal{H}_0 \bigcap \mathcal{H}_1 = \{\mathbf{0}\}$ any function $f \in \bigcup_{\alpha \in [0,1]} \mathcal{H}_\alpha$ has a unique decomposition $f = f_0 + f_1$ with $f_i \in \mathcal{H}_i$. Given the decomposition we can compute the norm of f in any particular $\mathcal{H}_\alpha$ via

$$\|f\|_\alpha^2 = \frac{1}{1-\alpha} \|f_0\|_0^2 + \frac{1}{\alpha} \|f_1\|_1^2, \quad \alpha \in (0,1) , \tag{9}$$

since for a scaled kernel $k' = \beta k$ the norm is rescaled as $\|f\|_{k'}^2 = \frac{1}{\beta} \|f\|_k^2$. We may define the following norm over $\mathcal{H}_0 + \mathcal{H}_1$.

Definition 1. *Given domain-compatible kernels k_0 and k_1 such that $\mathcal{H}_0 \bigcap \mathcal{H}_1 = \{\mathbf{0}\}$ let $k_\alpha = (1-\alpha)k_0 + \alpha k_1$ then given $f \in \mathcal{H}_0 + \mathcal{H}_1$. Define $\mathcal{C}(f)$ by*

$$\mathcal{C}^2(f) = \inf_{\alpha \in [0,1]} \|f\|_\alpha^2 . \tag{10}$$

The following theorem gives a canonical form for $\mathcal{C}(f)$.

Theorem 3. *Given $f = f_0 + f_1$ such that $f_i \in \mathcal{H}_i$ and $\mathcal{H}_0 \bigcap \mathcal{H}_1 = \{\mathbf{0}\}$ then*

$$\mathcal{C}^2(f) = (\|f_0\|_0 + \|f_1\|_1)^2 . \tag{11}$$

Proof. The theorem immediately follows from the substitution of the minimizer $\alpha = \frac{\|f_1\|}{\|f_0\| + \|f_1\|}$ into (9). $\square$

A recent generalization of this canonical form is given in [15, Lemma A.2].

Theorem 4. *Given the* K-LMS-NET *algorithm tuned with learning rate η, an outcome range $[r_1, r_2]$, parameterized kernel $k_\alpha = (1 - \alpha)k_0 + \alpha k_1$ constructed from two domain-compatible kernels k_0 and k_1 such that $\mathcal{H}_0 \cap \mathcal{H}_1 = \{0\}$, a data sequence $\langle (x_1, y_1), (x_2, y_2), \dots, (x_\ell, y_\ell) \rangle \in (\mathcal{X}, [r_1, r_2])^\ell$ then the total loss of the algorithm satisfies*

$$\sum_{t=1}^{\ell} L(y_t, \hat{y}_t) \leq \sum_{t=1}^{\ell} L(y_t, h(x_t)) + 2\sqrt{\hat{L}}\hat{H}\hat{X} + \hat{H}^2\hat{X}^2$$

$$+ 2(r_2 - r_1)^2 \max(2 \ln \mathcal{C}(h) + \ln \frac{1}{c} + \ln \frac{4}{3}, \ln 4) \quad (12)$$

for all $h \in \mathcal{H}_0 + \mathcal{H}_1$ and all constants $\hat{L}, \hat{H}, \hat{X}$, and $c \in (0, 1]$ such that the following four conditions hold: $\eta = [(1 + \frac{\sqrt{\hat{L}}}{\hat{H}\hat{X}})]^{-1}$, and

$$\mathcal{C}^2(h) + c \leq \hat{H}^2, \quad \sum_{t=1}^{\ell} L(y_t, h_\alpha(\mathbf{x}_t)) \leq \hat{L}, \quad \text{and} \quad \sup_{\{t \in [1, \dots, \ell], \alpha \in [0,1]\}} k_\alpha(x_t, x_t) \leq \hat{X}^2.$$

$$(13)$$

Predicting Almost as Well as the Best Width of a Gaussian Kernel.
In the following we define the surfeit of a function. In this abstract we avoid the technicalities of defining the surfeit for the complete Hilbert space $\mathcal{H}_k$; we consider the definition only on the prehilbert space H_k.

Definition 2. *Given a positive kernel $(\forall x, y \in \mathcal{X}^2 : k(x, y) \geq 0)$, let $f \in H_k$; then define the surfeit by*

$$\mathcal{S}^2(f) = \inf \left[\|f^+\|^2 + \|f^-\|^2 \right]. \quad (14)$$

The infimum is taken over all decompositions $f^+ + f^- = f$, where $f^+ = \sum_{i:\beta_i > 0} \beta_i k(x_i, \cdot)$ and $f^- = \sum_{i:\beta_i < 0} \beta_i k(x_i, \cdot)$ are a positive linear and negative linear combination of kernel functions, respectively, such that $f = f^+ + f^- = \sum_{i=1}^{m} \beta_i k(x_i, \cdot)$.

The infimum exists since $0 \leq \|f\|^2 \leq \mathcal{S}^2(f)$.

Theorem 5. *Given the* K-LMS-NET *algorithm with learning rate η, an outcome range $[r_1, r_2]$ with $\max(|r_1|, |r_2|) \geq 1$, a parameterized $(\alpha \in [0, 1])$ Gaussian kernel, $k_\alpha(\mathbf{v}_1, \mathbf{v}_2) = \exp(-s_0\alpha\|\mathbf{v}_1 - \mathbf{v}_2\|^2)$ with fixed scale constant $s_0 \geq 1$ over the domain $[x_1, x_2]^n \times [x_1, x_2]^n$ with associated prehilbert spaces H_α a data sequence $\langle (\mathbf{x}_1, y_1), (\mathbf{x}_2, y_2), \dots, (\mathbf{x}_\ell, y_\ell) \rangle \in ([x_1, x_2]^n, [r_1, r_2])^\ell$, and the constants $c \in (0, 1], s_0 \geq 1, \hat{L} \geq 0, \hat{H} \geq 1 + c$ and with $\eta = [(1 + \frac{\sqrt{\hat{L}}}{\hat{H}})]^{-1}$ then the total loss of the algorithm satisfies*

$$\sum_{t=1}^{\ell} L(y_t, \hat{y}_t) \leq \sum_{t=1}^{\ell} L(y_t, h_\alpha(\mathbf{x}_t)) + 2\sqrt{\hat{L}}\hat{H} + \hat{H}^2 + c + 2(r_2 - r_1)^2[\ln \ell + 2 \ln \mathcal{S}(h_\alpha)$$

$$+ \ln s_0 + \ln n + 2 \ln(x_2 - x_1) + \ln \max(|r_1|, |r_2|) + \ln \frac{1}{c} + \ln 5] \quad (15)$$

for all $h_\alpha \in \bigcup_{\alpha \in [0,1]} H_\alpha$ *such that* $\|h_\alpha\|_\alpha^2 + c \leq \hat{H}^2$, $\sum_{t=1}^\ell L(y_t, h_\alpha(\mathbf{x}_t)) + c \leq \hat{L}$,

$$and\ \alpha \in \left[0, 1 - \frac{c}{5s_0\ell \max(|r_1|, |r_2|)n(x_2 - x_1)^2 \mathcal{S}^2(h_\alpha)}\right]. \tag{16}$$

The previous bound is given without regard of the computability of the predictions. If we restrict the data sequence to a discretization of the unit interval we can then apply the methods of Sect. 3 (in particular see Claim 2) to obtain polynomially tractable approximate predictions.

3   Computing the Predictions of K-LMS-NET

In the previous section we gave both a generic bound, and bounds for two specific applications of the K-LMS-NET algorithm. Here we consider how the predictions may be computed. Rather than computing the predictions exactly we give a polynomial-time absolute ϵ-approximation scheme to the predictions (see (5)) of the K-LMS-NET algorithm. The scheme is a deterministic sampling algorithm that separately approximates the numerator and denominator of the quotient of integrals that define the predictions of the K-LMS-NET algorithm.

The sampling methodology builds on the following three ideas. First, by obtaining a relative ϵ-approximation on an integral; this automatically gives a relative ϵ-approximation for a quotient of integrals (cf. (5)) since relative error approximations (aka "significant digits") are closed under division. A good relative error approximation is also a good absolute error approximation up to a magnitude scaling constant. Second, to minimize the number of required samples we must concentrate samples in areas of large magnitude. Third, since the areas of large magnitude are co-determined by the critical points of the function to be approximated, the inspection of the analytic form gives both a bound on the number of the critical points and a method to find the critical points (areas of large magnitude).

In the following we first consider the cost in terms of relative loss bounds for using approximate predictions. We then consider the analytic forms of the functions to be integrated, both in general and then for our particular applications. Finally we give the details of our sampling methodology.

3.1   Additional Regret for Approximate Predictions

Rather than fixing the quality of the absolute ϵ accuracy of our approximate predictions, we advocate using a schedule $\{\epsilon_t\}$. In the following we see that a schedule which gradually increases the accuracy of our approximate predictions allows the additional cumulative regret incurred to be bounded by an $O(1)$ term.

When an exact prediction of the K-LMS-NET algorithm is replaced by absolute ϵ_t-approximate prediction on trial t the additional "approximation regret" incurred on that trial may be bounded by $2\epsilon_t|y_t - \hat{y}_t| + \epsilon_t^2$. Therefore we may bound the additional cumulative regret for using approximate predictions by $\epsilon_0 \in (0, 1)$ with a decreasing schedule for $\{\epsilon_t\}$ of $\epsilon_t = \frac{\epsilon_0}{6.5 \max([r_2-r_1], 1)(t+1) \ln^2(t+1)}$, recalling that the outcomes and predictions are contained in $[r_1, r_2]$. Thus with the above schedule of $\{\epsilon_t\}$, and given that the approximate predictions are obtainable in time polynomial in $O(\frac{1}{\epsilon_t})$ on trial t, then the additional cumulative regret is bounded by $0 < \epsilon_0 < 1$ and the cumulative running time of the algorithm is polynomial in the number of trials.

3.2   Analytic Forms of the Prediction and Loss Lunctions

We compute the predictions $\hat{y}_t$ of the K-LMS-NET algorithm (cf. (5)) by maintaining explicit symbolic representations of $\mathbf{w}_{\alpha,t}^i(x)$, $\hat{\mathbf{y}}_t^i(\alpha)$ and $L_{[1,t]}(\alpha)$; the symbolic representations may then be exploited to find the critical points.

Below we give an explicit representation of $\mathbf{w}_{\alpha,t+1}^i(x)$ (omitting $\hat{\mathbf{y}}_t^i(\alpha)$ and $L_{[1,t]}(\alpha)$ as they follow directly) by expanding the recurrence (6) giving the $2^t - 1$ terms below

$$\mathbf{w}_{\alpha,t+1}^i(x) = \sum_{k=1}^{t} (-1)^{k+1} \eta^k T_{t,k}(x) \text{ where } T_{t',k}(x) = \sum_{\{(i_1,i_2,\dots,i_k)|1\leq i_1<\dots<i_k\leq t'\}} S_{(i_1,i_2,\dots,i_k)}(x),$$

$$\text{and } S_{(i_1,i_2,\dots,i_k)}(x) = y_{i_1} k_\alpha(x_{i_1}, x_{i_2}) \times \dots \times k_\alpha(x_{i_{k-1}}, x_{i_k}) k_\alpha(x_{i_k}, x) \ . \quad (17)$$

For example, $\mathbf{w}_{\alpha,4}^i(x) = \eta \sum_{i=1}^3 y_i k_\alpha(x_i, x) + \eta^3 y_1 k_\alpha(x_1, x_2) k_\alpha(x_2, x_3) k_\alpha(x_3, x) - \eta^2 [y_1 k_\alpha(x_1, x_2) k_\alpha(x_2, x) + y_1 k_\alpha(x_1, x_3) k_\alpha(x_3, x) + y_2 k_\alpha(x_2, x_3) k_\alpha(x_3, x)]$. Clearly we cannot expect to give a polynomial time algorithm if we manipulate this representation directly, thus the applications we consider are cases where (17) algebraically collapses to a polynomial-sized representation.

In the following claims we give the representations of the functions needed to compute the predictions of the K-LMS-NET algorithm from the applications of Theorems 4 and 5. The proofs of these claims are straightforward and are omitted for reasons of brevity.

Claim 1 *In the K-LMS-NET algorithm with a kernel $k_\alpha = (1 - \alpha)k_0 + \alpha k_1$, the first layer weight function may be expressed as*

$$\mathbf{w}_{\alpha,t}^i(x) = \sum_{i=1}^{t-1} p_{t,i}(\alpha) k_0(x_i, x) + q_{t,i}(\alpha) k_1(x_i, x)$$

where $p_{t,i}(\alpha)$ and $q_{t,i}(\alpha)$ are polynomials of degree i in α. Therefore, the functions $\hat{\mathbf{y}}_t^i(\alpha)$ and $L_{[1,t]}(\alpha)$ may be expressed as polynomials in α of degree $t-1$ and $2t-2$ respectively.

We discretize the input data to obtain a tractable method to predict with a Gaussian kernel. The following claim quantifies the size of the representation of the functions to be sampled by the degree of discretization of the input data.

Claim 2 *In the K-LMS-NET algorithm with the parameterized Gaussian kernel $k_\alpha(\mathbf{v}, \mathbf{x}) = e^{-s_0 \alpha \|\mathbf{v} - \mathbf{x}\|^2}$ with fixed scale constant $s_0 \in \mathbb{R}^+$ and with the discretized interval $\mathcal{X} = \{0, \frac{1}{m}, \dots, \frac{m-1}{m}, 1\}^n$, the first layer weight function may be expressed as*

$$\mathbf{w}_{\alpha,t}^i(\mathbf{x}) = \sum_{i=1}^{t-1} p_{t,i}(\alpha)e^{-s_0\alpha\|\mathbf{x}_i - \mathbf{x}\|^2} \text{ where } p_{t,i}(\alpha) = \sum_{j=0}^{nm^2(i-1)} c_{t,i,j}\left[e^{\frac{-s_0\alpha}{m^2}}\right]^j ,$$

with each $c_{t,i,j} \in \mathbb{R}$. Applying the change in variable $\sigma = e^{\frac{-s_0\alpha}{m^2}}$ to the functions $\hat{\mathbf{y}}_t^i(\alpha)$ and $L_{[1,t]}(\alpha)$ gives polynomials in σ of degree $nm^2(t-1)$ and $2nm^2(t-1)$ respectively.

3.3   Finding Critical Points

We proceed by dividing functions into piecewise monotonic intervals. This means finding their critical points, or the zeros of the derivative. The problem of finding zeros of a polynomial has been called the *Fundamental Computational Problem of Algebra* [24]. There is a vast literature regarding this problem some general references are [17,24,3]. We do not need to actually find the zeros, we only need to *isolate* them as defined below.

Definition 3. *The k-isolation of measure δ of the zeros of a function $f : [a, b] \to \mathbb{R}$ is a list of $j \le k$ intervals $\{[a_1, b_1], \ldots, [a_j, b_j]\}$ such that if $f(r) = 0$ then there exists an i s.t. $r \in [a_i, b_i]$, and also the sum total measure of the intervals is δ.*

Observe that in the above we do not precisely find roots but *isolate* them as some intervals could have multiple roots and others none.

Definition 4. *The composition of functions $f(\sigma(\cdot))$ is called a σ-polynomial (polynomial after a change in variable to σ) if f is a polynomial and $\sigma : \mathbb{R} \to \mathbb{R}$ is continuously differentiable and $\forall x \in \mathbb{R} : \sigma'(x) \ne 0$ (σ is then strictly monotone without inflection). The degree of a σ-polynomial $f(\sigma(\cdot))$ is the degree of f.*

Every polynomial is a σ-polynomial where σ is identity function.

Claim 3 *Given a σ-polynomial $f(\sigma(\cdot)) : [0, 1] \to \mathbb{R}$ of degree s, there exists an s-isolation of the zeros of measure 2^{-p}, the isolation is computable in time polynomial in p and in s.*

Any algorithm that can efficiently act as a *root-existence* oracle for an interval $[a, b]$ of a polynomial which returns TRUE if there exists roots in $[a, b]$ and FALSE otherwise can be subordinated within a bisection algorithm to compute an s-isolation. In this abstract, we do not actually give an algorithm to compute an s-isolation efficiently (see [17,24,3] for algorithms where, e.g., the Euclidean Algorithm may efficiently serve as an oracle), for reasons of brevity.

Corollary 1. *Given σ-polynomials $f(\sigma(\cdot)) : [0, 1] \to \mathbb{R}$ and $g(\sigma(\cdot)) : [0, 1] \to \mathbb{R}$ of degree s_1 and s_2 respectively, and letting $l = e^{f(\sigma)}$ and $m = g(\sigma)e^{f(\sigma)}$, then there exists a $s_1 - 1$ and $s_2(s_1 - 1)$ isolation of l' and m' respectively of measure 2^{-p} computable in time polynomial in s_1, s_2 and p.*

Proof. Omitted for the sake of brevity.

3.4   Deterministic Piecewise Monotone Sampling

Our sampler functions as follows. The quantity we wish to estimate is a quotient of integrals. Relative error approximations (i.e., "significant digits") are closed under division. Hence we develop a sampler for a single integral for which we can give a relative ϵ-approximation scheme. Our intuition from absolute error approximations may suggest that a quantity to bound is the maximal slope of the function to be integrated; this quantity is of less use than the *relative variation* of a positive function, i.e., $\frac{\max_x f(x)}{\min_x f(x)}$. For a positive monotone function we will require a quantity of samples logarithmic in the relative variation. With a bound for monotone functions we can generalize to piecewise monotone, this requires that we isolate the critical points of our function. In the previous section, the applications chosen lead to functions for which it is easy to find the critical points. This leads to a method that samples exponentially more often in areas of large volume. We note that the sampler here has been designed to directly "prove a bound"; using the techniques here it is possible to design a sampler that also proves the bound, but which is considerable more adaptive (uses fewer samples), and hence more useful in practice.

In the following three lemmas we give simple algebraic results about ϵ-approximations.

Lemma 1. *Suppose* $\hat{a} \overset{r}{\approx}_\epsilon a$ *and* $\hat{b} \overset{r}{\approx}_\epsilon b$ *then* $(\hat{a} + \hat{b}) \overset{r}{\approx}_\epsilon (a + b)$.

Lemma 2. *Suppose* $\hat{b} \overset{r}{\approx}_\epsilon b$ *and* $b \leq B$ *then* $\hat{b} \overset{a}{\approx}_{2B\epsilon} b$.

Lemma 3. *Suppose* $\hat{a} \overset{r}{\approx}_\epsilon a$ *and* $\hat{b} \overset{r}{\approx}_\epsilon b$ *then* $\frac{\hat{a}}{\hat{b}} \overset{r}{\approx}_{3\epsilon} \frac{a}{b}$ *for all* $\epsilon \in (0, \frac{1}{3})$.
The following scale-invariant theorem is the key to our sampling methodology.

Theorem 6. *Given a continuous nondecreasing function* $f : [a, b] \to \mathbb{R}^+$, *let* $y = \int_a^b f(\alpha)d\alpha$. *Define* $z = \frac{f(b)}{f(a)}$; *then there exists a relative* ϵ-*approximation for* y *which requires* $\left\lceil \frac{1}{2}\left(\frac{1}{\epsilon} + 1\right) \ln z \right\rceil + 2$ *samples (evaluations) of* f.

The proof in Appendix A details how the samples are chosen.

The following lemma demonstrates that a good relative ϵ-approximation may be obtained by well-approximating a function on a subset of its domain if the measure of the non-approximated subset times the function's relative variation is sufficiently small.

Lemma 4. *Given measurable sets* $E' \subset E$ *with* $\mu(E) = 1$ *and a continuous function* f, *such that* $\forall x \in E : 0 < a \leq f(x) \leq b$, *define* $\Delta = \mu(E - E')$ *and* $z = \frac{b}{a}$. *Then if* $\hat{y} \overset{r}{\approx}_{\epsilon'} \int_{E'} f d\mu$ *it is also case that* $\hat{y} \overset{r}{\approx}_\epsilon \int_E f d\mu$ *when* $\epsilon' + \Delta z \leq \epsilon$.

Proof. Omitted for the sake of brevity.

We now summarize the process for approximating $\int_E f d\mu$: i) we divide f into monotonic regions by isolating the critical points in sufficiently small intervals (cf. Claim 3 and Corollary 1); ii) the integral of each monotonic regions is then separately approximated (cf. Theorem 6); and iii) the separate approximations are then summed without the isolated intervals (cf. Lemma 4) to obtain a $\hat{y} \overset{r}{\approx}_\epsilon \int_E f d\mu$. In Appendix A Lemmas 8 and 9 are given. These detail the separate approximation of the denominator and numerator of (5). Their proofs follow the basic sketch above except that additional points of the functions need to be isolated in order to properly clip the functions. The following theorem combines Lemmas 8 and 9 to demonstrate the computation of an absolute ϵ-approximation to a prediction of K-LMS-NET.

Theorem 7. *Given a σ-polynomial $f(\sigma(\cdot)) : [0,1] \rightarrow [0,\infty)$ of degree s and $z \in (1,\infty)$, and a σ-polynomial $g(\sigma(\cdot)) : [0,1] \rightarrow (-\infty,\infty)$ of degree t we may compute an absolute ϵ-approximation*

$$\bar{y} \overset{a}{\approx}_\epsilon \frac{\int_0^1 \max(r_1, \min(g(\sigma(\alpha)), r_2)) \max(e^{-f(\sigma(\alpha))}, z^{-1}) d\alpha}{\int_0^1 \max(e^{-f(\sigma(\alpha))}, z^{-1}) d\alpha} \tag{18}$$

in time polynomial in s, t, $\ln(z(1 + r_2 - r_1))$, and ϵ^{-1} .

Acknowledgments. I thank Massimiliano Pontil for valuable discussions and for pointing out the inspirational kernel sum theorem from Aronszajn [2].

References

[1] C. Andrieu, N. de Freitas, A. Doucet, and M. I. Jordan. An introduction to MCMC for machine learning. *Machine Learning*, 50(1-2):5–43, 2003.

[2] N. Aronszajn. Theory of reproducing kernels. *Trans. Amer. Math. Soc.*, 68:337–404, 1950.

[3] L. Blum, F. Cucker, M. Shub, and S. Smale. *Complexity and real computation*. Springer-Verlag, 1998.

[4] N. Cesa-Bianchi, P. Long, and M. Warmuth. Worst-case quadratic loss bounds for on-line prediction of linear functions by gradient descent. *IEEE Transactions on Neural Networks*, 7(2):604–619, May 1996.

[5] N. Cristianini and J. Shawe-Taylor. *An Introduction to Support Vector Machines*. Cambridge University Press, Cambridge, UK, 2000.

[6] L. Csató and M. Opper. Sparse on-line gaussian processes. *Neural Computation*, 14(3):641–668, 2002.

[7] Y. Freund. Predicting a binary sequence almost as well as the optimal biased coin. In *Proc. of COLT.*, pages 89–98. ACM Press, New York, NY, 1996.

[8] M. Gibbs and D. MacKay. Efficient implementation of gaussian processes (draft manuscript), 1996.

[9] M. Herbster. Learning additive models online with fast evaluating kernels. In *COLT 2001, Proceedings*, volume 2111 of *LNAI*, pages 444–460. Springer, 2001.

[10] W. Hoeffding. Probability inequalities for sums of bounded random variables. *Journal of the American Statistical Association*, 58(301):13–30, Mar. 1963.

[11] J. Kivinen, A. J. Smola, and R. C. Williamson. Online learning with kernels. In *NIPS 14*, Cambridge, MA, 2002. MIT Press.

[12] J. Kivinen and M. K. Warmuth. Averaging expert predictions. *Lecture Notes in Computer Science (EUROCOLT)*, 1572:153–167, 1999.

[13] N. Littlestone. Learning when irrelevant attributes abound: A new linear-threshold algorithm. *Machine Learning*, 2:285–318, 1988.

[14] N. Littlestone and M. K. Warmuth. The weighted majority algorithm. *Informa-tion and Computation*, 108(2):212–261, 1994.

[15] C. Micchelli and M. Pontil. Learning the kernel function via regularization, Dept. of Computer Science, University College London, Research Note: RN/04/12, 2004.

[16] C. S. Ong, A. J. Smola, and R. C. Williamson. Hyperkernels. In *Neural Informa-tion Processing Systems*, volume 15. MIT Press, 2002.

[17] V. Y. Pan. Solving a polynomial equation: Some history and recent progress. *SIAM Review*, 39(2):187–220, 1997.

[18] J. F. Traub and A. G. Werschulz. *Complexity and Information*. Cambridge University Press, Cambridge, 1998.

[19] J. Vermaak, S. J. Godsill, and A. Doucet. Sequential bayesian kernel regression. In *NIPS 16*. MIT Press, Cambridge, MA, 2004.

[20] V. Vovk. Aggregating strategies. In *Proc. 3rd Annu. Workshop on Comput. Learning Theory*, pages 371–383. Morgan Kaufmann, 1990.

[21] V. Vovk. Competitive on-line statistics. *Bull. of the International Stat. Inst.*, 1999.

[22] C. K. I. Williams and C. E. Rasmussen. Gaussian processes for regression. In *NIPS 1995*, Cambridge, Massachusetts, 1996. MIT Press.

[23] Q. Wu, Y. Ying, and D.-X. Zhou. Multi-kernel regularized classifiers. Submitted to *Journ. of Complexity*, 2004.

[24] C. K. Yap. *Fundamental problems of algorithmic algebra*. Oxford Uni. Press, 2000.

A   Additional Proofs

Lemma 5. *Given domain-compatible kernels k_0 and k_1 such that $\mathcal{H}_0 \cap \mathcal{H}_1 = \{0\}$, let $k_\alpha = (1 - \alpha)k_0 + \alpha k_1$. Then given $f \in \mathcal{H}_0 + \mathcal{H}_1$, we have $\forall c \in (0, 1]$: $\forall \delta \in [0, \min(\frac{1}{4}, \frac{3c}{4\mathcal{C}^2(f)})]$ that there exists $0 \leq \alpha' < \alpha'' \leq 1$ with $\alpha'' - \alpha' = \delta$ such that $\forall \alpha \in [\alpha', \alpha'']$, it is the case that $\|f\|_\alpha^2 \leq \mathcal{C}^2(f) + c$.*

Proof. Let $f_0 + f_1$ with $f_i \in \mathcal{H}_i$. Without loss of generality assume that $\|f_1\|_1 \leq \|f_0\|_0$. Set $\alpha' = \frac{\|f_1\|_1}{\|f_1\|_1 + \|f_0\|_0}$, recalling that $\|f\|_{\alpha'}^2 = \inf_{\alpha \in [0,1]} \|f\|_\alpha^2 = \mathcal{C}^2(f)$. Let $x = \|f\|_{\alpha' + \delta}^2 - \|f\|_{\alpha'}^2$; by substituting $\alpha' = \frac{\|f_1\|_1}{\|f_1\|_1 + \|f_0\|_0}$ into (9) we have that

$$x = \delta(\|f_1\|_1 + \|f_0\|_0)^2 \left[\frac{\frac{\|f_0\|_0\|f_1\|_1}{\delta} + \|f_0\|_0^2 - \|f_1\|_1^2}{(\|f_0\|_0 + \|f_1\|_1)^2} - \delta \right]^{-1} . \tag{19}$$

As we are upper bounding x let us separately upper bound

$$p(\|f_0\|_0, \|f_1\|_1, \delta) = \left[\frac{\frac{\|f_0\|_0\|f_1\|_1}{\delta} + \|f_0\|_0^2 - \|f_1\|_1^2}{(\|f_0\|_0 + \|f_1\|_1)^2} - \delta \right]^{-1} . \tag{20}$$

As a function of $\|f_1\|_1$ through routine calculations it can be shown that p obtains its maximum (for $\delta \in [0, 1/4]$) on either the boundary $\|f_1\|_1 = 0$ or $\|f_1\|_1 = \|f_0\|_0$. Thus substituting, $p(\|f_0\|_0, 0, \delta) = \frac{1}{1-\delta}$ and $p(\|f_0\|_0, \|f_0\|_0, \delta) = \frac{4\delta}{1-4\delta^2}$. Therefore, for all $\delta \in [0, 1/4]$, we have $p(\|f_0\|_0, \|f_0\|_0, \delta) \leq p(\|f_0\|_0, 0, \delta) \leq \frac{4}{3}$. By combining the upper bound of $\frac{4}{3}$ with (19) we have that for $\delta \in [0, 1/4]$, $\|f\|_{\alpha' + \delta}^2 \leq \mathcal{C}^2(f) + \frac{4}{3}\delta\mathcal{C}^2(f)$; therefore with $\alpha'' = \alpha' + \delta$ we are done.   □

Lemma 6. *Let* $k_\alpha(\mathbf{v}_1, \mathbf{v}_2) = \exp(-s_0\alpha\|\mathbf{v}_1 - \mathbf{v}_2\|^2)$ *denote a parameterized* $(\alpha \in [0,1])$ *Gaussian kernel with fixed scale constant* $s_0 \geq 1$ *over the domain* $[x_1, x_2]^n \times [x_1, x_2]^n$ *with associated prehilbert spaces* H_α. *Given a function* $h_{\alpha'} \in H_{\alpha'}$ *such that* $\|h_{\alpha'}\|_{\alpha'} \geq 1$ *with representation* $h_{\alpha'}(\cdot) = \sum_{i=1}^m \beta_i k_{\alpha'}(\mathbf{v}_i, \cdot)$ *then set* $h_{\alpha'+\delta}(\cdot) = \sum_{i=1}^m \beta_i k_{\alpha'+\delta}(\mathbf{v}_i, \cdot)$. *Then the square loss and squared norm of* $h_{\alpha'+\delta}$ *may be bounded by those of* $h_{\alpha'}$ *plus any constant* $0 < c < 1$ *for all sequences* $\langle(\mathbf{x}_1, y_1), (\mathbf{x}_2, y_2), \ldots, (\mathbf{x}_\ell, y_\ell)\rangle \in ([x_1, x_2]^n, [r_1, r_2])^\ell$ *where* $\max(|r_1|, |r_2|) \geq 1$. *Hence* $\sum_{t=1}^\ell (y_t - h_{\alpha'+\delta}(\mathbf{x}_t))^2 \leq \sum_{t=1}^\ell (y_t - h_{\alpha'}(\mathbf{x}_t))^2 + c$ *and* $\|h_{\alpha'+\delta}\|_{\alpha'+\delta}^2 \leq \|h_{\alpha'}\|_{\alpha'}^2 + c$ *for all* $\delta \in [0, \frac{c}{5s_0\ell \max(|r_1|, |r_2|)n(x_2 - x_1)^2 S^2(h_{\alpha'})}]$.

Proof. Omitted in this abstract; see full version.

Proof (sketches of Theorems 4 and 5). The theorems follow directly from Theorem 1 with Lemmas 5 and 6 with $\mathcal{A}$ chosen so that in each $\mu(\mathcal{A}) = \delta$.

The following inequality is needed for Theorem 6.

Lemma 7. *Suppose* $r \geq 1$, *then* $r + \frac{1}{2} \geq \ln(1 + \frac{1}{r})^{-1}$.

Proof (of Theorem 6). Let $r = \frac{1}{2\epsilon}$ and choose n s.t.

$$\left\lceil \left(r + \frac{1}{2}\right)\ln z\right\rceil + 1 \leq n \tag{21}$$

where $n + 1$ is the total number of function samples. The function is sampled over n intervals with widths $\Delta_i = \frac{(b-a)\left(\frac{r}{r+1}\right)^{i-1}}{(1+r)\left(1-\left(\frac{r}{r+1}\right)^n\right)}$; the samples are denoted $f(a) = f_0, f_1, \ldots, f_n = f(b)$ where $f_i = f(a + \sum_{j=1}^i \Delta_i)$. We also need the following inequality relating r, n and z:

$$\left(\frac{r}{r+1}\right)^{n-1} \leq \frac{1}{z}. \tag{22}$$

From (21) and Lemma 7 it follows that, $\ln z \leq (n-1)\ln\frac{r+1}{r}$ which implies (22).

Define $M = \sum_{i=1}^{n-1} f_i \Delta_i$; now define lower and upper bounds of y, L and U by $L = f_0\Delta_1 + \frac{r}{r+1}M \leq y \leq M + f_n\Delta_n = U$. We proceed to show that $\hat{y} = \frac{1}{2}(L + U)$ is a relative ϵ-approximation of y, since U and L are upper and lower bounds if we can show $U(1 - \epsilon) \leq \hat{y} \leq L(1 + \epsilon)$ which is equivalent to the conjunction of conditions $\frac{1}{2}\frac{U-L}{L} \leq \epsilon$, and $\frac{1}{2}\frac{U-L}{U} \leq \epsilon$. This will prove that $\hat{y}$ is an ϵ-approximation of y. However, since $L \leq U$ we need only show $\frac{1}{2}\frac{U-L}{L} \leq \epsilon$. Thus,

$$\frac{1}{2}\frac{U-L}{L} = \frac{1}{2}\frac{M + f_n\Delta_n - f_0\Delta_1 - \frac{r}{r+1}M}{f_0\Delta_1 + \frac{r}{r+1}M} \tag{23}$$

$$\leq \frac{1}{2}\frac{\frac{1}{r+1}\sum_{i=1}^{n-1}\left(\frac{r}{r+1}\right)^i f_i}{f_0 + \frac{r}{r+1}\sum_{i=1}^{n-1}\left(\frac{r}{r+1}\right)^i f_i} \leq \frac{1}{2}\frac{1}{r} \tag{24}$$

where (24) follows from (22). Hence $\hat{y}$ is an ϵ-approximation of y with the requisite number of samples. $\qquad\square$

The following two lemmas give a method to obtain relative ϵ-approximations of the denominator and the numerator of the predictions (5) K-LMS-NET.

Lemma 8. *Given a σ-polynomial $f(\sigma(\cdot)):[0,1]\rightarrow[0,\infty)$ of degree s and a $z \in (1,\infty)$, we may compute a relative ϵ-approximation $\hat{y}\overset{r}{\approx}_\epsilon \int_0^1 \max(e^{-f(\sigma(\alpha))}, z^{-1})d\alpha$ in time polynomial in s, $\ln(z)$ and ϵ^{-1} .*

Proof. Let $l = e^{-f(\sigma(\alpha))}$. By Corollary 1, we may puncture the interval $[0,1]$ into no more than $r \le s$ regions with the (up to) $s-1$ of the critical points l isolated into a total measure of no more than 2^{-p}. By construction in each of the r regions $\min(l, z^{-1})$ is monotonic; thus we may apply Theorem 6 to each of the r regions (with $\epsilon = \epsilon'/2$) since relative ϵ-approximations add (cf Lemma 1). The estimator formed by adding the r estimators is a relative $\epsilon'/2$-approximation to $\int_{E'} \max(l, z^{-1})d\alpha$ where E' is the interval $[0,1]$ minus the isolates. However if we set $p = 1 + \log(z/\epsilon')$ by Lemma 4 we have a relative ϵ'-approximation to $\int_0^1 \max(l, z^{-1})d\alpha$. $\qquad\square$

Lemma 9. *Given a σ-polynomial $f(\sigma(\cdot)) : [0,1]\rightarrow[0,\infty)$ of degree s and $z \in (1,\infty)$, and σ-polynomial $g(\sigma(\cdot)) : [0,1]\rightarrow(-\infty,\infty)$ of degree t we may compute a relative ϵ-approximation $\hat{y}\overset{r}{\approx}_\epsilon \int_0^1 \max(1, \min(g(\sigma(\alpha)), 1+r)) \max(e^{-f(\sigma(\alpha))}, \frac{1}{z})d\alpha$ in time polynomial in s, t, $\ln(z(1+r))$, and ϵ^{-1} .*

Proof. We sketch the proof for reasons of brevity and the fact that it closely follows the proof of Lemma 8. The key difference is the need to create additional isolates since it is subtle to clip $g(\sigma(\alpha))$ and $e^{-f(\sigma(\alpha))}$ independently. In fact we need to isolate the critical points of $g(\sigma(\alpha))e^{-f(\sigma(\alpha))}$, $g(\sigma(\alpha))$, and $e^{-f(\sigma(\alpha))}$; and the zeroes of $g(\sigma(\alpha)) = 1$, $g(\sigma(\alpha)) = 1+r$, and $e^{-f(\sigma(\alpha))} = z^{-1}$. Now we can ensure that we can correctly clip and also for each region between isolates that the function $\max(1, \min(g(\sigma(\alpha)), 1+r)) \max(e^{-f(\sigma(\alpha))}, z^{-1})$ is monotonic. We observe that the number of isolates is polynomial in s and t. $\qquad\square$

We compute a shifted version of the quotient (5) so that the predictions and outcomes may have both positive and negative values.

Proof (of Theorem 7). Apply Lemmas 9 and 8 to give relative ϵ'-approximations $\hat{n}\overset{r}{\approx}_{\epsilon'} \int_0^1 \max(1, \min(g(\sigma(\alpha)) + 1 - r_1, 1 + r_2 - r_1)) \max(e^{-f(\sigma(\alpha))}, z^{-1})d\alpha$, and $\hat{d}\overset{r}{\approx}_{\epsilon'} \int_0^1 \max(e^{-f(\sigma(\alpha))}, z^{-1})d\alpha$ with $\epsilon' = \frac{\epsilon}{6(1+r_2-r_1)}$. Observe that

$$y' = \frac{\int_0^1 \max(1, \min(g(\sigma(\alpha)) + 1 - r_1, 1 + r_2 - r_1)) \max(e^{-f(\sigma(\alpha))}, z^{-1})d\alpha}{\int_0^1 \max(e^{-f(\sigma(\alpha))}, z^{-1})d\alpha} \quad (25)$$

is an expectation of a quantity bounded by 1 and $1+r_2-r_1$, hence $y' \le 1+r_2-r_1$. Therefore by Lemmas 2 and 3 $\frac{\hat{n}}{\hat{d}}\overset{a}{\approx}_\epsilon y'$. Since $y' = \bar{y} + 1 - r_1$, we conclude that $\frac{\hat{n}}{\hat{d}} - (1 - r_1)\overset{a}{\approx}_\epsilon \bar{y}$. $\qquad\square$

On the Complexity of Working Set Selection[*]

Hans Ulrich Simon

Fakultät für Mathematik, Ruhr-Universität Bochum, D-44780 Bochum, Germany
simon@lmi.rub.de

Abstract. The decomposition method is currently one of the major
methods for solving the convex quadratic optimization problems being
associated with Support Vector Machines (SVM-optimization). A key issue in this approach is the policy for working set selection. We would like
to find policies that realize (as good as possible) three goals simultaneously: "(fast) convergence to an optimal solution", "efficient procedures
for working set selection", and "high degree of generality" (including
typical variants of SVM-optimization as special cases). In this paper, we
study a general policy for working set selection that has been proposed
quite recently. It is known that it leads to convergence for any convex
quadratic optimization problem. Here, we investigate its computational
complexity when it is used for SVM-optimization. We show that it poses
an NP-complete working set selection problem, but a slight variation
of it (sharing the convergence properties with the original policy) can
be solved in polynomial time. We show furthermore that so-called "rate
certifying pairs" (introduced by Hush and Scovel) can be found in linear time, which leads to a quite efficient decomposition method with a
polynomial convergence rate for SVM-optimization.

1   Introduction

Support vector machines (SVMs) introduced by Vapnik and co-workers [1,23]
are a promising technique for classification, function approximation, and other
key problems in statistical learning theory. In this paper, we consider the optimization problems that are induced by SVMs, which are special cases of convex
quadratic optimization.

The difficulty of solving problems of this kind is the density of the matrix
that represents the "quadratic part" of the cost function. Thus, a prohibitive
amount of memory is required to store the matrix and traditional optimization
algorithms (such as Newton, for example) cannot be directly applied. Several
authors have proposed (different variants of) a decomposition method to overcome this difficulty [20,6,21,22,17,18,2,9,13,19,10,8,14,15,11,3,12,4]. This method
keeps track of a current feasible solution which is iteratively improved. In each

[*] This work was supported in part by the IST Programme of the European Community, under the PASCAL Network of Excellence, IST-2002-506778. This publication
only reflects the authors' views. This work was furthermore supported by the Deut-
sche Forschungsgemeinschaft Grant SI 498/7-1.

S. Ben-David, J. Case, A. Maruoka (Eds.): ALT 2004, LNAI 3244, pp. 324–337, 2004.

iteration the variable indices are split into a "working set" $I \subseteq \{1, \ldots, m\}$ and its complement $J = \{1, \ldots, m\} \setminus I$. Then, the subproblem with variables x_i, $i \in I$, is solved, thereby leaving the values for the remaining variables x_j, $j \in J$, unchanged. The success of the method depends in a quite sensitive manner on the policy for the selection of the working set I (whose size is typically bounded by a small constant). Ideally, the selection procedure should be computationally efficient and, at the same time, effective in the sense that the resulting sequence of feasible solutions converges (with high speed) to an optimal limit point. Clearly, these goals are conflicting in general and trade-offs are to be expected.

Our results and their relation to previous work. We study a general policy for working set selection that has been proposed quite recently [16]. It is known that it leads to convergence for any convex quadratic optimization problem. Here, we investigate its computational complexity when it is used for SVM-optimization. As a "test-case", we discuss one of the most popular and well-studied SVM-optimization problems.[1] We show that the application of the general policy poses an NP-hard working set selection problem (see Section 4). Although this looks frustrating at first glance, it turns out that a slight variation of the general policy (replacing in some sense "exact working set selection" by "approximate working set selection") allows still for a general convergence proof (valid for convex quadratic optimization in general; see Section 3) and poses an efficiently solvable working set selection problem as far as SVM-optimization is concerned (see Section 5).

It would be clearly desirable to achieve a high convergence speed. Hush and Scovel [4] proved recently that the decomposition method (when applied to the same SVM-optimization problem that we discuss in our paper) leads to a polynomial convergence rate if the working set always contains a so-called "rate certifying pair". They also provided an $O(m \log m)$ algorithm for finding such a pair. We design a new algorithm that finds a rate certifying pair in linear time. This leads (to the best of our knowledge) to the first working set selection procedure that is (almost) as efficient as Joachim's method [6] used in the software package SVM^{light} and has (on top of being efficient) a provable polynomial convergence rate.

More relations to previous work will be discussed in the full paper.

2   Preliminaries

Throughout this paper,

$$f(x) = \frac{1}{2} x^\top Q x - w^\top x = \frac{1}{2} \sum_{i=1}^{m} \sum_{j=1}^{m} Q_{i,j} x_i x_j - \sum_{i=1}^{m} w_i x_i \tag{1}$$

denotes a convex cost function, where $Q \in \mathbb{R}^{m \times m}$ is a positive semi-definite matrix over the reals. We are interested in optimization problems of the following

---

[1] The dual problem to maximum margin classification with the 1-norm soft margin criterion

general form $\mathcal{P}$:

$$\min_x f(x) \text{ s.t. } Ax = b, l \le x \le r \tag{2}$$

Here, $A \in \mathbb{R}^{k \times m}$, $b \in \mathbb{R}^k$, $l, r \in \mathbb{R}^m$, and $l \le x \le r$ is the short-notation for the "box constraints"

$$\forall i = 1, \ldots, m : l_i \le x_i \le r_i .$$

In the sequel,

$$R(\mathcal{P}) = \{x \in \mathbb{R}^m | \; Ax = b, l \le x \le r\}$$

denotes the compact set of feasible points for $\mathcal{P}$.

We briefly note that any bounded[2] optimization problem with cost function $f(x)$ and linear equality- and inequality-constraints can be brought into the form (2) because we may convert the linear inequalities into linear equations by introducing non-negative slack variables. By the compactness of the region of feasible points, we may also put a suitable upper bound on each slack variable such that finally all linear inequalities take the form of box constraints.

Example 1. A popular (and actually one of the most well studied) variant of Support Vector Machines leads to an optimization problem of the following form $\mathcal{P}_0$:

$$\min_x f(x) \text{ s.t. } y^\top x = 0 , \; l \le x \le r \tag{3}$$

Here, $y \in \{-1, 1\}^m$ is a vector whose components represent binary classification labels. Note that we may "normalize" $\mathcal{P}_0$ by substituting $y_i x_i$ for x_i. This leads to a problem of the same form as $\mathcal{P}_0$ but with $y = \bar{1}$, where $\bar{1}$ denotes the "all-ones" vector. (An analogous notational convention is used for any other constant.) The main difference between $\mathcal{P}_0$ and the general problem $\mathcal{P}$ is that $\mathcal{P}_0$ has only the single equality constraint $y^\top x = 0$.[3]

The *decomposition method* with working sets of size at most q proceeds iteratively as follows: given a feasible solution $x \in R(\mathcal{P})$ (chosen arbitrarily in the beginning), a so-called working set $I \subseteq \{1, \ldots, m\}$ of size at most q is selected. Then x is updated by the optimal solution for the subproblem with variables x_i, $i \in I$ (leaving the values x_j with $j \notin I$ unchanged). The policy for working set selection is a critical issue that we briefly discuss in the next section.

3   Working Set Selection and Convergence

Consider the situation where we attack a problem $\mathcal{P}$ of the general form (2) by means of the decomposition method. As explained below, the selection of a

---

[2] Here, "bounded" means that the region of feasible points is compact (or can be made compact without changing the smallest possible cost).

[3] As far as the SVM-application is concerned, we could also set $w = \bar{1}$, $l = \bar{0}$, and $r = \bar{C}$ for some constant $C > 0$. Since these settings do not substantially simplify the problem, we prefer the more general notation.

working set $I \subseteq \{1, \ldots, m\}$ of size at most q can be guided by a function family $C_I(x)$. For instance, the following family was considered in [16]:

$$C_I(x) := \inf_{h \in \mathbb{R}^k} \sum_{i \in I} (x_i - l_i) \max\{0, \nabla f(x)_i - A_i^\top h\} + (r_i - x_i) \max\{0, A_i^\top h - \nabla f(x)_i\}$$

(4)

Here, A_i denotes the i'th column of A and $A_i^\top$ its transpose.

The following results, being valid for any optimization problem $\mathcal{P}$ of the form (2), were shown in [16]:

1. The function family $C_I(x)$ defined in (4) satisfies the following conditions:
   (C1) For each $I \subseteq \{1, \ldots, m\}$ such that $|I| \leq q$, $C_I(x)$ is continuous on $R(\mathcal{P})$.
   (C2) If $|I| \leq q$ and x' is an optimal solution for the subproblem induced by the current feasible solution x and working set I, then $C_I(x') = 0$.
   (C3) If x is not an optimal solution for $\mathcal{P}$, then there exists an $I \subseteq \{1, \ldots, m\}$ such that $|I| \leq q$ and $C_I(x) > 0$ provided that $q \geq k + 1$.
2. Let $q \geq k + 1$ (where k is the number of equality constraints in $\mathcal{P}$). Assume that $Q \in \mathbb{R}^{m \times m}$ (the matrix from the definition of the cost function in (1)) has positive definite submatrices $Q_{I,I}$ for all subsets $I \subseteq \{1, \ldots, m\}$ of size at most q.[4] Let $C_I(x)$ be a family of functions[5] that satisfies conditions (C1),(C2),(C3). Let a *decomposition method induced by* $C_I(x)$ be an algorithm that, given the current feasible solution x, always chooses a working set $I \subseteq \{1, \ldots, m\}$ of size at most q that maximizes $C_I(x)$. Then this method converges to an optimal solution.

We will show in Section 4 that the working set selection induced by the family $C_I(x)$ from (4) is (unfortunately) an NP-complete problem already for the (comparably simple) SVM-optimization problem $\mathcal{P}_0$ from (3). We will, however, design a polynomially time-bounded algorithm that, given the current feasible solution x, always finds a working set $I \subseteq \{1, \ldots, m\}$ of size at most q that maximizes $C_I(x)$ up to factor 4. This raises the question whether convergence can still be granted when the selection of a working set that maximizes $C_I(x)$ (referred to as "Exact Working Set Selection") is replaced by the selection of a working set that maximizes $C_I(x)$ only up to a constant factor (referred to as "Approximate Working Set Selection"). It turns out, fortunately, that this is true:

Theorem 1. *Let $\mathcal{P}$ be the optimization problem given by (2) and (1), and let $q \geq k + 1$. Assume that $Q \in \mathbb{R}^{m \times m}$ is a matrix with positive definite submatrices $Q_{I,I}$ for all subsets $I \subseteq \{1, \ldots, m\}$ of size at most q. Let $C_I(x)$ be a family*

---

[4] This assumption does not follow automatically from the positive semi-definiteness of Q (though it would follow from positive definiteness of Q). It is however (at least for SVM-applications) often satisfied. For some kernels like, for example, the RBF-kernel, it is certainly true; for other kernels it typically satisfied provided that q is sufficiently small. See also the discussion of this point in [13].

[5] Not necessarily identical to the family defined in (4)

of functions that satisfies conditions (C1),(C2),(C3). Let an approximate de-
composition method induced by $C_I(x)$ be an algorithm that, given the current
feasible solution x, always chooses a working set $I \subseteq \{1, \ldots, m\}$ of size at most
q that maximizes $C_I(x)$ up to a constant factor. Then this method converges to
an optimal solution.

Theorem 1 (whose proof is similar to the original proof of convergence in [16] and therefore omitted in this abstract) provides a justification to pass from "Exact Working Set Selection" to "Approximate Working Set Selection".

4   Complexity of Exact Working Set Selection

The function family from (4) can be expressed in a simpler fashion when we consider the special optimization problem $\mathcal{P}_0$ from (3) in its "normalized version" (with $y = \bar{1}$):

$$C_I(x) = \inf_{t \in \mathbb{R}} \sum_{i \in I} (x_i - l_i) \max\{0, \nabla f(x)_i - t\} + (r_i - x_i) \max\{0, t - \nabla f(x)_i\}$$

This leads us to the following (purely combinatorial) problem:[6]

EXACT WORKING SET SELECTION (EWSS). Given numbers $a_1 \leq \cdots \leq a_m$, non-negative weight parameters $w_1, w_1', \ldots, w_m, w_m'$ and a non-negative number q, find a "working set" $I \subseteq \{1, \ldots, m\}$ of size at most q that maximizes the "gain"

$$\inf_{t \in \mathbb{R}} \sum_{i \in I: a_i < t} w_i'(t - a_i) + \sum_{i \in I: a_i > t} w_i(a_i - t) \ .$$

When we consider EWSS as a decision problem, we assume that the input contains an additional bound B. The question is whether there exists a working set that achieves a gain of at least B.

We may think of $a_1, \ldots, a_m$ as points on the real line that are ordered from left to right. EWSS corresponds to a game between two players:

1. Player 1 selects $q' \leq q$ points. Intuitively, this means that she commits herself to a working set $I \subseteq \{1, \ldots, m\}$ of size q'.
2. Player 2 selects a threshold t and pays an amount of $\sum_{i \in I: a_i < t} w_i'(t - a_i) + \sum_{i \in I: a_i > t} w_i(a_i - t)$ to player 1.

Given I (the move of player 1), the optimal move of player 2 is easy to determine. We say that threshold t is in a *balanced position* if the following holds:

1. If $t \notin \{a_1, \ldots, a_m\}$, then $\sum_{i \in I: a_i < t} w_i' = \sum_{i \in I: a_i > t} w_i$.

---

[6] The correspondence is as follows. Assume that $\nabla f(x)_1 \leq \cdots \leq \nabla f(x)_m$ (after reindexing if necessary). Now, a_i represents $\nabla f(x)_i$, w_i represents $x_i - l_i$, w_i' represents $r_i - x_i$.

2. If $t = a_j$ for some $j \in \{1, \ldots, m\}$, then $\sum_{i=1}^{j} w_i' \geq \sum_{i=j+1}^{m} w_i$ and $\sum_{i=j}^{m} w_i \geq \sum_{i=1}^{j-1} w_i'$.

Lemma 1. *Given I, the balanced positions of threshold t form either an interval $[a_j, a_{j+1}]$ or a singleton set $\{a_j\}$. Furthermore, threshold t represents an optimal move of player 2 iff it is in a balanced position.*

Proof. The first statement ist easy to see. We omit the straightforward proof in this abstract. The second statement is based on the following observations (valid for some sufficiently small $\delta > 0$):

1. If we replace t by $t - \delta$, then the gain of player 1 changes by an amount of

$$\left(\sum_{i:a_i \geq t} w_i - \sum_{i:a_i < t} w_i' \right) \delta \ .$$

2. If we replace t by $t + \delta$, then the gain of player 1 changes by an amount of

$$\left(\sum_{i:a_i \leq t} w_i' - \sum_{i:a_i > t} w_i \right) \delta \ .$$

It follows that a theshold t in an unbalanced position cannot be an optimal move of player 2 because the gain of player 1 could be reduced by moving t in direction to the side with the larger total weight. Thus, a unique balanced position of the form $t = a_j$ is an optimal move. If all positions in an interval $[a_j, a_{j+1}]$ are balanced, then any move $t \in [a_j, a_{j+1}]$ leads to the same gain of player 1. Thus, any such threshold represents an optimal move of player 2. □

Corollary 1. *Given I, a threshold $t \in \{a_1, \ldots, a_m\}$ in balanced position is found in linear time.*

Proof. Let t run through the sorted list $a_1 \leq \cdots \leq a_m$ and keep track of the total w'-weight of $\{a_i | a_i < t\}$ and the total w-weight of $\{a_i | a_i > t\}$. Stop when the balance condition is satisfied. □

We say that t is an *S-unificator* for some $S > 0$ if

$$S = w_{i'}'(t - a_{i'}) = w_i(a_i - t)$$

holds for all $i, i' \in \{1, \ldots, m\}$ such that $a_{i'} < t$ and $a_i > t$.

Lemma 2. *If t is an S-unificator, then*

$$\max_{I \subseteq \{1, \ldots, m\} : |I| \leq q} \inf_{t \in \mathbb{R}} \sum_{i \in I : a_i < t} w_i'(t - a_i) + \sum_{i \in I : a_i > t} w_i(a_i - t) \leq qS$$

with equality iff there exists a working set I of size q that puts t in a balanced position.

Proof. If player 2 chooses threshold t, then the gain for player 1 is $|I|S \leq qS$ (no matter which working set I was chosen). Thus, qS is the largest gain player 1 can hope for. If she finds a working set I of size q that puts t in a balanced position, the gain qS is achieved (since player 2 will find no threshold superior to t). If not, player 2 can reduce the gain from qS to a strictly smaller value by shifting t into the direction of the "heavier" side.   □

Recall that SUBSET SUM is the following NP-complete problem:
Given non-negative integers $s_1 \leq \cdots \leq s_m \leq S$, decide whether there exist an $I \subseteq \{1, \ldots, m\}$ such that $\sum_{i \in I} s_i = S$.
We consider here a variant of SUBSET SUM where the input contains an additional parameter $q \leq m$ and the question is whether there exists an $I \subseteq \{1, \ldots, m\}$ such that $|I| = q$ and $\sum_{i \in I} s_i = S$. We refer to this problem as "SUBSET SUM with bounded subsets".

Lemma 3. *The problem "SUBSET SUM with bounded subsets" is NP-complete.*

Proof. The problem clearly belongs to NP. NP-hardness basically follows from a close inspection of Karp's [7] polynomial reduction from 3-DIMENSIONAL MATCHING to PARTITION. We omit the details in this abstract.   □

Theorem 2. *"Exact Working Set Selection" (viewed as a decision problem) is NP-complete.*

Proof. Since the optimal threshold t for a given working set I can be found efficiently (and the appropriate working set can be guessed), the problem clearly belongs to NP. We complete the proof by presenting a polynomial reduction from "SUBSET SUM with bounded subsets" to EWSS. From the input parameters $s_1 \leq \cdots \leq s_m \leq S$ and q of "SUBSET SUM with bounded subsets", we derive the following input parameters of EWSS:

- $a_0 = -1$ and $a_i = S/s_i$ for $i = 1, \ldots, m$.
- $(w_0, w_0') = (0, S)$ and $(w_i, w_i') = (s_i, S - s_i)$ for $i = 1, \ldots, m$.
- Parameter $q' = q + 1$ is considered as the bound on the size of the working set and $B = q'S$.

Note that threshold $t = 0$ is an S-unificator. Thus, the largest possible gain for player 1 is $B = q'S$. This gain can be achieved iff there exists a working set S of size q' that puts threshold 0 in a balanced position. Since $0 \notin \{a_0, a_1, \ldots, a_m\}$, 0 is in a balanced position iff

$$\sum_{i \in I: a_i < 0} w_i' = \sum_{i \in I: a_i > 0} w_i \ . \tag{5}$$

According to the choice of the input parameters for EWSS, condition (5) implies that $\sum_{i \in I: a_i < 0} w_i' = w_0' = S$ and $\sum_{i \in I: a_i > 0} w_i = \sum_{i \in I: a_i > 0} s_i$, where the latter sum contains q terms.

This discussion can be summarized as follows: player 1 can achieve gain at least $B = q'S$ iff there exist q terms from $s_1, \ldots, s_n$ that sum-up to S. This shows that "SUBSET SUM with bounded subsets" can be polynomially reduced to EWSS.   □

5   Complexity of Approximate Working Set Selection

Recall that KNAPSACK is the following NP-complete problem:
Given a finite set M of items, a "weight" $w(i) > 0$ and a "value" $v(i) > 0$ for each $i \in M$, a "weight bound" $W > 0$ and a "value goal" $V > 0$, decide whether there exists a subset $\mathcal{I} \subseteq M$ such that

$$W_{\mathcal{I}} := \sum_{i \in \mathcal{I}} w(i) \leq W \text{ and } V_{\mathcal{I}} := \sum_{i \in \mathcal{I}} v(i) \geq V \ .$$

In order to view KNAPSACK as optimization problem, we may drop the value constraint $V_{\mathcal{I}} \geq V$ and ask for a subset $\mathcal{I}$ that leads to the largest possible total value $V_{\mathcal{I}}$ subject to the weight constraint $W_{\mathcal{I}} \leq W$.

We consider here a variant of KNAPSACK where the input contains an additional parameter $q \leq n$ and the constraint $|\mathcal{I}| \leq q$ is put on top of the weight constraint. We refer to this problem as "KNAPSACK with a bounded number of items".

Lemma 4. *"KNAPSACK with a bounded number of items" can be solved by a full approximation scheme within $O(kq^4|M|^2)$ steps, i.e., there exists an algorithm that, on input (M, w, v, W, q, k), runs for $O(kq^4|M|^2)$ steps and outputs a (legal) solution $\mathcal{I}$ whose total value $V_{\mathcal{I}}$ is within factor $1 + 1/k$ of the optimum.*

There exists a full approximation scheme for KNAPSACK due to Ibarra and Kim [5] that is based on "Rounding and Scaling". The full approximation scheme for "KNAPSACK with a bounded number of items" can be designed and analysed in a similar fashion. We omit the proof of Lemma 4 in this abstract.

Theorem 3. *Any algorithm that solves "KNAPSACK with a bounded number of items" within $T(|M|, q)$ steps and outputs a solution whose total value is within factor c of the optimum can be converted into an algorithm that solves "Approximate Working Set Selection" within $O(qmT(m, q))$ steps and outputs a solution that is within factor $2c$ of the optimum.*

Proof. Let I_* denote a working set that leads to the largest possible gain, say g_*, for player 1 and t_* the corresponding threshold (being in a balanced position w.r.t. I_*). According to Lemma 1, we may assume without loss of generality that $t_* \in \{a_1, \ldots, a_m\}$. Define

$$M = \{1, \ldots, m\}, \ M'_* = \{i \in M | \ a_i < t_*\} \text{ and } M''_* = \{i \in M | \ a_i > t_*\}$$

and

$$I'_* = M'_* \cap I_* \text{ and } I''_* = M''_* \cap I_* \ .$$

Note that $g_* = g'_* + g''_*$ where

$$g'_* = \sum_{i \in I'_*} w_i(t - a_i) \text{ and } g''_* = \sum_{i \in I''_*} w_i(a_i - t) \ .$$

Consider the following non-deterministic[7] algorithm:

---
[7] We will later remove non-determinism by means of exhaustive search.

1. Guess $j \in M$ such that $t_* = a_j$, guess $q' = |I'_*|$, and guess whether $g'_* \geq g''_*$.
2. If $g''_* \geq g'_*$, then proceed as follows:
   a) Pick a set $I' \subseteq M'_*$ of size q' such that the parameters w'_i with $i \in I'$ are the q' largest weight parameters in $(w'_i)_{i \in M'_*}$. Compute the total weight $W' = \sum_{i \in I'} w'_i$.
   b) For every $i \in M''_*$, set $v_i = w_i(a_i - t_*)$. Intuitively, v_i represents the gain that results from putting i into the working set. Apply the given algorithm, say A, for "KNAPSACK with a bounded number of items" to the following problem instance:
      - M''_* is the set of items.
      - w_i is the weight and v_i the value of item $i \in M''_*$.
      - $W' + w_j$ is the weight bound and $q'' = q - q'$ is the bound on the number of items.
      Let I'' be the set of indices that is returned by A.
3. If $g''_* < g'_*$, then apply the analogous procedure.
4. Output working set $I = I' \cup I''$.

Let's see how to remove the initial non-deterministic guesses. In a deterministic implementation, the algorithm performs exhaustive search instead of guessing: it loops through all $j \in M$ and $q' \in \{0, \ldots, q\}$, and it explores both possible values (TRUE and FALSE) of the Boolean expression $g''_* \geq g'_*$. Clearly, all but one runs through these loops are based on "wrong guesses". A wrong guess may even lead to an inconsistency. (For example, there might be less than q' points left of a_j.) Whenever such an inconsistency is detected, the algorithm aborts the current iteration and proceeds with the next. Each non-aborted iteration (including the iteration with the correct guesses) leads to a candidate working set. A candidate set leading to the highest gain for player 1 is finally chosen. Observe now that I''_* is a legal solution for the knapsack problem since it is a subset of M'' of size at most $q'' = q - q'$ and

$$\sum_{i \in I''_*} w_i \leq w_j + \sum_{i \in I'_*} w'_i \leq w_j + W' \ .$$

The first inequality holds because t_* is in a balanced position; the second-one holds because W' is the total weight of the q' "heaviest" points left of t_*. Let's now argue that the solution $I = I' \cup I''$ obtained in the iteration with the correct guesses leads to a gain $g \geq g_*/(2c)$. Let g' and g'' denote the gains represented by I' and I'', respectively (such that $g = g' + g''$). For reasons of symmetry, we may assume that $g''_* \geq g'_*$. Then, the following holds:

$$g \geq g'' \geq \frac{1}{c} \max \left\{ \sum_{i \in \mathcal{I}} v_i \ \middle|\ \mathcal{I} \subseteq M'', |\mathcal{I}| \leq q'', \sum_{i \in \mathcal{I}} w_i \leq w_j + W' \right\}$$

$$\geq \frac{1}{c} \sum_{i \in I''_*} v_i = \frac{g''_*}{c} \geq \frac{g_*}{2c} \ .$$

Note that $\mathcal{I}$ is the variable running through all legal solutions for the knapsack problem instance. The second inequality holds because, by assumption, A has performance ratio c. The third inequality holds because I''_* is a legal solution for the knapsack problem instance. The final inequality is valid since $g''_* \geq g'_*$. The time bound $O(qmT(m,q))$ is obvious since there are basically $O(qm)$ calls of the given algorithm A with time bound T.   □

Combining Lemma 4 and Theorem 3 (thereby setting $k = 1$ and $c = 1 + 1/k = 2$ for sake of simplicity), we get

Corollary 2. *There exists an algorithm for "Approximate Working Set Selection" that runs in time $O(q^5 m^3)$ and finds a working set whose gain is within factor 4 of the optimum.*

We briefly note the following

Theorem 4. *There exists a full approximation scheme for "Approximate Working Set Selection".*

The proof will be found in the full paper.

6 Linear Time Construction of a Rate Certifying Pair

We consider again the optimization problem $\mathcal{P}_0$ from (3). Let $x \in R(\mathcal{P}_0)$ be a feasible solution and $x_* \in R(\mathcal{P}_0)$ an optimal feasible solution. Define

$$\sigma(x) := \sup_{x' \in R(\mathcal{P}_0)} \nabla f(x)^\top (x - x') \tag{6}$$

$$\sigma(x|i_1, i_2) := \sup_{x' \in R(\mathcal{P}_0):\, x'_i = x_i \text{ for } i \neq i_1, i_2} \nabla f(x)^\top (x - x') \ . \tag{7}$$

As already noted by Hush and Scovel [4], the following holds:[8]

$$f(x) - f(x_*) \leq \nabla f(x)^\top (x - x_*) \leq \sigma(x) \ . \tag{8}$$

(i_1, i_2) is called an α-*rate certifying pair* for x if

$$\sigma(x|i_1, i_2) \geq \alpha(f(x) - f(x_*)) \ . \tag{9}$$

An α-*rate certifying algorithm* is a decomposition algorithm for $\mathcal{P}_0$ that always includes an α-rate certifying pair for the current feasible solution in the working set. Hush and Scovel [4] have shown that any α-rate certifying algorithm has a polynomial rate of convergence. Furthermore, they provided an algorithm that, given x and $\nabla f(x)$, finds an $(1/m^2)$-rate certifying pair for x in $O(m \log m)$ steps. We can improve on the latter result as follows:

Theorem 5. *There exists a decomposition algorithm for $\mathcal{P}_0$ that, given the current feasible solution x and $\nabla f(x)$ in the beginning of the next iteration, computes an $(1/m^2)$-rate certifying pair for x in $O(m)$ steps.*

---

[8] The first inequality follows from a convexity argument; the second-one is trivial.

Proof. Without loss of generality, we may assume that $\mathcal{P}_0$ is normalized, i.e., y in (3) is the all-ones vector. According to (8),

$$\sigma(x|i_1, i_2) \geq \alpha\sigma(x) \tag{10}$$

is a sufficient condition for (9). Chang, Hsu, and Lin [2] have shown that, for every $x \in R(\mathcal{P}_0)$, there exists a pair (i_1, i_2) that satisfies the stronger condition (10) for $\alpha = 1/m^2$. In order to find an $(1/m^2)$-rate certifying pair for x, it is therefore sufficient to construct a pair (i_1, i_2) that maximizes $\sigma(x|i_1, i_2)$. To this end, we define the quantities

$$\mu_i^+ := x_i - l_i \text{ and } \mu_i^- := r_i - x_i .$$

It is not hard to see that the following holds:

Claim 1. If $\nabla f(x)_{i_1} \geq \nabla f(x)_{i_2}$ then

$$\sigma(x|i_1, i_2) = (\nabla f(x)_{i_1} - \nabla f(x)_{i_2}) \min\{\mu_{i_1}^+, \mu_{i_2}^-\} .$$

Proof of Claim 1. According to (7), we may choose x' such that $\bar{1}^\top x' = 0$, $l \leq x' \leq r$, $x_i' = x_i$ for every $i \neq i_1, i_2$, and

$$\sigma(x|i_1, i_2) = \nabla f(x)_{i_1}(x_{i_1} - x_{i_1}') + \nabla f(x)_{i_2}(x_{i_2} - x_{i_2}') .$$

Recall that x (as a member of $R(\mathcal{P}_0)$) also satisfies $\bar{1}^\top x = 0$ and $l \leq x \leq r$. Thus,

$$0 = \bar{1}^\top(x - x') = (x_{i_1} - x_{i_1}') + (x_{i_2} - x_{i_2}') ,$$

which implies that

$$d := x_{i_1} - x_{i_1}' = x_{i_2}' - x_{i_2} \tag{11}$$

and

$$\sigma(x|i_1, i_2) = d \cdot (\nabla f(x)_{i_1} - \nabla f(x)_{i_2}) .$$

Since, by assumption, $\nabla f(x)_{i_1} - \nabla f(x)_{i_2} \geq 0$, it follows that x' was chosen such as to maximize d from (11) without violating the box-constraints. The largest possible value for d is obviously

$$d = \min\{x_{i_1} - l_{i_1}, r_{i_2} - x_{i_2}\} = \min\{\mu_{i_1}^+, \mu_{i_2}^-\} ,$$

which concludes the proof of Claim 1.

Claim 2. For $\mu \in M := \{x_i - l_i, r_i - x_i|\ i = 1, \ldots, m\}$, define

$$\sigma_\mu(x) = \left(\max_{i_1: \mu_{i_1}^+ \geq \mu} \nabla f(x)_{i_1} - \min_{i_2: \mu_{i_2}^- \geq \mu} \nabla f(x)_{i_2} \right) \mu .$$

Then, the following holds:

$$\max_{i_1, i_2} \sigma(x|i_1, i_2) = \max_\mu \sigma_\mu(x) .$$

Proof of Claim 2. We first show that

$$\max_{i_1,i_2} \sigma(x|i_1, i_2) \leq \max_{\mu} \sigma_\mu(x) \ .$$

According to Claim 1, we may choose i_1^*, i_2^* such that

$$0 \leq \max_{i_1,i_2} \sigma(x|i_1, i_2) = \left(\nabla f(x)_{i_1^*} - \nabla f(x)_{i_2^*}\right) \min\{\mu_{i_1^*}^+, \mu_{i_2^*}^-\} \ .$$

Setting

$$\mu^* := \min\{\mu_{i_1^*}^+, \mu_{i_2^*}^-\} \ ,$$

we may proceed as follows:

$$\max_{i_1,i_2} \sigma(x|i_1, i_2) = \left(\nabla f(x)_{i_1^*} - \nabla f(x)_{i_2^*}\right) \mu_*$$

$$\leq \max_{\mu} \left(\max_{i_1 : \mu_{i_1}^+ \geq \mu} \nabla f(x)_{i_1} - \min_{i_2 : \mu_{i_2}^- \geq \mu} \nabla f(x)_{i_2} \right)$$

The last inequality is valid because $\mu := \mu^*$ and $i_1 := i_1^*, i_2 := i_2^*$ is among the possible choices for μ, i_1, i_2.
The reverse inequality

$$\max_{\mu} \sigma_\mu(x) \leq \max_{i_1,i_2} \sigma(x|i_1, i_2)$$

can be shown is a similar fashion. Choose μ^* and i_1^*, i_2^* such that

$$\mu_{i_1^*}^+ \geq \mu^* \text{ and } \mu_{i_2^*}^- \geq \mu^*$$

and

$$\max_{\mu} \sigma_\mu(x) = \left(\nabla f(x)_{i_1^*} - \nabla f(x)_{i_2^*}\right) \mu_*$$

$$\leq \left(\nabla f(x)_{i_1^*} - \nabla f(x)_{i_2^*}\right) \min\{\mu_{i_1^*}^+, \mu_{i_2^*}^-\}$$

$$\leq \max_{i_1,i_2} \sigma(x|i_1, i_2) \ .$$

This concludes the proof of Claim 2.

In order to compute the pair (i_1, i_2) that maximizes $\sigma(x|i_1, i_2)$, we may apply Claim 2 and proceed as follows:
Consider the values $\mu \in M$ in decreasing order, thereby keeping track of the index $i_1(\mu)$ that maximizes $\nabla f(x)_{i_1}$ subject to $\mu_{i_1}^+ \geq \mu$ and of the index $i_2(\mu)$ that minimizes $\nabla f(x)_{i_2}$ subject to $\mu_{i_2}^- \geq \mu$. Finally, pick the value μ_* that maximizes $\left(\nabla f(x)_{i_1(\mu)} - \nabla f(x)_{i_2(\mu)}\right) \mu$ and output $(i_1(\mu_*), i_2(\mu_*))$.
It is not hard to see that this procedure can be implemented within $O(m)$ steps if we maintain two lists. The first-one contains the items $(i, x_i - l_i)$ and the second-one the items $(i, r_i - x_i)$. Both lists are sorted non-increasingly according to their second component with i ranging from 1 to m.[9] $\square$

---

[9] Note that this data structure can be efficiently updated because two subsequent feasible solutions differ in only two components.

Final Remarks. The time-bound from Lemma 4 for the full approximation scheme for "KNAPSACK with a bounded number of items" is polynomial, but probably leaves space for improvement. According to Theorem 3, any improvement on this time bound immediately leads to more efficient algorithms for "Approximate Working Set Selection".

The central object of our future research is the design of policies that lead to fast convergence to the optimum and, at the same time, can be efficiently implemented for a wide range of optimization problems.

References

[1] Bernhard E. Boser, Isabelle M. Guyon, and Vladimir N. Vapnik. A training algorithm for optimal margin classifiers. In *Proceedings of the 5th Annual ACM Workshop on Computational Learning Theory*, pages 144–152. ACM Press, 1992.

[2] Chih-Chung Chang, Chih-Wei Hsu, and Chih-Jen Lin. The analysis of decomposition methods for support vector machines. *IEEE Transactions on Neural Networks*, 11(4):248–250, 2000.

[3] Chih-Wei Hsu and Chih-Jen Lin. A simple decomposition method for support vector machines. *Machine Learning*, 46(1–3):291–314, 2002.

[4] Don Hush and Clint Scovel. Polynomial-time decomposition algorithms for support vector machines. *Machine Learning*, 51:51–71, 2003.

[5] Oscar H. Ibarra and Chul E. Kim. Fast approximation algorithms for knapsack and sum of subset problem. *Journal of the Association on Computing Machinery*, 22(4):463–468, 1975.

[6] Thorsten Joachims. Making large scale SVM learning practical. In Bernhard Schölkopf, Christopher J. C. Burges, and Alexander J. Smola, editors, *Advances in Kernel Methods—Support Vector Learning*, pages 169–184. MIT Press, 1998.

[7] Richard M. Karp. Reducibility among combinatorial problems. In R. E. Miller and J. W. Thatcher, editors, *Complexity of Computer Computations*, pages 85–103. Plenum Press, 1972.

[8] S. S. Keerthi and E. G. Gilbert. Convergence of a generalized SMO algorithm for SVM classifier design. *Machine Learning*, 46:351–360, 2002.

[9] S. S. Keerthi, S. Shevade, C. Bhattacharyya, and K. Murthy. Improvements to SMO algorithm for SVM regression. *IEEE Transactions on Neural Networks*, 11(5):1188–1193, 2000.

[10] S. S. Keerthi, S. Shevade, C. Bhattacharyya, and K. Murthy. Improvements to Platt's SMO algorithm for SVM classifier design. *Neural Computation*, 13:637–649, 2001.

[11] P. Laskov. An improved decomposition algorithm for regression support vector machines. *Machine Learning*, 46:315–350, 2002.

[12] S.-P. Liao, H.-T. Lin, and Chih-Jen Lin. A note on the decomposition methods for support vector regression. *Neural Computation*, 14:1267–1281, 2002.

[13] Chih-Jen Lin. On the convergence of the decomposition method for support vector machines. *IEEE Transactions on Neural Networks*, 12:1288–1298, 2001.

[14] Chih-Jen Lin. Asymptotic convergence of an SMO algorithm without any assumptions. *IEEE Transactions on Neural Networks*, 13:248–250, 2002.

[15] Chih-Jen Lin. A formal analysis of stopping criteria of decomposition methods for support vector machines. *IEEE Transactions on Neural Networks*, 13:1045–1052, 2002.

[16] Niko List and Hans Ulrich Simon. A general convergence theorem for the decomposition method. In *Proceedings of the 17th Annual Conference on Computational Learning Theory*, pages 363–377 . Springer Verlag, 2004.

[17] O. L. Mangasarian and David R. Musicant. Successive overrelaxation for support vector machines. *IEEE Transactions on Neural Networks*, 10:1032–1037, 1999.

[18] O. L. Mangasarian and David R. Musicant. Active support vector machine classification. In *Advances in Neural Information Processing Systems 12*, pages 577–583. MIT Press, 2000.

[19] O. L. Mangasarian and David R. Musicant. Lagrangian support vector machines. *Journal of Machine Learning Research*, 1:161–177, 2001.

[20] Edgar E. Osuna, Robert Freund, and Federico Girosi. Training support vector machines: an application to face detection. In *Proceedings of IEEE Conference on Computer Vision and Pattern Recognition*, pages 130–136, 1997.

[21] John C. Platt. Fast training of support vector machines using sequential minimal optimization. In Bernhard Schölkopf, Christopher J. C. Burges, and Alexander J. Smola, editors, *Advances in Kernel Methods—Support Vector Learning*, pages 185–208. MIT Press, 1998.

[22] C. Saunders, M. O. Stitson, J. Weston, L. Bottou, Bernhard Schölkopf, and Alexander J. Smola. Support vector machine reference manual. Technical Report CSD-TR-98-03, Royal Holloway, University of London, Egham, UK, 1998.

[23] Vladimir Vapnik. *Statistical Learning Theory*. Wiley Series on Adaptive and Learning Systems for Signal Processing, Communications, and Control. John Wiley & Sons, 1998.

Convergence of a Generalized Gradient Selection Approach for the Decomposition Method[*]

Nikolas List

Fakultät für Mathematik, Ruhr-Universität Bochum, 44780 Bochum, Germany
Niko.List@gmx.de

Abstract. The decomposition method is currently one of the major methods for solving the convex quadratic optimization problems being associated with support vector machines. For a special case of such problems the convergence of the decomposition method to an optimal solution has been proven based on a working set selection via the gradient of the objective function. In this paper we will show that a generalized version of the gradient selection approach and its associated decomposition algorithm can be used to solve a much broader class of convex quadratic optimization problems.

1 Introduction

In the framework of Support–Vector–Machines (SVM) introduced by Vapnik et al. [1] special cases of convex quadratic optimization problems have to be solved. A popular variant of SVM is the C–Support–Vector–Classification (C–SVC) where we try to classify m given data points with binary labels $y \in \{\pm 1\}^m$. This setting induces the following convex optimization problem:

$$\min_x f_C(x) := \frac{1}{2} x^\top Q x - e^\top x \quad \text{s.t.} \quad 0 \leq x_i \leq C, \, \forall i = 1, \dots, m, \, y^\top x = 0 \ , \quad (1)$$

where $x \in \mathbb{R}^m$, C is a real constant and e is the m–dimensional vector of ones. $Q \in \mathbb{R}^{m \times m}$ is a positive semi–definite matrix whose entries depend on the data points and the used kernel[1].

In general, the matrix Q is dense and therefore a huge amount of memory is necessary to store it if traditional optimization algorithms are directly applied to it. A solution to this problem, as proposed by Osuna et al. [4], is to decompose the large problem in smaller ones which are solved iteratively. The key idea is to select a working set B^k in each iteration based on the currently „best" feasible x^k. Then the subproblem based on the variables $x_i, i \in B^k$ is solved and the new solution x^{k+1} is updated on the selected indices while it remains unchanged on

---

[*] This work was supported in part by the IST Programm of the European Community, under the PASCAL Network of Excellence, IST-2002-506778. This publication only reflects the authors views.
[1] The reader interested in more background information concerning SVM is referred to [2,3].

S. Ben-David, J. Case, A. Maruoka (Eds.): ALT 2004, LNAI 3244, pp. 338–349, 2004.

the complement of B^k. This strategy has been used and refined by many other authors [5,6,7].

A key problem in this approach is the selection of the working set B^k. One widely used technique is based on the gradient of the objective function at x^k [5][2]. The convergence of such an approach to an optimal solution has been proven by Lin [8][3]. A shortcoming of the proposed selection and the convergence proof of the associated decomposition method in [8] is that they have only been formulated for the special case of (1) or related problems with only one equality constraint. Unfortunately ν-SVM introduced by Schölkopf et al. [10] leads to optimization problems with two such equality constraints (see e. g. [11]). Although there is an extension of the gradient algorithm to the case of ν-SVM [12] no convergence proof for this case has been published.

1.1   Aim of This Paper

There exist multiple formulations of SVM which are used in different classification and regression problems as well as quantile estimation and novelty detection[4] which all lead to slightly different optimization problems. Nonetheless all of them can be viewed as special cases of a general convex quadratic optimization problem (2, see below). As the discussion concerning the decomposition method has mainly focused on the single case of C–SVC, it may be worth studying under which circumstances the decomposition method is applicable to solve such general problems and when such a strategy converges to an optimal solution. Recently Simon and List have investigated this topic. They prove a very general convergence theorem for the decomposition method, but for the sake of generality no practical selection algorithm is given [13].

The aim of this paper is to show that the well known method of gradient selection as implemented e. g. in SVM^{light} [5] can be extended to solve a far more general class of quadratic optimization problems. In addition, the achieved theoretical foundation, concerning the convergence and efficiency of this selection method, is preserved by adapting Lin's convergence theorem [8] to the decomposition algorithm associated with the proposed general gradient selection.

We want to point out that not necessarily all cases covered by the given generalization arise in SVM but the class of discussed optimization problems subsumes all the above mentioned versions of SVM. The proposed selection algorithm is therefore useful for the decomposition of all such problems and gives a unified approach to the convergence proof of the decomposition method associated with this selection.

---

[2] Platts' SMO [6] with the extension of Keerthi et al. [7] can be viewed as a special case of that selection.

[3] For the special case of SMO Keerthi and Gilbert have proven the convergence [9].

[4] [2,3] both give an overview.

2   Definitions and Notations

2.1   Notations

The following naming conventions will be helpful: If $A \in \mathbb{R}^{n \times m}$ is a matrix, $A_i, i \in \{1, \dots, m\}$ will denote the ith column. Vectors $x \in \mathbb{R}^m$ will be considered column vectors so that their transpose $x^\top$ is a row vector. We will often deal with a partitioning of $\{1, \dots, m\}$ in two disjunct sets B and N and in this case the notion A_B will mean the matrix consisting only of columns A_i with $i \in B$. Ignoring permutation of columns we therefore write $A = [\, A_B \ A_N \,]$. The same shall hold for vectors $x \in \mathbb{R}^m$ where x_B denotes the vector consisting only of entries x_i with $i \in B$. We can therefore expand $Ax = d$ to $[\, A_B \ A_N \,] \left(\begin{smallmatrix} x_B \\ x_N \end{smallmatrix} \right) = d$. A matrix $Q \in \mathbb{R}^{m \times m}$ can then be decomposed to four block matrices Q_{BB}, Q_{BN}, Q_{NB} and Q_{NN} accordingly.

Inequalities $l \leq r$ of two vectors $l, r \in \mathbb{R}^m$ will be short for $l_i \leq r_i, \forall i \in \{1, \dots, m\}$. In addition we will adopt the convention that the maximum over an empty set will be $-\infty$ and the minimum ∞ accordingly.

Throughout the paper, we will be concerned with the following convex quadratic optimization problem $\mathcal{P}$:

$$\min_x f(x) := \frac{1}{2} x^\top Q x + c^\top x \text{ s.t. } l \leq x \leq u, \ Ax = d \qquad (2)$$

where Q is a positive semi-definite matrix and $A \in \mathbb{R}^{n \times m}$, $l, u, x, c \in \mathbb{R}^m$ and $d \in \mathbb{R}^n$. The feasibility region of $\mathcal{P}$ will be denoted by $\mathcal{R}(\mathcal{P})$.

2.2   Selections, Subproblems, and Decomposition

Let us now define the notions used throughout this paper.

Definition 1 (Selection). *Let $q < m$. A map $B : \mathbb{R}^m \longrightarrow \mathfrak{P}(\{1, \dots, m\})$ such that $|B(x)| \leq q$ for any x and $\hat{x}$ is optimal wrt. $\mathcal{P}$ iff $B(\hat{x}) = \emptyset$ is called (q-)significant selection wrt. $\mathcal{P}$.*[5]

Definition 2 (Subproblem). *For a given set $B \subset \{1, \dots, m\}$ with $|B| \leq q$, $N := \{1, \dots, m\} \backslash B$ and a given $x \in \mathcal{R}(\mathcal{P})$ we define $f_{B,x_N}(x') := \frac{1}{2} x'^\top Q_{BB} x' + (c_B + Q_{BN} x_N)^\top x'$ for every $x' \in \mathbb{R}^q$. The following optimization problem $\mathcal{P}_{B,x_N}$*

$$\min_{x'} f_{B,x_N}(x') \text{ s.t. } l_B \leq x' \leq u_B, \ A_B x' = d - A_N x_N \qquad (3)$$

*will be called the **subproblem** induced by B.*[6]

We are now in the position to define the decomposition method formally:

Algorithm 1 (Decomposition Method). *The following algorithm can be associated with every significant selection wrt. $\mathcal{P}$*

---

[5] If x is evident from the context we often write B instead of $B(x)$.
[6] Note, that $\mathcal{P}_{B,x_N}$ is a special case of $\mathcal{P}$.

1: **Initialize:** $k \leftarrow 0$ and $x^0 \in \mathcal{R}(\mathcal{P})$
2: $B \leftarrow B(x^k)$
3: **while** $B \neq \emptyset$ **do**
4:     $N \leftarrow \{1, \dots, m\} \setminus B$
5:     Find x' as an optimal solution of $\mathcal{P}_{B, x_N^k}$
6:     Set $x^{k+1} \leftarrow \begin{pmatrix} x' \\ x_N^k \end{pmatrix}$
7:     $k \leftarrow k+1$, $B \leftarrow B(x^k)$
8: **end while**

This algorithm shall be called the **decomposition method** of $\mathcal{P}$ induced by B.

3   Gradient Selection

The idea of selecting the indices via an ordering according to the gradients of the objective function has been motivated by the idea to select indices which contribute most to the steepest descent in the gradient field (see [5]). We would like to adopt another point of view in which indices violating the KKT–conditions of the problem $\mathcal{P}$ are selected. This idea has been used e. g. in [7] and [11].

To motivate this we will first focus on the well–known problem of C–SVC (Sec. 3.1) and later enhance this strategy to a more general setting (Sec. 3.2).

3.1 C-SVC and KKT–Violating Pairs

In the case of C–SVC a simple reformulation of the KKT–conditions leads to the following optimality criterion: $\hat{x}$ is optimal wrt. (1) iff there exists a $b \in \mathbb{R}$ such that for any $i \in \{1, \dots, m\}$

$$\left(\hat{x}_i > 0 \Rightarrow \nabla f(\hat{x})_i - by_i \leq 0\right) \quad \text{and} \quad \left(\hat{x}_i < C \Rightarrow \nabla f(\hat{x})_i - by_i \geq 0\right) . \quad (4)$$

Following [8] (4) can be rewritten as

$$\left(i \in \overline{I_{bot}}(\hat{x}) \Rightarrow y_i \nabla f(\hat{x})_i \geq b\right) \quad \text{and} \quad \left(i \in \overline{I_{top}}(\hat{x}) \Rightarrow y_i \nabla f(\hat{x})_i \leq b\right) ,$$

where

$$\overline{I_{top}}(x) := \{i \mid (x_i < C, y_i = -1) \wedge (x_i > 0, y_i = 1)\}$$
$$\overline{I_{bot}}(x) := \{i \mid (x_i > 0, y_i = -1) \wedge (x_i < C, y_i = 1)\} .$$

The KKT–conditions can therefore be collapsed to a simple inequality[7]: $\hat{x}$ is optimal iff

$$\max_{i \in \overline{I_{top}}(x)} y_i \nabla f(x)_i \leq \min_{i \in \overline{I_{bot}}(x)} y_i \nabla f(x)_i \quad (5)$$

---

[7] Note, that if one of the sets is empty, it's easy to fulfill the KKT–conditions by choosing an arbitrarily large or small b.

Given a non–optimal feasible x, we can now identify indices $(i,j) \in \overline{I_{top}}(x) \times \overline{I_{bot}}(x)$ that satisfy the following inequality:

$$y_i \nabla f(x)_i > y_j \nabla f(x)_j$$

Such pairs do not admit the selection of a $b \in \mathbb{R}$ according to (4). Following [9], such indices are therefore called KKT–violating pairs .

From this point of view the selection algorithm proposed by Joachims chooses pairs of indices which violate this inequality the most. As this strategy, implemented for example in SVM^{light} [5], selects the candidates in $\overline{I_{top}}(x)$ from the top of the list sorted according to the value of $y_i \nabla f(x)_i$, Lin calls indices in $\overline{I_{top}}(x)$,,top–candidates" (see [8]). Elements from $\overline{I_{bot}}(x)$ are selected from the bottom of this list and are called ,,bottom–candidates". We will adopt this naming convention here.

3.2   General KKT–Pairing

We will now show that a pairing strategy, based on a generalized version of the KKT–conditions in (5), can be extended to a more general class of convex quadratic optimization problems. The exact condition is given in the following definition:

Definition 3. *Let $\mathcal{P}$ be a general convex quadratic optimization problem as given in (2). If any selection of pairwise linearly independent columns $A_i \in \mathbb{R}^n$ of the equality constraint matrix A is linearly independent, we call the problem $\mathcal{P}$ **decomposable by pairing**.*

Note, that most variants of SVM, including ν–SVM, fulfill this restriction. We may then define an equivalence relation on the set of indices $i \in \{1, \ldots, m\}$ as follows:

$$i \sim j \Leftrightarrow \exists \lambda_{i,j} \in \mathbb{R} \setminus \{0\} : \lambda_{i,j} A_i = A_j \tag{6}$$

Let $\{i_r \mid r = 1, \ldots, s\}$ be a set of representatives of this relation. The subset of corresponding columns

$$\{a_r := A_{i_r} \mid r = 1, \ldots, s\} \subset \{A_i \mid i = 1, \ldots, m\}$$

therefore represents the columns of A up to scalar multiplication. Additionally, we define $\lambda_i := \lambda_{i,i_r}$ for any $i \in [i_r]$. Thus $\lambda_i A_i = a_r$ if $i \in [i_r]$.

From Definition 3 we draw two simple conclusions for such a set of representatives: As all $\{a_r \mid r = 1, \ldots, s\}$ are pairwise linearly independent by construction, they are linearly independent and it follows that $s = \dim\langle a_r \mid r = 1, \ldots, s\rangle \leq \operatorname{rank} A \leq n$.

To formulate the central theorem of this section we define our generalized notion of ,,top" and ,,bottom" candidates first:

Definition 4. *Let* $\{i_1, \ldots, i_s\}$ *be a set of representatives for the equivalence relation* (6). *For any* $r \in \{1, \ldots, s\}$ *we define:*

$$\overline{I_{top,r}}(x) := [i_r] \cap \{j \mid (x_j > l_j \wedge \lambda_j > 0) \vee (x_j < u_j \wedge \lambda_j < 0)\}$$

$$\overline{I_{bot,r}}(x) := [i_r] \cap \{j \mid (x_j > l_j \wedge \lambda_j < 0) \vee (x_j < u_j \wedge \lambda_j > 0)\}$$

Indices in $\overline{I_{top,r}}(x)$ $(\overline{I_{bot,r}}(x))$ *are called* **top candidates (bottom candidates)**. *Top candidates for which* $x_i = l_i$ *or* $x_i = u_i$ *are called* **top–only** *candidates. The notion* **bottom–only** *candidate is defined accordingly. We use the following notation:*

$$I_{top,r}(x) := \{i \in \overline{I_{top,r}}(x) \mid x_i \in \{l_i, u_i\}\} ,$$

$$I_{bot,r}(x) := \{i \in \overline{I_{bot,r}}(x) \mid x_i \in \{l_i, u_i\}\}$$

The following naming convention will be helpful:

$$\overline{I_{top}}(x) := \bigcup_{r \in \{i_1, \ldots, i_s\}} \overline{I_{top,r}}(x) .$$

$\overline{I_{bot}}(x)$, $I_{top}(x)$ *and* $I_{bot}(x)$ *are defined accordingly.*

We will now generalize (5) to problems $\mathcal{P}$ decomposable by pairing. The KKT–conditions of such a problem $\mathcal{P}$ say that $\hat{x}$ is optimal wrt. $\mathcal{P}$ iff there exists an $h \in \mathbb{R}^n$ such that for any $i \in \{1, \ldots, m\}$

$$\left(\hat{x}_i > l_i \Rightarrow \nabla f(\hat{x})_i - A_i^\top h \leq 0\right) \quad \text{and} \quad \left(\hat{x}_i < u_i \Rightarrow \nabla f(\hat{x})_i - A_i^\top h \geq 0\right) .$$

Given a set of representatives $\{i_r \mid r = 1, \ldots, s\}$ and $A_i = \frac{1}{\lambda_i} a_r$ for $i \in [i_r]$ this condition can be written as follows: $\hat{x}$ is optimal wrt. $\mathcal{P}$ iff there exists an $h \in \mathbb{R}^n$ such that for any $i \in \{1, \ldots, m\}$

$$\left(i \in \overline{I_{top,r}}(\hat{x}) \Rightarrow \lambda_i \nabla f(\hat{x})_i \leq a_r^\top h\right) \text{ and } \left(i \in \overline{I_{bot,r}}(\hat{x}) \Rightarrow \lambda_i \nabla f(\hat{x})_i \geq a_r^\top h\right) \quad (7)$$

The following theorem will show that the KKT–conditions of such problems can be collapsed to a simple inequality analogous to (5):

Theorem 1. *If problem* $\mathcal{P}$ *is decomposable by pairing and a set of representatives* $\{i_1, \ldots, i_r\}$ *for the equivalence relation* (6) *is given, the KKT–conditions can be stated as follows:* $\hat{x}$ *is optimal wrt.* $\mathcal{P}$ *iff for all* $r \in \{1, \ldots, s\}$

$$\max_{i \in \overline{I_{top,r}}(\hat{x})} \lambda_i \nabla f(\hat{x})_i \leq \min_{i \in \overline{I_{bot,r}}(\hat{x})} \lambda_i \nabla f(\hat{x})_i \quad (8)$$

Proof. For an optimal $\hat{x}$ *equation* (8) *follows immediately from* (7).
    To prove the opposite direction we define $h_{top}^r := \max_{i \in \overline{I_{top,r}}(x)} \lambda_i \nabla f(x)_i$ *and* $h_{bot}^r := \min_{i \in \overline{I_{bot,r}}(x)} \lambda_i \nabla f(x)_i$ *for any* $r \in \{1, \ldots, s\}$. *By assumption* $h_{top}^r \leq h_{bot}^r$

and we can choose $\bar{h}^r \in [h^r_{top}, h^r_{bot}]$. As $\mathcal{P}$ is decomposable by pairing, it follows that $(a_1, \dots, a_s)^\top \in \mathbb{R}^{s \times n}$ represents a surjective linear mapping from $\mathbb{R}^n$ to $\mathbb{R}^s$. Thus there exists an $h \in \mathbb{R}^n$ such that for all $r \in \{1, \dots, s\} : a_r^\top h = \bar{h}^r$. We conclude that

$$\lambda_i \nabla f(x)_i \leq h^r_{top} \leq \bar{h}^r = a_r^\top h \ \ if \ i \in \overline{I_{top,r}}(x)$$
$$\lambda_i \nabla f(x)_i \geq h^r_{bot} \geq \bar{h}^r = a_r^\top h \ \ if \ i \in \overline{I_{bot,r}}(x)$$

holds for all $i \in \{1, \dots, m\}$. Therefore the KKT–conditions (7) are satisfied and $\hat{x}$ is an optimal solution.   □

3.3   Selection Algorithm

Given a set of representatives $\{i_1, \dots, i_s\}$ and the corresponding λ_i for all $i \in \{1, \dots, m\}$ we are now able to formalize a generalized gradient selection algorithm. For any $x \in \mathcal{R}(\mathcal{P})$ we call the set

$$\mathcal{C}(x) := \{(i,j) \in \overline{I_{top,r}}(x) \times \overline{I_{bot,r}}(x) \mid \lambda_i \nabla f(x)_i - \lambda_j \nabla f(x)_j > 0, r = 1, \dots, s\}$$

selection candidates wrt. x.

Algorithm 2. *Given a feasible x, we can calculate a $B(x) \subset \{1, \dots, m\}$ for an even q as follows:*

1: **Initialize:** $\mathcal{C} \leftarrow \mathcal{C}(x)$, $B \leftarrow \emptyset$, $l \leftarrow q$.
2: **while** $(l > 0)$ *and* $(\mathcal{C} \neq \emptyset)$ **do**
3:     *Choose* $(i,j) = \mathrm{argmax}_{(i,j) \in \mathcal{C}} \ \lambda_i \nabla f(x)_i - \lambda_j \nabla f(x)_j$
4:     $B \leftarrow B \cup \{i,j\}$.
5:     $\mathcal{C} \leftarrow \mathcal{C} \setminus \{i,j\}^2$, $l \leftarrow l - 2$.
6: **end while**
7: **return** B

We note that the selection algorithms given in [5,8,11,12,7] can be viewed as special cases of this algorithm. This holds as well for the extensions to ν–SVM.

4   Convergence of the Decomposition Method

Theorem 1 implies that the mapping B returned by Algorithm 2 is a significant selection in the sense of Definition 1 and therefore induces a decomposition method. Such a decomposition method converges to an optimal solution of $\mathcal{P}$ as stated in the following theorem:

Theorem 2. *Let $\mathcal{P}$ be a convex quadratic optimization problem decomposable by pairing. Then any limit point $\bar{x}$ of a sequence $(x_n)_{n \in \mathbb{N}}$ of iterative solutions of a decomposition method induced by a general gradient selection according to Algorithm 2 is an optimal solution of $\mathcal{P}$.*

The proof is given in the following sections and differs only in some technical details from the one given in [8].

4.1   Technical Lemmata

Let us first note that $\mathcal{R}(\mathcal{P})$ is compact and therefore, for any sequence $(x_n)_{n \in \mathbb{N}}$ of feasible solutions such a limit point $\bar{x}$ exists. Let, in the following, $(x_k)_{k \in \mathcal{K}}$ be a converging subsequence such that $\bar{x} = \lim_{k \in \mathcal{K}, k \to \infty} x_k$.

If we assume that the matrix Q satisfies the equation $\min_I \lambda_{min}(Q_{II}) > 0$ where I ranges over all subsets of $\{1, \dots, m\}$ such that $|I| \leq q$ we can prove the following Lemma[8]:

Lemma 1. *Let $(x^k)_{k \in \mathcal{K}}$ be a converging subsequence. There exists an $\sigma > 0$ such that*

$$f(x^k) - f(x^{k+1}) \geq \sigma \|x^{k+1} - x^k\|^2$$

Proof. Let B^k denote $B(x^k)$, $N^k = \{1, \dots, m\} \setminus B^k$ and $d := x^k - x^{k+1}$. Since f is a quadratic function Taylor-expansion around x^{k+1} yields

$$f(x^k) = f(x^{k+1}) + \nabla f(x^{k+1})^\top d + \frac{1}{2} d^\top Q d . \tag{9}$$

As x^{k+1} is an optimal solution of the convex optimization problem $\mathcal{P}_{B^k, x^k_{N^k}}$ we can conclude that the line segment L between x^k and x^{k+1} lies in the feasibility region $\mathcal{R}(\mathcal{P}_{B^k, x^k_{N^k}})$ of the subproblem induced by B^k and therefore $f(x^{k+1}) = \min_{x \in L} f(x)$. Thus, the gradient at x^{k+1} in direction to x^k is ascending, i.e.

$$\nabla f(x^{k+1})^\top d \geq 0 . \tag{10}$$

If $\sigma := \frac{1}{2} \min_I \lambda_{min}(Q_{II}) > 0$, the Courant-Fischer Minimax Theorem [15] implies

$$d^\top Q d \geq 2\sigma \|d\|^2 . \tag{11}$$

From (9), (10) and (11), the lemma follows.   □

Lemma 2. *For any $l \in \mathbb{N}$ the sequence $(x^{k+l})_{k \in \mathcal{K}}$ converges with limit point $\bar{x}$ and, as $\lambda_i \nabla f(x)$ is continuous in x, $(\lambda_i \nabla f(x^{k+l})_i)_{k \in \mathcal{K}}$ converges accordingly with limit point $\lambda_i \nabla f(\bar{x})_i$ for all $i \in \{1, \dots, m\}$*

Proof. According to Lemma 1, $(f(x^k))_{k \in \mathcal{K}}$ is a monotonically decreasing sequence on a compact set and therefore converges and we are thus able to bound $\|x^{k+1} - \bar{x}\|$ for $k \in \mathcal{K}$ as follows:

$$\|x^{k+1} - \bar{x}\| \leq \|x^{k+1} - x^k\| + \|x^k - \bar{x}\|$$

$$\leq \sqrt{\frac{1}{\sigma}(f(x^k) - f(x^{k+1}))} + \|x^k - \bar{x}\|$$

---

[8] This holds if Q is positive definite. With respect to problems induced by SVM this tends to hold for small q or special kernels like for example RBF-kernels. For the special case of SMO ($q = 2$) Lemma 1 has been proven without this assumption [14].

As $f(x^k)$ is a cauchy sequence and $x^k \xrightarrow{k \in \mathcal{K}, k \to \infty} \bar{x}$, this term converges to zero for $k \in \mathcal{K}$ and $k \to \infty$. Therefore $(x^{k+1})_{k \in \mathcal{K}}$ converges with limit $\bar{x}$. By induction the claim follows for any $l \in \mathbb{N}$. $\square$

Lemma 3. For any $i, j \in \{1, \ldots, m\}$ such that $i \sim j$ and $\lambda_i \nabla f(\bar{x})_i > \lambda_j \nabla f(\bar{x})_j$ and all $l \in \mathbb{N}$ there exists a $k \in \mathcal{K}$ such that for the next l iterations $k' \in \{k, \ldots, k+l\}$ the following holds:
If i, j are both selected in iteration k', either i becomes bottom–only or j becomes top–only for the next iteration $k' + 1$.

Proof. According to Lemma 2 we can find for any given $l \in \mathbb{N}$ a $k \in \mathcal{K}$ such that for any $k' \in \{k, \ldots, k+l\}$ the following inequality holds:

$$\lambda_i \nabla f(x^{k'+1})_i > \lambda_j \nabla f(x^{k'+1})_j . \tag{12}$$

Assume that $i, j \in B(x^{k'})$ for any $k' \in \{k, \ldots, k+l\}$. As both indices are in the working set, $x^{k'+1}$ is an optimal solution of $\mathcal{P}_{B(x^{k'}), x_{N(k')}^{k'}}$. For sake of contradiction we assume that i is top candidate and j bottom candidate in iteration $k'+1$ at the same time, i.e. $i \in \overline{I_{top,r}}(x^{k'+1})$ and $j \in \overline{I_{bot,r}}(x^{k'+1})$ for an $r \in \{1, \ldots, s\}$[9]. In this case, as $\mathcal{P}_{B(x^{k'}), x_{N(k')}^{k'}}$ is decomposable by pairing, Theorem 1 implies

$$\lambda_i \nabla f(x^{k'+1})_i \leq \lambda_j \nabla f(x^{k'+1})_j .$$

This contradicts to (12) and the choice of k'. $\square$

4.2 Convergence Proof

We are now in the position to state the main proof of the convergence theorem. For sake of contradiction, we assume there exists a limit point $\bar{x}$ which is not optimal wrt. $\mathcal{P}$.

In the following, we will concentrate on the set $\mathcal{C}_> := \{r \mid [i_r]^2 \cap C(\bar{x}) \neq \emptyset\} \subset \{1, \ldots, s\}$ of equivalence classes which contribute to the selection candidates $C(\bar{x})$ on the limit point $\bar{x}$. As $\bar{x}$ is not optimal $\mathcal{C}_> \neq \emptyset$. For any such equivalence class we select the most violating pair (ι_r, κ_r) as follows:

$$(\iota_r, \kappa_r) = \text{argmax}_{(i,j) \in \mathcal{C}(\bar{x}) \cap [i_r]^2} \lambda_i \nabla f(\bar{x})_i - \lambda_j \nabla f(\bar{x})_j$$

Based on these pairs, we define the following two sets for any $r \in \mathcal{C}_>$:

$$\mathcal{I}_r := \{i \in [i_r] \mid \lambda_i \nabla f(\bar{x})_i \geq \lambda_{\iota_r} \nabla f(\bar{x})_{\iota_r}\}$$
$$\mathcal{K}_r := \{i \in [i_r] \mid \lambda_i \nabla f(\bar{x})_i \leq \lambda_{\kappa_r} \nabla f(\bar{x})_{\kappa_r}\}$$

For any iteration $k \in \mathbb{N}$ an index $i \in \mathcal{I}_r \setminus \{\iota_r\}$ will then be called dominating ι_r in iteration k iff $i \in \overline{I_{top,r}}(x^k)$. An index $j \in \mathcal{K}_r \setminus \{\kappa_r\}$ will be called dominating κ_r

---

[9] As $i \sim j$ such an r must exist

iff $j \in \overline{I_{bot,r}}(x^k)$ accordingly. d^k will denote the number of all dominating indices in iteration k. Note that, as no $i \in [i_r]$ can dominate ι_r as well as κ_r in one iteration, d^k is bounded by $m - 2|\mathcal{C}_>|$. We now claim, that there exists a $k \in \mathcal{K}$ such that, for the next $m_{\mathcal{C}} := m - 2|\mathcal{C}_>| + 1$ iterations $k' \in \{k, \dots, k + m_{\mathcal{C}}\}$, the following two conditions hold: 1) $d^{k'} > 0$ and 2) $d^{k'+1} < d^{k'}$ which leads to the aspired contradiction.

The $k \in \mathcal{K}$ we are looking for can be chosen, according to Lemma 2, such that for the next $m_{\mathcal{C}} + 1$ iterations all inequalities on $\bar{x}$ will be preserved, i.e. for $k' \in \{k, \dots, k + m_{\mathcal{C}} + 1\}$ the following holds:

$$\forall (i,j) \in \{1, \dots, m\}^2 : \lambda_i \nabla f(\bar{x})_i < \lambda_j \nabla f(\bar{x})_j \Rightarrow \lambda_i \nabla f(x^{k'})_i < \lambda_j \nabla f(x^k)_j ,$$

$$\bar{x}_i > l_i \Rightarrow x^{k'} > l_i \quad \text{and} \quad \bar{x}_i < u_i \Rightarrow x^{k'} < u_i .$$

Note that $(\iota_r, \kappa_r) \in \overline{I_{top,r}}(x^{k'}) \times \overline{I_{bot,r}}(x^{k'})$ for any such k' and thus, due to Lemma 3, they cannot be select at the same time. Let us now prove the two conditions introduced earlier for the selected k:

1) As $d^{k'} = 0$ would imply, that for any $r \in \mathcal{C}_>$

$$(\iota_r, \kappa_r) = \mathrm{argmax}_{(i,j) \in \mathcal{C}(x^{k'})} \lambda_i \nabla f(x^{k'})_i - \lambda_j \nabla f(x^{k'})_j$$

at least one pair (ι_r, κ_r) would be selected in the next iteration $k' + 1$ which is, by choice of k, not possible for any $k' \in \{k, \dots, k + m_{\mathcal{C}}\}$. Therefore $d^{k'} > 0$ holds for all such k' as claimed.

2) To prove that $d^{k'}$ will decrease in every iteration $k' \in \{k, \dots, k + m_{\mathcal{C}}\}$ by at least one, we have to consider two aspects: First, there have to be vanishing dominating indices, i.e. a top candidate from $\mathcal{I}_r$ has to become bottom–only or a bottom candidate from $\mathcal{K}_r$ has to become top–only. Second, we have to take care that the number of non-dominating indices, which become dominating in the next iteration, is strictly bounded by the number of vanishing dominating indices.

Note, that the state of an index i, concerning domination, only changes if i is selected, i.e. $i \in B(x^{k'})$. As we will only be concerned with such selected indices, let us define the following four sets:

$$\mathcal{I}_r^+ := \mathcal{I}_r \cap \overline{I_{top,r}}(x^{k'}) \cap B(x^{k'}) , \quad \mathcal{I}_r^- := \mathcal{I}_r \setminus \{\iota_r\} \cap I_{bot,r}(x^{k'}) \cap B(x^{k'}) ,$$

$$\mathcal{K}_r^+ := \mathcal{K}_r \cap \overline{I_{bot,r}}(x^{k'}) \cap B(x^{k'}) , \quad \mathcal{K}_r^- := \mathcal{K}_r \setminus \{\iota_r\} \cap I_{top,r}(x^{k'}) \cap B(x^{k'})$$

$\mathcal{I}_r^+$ contains the selected indices dominating ι_r in the current iteration while $\mathcal{I}_r^-$ contains the selected indices from $\mathcal{I}_r \setminus \{\iota_r\}$ currently not dominating ι_r. $\mathcal{K}_r^+$ and $\mathcal{K}_r^-$ are defined accordingly. Let us first state a simple lemma concerning vanishing dominating indices:

Lemma 4. *In the next iteration all indices from $\mathcal{I}_r^+$ will become bottom–only or all indices from $\mathcal{K}_r^+$ will become top–only.*
In particular, if $\mathcal{I}_r^+ \neq \emptyset$ and $\mathcal{K}_r^+ = \emptyset$ κ_r is selected and all indices from $\mathcal{I}_r^+$ will become bottom–only. The same holds for $\mathcal{K}_r^r \neq \emptyset$ and $\mathcal{I}_r^+ = \emptyset$ accordingly.

Proof. If both sets are empty there's nothing to show. Without loss of generality we assume $\mathcal{I}_r^+ \neq \emptyset$. In this case there have to be selected bottom candidates from $[i_r]$ as the indices are selected pairwise.

If $\mathcal{K}_r^+ = \emptyset$, by choice of k, the first selected bottom candidate has to be κ_r. As κ_r is a bottom candidate in the next iteration as well, the claim follows according to Lemma 3.

If $\mathcal{K}_r^+ \neq \emptyset$, the assumption that a pair $(i,j) \in \mathcal{I}_r^+ \times \mathcal{K}_r^+$ exists, such that i will be top and j will be bottom candidate in the next iteration, contradicts to Lemma 3. □

The next lemma will deal with indices currently non–dominating but, in the next iteration, eventually becoming dominating:

Lemma 5. *If $\mathcal{I}_r^- \neq \emptyset$ the following two conditions hold[10]: $|\mathcal{I}_r^-| < |\mathcal{I}_r^+|$ and $\mathcal{K}_r^- = \emptyset$. The same holds for $\mathcal{K}_r^-$ respectively.*

Proof. If $\mathcal{I}_r^- \neq \emptyset$ all selected top candidates dominate ι_r and $\mathcal{K}_r^-$ is therefore empty. As the indices are selected pairwise in every class, it holds that $2|\mathcal{I}_r^+| = |B(x^{k'}) \cap [i_r]| > 0$. In addition, $\kappa_r \in B(x^{k'}) \cap [i_r]$ and it therefore follows that at least one selected bottom candidate is not in $\mathcal{I}_r$ and thus $|\mathcal{I}_r^-| + 1 \leq |\mathcal{I}_r^+|$. □

To finalize the proof, we note that for at least one $r \in \mathcal{C}_>$ there have to be dominating indices, i.e. $\mathcal{I}_r^+ \neq \emptyset$ or $\mathcal{K}_r^+ \neq \emptyset$. Otherwise, by choice of k, (ι_r, κ_r) would be selected for some r.

Thus, according to Lemma 4, the number of vanishing dominating indices is strictly positive and, according to Lemma 5, the number of non–dominating indices, eventually becoming dominating, is strictly smaller. This proves condition 2) and, with condition 1), leads to a contradiction as mentioned above.

Thus the assumption that a limit point $\bar{x}$ is not optimal has to be wrong and the decomposition method, based on the generalized gradient selection, converges for problems decomposable by pairing. □

5   Final Remarks and Open Problems

We have shown that the well–known method of selecting the working set according to the gradient of the objective function can be generalized to a larger class of convex quadratic optimization problems. The complexity of the given extension is equal to Joachims' selection algorithm except for an initialization overhead for the calculation of the classes of indices and the λ_i. Thus implementations like SVM^{light} [5] can easily be extended to solve such problems with little extra cost.

We would like to point out that the given selection algorithm and the extended convergence proof hold for most variants of SVM including the ν-SVM for which the proof of convergence of a decomposition method with a gradient selection strategy (e.g. [12]) has not been published yet.

It would be interesting to eliminate the restriction on the matrix Q (see footnote 8) and to extend the proof in [14] to working sets with more than two

---

[10] We briefly note, that such candidates might only exist if ι_r is top–only.

indices. A more interesting topic for future research would be the extension of known results concerning speed of convergences (e.g. [16], [17]) to the extended gradient selection approach proposed in this paper.

Acknowledgments. Thanks to Hans Simon for pointing me to a more elegant formulation of Definition 3 and to a simplification in the main convergence proof. Thanks to Dietrich Braess for pointing out the simpler formulation of the proof of Lemma 1.

References

[1] Boser, B.E., Guyon, I.M., Vapnik, V.N.: A Training Algorithm for Optimal Margin Classifiers. In: Proceedings of the 5th Annual Workshop on Computational Learning Theory, ACM Press (1992) 144–153
[2] Christianini, N., Shawe-Taylor, J.: An Introduction to Support Vector Machines. 5. edn. Cambridge University Press (2003)
[3] Schölkopf, B., Smola, A.J.: Learning with Kernels. 2. edn. MIT Press (2002)
[4] Osuna, E., Freund, R., Girosi, F.: An Improved Training Algorithm for Support Vector Machines. In Principe, J., Gile, L., Morgan, N., Wilson, E., eds.: Neural Networks for Signal Processing VII – Proceedings of the 1997 IEEE Workshop, New York, IEEE (1997) 276–285
[5] Joachims, T.: 11. [18] 169–184
[6] Platt, J.C.: 12. [18] 185–208
[7] Keerthi, S.S., Shevade, S.K., Bhattacharyya, C., Murthy, K.R.K.: Improvements to Platt's SMO algorithm for SVM classifier design. Neural Computation **13** (2001) 637–649
[8] Lin, C.J.: On the Convergence of the Decomposition Method for Support Vector Machines. IEEE Transactions on Neural Networks **12** (2001) 1288–1298
[9] Keerthi, S.S., Gilbert, E.G.: Convergence of a generalized SMO algorithm for SVM classifier design. Machine Learning **46** (2002) 351–360
[10] Schölkopf, B., Smola, A.J., Williamson, R., Bartlett, P.: New Support Vector Algorithms. Neural Computation **12** (2000) 1207–1245
[11] Chen, P.H., Lin, C.J., Schölkopf, B.: A Tutorial on ν–Support Vector Machines. (http://www.csie.ntu.edu.tw/~cjlin/papers/nusvmtutorial.pdf)
[12] Chang, C.C., Lin, C.C.: Training ν- Support Vector Classifiers: Theory and Algorithms. Neural Computation **10** (2001) 2119–2147
[13] Simon, H.U., List, N.: A General Convergence Theorem for the Decomposition Method. In Shawe-Taylor, J., Singer, Y., eds.: Proceedings of the 17th Annual Conference on Learning Theory, COLT 2004. Volume 3120/2004 of Lecture Notes in Computer Science., Heidelberg, Springer Verlag (2004) 363–377
[14] Lin, C.J.: Asymptotic Convergence of an SMO Algorithm without any Assumptions. IEEE Transactions on Neural Networks **13** (2002) 248–250
[15] Golub, G.H., Loan, C.F.: Matrix Computations. 3. edn. The John Hopkins University Press (1996)
[16] Lin, C.C.: Linear Convergence of a Decomposition Method for Support Vector Machines. (http://www.csie.ntu.edu.tw/~cjlin/papers/linearconv.pdf)
[17] Hush, D., Scovel, C.: Polynomial-time Decomposition Algorithms for Support Vector Machines. Machine Learning **51** (2003) 51–71
[18] Schölkopf, B., Burges, C.J.C., Smola, A.J., eds.: Advances in Kernel Methods – Support Vector Learning. MIT Press, Cambridge, MA (1999)

Newton Diagram and Stochastic Complexity in Mixture of Binomial Distributions

Keisuke Yamazaki and Sumio Watanabe

Precision and Intelligence Laboratory, Tokyo Institute of Technology
4259 Nagatsuda, Midori-ku, Yokohama, 226-8503 Japan
Mailbox R2-5
{k-yam,swatanab}@pi.titech.ac.jp

Abstract. Many singular learning machines such as neural networks and mixture models are used in the information engineering field. In spite of their wide range applications, their mathematical foundation of analysis is not yet constructed because of the singularities in the parameter space.

In recent years, we developed the algebraic geometrical method that shows the relation between the efficiency in Bayesian estimation and the singularities. We also constructed an algorithm in which the Newton diagram is used to search of desingularization maps. Using the Newton diagram, we are able to reveal the exact value of the asymptotic stochastic complexity, which is a criterion of the model selection.

In this paper, we apply the method and the algorithm to a mixture of binomial distributions and clarify its stochastic complexity. Since our result is given by the mathematically rigorous way, it can contribute to the evaluation of the conventional approximations for calculating the stochastic complexity, such as the Markov Chain Monte Carlo and Variational Bayes methods.

1 Introduction

In the information engineering field, many kinds of learning machines such as neural networks, mixture models and Bayesian networks are being used. In spite of the wide-range applications and technical learning algorithms, their mathematical properties are not yet clarified.

All learning models(or learning machines) belong to either category, *identifiable* or *non-identifiable*. A learning model is generally represented as a probability density function $p(x|w)$, where w is a parameter and x is a feature vector of data. When a machine learns from sample data, its parameter is optimized. Thus, the parameter determines the probability distribution of the model. If the mapping from the parameter to the distribution is one-to-one, the model is *identifiable*, otherwise, *non-identifiable*.

There are many difficulties in analyzing non-identifiable models using the conventional method. If the learning model attains the true distribution, the parameter space contains the true parameter(s). In non-identifiable models, the

S. Ben-David, J. Case, A. Maruoka (Eds.): ALT 2004, LNAI 3244, pp. 350–364, 2004.
© Springer-Verlag Berlin Heidelberg 2004

set of true parameters is not one point but an analytic set in the parameter space. Because the set includes many singularities, the Fisher information matrices are not positive definite. Thus, the log likelihood cannot be approximated by any quadratic form of the parameters in the neighborhood of singularities [2],[21]. That is one of the reasons why the non-identifiable model cannot be clarified. We refer to this model as a singular model.

In Bayesian estimation, the stochastic complexity [12], which is equal to the free energy or the minus marginal likelihood, is very important. Using this observable, we can select the optimal size of the model and derive its generalization error. It is well known that the stochastic complexity is equivalent to BIC in identifiable (statistical regular) models [13]. However, it does not hold in singular models.

The importance of the analysis for the non-identifiable model has been recently pointed out [9]. In some models such as mixture models, the maximum likelihood estimator often diverges. Dacunha-Castelle and Gassiat proposed that the asymptotic behavior of the log likelihood ratio of the maximum likelihood method can be analyzed based on the theory of empirical processes by choosing a locally conic parameterization [4]. Hagiwara has shown that the maximum likelihood method makes training errors very small, but conjectured that it makes generalization errors very large [8]. It is well known by many experiments that the Bayesian estimation is more useful than the maximum likelihood method [1], [11].

In recent years, we have proven that the singularities in the parameter space strongly relate to the efficiency of the Bayesian estimation based on algebraic geometry. This relation reveals that the stochastic complexity is determined by the zeta function of the Kullback information from the true distribution to the learning model and of an a priori distribution. The analysis of the stochastic complexity results in finding the largest pole of the zeta function. Using this method, we have clarified the upper bounds of the stochastic complexities in concrete models, such as multi-layered perceptrons, mixture models, Bayesian networks and hidden Markov models [22], [23], [24]. Though we are actually able to analyze these singular models, it is not easy to find the largest pole. Finding the largest pole is equivalent to finding a resolution of singularities in the Kullback information according to the algebraic geometrical method [14]. However, if the Kullback information satisfies a non-degenerate condition (Definition 3 in Section 3), we can systematically derive a desingularization based on the Newton diagram [3], [5], [6]. The problem is that almost all singular models do not satisfy the condition. It seemed impossible to apply the method of the Newton diagram to these models by choosing an appropriate variable. However, we constructed an algorithm to make the Kullback information satisfy the condition [25].

In this paper, we apply the algorithm to a real, concrete and practical model, a mixture of binomial distribution, and reveal the stochastic complexity. The result of this paper is not its upper bound but the exact value. This would construct a new criterion to select the optimal sized model in terms of the marginal likelihood. Moreover, the procedure of the proof shows advantages of the method with the Newton diagram to analyze other singular models.

2   Bayesian Learning and Stochastic Complexity

In this section, we introduce the standard framework of Bayesian estimation. They are well known in statistical learning theory.

Let $X^n = (X_1, X_2, \cdots, X_n)$ be a set of training samples that are independently and identically distributed. The number of training samples is n. These and the testing samples are taken from the true probability distribution $q(x)$. Let $p(x|w)$ be a learning machine. The a priori probability distribution $\varphi(w)$ is given on the set of parameters W. Then, the a posteriori probability distribution is defined by

$$p(w|X^n) = \frac{1}{Z_0(X^n)} \varphi(w) \prod_{i=1}^{n} p(X_i|w),$$

where $Z_0(X^n)$ is a normalizing constant. The empirical Kullback information is given by

$$H_n(w) = \frac{1}{n} \sum_{i=1}^{n} \log \frac{q(X_i)}{p(X_i|w)}.$$

Then, $p(w|X^n)$ is rewritten as

$$p(w|X^n) = \frac{1}{Z(X^n)} \exp(-nH_n(w)) \, \varphi(w),$$

where the normalizing constant $Z(X^n)$ is given by

$$Z(X^n) = \int \exp(-nH_n(w))\varphi(w)dw.$$

The stochastic complexity is defined by

$$F(X^n) = -\log Z(X^n).$$

We can select the optimal model and hyperparameters by minimizing $-\log Z_0(X^n)$. This is equivalent to minimizing the stochastic complexity, since

$$-\log Z_0(X^n) = -\log Z(X^n) + S(X^n),$$

$$S(X^n) = -\sum_{i=1}^{n} \log q(X_i),$$

where the empirical entropy $S(X^n)$ is independent of the learners. The average stochastic complexity $F(n)$ is defined by

$$F(n) = -E_{X^n}\left[\log Z(X^n)\right], \tag{1}$$

where $E_{X^n}[\cdot]$ stands for the expectation value over all sets of training samples.

The Bayesian predictive distribution $p(x|X^n)$ is given by

$$p(x|X^n) = \int p(x|w)p(w|X^n)dw.$$

The generalization error $G(n)$ is the average Kullback information from the true distribution to the Bayesian predictive distribution,

$$G(n) = E_{X^n}\left[\int q(x) \log \frac{q(x)}{p(x|X^n)} dx\right].$$

Clarifying the behavior of $G(n)$, when the number of training samples is sufficiently large, is very important. The relation between $G(n)$ and $F(n)$ is

$$G(n) = F(n+1) - F(n). \tag{2}$$

This relation is well known [10], [14], [20] and allows that the generalization error is calculated from the average stochastic complexity. If $F(n)$ is obtained as

$$F(n) = \lambda \log n,$$

and the generalization error has the asymptotic expansion, it is given by

$$G(n) = \frac{\lambda}{n} + o\left(\frac{1}{n}\right).$$

This λ is referred to as the learning coefficient.

If a learning machine is an identifiable and regular statistical model, it is proven [13] that asymptotically

$$F(n) = \frac{d}{2} \log n + const.$$

holds, where d is the dimension of the parameter space W. However, for models that are non-identifiable and non-regular such as artificial neural networks and mixture models, the different results are derived [21]. We define the Kullback information from the true distribution $q(x)$ to the learner $p(x|w)$ by

$$H(w) = \int q(x) \log \frac{q(x)}{p(x|w)} dx, \tag{3}$$

and assume that it is an analytic function. The asymptotic expansion of $F(n)$ is

$$F(n) = \lambda \log n - (m-1) \log \log n + const,$$

where the rational number $(-\lambda)$ and the natural number m are respectively equal to the largest pole and its order of the zeta function of the Kullback information and the a priori distribution [15] defined by

$$J(z) = \int H(w)^z \varphi(w) dw, \tag{4}$$

where z is a complex variable. The zeta function is holomorphic in the region $Re(z) > 0$, and can be analytically continued to the meromorphic function on the entire complex plane, whose poles are all real, negative and rational numbers.

We can calculate λ and m by using a resolution of singularities in algebraic geometry [15]. By finding the resolution map $g(\cdot)$, we can represent the Kullback information eq. (3) as

$$H(g(u)) = u_1^{\alpha_1} u_2^{\alpha_2} \cdots u_d^{\alpha_d}. \tag{5}$$

Then, the largest pole λ and its order m are found by integrating eq. (4). However, it is not easy to find the largest pole since it is generally difficult to find the resolution map $g(\cdot)$. Instead of the largest one, we can find a pole of $J(z)$ using a partial resolution map that is given by a blow-up. It is known that a pole determines an upper bound of λ. Then, upper bounds can be derived in some models such as multi-layer neural networks [16], mixture models [22], Bayesian networks [23] and hidden Markov models [24]. In this paper, the largest pole in a mixture of binomial distributions is clarified by using the Newton diagram. The result shows not an upper bound but the exact asymptotic expansion of the stochastic complexity.

3 Newton Diagram and Resolution of Singularities

In this section, we introduce the Newton diagram and its relation to a resolution of singularities. According to this method, we can write the analytic function eq. (3) as an expression eq. (5) and find the largest pole of the zeta function.

Let the Taylor expansion of an analytic function $H(w)$ be

$$H(w) = \sum_v c_v w^v,$$

where $w = (w_1, \cdots, w_d) \in R^d$, $v = (v_1, \cdots, v_d) \in Q \subset Z^d$ and c_v is a constant. We use the notation that

$$w^v \equiv w_1^{v_1} w_2^{v_2} \cdots w_d^{v_d}.$$

Definition 1. *The convex hull of the subset*

$$\{v + v'; c_v \neq 0, v' \in R_+^d\}$$

is referred to as the Newton diagram $\Gamma_+(H)$.

Example 1. Assume $H(w)$ is defined by

$$H(w) = w_1^5 + w_1^3 w_2^3 + w_1^2 w_2^2 + w_2^5,$$

where $w = (w_1, w_2)$, $v = (5,0), (3,3), (2,2), (0,5)$ and $c_v = 1$. Then, the Newton diagram is depicted by the shaded area (Fig. 1 (a)).

For a given constant vector $a \in Z^d$, we define $l(a)$ by

$$l(a) \equiv \min\{\langle v, a \rangle; v \in \Gamma_+(H)\},$$

where $\langle, \rangle$ is the inner product, $\langle v, a \rangle = \sum_{i=1}^d a_i v_i$.

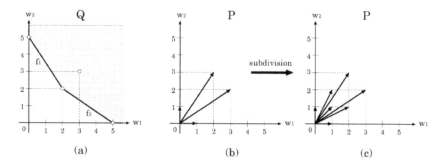

Fig. 1. (a) The Newton diagram, (b) the fan, (c) the subdivided fan

Definition 2. *A face of $\Gamma_+(H)$ is defined by*

$$\gamma(a) \equiv \{v \in \Gamma_+(H); \langle v, a \rangle = l(a)\}.$$

Intuitively, the face is the border of the Newton diagram.

Example 2. On the condition of Example 1, the Newton diagram has four faces, $f_1 = [(0,5),(2,2)]$, $f_2 = [(2,2),(5,0)]$, $[(0,5),(0,\infty)]$, $[(5,0),(\infty,0)]$. (Figure 1 (a)).

Depending on a face γ, a polynomial f_γ is defined by

$$f_\gamma(w) \equiv \sum_{v \in \gamma} c_v w^v.$$

Definition 3. *The function $H(w)$ is said to be non-degenerate if and only if*

$$\left\{ w \in R^d; \frac{\partial f_\gamma}{\partial w_1}(w) = \cdots = \frac{\partial f_\gamma}{\partial w_d}(w) = 0 \right\} \subset \{w_1 \cdots w_d = 0\}$$

for an arbitrary compact face γ of $\Gamma_+(H)$. If otherwise, $H(w)$ is said to be degenerate.

Example 3. It is easy to show the function $H(w)$ in Example 1 is non-degenerate.

Consider the dual space $P \subset Z^d$ of Q.

Definition 4. *The set of the orthogonal vectors to the faces are called a fan.*

Consider the parallelogram constituted by arbitrary two vectors of the fan. If it includes a point of P, add the vector from the origin to the point.

Definition 5. *Subdivision of $\Gamma_+(H)$ is defined by adding the vectors until there is no point in the parallelograms.*

Example 4. The fan and the subdivided one of the Newton diagram in Example 1 are respectively depicted by Fig. 1 (b) and (c).

For a matrix

$$A = \begin{pmatrix} a_1^1 & \cdots & a_1^d \\ \vdots & \ddots & \vdots \\ a_d^1 & \cdots & a_d^d \end{pmatrix},$$

and $w, u \in R^d$, we define

$$w = u^A \Leftrightarrow \begin{cases} w_1 = u_1^{a_1^1} \cdots u_d^{a_1^d} \\ \quad\vdots \\ w_d = u_1^{a_d^1} \cdots u_d^{a_d^d} \end{cases},$$

where a set, $a_1 = (a_1^1, \cdots, a_d^1), \cdots, a_d = (a_1^d, \cdots, a_d^d)$ is a part of the subdivided fan. By using the above definitions, the theorem is known which relates the Newton diagram to a resolution of singularities [5], [6].

Theorem 1. *The map $\pi(u) : w = u^A$, where $\det A = \pm 1$ is called a real toric modification. The map $\pi^{-1}(U_0) \to W$ for the neighborhood $U_0 \subset R^d$ of the origin is a resolution of singularities if the function $H(w)$ is non-degenerate.*

Example 5. According to the subdivided fan in Example 1, we can select two vectors, $(3, 2), (1, 1)$. Then, the map $g(u_1, u_2)$ is defined by

$$\begin{cases} w_1 = u_1^3 u_2^1 \\ w_2 = u_1^2 u_2^1 \end{cases}.$$

This gives an expression of eq. (5),

$$H(g(u)) = u_1^{10} u_2^4 (u_1^5 u_2 + u_1^5 u_2^2 + 1 + u_2).$$

We can find a resolution of singularities at the origin considering all sets of vectors such that $\det A = \pm 1$. Each A provides local coordinates.

In order to find the largest pole of the zeta function determined by the eq. (4), the problem comes down to find an efficient vector of the subdivided fan in the Newton diagram. The largest pole depends on the ratio between the Jacobian $|g'(u)|$ and the power of the common factor in $H(g(u))$. If a vector of the subdivided fan is a_j and $H(g(u))$ has the common factor u_j^β, it settles a pole $-\alpha/\beta$, where $\alpha = \sum_i a_i^j$.

4   Main Result

In this section, let us introduce mixtures of binomial distributions and our result.

4.1   Mixture of Binomial Distributions

A mixture of binomial distributions is formulated by

$$p(x = k|w) = \binom{N}{k} \left\{ \sum_{i=1}^{K} a_i p_i^k (1 - p_i)^{N-k} \right\}, \tag{6}$$

where N, K are integers such that $K < N$, $k = 0, 1, \cdots, N$, $(N\ k)^T$ is the number of combination of N elements taken k at a time, and

$$w = (\{a_i\}_{i=1}^{K-1}, \{p_i\}_{i=1}^{K})$$

is a parameter such that $0 < p_i \le 1/2$, $a_i \ge 0$, and

$$a_{K+1} = 1 - \sum_{i=1}^{K-1} a_i.$$

A binomial distribution is defined by

$$\binom{N}{k} \bar{p}^k (1 - \bar{p})^{N-k},$$

where $1 < \bar{p} \le 1/2$. Thus, the mixture eq. (6) has K components.
   This learning machine is used for the gene analysis and the mutational spectrum analysis [7].

4.2   Main Result

We use the notation,

$$f(x) \asymp g(x),$$

where there are positive constants C_1, C_2 such that

$$C_1 g(x) \le f(x) \le C_2 g(x).$$

Assume that the true distribution consists of K_0 components,

$$q(x = k) = \binom{N}{k} \left\{ \sum_{i=1}^{K_0} a_i^* p_i^{*k} (1 - p_i^*)^{N-k} \right\}, \tag{7}$$

where $0 < p_i^* \le 1/2$ are constants, $p_1^* < p_2^* < \cdots < p_{K_0}^*$, $a_i^* > 0$ and $a_{K_0}^* = 1 - \sum_{i=1}^{K_0-1} a_i^*$.

Theorem 2. *If the learning machine is given by the eq. (6) and the true distribution is given by the eq. (7), the Kullback information eq. (3) satisfies*

$$H(w) \asymp \sum_{k=1}^{N} \left\{ \sum_{j=1}^{K} a_j p_j^k - \sum_{j=1}^{K_0} a_j^* p_j^{*k} \right\}^2.$$

Proof. Using the notation, we can express the Kullback information eq. (3) as

$$H(w) \asymp \sum_{k=0}^{N} [p(x=k|w) - q(x=k)]^2 .$$

According to Fourier transform and Parseval's identity, it is rewritten as

$$H(w) \asymp \sum_{t=0}^{N} \left| \sum_{k=0}^{N} \exp\left(\frac{2\pi it}{N+1} k \right) \right.$$

$$\times \left. \left\{ \sum_{j=1}^{K} a_j (1-p_j)^{N-k} p_j^k - \sum_{j=1}^{K_0} a_j^*(1-p_j^*)^{N-k} p_j^{*k} \right\} \right|^2 .$$

Because of the orthogonality of $\left\{ \exp\left(\frac{2\pi it}{N+1} k \right) \right\}_{k=0}^{N}$,

$$H(w) \asymp \sum_{k=0}^{N} \left\{ \sum_{j=1}^{K} a_j(1-p_j)^{N-k} p_j^k - \sum_{j=1}^{K_0} a_j^*(1-p_j^*)^{N-k} p_j^{*k} \right\}^2$$

$$\asymp \sum_{k=1}^{N} \left\{ \sum_{j=1}^{K} a_j p_j^k - \sum_{j=1}^{K_0} a_j^* p_j^{*k} \right\}^2 .$$

□

The following is the main result of this paper.

Theorem 3. *If the learning machine eq. (6) has $K+1$ components and the true distribution eq. (7) has K components, then, for a sufficiently large natural number n, the stochastic complexity satisfies the equation,*

$$F(n) = \left(K - \frac{1}{4} \right) \log n + C,$$

where C is a constant independent of n.

Proof. According to Theorem 2, the Kullback information satisfies

$$H(w) \asymp \sum_{k=1}^{N} \left\{ \sum_{j=1}^{K+1} a_j p_j^k - \sum_{j=1}^{K} a_j^* p_j^{*k} \right\}^2 .$$

We define the map $\Theta_1 : w \to w_1$, such that

$$a_j' \equiv a_j - a_{j-1}^* \quad (j = 2, \cdots, K+1),$$
$$p_j' \equiv p_j - p_{j-1}^* \quad (j = 2, \cdots, K+1),$$
$$a_1' \equiv a_1,$$
$$p_1' \equiv p_1 - p_1^*,$$

in order to shift the singularities to the origin. We write these variables, a'_j and p'_j as a_j and p_j respectively to avoid the complicated notation. Then,

$$
H(\Theta_1^{-1}(w_1)) \asymp \mathcal{H}(w_1) \equiv \sum_{k=1}^{N} \left\{ c_2(k)(a_1 + a_2) + \sum_{j=3}^{K} c_j(k)a_j \right.
$$
$$
+ c_1(k)(a_1 p_1 + (a_2 + a_1^*)p_2)
$$
$$
+ d_1(k)(a_1 p_1^2 + (a_2 + a_1^*)p_2^2)
$$
$$
\left. + \sum_{j=2}^{K+1} d_j p_j + f_r(k, w) \right\}^2 ,
$$

where

$$
c_2(k) = p_1^{*k} - p_K^{*k},
$$
$$
c_j(k) = p_j^{*k} - p_K^{*k} \quad (j = 3, \cdots, K),
$$
$$
c_1(k) = k p_1^{*k-1},
$$
$$
d_1(k) = \binom{k}{2} p_1^{*k-2} \quad (d_1(1) = 0),
$$
$$
d_j(k) = a_{j-1}^* k p_{j-1}^{*k-1} \quad (j = 2, \cdots, K),
$$
$$
d_{K+1}(k) = k \left(1 - \sum_{j=1}^{K-1} a_j^* \right) p_K^{*k-1}
$$

and $f_r(k, w)$ is the sum of the remaining terms in $\mathcal{H}(w_1)$. In order to find the faces, we rewrite the function as

$$
\mathcal{H}(w_1) = h_1(w_1)^2 + 2h_1(w_1)h_2(w_1) + h_2(w_1)^2,
$$

where

$$
h_1(w_1) = \sum_{k=1}^{N} \left\{ c_2(k)(a_1 + a_2) + \sum_{j=3}^{K} c_j(k)a_j + \sum_{j=2}^{K+1} d_j(k)p_j \right\},
$$
$$
h_2(w_1) = \sum_{k=1}^{N} \{ c_1(k)(a_1 p_1 + (a_2 + a_1^*)p_2)
$$
$$
+ d_1(k)(a_1 p_1^2 + (a_2 + a_1^*)p_2^2) + f_r(k, w) \}.
$$

The terms in $h_2(w_2)$ are higher order than that of $h_1(w_1)$. Because the vectors are linearly independent,

$$
\{(c_2(k), \cdots, c_K(k), d_2(k), \cdots, d_{K+1}(k))\}_{k=1}^{N},
$$
$$
h_1(w_1)^2 \asymp \sum_{k=1}^{N} \{c_2(k)^2\}(a_1 + a_2)^2 + \sum_{k=1}^{N} \left\{ \sum_{j=3}^{K} c_j(k)^2 \right\} a_j^2 + \sum_{k=1}^{N} \left\{ \sum_{j=2}^{K+1} d_j(k)^2 \right\} p_j^2.
$$

Thus, the faces in the Newton diagram of $\mathcal{H}(w_1)$ consist of the terms,

$$(a_1 + a_2)^2,$$
$$a_j^2 \quad (j = 3, \cdots, K),$$
$$p_j^2 \quad (j = 2, \cdots, K+1).$$

Because of the term, $(a_1 + a_2)^2$, the function $\mathcal{H}(w_1)$ is degenerate. We define the map $\Theta_2 : w_1 \to w_2$,

$$a_2' \equiv a_1 + a_2,$$
$$a_j' \equiv a_j \quad (j = 1, 3, 4, \cdots, K),$$
$$p_j' \equiv p_j \quad (j = 1, 2, \cdots, K+1).$$

We write these variables, a_j' and p_j' as a_j and p_j respectively to avoid the complicated notation. Then, $\mathcal{H}(w_1)$ is rewritten as

$$\mathcal{H}(\Theta_2^{-1}(w_2)) = h_1'(w_2)^2 + 2h_1'(w_2)h_2'(w_2) + h_2'(w_2)^2,$$

where

$$h_1'(w_2) = \sum_{k=1}^{N} \left\{ c_2(k)a_2 + \sum_{j=3}^{K} c_j(k)a_j \right.$$
$$\left. + \sum_{j=3}^{K+1} d_j(k)p_j + c_1(k)(a_1 p_1 + (a_2 - a_1 + a_1^*)p_2) \right\},$$

$$h_2'(w_2) = \sum_{k=1}^{N} \left\{ d_1(k)(a_1 p_1^2 + (a_2 - a_1 + a_1^*)p_2^2) + f_r'(k, w) \right\},$$

and $f_r'(k, w)$ is the sum of the remaining terms in $\mathcal{H}(\Theta_2^{-1}(w_2))$. The terms in $h_2'(w_2)$ are higher order than that of $h_1'(w_2)$. According to the linear independency of the vectors,

$$\{(c_1(k), \cdots, c_K(k), d_2(k), \cdots, d_{K+1}(k))\}_{k=1}^{N},$$

$$h_1'(w_2)^2 \asymp \sum_{k=1}^{N} \left\{ c_2(k)^2 \right\} a_2^2 + \sum_{k=1}^{N} \left\{ \sum_{j=3}^{K} c_j(k)^2 \right\} a_j^2 + \sum_{k=1}^{N} \left\{ \sum_{j=3}^{K+1} d_j(k)^2 \right\} p_j^2$$
$$+ \sum_{k=1}^{N} \left\{ c_1(k)^2 \right\} (a_1 p_1 + (a_2 - a_1 + a_1^*)p_2)^2.$$

Thus, the faces in the Newton diagram of $\mathcal{H}(\Theta_2^{-1}(w_2))$ consist of the terms,

$$(a_1 p_1 + a_1^* p_2)^2,$$
$$a_j^2 \quad (j = 3, \cdots, K),$$
$$p_j^2 \quad (j = 3, \cdots, K+1).$$

Because of the term, $(a_1p_1 + a_1^*p_2)^2$, the function $\mathcal{H}(\Theta_2^{-1}(w_2))$ is degenerate. Thus, we define the map $\Theta_3 : w_2 \to w_3$,

$$a_j' \equiv a_j \quad (j = 1, \cdots, K),$$
$$p_2' \equiv a_1p_1 + (a_2 - a_1 + a_1^*)p_2,$$
$$p_j' \equiv p_j \quad (j = 1, 3, 4, \cdots, K + 1).$$

We write these variables, a_j' and p_j' as a_j and p_j respectively to avoid the complicated notation. Then, $\mathcal{H}(\Theta_2^{-1}(w_2))$ is rewritten as

$$\mathcal{H}(\Theta_2^{-1}\Theta_3^{-1}(w_3)) = h_1''(w_3)^2 + 2h_1''(w_3)h_2''(w_3) + h_2''(w_3)^2,$$

where

$$h_1''(w_3) = \sum_{k=1}^{N} \left\{ c_2(k)a_2 + \sum_{j=3}^{K} c_j(k)a_j + \sum_{j=3}^{K+1} d_j(k)p_j + c_1(k)p_2 \right.$$
$$\left. + d_1(k)(a_1p_1^2 + \frac{(p_2 - a_1p_1)^2}{a_2 - a_1 + a_1^*}) \right\},$$

$$h_2''(w_3) = \sum_{k=1}^{N} f_r''(k, w),$$

and $f_r''(k, w)$ is the sum of the remaining terms in $\mathcal{H}(\Theta_2^{-1}\Theta_3^{-1}(w_3))$. The terms in $h_2''(w_3)$ are higher order than that of $h_1''(w_3)$. According to the linear independency of the vectors,

$$\{(c_1(k), \cdots, c_K(k), d_1(k), \cdots, d_{K+1}(k))\}_{k=1}^{N},$$

$$h_1''(w_3)^2 \asymp \sum_{k=1}^{N} \left\{ c_2(k)^2 \right\} a_2^2 + \sum_{k=1}^{N} \left\{ \sum_{j=3}^{K} c_j(k)^2 \right\} a_j^2 + \sum_{k=1}^{N} \left\{ \sum_{j=3}^{K+1} d_j(k)^2 \right\} p_j^2$$
$$+ \sum_{k=1}^{N} \left\{ c_1(k)^2 \right\} p_2^2 + \sum_{k=1}^{N} \left\{ d_1(k)^2 \right\} \left(a_1p_1^2 + \frac{(p_2 - a_1p_1)^2}{a_2 - a_1 + a_1^*} \right)^2.$$

Thus, the faces in the Newton diagram of $\mathcal{H}(\Theta_2^{-1}\Theta_3^{-1}(w_3))$ consist of the terms,

$$a_1^2p_1^4,$$
$$a_j^2 \quad (j = 2, \cdots, K),$$
$$p_j^2 \quad (j = 2, \cdots, K + 1).$$

Finally, the function $\mathcal{H}(\Theta_2^{-1}\Theta_3^{-1}(w_3))$ is non-degenerate. Then, we are able to find the efficient vector,

$$(a_1, a_2, \cdots, a_K, p_1, p_2, \cdots, p_{K+1}) = (0, 2, \cdots, 2, 1, 2, \cdots, 2).$$

According to the fan, a resolution of singularities $g(u)$, where

$$u = (u_1, u_2, \cdots, u_K, v_1, v_2, \cdots, v_{K+1})$$

is derived as

$$a_1 \equiv u_1,$$
$$a_j \equiv u_j v_1^2 \quad (j = 2, \cdots, K),$$
$$p_1 \equiv v_1,$$
$$p_j \equiv v_j^2 \quad (j = 2, \cdots, K+1).$$

The Jacobian of $g(u)$ is

$$|g(u)| = v_1^{4K-2},$$

and the common factor of $\mathcal{H}(\Theta_2^{-1}\Theta_3^{-1}(w_3))$ is v_1^4. Therefore, the largest pole λ' of

$$\int \mathcal{H}(\Theta_2^{-1}\Theta_3^{-1}(g(u)))^z |g(u)| du$$

is

$$\lambda' = K - \frac{1}{4}.$$

The Jacobians of maps $\Theta_1, \Theta_2, \Theta_3$ are not equal to zero. Therefore, the largest pole of eq. (4) is same as λ'.   □

5 Discussion and Conclusion

First, let us summarize the advantages of the method to use the Newton diagram. There are two advantages for the analysis of singular learning machines. (a) We are able to ignore higher-order terms which are inside of the Newton diagram. (b) A resolution of singularities is systematically found by using the fan. In some examples of Section 3, we focused not the whole diagram but only the faces and the corresponding orthogonal vectors to find a resolution of singularities. For instance, the term $w_1^3 w_2^3$ of $H(w)$ in Example 1 does not affect the resolution of singularities in Example 5. In the proof of Theorem 3, we ignored f_r, f_r', f_r''. This makes the analysis much simple. This means we need to consider only the terms in the faces of the Kullback information. In general, it is not easy to find which terms determine a resolution or to derive a resolution of singularities from all terms in the Kullback information. Moreover, the number of resolutions exponentially grows when the dimension of the parameter increases. This is one of the reasons to use a partial resolution (blow-up) in the previous studies [22], [23], [24]. Based on these advantages, we revealed not an upper bound but the exact value of λ, the coefficient of the leading term in the stochastic complexity. The process of the proof claims that they are effective in the real, concrete and practical models like the mixture. It is expected the method with the Newton diagram can be applied to other singular models. For example, we obtained an upper bound of general mixture models [22]. If the components are binomial distributions, the upper bound is $\lambda \le K + 1/2$. Our result shows that it can be tighter on some conditions.

Second, let us talk about the degenerate Kullback information. As above stated, the method with the Newton diagram is useful to analyze learning machines with singularities. However, it assumes that the Kullback information is non-degenerate. In fact, most Kullback informations of the non-regular models are degenerate. It depends on the coordinate of the parameter whether a function is degenerate or not. Then, we constructed the algorithm that makes the Kullback information non-degenerate [25]. This means that there exist simple and complicated degenerate functions. In the Kullback information, the fans of the Newton diagram generally include the polynomial $f(w)^2$. If $f(w)$ has a primary expression such that $f(w) = a + bc + \cdots$, we can apply the algorithm. This is a simple degenerate function. On the other hand, we cannot do it if the smallest order term of $f(w)$ is a quadratic expression. This is a complicated degenerate function. A mixture of binomial distribution in the main theorem belongs to a simple one. However, the Kullback information is complicated degenerate if the number of component is general. It is still an open problem to classify singular machines into two categories, simple and complicated degenerate functions. It is equivalent to finding how generally applicable the algorithm is.

At last, let us discuss the model selection problem. We clarified the stochastic complexity in a mixture of binomial distributions using the algebraic geometrical method and the Newton diagram. As we mentioned in Section 2, the stochastic complexity is a criterion of the model selection. In statistical regular models, it is equivalent to the well known BIC [13]. However, it is not in non-regular models. The dimension of the parameter w is $d = 2K - 1$. So, the coefficient λ is smaller than $d/2$. Furthermore, by using our result, the conventional approximations to calculate the stochastic complexity such as Markov Chain Monte Carlo and Variational Bayes methods can be evaluated.

Acknowledgment. This work was partially supported by the Ministry of Education, Science, Sports, and Culture in Japan, Grant-in-aid for scientific research 15500130, 2004.

References

[1] Akaike,H. : Likelihood and Bayes procedure. Bayesian Statistics, (Bernald J.M. eds.) University Press, Valencia, Spain, (1980) 143-166

[2] Amari, S. and Ozeki, T. : Differential and algebraic geometry of multilayer perceptrons. IEICE Trans, E84-A **1**, (2001) 31-38

[3] Aranson, A. B. : Computation and applications of the Newton polyhedrons. Mathematics and Computers in Simulation, **57**, (2001) 155-160

[4] Dacunha-Castelle, D. and Gassiat, E. : Testing in locally conic models, and application to mixture models. Probability and Statistics, **1** (1997) 285-317

[5] Ewald, G : Combinatorial convexity and algebraic geometry. Graduate texts in mathematics, **168**, Springer-Verlag New York (1996)

[6] Fulton, W. : Introduction to toric varieties. Annals of Mathematics Studies, **131**, Princeton University Press (1993)

[7] Glazko, G. B., Milanesi, L. and Rogozin, I. B. : The subclass approach for mutational spectrum analysis: Application of the SEM algorithm. Journal of Theor. Biology, **192** (1998) 475-487

[8] Hagiwara, K. : On the problem in model selection of neural network regression in overrealizable scenario. Neural Computation, **14** (2002) 1979-2002

[9] Hartigan, J. A. : A Failure of likelihood asymptotics for normal mixtures. Proceedings of the Berkeley Conference in Honor of J.Neyman and J.Kiefer, **2** (1985) 807-810

[10] Levin, E., Tishby, N., and Solla,S.A. : A statistical approaches to learning and generalization in layered neural networks. Proc. of IEEE, **78 (10)** (1990) 1568-1674

[11] Mackay, D. J. : Bayesian interpolation. Neural Computation, **4 (2)** (1992) 415-447

[12] Rissanen, J. : Stochastic complexity and modeling. Annals of Statistics, **14** (1986) 1080-1100

[13] Schwarz, G. : Estimating the dimension of a model. Annals of Statistics, **6 (2)** (1978) 461-464

[14] Watanabe, S. : Algebraic analysis for singular statistical estimation. Lecture Notes on Computer Science, **1720** (1999) 39-50, Springer

[15] Watanabe, S. : Algebraic analysis for non-identifiable learning machines. Neural Computation, **13 (4)** (2001) 899-933

[16] Watanabe, S. : Algebraic geometrical methods for hierarchical learning machines. Neural Networks, **14 (8)** (2001) 1049-1060

[17] Watanabe, S. : Algebraic information geometry for learning machines with singularities. Advances in Neural Information Processing Systems, MIT Press, **14** (2001) 329-336

[18] Watanabe, S.: Resolution of singularities and weak convergence of Bayesian stochastic complexity. Proc. of International Workshop on Singular Models and Geometric Methods in Statistics. Institute of Statistical Mathematics (2002) 156-165

[19] Watanabe, S. and Fukumizu, K. : Probabilistic design of layered neural networks based on their unified framework. IEEE Trans. on Neural Networks, **6 (3)** (1995) 691-702

[20] Yamanishi, K. : A decision-theoretic extension of stochastic complexity and its applications to learning. IEEE Trans. on Information Theory, **44 (4)** (1998) 1424-1439

[21] Yamazaki, K. and Watanabe, S. : A probabilistic algorithm to calculate the learning curves of hierarchical learning machines with singularities, Trans. on IEICE, J85-D-2 **3** (2002) 363-372, the English version will appear in Electronics and Communications in Japan.

[22] Yamazaki, K. and Watanabe, S. : Singularities in mixture models and upper bounds of stochastic complexity. International Journal of Neural Networks, **16** (2003) 1029-1038

[23] Yamazaki, K. and Watanabe, S. : Stochastic complexity of Bayesian networks. Proc. of UAI 2003 (2003) 592-599

[24] Yamazaki, K. and Watanabe, S. : Stochastic complexities of hidden Markov models. Proc. of NNSP 2003 (2003) 179-188

[25] Yamazaki, K., Aoyagi, M. and Watanabe, S. : Stochastic complexity and Newton diagram. Proc. of International Symposium on Information Theory and its Applications, ISITA2004 to appear

Learnability of Relatively Quantified Generalized Formulas

Andrei Bulatov[1], Hubie Chen[2], and Víctor Dalmau[3]

[1] Computing Laboratory
Oxford University
Oxford, UK
Andrei.Bulatov@comlab.ox.ac.uk
[2] Department of Computer Science
Cornell University
Ithaca, NY 14853, USA
hubes@cs.cornell.edu
[3] Departament de Tecnologia
Universitat Pompeu Fabra
Barcelona, Spain
victor.dalmau@upf.edu

Abstract. In this paper we study the learning complexity of a vast class of quantifed formulas called *Relatively Quantified Generalized Formulas*. This class of formulas is parameterized by a set of predicates, called a basis. We give a complete classification theorem, showing that every basis gives rise to quantified formulas that are either polynomially learnable with equivalence queries, or not polynomially predictable with membership queries under some cryptographic assumption. We also provide a simple criteria distinguishing the learnable cases from the non-learnable cases.

1 Introduction

The problem of learning an unknown formula has been widely studied. It is well-known that the general problem of learning an arbitrary formula is hard, even in the case of propositional formulas, under the usual learning models [3,16]. This general non-learnability motivates the research program of distinguishing restricted classes of formulas that are learnable from those that are not learnable. Towards this end, a number of efficiently learnable classes of propositional formulas have been identified, for instance [1,2,6,14].

An attractive framework of formula classes was studied by Schaefer [21]; he considered *generalized formulas*, defined as conjunctions of predicates, and considered restricted classes of generalized formulas where the predicates must come from a restricted predicate set, called a *basis*. Schaefer proved a now classic dichotomy theorem: for any basis over a two-element (boolean) domain, the problem of deciding if a generalized formula over the basis is true (that is, has a model) is either polynomial time solvable or NP-complete. He also provided a simple criterion to distinghish the tractable cases from those that are not. Generalized formulas have, since Schaefer's theorem, been heavily studied in several

S. Ben-David, J. Case, A. Maruoka (Eds.): ALT 2004, LNAI 3244, pp. 365–379, 2004.

different contexts [4,7,8,9,10,17,18]; they are widely acknowledged as a useful way of obtaining restricted versions of logical formulas in order to systematically study the distinction between tractability and intractability.[1]

In the context of learning, Dalmau [12], along with Jeavons in [13], has studied the learnability of such formula classes. In particular, Dalmau [12] proved an analog of Schaefer's theorem in the setting of learnability. The case of bases over domains of size greater than two was considered by Dalmau and Jeavons [13]: they established general algebraic technology for studying learnability of generalized formulas, and gave some broad sufficient conditions for learnability.

In this paper, we continue this line of investigation by proving a classification theorem on the learnability of an very broad class of quantified generalized formulas. We consider *relatively quantified generalized formulas*, where quantification is allowed over any subset of the domain of a variable. We prove a full classification theorem on such relatively quantified formulas, showing that for *any* basis over a finite domain, the concept class consisting of relatively quantified formulas over the basis is either learnable in the exact model with equivalence queries, or non-learnable in the PAC-prediccion model with membership queries. Our classification theorem thus demonstrates an extremely sharp dichotomy on a diverse family of concept classes: none of the concept classes characterize any of the learning models intermediate between the two that we have just named, such as exact learning with equivalence and membership queries, or PAC learning (either with or without membership queries).

One of the primary tools we use to obtain our classification theorem is the algebraic approach to studying learnability of formulas [13]. This approach has demonstrated that the learnability of generalized formulas over a basis depends only on a set of operations called the *polymorphisms* of the basis. Our main theorem states that relatively quantified formulas over a basis are learnable if and only if the basis has a particular type of polymorphism which we call a *generalized majority-minority (GMM) operation*. Our positive learnability results demonstrate that quantified formulas with a GMM polymorphism have a novel, compact representation which we call a *signature*. Our negative results use algebraic techniques to show that quantified formulas without a GMM polymorphism must have a two-element domain that is non-learnable by the dichotomy theorem of Dalmau [12]. We believe it remarkable that our negative results, which can be applied to bases over domains of arbitrary size, can ultimately be derived from the negative results for two-element bases.

2   Preliminaries

2.1   Formulas

We use $[n]$ to denote the set containing the first n positive integers, that is, $\{1, \dots, n\}$. Let $V = \{x_1, x_2, \dots\}$ be a countably infinite set of variables and let A be a finite set called the *domain*. A k-ary *relation* (k integer) on A is a subset

---

[1]   See [11] for a monograph on boolean generalized formulas.

of A^k where k is called the *rank* or *arity* of the relation. The set $\{1, \ldots, k\}$ is referred to as the set of *indices* or *coordinates* of R.

We use the term *formula* in a wide sense, to mean any well-formed formula, formed from variables, logical connectives, parentheses, relation symbols, and existential and universal quantifiers.

Definition 1 ([13]). *Let A be any finite set and let $\Gamma = \{R_1, R_2, \ldots\}$ be any set of relations over A, where each R_i has rank k_i. (R_i denotes both the relation and its symbol.)*

The set of quantified generalized formulas *over the basis Γ, denoted by $\forall\exists$-Form(Γ), is the smallest set of formulas such that:*

(a) *For all $R \in \Gamma$ of rank k, $R(y_1, \ldots, y_k) \in \forall\exists$-Form($\Gamma$) where $y_i \in V$ for $1 \le i \le k$.*
(b) *For all $\Phi, \Psi \in \forall\exists$-Form($\Gamma$), $\Phi \wedge \Psi \in \forall\exists$-Form($\Gamma$).*
(c) *For all $\Phi \in \forall\exists$-Form(Γ) and for all $x \in V$, $\exists x\Phi \in \forall\exists$-Form($\Gamma$).*
(d) *For all $\Phi \in \forall\exists$-Form(Γ) and for all $x \in V$, $\forall x\Phi \in \forall\exists$-Form($\Gamma$).*

If we remove condition (d) *in the previous definition we obtain a reduced class of formulas called* existentially quantified generalized formulas over the basis Γ, *denoted by $\exists$-Form(Γ).*

In this paper we focus our attention on a related family of formulas, called *relatively quantified generalized formulas over the basis Γ*, and denoted $\forall\exists_r$-Form(Γ). In a $\forall\exists_r$-Form(Γ) formula, every occurrence of a quantifier $Q \in \{\exists, \forall\}$ is followed by an expression of the form $(x \in B)$ where B is a subset of A. The intended meaning of the expression $(x \in B)$ is to indicate that the quantification of x is relative to the elements from B. That is, the semantics of $\exists(x \in B)\Phi$ is "there exists a b in B such that Φ holds when x is substituted with b", similarly, $\forall(x \in B)\Phi$ is interpreted as "for all b in B, Φ holds when x is substituted with b". The *relatively existentially quantified generalized formulas* $\exists_r$-Form(Γ) are defined similarly.

It can be immediately observed that usual quantification can be simulated by performing all quantification relative to A, and hence $\forall\exists$-Form(Γ) is contained in $\forall\exists_r$-Form(Γ) for each Γ. Indeed, the relationship between $\forall\exists$-Form(Γ) and $\forall\exists_r$-Form(Γ) is even closer, as one can easily observe the following:

Proposition 1. *Let Γ be any finite set of relations containing every unary relation. Then $\forall\exists_r$-Form(Γ) ($\exists_r$-Form(Γ)) and $\forall\exists$-Form(Γ) ($\exists$-Form(Γ))) are equivalent.*

Proof. Clearly, $\forall\exists$-Form(Γ) $\subseteq \forall\exists_r$-Form($\Gamma$). We prove the converse by induction on the structure of a formula Φ. The base case of induction, $\Phi \in \Gamma$, is obvious. Now, if $\Phi, \Psi \in \forall\exists$-Form($\Gamma$), then $\Phi \wedge \Psi \in \forall\exists$-Form($\Gamma$); $\exists(x \in B)\Phi$ is equivalent to $\exists x(\Phi \wedge B(x))$, where B is the predicate interpreted as the unary relation B; and $\forall(x \in B)\Phi$, $B = \{b_1, \ldots, b_k\}$, is equivalent to

$$(\exists x \ \Phi \wedge b_1'(x)) \wedge \ldots \wedge (\exists x \ \Phi \wedge b_k'(x)),$$

where the $b_i'(x)$ is a predicate interpreted as the unary relation $\{(b_i)\}$.   □

In our analysis the size of our formulas will be relevant. By *the size* of a formula Φ, denoted by $|\Phi|$, we mean the length of a string that encodes it (in any reasonable encoding). Let F, G be two families of formulas. We shall say that F is polynomially contained in G if there exists a polynomial p such that for each formula Φ in F there exists an equivalent formula Ψ in G such that $|\Psi| \leq p(|\Phi|)$. If furthermore G is polynomially contained in F then we say that F and G are polynomially equivalent. By looking at Proposition 1 with this definitions on hand we can easily infer that for each Γ, $\forall\exists$-Form(Γ) is polynomially contained in $\forall\exists_r$-Form(Γ). Furthermore, if Γ contains all unary relations then $\exists$-Form(Γ) and $\exists_r$-Form(Γ) are polynomially equivalent.

Each formula Φ defines a relation R_Φ if we apply the usual semantics of first-order logic, and the variables are taken in lexicographical order. More formally, let Φ be a formula over the free variables $x_{i_1}, x_{i_2}, \ldots, x_{i_m}$ where $i_1 < i_2 < \cdots < i_m$; we define

$$R_\Phi = \{(a_1, a_2, \ldots, a_m) : x_{i_j} = a_j \ (1 \leq j \leq m) \text{ satisfies } \Phi\}$$

Example 1. Consider the problem of learning a boolean formula formed by a quantified conjunction of clauses with three literals per clause. Every such formula can be expressed as a formula in $\forall\exists_r$-Form(Γ) with the set of logical relations $\Gamma = \{R_0, R_1, R_2, R_3\}$, defined by:

$$R_0(x, y, z) \equiv x \vee y \vee z,$$
$$R_1(x, y, z) \equiv \overline{x} \vee y \vee z,$$
$$R_2(x, y, z) \equiv \overline{x} \vee \overline{y} \vee z,$$
$$R_3(x, y, z) \equiv \overline{x} \vee \overline{y} \vee \overline{z}.$$

Indeed, formulas in $\forall\exists_r$-Form(Γ) have even a bit more of expressivity power (due to the relativized quantification). As an example, let Φ be following formula:

$$\Phi = \exists(x_1 \in \{0\})\exists(x_2 \in \{1\})\forall(x_3 \in \{0,1\})\exists(x_4 \in \{0,1\})\forall(x_5 \in \{0,1\})$$
$$R_1(x_3, x_4, x_5) \wedge R_1(x_6, x_5, x_4) \wedge R_2(x_6, x_7, x_1) \wedge R_3(x_2, x_8, x_4)$$

Φ is a formula in $\forall\exists_r$-Form Γ over the free variables x_6, x_7, and x_8. R_Φ contains exactly all the assignments over these variables satisfying Φ:

$$R_\Phi = \{(0,0,0), (0,1,0), (1,0,0)\}$$

Let R be an n-ary relation on a finite set A. For a set $I = \{i_1, \ldots, i_m\} \subseteq \{1, \ldots, n\}$, $1 \leq i_1 < \cdots < i_m \leq n$ we define the projection of a tuple $\mathbf{a} = (a_1, \ldots, a_n)$ over I to be the tuple $\text{pr}_I \mathbf{a} = (a_{i_1}, \ldots, a_{i_m})$, and the projection of R over I to be the relation $\text{pr}_I = \{\text{pr}_I \mathbf{a} \mid \mathbf{a} \in R\}$.

2.2   Learning Preliminaries

We use two models of learning, both of them fairly standard: the model of exact learning with equivalence queries defined by Angluin [1] and the model of PAC-prediction with membership queries as defined by Angluin and Kharitonov [3]. We have chosen these models because each of them represents an opposite extreme in the spectrum of the usual learning models. Consequently, by proving our positive results in the model of exact learning with equivalence queries and our negative learnability results in the model of PAC-prediction with membership queries, we obtain results that are also valid for the many learning models lying in between, such as the PAC model [23], exact learning with equivalence and membership queries [1], or the PAE model [5], all of them among the most studied in computational learning theory.

In our setting a concept c from a concept class C is merely a subset of a domain space X, paired with an encoding of c. A learning algorithm A has the goal of identifying a target concept t. It may make any number of queries or requests to a teacher or oracle, who is commited to answer according to t, although not necessarily in a collaborative way. In the Exact model with equivalence queries [1] the learner supplies the oracle with a hypothesis h and the oracle either says equivalent or returns a counterexample $x \in h \bigtriangleup t$. If the hypothesis provided, h, does not belong to the concept class C then we speak of *improper* equivalence queries. We say that A learns a concept class C if for every target concept t, A halts with an output concept v equivalent to c. A runs in polynomial time if its running time is bounded by a polynomial on the size of the representation of t and the size of the largest counterexample.

In the PAC-prediction with membership queries [3] the oracle also holds a probability distribution D on the space of examples X. The learner is allowed to make two kinds of oracle calls. In a membership query the learner supplies some $x \in X$ and the oracle answers "yes" if $x \in t$ and "no" otherwise. In a request for a random classified example the oracle returns a pair (x, b) where x is choosen according to D and b is 1 if $x \in t$ and 0 otherwise. The learning algorithm A must eventually make one request for an element to predict and halt with an output of 1 or 0. We say that A leans a concept class C if for every target concept t and for every distribution probability D on S, A predicts the correct classification of the requested example with probability at least $1 - \epsilon$, for some accuracy bound ϵ. We say that A runs in polynomial time if its running time is bounded by a polynomial on the size of the representation of t, the size of the largest counterexample, and $1/\epsilon$. We shall say that a concept class C is polynomially learnable in any of the models if there exists a learning algorithm A that learns C and runs in polynomial time.

We use families of formulas as concept clases. The concept represented by a formula Φ is the set of all assignments (over the free variables of Φ) that satisfy the formula. We shall use throughout the paper the following observation: when F_1 and F_2 are families of formulas such that F_1 is polynomially contained in F_2, if F_2 is polynomially learnable in any of the previous models then so is F_1.

2.3   Polymorphisms

Every set of relations Γ on a set A has a collection of associated operations on A, called the *polymorphisms* of Γ. We will use the polymorphisms of Γ in a crucial way to study Γ. An n-ary operation f *preserves* an m-ary relation R (or f is a *polymorphism* of R, or R is *invariant* under f) if, for any $\mathbf{a_1} = (a_{11}, \ldots, a_{m1}), \ldots, \mathbf{a_n} = (a_{1n}, \ldots, a_{mn}) \in R$, the tuple $f(\mathbf{a_1}, \ldots, \mathbf{a_n})$ defined as $(f(a_{11}, \ldots, a_{1n}), \ldots, f(a_{m1}, \ldots, a_{mn}))$ belongs to R. If f preserves every relation from the set Γ, we say that f is a polymorphism of Γ. The set of all polymorphisms of Γ is denoted by $\mathrm{Pol}(\Gamma)$.

Example 2. Let R_1 be the 2-ary relation over the boolean domain $A = \{0,1\}$ that is given by

$$R_1 = \{(0,1), (1,0), (1,1)\}$$

That is, $R_1(x,y)$ is equivalent to $x \vee y$.

Let $m : \{0,1\}^3 \to \{0,1\}$ be the ternary operation on $\{0,1\}$ that returns the majority of its arguments. That is,

$$m(x,y,z) = \begin{cases} x \text{ if } x = y \\ z \text{ otherwise} \end{cases}$$

It is not difficult to verify that m is a polymorphism of R_1. We only need to check that for every three (not necessarily different) tuples in R_1, for example $(0,1), (0,1), (1,1)$, the tuple obtained by applying m component-wise, which in our example is $(m(0,0,1), m(1,1,1)) = (0,1)$, belongs to R_1.

Indeed, it is easy to see that m is also a polymorphism of R_2 and R_3 where $R_2(x,y) \equiv \overline{x} \vee y$ and $R_3(x,y) \equiv \overline{x} \vee \overline{y}$. Consequently, m is a polymorphism of $\Gamma = \{R_1, R_2, R_3\}$.

The next theorem amounts to say that the learnability and non-learnability of a set of formulas can be expressed in terms of polymorphisms.

Theorem 1 ([13]). *Let Γ, Γ_0 be sets of relations on a finite set A with Γ_0 finite. Then:*

1. *If $\mathrm{Pol}(\Gamma) \subseteq \mathrm{Pol}(\Gamma_0)$ and $\exists$-$\mathrm{Form}(\Gamma)$ is polynomially predictable with membership queries then so is $\exists$-$\mathrm{Form}(\Gamma_0)$.*
2. *If $\mathrm{Pol}(\Gamma) \subseteq \mathrm{Pol}(\Gamma_0)$ and $\forall\exists$-$\mathrm{Form}(\Gamma)$ is polynomially predictable with membership queries then so is $\forall\exists$-$\mathrm{Form}(\Gamma_0)$.*

In the same paper, it was shown that two types of polymorphisms guarantee the learnability of a class of formulas. An operation $f : A^k \to A$ with $k \geq 3$ is said to be a *near-unanimity* operation if

$$f(x,y,\ldots,y) = \cdots = f(y,\ldots,y,x) = y$$

for all $x, y \in A$. In this paper, it will be convenient for us to call such an operation *generalized majority*. The operation $x \cdot y^{-1} \cdot z$, where $\cdot$ and $^{-1}$ are the operations of a certain finite group, is called a *coset generating* operation. Note that every affine operation is a coset generating operation arising from an Abelian group.

Theorem 2 ([13]). *Let Γ be a set of relations on a finite set A. If Γ has a polymorphism f such that f is either a near-unanimity or coset generating operation, then $\forall\exists$-Form(Γ) is polynomially exactly learnable with equivalence queries.*

Example 3. Every quantified 2-CNF formula can be expressed as a $\forall\exists$-Form(Γ) formula where Γ is the basis of Example 2. Furthermore it is easy to observe that the operation m defined also in Example 2 is a near-unanimity operation. Consequently, we can infer that $\forall\exists$-Form(Γ), and hence the family of quantified 2-CNFs, is polynomially exactly learnable with equivalence queries.

Example 4. Let R be the solution space of a system of linear equations over a field F. Then the operation $m(x, y, z) = x - y + z$ is a polymorphism of R. Indeed, let $A \cdot \mathbf{x} = \mathbf{b}$ be the system defining R, and $\mathbf{x}, \mathbf{y}, \mathbf{z} \in R$. Then

$$A \cdot m(\mathbf{x}, \mathbf{y}, \mathbf{z}) = A \cdot (\mathbf{x} - \mathbf{y} + \mathbf{z}) = A \cdot \mathbf{x} - A \cdot \mathbf{y} + A \cdot \mathbf{z} = \mathbf{b}.$$

In fact, the converse can also be shown: if R is invariant under m then it is the solution space of a certain system of linear equations.

The operation $x - y + z$ is called an *affine* opeartion. A similar operation $x \cdot y^{-1} \cdot z$, where $\cdot$ and $^{-1}$ are operations of a group is called a *coset generating operation*. If F is a 2-element field, then $m(x, y, z) = x - y + z$ (and equal also $x + y + z$) is called a *minority* operation, because it satisfies the indentities $m(x, x, y) = m(x, y, x) = m(y, x, x) = y$.

3   Main Result

The class of operations we introduce here generalizes both near-unanimity and coset generating operations.

Definition 2. *An operation $f : A^k \to A$ with k odd and $k \geq 3$ is a* generalized majority-minority *(GMM) operation if for all $a, b \in A$, either*

$$(1)\quad f(x, y, .., y, y) = f(y, x, .., y, y) = \cdots = f(y, y, .., y, x) = y, \quad \text{for } x, y \in \{a, b\}$$

or

$$(2)\quad f(x, y, .., y, y) = f(y, x, .., y, y) = \cdots = f(y, y, .., y, x) = x, \quad \text{for } x, y \in \{a, b\}.$$

A GMM operation f is called conservative *if, for any $x_1, \ldots, x_k$, $f(x_1, \ldots, x_k) \in \{x_1, \ldots, x_k\}$.*

Let us fix a GMM operation on a set A. A pair $a, b \in A$ is said to be a *majority* pair if f on a, b satisfies (1). It is said to be a *minority* pair if f satisfies (2).

Theorem 3. *Let A be a finite set and let Γ be a finite set of relations on A. Then $\forall\exists_r$-Form(Γ) is polynomially exactly learnable with (improper) equivalence queries if and only if Γ is invariant under a conservative GMM operation. Otherwise $\exists_r$-Form(Γ) is not polynomially predictable with membership queries under the assumption that public key encryption systems secure against chosen ciphertext attack exists.*

As it has been mentioned in Section 2, for each Γ, $\forall\exists$-Form(Γ) is polynomially contained in $\forall\exists_r$-Form(Γ). Consequently, the positive learnability results also hold for the class of generalized quantified formulas, i.e., $\forall\exists$-Form(Γ) is polynomially exactly learnable if Γ is invariant under a conservative GMM operation. However, the negative learnability results do not hold in general for the class of generalized quantified formulas. We can however extend the negative results to $\exists$-Form(Γ) by imposing some assumptions on Γ. Since for each Γ containing every unary relation, we have that $\exists_r$-Form(Γ) is polynomially contained in $\exists$-Form(Γ) we can infer that, for every such Γ, if $\exists$-Form(Γ) is polynomially predictable with membership queries, then Γ must be invariant under a conservative GMM operation. In fact we are able to strenghten this result by only requiring that the basis Γ contains all unary relations of cardinality at most 2. In this case we can remove the condition of conservativity of a GMM operation.

Theorem 4. *Let A be a finite set and let Γ be a set of relations containing all unary relations of cardinality at most 2 such that $\exists$-Form(Γ) is polynomially predictable with membership queries. If there exists public key encryption systems secure against chosen ciphertext attack then Γ must be invariant under a GMM operation.*

Thus we have

Corollary 1. *Let A be a finite set and let Γ be a finite set of relations on A containing all unary relations of cardinality at most 2. Then $\forall\exists$-Form(Γ) is polynomially exactly learnable with (improper) equivalence queries if and only if Γ is invariant under a GMM operation. Otherwise $\exists$-Form(Γ) is not polynomially predictable with membership queries under the assumption that public key encryption systems secure against chosen ciphertext attack exists.*

The positive learnability results are shown in Section 4. Due to space restrictions we could not include the negative learnability results in the body of the paper. They can be found in the full version of the paper which can be downloaded from `http::/www.tecn.upf.es/~vdalmau`.

4   Positive Learnability Results

Let Γ be a set of relations on a finite set A and let $f : A^k \to A$ will be a GMM operation, k odd. In this section we shall show that if f is a polymorphism of Γ, then $\forall\exists_r$-Form(Γ) is polynomially learnable in the exact model with equivalence queries. Our learning algorithm will make use of an alternative and compact representation for relatively quantified generalized formulas called *signature*. The equivalence queries and the output of the learning algorithm will be signatures.

This section contains three subsections. In the first subection we introduce signatures and we show that for every relation concept expressed by a formula in $\forall\exists_r$-Form(Γ) there exists a succint representation (of the size bounded by a polynomial in the arity of R) in the form of a signature. In the second subsection we prove that signatures are polynomially evaluable, that is, we can decide in polynomial time whether given a signature and a tuple $\mathbf{a}$, whether $\mathbf{a}$ belongs to the relation represented by the signature. Finally, in the third subsection, we present an algorithm that polynomially learns signatures with equivalence queries. We want to stress out that all results in this section assume that the basis Γ under consideration has a GMM polymorphism f.

4.1   Signatures

Our approach relies in the following result.

Lemma 1. *Let Γ be a set of relations on a finite set A invariant under a GMM operation f.*

1. *Every relation represented by a formula from $\forall\exists$-Form(Γ) is also invariant under f.*

2. *If furthermore f is conservative, then every relation represented by a formula from $\forall\exists_r$-Form(Γ) is invariant under f*

Proof. We shall only sketch the proof of (1) (the proof of (2) is similar). We shall proof that for every formula Ψ in $\forall\exists$-Form(Γ), R_Ψ is invariant under f. It is proven by structural induction on Ψ (see also [13,4]). The only non entirely straightforward case is when Ψ is obtained by means of universal quantification $\Psi = \forall x \Phi$. In this case we use the fact, stated in the proof of Proposition 1, that Ψ is equivalent to

$$(\exists x \ \Phi \wedge a'_1(x)) \wedge \cdots \wedge (\exists x \ \Phi \wedge a'_r(x)),$$

where $\{a_1, \ldots, a_r\}$ are the elements of A and a'_i, $1 \leq i \leq r$ is the unary relation $\{(a_i)\}$. It is worth mentioning that (1) holds for every function f satisfying $f(x, x, \ldots, x) = x$ and that (2) holds for every conservative f (not merely if f is a GMM operation). $\qquad\square$

Consequently from now on we shall view concepts as relations invariant under f. Signatures will be a compact representation of such relations.

In what follows, A (the domain), f (the GMM operation on A), and k (its arity) are fixed. A signature of arity n is a triple (Pro, Rec, Wit) where

– Pro is a collection of pairs $(I, \mathbf{a})$ where I is a subset of $[n]$ of cardinality at most $k - 1$ and $\mathbf{a}$ is a tuple on A whose arity matches the cardinality of I.

- Rec is a collection of triples (i, a, b) where $1 \leq i \leq n$ and $a, b \in A$ is a minority pair.
- Wit is a collection of n-ary tuples on A.

Furthermore Pro, Rec and Wit must satisfy the following conditions:

- For every $(I, \mathbf{a}) \in$ Pro, Wit contains some tuple $\mathbf{x}$ such that $\mathrm{pr}_I \mathbf{x} = \mathbf{a}$.
- For every $(i, a, b) \in$ Rec, Wit contains some tuples $\mathbf{a}, \mathbf{b} \in R$ such that $\mathrm{pr}_{\{1,\dots,i-1\}} \mathbf{a} = \mathrm{pr}_{\{1,\dots,i-1\}} \mathbf{b}$, $\mathrm{pr}_i \mathbf{a} = a$, and $\mathrm{pr}_i \mathbf{b} = b$.
- $|\mathsf{Wit}| \leq |\mathsf{Pro}| + |\mathsf{Rec}|$

We shall denote by Sig_n the set of all signatures of arity n and by Sig the set $\bigcup_{n \geq 0} \mathrm{Sig}_n$.

Let R be an n-ary relation and let (Pro, Rec, Wit) be a signature. We say that (Pro, Rec, Wit) represents R ((Pro, Rec, Wit) is a signature of R) if the three following conditions are satisfied:

- For every $1 \leq k' \leq k$, for every $I \subseteq [n]$ such that $|I| \leq k' - 1$ and for every $(k' - 1)$-ary typle $\mathbf{a}$ on A, $(I, \mathbf{a}) \in$ Pro if and only if $\mathbf{a} \in \mathrm{pr}_I R$.
- For every $1 \leq i \leq n$ and for every minority pair $a, b \in A$, $(i, a, b) \in$ Rec if and only if there are $\mathbf{a}, \mathbf{b} \in R$ such that $\mathrm{pr}_{\{1,\dots,i-1\}} \mathbf{a} = \mathrm{pr}_{\{1,\dots,i-1\}} \mathbf{b}$, $\mathrm{pr}_i \mathbf{a} = a$, and $\mathrm{pr}_i \mathbf{b} = b$.
- Wit is contained in R.

For a set of tuples T, we denote by $\langle T \rangle$ the smallest relation invariant under f and containing T. We refer to this relation as to the *relation generated by* T.

Theorem 5. *Let R and S be n-ary relations on A invariant under f with signatures* (Pro$_R$, Rec$_R$, Wit$_R$) *and* (Pro$_S$, Rec$_S$, Wit$_S$). *If the signatures are identical then $R = S$.*

Proof. We start with an auxiliary statement.

CLAIM. If $S \subseteq R$ then $R = S$.

We shall show that $R \subseteq S$. In particular, we shall show by induction on i that $\mathrm{pr}_{\{1,\dots,i\}} R \subseteq \mathrm{pr}_{\{1,\dots,i\}} S$. Take $i \leq n$. If $i \leq k - 1$ then the required inclusion easily follows from Pro$_R$ = Pro$_S$. So let $i \geq k$ and $R' = \mathrm{pr}_{\{1,\dots,i\}} R$, $S' = \mathrm{pr}_{\{1,\dots,i\}} S$ and $\mathbf{a} = (a_1, \dots, a_i) \in R'$. By induction hypothesis, for some b_i, the tuple $(a_1, \dots, a_{i-1}, b_i) = \mathbf{a}'$ belongs to S'.

We consider two cases.

Case 1. $\{a_i, b_i\}$ is majority.

In this case we show that, for every $I \subseteq \{1, \dots, i\}$, $\mathrm{pr}_I \mathbf{a} \in \mathrm{pr}_I S'$. We show it by induction on the cardinality m of I. The result is true for $m \leq k - 1$ due to the fact that Pro$_R$ = Pro$_S$. It is also true for every set I that does not contain i, since $\mathbf{a}' \in S'$ certifies it. Thus let $I = \{j_1, \dots, j_m\}$ be any set of indices $1 \leq j_1 < j_2 < \dots < j_m = i$ with $m \geq k$ and also let $S'' = \mathrm{pr}_I S'$ and $\mathbf{a}^* = \mathrm{pr}_I \mathbf{a}$. To simplify the notation let us denote $\mathbf{a}^* = (c_1, \dots, c_m)$. By induction hypothesis, S'' contains the tuples $\mathbf{d_1} = (d_1, c_2, \dots, c_m)$, $\mathbf{d_2} = (c_1, d_2, c_3, \dots, c_m)$, $\dots$, $\mathbf{d_m} =$

$(c_1, \ldots, c_{m-1}, d_m)$ for some $d_1, \ldots, d_m \in A$. If for some i, $c_i = d_i$ then we are done. Otherwise, we can assume that $d_m = b_i$ and $c_m = a_i$ and henceforth $\{d_m, c_m\}$ is majority. If for some j, the pair $\{d_j, c_j\}$ is minority then we are done, because $f(\mathbf{d_j}, \mathbf{d_j}, \ldots, \mathbf{d_j}, \mathbf{d_m}) = \mathbf{a}^*$. Otherwise, $\{d_j, c_j\}$ is majority for any j. In this case we have $f(\mathbf{d_1}, \ldots, \mathbf{d_k}) = \mathbf{a}^*$.

Case 2. $\{a_i, b_i\}$ is minority.

Since $\mathbf{a}' \in S'$ and $S \subseteq R$, we have $\mathbf{a}' \in R'$. Furthermore, since $\mathbf{a} \in R'$, we can conclude that (i, a_i, b_i) belongs to Rec_R and hence to Rec_S. Consequently, there are $c_1, \ldots, c_{i-1}$, such that $\mathbf{c} = (c_1, \ldots, c_{i-1}, a_i)$ and $\mathbf{c}' = (c_1, \ldots, c_{i-1}, b_i)$ are in S'. The tuples $\mathbf{e} = (d_1, \ldots, d_{i-1}, a_i) = f(\mathbf{a}', \mathbf{a}', \ldots, \mathbf{a}', \mathbf{c})$ and $\mathbf{d}' = (d_1, \ldots, d_{i-1}, b_i) = f(\mathbf{a}', \mathbf{a}', \ldots, \mathbf{a}', \mathbf{c}')$, belong to S'. If $\{c_j, a_j\}$ is majority for a certain j, then $d_j = a_j$. Therefore, if $d_j \neq a_j$ then $\{d_j, a_j\}$ is minority. Thus we have $f(\mathbf{d}, \mathbf{d}', \ldots, \mathbf{d}', \mathbf{a}') = \mathbf{a}$ belongs to S' and we are done.

Let $T = \langle \mathsf{Wit}_R \rangle$ (and $= \langle \mathsf{Wit}_S \rangle$). Observe that $(\mathsf{Pro}_S, \mathsf{Rec}_S, \mathsf{Wit}_S)$ is a signature of T. Since $T \subseteq S$ and T and S have the same signature, we have $S = T$. Similarly $R = T$ and we are done. $\square$

Consequently, a signature represents at most one relation invariant under f (it is possible however that a given signature does not represent any relation). Notice that the size of Pro and Rec (and hence of Wit) is always bounded by a polynomial in n (recall that f and hence k and A are fixed).

4.2   Signatures Are Polynomially Evaluable

Our learning algorithm will use signatures as its concept class. That is, both the equivalence queries and the output of the algorithm will be signatures. Consequently, in order to make sure that we can use the output of our algorithm in order to classify examples we must show that signatures are *polynomially evaluable*, i.e, we can decide in polynomial time, given a tuple $\mathbf{a}$ and a signature s, whether the tuple $\mathbf{a}$ belongs to the relation represented by the signature s.

Let R be an n-ary relation, let $s = (\mathsf{Pro}_R, \mathsf{Rec}_R, \mathsf{Wit}_R)$ be a signature of R, and let $a_1, \ldots, a_m \in A$, $m \leq n$. By $R_{a_1, \ldots, a_m}$ we denote the relation

$$\{(b_1, \ldots, b_{n-m}) \mid (a_1, \ldots, a_m, b_1, \ldots, b_{n-m}) \in R\}$$

A signature $s_{a_1, \ldots, a_m}$ of $R_{a_1, \ldots, a_m}$ can be efficiently computed as the following theorem shows.

Theorem 6. *Let R be an n-ary relation invariant under f and $a_1, \ldots, a_m \in A$. There exists an algorithm that, given a signature $s = (\mathsf{Pro}_R, \mathsf{Rec}_R, \mathsf{Wit}_R)$ of R computes a signature $s_{a_1, \ldots, a_m}$ of $R_{a_1, \ldots, a_m}$ with running time polynomial on n.*

Proof. Let d be any element in the universe A. We shall show an algorithm that contructs a signature $(\mathsf{Pro}_{R_d}, \mathsf{Rec}_{R_d}, \mathsf{Wit}_{R_d})$ of R_d.

The algorithm has two phases. In the first phase, it computes Pro_{R_d} and the elements of Wit_{R_d} witnessing the tuples from Pro_{R_d}. Let I be any set containing at most $k'-1$, $k' \leq k$ indices and let $\mathbf{a}$ be a k'-ary tuple on A. Let $J = \{1\} \cup \{i+1 : i \in I\}$ and $S = \langle \mathrm{pr}_J \mathsf{Wit}_R \rangle$; note that S is a relation of arity at most k. It is not difficult to see that S can be computed efficiently since the maximum possible total number of tuples in S is $|A|^k$. If $(d, \mathbf{a}) \notin S$, then we do not include $(I, \mathbf{a})$ in Pro_{R_d}. Otherwise, we can find easily a tuple $\mathbf{b}$ in the relation generated by Wit_R such that $\mathrm{pr}_J \mathbf{b} = (d, \mathbf{a})$. We include $\mathrm{pr}_{\{2,\ldots,n\}} \mathbf{b}$ in Wit_{R_d} and we include $(I, \mathbf{a})$ in Pro_{R_d}

In the second phase the algorithm computes Rec_{R_d} and the elements of Wit_{R_d} witnessing the tuples from Rec_{R_d}. If $(i+1, a, b) \notin \mathsf{Rec}_R$ then $(i, a, b) \notin \mathsf{Rec}_{R_d}$. Otherwise we do the following. Let $I = \{i\}$ be the set of indices containing exactly i. If $(I, a) \notin \mathsf{Pro}_{R_d}$ then $(i, a, b) \notin \mathsf{Rec}_{R_d}$. Otherwise, we include (i, a, b) in Rec_{R_d}. In order to find a couple of tuples that witness (i, a, b) we do the following: Let $\mathbf{e}' \in \mathsf{Wit}_{R_d}$ be the tuple with $a = \mathrm{pr}_i \mathbf{e}'$ that witnesses (I, a). The tuple $\mathbf{e} = (d, \mathbf{e}')$ belongs to R, $\mathrm{pr}_1 \mathbf{e} = d$, and $\mathrm{pr}_{i+1} \mathbf{e} = a$. Since $(i+1, a, b) \in \mathsf{Rec}_R$, there are $\mathbf{a}', \mathbf{b}' \in \mathsf{Wit}_R \subseteq R$ such that $\mathrm{pr}_i \mathbf{a}' = \mathrm{pr}_i \mathbf{b}'$, $\mathrm{pr}_{i+1} \mathbf{a}' = a$, and $\mathrm{pr}_{i+1} \mathbf{b}' = b$. If $\mathrm{pr}_1 \mathbf{a}' = d$ then we are done. So, we assume that $\mathrm{pr}_1 \mathbf{a}' \neq d$ and consider two cases depending on whether $\{\mathrm{pr}_1 \mathbf{a}', d\}$ is majority or minority. If $\{\mathrm{pr}_1 \mathbf{a}', d\}$ is majority then we set $\mathbf{a}^* = f(\mathbf{e}, \mathbf{e}, \ldots, \mathbf{e}, \mathbf{a}')$ and we set $\mathbf{b}^* = f(\mathbf{e}, \mathbf{e}, \ldots, \mathbf{e}, \mathbf{b}')$. It is not hard to see that $\mathbf{a}^*, \mathbf{b}^*$ are in R, $\mathrm{pr}_1 \mathbf{a}^* = \mathrm{pr}_1 \mathbf{b}^* = d$ and $\mathrm{pr}_{\{1,\ldots,i\}} \mathbf{a}^* = \mathrm{pr}_{\{1,\ldots,i\}} \mathbf{b}^*$. Since $\{a, b\}$ is minority, we have that $\mathrm{pr}_{i+1} \mathbf{a}^* = a$ and $\mathrm{pr}_{i+1} \mathbf{b}^* = b$. If $\{\mathrm{pr}_1 \mathbf{a}', d\}$ is minority then we set $\mathbf{a}^* = f(\mathbf{e}, \mathbf{a}', \ldots, \mathbf{a}', \mathbf{a}')$ and $\mathbf{b}^* = f(\mathbf{e}, \mathbf{a}', \ldots, \mathbf{a}', \mathbf{b}')$. Finally, we include $\mathrm{pr}_{2,\ldots,n} \mathbf{a}^*, \mathrm{pr}_{2,\ldots,n} \mathbf{b}^*$ into Wit_{R_d}.

It is easy to see that the running time of the algorithm is polynomial in n.

Let us prove that the algorithm contructs the right sets. It is straightforward to see that $\mathsf{Wit}_{R_d} \subseteq R_d$. Let us start with Pro_{R_d}. It suffices to show that, for every collection of indexes I of size $k'-1$, $k' \leq k$ and any $(k'-1)$-tuple $\mathbf{a}$ the pair $(I, \mathbf{a})$ belongs to Pro_{R_d} if and only if $\mathbf{a} \in \mathrm{pr}_I R_d$. To see this, first observe that $\mathbf{a} \in \mathrm{pr}_I R_d$ if and only if $(d, \mathbf{a}) \in \mathrm{pr}_J R$. By Theorem 5, $R = \langle \mathsf{Wit}_R \rangle$. Hence, $\mathrm{pr}_J R = \langle \mathrm{pr}_J \mathsf{Wit}_R \rangle$ and the required property follows from the construction of Pro_{R_d}.

Then we consider Rec_{R_d}. In this case we have to show that there exists some $d_1, \ldots, d_{i-1}$ such that $(d_1, \ldots, d_{i-1}, a), (d_1, \ldots, d_{i-1}, b) \in \mathrm{pr}_{\{1,\ldots,i\}} R_d$ if and only if $(i, a, b) \in \mathsf{Rec}_{R_d}$. If such tuples exist then $(d, d_1, \ldots, d_{i-1}, a), (d, d_1, \ldots, d_{i-1}, b) \in \mathrm{pr}_{\{1,\ldots,i+1\}} R$ and $(i+1, a, b) \in \mathsf{Rec}_R$. Then there is $\mathbf{c} \in R_d$ such that $\mathrm{pr}_i \mathbf{c} = a$. Therefore $(\{i\}, a) \in \mathsf{Pro}_R$ and consequently the algorithm includes (i, a, b) into Rec_{R_d} in phase 2. Conversely, if $(i, a, b) \in \mathsf{Rec}_{R_d}$ then, for some $d_1, \ldots d_{i-1}$, we get $(d, d_1, \ldots, d_{i-1}, a), (d, d_1, \ldots, d_{i-1}, b) \in \mathrm{pr}_{\{1,\ldots,i+1\}} R$ and, therefore we have $(d_1, \ldots, d_{i-1}, a), (d_1, \ldots, d_{i-1}, b) \in \mathrm{pr}_{\{1,\ldots,i\}} R_d$.

By iterating the process we can obtain for any given $a_1, \ldots, a_l \in A$, a signature of $R_{a_1,\ldots,a_l} = (\ldots (R_{a_1})_{a_2})\ldots)_{a_l}$. $\square$

By convention there exists one tuple of arity 0, denoted λ. Consequently there are only two relations of arity 0, the empty relation $\emptyset$ and the relation $\{\lambda\}$. This enables us to deal with signatures of relations of arity 0 in a natural way. If R is $\emptyset$ then $\mathsf{Pro}(R) = \mathsf{Rec}(R) = \mathsf{Wit}(R) = \emptyset$ whereas if R is $\{\lambda\}$ then $\mathsf{Pro}(R) = \{(\emptyset, \lambda)\}$, $\mathsf{Rec}(R) = \emptyset$, and $\mathsf{Wit}(R) = \{\lambda\}$.

Corollary 2. *Let R be an n-ary relation invariant under f. There exists an algorithm that, given a signature of R and a tuple $\mathbf{a} = (a_1, \ldots, a_n) \in A^n$, decides whether $\mathbf{a} \in R$ with running time polynomial in n.*

Proof. To check if a given tuple $(a_1, \ldots, a_n)$ belongs to R, it suffices to check whether the set $\mathsf{Wit}(R_{a_1, \ldots, a_n})$ contains λ. $\qquad\qquad\square$

It is important to notice here that the algorithm which certifies that signatures are polynomially evaluable does not necessary succeed when the signature that receives as input does not represent a relation. However, for every n-ary signature $(\mathsf{Pro}, \mathsf{Rec}, \mathsf{Wit})$ and every $a_1, \ldots, a_m$ we can define the signature $(\mathsf{Pro}_{a_1, \ldots, a_m}, \mathsf{Rec}_{a_1, \ldots, a_m}, \mathsf{Wit}_{a_1, \ldots, a_m})$ as the output of the algorithm introduced in the proof of Theorem 6 regardless on whether $(\mathsf{Pro}, \mathsf{Rec}, \mathsf{Wit})$ is the signature of a relation or not. The reason for this is that we are interested in regarding the set of all signatures as our representation class. In this case, we will assume that the relation represented by a signature s consists of all tuples $\mathbf{a}$ for which the algorithm with input s and $\mathbf{a}$ outputs "yes". It is easy to observe that the relation represented by a signature $(\mathsf{Pro}, \mathsf{Rec}, \mathsf{Wit})$ is allways a subset of $\langle \mathsf{Wit} \rangle$.

Step 1.	set $\mathsf{Pro}, \mathsf{Rec}, \mathsf{Wit} := \emptyset$
Step 2.	**while** $EQ((\mathsf{Pro}, \mathsf{Rec}, \mathsf{Wit})) =$ 'no' **do**
	let $\mathbf{a} = (a_1, \ldots, a_n)$ be the counterexample produced by EQ
Step 2.1	**if** for some $I = \{i_1, \ldots, i_{k'-1}\}$, $i_1 < i_2 < \cdots < i_{k'-1}$. $k' \leq k$, the pair $(I, \mathrm{pr}_I\, \mathbf{a}) \notin \mathsf{Pro}$ **then**
Step 2.1.1	set $\mathsf{Pro} := \mathsf{Pro} \cup (I, \mathrm{pr}_I\, \mathbf{a})$ and $\mathsf{Wit} := \mathsf{Wit} \cup \{\mathbf{a}\}$
Step 2.2	**else**
	For each $0 \leq i \leq n$ compute $(\mathsf{Pro}_{a_1, \ldots, a_i}, \mathsf{Rec}_{a_1, \ldots, a_i}, \mathsf{Wit}_{a_1, \ldots, a_i})$.
	Let i be the smallest integer such
	that $\lambda \notin \mathsf{Wit}_{a_1, \ldots, a_i}$ (such i must exist if $\mathbf{a}$ does not belong
	to the relation represented by $(\mathsf{Pro}, \mathsf{Rec}, \mathsf{Wit})$)
Step 2.2.1	**pick** an element $\mathbf{b} = (b_i, b_{i+1}, \ldots, b_n) \in \mathsf{Wit}_{a_1, \ldots, a_{i-1}}$
	($\{a_i, b_i\}$ must be a minority pair by Theorem 5)
Step 2.2.	set $\mathsf{Rec} := \mathsf{Rec} \cup \{(i, a_i, b_i)\}$ and
	$\mathsf{Wit} := \mathsf{Wit} \cup \{\mathbf{a}, (a_1, \ldots, a_{i-1}, b_i, b_{i+1}, \ldots, b_n)\}$
	endwhile
Step 3.	**return** $\mathsf{Pro}, \mathsf{Rec}, \mathsf{Wit}$

Fig. 1. Algorithm learning signatures with equivalence queries

4.3 Signatures Are Polynomially Learnable with Equivalence Queries

Making use of the algorithm presented in Theorem 6, it is not difficult to find an algorithm that learns signatures with equivalence queries. The algorithm is presented in Figure 1.

The target concept of the algorithm is an n-ary relation invariant under f. Recall that f, k and A are fixed. At any stage of the execution of the algorithm the relation represented by (Pro, Rec, Wit) is a subset of $\langle \text{Wit} \rangle \subseteq R$. This ensures that the algorithm is monotonic. Furthermore at every round of the algorithm, either Pro or Rec increases its size. Since Pro and Rec can have at most a polynomial number of elements we can ensure that the algorithm ends in a number of steps polynomial in n.

Theorem 7. *The class* Sig *is polynomially learnable with equivalence queries.*

Corollary 3. *Let A be a finite set and let Γ be a finite set of relation on A.*

- *If Γ is invariant under a GMM operation then $\forall \exists$-Form(Γ) is polynomially learnable with equivalence queries in* Sig.
- *If Γ is invariant under a conservative GMM operation then $\forall \exists_r$-Form(Γ) is polynomially learnable with equivalence queries in* Sig.

References

[1] D. Angluin. Queries and Concept Learning. *Machine Learning*, 2:319–342, 1988.
[2] D. Angluin, M. Frazier, and L. Pitt. Learning Conjunctions of Horn Clauses. *Machine Learning*, 9:147–164, 1992.
[3] D. Angluin and M. Kharitonov. When won't Membership Queries help. *Journal of Computer and System Sciences*, 50:336–355, 1995.
[4] F. Börner, A.A. Bulatov, P.G. Jeavons, and A.A. Krokhin. Quantified constraints and surjective polymorphisms. In *Proceedings of 17th International Workshop Computer Science Logic, CSL'03*, volume 2803 of *Lecture Notes in Computer Science*, pages 58–70. Springer-Verlag, 2003.
[5] N. Bshouty, J. Jackson, and C. Tamon. Exploiring Learnability between Exact and PAC. In *15th Annual ACM Conference on Computational Learning Theory, COLT'02*, pages 244–254, 2002.
[6] N.H. Bshouty. Exact Learning Boolean Functions via the Monotone Theory. *Information and Computation*, pages 146–153, November 1995.
[7] A.A. Bulatov. Tractable conservative constraint satisfaction problems. In *Proceedings of the 18th Annual IEEE Simposium on Logic in Computer Science*, pages 321–330, Ottawa, Canada, June 2003. IEEE Computer Society.
[8] H. Chen. Quantified constraint satisfaction problems: Closure properties, complexity, and algorithms. Technical report, Cornell University, 2003.
[9] N. Creignou. A Dichotomy Theorem for Maximum Generalized Satisfiability Problems. *Journal of Computer and System Sciences*, 51(3):511–522, 1995.
[10] N. Creignou and M. Hermann. Complexity of Generalized Satisfiability Counting Problems. *Information and Computation*, 125:1–12, 1996.

[11] N. Creignou, S. Khanna, and M. Sudan. *Complexity Classification of Boolean Constraint Satisfaction Problems*, volume 7 of *Monographs on Discrete Mathematics and Applications*. SIAM, 2001.

[12] V. Dalmau. A Dichotomy Theorem for Learning Quantified Boolean Formulas. *Machine Learning*, 35(3):207–224, 1999.

[13] V. Dalmau and P. Jeavons. Learnability of Quantified Formulas. *Theoretical Computer Science*, (306):485–511, 2003.

[14] Jeffrey C. Jackson. An Efficient Membership-query Algorithm for Learning DNF with respect to the Uniform Distribution. *Journal of Computer and System Sciences*, 55(3):414–440, December 1997.

[15] P. Jeavons, D. Cohen, and M.C. Cooper. Constraints, Consistency and Closure. *Artificial Intelligence*, 101:251–265, 1998.

[16] Michael Kearns and Leslie Valiant. Cryptographic limitations on learning Boolean formulae and finite automata. *Journal of the ACM*, 41(1):67–95, January 1994.

[17] S. Khanna, M. Sudan, and L. Trevisan. Constraint Satisfaction: The Approximability of Minimization Problems. In *12th IEEE Conference on Computational Complexity*, 1997.

[18] S. Khanna, M. Sudan, and P.D. Williamson. A Complete Classification of the Approximability of Maximation Problems Derived from Boolean Constraint Satisfaction. In *29th Annual ACM Symposium on Theory of Computing*, 1997.

[19] N. Pippenger. *Theories of Computability*. Cambridge University Press, 1997.

[20] E.L. Post. *The Two-Valued Iterative Systems of Mathematical Logic*, volume 5 of *Annals of Mathematics Studies*. Princeton, N.J, 1941.

[21] T.J. Schaefer. The Complexity of Satisfiability Problems. In *10th Annual ACM Symposium on Theory of Computing*, pages 216–226, 1978.

[22] A. Szendrei. *Clones in Universal Algebra*, volume 99 of *Seminaires de Mathématiques Supéreiores*. University of Montreal, 1986.

[23] L. Valiant. A Theory of the Learnable. *Comm. ACM*, 27(11):1134–1142, 1984.

Learning Languages Generated by Elementary Formal Systems and Its Application to SH Languages*

Yasuhito Mukouchi and Masako Sato

Department of Mathematics and Information Sciences
College of Integrated Arts and Sciences
Osaka Prefecture University, Sakai, Osaka 599-8531, Japan

Abstract. The *Elementary Formal Systems* (*EFSs*, for short) are originally introduced by Smullyan to develop his recursion theory. In a word, EFSs are a kind of logic programs which use strings instead of terms in first order logic, and they are shown to be natural devices to define languages.

In defining languages of EFSs, many studies assume that substitutions are nonerasing. A *substitution* or a *nonerasing substitution* is defined as a homomorphism from *nonempty* strings to *nonempty* strings that maps each constant symbol to itself, although an *erasing substitution* allows mapping of variables to the empty string.

In this paper, we investigate the learnability of language classes generated by *simple formal systems* (*SFSs*, for short) as well as *regular formal systems* (*RFSs*, for short). We show that the learnability of some classes of their languages varies according to whether or not erasing substitutions are allowed. Then we present a subclass of RFSs such that the corresponding class of languages is inferable in the limit from positive examples, even when erasing substitutions are allowed.

We also apply the obtained result to the learning problem of languages generated by simple H systems. The *simple H systems* (*SH systems*, for short) are introduced by Mateescu et al. by modeling the recombinant behavior of DNA sequences. We show that an SH system can be naturally converted into an RFS whose language coincides with the language generated by the original SH system. By using this conversion, we show that the class of languages generated by a certain subclass of SH systems is inferable in the limit from positive examples.

1 Introduction

The *Elementary Formal Systems* (*EFSs*, for short) are originally introduced by Smullyan [23] to develop his recursion theory. In a word, EFSs are a kind of logic programs which use strings instead of terms in first order logic (Yamamoto [25]), and they are shown to be natural devices to define languages (Arikawa

---

* Supported in part by Grant-in-Aid for Scientific Research (C) No. 15500093 from the Ministry of Education, Culture, Sports, Science and Technology, Japan.

S. Ben-David, J. Case, A. Maruoka (Eds.): ALT 2004, LNAI 3244, pp. 380–394, 2004.

[3] and Arikawa et al. [4]). Especially Arikawa et al. [4] presented various subclasses of EFSs whose language classes correspond to the four classes of Chomsky hierarchy.

By taking advantage of structural merits and flexibility of logic programs, many researchers discussed learning problems in the framework of EFSs (Arikawa et al. [4,5], Sakamoto et al. [18], Lange et al. [12] and so on). Especially, in the learning paradigm of identification in the limit due to Gold [8], Shinohara [21] showed that the language class generated by the so-called length-bounded EFSs with at most k axioms is inferable in the limit from positive examples for each $k \geq 0$. Angluin [1] introduced a *pattern* and its language and showed that the class of pattern languages is inferable in the limit from positive examples. The class of pattern languages is regarded as the class of languages generated by EFSs with just one axiom.

In defining models and languages of EFSs, many studies assume that substitutions are nonerasing. A *substitution* or a *nonerasing substitution* is defined as a homomorphism from *nonempty* strings to *nonempty* strings that maps each constant symbol to itself, although an *erasing substitution* allows mapping of variables to the empty string. However, in applying patterns or EFSs to real problems, there are many cases that erasing substitutions are more suitable (Arimura et al. [6], Shinohara [19] and so on). We call a language generated by an EFS using nonerasing substitutions (resp., erasing substitutions) an *EFS language* (resp., an *erasing EFS language*). Then an erasing EFS language generated by an EFS with just one axiom is called an *extended pattern language*. It is unknown whether or not the class of extended pattern languages is inferable in the limit from positive examples, although Reidenbach [17] showed that that class with just two constant symbols is not inferable in the limit from positive examples. Concerning erasing EFS languages, Uemura and Sato [24] showed that the class of the so-called erasing PFS languages is inferable in the limit from positive examples under a certain condition.

In this paper, we investigate the learnability of language classes generated by *simple formal systems* (*SFSs*, for short) as well as *regular formal systems* (*RFSs*, for short). We show that the learnability of their languages varies according to whether or not erasing substitutions are allowed. That is, we show that the class of EFS languages generated by SFSs or RFSs with at most k axioms is inferable in the limit from positive examples, but so is not the corresponding class of erasing EFS languages.

We also apply the obtained result to the learning problem of languages generated by simple H systems. *Simple H systems* (*SH systems*, for short) are introduced by Mateescu et al. [14] by modeling the recombinant behavior of DNA sequences. We show that an SH system can be naturally converted into an RFS whose erasing EFS language coincides with the language generated by the original SH system. By using this conversion, we show that the class of languages generated by SH systems with at most k segments is inferable in the limit from positive examples for each $k \geq 0$. Head [10] showed that the class of SH languages becomes a subclass of strictly locally testable languages. The obtained result presents a learnable subclass of strictly locally testable languages (Yoko-mori et al. [26], Garchia [7] and so on).

2   Preliminaries

In this section, we summarize basic notations and results necessary for our discussion.

Let Σ be a fixed finite alphabet. Each element of Σ is called a *constant symbol*. Let Σ^* be the set of constant strings over Σ and let Σ^+ be that of nonempty constant strings over Σ. Let us denote by ε the empty string, i.e., the string with length 0. Then $\Sigma^+ = \Sigma^* \setminus \{\varepsilon\}$ holds. A subset L of Σ^* is called a *language* over Σ. For a string $w \in \Sigma^*$, we denote by $|w|$ the length of w. For two strings $u, v \in \Sigma^*$, we denote by uv or $u \cdot v$ the concatenation of u and v.

In this paper, $\sharp S$ denotes the cardinality of a set S, and N denotes the set of nonnegative integers.

Definition 1 (Angluin [2]). *A class* $\mathcal{L} = \{L_i\}_{i \in N}$ *of languages is said to be an* indexed family of recursive languages, *if there is a total computable function* $f : N \times \Sigma^* \to \{0, 1\}$ *such that* $f(i, w) = 1$ *if and only if* $w \in L_i$.

Since we exclusively deal with an indexed family of recursive languages as a class of languages, we simply call it a class of languages without any notice.

Definition 2 (Gold [8]). *A* positive presentation, *or a* text, *of a language* $L \subseteq \Sigma^*$ *is an infinite sequence* $w_0, w_1, \cdots \in \Sigma^*$ *such that* $\{w_i \mid i \geq 0\} = L$.

In what follows, σ or δ denotes a positive presentation, and $\sigma[n]$ denotes the σ's initial segment of length $n \geq 0$.

An inductive inference machine *(IIM, for short) is an effective procedure, or a certain type of Turing machine, which requests inputs from time to time and produces indices from time to time. The outputs produced by the machine are called* guesses.

For an IIM M, for a positive presentation σ and for $n \geq 0$, by $M(\sigma[n])$, we denote the last guess produced by M which is successively presented examples in $\sigma[n]$ on its input requests.

An IIM M is said to converge *to an index i for a positive presentation σ, if there is an $n \geq 0$ such that for every $m \geq n$, $M(\sigma[m]) = i$.*

Then we define the learnability of a class of languages as follows:

Definition 3 (Gold [8] and Angluin [2]). *Let* $\mathcal{L} = \{L_i\}_{i \in N}$ *be a class of languages.*

An IIM M is said to infer *a language $L_i \in \mathcal{L}$ in the limit from positive examples, if for every positive presentation σ of L_i, M converges to an index j for σ such that $L_j = L_i$.*

An IIM M is said to infer *a class $\mathcal{L}$ in the limit from positive examples, if for every $L_i \in \mathcal{L}$, M infers L_i in the limit from positive examples.*

A class $\mathcal{L}$ is said to be inferable *in the limit from positive examples, if there is an IIM which infers $\mathcal{L}$ in the limit from positive examples.*

Angluin [2] presented a theorem characterizing for a class to be inferable in the limit from positive examples.

Definition 4 (Angluin [2]). *A set T of strings is a* finite tell-tale set *of a language L within a class $\mathcal{L}$, if (1) T is a finite subset of L and (2) there is no $L_i \in \mathcal{L}$ such that $T \subseteq L_i \subsetneq L$.*

Theorem 1 (Angluin [2]). *A class $\mathcal{L}$ is inferable in the limit from positive examples, if and only if there is an effective procedure which on input $i \geq 0$ enumerates a finite tell-tale set of $L_i \in \mathcal{L}$ within $\mathcal{L}$.*

We note that if a class $\mathcal{L}$ with some specific indexing is inferable in the limit from positive examples, so is the class with arbitrary indexing (cf., e.g., Lange and Zeugmann [11]). Additionally, we discuss inferability of each class using set-theoretic property of the class which is independent of indexing. Thus, in the present paper, we fix some suitable indexing for each class and do not pay much attention on indexing of the class.

By the theorem above, we see that the following lemma is valid:

Lemma 1. *Let $\mathcal{L}$ be a class of languages.*
Then if there exists a sequence $L_{i_0}, L_{i_1}, \cdots \in \mathcal{L}$ and a language $L_i \in \mathcal{L}$ such that

$$L_{i_0} \subsetneq L_{i_1} \subsetneq \cdots \quad and \quad \bigcup_{n \geq 0} L_{i_n} = L_i,$$

then $\mathcal{L}$ is not inferable in the limit from positive examples.

A class is called *super-finite*, if it contains every finite language and at least one infinite language. We note that each super-finite class satisfies the premise in the above lemma, and thus it is not inferable in the limit from positive examples (Gold [8]).

Wright [27] and Motoki et al. [15] showed a sufficient condition for a class to be inferable in the limit from positive examples.

Definition 5 (Wright [27] and Motoki et al. [15]). *A class $\mathcal{L}$ is said to have* infinite elasticity, *if there are two infinite sequences $L_{i_1}, L_{i_2}, \cdots \in \mathcal{L}$ and $w_0, w_1, \cdots \in \Sigma^*$ such that for every $n \geq 1$,*

$$\{w_0, w_1, \cdots, w_{n-1}\} \subseteq L_{i_n} \quad but \quad w_n \notin L_{i_n}.$$

A class $\mathcal{L}$ is said to have finite elasticity, *if $\mathcal{L}$ does not have infinite elasticity.*

By definition, it is easy to see that if a class $\mathcal{L}$ has a finite elasticity, then so does every subclass of $\mathcal{L}$.

Theorem 2 (Wright [27] and Motoki et al. [15]). *A class $\mathcal{L}$ is inferable in the limit from positive examples, if $\mathcal{L}$ has finite elasticity.*

3   Elementary Formal Systems and Their Languages

3.1   Definitions and Basic Properties

In this paper, we briefly recall EFSs and their languages. For detailed definitions and properties of EFSs, please refer to Smullyan [23], Arikawa [3], Arikawa et al. [4] and Yamamoto [25].

Let Σ be a finite alphabet. Let X and Π be nonempty sets. Elements in X and Π are called *variables* and *predicate symbols*, respectively. We assume that Σ, X and Π are mutually disjoint. By $x, y, x_1, x_2, \cdots$, we denote variables, and by $p, q, p_1, p_2, \cdots$, we denote predicate symbols. Each predicate symbol is associated with a positive integer which we call an *arity*.

Definition 6. *A* term *or a* pattern *is a possibly empty string over* $\Sigma \cup X$. *By* $\pi, \pi_1, \pi_2, \cdots$, *we denote terms. A term π is said to be* ground, *if π does not contain any variable. By $w, w_1, w_2, \cdots$, we denote ground terms.*

An atomic formula *(*atom, *for short) is an expression of the form* $p(\pi_1, \cdots, \pi_n)$, *where* $n \geq 1$, *$p \in \Pi$ is a predicate symbol with arity n, and $\pi_1, \cdots, \pi_n$ are terms. By $A, B, A_1, A_2, \cdots$, we denote atoms. An atom $p(\pi_1, \cdots, \pi_n)$ is said to be* ground, *if $\pi_1, \cdots, \pi_n$ are ground terms. We define the length of an atom $p(\pi_1, \cdots, \pi_n)$, denoted by $|p(\pi_1, \cdots, \pi_n)|$, as $\sum_{1 \leq i \leq n} |\pi_i|$.*

We define well-formed formulas and clauses in the ordinary ways [13].

Definition 7. *A* definite clause *is a clause of the form*

$$A \leftarrow B_1, \cdots, B_n,$$

where $n \geq 0$, and $A, B_1, \cdots, B_n$ are atoms. In case, $A, B_1, \cdots, B_n$ are all ground atoms, then we call the above clause a ground clause. *The atom A above is called the* head *of the clause, and the sequence $B_1, \cdots, B_n$ is called the* body *of the clause. By $C, D, C_1, C_2, \cdots$, we denote definite clauses. Then an EFS is a finite set of definite clauses, each of which is called an* axiom.

A substitution *is a homomorphism from terms to terms which maps each symbol $a \in \Sigma$ to itself and each variable $x \in X$ to nonempty term in $(\Sigma \cup X)^+$. In case we allow mapping of a variable to the empty string ε, we call such substitutions* erasing *substitutions. By $\theta, \delta, \theta_1, \theta_2, \cdots$, we denote substitutions.*

For a term π, the image of π by a substitution θ is denoted by $\pi\theta$. For a predicate symbol $p \in \Pi$ with arity n and for terms $\pi_1, \cdots, \pi_n$, the image of an atom $A = p(\pi_1, \cdots, \pi_n)$ by a substitution θ is defined as $A\theta = p(\pi_1, \cdots, \pi_n)\theta = p(\pi_1\theta, \cdots, \pi_n\theta)$. Furthermore for atoms $A, B_1, \cdots, B_n$, the image of a clause $C = A \leftarrow B_1, \cdots, B_n$ by a substitution θ is defined as $C\theta = (A \leftarrow B_1, \cdots, B_n)\theta = A\theta \leftarrow B_1\theta, \cdots, B_n\theta$.

Then for an EFS, we define its language as follows:

Definition 8. *Let Γ be an EFS. We define the relation $\Gamma \vdash C$ for a clause C inductively as follows:*

(1) If $C \in \Gamma$, then $\Gamma \vdash C$.

(2) If $\Gamma \vdash C$, then $\Gamma \vdash C\theta$ for every substitution θ.

(3) If $\Gamma \vdash A \leftarrow B_1, \cdots, B_{n+1}$ and $\Gamma \vdash B_{n+1} \leftarrow$, then $\Gamma \vdash A \leftarrow B_1, \cdots, B_n$.

We also define the relation $\Gamma \vdash_\varepsilon C$ similarly but allowing erasing substitutions in (2). Therefore $\Gamma \vdash C$ implies $\Gamma \vdash_\varepsilon C$, but the converse is not always true.

For an EFS Γ and for a unary predicate symbol $p \in \Pi$, we define the languages $L(\Gamma, p)$ and $L_\varepsilon(\Gamma, p)$ as follows:

$$L(\Gamma, p) = \{w \in \Sigma^* \mid \Gamma \vdash p(w) \leftarrow\} \quad and \quad L_\varepsilon(\Gamma, p) = \{w \in \Sigma^* \mid \Gamma \vdash_\varepsilon p(w) \leftarrow\}.$$

A language L is called an EFS language *(resp., an* erasing EFS language*), if there is an EFS Γ and a unary predicate symbol $p \in \Pi$ such that $L = L(\Gamma, p)$ (resp., $L = L_\varepsilon(\Gamma, p)$).*

Arikawa et al. [4] has introduced subclasses of EFSs whose language classes correspond to the four classes of Chomsky hierarchy. In the present paper, we concentrate our attention to the subclasses of EFSs called simple formal systems (Arikawa [3]) and regular formal systems (Shinohara [20]) defined as follows:

Definition 9. *An EFS Γ is called a* simple formal system *(an* SFS*, for short), if every axiom of Γ is of the form*

$$p(\pi) \leftarrow q_1(x_1), \cdots, q_n(x_n),$$

where $n \geq 0$, $p, q_1, \cdots, q_n \in \Pi$ are unary predicate symbols, π is a term, and $x_1, \cdots, x_n$ are mutually distinct variables appearing in π.

A term π is called regular*, if every variable appears at most once in π. An SFS Γ is called a* regular formal system *(an* RFS*, for short), if every term appearing in Γ is regular.*

A language L is called an SFS language *(resp., an* erasing SFS language*), if L is an EFS language (resp., an erasing EFS language) generated by an SFS. We also define an RFS language and an erasing RFS language similarly.*

We denote by $\mathcal{SFS}$ the class of SFSs, by $\mathcal{SFSL}$ that of SFS languages, and by $e\mathcal{SFSL}$ that of erasing SFS languages. We also define the classes $\mathcal{RFS}$, $\mathcal{RFSL}$ and $e\mathcal{RFSL}$ similarly.

Arikawa [3] and Arikawa et al. [4] showed the powers of SFSs and RFSs:

Theorem 3 (Arikawa [3] and Arikawa et al. [4]). *The following relations hold:*

$$\mathcal{CFL} = \mathcal{RFSL} \subsetneqq \mathcal{SFSL} \subsetneqq \mathcal{CSL},$$

where $\mathcal{CFL}$ and $\mathcal{CSL}$ represent the class of context-free languages and that of context-sensitive languages, respectively.

Furthermore, on erasing SFS or RFS languages, we have the following theorem:

Theorem 4. *The following relations hold:*
   (1) $e\mathcal{SFSL} = \mathcal{SFSL}$ holds.
   (2) $e\mathcal{RFSL} = \mathcal{RFSL}$ holds.

Proof. (I) Let $L \in e\mathcal{SFSL}$. Then there is an SFS Γ and a unary predicate symbol $p \in \Pi$ such that $L = L_\varepsilon(\Gamma, p)$.

For a clause C, let us put $\mathrm{var}(C)$ the set of all variables appearing in C. For a set Y of variables, we put $\theta_\varepsilon(Y) = \{x := \varepsilon \mid x \in Y\}$, that is, $\theta_\varepsilon(Y)$ is the erasing substitution that maps every variable $x \in Y$ to the empty string ε.

Then let us put $\Gamma' = \{C\theta_\varepsilon(Y) \mid C \in \Gamma, Y \subseteq \mathrm{var}(C)\}$. We note that Γ' is an EFS but may not be an SFS, because Γ' may contain a clause whose body has an atom of the form $q(\varepsilon)$.

Let $\Gamma'' = \Gamma'$. Then we delete from Γ'' every clause C whose body contains an atom $q(\varepsilon)$ with $\Gamma' \nvdash q(\varepsilon) \leftarrow$. Finally, we delete all atoms of the form $q(\varepsilon)$ appearing in the bodies of the clauses in Γ''. Then Γ'' is an SFS such that $L = L_\varepsilon(\Gamma, p) = L(\Gamma'', p)$, and thus $L \in \mathcal{SFSL}$ holds.

This means that $e\mathcal{SFSL} \subseteq \mathcal{SFSL}$.

(II) Let $L \in \mathcal{SFSL}$. Then there is an SFS Γ and a unary predicate symbol $p \in \Pi$ such that $L = L(\Gamma, p)$.

First, we put

$$
\Gamma_0 = \left\{ C' \; \middle| \; \begin{array}{l} C' \text{ is obtained from some } C \in \Gamma \text{ by replacing every} \\ \text{variable } x \text{ that appears only in the head of } C \text{ with} \\ ax \text{ for some } a \in \Sigma. \end{array} \right\}.
$$

Let $p_1, \cdots, p_n$ be all the predicate symbols such that $\Gamma \vdash p_i(\varepsilon) \leftarrow$. Then we define Γ_i's $(1 \leq i \leq n)$ as follows:

$$
\Gamma_i = \Gamma_{i-1} \cup \left\{ C' \; \middle| \; \begin{array}{l} C' \text{ is obtained from some } C \in \Gamma_{i-1} \text{ by delet-} \\ \text{ing the atom } p_i(x) \text{ in the body of } C \text{ and} \\ \text{deleting every appearance of variable } x \text{ in the} \\ \text{head of } C, \text{ where } x \text{ is the variable appearing} \\ \text{in the body associated with } p_i. \end{array} \right\}.
$$

Then Γ_n is an SFS such that $L = L(\Gamma, p) = L_\varepsilon(\Gamma_n, p)$, and thus $L \in e\mathcal{SFSL}$ holds.

This means that $\mathcal{SFSL} \subseteq e\mathcal{SFSL}$.

By (I) and (II), we conclude that $\mathcal{SFSL} = e\mathcal{SFSL}$ is valid. The above proof is also a proof for $\mathcal{RFSL} = e\mathcal{RFSL}$. □

3.2   Learnability of EFS Languages

In the present paper, we consider learnability of languages generated by SFSs, RFSs and SH systems. Since these systems are recursively enumerable and their languages are recursive, we can regard these language classes as indexed families of recursive languages.

As easily seen, the classes $\mathcal{SFSL}$, $\mathcal{RFSL}$, $e\mathcal{SFSL}$ and $e\mathcal{RFSL}$ are superfinite, and thus we have the following theorem:

Theorem 5. *The classes $\mathcal{SFSL}$, $\mathcal{RFSL}$, $e\mathcal{SFSL}$ and $e\mathcal{RFSL}$ are not inferable in the limit from positive examples.*

For each $k \geq 0$, we define the subclass $\mathcal{SFS}^{\leq k}$ of $\mathcal{SFS}$ as the class of SFSs with at most k axioms. Then we denote by $\mathcal{SFSL}^{\leq k}$ the class of SFS languages generated by SFSs in $\mathcal{SFS}^{\leq k}$ and by $e\mathcal{SFSL}^{\leq k}$ that of erasing SFS languages generated by SFSs in $\mathcal{SFS}^{\leq k}$. We also define the classes $\mathcal{RFS}^{\leq k}$, $\mathcal{RFSL}^{\leq k}$ and $e\mathcal{RFSL}^{\leq k}$ similarly.

Shinohara [21,22] showed that for each $k \geq 0$, the class of languages generated by the so-called length-bounded EFSs with at most k axioms has finite elasticity, and thus it is inferable in the limit from positive examples. Since $\mathcal{SFSL}^{\leq k}$ and $\mathcal{RFSL}^{\leq k}$ are subclasses of the class, we see that the following theorem holds:

Theorem 6. *Let $k \geq 0$.*
Then the classes $\mathcal{SFSL}^{\leq k}$ and $\mathcal{RFSL}^{\leq k}$ have finite elasticity, and thus they are inferable in the limit from positive examples.

In the rest of this section, we consider learnability of the classes $e\mathcal{SFSL}^{\leq k}$ and $e\mathcal{RFSL}^{\leq k}$.

Theorem 7. *Let $\sharp \Sigma \geq 1$ and let $k \geq 3$.*
Then the classes $e\mathcal{RFSL}^{\leq k}$ and $e\mathcal{SFSL}^{\leq k}$ are not inferable in the limit from positive examples.

Proof. We consider the following RFSs:

$$
\Gamma_n = \begin{cases} p(x_1 \cdots x_n) \leftarrow q(x_1), \cdots, q(x_n); \\ q(a) \leftarrow; \\ q(\varepsilon) \leftarrow \end{cases} \quad (n \geq 0),
$$
$$
\Gamma_\infty = \begin{cases} p(ax_1) \leftarrow p(x_1); \\ p(\varepsilon) \leftarrow \end{cases}.
$$

Then, as easily seen,

$$
L_\varepsilon(\Gamma_n, p) = \{a^i \mid 0 \leq i \leq n\} \quad (n \geq 0),
$$
$$
L_\varepsilon(\Gamma_\infty, p) = \{a^i \mid i \geq 0\}
$$

hold, and thus

$$
L_\varepsilon(\Gamma_0, p) \subsetneqq L_\varepsilon(\Gamma_1, p) \subsetneqq \cdots \quad \text{and} \quad \bigcup_{n \geq 0} L_\varepsilon(\Gamma_n, p) = L_\varepsilon(\Gamma_\infty, p)
$$

hold. Therefore, by Lemma 1, the class $e\mathcal{RFSL}^{\leq k}$ is not inferable in the limit from positive examples.

Since the above EFSs are also SFSs, we see that the class $e\mathcal{SFSL}^{\leq k}$ is also not inferable in the limit from positive examples. $\qquad\square$

We note that Shinohara [19] showed that the class of the so-called extended regular pattern languages, which coincides with $e\mathcal{RFSL}^{\leq 1}$, is inferable in the limit from positive examples. On the other hand, Uemura and Sato [24] showed that the class of the so-called erasing primitive formal languages, which is a subclass of $e\mathcal{RFSL}^{\leq 2}$, is inferable in the limit from positive examples under a certain condition.

Furthermore, the following example shows that the class of *infinite* languages in $e\mathcal{RFSL}^{\leq k}$ with $k \geq 5$ and the class $e\mathcal{SFSL}^{\leq k}$ with $k \geq 2$ are also not inferable in the limit from positive examples.

Example 1. (1) Let $k \geq 5$, let $\sharp\Sigma \geq 2$, and let $a, b \in \Sigma$ be two distinct constant symbols.

We consider the following RFSs:

$$
\Gamma_n = \left\{
\begin{array}{l}
r(x_1 x_2 b) \leftarrow r(x_1), p(x_2); \\
r(\varepsilon) \leftarrow; \\
p(x_1 \cdots x_n) \leftarrow q(x_1), \cdots, q(x_n); \\
q(a) \leftarrow; \\
q(\varepsilon) \leftarrow
\end{array}
\right\} \quad (n \geq 0),
$$

$$
\Gamma_\infty = \left\{
\begin{array}{l}
r(x_1 x_2 b) \leftarrow r(x_1), p(x_2); \\
r(\varepsilon) \leftarrow; \\
p(a x_1) \leftarrow p(x_1); \\
p(\varepsilon) \leftarrow
\end{array}
\right\}.
$$

Then, as easily seen,

$$
\begin{array}{ll}
L_\varepsilon(\Gamma_n, r) = \{a^{i_1} b a^{i_2} b \cdots a^{i_m} b \mid m \geq 0, \ 0 \leq i_1, i_2, \cdots, i_m \leq n\} & (n \geq 0), \\
L_\varepsilon(\Gamma_\infty, r) = \{a^{i_1} b a^{i_2} b \cdots a^{i_m} b \mid m \geq 0, \ i_1, i_2, \cdots, i_m \geq 0\}
\end{array}
$$

hold, and thus by Lemma 1, the class of infinite languages in $e\mathcal{RFSL}^{\leq k}$ is not inferable in the limit from positive examples.

(2) Let $k \geq 2$ and let $\sharp\Sigma \geq 2$.

We consider the following SFSs:

$$
\Gamma_n = \{p(x_1 x_2 \cdots x_n x_n \cdots x_2 x_1) \leftarrow\} \quad (n \geq 0),
$$

$$
\Gamma_\infty = \left\{
\begin{array}{l}
p(x_1 x_2 x_1) \leftarrow p(x_2); \\
p(x_1 x_1) \leftarrow
\end{array}
\right\}.
$$

For each $n \geq 0$,

$$
p(x_1 x_2 \cdots x_n x_{n+1} x_{n+1} x_n \cdots x_2 x_1)\{x_{n+1} := \varepsilon\} = p(x_1 x_2 \cdots x_n x_n \cdots x_2 x_1)
$$

holds, and thus we have $L_\varepsilon(\Gamma_n, p) \subseteq L_\varepsilon(\Gamma_{n+1}, p)$.

Let $a, b \in \Sigma$ be two distinct constant symbols. For each $n \geq 0$, we put $w_n = a b^n$ and $w'_n = w_0 w_1 \cdots w_n w_n \cdots w_1 w_0$. Then, as easily seen, for each $n \geq 0$, $w'_{n+1} \in L_\varepsilon(\Gamma_{n+1}, p) \setminus L_\varepsilon(\Gamma_n, p)$ holds. Thus it is easy to see that these languages satisfy the conditions of Lemma 1. Therefore the class $e\mathcal{SFSL}^{\leq k}$ is not inferable in the limit from positive examples.

Now, we introduce a subclass of $e\mathcal{RFSL}^{\leq k}$ that is inferable in the limit from positive examples.

Definition 10. *A regular term π is called* canonical, *if $\pi = w_0 x_1 w_1 x_2 \cdots x_n w_n$ for some $n \geq 0$, $w_0, w_n \in \Sigma^*$ and $w_1, \cdots, w_{n-1} \in \Sigma^+$.*

An RFS Γ is called canonical, *if all regular terms appearing in Γ are canonical. We denote by $\mathcal{CRFS}$ the class of canonical RFSs, by $\mathcal{CRFSL}$ that of canonical RFS languages, and by $e\mathcal{CRFSL}$ that of erasing canonical RFS languages. Furthermore, for each $k \geq 0$, we define $\mathcal{CRFS}^{\leq k}$, $\mathcal{CRFSL}^{\leq k}$ and $e\mathcal{CRFSL}^{\leq k}$ similarly to $\mathcal{RFS}^{\leq k}$, $\mathcal{RFSL}^{\leq k}$ and $e\mathcal{RFSL}^{\leq k}$.*

Shinohara [19] showed that the so-called extended pattern language definable by an arbitrary regular pattern is also definable by a *canonical* regular pattern.

Lemma 2. *Let π be a term and let τ be a canonical regular term.*
Then if $\pi = \tau\theta$ for some erasing substitution θ, then $|\tau| \leq 2|c(\pi)| + 1$ holds, where $c(\pi)$ denotes the constant string obtained from π by deleting all variables in π.

Proof. Assume $\pi = \tau\theta$ for some erasing substitution θ. Then, as easily seen, $c(\tau)$ is a subsequence of $c(\pi)$, and thus $|c(\tau)| \leq |c(\pi)|$ holds. Let us put $c(\tau) = c_1 c_2 \cdots c_m$, where $m = |c(\tau)|$ and $c_1, c_2, \cdots, c_m \in \Sigma$. Since τ is a canonical regular term, τ must be of the form $\alpha_1 c_1 \alpha_2 c_2 \cdots c_m \alpha_{m+1}$, where α_i is either a variable or the empty string $(1 \leq i \leq m+1)$. Therefore we have $|\tau| \leq 2m + 1 = 2|c(\tau)| + 1 \leq 2|c(\pi)| + 1$. $\qquad\square$

Definition 11. *Let Γ be an EFS and let C be a clause.*
An axiom D of Γ is said to be used in proving C, *if $\Gamma \vdash_\varepsilon C$ but $\Gamma \backslash \{D\} \nvdash_\varepsilon C$.*

Lemma 3. *Let $p(w)$ be a ground atom and let Γ be a canonical RFS such that $\Gamma \vdash_\varepsilon p(w) \leftarrow$.*
Then the length of the head of each axiom of Γ used in proving $p(w) \leftarrow$ is not greater than $2|w| + 1$.

Proof. A clause C is said to be a *ground instance* of a clause D, if C is a ground clause such that $C = D\theta$ for some erasing substitution θ.

First, we define the relation $\Gamma \vdash'_\varepsilon C$ for a clause C as follows:
(1) If C is a ground instance of an axiom of Γ, then $\Gamma \vdash'_\varepsilon C$.
(2) If $\Gamma \vdash'_\varepsilon A \leftarrow B_1, \cdots, B_{n+1}$ and $\Gamma \vdash'_\varepsilon B_{n+1} \leftarrow$, then $\Gamma \vdash'_\varepsilon A \leftarrow B_1, \cdots, B_n$.
In case C is a ground clause, we can show that $\Gamma \vdash_\varepsilon C$ if and only if $\Gamma \vdash'_\varepsilon C$.
Since Γ is an SFS, for every ground instance C of an axiom of Γ, the length of the head of C is greater than or equal to the length of each atom in the body of C.

Assume that $\Gamma \vdash'_\varepsilon p(w) \leftarrow$ is witnessed by a sequence $\Gamma \vdash'_\varepsilon C_1, \cdots, \Gamma \vdash'_\varepsilon C_n$. Without loss of generality, we can assume that every clause C_i with $1 \leq i < n$ is used by (2) in deriving C_j for some j with $i < j \leq n$. (Otherwise, we can eliminate $\Gamma \vdash'_\varepsilon C_i$.)

Then, as easily seen, the length of every head of C_i with $1 \leq i < n$ is not greater than the length of $p(w)$. Therefore, by Lemma 2, the head of every axiom of Γ used by (1) is not greater than $2|w| + 1$.

This means that the length of the head of each axiom of Γ used in proving $p(w) \leftarrow$ is not greater than $2|w| + 1$. $\qquad\square$

By this lemma, in a similar way to Shinohara [21,22], we can show the following theorem:

Theorem 8. *Let $k \geq 0$.*
Then the class $e\mathcal{CRFSL}^{\leq k}$ has finite elasticity, and thus it is inferable in the limit from positive examples.

4 Simple H Systems

4.1 Definitions and Basic Properties

According to Mateescu et al. [14], we define simple H systems[1] and their languages.

For three strings $x, y, z \in \Sigma^*$ and for a constant symbol $a \in \Sigma$, we define the relation $(x, y) \vdash^a z$ as follows:

$$(x, y) \vdash^a z \iff \exists x_1, x_2, y_1, y_2 \in \Sigma^* \text{ s.t. } x = x_1 a x_2, \ y = y_1 a y_2, \ z = x_1 a y_2.$$

In this relation, we call the symbol a a *marker*.

For sets $M \subseteq \Sigma$ and $S \subseteq \Sigma^*$, we define the sets $\sigma_M(S), \sigma_M^i(S) \subseteq \Sigma^*$ ($i \in N \cup \{*\}$) as follows:

$$
\begin{aligned}
\sigma_M(S) &= S \cup \{z \in \Sigma^* \mid \exists x, y \in S, \exists a \in M \text{ s.t. } (x, y) \vdash^a z\}, \\
\sigma_M^0(S) &= S, \\
\sigma_M^{i+1}(S) &= \sigma_M(\sigma_M^i(S)) \qquad (i \geq 0), \\
\sigma_M^*(S) &= \bigcup_{i \geq 0} \sigma_M^i(S).
\end{aligned}
$$

Definition 12 (Mateescu et al. [14]). *A simple H system is a triple $G = (\Sigma, M, A)$, where Σ is a finite alphabet, $M \subseteq \Sigma$, and $A \subseteq \Sigma^*$ is a finite set. The elements of M are called* markers *and those of A are called* axioms.

For a simple H system $G = (\Sigma, M, A)$, the language $L(G)$ generated by G is defined by

$$L(G) = \sigma_M^*(A).$$

Hereafter, we call a simple H system an *SH system* simply, and by $\mathcal{SHS}$, we denote the class of SH systems. Furthermore, a language L is called an *SH language*, if there is an SH system G such that $L = L(G)$. By $\mathcal{SHL}$, we denote the class of SH languages.

---

[1] Mateescu et al. [14] called the splicing systems *H systems* in honor of the originator, Tom Head [9], of this field.

Proposition 1 (Mateescu et al. [14]). *Every SH language is a regular language, and the converse is not always true. That is,* $\mathcal{SHL} \subsetneq \mathcal{REG}$ *holds, where* $\mathcal{REG}$ *represents the class of regular languages.*

4.2   SH Languages and Erasing RFS Languages

In the present section, we consider converting an SH system into an RFS.

First, we prepare two special markers $\langle$ and $\rangle$ that express the beginning and the end of a string. We assume that these markers $\langle$ and $\rangle$ do not belong to a finite alphabet Σ. For a set $S \subseteq \Sigma^*$, we put $\langle S \rangle = \{\langle w \rangle \mid w \in S\}$.

For a string w, let us denote by $\mathrm{Sub}(w)$ the set of substrings of w, and for a set S of strings, we put $\mathrm{Sub}(S) = \bigcup_{w \in S} \mathrm{Sub}(w)$.

For sets $S \subseteq \Sigma^*$ and $M \subseteq \Sigma$, we define the set $\mathrm{Seg}_M(S) \subseteq \mathrm{Sub}(\langle S \rangle)$ as follows:

$$\mathrm{Seg}_M(S) = \{w \in \mathrm{Sub}(\langle S \rangle) \mid w \in (M \cup \{\langle\}) \cdot (\Sigma \setminus M)^* \cdot (M \cup \{\rangle\})\}.$$

For example, let $\Sigma = \{a, b\}$, $M = \{a\}$ and $S = \{aab, bbabbb, bb\}$. Then $\langle S \rangle = \{\langle aab \rangle, \langle bbabbb \rangle, \langle bb \rangle\}$ and $\mathrm{Seg}_M(S) = \{\langle a, aa, ab \rangle, \langle bba, abbb \rangle, \langle bb \rangle\}$.

In general, a finite subset of the set $(M \cup \{\langle\}) \cdot (\Sigma \setminus M)^* \cdot (M \cup \{\rangle\})$ for some $M \subseteq \Sigma$ is called a *segment set*. We can show that a segment set can directly define an SH language and that a segment set can be converted into an SH system (Mukouchi et al. [16]). We call a segment set $\mathrm{Seg}_M(A)$ a *segmental representation* of an SH system $G = (\Sigma, M, A)$.

By Proposition 1 and Theorem 3, we see that $\mathcal{SHL} \subsetneq e\mathcal{RFSL}$ holds.

In fact, for a given SH system $G = (\Sigma, M, A)$, we can obtain an RFS Γ such that $L(G) = L_\varepsilon(\Gamma, p_\rangle)$ as follows:

(1) Let $\Pi = \{p_a \mid a \in M \cup \{\rangle\}\}$ be the set of unary predicate symbols.

(2) Let us define an RFS Γ as follows:

$$\Gamma = \{p_b(xaw) \leftarrow p_a(x) \mid a \in M, \ b \in M \cup \{\rangle\}\}, \ awb \in \mathrm{Seg}_M(A)\}$$
$$\cup \{p_b(w) \leftarrow \mid b \in M \cup \{\rangle\}\}, \ \langle wb \in \mathrm{Seg}_M(A)\}.$$

Example 2. Let $\Sigma = \{a, b\}$, $M = \{a\}$ and $A = \{aab, bbabbb, bb\}$. Then let $G = (\Sigma, M, A)$ be an SH system. Then $\mathrm{Seg}_M(A) = \{\langle a, aa, ab \rangle, \langle bba, abbb \rangle, \langle bb \rangle\}$.

Let $\Pi = \{p_a, p_\rangle\}$ be the set of unary predicate symbols. Then let us put

$$\Gamma = \left\{ \begin{array}{l} p_a(\varepsilon) \leftarrow; \\ p_a(xa) \leftarrow p_a(x); \\ p_\rangle(xab) \leftarrow p_a(x); \\ p_a(bb) \leftarrow; \\ p_\rangle(xabbb) \leftarrow p_a(x); \\ p_\rangle(bb) \leftarrow \end{array} \right\}.$$

Then we can show that for each string $w \in \Sigma^*$, $w \in L(G)$ if and only if $\Gamma \vdash_\varepsilon p_\rangle(w) \leftarrow$ by a mathematical induction on the numbers of markers appearing in w. Thus we have $L(G) = L_\varepsilon(\Gamma, p_\rangle)$.

4.3   Learnability of SH Languages

Since every finite language $L \subseteq \Sigma^*$ is generated by an SH system $G = (\Sigma, \phi, L)$, we see that the class $\mathcal{SHL}$ is super-finite, and thus we have the following theorem:

Theorem 9. *The class $\mathcal{SHL}$ is not inferable in the limit from positive examples.*

On the other hand, the following example shows that the class of *infinite* SH languages is also not inferable in the limit from positive examples.

Example 3. Let $\sharp\Sigma \geq 2$ and let $a, b \in \Sigma$ be two distinct constant symbols.
First, for each $n \geq 0$, let $G_n = (\Sigma, \{a\}, A_n)$ be an SH system with

$$A_n = \{aababba \cdots ab^n a\}.$$

Then, as easily seen,

$$L(G_n) = \{ab^{i_1} ab^{i_2} a \cdots ab^{i_m} a \mid m \geq 1,\ 0 \leq i_1, i_2, \cdots, i_m \leq n\}$$

holds. On the other hand, let $G_\infty = (\Sigma, \{a, b\}, A_\infty)$ be an SH system with

$$A_\infty = \{aabba\}.$$

Then

$$L(G_\infty) = \{ab^{i_1} ab^{i_2} a \cdots ab^{i_m} a \mid m \geq 1,\ i_1, i_2, \cdots, i_m \geq 0\}$$

holds. Thus it is easy to see that these languages satisfy the conditions of Lemma 1. Therefore the class of infinite SH languages is not inferable in the limit from positive examples.

By this example, we see that even if the number of axioms is restricted to a fixed number, $\mathcal{SHL}$ is also not inferable in the limit from positive examples.

Now, we introduce a subclass of $\mathcal{SHL}$ that is inferable in the limit from positive examples.

For each $k \geq 0$, we define the subclass $\mathcal{SHS}^{\leq k}$ of $\mathcal{SHS}$ as the class of SH systems $G = (\Sigma, M, A)$ with $\sharp \mathrm{Seg}_M(A) \leq k$. Then we denote by $\mathcal{SHL}^{\leq k}$ the class of SH languages generated by SH systems in $\mathcal{SHS}^{\leq k}$.

By the conversion method shown in the previous section, for a given SH system $G \in \mathcal{SHS}^{\leq k}$, it is converted into a canonical RFS $\Gamma \in \mathcal{CRFS}^{\leq k}$ such that $L(G) = L_\varepsilon(\Gamma, p)$ for some unary predicate symbol p. This means that $\mathcal{SHL}^{\leq k} \subseteq e\mathcal{CRFSL}^{\leq k}$.

Since $e\mathcal{CRFSL}^{\leq k}$ has finite elasticity, we have the following theorem:

Theorem 10. *Let $k \geq 0$.*
Then the class $\mathcal{SHL}^{\leq k}$ has finite elasticity, and thus it is inferable in the limit from positive examples.

We note that we can also show the above theorem by using the framework of the so-called monotonic formal system due to Shinohara [22].

5   Concluding Remarks

We have discussed the influence of allowing erasing substitution upon inferability of classes of EFS languages. Especially we presented a subclass of erasing EFS languages that is inferable in the limit from positive examples.

Then we showed that each SH system can be converted into a canonical RFS whose erasing EFS language coincides with the SH language of the original SH system. By using this conversion, we showed that the subclass of SH languages generated by SH systems with at most k segments is inferable in the limit from positive examples for each $k \geq 0$.

As easily seen, even if erasing substitutions are not allowed, each SH system can be converted into an RFS, but the axioms become more complicated form and more number of axioms are needed. There seem to be many cases that allowing erasing substitutions are more suitable.

References

[1] D. Anguluin: *Finding a pattern common to a set of strings*, Journal of Computer and System Sciences **21**(1) (1980) 46–62.

[2] D. Anguluin: *Inductive inference of formal languages from positive data*, Information and Control **45** (1980) 117–135.

[3] S. Arikawa: *Elementary formal systems and formal languages – simple formal systems*, Memoirs of Faculty of Science, Kyushu University, Series A, Mathematics **24** (1970) 47–75.

[4] S. Arikawa, T. Shinohara and A. Yamamoto: *Learning elementary formal systems*, Theoretical Computer Science **95** (1992) 97–113.

[5] S. Arikawa, M. Sato, A. Shinohara and T. Shinohara: *Developments in computational learning and discovery theory within the framework of elementary formal systems*, Machine Intelligence **15** (1995) 227–247.

[6] H. Arimura, R. Fujino, T. Shinohara and S. Arikawa: *Protein motif discovery from positive examples by minimal multiple generalization over regular patterns*, Genome Informatics **5** (1994) 39–48.

[7] P. García, E. Vidal and J. Oncina: *Learning locally testable languages in the strict sense*, Proceedings of the 1st International Workshop on Algorithmic Learning Theory (1990) 325–338.

[8] E.M. Gold: *Language identification in the limit*, Information and Control **10** (1967) 447–474.

[9] T. Head: *Formal language theory and DNA: an analysis of the generative capacity of specific recombinant behaviors*, Bulletin of Mathematical Biology **49** (1987) 737–759.

[10] T. Head: *Splicing representations of strictly locally testable languages*, Discrete Applied Mathematics **87**(1–3) (1998) 139–147.

[11] S. Lange and T. Zeugmann: *Language learning in dependence on the space of hypotheses*, Proceedings of the 6th Annual ACM Conference on Computational Learning Theory (1993) 127–136.

[12] S. Lange, G. Grieser and K.P. Jantke: *Advanced elementary formal systems*, Theoretical Computer Science **298**(1) (2003) 51–70.

[13] J.W. Lloyd: "Foundations of logic programming," Springer-Verlag, 1984.

[14] A. Mateescu, Gh. Păun, G. Rozenberg and A. Salomaa: *Simple splicing systems*, Discrete Applied Mathematics **84** (1998) 145–163.

[15] T. Motoki, T. Shinohara and K. Wright: *The correct definition of finite elasticity: corrigendum to identification of unions*, Proceedings of the 4th Annual ACM Workshop on Computational Learning Theory (1991) 375–375.

[16] Y. Mukouchi, R. Takaishi and M. Sato: *Properties of SH systems and their languages*, in preparation.

[17] D. Reidenbach: *A negative result on inductive inference of extended pattern languages*, Proceedings of the 12th International Conference on Algorithmic Learning Theory, Lecture Notes in Artificial Intelligence **2533** (2002) 308–320.

[18] H. Sakamoto, K. Hirata and H. Arimura: *Learning elementary formal systems with queries*, Theoretical Computer Science **298**(1) (2003) 21–50.

[19] T. Shinohara: *Polynomial time inference of extended regular pattern languages*, Proceedings of RIMS Symposium on Software Science and Engineering, Lecture Notes in Computer Science **147** (1982) 115–127.

[20] T. Shinohara: *Inductive inference of formal systems from positive data*, Bulletin of Informatics and Cybernetics **22** (1986) 9–18.

[21] T. Shinohara: *Rich classes inferable from positive data: length-bounded elementary formal systems*, Information and Computation **108** (1994) 175–186.

[22] T. Shinohara: *Inductive inference of monotonic formal systems from positive data*, New Generation Computing **8**(4) (1991) 371–384.

[23] R.M. Smullyan: "Theory of formal systems," Princeton University Press, 1961.

[24] J. Uemura and M. Sato: *Learning of erasing primitive formal systems from positive examples*, Proceedings of the 14th International Conference on Algorithmic Learning Theory, Lecture Notes in Artificial Intelligence **2842** (2003) 69–83.

[25] A. Yamamoto: *Procedural semantics and negative information of elementary formal system*, Journal of Logic Programming **13**(4) (1992) 89–98.

[26] T. Yokomori, N. Ishida and S. Kobayashi: *Learning local languages and its application to protein α-chain identification*, Proceedings of the 27th Hawaii International Conference on System Sciences **5** (1994) 113–122.

[27] K. Wright: *Identification of unions of languages drawn from an identifiable class*, Proceedings of the 2nd Annual ACM Workshop on Computational Learning Theory (1989) 328–333.

New Revision Algorithms

Judy Goldsmith[1*], Robert H. Sloan[2**], Balázs Szörényi[3], and
György Turán[2,3,4**]

[1] University of Kentucky, Lexington, KY 40506-0046, USA,
goldsmit@cs.uky.edu.
[2] University of Illinois at Chicago, Chicago, IL 60607, USA,
sloan@uic.edu,
http://www.cs.uic.edu/~sloan
[3] Hungarian Academy of Sciences and University of Szeged, Research Group on
Artificial Intelligence, Szeged, Hungary,
szorenyi@rgai.hu
[4] gyt@uic.edu

Abstract. A revision algorithm is a learning algorithm that identifies
the target concept, starting from an initial concept. Such an algorithm
is considered efficient if its complexity (in terms of the resource one is
interested in) is polynomial in the syntactic distance between the initial
and the target concept, but only polylogarithmic in the number of variables in the universe. We give efficient revision algorithms in the model
of learning with equivalence and membership queries. The algorithms
work in a general revision model where both deletion and addition type
revision operators are allowed. In this model one of the main open problems is the efficient revision of Horn sentences. Two revision algorithms
are presented for special cases of this problem: for depth-1 acyclic Horn
sentences, and for definite Horn sentences with unique heads. We also
present an efficient revision algorithm for threshold functions.

1 Introduction

Efficient learnability has been studied from many different angles in computational learning theory for the last two decades, for example, in both the PAC
and query learning models, and by measuring complexity in terms of sample size,
the number of queries or running time. Attribute-efficient learning algorithms
are required to be efficient (polynomial) in the number of relevant variables, and
"super-efficient" (polylogarithmic) in the total number of variables [1,2]. It is
argued that practical and biologically plausible learning algorithms need to be
attribute efficient.

A related notion, *efficient revision algorithms*, originated in machine learning
[3,4,5,6], and has received some attention in computational learning theory as
well. A revision algorithm is applied in a situation where learning does not start

---

[*] Partially supported by NSF grants CCR-0100040 and ITR-0325063.
[**] Partially supported by NSF grant CCR-0100336.

S. Ben-David, J. Case, A. Maruoka (Eds.): ALT 2004, LNAI 3244, pp. 395–409, 2004.

from scratch, but there is an initial concept available, which is a reasonable approximation of the target concept. The standard example is an initial version of an expert system provided by a domain expert. The efficiency criterion in this case is to be efficient (polynomial) in the *distance* from the initial concept to the target (whatever distance means; we get back to this in a minute), and to be "super-efficient" (polylogarithmic) in the total size of the initial formula. Again, it is argued that this is a realistic requirement, as many complex concepts can only be hoped to be learned efficiently if a reasonably good initial approximation is available. The notion of distance usually considered is a syntactic one: the number of edit operations that need to be applied to the initial representation in order to get a representation of the target. The particular edit operations considered depend on the concept class. Intuitively, attribute-efficient learning is a special case of efficient revision, when the initial concept has an empty representation. In machine learning, the study of revision algorithms is referred to as theory revision; detailed references to the literature are given in Wrobel's overviews of theory revision [7,8] and also in our recent papers [9,10].

The theoretical study of revision algorithms was initiated by Mooney [11] in the PAC framework. We have studied revision algorithms in the model of learning with equivalence and membership queries [9,10] and in the mistake-bound model [12].

It is a general observation both in practice and in theory that those edit operations which delete something from the initial representation are easier to handle than those which add something to it. We have obtained efficient revision algorithms for monotone DNF with a bounded number of terms when both deletion and addition type revisions are allowed, but for the practically important case of Horn sentences we found an efficient revision algorithm only for the deletions-only model. We also showed that efficient revision of general (or even monotone) DNF is not possible, even in the deletions-only model. Finding an efficient revision algorithm for Horn sentences with a bounded number of terms in the general revision model (deletions and additions) emerged as perhaps the main open problem posed by our previous work on revision algorithms. The work presented here extends that of Doshi [13], who gave a revision algorithm for "unique explanations", namely depth-1, acyclic Horn formulas with unique, non-**F**, and unrevisable heads. Horn revision also happens to be the problem that most practical theory revision systems address. It is to be noted here that the notions of learning and revising Horn formulas are open to interpretation, as discussed in [10]; the kind of learnability result that we wish to extend to revision in this paper is Angluin et al.'s for propositional Horn sentences [14].

It seems to be an interesting general question whether attribute-efficiently learnable classes can also be revised efficiently. The monotone DNF result mentioned above shows that the answer is negative in general. We gave a positive answer for parity functions in [9] and for projective DNF in [12]. Projective DNF is a class of DNF introduced by Valiant [15], as a special case of his projective learning model, and as part of a framework to formulate expressive and biologically plausible learning models. In biological terms revision may be relevant for learning when some information is hard-wired from birth; see, e.g., Pinker [16] for recent arguments in favor of hereditary information in the brain.

Valiant showed that projective DNF are attribute-efficiently learnable in the mistake-bound model, and we extended his result by showing that they are efficiently revisable. Our algorithm was based on showing that a natural extension of the Winnow algorithm is in fact an efficient revision algorithm for disjunctions even in the presence of attribute errors.

Valiant's related models [17,18] also involve threshold functions, and as threshold functions are also known to be attribute-efficiently learnable, this raises the question whether threshold functions can be revised efficiently. Threshold functions (also called Boolean threshold functions or zero-one threshold functions in the literature) form a much studied concept class in computational learning theory. Winnow is an attribute-efficient mistake-bounded learning algorithm [19]. Attribute-efficient proper query learning algorithms are given in Uehara et al. [20] and Hegedűs and Indyk [21]. Further related results are given in [22,23,24,25].

Results. In this paper we present results for the two revision problems outlined above: the revision of Horn sentences and threshold functions, in the general revision model allowing both deletions and additions (more precise definitions are given in Section 2). We use the model of learning with membership and equivalence queries.

For Horn sentences, we show that one can revise two subclasses of Horn sentences with respect to both additions and deletions of variables. The new algorithms make use of our previous, deletions-only revision algorithm for Horn sentences [10] and new techniques which could be useful for the general question as well.

The first of the two classes is depth-1 acyclic Horn sentences. The class of acyclic Horn sentences was introduced by Angluin [26] in a paper that presented the first efficient learning algorithm for a class of Horn sentences, and was studied from the point of view of minimization and other computational aspects (see, e.g., [27]), and in the context of predicate logic learning [28]. We consider the subclass of depth-1 acyclic Horn sentences, where, in addition to assuming that the graph associated with the Horn sentence is acyclic, we also require this graph to have depth 1. One of our main results, Theorem 1, shows that this class can be revised using $O(dist(\varphi, \psi) \cdot m^3 \cdot \log n)$ queries, where n is the number of variables, φ is the m-clause initial formula, ψ is the target formula, and *dist* is the revision distance, which will be defined formally in Section 2.

We also give a revision algorithm for definite Horn sentences with unique heads, meaning that no variable ever occurs as the head of more than one Horn clause. For this class, we revise with query complexity $O(m^4 + dist(\varphi, \psi) \cdot (m^3 + \log n))$, where again φ is the initial formula and ψ is the target function (Theorem 2).

For threshold functions we give a revision algorithm using $O(dist(\varphi, \psi) \cdot \log n)$ queries (Theorem 3). In this algorithm the pattern mentioned above is reversed, and it turns out to be easier to handle additions than deletions. It is also shown that both query types are necessary for efficient revision, and that the query complexity of the algorithm is essentially optimal up to order of magnitude. Another interesting point is that the natural extension of Winnow mentioned above does not work in this more general context.

Organization of paper. Preliminaries are given in Section 2, Horn formula revisions in Section 3, threshold functions in Section 4. Due to space constraints, complete proofs are deferred to the full version of the paper.

2   Preliminaries

We use standard notions from propositional logic such as variable, literal, term (or conjunction), clause (or disjunction), etc. The set of variables for n-variable formulas and functions is $X_n = \{x_1, \ldots, x_n\}$. (In this paper, n will always be the total number of variables.) *Instances* or *vectors* are elements $\mathbf{x} \in \{0,1\}^n$. When convenient we treat $\mathbf{x}$ as a subset of $[n]$ or X_n, corresponding to the components, resp. the variables, which are set to true in $\mathbf{x}$. Given a set $Y \subseteq [n] = \{1, \ldots, n\}$, we write $\chi_Y = (\alpha_1, \ldots, \alpha_n) \in \{0,1\}^n$ for the characteristic vector of Y. We write $\mathbf{x} = (x_1, \ldots, x_n) \leq \mathbf{y} = (y_1, \ldots, y_n)$ if $x_i \leq y_i$ for every $i = 1, \ldots, n$.

A *Horn clause* is a disjunction with at most one unnegated variable; we will usually think of it as an implication and call the clause's unnegated variable its *head*, and its negated variables its *body*. We write body(c) and head(c) for the body and head of c, respectively. A clause with an unnegated variable is called *definite* (or positive). We will consider clauses with no unnegated variables to have head $\mathbf{F}$, and will sometimes write them as $(body \rightarrow \mathbf{F})$. A *Horn sentence* is a conjunction of Horn clauses. A Horn sentence is definite if all its clauses are definite. A Horn sentence has *unique heads* if no two clauses have the same head.

We define the *graph* of a Horn sentence to be a directed graph on the variables together with $\mathbf{T}$ and $\mathbf{F}$, with an edge from variable u to variable v (resp. $\mathbf{F}$ iff there is a clause with head v (resp. $\mathbf{F}$) having u in its body, and an edge from $\mathbf{T}$ to variable v if there is a clause consisting solely of variable v. A Horn sentence is *acyclic* if its graph is acyclic; the *depth* of an acyclic Horn sentence is the maximum path length in its graph [26].

For example, the Horn sentence

$$(x_1 \wedge x_2 \rightarrow x_3) \wedge (x_1 \wedge x_4 \rightarrow x_5) \wedge (x_4 \wedge x_6 \rightarrow \mathbf{F})$$

is depth-1 acyclic. Its graph has the edges (x_1, x_3), (x_2, x_3), (x_1, x_5), (x_4, x_5), $(x_4, \mathbf{F})$, and $(x_6, \mathbf{F})$ and this graph is acyclic with depth 1.

If $\mathbf{x}$ satisfies the body of Horn clause c, considered as a term, we say $\mathbf{x}$ *covers* c. Notice that $\mathbf{x}$ *falsifies* c if and only if $\mathbf{x}$ covers c and head$(c) \notin \mathbf{x}$. (By definition, $\mathbf{F} \notin \mathbf{x}$.)

For Horn clause body b (or any monotone term) and vector $\mathbf{x}$, we use $b \cap \mathbf{x}$ for the monotone term that has those variables of b that correspond to 1's in $\mathbf{x}$. As an example, $x_1 x_4 \cap 1100 = x_1$.

An n-variable *threshold function* TH_U^t is specified by a set $U \subseteq [n]$ and a *threshold* $0 \leq t \leq n$, such that for a vector $\mathbf{x} = (x_1, \ldots, x_n) \in \{0,1\}^n$ it holds that $\text{TH}_U^t(\mathbf{x}) = 1$ iff at least t of the variables with subscripts in U are set to 1 in $\mathbf{x}$. In other words, $\text{TH}_U^t(\mathbf{x}) = 1$ iff $\sum_{i=1}^n \alpha_i x_i \geq t$, where $\chi_U = (\alpha_1, \ldots, \alpha_n)$. We say that S is a *positive* (resp., *negative*) set if χ_S is a positive (resp., negative) example of the target threshold function. (As the number of variables is clear from the context, we do not mention it in the notation.) Note that for every non-constant threshold function its set of relevant variables and its threshold are well defined, thus every non-constant function has a unique representation. The variables with indices in U (resp., outside of U) are the *relevant* (resp., *irrelevant*) variables of TH_U^t. As noted in the introduction, functions of this type are also called Boolean threshold functions and 0-1-threshold functions, in order to distinguish them from the more general kind of threshold functions where the coefficients α_i can be arbitrary reals. We simply call them threshold functions, as we only consider this restricted class.

We use the standard model of membership and equivalence queries (with counterexamples), denoted by MQ and EQ [29]. In an equivalence query, the learning algorithm proposes a *hypothesis*, a concept h, and the answer depends on whether $h \equiv c$, where c is the target concept. If so, the answer is "correct", and the learning algorithm has succeeded in its goal of exact identification of the target concept. Otherwise, the answer is a *counterexample*, any instance $\mathbf{x}$ such that $c(\mathbf{x}) \neq h(\mathbf{x})$.

2.1   Revision

The *revision distance* between a formula φ and a concept C is defined to be the minimum number of applications of a specified set of syntactic revision operators to φ needed to obtain a formula for C. The revision operators may depend on the concept class one is interested in. Usually, a revision operator can either be *deletion-type* or *addition-type*.

For disjunctive or conjunctive normal forms, the deletion operation can be formulated as *fixing an occurrence of a variable* in the formula to a constant. In the *general model*, studied in this paper, we also allow additions. The addition operation is to *add a new literal to one of the terms or clauses of the formula*. (Adding a new literal to open up a new clause or term would be an even more general addition-type operator, which we have not considered so far.) In the case of Horn sentences the new literals must be added to the body of a clause.

In the case of threshold functions, deletions mean deleting a relevant variable and additions mean adding a new relevant variable. In the *general model* for this class we also allow the *modification of the threshold*. We consider the modification of the threshold by any amount to be a single operation (as opposed to changing it by one); as we are going to prove upper bounds, this only makes the results stronger. Thus, for example, the revision distance between $\varphi = \text{TH}_{\{x_1,x_2,x_4\}}^1$ and $\text{TH}_{\{x_1,x_2,x_3,x_5\}}^3$ is 4 in the general model.

We use $dist(\varphi, \psi)$ to denote the revision distance from φ to ψ whenever the revision operators are clear from context. In general, the distance is not symmetric.

A *revision algorithm* for a formula φ has access to membership and equivalence oracles for an unknown target concept and must return some representation of the target concept. Our goal is to find revision algorithms whose query complexity is polynomial in $d = dist(\varphi, \psi)$, but at most *polylogarithmic* in n, the number of variables in the universe. Dependence on other parameters may depend on the concept class. For DNF (resp. CNF) formulas, we will allow polynomial dependence on the number of terms (resp. clauses) in φ; it is impossible to do better even for arbitrary monotone DNF in the deletions-only model of revision [9].

We state only query bounds in this paper; all our revision algorithms are computable in polynomial time, given the appropriate oracles.

2.2   Binary Search for New Variables

Many of our revision algorithms use a kind of binary search, often used in learning algorithms involving membership queries, presented as Algorithm 1. The starting points of the binary search are two instances, a negative instance **neg** and a positive instance **pos** such that **neg** $\leq$ **pos**. The algorithm returns two items: the first is a set of variables that when added to **neg** make a positive instance; the second is a variable that is critical in the sense that the first component plus **neg** becomes a negative instance if that variable is turned off.

Algorithm 1 BINARYSEARCH(**neg**, **pos**).

Require: MQ(**neg**) $==$ 0 and MQ(**pos**) $==$ 1 and **neg** $\leq$ **pos**
  1: **neg**$_0$:= **neg**
  2: **while neg** and **pos** differ in more than 1 position **do**
  3:     Partition **pos** \ **neg** into approximately equal-size sets d_1 and d_2.
  4:     Put **mid** := **neg** with positions in d_1 switched to 0
  5:     **if** MQ(**mid**) $==$ 0 **then**
  6:         **neg** := **mid**
  7:     **else**
  8:         **pos** := **mid**
  9: v := the one variable on which **pos** and **neg** differ
 10: **return** ((**pos** \ **neg**$_0$), v)

---

3   Revising Horns

In this section we give algorithms for revising two different classes of Horn sentences when addition of new variables into the bodies is allowed as well as deletion of variables.

3.1   Depth-1 Acyclic Horn Sentences

We show here how to revise depth-1 acyclic Horn sentences. Depth-1 acyclic Horn sentences are precisely those where variables that occur as heads never occur in the body of any clause. Notice that such formulas are a class of unate CNF. Previously we gave a revision algorithm for unate DNF (which would dualize to unate CNF) that was exponential in the number of clauses [9]. Here we give an algorithm for an important subclass of unate CNF that is polynomial in the number of clauses.

The general idea of the algorithm is to maintain a one-sided hypothesis, in the sense that all equivalence queries using the hypothesis must return negative counterexamples until the hypothesis is correct.

Each negative counterexample can be associated with one particular head of the target clause, or else with a headless target clause. We do this with a negative counterexample $\mathbf{x}$ as follows.

For a head variable v and instance $\mathbf{x}$, we will use the notation $\mathbf{x}^v$ to refer to $\mathbf{x}$ modified by setting all head variables *other than* v to 1. Note that $\mathbf{x}^v$ cannot falsify any clause with a head other than v. Since v will normally be the head of a Horn clause and we use $\mathbf{F}$ to denote the "head" of a headless Horn clause, we will use $\mathbf{x}^{\mathbf{F}}$ to denote $\mathbf{x}$ modified to set *all* head variables to 1.

The algorithm begins with an assumption that the revision distance from the initial theory to the target theory is e. If the revision fails, then e is doubled and the algorithm is repeated. Since the algorithm is later shown to be linear in e, this series of attempts does not affect the asymptotic complexity. We give a brief overview of the algorithm, followed by somewhat more detail, and the pseudocode, as Algorithm 2.

We maintain a hypothesis that is, viewed as the set of its satisfying vectors, always a superset of the target. Thus each time we ask an equivalence query, if we have not found the target, we get a negative counterexample $\mathbf{x}$. Then the first step is to ask a membership query on $\mathbf{x}$ modified to turn on *all* of the head positions. If that returns 0, then the modified $\mathbf{x}$ must falsify a headless target clause. Otherwise, for each head position h that is 0 in the original $\mathbf{x}$, ask a membership query on $\mathbf{x}^h$. We stop when the first such membership query returns 0; we know that $\mathbf{x}$ falsifies a clause with head h. In our pseudocode, we refer to the algorithm just described as ASSOCIATE.

Once a negative counterexample is associated with a head, we first try to use it to make deletions from an existing hypothesis clause with the same head. If this is not possible, then we use the counterexample to add a new clause to the hypothesis. We find any necessary additions when we add a new clause.

If $\mathbf{x}^h \cap \text{body}(c)^h$ is a negative instance, which we can determine by a membership query, then we can create a new smaller hypothesis clause whose body is $\mathbf{x} \cap \text{body}(c)$. (Notice that $\mathbf{x} \cap \text{body}(c) \subset \text{body}(c)$ because as a negative *counterexample*, $\mathbf{x}$ must satisfy c.)

To use $\mathbf{x}$ to add a new clause, we then use an idea from the revision algorithm for monotone DNF [9]. For each initial theory clause with the same head as we have associated (which for $\mathbf{F}$ is *all* initial theory clauses, since deletions of heads are allowed), use binary search from **x** intersect (the initial clause with the other heads set to 1) up to **x**. If we get to something negative with fewer than e additions, we update **x** to this negative example.

Whether or not **x** is updated, we keep going, trying all initial theory clauses with the associated head. This guarantees that in particular we try the initial theory clause with smallest revision distance to the target clause that **x** falsifies. All necessary additions to this clause are found by the calls to BINARYSEARCH; later only deletions will be needed.

Algorithm 2 HORNREVISEUPTOE(φ, e). Revises depth-1 acyclic Horn Sentence φ if possible using $\leq e$ revisions; otherwise returns failure.

1: $H :=$ everywhere-true empty conjunction
2: **while** ($\mathbf{x} := EQ(H)$) $\neq$ "Correct!" **and** $e > 0$ **do**
3:    $h :=$ASSOCIATE($\mathbf{x}, \varphi$)
4:    **for all** clauses $c \in H$ with head h **do**
5:       **if** MQ($\mathbf{x}^h \cap \text{body}(c)^h$) $== 0$ **then** {delete vars from c}
6:          $\text{body}(c) = \text{body}(c) \cap \mathbf{x}$
7:          $e = e-$number of variables removed
8:    **if** no vars. were deleted from any clause **then** {find new clause to add}
9:       $min = e$
10:       $FoundAClause=false$
11:       **for all** $c \in \varphi$ with head h (or all $c \in \varphi$ if $h ==$ **F**) **do**
12:          $\mathbf{new} = \text{body}(c)^h \cap \mathbf{x}^h$
13:          $numAddedLits = 0$ {# additions for this c}
14:          **while** MQ($\mathbf{new}$) $== 1$ **and** $numAddedLits < e$ **do**
15:             $l :=$ BINARYSEARCH($\mathbf{new}, \mathbf{x}^h$)
16:             $\mathbf{new} := \mathbf{new} \cup \{l\}$
17:             $numAddedLits = numAddedLits + 1$
18:             **if** MQ($\mathbf{x} - \{l\}$) $== 0$ **then** {($\mathbf{x} - \{l\}$) is "Pivot"}
19:                {i.e., $\mathbf{x} - \{l\}$ is counterexample falsifying fewer target clauses}
20:                $\mathbf{x} = \mathbf{x} - \{l\}$
21:                **restart** the **for all** c loop with this $\mathbf{x}$ by backing up to Line 11 to reset other parameters
22:          **if** MQ($\mathbf{new}$) $== 0$ **then**
23:             $\mathbf{x} := \mathbf{new}$
24:             $FoundAClause = true$
25:             $min := \min(numAddedLits, min)$
26:       **if not** $FoundAClause$ **then**
27:          **return** "Failure"
28:       **else**
29:          $H := H \wedge (x \rightarrow h)$ {treating x as monotone disjunction}
30:          $e := e - min$
31: **if** $x ==$ "Correct!" **then**
32:    **return** H
33: **return** "Failure"

Theorem 1. *There is a revision algorithm for depth-1 acyclic Horn sentences with query complexity $O(d \cdot m^3 \cdot \log n)$, where d is the revision distance and m is the number of clauses in the initial formula.*

Proof sketch: We give here some of the highlights of the proof of correctness and query complexity of the algorithm; space does not permit detailed proofs. Relatively straightforward calculation shows that the query complexity of HORN-REVISEUPTOE for revising an initial formula of m clauses on a universe of n variables is polynomial in m, $\log n$, and the parameter e. Thus, if we can argue that when e is at least the revision distance the algorithm succeeds in finding the target, we are done.

The result follows from a series of lemmas. The first two lemmas give qualitative information. The first shows that the hypothesis is always one-sided (i.e., only negative counterexamples can ever be received), and the second says that newly added hypothesis clauses are not redundant.

Lemma 1. *The algorithm maintains the invariant that its hypothesis is true for every instance that satisfies the target function.*

Proof. Formally the proof is by induction on number of changes to the hypothesis. The base case is true, because the initial hypothesis is everywhere true.

For the inductive step, consider how we update the hypothesis, either by adding a new clause or deleting variables from the body of an existing clause.

Before creating or updating a clause to have head h and body $\mathbf{y}$, we have ensured that $\mathrm{MQ}(\mathbf{y}^h) = 0$, that is, that $\mathbf{y}^h$ is a negative instance. Because of that, $\mathbf{y}^h$ must falsify some clause, and because of its form and the syntactic form of the target, it must be a clause with head h. None of the heads in $\mathbf{y}^h \setminus \mathbf{y}$ can be in any body, so $\mathbf{y}$ must indeed be a superset of the variables of some target clause with head h, as claimed.

Lemma 2. *If negative counterexample $\mathbf{x}$ is used to add a new clause with head h to the hypothesis, then the body of the new clause does not cover any target clause body covered by any other hypothesis clause with head h.*

Proof. Recall that head h was associated with $\mathbf{x}$. If $\mathbf{x}$ falsified the same target clause as an existing hypothesis clause body, then $\mathbf{x}$ would be used to delete variables from that hypothesis clause body. Therefore $\mathbf{x}$ does not falsify the same target clause as any existing hypothesis clause with the same head, and the newly added hypothesis clause's body is a subset of $\mathbf{x}$.

The following two lemmas, whose proof will be given in the journal version of this paper, complete the proof.

Lemma 3. HORNREVISEUPTOE(φ, e) *succeeds in finding the target Horn sentence ψ if it has revision distance at most e from initial formula φ.*

Lemma 4. *The query complexity of* HORNREVISEUPTOE *is $O(m^3 \cdot e \cdot \log n)$, where the initial formula has m clauses and there are n variables in the universe.*

3.2   Definite Horn Sentences with Unique Heads

We give here a revision algorithm for definite Horn sentences with unique heads. Since we are considering only definite Horn sentences, note that the head variables cannot be fixed to 0. We use the algorithm for revising Horn sentences in the deletions-only model presented in [10] as a subroutine. Its query complexity is $O(dm^3 + m^4)$, where d is the revision distance and m is the number of clauses in the initial formula.

This algorithm has a first phase that finds all the variables that need to be added to the initial formula. That partially revised formula is then passed as an initial formula to the known algorithm [10] for revising Horn sentences in the deletions-only model of revision.

To find all necessary additions to the body b of clause $c = (b \to h)$, we first construct the instance $\mathbf{x}_c$ as follows: in the positions of the heads of the initial formula, instance $\mathbf{x}_c$ has 1's, except for a 0 in position h. Furthermore, instance $\mathbf{x}_c$ has 1's in all the positions corresponding to a variable in the clause's body, and 0 in all positions not yet specified.

Next, the query $\mathrm{MQ}(\mathbf{x}_c)$ is asked. If $\mathrm{MQ}(\mathbf{x}_c) = 0$, then no variables need to be added to the body of c. If $\mathrm{MQ}(\mathbf{x}_c) = 1$, the necessary additions to the body of c are found by repeated use of BINARYSEARCH. To begin the binary search, $\mathbf{x}_c$ is the known positive instance that must satisfy the target clause c_* derived from c, and the assignment with a 0 in position h and a 1 everywhere else is the known negative instance that must falsify c_*.

Each variable returned by BINARYSEARCH is added to the body of the clause, and $\mathbf{x}_c$ is updated by setting the corresponding position to 1. The process ends when $\mathbf{x}_c$ becomes a negative instance.

Once the necessary additions to every clause in the initial theory are found, a Horn sentence needing only deletions has been produced, and the deletions-only algorithm from [10] can be used to complete the revisions.

Theorem 2. *There is a revision algorithm for definite Horn sentences with unique heads in the general model of revision with query complexity $O(m^4 + dm^3 + d\log n)$, where d is the revision distance from the initial formula to the target formula.*

Proof sketch.   The key part is adding variables to one initial clause $c = (b \to h)$. Let c_* be the target clause derived from c.

Lemma 5. *Every variable added to a clause c must occur in the target clause c_* that is derived from c.*

(Proof of lemma omitted.)

This is enough to allow us to use the earlier algorithm for learning in the deletions-only model.

The query complexity for the part of the algorithm that finds necessary additions is at most the $O(\log n)$ per added variable, which contributes a factor of $O((\varphi, \psi) \cdot \log n)$. The deletions-only algorithm has complexity $(m^4 + dm^3)$, where d is the revision distance. Combining these two gives us $O(m^4 + dm^3 + d\log n)$.

$\square$

4   Revising Threshold Functions

We present a threshold revision algorithm REVISETHRESHOLD. The overall revision algorithm is given as Algorithm 3, using the procedures described in Algorithms 4 and 5. Algorithm REVISETHRESHOLD has three main stages. First we identify all the variables that are irrelevant in φ but relevant in ψ (Algorithm FINDADDITIONS). Then we identify all the variables that are relevant in φ but irrelevant in ψ (Algorithm FINDDELETIONS). Finally, we determine the target threshold. (In our pseudocode this third step is built into Algorithm FINDDELETIONS, as the last iteration after the set of relevant variables of the target function is identified.)

Algorithm 3 The procedure REVISETHRESHOLD(φ)

1: {function to be revised is $\varphi = \mathrm{TH}_U^t$}
2: Use 2 EQ's to determine if target is constant 0 or 1; if so **return**
3: $V := $ FINDADDITIONS(U)
4: **return** FINDDELETIONS(U, V)

The main result of the section is the following.

Theorem 3. REVISETHRESHOLD *is a threshold function revision algorithm of query complexity* $O(d \log n)$, *where d is the revision distance between the initial formula φ and the target function ψ.*

Proof sketch.   Throughout, let $\varphi = TH_U^t$ and $\psi = TH_R^\theta$.

Algorithm 4 The procedure FINDADDITIONS(U)

Require: the target function is not constant
1: $Potentials := X_n \setminus U$; $NewRelevants := \emptyset$
2: **if** MQ(χ_U) $== 0$ **then**
3:    $Base := U$
4: **else**
5:    $(Base, x) := $ BINARYSEARCH($\emptyset, U$), $Base := Base \setminus \{x\}$
6:    **if** MQ($\chi_{Base \cup Potentials}$) $== 0$ **then**
7:       **return** $\emptyset$
8: **repeat**
9:    $(Y, y) := $ BINARYSEARCH($Base, Base \cup Potentials$)
10:    $NewRelevants := NewRelevants \cup \{y\}$
11:    $Potentials := Potentials \setminus \{y\}$
12:    **if** MQ($\chi_{Base \cup Potentials}$) $== 0$ **then**
13:       $Base := Base \cup \{y\}$
14: **until** MQ(χ_{Base}) $== 1$
15: **return** $NewRelevants$

A set S is *critical for the target function* ψ, or simply *critical*, if $|S \cap R| = \theta - 1$. It is clear from the definition that if S is critical, then for every $Z \subseteq X_n \setminus S$ it holds that Z contains at least one relevant variable of ψ iff $\mathrm{MQ}(\chi_{S \cup Z}) = 1$.

Algorithm 5 The procedure $\text{FINDDELETIONS}(U, V)$

Require: U, V disjoint; $V \subseteq R$ and $R \subseteq U \cup V$ ($R =$ relevant variables in target)
1: $\hat{U} := U$;
2: $u := |\hat{U}| + |V|$; $\ell := 1$
3: **if** $(\varphi' := \text{TESTEXTREME}(N, P, \hat{U} \cup V)) \neq constant$ **then**
4:     **return** φ'
5: **while** $u > \ell + 1$ **do**
6:     $m := \lceil (u + \ell)/2 \rceil$
7:     **if** $(\mathbf{x} := \text{EQ}(\text{TH}^m_{\hat{U} \cup V})) == YES$ **then**
8:        **return** $\text{TH}^m_{\hat{U} \cup V}$
9:     let $C := \mathbf{x} \cap (\hat{U} \cup V)$
10:    **if** $\mathbf{x}$ is a positive counterexample **then**
11:      $P := C$ and $u := m$
12:    **else**
13:      $N := C$ and $\ell := m$
14: $(P, p) := \text{BINARYSEARCH}(\emptyset, P)$
15: $Base := P \cap N$, $P' := P \setminus Base$, $N' := N \setminus Base$
    {Now the key property holds for $Base$, N' and P'}
16: $Test := (Base \cup P') \setminus \{p\}$
    {For any $i \in N'$, $\mathrm{MQ}(\chi_{Test \cup \{i\}}) = 1$ iff i is relevant}
17: **while** $|P'| > 1$ **do**
18:    $i := \text{MAKEEVEN}(N', P', Base)$
    {Make $|N'|$ and $|P'|$ be even without spoiling the key property}
19:    **if** $\mathrm{MQ}(\chi_{Test \cup i}) == 0$ **then**
20:      $\hat{U} := \hat{U} - i$ and goto Line 2
21:    Let N_0, N_1 (resp. P_0, P_1) be an equal-sized partition of N' (resp. P')
22:    Ask $\mathrm{MQ}(\chi_{Base \cup N_j \cup P_k})$ for $j, k = 0, 1$
23:    Let j and k be indices s.t. $\mathrm{MQ}(\chi_{Base \cup N_j \cup P_k}) = 0$ {such j and k exist}
24:    $Base := Base \cup P_k$, $P' := P_{1-k}$, $N' := N_i$
25: $\hat{U} := \hat{U} \setminus N'$
26: **goto** Line 2

Procedure FINDADDITIONS (Algorithm 4) finds the new relevant variables; that is, the elements of $R \cap \bar{U}$, where $\bar{U} = X_n \setminus U$. It stores the uncertain but potentially relevant variables in the set *Potentials* (thus *Potentials* is initially set to $X_n \setminus U$). The procedure first determines a set $Base \subseteq U$ such that $Base$ is negative, and $Base \cup Potentials$ is positive (unless *Potentials* contains no relevant variables—in which case there are no new relevant variables used by ψ, so we quit). Then the search for the new relevant variables starts. We use $\text{BINARYSEARCH}(Base, Base \cup Potentials)$ to find one relevant variable. This variable is removed from *Potentials*, and the process is repeated, again using BINARYSEARCH. After removing a certain number of relevant variables from

Potentials, the instance *Base* ∪ *Potentials* must become critical. After reaching this point, we do not simply remove any newly found relevant variables from *Potentials*, but we also add them to the set *Base*. This way from then on it holds that $|(Base \cup Potentials) \cap R| = \theta$. Thus the indicator that the last relevant variable has been removed from *Potentials* is that *Base* becomes positive $(\mathrm{MQ}(\chi_{Base}) = 1)$.

Let us assume that we have identified a set of variables that is known to contain all the relevant variables of the target function, and possibly some additional irrelevant variables. Consider threshold functions with the set of variables above, and all possible values of the threshold. Let us perform a sequence of equivalence queries with these functions, doing a binary search over the threshold value (moving down, resp. up, if a positive, resp. negative, counterexample is received). In algorithm FINDDELETIONS this is done by the first **while** loop starting at Line 5 and the use of TESTEXTREME right before it at Line 3 (the latter is needed to ensure the full range of search; it performs the test for the two extreme cases in the binary search, which the while loop might miss: the conjunction and the disjunction of all the variables). In case the relevant variables of the target functions are exactly those that we currently use, then one can see that this binary search will find ψ. Otherwise (i. e. when some of the currently used variables are irrelevant in ψ) it can be shown that after the above binary search we always end up with a "large" negative example (χ_N) and a "small" positive example (χ_P); more precisely they satisfy $|P| \le |N|$. Using these sets one easily obtains three sets *Base*, N' and P' that have the *key property*:

Key property: *Sets Base, N', and P' satisfy the key property if they are pairwise disjoint, and it holds that $Base \cup N'$ is negative, $|(Base \cup P') \cap R| = \theta$, and $|N'| \ge |P'|$.*

The following claim gives two important features of this definition.

Claim 1 a) *If Base, N' and P' satisfy the key property then N' contains an irrelevant variable and P' contains a relevant variable.*

b) *If Base, N' and P' satisfy the key property and $|P'| = 1$ then every element of N' is irrelevant.*

From now on we maintain these three sets in such a manner that they preserve the key property, but in each iteration the size of N' and P' get halved. For this we split up N' (respectively P') into two equal sized disjoint subsets N_1 and N_2 (resp. P_1 and P_2). When both $|N'|$ and $|P'|$ are even then we can do this without any problem; otherwise we have to make some adjustments to N' and/or to P', that will be taken care of by procedure MAKEEVEN (the technical details are omitted due to space limitations). Using the notation $\theta' = \theta - |R \cap Base|$ we have $|R \cap (N_1 \cup N_2)| < \theta'$ and $|R \cap (P_1 \cup P_2)| = \theta'$. Thus for some $j, k \in \{0, 1\}$ we have $|R \cap (N_j \cup P_k)| < \theta'$ (equivalently $\mathrm{MQ}(\chi_{Base \cup N_j \cup P_k}) = 0$). Note that the sets $Base := Base \cup P_k$, $N' := N_j$ and $P' := P_{1-k}$ still have the key property, but the size of N' and P' is reduced by half. Thus after at most $\log n$ steps P' is reduced to a set consisting of a single (relevant) variable. Thus N' is a nonempty set of irrelevant variables (part *b)* of Claim 1). □

We mention some additional results showing that both types of queries are necessary for efficient revision, the query bound of algorithm REVISETHRESHOLD cannot be improved in general and that Winnow (see [19]) cannot be used for revising threshold functions (at least in its original form).

Theorem 4. a) *Efficient revision is not possible using only membership queries, or only equivalence queries.*

b) *The query complexity of any revision algorithm for threshold functions is $\Omega\left(d\log\frac{n}{d}\right)$ queries, where d is the revision distance.*

c) *Winnow is not an efficient revision algorithm for threshold functions because it may make too many mistakes. More precisely, for any weight vector representing the initial threshold function* $\mathrm{TH}^1_{x_1,\ldots,x_n}$, *Winnow can make n mistakes when the target function is* $\mathrm{TH}^2_{x_1,\ldots,x_n}$.

Proofs will be given in the full version of this paper.

References

[1] Blum, A., Hellerstein, L., Littlestone, N.: Learning in the presence of finitely or infinitely many irrelevant attributes. J. of Comput. Syst. Sci. **50** (1995) 32–40 Earlier version in 4th COLT, 1991.

[2] Bshouty, N., Hellerstein, L.: Attribute-efficient learning in query and mistake-bound models. J. of Comput. Syst. Sci. **56** (1998) 310–319

[3] Koppel, M., Feldman, R., Segre, A.M.: Bias-driven revision of logical domain theories. Journal of Artificial Intelligence Research **1** (1994) 159–208

[4] Ourston, D., Mooney, R.J.: Theory refinement combining analytical and empirical methods. Artificial Intelligence **66** (1994) 273–309

[5] Richards, B.L., Mooney, R.J.: Automated refinement of first-order Horn-clause domain theories. Machine Learning **19** (1995) 95–131

[6] Towell, G.G., Shavlik, J.W.: Extracting refined rules from knowledge-based neural networks. Machine Learning **13** (1993) 71–101

[7] Wrobel, S.: Concept Formation and Knowledge Revision. Kluwer (1994)

[8] Wrobel, S.: First order theory refinement. In De Raedt, L., ed.: Advances in ILP. IOS Press, Amsterdam (1995) 14–33

[9] Goldsmith, J., Sloan, R.H., Turán, G.: Theory revision with queries: DNF formulas. Machine Learning **47** (2002) 257–295

[10] Goldsmith, J., Sloan, R.H., Szörényi, B., Turán, G.: Theory revision with queries: Horn, read-once, and parity formulas. Artificial Intelligence **156** (2004) 139–176

[11] Mooney, R.J.: A preliminary PAC analysis of theory revision. In Petsche, T., ed.: Computational Learning Theory and Natural Learning Systems. Volume III: Selecting Good Models. MIT Press (1995) 43–53

[12] Sloan, R.H., Szörényi, B., Turán, G.: Projective DNF formulae and their revision. In: Learning Theory and Kernel Machines, 16th Annual Conference on Learning Theory and 7th Kernel Workshop, COLT/Kernel 2003, Washington, DC, USA, August 24-27, 2003, Proceedings. Volume 2777 of Lecture Notes in Artificial Intelligence., Springer (2003) 625–639

[13] Doshi, J.U.: Revising Horn formulas. Master's thesis, Dept. of Computer Science, University of Kentucky (2003)

[14] Angluin, D., Frazier, M., Pitt, L.: Learning conjunctions of Horn clauses. Machine Learning **9** (1992) 147–164

[15] Valiant, L.G.: Projection learning. Machine Learning **37** (1999) 115–130

[16] Pinker, S.: The Blank Slate: The Modern Denial of Human Nature. Viking Press (2002)

[17] Valiant, L.G.: A neuroidal architecture for cognitive computation. Journal of the ACM **47** (2000) 854–882

[18] Valiant, L.G.: Robust logics. Artificial Intelligence **117** (2000) 231–253

[19] Littlestone, N.: Learning quickly when irrelevant attributes abound: A new linear-threshold algorithm. Machine Learning **2** (1988) 285–318

[20] Uehara, R., Tsuchida, K., Wegener, I.: Optimal attribute-efficient learning of disjunction, parity, and threshold functions. In: Computational Learning Theory, Third European Conference, EuroCOLT '97, Jerusalem, Israel, March 1997, Proceedings. Volume 1208 of Lecture Notes in Artificial Intelligence., Springer (1997) 171–184

[21] Hegedűs, T., Indyk, P.: On learning disjunctions of zero-one threshold functions with queries. In: Algorithmic Learning Theory, 8th International Workshop, ALT '97, Sendai, Japan, October 1997, Proceedings. Volume 1316 of Lecture Notes in Artificial Intelligence., Springer (1997) 446–460

[22] Hegedűs, T.: On training simple neural networks and small-weight neurons. In: Computational Learning Theory: EuroColt '93. Volume New Series Number 53 of The Institute of Mathematics and its Applications Conference Series., Oxford, Oxford University Press (1994) 69–82

[23] Pitt, L., Valiant, L.G.: Computational limitations on learning from examples. J. ACM **35** (1988) 965–984

[24] Schmitt, M.: On methods to keep learning away from intractability. In: Proc. International Conference on Artifical Neural Networks (ICANN) '95. Volume 1. (1995) 211–216

[25] Sloan, R.H., Turán, G.: Learning from incomplete boundary queries using split graphs and hypergraphs. In: Computational Learning Theory, Third European Conference, EuroCOLT '97, Jerusalem, Israel, March 1997, Proceedings. Number 1208 in Lecture Notes in Artificial Intelligence, Springer (1997) 38–50

[26] Angluin, D.: Learning propositional Horn sentences with hints. Technical Report YALEU/DCS/RR-590, Department of Computer Science, Yale University (1987)

[27] Hammer, P.L., Kogan, A.: Quasi-acyclic propositional Horn knowledge bases: optimal compression. IEEE Trans. Knowl. Data Eng. **7** (1995) 751–762

[28] Arimura, H.: Learning acyclic first-order Horn sentences from entailment. In: Algorithmic Learning Theory, 8th International Workshop, ALT '97, Sendai, Japan, October 1997, Proceedings. Volume 1316 of Lecture Notes in Artificial Intelligence., Springer (1997) 432–445

[29] Angluin, D.: Queries and concept learning. Machine Learning **2** (1988) 319–342

The Subsumption Lattice and Query Learning[*]

Marta Arias and Roni Khardon

Department of Computer Science, Tufts University
Medford, MA 02155, USA
{marias,roni}@cs.tufts.edu

Abstract. The paper identifies several new properties of the lattice induced by the subsumption relation over first-order clauses and derives implications of these for learnability. In particular, it is shown that the length of subsumption chains of function free clauses with bounded size can be exponential in the size. This suggests that simple algorithmic approaches that rely on repeating minimal subsumption-based refinements may require a long time to converge. It is also shown that with bounded size clauses the subsumption lattice has a large branching factor. This is used to show that the class of first-order length-bounded monotone clauses is not properly learnable from membership queries alone. Finally, the paper studies pairing, a generalization operation that takes two clauses and returns a number of possible generalizations. It is shown that there are clauses with an exponential number of pairing results which are not related to each other by subsumption. This is used to show that recent pairing-based algorithms can make exponentially many queries on some learning problems.

1 Introduction

The field of Inductive Logic Programming (ILP) is concerned with developing theory and methods that allow for efficient learning of classes of concepts expressed in the language of first-order logic. Subsumption is a generality relation over first order clauses that induces a quasi-order on the set of clauses. The subsumption lattice is of crucial importance since many ILP algorithms perform a search over this space and as a result the lattice has been investigated extensively in the literature (see survey in [15]). The paper contributes to this study in two ways. First, we expose and prove new properties of the subsumption lattice of first-order clauses. Second, we use these properties to prove negative learning results in the model of exact learning from queries. These results illustrate the connection between the subsumption lattice and learning.

This work arises from the study of query complexity of learning in first order logic. Several positive learnability results exist in the model of exact learning from queries [1]. However, except for a "monotone-like case" [19] the query complexity is either exponential in one of the crucial parameters (e.g. the number of universally quantified variables) [13,3] or the algorithms use additional syntax-based oracles [7,20,18]. It is not clear whether the exponential dependence is

---

[*] This work has been partly supported by NSF Grant IIS-0099446

S. Ben-David, J. Case, A. Maruoka (Eds.): ALT 2004, LNAI 3244, pp. 410–424, 2004.

necessary or not. Previous work in [4] showed that the VC-dimension cannot resolve this question. The current paper explores how properties of subsumption affect this question.

We start by considering the length of proper subsumption chains $c_1 \prec c_2 \prec .. \prec c_n$ of first order clauses of restricted size. This is motivated by two issues. First, many ILP algorithms (e.g. [21,17,8]) use refinement of clauses where in each step the clause is modified using a minimal subsumption step. Thus the length of subsumption chains hinges on convergence of such approaches. A second motivation comes from the use of certificates [12,11] to study query complexity. It is known [12,11] that a class C is learnable from equivalence and membership queries if and only if the class C has polynomial certificates. Previous work in [6] developed certificates for propositional classes. In particular, one of the constructions of certificates for Horn expressions uses the fact that all proper subsumption chains of propositional Horn clauses are short. Hence any generalization of this construction to first order logic relies on the length of such chains.

Section 3 shows that subsumption chains can be exponentially long (in number of literals and variables) even with function free clauses with a bounded number of literals. This result suggests that simple algorithmic approaches that rely only on minimal refinement steps may require a long time to converge and excludes simple generalizations of the certificate construction. We also show that if one imposes inequalities on all terms in a clause then subsumption chains are short. This further supports the use and study of inequated expressions as done e.g. in [13,3,9].

The chain length result gives an informal argument against certain approaches. Section 4 uses a similar construction to show that the class of length-bounded monotone first order clauses is not properly learnable using membership queries only. This result is derived by studying the lattice structure of length bounded clauses and using it to show that the *teaching dimension* [2,10] is exponential in the size. The result follows since the teaching dimension gives a lower bound for the number of membership queries required to learn a class [2,10].

Finally in Section 5 we address the complexity of the algorithms given in [13, 3] discussed above. One of the sources of exponential dependence on the number of variables is the number of pairings. Intuitively, a pairing is an operation that, given two first-order clauses, results in a new clause which is more general than the initial ones; two clauses have many pairings and the algorithm enumerates these in the process of learning. Results in [13,3] gave an upper-bound on the number of pairings, but left it open whether a large number of pairings can actually occur in examples. We give an exponential lower bound (in number of variables) on the number of pairings and construct an explicit example showing that the algorithm can be forced to make an exponential number of queries.

Due to space limitations several proofs are omitted from the paper; they can be found in [5].

2   Preliminaries

We assume familiarity with basic concepts in first order logic as described e.g. in [14,15]. We briefly review notions relevant to this paper.

A signature S consists of a finite set of predicates P and a finite set of functions F, both with their associated arities. Constants are functions with arity 0. A countable set of variables $x_1, x_2, x_3, \ldots$ is used to construct expressions. A variable is a *term*. If $t_1, \ldots, t_n$ are terms and $f \in F$ is a function symbol of arity n, then $f(t_1, ..., t_n)$ is a term. An *atom* is an expression $p(t_1, ..., t_n)$ where $p \in P$ is a predicate symbol of arity n and $t_1, ..., t_n$ are terms. An atom is called a *positive literal*. A *negative literal* is an expression $\neg l$ where l is a positive literal. A *clause* is a disjunction of literals where all variables are universally quantified. A *Horn clause* has at most one positive literal and an arbitrary number of negative literals. A Horn clause $\neg p_1 \vee ... \vee \neg p_n \vee p_{n+1}$ is equivalent to its implicational form $p_1 \wedge ... \wedge p_n \to p_{n+1}$. We call $p_1 \wedge ... \wedge p_n$ the *antecedent* and p_{n+1} the *consequent* of the clause. A *meta-clause* is a pair of the form $[s, c]$, where both s and c are sets of atoms such that $s \cap c = \emptyset$; s is the *antecedent* of the meta-clause and c is the *consequent*. Both are interpreted as the conjunction of the atoms they contain. Therefore, the meta-clause $[s, c]$ is interpreted as the logical expression $\bigwedge_{b \in c} s \to b$. An ordinary clause $C = s_c \to b_c$ corresponds to the meta-clause $[s_c, \{b_c\}]$. Fully inequated clauses [3] are clauses whose terms are forced to be always distinct. That is, any instance of a fully inequated clause is not allowed to unify any of its terms. This can be done by adding explicit inequalities on all terms as in: $E = [x \neq f(x)] \wedge [x \neq a] \wedge [a \neq f(x)] \wedge p(x, f(x)) \wedge p(a, x) \to q(a)$.

We use the symbol '$\models$' to denote logical implication which is defined following the standard semantics of first-order logic.

We need several parameters to quantify the complexity of a first-order expressions; we use the first-order expression $E = \neg p(x, f(x)) \vee \neg p(a, b) \vee q(b)$ to illustrate these. $NTerms(\cdot)$: counts the number of distinct terms in the input expression. Hence, $NTerms(E) = 4$ corresponding to the term set $\{x, a, f(x), b\}$. $WTerms(\cdot)$: similar to $NTerms$, with the only difference that functional terms are given twice as much weight as variables. Hence, $WTerms(E) = 7$ since terms in $\{a, f(x), b\}$ contribute 2 and x contributes 1. $NLiterals(\cdot)$: counts the number of literals in the input expression. Hence, $NLiterals(E) = 3$.

Let C, D be two arbitrary first-order clauses. We say that a clause C *subsumes* a clause D and denote this by $C \preceq D$ if there is a substitution θ such that $C \cdot \theta \subseteq D$. Moreover, they are *subsume-equivalent*, denoted $C \sim D$, if $C \preceq D$ and $D \preceq C$. We say that C *strictly* or *properly subsumes* D, denoted $C \prec D$, if $C \preceq D$ but $D \not\preceq C$. The relation $\preceq$ is reflexive and transitive and hence it induces a quasi-order on the set of clauses.

3   On the Length of Proper Chains

In this section we study the length of proper subsumption chains of clauses $c_1 \prec c_2 \prec .. \prec c_n$. It is known that infinite chains exist if one does not restrict clause size [16,15] but bounds for clauses of restricted size (which are necessarily finite) were not known before. We show that in the case of fully inequated clauses, the length of any proper chain is polynomial in the number of literals and the number of terms in the clauses involved. On the other hand, if clauses are not fully inequated, then chains of length exponential in the number of variables (or literals) exist, even if clauses are function free.

3.1   Subsumption Chains for Fully Inequated Clauses Are Short

We say that a substitution θ is unifying w.r.t. a clause c_1 if there exist two distinct terms t, t' in c_1 that have been syntactically unified i.e. $t \cdot \theta = t' \cdot \theta$. It is easy to verify the following lemma:

Lemma 1. *Let c_1, c_2 be two fully inequated clauses. If $c_1 \preceq c_2$, then (1) it must be via a non-unifying substitution w.r.t. c_1, (2) $WTerms(c_1) \leq WTerms(c_2)$, and (3) $NLiterals(c_1) \leq NLiterals(c_2)$.*

Lemma 2. *Let c_1, c_2 be fully inequated clauses such that $c_1 \prec c_2$. Then, either $NLiterals(c_1) < NLiterals(c_2)$ or $WTerms(c_1) < WTerms(c_2)$.*

Proof. By the previous lemma we only need to disprove the possibility that both $NLiterals(c_1) = NLiterals(c_2)$ and $WTerms(c_1) = WTerms(c_2)$. Suppose so, and let θ be the substitution such that $c_1\theta \subseteq c_2$. Then θ induces a 1-1 mapping of terms. Now if θ maps a variable to a non-variable term then $WTerms(c_1) < WTerms(c_2)$. So θ must be a variable renaming. If θ is a variable renaming and $NLiterals(c_1) = NLiterals(c_2)$, then c_1 and c_2 must be syntactic variants, contradicting the assumption that $c_2 \not\preceq c_1$. ☐

As a result each step in a strict subsumption chain reduces one of $NLiterals$ or $WTerms$ and since these are bounded by $2t$ and l respectively we get:

Theorem 1. *The longest proper subsumption chain of fully inequated clauses with at most t terms and l literals is of length at most $2t + l$.*

3.2   Function Free Clauses Have Long Proper Chains

In this section we demonstrate that function free first-order clauses can produce chains of exponential length. We start with a simple construction where the arity of predicates is not constant.

Let p be a predicate symbol of arity a. The chain $d_1 \succ d_2 \succ .. \succ d_n$ is defined inductively. The first clause is $d_1 = p(z, .., z)$, and given a clause $d_i = p_1, p_2, .., p_k$, we define the next clause d_{i+1} as follows: (1) if p_1 contains only two occurrences of the variable z, then $d_{i+1} = p_2, .., p_k$, or else (2) if p_1 contains $c \geq 3$ occurrences of the variable z, replace the atom p_1 by a new set of atoms $p'_1, .., p'_{k'}$ such that $k' = min(c, l - k + 1)$, and every new atom p'_j for $1 \leq j \leq k'$ is a copy of p_1 in which the j'th occurrence of the variable z has been replaced by a new fresh variable not appearing in d_i (the same variable for all copies).

Example 1. Suppose p has arity 4 and that $l = 3$. The construction produces the following chain of length 11:

$$p(z, z, z, z)$$
$$\succ \quad p(x_1, z, z, z), p(z, x_1, z, z), p(z, z, x_1, z)$$
$$\succ \quad p(x_1, x_2, z, z), p(z, x_1, z, z), p(z, z, x_1, z)$$
$$\succ \qquad p(z, x_1, z, z), p(z, z, x_1, z)$$
$$\succ \quad p(x_2, x_1, z, z), p(z, x_1, x_2, z), p(z, z, x_1, z)$$
$$\succ \qquad p(z, x_1, x_2, z), p(z, z, x_1, z)$$
$$\succ \qquad p(z, z, x_1, z)$$
$$\succ \quad p(x_2, z, x_1, z), p(z, x_2, x_1, z), p(z, z, x_1, x_2)$$
$$\succ \qquad p(z, x_2, x_1, z), p(z, z, x_1, x_2)$$
$$\succ \qquad p(z, z, x_1, x_2)$$
$$\succ \qquad \emptyset$$

Let $N(c, s)$ be the number of subsumption generalizations that can be produced by this method when starting with a singleton clause which is allowed to expand on s literals (i.e., $l = s+1$) and whose only atom has $c \geq 2$ occurrences of the variable z. Then, the following relations hold: (A) $N(2, s) = 1$, for all $s \geq 0$. To see this note that when there are only 2 occurrences of the variable z, the only possible step is to remove the atom, thus obtaining the empty clause. (B) $N(c, 0) = c - 1$, for all $c \geq 2$. This is derived by observing that when we have $c \geq 2$ occurrences of the distinguished variable z and no expansion on the number of literals is possible, we can apply $c-2$ steps that replace occurrences of z by new variables, and a final step that drops the literal. After this, no more generalizations are possible. (C) $N(c, s) = 1+\sum_{i=\max(0, s-c+1)}^{s} N(c-1, i)$, for all $c > 2, s > 0$. This recurrence is obtained by observing that the initial clause containing our single atom can be replaced by $\min(c, s+1)$ "copies" in a first generalization step leaving $q = \max(0, s - c + 1)$ empty slots. After this, each of these copies which contain $c - 1$ occurrences of the distinguished variable z, go through the series of generalizations: the left-most atom has q positions to use for its expansion and is generalized $N(c-1, q)$ times until it is finally dropped; the next atom has $q + 1$ position to expand since the left-most atom has been dropped, and hence it produces $N(c - 1, q + 1)$ generalization steps until it is finally dropped, and so on. The next lemma can be proved by induction on c and s.

Lemma 3. $N(c, s) \geq \binom{c}{s+1} - 1$ for $c \geq 2$ and $s \geq 0$.

It remains to show that this is a proper chain. First, we investigate key structural properties of the clauses participating in our chain. The following three lemmas can be proved by induction on the updates of d_i.

Lemma 4. Let $Vars(p)$ be the variables occurring in the atom p. For all $d_i = p_1, .., p_k$ the following properties hold: (1) Every atom $p_j \in d_i$ contains no repeated occurrences of variables, with the exception of z, which appears at least twice in each atom. (2) $Vars(p_j) \supseteq Vars(p_{j+1})$ for all $j = 1, .., k - 1$.

From the properties stated in the previous lemma, it follows that we can view any clause d_i as a sequence of blocks of atoms $B_1, B_2, .., B_m$ such that all the atoms in a single block contain exactly the same variables, and variables appearing in neighboring blocks are such that $Vars(B_j) \supset Vars(B_{j+1})$.

Lemma 5. *Fix some clause d_i, and let p be an atom in any block B. If $p \cdot \theta \in B$, then θ does not change variables in p.*

Lemma 6. *Let d_i be any clause in the sequence and let $B_1, .., B_m$ be its blocks. Then, for any pair of blocks B_{i_1} and B_{i_2} s.t. $i_1 < i_2$, there exists some variable in $Vars(B_{i_2}) \setminus \{z\}$ that is in the same position j in all the atoms in B_{i_1} but in all the atoms in B_{i_2} it appears in different positions, always different from the one in B_{i_1}. Moreover, all the atoms in B_{i_2} contain the variable z at position j.*

Lemma 7. *Fix some clause $d_i = p_1, .., p_k$ with at least 2 atoms (i.e., $k \geq 2$). Then $(p_2, .., p_k) \cdot \theta \subseteq d_i$ only if θ does not change variables in p_2.*

Proof. Let $d_i = B_1, .., B_m$. Let p be any atom in any block B_j and assume $p \cdot \theta \in d_i$. Notice that $p \cdot \theta \notin B_1, .., B_{j-1}$ since atoms in blocks $B_1, .., B_{j-1}$ contain strictly more variables than $p \cdot \theta$. Hence $p \cdot \theta \in B_j, .., B_m$. We first claim that if θ does not change variables in $B_{j+1}, .., B_m$ then θ does not change variables in B_j. To prove the claim note that if $p \cdot \theta \in B_j$ then Lemma 5 applies. On the other hand if $p \cdot \theta \in B_{j'}$ for $j < j'$ then Lemma 6 guarantees that there exists some variable $x \in Vars(B_{j'})$ that appears in a position in p in which atoms in $B_{j'}$ contain the variable z. Since by assumption θ does not change this variable this implies that $p \cdot \theta \notin B_{j'}$ leading to a contradiction.

Finally if $(p_2, .., p_k) \cdot \theta \subseteq d_i$ then we have an atom p as above from each block. Therefore we can apply the claim inductively starting with $j = m$ and until $j = i_2$ where i_2 is the block index of p_2. This implies that θ does not change variables that appear in the leftmost block of $p_2, .., p_k$, and hence in p_2 as required. $\square$

Lemma 8. *For all $i = 1, .., n - 1$ we have that $d_i \succ d_{i+1}$.*

Proof. Suppose that $d_i = p_1, .., p_k$. We have the following possible transitions from d_i to d_{i+1}:

Case 1. $d_{i+1} = p_2, .., p_k$. Clearly, $d_i \supset d_{i+1}$, and hence $d_i \succeq d_{i+1}$ via the empty substitution. Suppose by way of contradiction that $d_i \preceq d_{i+1}$, so there must be a substitution θ s.t. $d_i \cdot \theta \subseteq d_{i+1}$. Clearly, $i + 1 \neq n$ since otherwise we could not satisfy $d_i \cdot \theta \subseteq d_{i+1} = \emptyset$. Therefore, $d_{i+1} \neq \emptyset$ and d_i contains at least 2 atoms. The fact $d_i \cdot \theta \subseteq d_{i+1}$ implies that $(p_2 .., p_k) \cdot \theta \subseteq d_i$, and by Lemma 7, θ must not change variables in p_2. If p_1 and p_2 are in the same block, then $p_1 \cdot \theta = p_1 \notin d_{i+1}$. If p_1 and p_2 are in different blocks, then Lemma 6 guarantees that for every atom in $p_2, .., p_k$ there is a variable that appears in a different location in p_1 and as above this variable cannot be changed by θ. Hence, $p_1 \cdot \theta \not\subseteq d_{i+1}$, contradicting our assumption that $d_i \preceq d_{i+1}$.

Case 2. $d_{i+1} = p_1', .., p_{k'}', p_2, .., p_k$. Let x be the newly introduced variable. Then, $d_{i+1} \cdot \{x \mapsto z\} \subseteq d_i$ and hence $d_i \succeq d_{i+1}$. To see that $d_i \not\preceq d_{i+1}$, suppose that this is not the case. Hence, there must be a substitution θ such that $d_i \cdot \theta \subseteq d_{i+1}$. If $d_i = p_1$, (i.e., d_i contains one atom only), then $p_1 \cdot \theta \subseteq p_1', .., p_{k'}'$. In this case, θ must map z into the new variable x but this results in multiple occurrences of x, and hence $p_1 \cdot \theta \not\subseteq p_1', .., p_{k'}'$. Hence, d_i must contain at least two atoms and the substitution θ must satisfy that $(p_1, .., p_k) \cdot \theta \subseteq p_1', .., p_{k'}', p_2, .., p_k$. The new atoms $p_1', .., p_{k'}'$ contain more variables than $p_1, .., p_k$, therefore $(p_1, .., p_k) \cdot \theta \subseteq p_2, .., p_k$. By the same reasoning as in the previous case, we conclude that $d_i \succ d_{i+1}$. □

Now Lemma 3 and Lemma 8 imply:

Theorem 2. *Let p be a predicate symbol of arity $\alpha \geq 1$. There exists a proper subsumption chain of length $\binom{\alpha}{l}$ of function free clauses using at most α variables and l literals.*

The construction above can be improved to use predicates of arity 3 as follows.

Definition 1. *Let d be any clause. Let $Trans(d)$ be the clause obtained by replacing each literal $p(t_1, .., t_a)$ with a new set $\{p(y_i, y_{i+1}, t_i) \mid 1 \leq i \leq a\}$, where all $y_1, .., y_{a+1}$ are new variables not appearing in d. The new variables $y_1, .., y_{a+1}$ are different for each atom in d.*

Example 2. The clause $p(z, x_1, x_2, z), p(z, z, x_1, z)$ is transformed into the clause $p(y_1, y_2, z), p(y_2, y_3, x_1), p(y_3, y_4, x_2), p(y_4, y_5, z), p(y_1', y_2', z), p(y_2', y_3', z), p(y_3', y_4', x_1), p(y_4', y_5', z)$.

Consider a function free clause d with predicate symbols of arity at most a, containing v variables and l literals. Then, $Trans(d)$ uses predicates of arity 3, has $l(a+1)+v$ variables and al literals. The next lemma gives the main property of this transformation:

Lemma 9. *Let d_1, d_2 be clauses. Then, $d_1 \preceq d_2$ iff $Trans(d_1) \preceq Trans(d_2)$.*

Proof. Assume first that $d_1 \preceq d_2$, i.e., there is a substitution θ from variables in d_1 into terms of d_2 such that $d_1 \cdot \theta \subseteq d_2$. Obviously, θ does not alter the value of the new variables added to $Trans(d_1)$, and hence $Trans(d_1) \cdot \theta = Trans(d_1 \cdot \theta) \subseteq Trans(d_2)$, so that $Trans(d_1) \preceq Trans(d_2)$.

For the other direction, assume that there exists a substitution θ such that $Trans(d_1) \cdot \theta \subseteq Trans(d_2)$. Let $d_1 = l_1^1 \vee l_1^2 \vee .. \vee l_1^{k_1}$ and let $\{y_1^j, .., y_{arity(l_1^j)+1}^j\}$ be the variables used in the transformation for literal l_1^j in d_1, for $1 \leq j \leq k_1$. Similarly, let $d_2 = l_2^1 \vee l_2^2 \vee .. \vee l_2^{k_2}$ and let $\{y'_1^j, .., y'^j_{arity(l_2^j)+1}\}$ be the variables used in the transformation for literal l_2^j in d_2, for $1 \leq j \leq k_2$. First we show that θ must map blocks of auxiliary variables in $Trans(d_1)$, $\{y_1^j, .., y_{arity(l_1^j)+1}^j\}$ into blocks of auxiliary variables in $Trans(d_2)$, $\{y'^{j'}_1, .., y'^{j'}_{arity(l^{j'}_2)+1}\}$ so that the predicate symbol of l^j_1 coincides with the predicate symbol of $l^{j'}_2$. Moreover, the order of the variables is preserved, i.e., θ maps each $y^j_i \mapsto y'^{j'}_i$, for all $1 \leq i \leq arity(l^{j'}_2)$. By way of contradiction, suppose that there exists a pair of variables in $Trans(d_1)$, y^j_i and y^j_{i+1}, that have been mapped into y''^a_* and y''^b_*, respectively, where $a \neq b$. Then, $p(y^j_i, y^j_{i+1}, *) \cdot \theta = p(y''^a_*, y''^b_*, *) \in Trans(d_2)$. This contradicts the fact that, by construction, all literals in $Trans(d_2)$ are such that the superscripts of the first two auxiliary variables coincide.

Suppose now that some y^j_i has been mapped into $y'^{j'}_{i'}$ where $i \neq i'$ and i is the smallest such index. Assume also that the predicate symbol corresponding to literal l^j_1 is p. If $i > 1$, then $p(y^j_{i-1}, y^j_i, *) \cdot \theta = p(y'^{j'}_{i-1}, y'^{j'}_{i'}, *) \in Trans(d_2)$. But this is a contradiction since all literals in $Trans(d_2)$ are such that its two initial arguments have the form $p(y''^*_h, y''^*_{h+1}, *)$ and here $(i-1)+1 \neq i'$. If $i = 1$, then since $i' > 1$ there must be an index h s.t. θ maps $y^j_{i+h} \mapsto y'^{j'}_{i'+h}$ but θ does not map $y^j_{i+h+1} \mapsto y'^{j'}_{i'+h+1}$. Thus we arrive to the same contradiction as in the previous case.

Now, the fact that each $y^j_i \mapsto y'^{j'}_i$ implies that θ maps arguments of literals in d_1 into arguments in the same position of literals in d_2. Moreover, since blocks of variables are not mixed, all arguments from a literal in d_1 are mapped into all the arguments of a fixed literal in d_2, so we conclude that $d_1 \cdot \theta \subseteq d_2$.   □

Theorem 3. *If there is a predicate symbol of arity at least 3, then there exist proper subsumption chains of length at least $2^{\sqrt{v}/2}$ of function free clauses using at most v variables and $\frac{v}{2}$ literals, where $v \geq 9$.*

Proof. Theorem 2 shows that there exists a chain of length $\binom{a}{l} = \binom{\sqrt{v}}{\sqrt{v}/2} > 2^{\sqrt{v}/2}$ if we use predicate symbols of arity $\sqrt{v}$, $\sqrt{v}$ variables and $\frac{\sqrt{v}}{2}$ atoms per clause. Consider the chain $Trans(d_1) \succ Trans(d_2) \succ .. \succ Trans(d_n)$. Lemma 9 guarantees that this is also a proper chain. The chain has clauses with $\frac{\sqrt{v}}{2}(\sqrt{v}+1) + \sqrt{v} = \frac{v}{2} + \frac{3\sqrt{v}}{2} \leq v$ variables (here we use $v \geq 9$) and $\sqrt{v}\frac{\sqrt{v}}{2} = \frac{v}{2}$ literals.   □

4   Learning from Membership Queries Only

The previous result suggests that simple use of minimal refinement steps may require long time to converge. We next use a related construction to show that there can be no polynomial algorithm that properly learns the class of monotone function-free and length-bounded clauses from membership queries only. We use a combinatorial notion, the *teaching dimension* [2,10], that is known to be a lower bound for the complexity of exact learning from membership queries only.

Definition 2. *The teaching dimension of a class $\mathcal{T}$ is the minimum integer d such that for each expression $f \in \mathcal{T}$ there is a set T of at most d examples (the* teaching set*) with the property that any expression $g \in \mathcal{T}$ different from f is not consistent with f over the examples in T.*

Let k be such that $\log_2 k$ is an integer. Then $\langle t_1, .., t_k \rangle$ denotes the term represented by a complete binary tree of applications of a binary function symbol f of depth $\log k$ with leaves $t_1, .., t_k$. For example, $\langle 1, 2, 3, 4, 5, 6, 7, 8 \rangle$ represents the term $f(f(f(1, 2), f(3, 4)), f(f(5, 6), f(7, 8)))$. Notice that the number of distinct terms in $\langle t_1, .., t_k \rangle$ is at most $k + \sum_{i=1}^{k} NTerms(t_i)$. In particular, if each t_i is either a variable or a constant, then $NTerms(\langle t_1, .., t_k \rangle) \leq 2k$.

Let p be a unary predicate symbol. Consider the clause $p(\langle a, .., a \rangle)$, where the constant a occurs k times. We consider all the possible minimal generalizations of $p(\langle a, .., a \rangle)$. That is, clauses C that are strict generalizations of $p(\langle a, .., a \rangle)$ for which no other clause C' is such that $p(\langle a, .., a \rangle) \succ C' \succ C$. Among them we find the clauses

$$C_k = p(\langle x, .., x \rangle)$$
$$C_{k-1} = p(\langle a, x, .., x \rangle) \vee p(\langle x, a, x, .., x \rangle) \vee .. \vee p(\langle x, .., x, a \rangle)$$
$$C_{k-2} = p(\langle a, a, x, .., x \rangle) \vee p(\langle a, x, a, x.., x \rangle) \vee .. \vee p(\langle x, .., x, a, a \rangle)$$
$$\vdots$$
$$C_{k/2} = p(\langle a, .., a, x, .., x \rangle) \vee .. \vee p(\langle x, .., x, a, .., a \rangle)$$
$$\vdots$$
$$C_1 = p(\langle a, .., a, x \rangle) \vee p(\langle a, .., a, x, a \rangle) \vee .. \vee p(\langle x, a, .., a \rangle)$$

where each C_i includes all possibilities of replacing i positions with a variable. Clearly, $|C_i| = \binom{k}{i}$. In particular, $\left| C_{k/2} \right| = \binom{k}{k/2} > 2^{k/2}$.

We next define the learning problem for which we find an exponential lower bound. The signature $\mathcal{S}$ consists of the function symbol f of arity 2, two constants a, b, and a single predicate symbol p of arity 1. Fix l to be some integer. Let the (representation) concept class be $\mathcal{C} = \{$first-order monotone $\mathcal{S}$-clauses with at most l atoms$\}$ and the set of examples be $\mathcal{E} = \{$first order ground monotone $\mathcal{S}$-clauses with at most l atoms$\}$.

We identify the representation concept class $\mathcal{C}$ with its denotations in the following way. The concept represented by $C \in \mathcal{C}$ is $\{E \in \mathcal{E} \mid C \models E\}$ which in this case coincides with $\{E \in \mathcal{E} \mid C \preceq E\}$. Thus, this problem is cast in the framework of learning from entailment.

Suppose that the target concept is $f = p(\langle a, .., a \rangle)$ and that $l \leq \frac{\binom{k}{k/2}}{2}$. We want to find a minimal teaching set T for f. The cardinality of a minimal teaching set for f is clearly a lower bound on the teaching dimension of $\mathcal{C}$. By definition, the examples in T have to eliminate every other expression in $\mathcal{C}$. In other words, for every expression g in $\mathcal{C}$ other than f, T must include an example E such that $f \preceq E$ and $g \not\preceq E$ or vice versa.

We first observe that the clause $C_{k/2}$ is not included in our concept class $\mathcal{C}$ because it contains too many literals: $l \leq \frac{\binom{k}{k/2}}{2} = \frac{|C_{k/2}|}{2} < |C_{k/2}|$. However, subsets of $C_{k/2}$ with exactly l atoms are included in C because they are monotone S-clauses of at most l literals. Note also that each clause includes $\leq 2kl$ terms. There are $K = \binom{k/2}{l} > (\frac{2^{k/2}}{l})^l = 2^{\Omega(lk)}$ such subsets where we use an additional restriction that $l \leq k$. Let these be $C_{k/2}^1, .., C_{k/2}^K$. By definition, the teaching set T has to reject each one of these K clauses.

   Notice that $C_{k/2}^j \preceq f = p(\langle a, .., a\rangle)$ for each $j = 1, .., K$ (consider the witnessing substitution $\{x \mapsto a\}$). Now, to reject an arbitrary $C_{k/2}^j$, T has to include some example $E \in \mathcal{E}$ s.t. $C_{k/2}^j \preceq E$ but $p(\langle a, .., a\rangle) \npreceq E$. The only example in $\mathcal{E}$ that qualifies is $E^j = C_{k/2}^j \cdot \{x \mapsto b\}$. Hence, for each $C_{k/2}^j$ the example E^j must be included in T and these examples are distinct. Hence, T must contain all the examples in $E^1, .., E^K$. Substituting $k = \sqrt{t}$ and $l \leq \frac{\sqrt{t}}{2}$ so that $2kl \leq t$ we obtain:

Theorem 4. *Let C be the class of monotone clauses built from a signature containing 2 constants, a binary function symbol and a unary predicate symbol with at most $l \leq \frac{\sqrt{t}}{2}$ literals and t terms per clause. Then, the teaching dimension of C is $2^{\Omega(l\sqrt{t})}$.*

5   On the Number of Pairings

Plotkin [16] (see also [15]) defined the *least general generalization* (*lgg*) of clauses w.r.t. subsumption and gave an algorithm to compute it. The *lgg* of C_1, C_2 is a clause C that subsumes both clauses, namely $C \preceq C_1$, $C \preceq C_2$, and is the least such clause, that is $D \preceq C$ for any D that subsumes both clauses. The algorithm essentially takes a cross product of atoms with the same predicate symbol in the two clauses and generalizes arguments bottom up. Generalization of arguments is defined as follows. The lgg of two terms $f(s_1, ..., s_n)$ and $g(t_1, ..., t_m)$ is the term $f(lgg(s_1, t_1), ..., lgg(s_n, t_n))$ if $f = g$ and $n = m$. Otherwise, it is a new variable x, where x stands for the *lgg* of that pair of terms throughout the computation of the *lgg*. This information is kept in what we call the *lgg* table.

Example 3. Let $C_1 = \{p(a, f(b)), p(g(a, x), c), q(a)\}$ and $C_2 = \{p(z, f(2)), q(z)\}$. Their pairs of compatible literals are $\{p(a, f(b)) - p(z, f(2)),\quad p(g(a, x), c) - p(z, f(2)),\quad q(a) - q(z)\}$. Their lgg is $lgg(C_1, C_2) = \{p(X, f(Y)), p(Z, V), q(X)\}$. The *lgg table* produced during the computation of $lgg(C_1, C_2)$ is

```
[ a - z => X ]              (from p(a, f(b)) with p(z, f(2)))
[ b - 2 => Y ]              (from p(a, f(b)) with p(z, f(2)))
[ f(b) - f(2) => f(Y) ]    (from p(a, f(b)) with p(z, f(2)))
[ g(a,x) - z => Z ]        (from p(g(a, x), c) with p(z, f(2)))
[ c - f(2) => V ]          (from p(g(a, x), c) with p(z, f(2)))
```

   The number of literals in the *lgg* of two clauses can be as large as the product of the number of literals in the two clauses and repeated application of *lgg* can lead to an exponential increase in size. Pairings are subsets of the *lgg* that avoid this explosion in size by imposing an additional constraint requiring that each literal in the original clauses is *paired* at most once with a compatible literal of the other clause. In Example 3, we have the literal $p(z, f(2)) \in C_2$ paired to the literals $p(a, f(b))$ and $p(g(a, x), c)$ of C_1. A pairing disallows this by including just one copy in the result. Naturally, given two clauses we now have many possible pairings instead of a single *lgg*.

Pairings are defined in [13,3] by way of matchings of terms. Notice that the first two columns of the *lgg* table define a matching between terms in the two clauses. In our example this matching is not 1-1 since the term $f(2)$ in C_2 has been used in more than one entry of the matching, in particular, in entries $f(b) - f(2)$ and $c - f(2)$. This reflects the fact that the atom $p(z, f(2))$ of C_2 is paired with two atoms in C_1 in the *lgg*. Every 1-1 matching corresponding to a 1-1 restriction of the *lgg* table induces a pairing.

5.1   General Clauses

We first show that general clauses allowing the use of arbitrary terms can have an exponential number of pairings. Fix v such that $\log_2 v$ is an integer. Let $t_{i,j}$ be a ground term that is unique for every pair of integers $0 \le i, j \le v - 1$. For example, $t_{i,j}$ could use two unary function symbols f_0 and f_1 and a constant a and we define $t_{i,j}$ as a string of applications of f_0 or f_1 of length $2 \log v$, finalized with the constant a such that the first $\log v$ function symbols encode the binary representation of i and the last $\log v$ function symbols encode j. For example, if $v = 8$, then the term $t_{5,3}$ can be encoded as $\underbrace{f_1(f_0(f_1}_{5}(\underbrace{f_0(f_1(f_1}_{3}(a))))))$. The size of such a term (in terms of symbol occurrences) is exactly $2 \log v + 1$. Let $x_0, .., x_{v-1}$ and $y_0, .., y_{v-1}$ be variables. We define

$$C_1 = \bigvee_{\substack{0 \le i,j < v \\ 0 \le l < v-1}} p(t_{i,j}, x_l, x_{l+1})$$

$$C_2 = \bigvee_{0 \le i,j < v} p(t_{i,j}, y_i, y_j).$$

Notice that $|C_1| = v^2(v - 1)$ and $|C_2| = v^2$, and they use a single predicate symbol of arity 3.

Any 1-1 matching between the variables in C_1 and C_2 can be represented by a permutation π of $\{0, .., v - 1\}$: each variable x_i in C_1 is matched to $y_{\pi(i)}$ in C_2. All the matchings considered in this section map the common ground terms of C_1 and C_2 to one another, i.e., the extended matchings also contain all entries $[t - t \Rightarrow t]$, where t is any ground term appearing in both C_1 and C_2. Let the extended matching induced by permutation π be

$$\left\{ x_i - y_{\pi(i)} \Rightarrow X_{\pi(i)} \mid 0 \le i \le v - 1 \right\} \cup \{t - t \Rightarrow t \mid t \in Terms(C_1) \cap Terms(C_2)\}.$$

First we study $lgg_\pi(C_1, C_2)$, the pairing induced by the 1-1 matching represented by π. A literal $p(t_{i,j}, X_a, X_b)$ is included in $lgg_\pi(C_1, C_2)$ iff $a = \pi(l)$

and $b = \pi(l + 1)$ for some $l \in \{0, .., v - 2\}$ (this is the condition imposed by C_1), and $i = a, j = b$ (this is the condition imposed by C_2). Therefore, $lgg_\pi(C_1, C_2) = \bigvee_{0 \le l < v-1} p(t_{\pi(l),\pi(l+1)}, X_{\pi(l)}, X_{\pi(l+1)})$.

Finally we see that different permutations yield pairings that are subsumption inequivalent, i.e., $lgg_\pi(C_1, C_2) \not\preceq lgg_{\pi'}(C_1, C_2)$ for any $\pi \ne \pi'$. It is sufficient to observe that since π and π' are distinct, there must exist some term $t_{\pi(l),\pi(l+1)}$ in $lgg_\pi(C_1, C_2)$ that is not present in $lgg_{\pi'}(C_1, C_2)$. This holds since a distinct pair of consecutive indices exists for any two permutations. Since the terms $t_{*,*}$ are ground, subsumption is not possible. There are $v!$ distinct permutations of $\{0, .., v - 1\}$ and therefore:

Theorem 5. *Let S be a signature containing a predicate symbol of arity at least 3, two unary function symbols and a constant. The number of distinct pairings between a pair of S-clauses using v variables, $O(v^3)$ literals and terms of size $O(\log v)$ can be $\Omega(v!)$.*

5.2   Function Free Clauses

We next generalize the construction to use function free clauses. We start with a construction using non-fixed arity. Our construction mimics the behavior of pairing ground terms in the previous section by using 2 additional variables, z_0 and z_1, that encode the integers i and j in a similar way to $t_{i,j}$. By looking at matchings π that match the variables z_0 and z_1 to themselves, we guarantee that the resulting lgg_π contains the correct encoding of the variables in the last and previous-to-last positions of the atoms. Let

$$C_1 = \bigvee_{\substack{(i_1,...,i_{\log v}) \in \{0,1\}^{\log v} \\ (j_1,...,j_{\log v}) \in \{0,1\}^{\log v} \\ 0 \le l < v-1}} p(z_{i_1}, .., z_{i_{\log v}}, z_{j_1}, .., z_{j_{\log v}}, x_l, x_{l+1})$$

$$C_2 = \bigvee_{\substack{(i_1,...,i_{\log v}) = binary(i) \\ (j_1,...,j_{\log v}) = binary(j) \\ 0 \le i,j < v}} p(z_{i_1}, .., z_{i_{\log v}}, z_{j_1}, .., z_{j_{\log v}}, y_i, y_j)$$

where we use $binary(n)$ to denote the tuple $z_{n_1}, .., z_{n_{\log v}}$ encoding n in its binary representation using z_0, z_1. For example, assuming $v = 8$, $binary(6) = z_1, z_1, z_0$. Notice that $|C_1| = v^2(v - 1)$ and $|C_2| = v^2$, the clauses use a single predicate symbol of arity $2 \log v + 2$, and both clauses use exactly $v + 2$ variables.

Any 1-1 matching between the variables $x_0, .., x_{v-1}$ in C_1 and $y_0, .., y_{v-1}$ in C_2 can be represented by a permutation π of $\{0, .., v - 1\}$: each variable x_i in C_1 is matched to $y_{\pi(i)}$ in C_2. Let the matching induced by permutation π be

$$\{x_i - y_{\pi(i)} \Rightarrow X_{\pi(i)} \mid 0 \le i < v\}.$$

First we study $lgg_{\pi \cup \{z_0 - z_0, z_1 - z_1\}}(C_1, C_2)$, the pairing induced by the 1-1 matching represented by π augmented with z_0 and z_1 matched to themselves. A literal $p(z_{i_1}, .., z_{i_{\log v}}, z_{j_1}, .., z_{j_{\log v}}, X_a, X_b)$ is included in $lgg_\pi(C_1, C_2)$

iff $a = \pi(l)$ and $b = \pi(l+1)$ for some $l \in \{0, .., v-2\}$ (this is the condition imposed by C_1), and $(i_1, .., i_{\log v}) = binary(a), (j_1, .., j_{\log v}) = binary(b)$ (this is the condition imposed by C_2). Therefore, $lgg_{\pi \cup \{z_0 - z_0, z_1 - z_1\}}(C_1, C_2) = \bigvee_{0 \leq l \leq v-1} p(binary(\pi(l)), binary(\pi(l+1)), X_{\pi(l)}, X_{\pi(l+1)})$.

Finally, we want to check whether different permutations yield pairings that are subsumption inequivalent, i.e., if for any $\pi \neq \pi'$

$$lgg_{\pi \cup \{z_0 - z_0, z_1 - z_1\}}(C_1, C_2) \preceq lgg_{\pi' \cup \{z_0 - z_0, z_1 - z_1\}}(C_1, C_2).$$

To this end, we investigate which substitutions θ satisfy

$$lgg_{\pi \cup \{z_0 - z_0, z_1 - z_1\}}(C_1, C_2) \cdot \theta \subseteq lgg_{\pi' \cup \{z_0 - z_0, z_1 - z_1\}}(C_1, C_2).$$

If θ does not change the values of z_0, z_1, then as before some atom

$$p(binary(\pi(l)), binary(\pi(l+1)), *, *) \cdot \theta = p(binary(\pi(l)), binary(\pi(l+1)), *, *)$$

in $lgg_{\pi \cup \{z_0 - z_0, z_1 - z_1\}}(C_1, C_2) \cdot \theta$ does not occur in $lgg_{\pi' \cup \{z_0 - z_0, z_1 - z_1\}}(C_1, C_2)$. If θ maps both variables z_0, z_1 to the same value (either z_1 or z_0), then inclusion cannot happen since $lgg_{\pi' \cup \{z_0 - z_0, z_1 - z_1\}}(C_1, C_2)$ contains no atoms of the form $p(z_0, .., z_0, *, *)$ or $p(z_1, .., z_1, *, *)$. Obviously, if z_0 or z_1 are mapped into any other variable X_*, then the inclusion is not possible either. Hence, θ must exchange the values of z_0, z_1, and:

$$p(binary(\pi(l)), binary(\pi(l+1)), *, *) \cdot \theta = p(\overline{binary(\pi(l))}, \overline{binary(\pi(l+1))}, *, *)$$

where $\overline{binary(n)}$ is the "complement" of $binary(n)$. For example, assuming $v = 8$, $\overline{binary(6)} = z_0, z_0, z_1$. More precisely, $\overline{binary(n)} = binary(v - 1 - n)$. We have seen that there is only one permutation $\pi' = \overline{\pi}$ for which there exists some θ s.t. $lgg_{\pi \cup \{z_0 - z_0, z_1 - z_1\}}(C_1, C_2) \cdot \theta \subseteq lgg_{\pi' \cup \{z_0 - z_0, z_1 - z_1\}}(C_1, C_2)$. Moreover, θ is exactly $\{z_0 \mapsto z_1, z_1 \mapsto z_0\} \cup \{X_l \mapsto X_{v-1-l} \mid 0 \leq l < v\}$. We therefore get:

Theorem 6. *Let S be a signature containing a predicate symbol of arity at least $2 \log v + 2$. The number of distinct pairings between a pair of function free S-clauses using $v + 2$ variables, $O(v^3)$ literals can be $\Omega(v!)$.*

As in the previous section we can generalize the result to use predicates with fixed arity:

Theorem 7. *Let S be a signature containing a predicate symbol of arity at least 3. The number of distinct pairings between a pair of function free S-clauses using at most v variables and v literals can be $\Omega(2^{v/4})$.*

5.3   Implications for Learnability

The Algorithms in [13,3] are shown to learn first order classes from equivalence and membership queries. The algorithms use pairings in the process of learning and a t^v upper bound on the number of these is used. No explicit lower bound was given leaving open the possibility that better analysis might yield better upper bounds. The results above can be used to give a concrete example where an exponential number of queries is indeed used. We sketch the details here for the algorithm in [3]. Let the target be T. The algorithm maintains a set of meta-clauses as its hypothesis. Two major steps in the algorithm are minimization and pairing. In minimization, given a counter example clause C s.t. $T \models C$ the algorithm iterates dropping one object at a time and asking an entailment membership query to check whether it is correct. For example given $p(x_1, x_2), p(x_2, x_3), p(x_1, x_3), p(x_3, x_4) \rightarrow q(x_3, x_3)$ dropping x_2 (and all atoms using it) yields $p(x_1, x_3), p(x_3, x_4) \rightarrow q(x_3, x_3)$. In this way a counter example with a minimal set of variables is obtained. Then the algorithm tries to find a pairing of the minimized example and a meta-clause in the hypothesis which yields an implied clause of smaller size. This is done by enumerating all "basic" pairings. If no such pairing is found then the clause is added as a new meta-clause to the hypothesis. Therefore in order to show that the algorithm makes an exponential number of queries it suffices to show a target $T = D_1 \wedge D_2$ where (1) each of D_1, D_2 is already minimal so that minimization does not alter them, (2) D_1, D_2 have an exponential number of "basic" pairings, and (3) $T \not\models C$ for any C which is a pairing of D_1, D_2. If this holds then we can give the clause D_1 to the algorithm as a counter example and then follow with D_2. The algorithm will ask a membership query on all the pairings getting an answer of No every time and eventually add D_2 to its hypothesis. We omit the technical definition of "basic" pairings but note that all pairings constructed in the previous section are "basic" since they map variables to variables.

Let $f()$ be a nullary predicate symbol, and $q()$ and $r()$ binary predicates. Let N_1, N_2 be the number of variables used in C_1, C_2 in the construction above respectively, and rename these variables (in any order) so that C_1 uses variables $v_1, \ldots, v_{N_1}$, and C_2 uses variables $w_1, \ldots, w_{N_2}$. Then we use $q()$ and $r()$ to define chains of variables touching all variables in C_1, C_2: $Q = \wedge_{1 \leq l < N_1} q(v_l, v_{l+1})$ and $R = \wedge_{1 \leq l < N_2} r(w_l, w_{l+1})$. Now define C_1', C_2' to be the conjunction of the atoms from C_1, C_2 above (we used disjunction above) and let $D_1 = C_1' \wedge Q \rightarrow f()$ and $D_2 = C_2' \wedge R \rightarrow f()$. Finally $T = D_1 \wedge D_2$. Since a linear chain formed as in Q, R never subsumes any subchains and since Q, R use different predicate symbols we can show the following:

Lemma 10. *Let $T = D_1 \wedge D_2$ as defined above and let C be any clause.*
(1) $D_1 \not\preceq D_2$ and hence $D_1 \not\models D_2$. $D_2 \not\preceq D_1$ and hence $D_2 \not\models D_1$.
(2) If $T \models C$ then it is the case that either $D_1 \preceq C$ or $D_2 \preceq C$.
(3) If D is a result of dropping any object from D_1 or D_2 then $T \not\models D$.

Theorem 8. *The algorithm of [3] can make $\Omega(2^{v/4})$ queries on some targets.*

References

[1] D. Angluin. Queries and concept learning. *Machine Learning*, 2(4):319–342, April 1988.

[2] Dana Angluin. Queries revisited. In *Proceedings of the International Conference on Algorithmic Learning Theory*, volume 2225 of *Lecture Notes in Computer Science*, pages 12–31, Washington, DC, USA, November 25-28 2001. Springer.

[3] M. Arias and R. Khardon. Learning closed Horn expressions. *Information and Computation*, 178:214–240, 2002.

[4] M. Arias and R. Khardon. Complexity parameters for first-order structures. In *Proceedings of the 13th International Conference on Inductive Logic Programming*, pages 22–37. Springer-Verlag, 2003. LNAI 2835.

[5] M. Arias and R. Khardon. The subsumption lattice and query learning. Technical Report 2004-7, Department of Computer Science, Tufts University, 2004.

[6] M. Arias, R. Khardon, and R. A. Servedio. Polynomial certificates for propositional classes. In *Proceedings of the Conference on Computational Learning Theory*, pages 537–551. Springer-Verlag, 2003. LNAI 2777.

[7] Hiroki Arimura. Learning acyclic first-order Horn sentences from entailment. In *Proceedings of the International Conference on Algorithmic Learning Theory*, Sendai, Japan, 1997. Springer-Verlag. LNAI 1316.

[8] L. De Raedt and W. Van Laer. Inductive constraint logic. In *Proceedings of the 6th Conference on Algorithmic Learning Theory*, volume 997. Springer-Verlag, 1995.

[9] F. Esposito, N. Fanizzi, S. Ferilli, and G. Semeraro. Ideal theory refinement under object identity. In *Proceedings of the International Conference on Machine Learning*, pages 263–270, 2000.

[10] Sally A. Goldman and Michael Kearns. On the complexity of teaching. *Journal of Computer and System Sciences*, 50:20–31, 1995.

[11] T. Hegedus. On generalized teaching dimensions and the query complexity of learning. In *Proceedings of the Conference on Computational Learning Theory*, pages 108–117, New York, NY, USA, July 1995. ACM Press.

[12] L. Hellerstein, K. Pillaipakkamnatt, V. Raghavan, and D. Wilkins. How many queries are needed to learn? *Journal of the ACM*, 43(5):840–862, September 1996.

[13] R. Khardon. Learning function free Horn expressions. *Machine Learning*, 37:241–275, 1999.

[14] J. W. Lloyd. *Foundations of logic programming; (2nd extended ed.)*. Springer-Verlag New York, Inc., 1987.

[15] S. Nienhuys-Cheng and R. De Wolf. *Foundations of Inductive Logic Programming*. Springer-verlag, 1997. LNAI 1228.

[16] G. D. Plotkin. A note on inductive generalization. *Machine Intelligence*, 5:153–163, 1970.

[17] J. R. Quinlan. Learning logical definitions from relations. *Machine Learning*, 5:239–266, 1990.

[18] K. Rao and A. Sattar. Learning from entailment of logic programs with local variables. In *Proceedings of the International Conference on Algorithmic Learning Theory*, Otzenhausen, Germany, 1998. Springer-verlag. LNAI 1501.

[19] C. Reddy and P. Tadepalli. Learning Horn definitions with equivalence and membership queries. In *International Workshop on Inductive Logic Programming*, pages 243–255, Prague, Czech Republic, 1997. Springer. LNAI 1297.

[20] C. Reddy and P. Tadepalli. Learning first order acyclic Horn programs from entailment. In *International Conference on Inductive Logic Programming*, pages 23–37, Madison, WI, 1998. Springer. LNAI 1446.

[21] E. Y. Shapiro. *Algorithmic Program Debugging*. MIT Press, Cambridge, MA, 1983.

Learning of Ordered Tree Languages with Height-Bounded Variables Using Queries

Satoshi Matsumoto[1] and Takayoshi Shoudai[2]

[1] Department of Mathematical Sciences, Tokai University, Hiratsuka 259-1292, JAPAN.
matumoto@ss.u-tokai.ac.jp
[2] Department of Informatics, Kyushu University, Kasuga 816-8580, JAPAN
shoudai@i.kyushu-u.ac.jp

Abstract. We consider the polynomial time learnability of ordered tree patterns with internal structured variables, in the query learning model of Angluin (1988). An ordered tree pattern with internal structured variables, called a term tree, is a representation of a tree structured pattern in semistructured or tree structured data such as HTML/XML files. Standard variables in term trees can be substituted by an arbitrary tree of arbitrary height. In this paper, we introduce a new type of variables, which are called height-bounded variables. An i-height-bounded variable can be replaced with any tree of height at most i. By this type of variables, we can define tree structured patterns with rich structural features. We assume that there are at least two edge labels. We give a polynomial time algorithm for term trees with height-bounded variables using membership queries and one positive example. We also give hardness results which indicate that one positive example is necessary to learn term trees with height-bounded variables.

1 Introduction

Semistructured data such as HTML/XML files have no rigid structure but have tree structures. Such semistructured data are called tree structured data, in general. Tree structured data are represented by rooted trees t such that all children of each internal vertex of t are ordered and t has edge labels [1]. In the fields of data mining and knowledge discovery, many researchers have developed techniques based on machine learning for analyzing tree structured data, and some types of tree structured patterns have been proposed. For example, an *ordered term tree* [6,7,8,10], simply called a *term tree*, can directly represent not only associations but also structural relations between substructures common to tree structured data, because a term tree is a tree structured pattern with ordered children and structured variables which can be substituted by arbitrary trees. A variable in a term tree t has a variable label and is represented by a list $[u_0, u_1, \ldots, u_\ell]$ ($\ell \geq 1$) where u_0 is an internal vertex of t and $u_1, \ldots, u_\ell$ are consecutive children of u_0. A variable can be replaced with an arbitrary tree T so that the root of T is identified with u_0 and ℓ leaves of T are identified with

S. Ben-David, J. Case, A. Maruoka (Eds.): ALT 2004, LNAI 3244, pp. 425–439, 2004.
© Springer-Verlag Berlin Heidelberg 2004

$u_1, \ldots, u_\ell$. We say that a variable $[u_0, u_1, \ldots, u_\ell]$ is a *multi-child-port variable* if $\ell \geq 2$, a *single-child-port variable* if $\ell = 1$. For example, in Fig. 1, we give the term tree s such that T_1, T_2 and T_3 shown in Fig. 1 are obtained from s by replacing variables labeled with "x", "y" and "z" with appropriate trees.

In [11], we introduce a new kind of variables, called (i, j)-*height-constrained variables* $(1 \leq i \leq j)$, to a term tree, in order to present a tree structured pattern which can also have distance relations between substructures common to tree structured data. An (i, j)-height-constrained variable $[u_0, u_1, \ldots, u_\ell]$ can be replaced with a tree T if the following two conditions hold: (1) the minimum depth of ℓ leaves of T which are identified with $u_1, \ldots, u_\ell$ is at least i, and (2) the height of T is at most j. For example, in Fig.1, the tree T_3 can be obtained from t by replacing the (1,1)-height-constrained variable having label "$x(1,1)$", the (2,3)-height-constrained variable having label "$y(2,3)$" and the (1,2)-height-constrained variable "$z(1,2)$" of the term tree t with the trees g_1, g_2 and g_3, respectively. However, neither the trees T_1 nor T_2 given in Fig. 1 can be obtained from t. By using term trees having height-constrained variables as tree structured patterns and setting appropriate values for height-constrained variables, we can design data mining tools which can extract rare interesting substructures from tree structured data. For any $j \geq 1$, we call a (1, j)-height-constrained variable a j-*height-bounded variable*. In this paper, we consider the learnabilities of some classes of term trees having height-bounded variables.

We say that a term tree t is *linear* (or *regular*) if all variable labels in t are mutually distinct. For a set of edge labels Λ, the *term tree language* of a term tree t, denoted by $L_\Lambda(t)$, is the set of all edge-labeled trees which are obtained from t by replacing substitutable trees for all variables in t. For a linear term tree t, we say that $L_\Lambda(t)$ is a *linear term tree language* of t. Let $\mathcal{OTT}_\Lambda^{\mathcal{H}}$ be the set of all linear term trees each of whose variables is either a height-bounded multi-child-port variable or a height-bounded single-child-port variable. We denote by $\mathcal{OTT}_\Lambda^{\mathcal{H},1}$ the set of all linear term trees in $\mathcal{OTT}_\Lambda^{\mathcal{H}}$ each of whose variables is a height-bounded single-child-port variable. In this paper, we show that the classes $\mathcal{OTT}_\Lambda^{\mathcal{H},1}$ and $\mathcal{OTT}_\Lambda^{\mathcal{H}}$ are learnable in polynomial time in the exact learning model of Angluin [3]. In this model, a learning algorithm is said to *exactly identify* a target r_* if the algorithm outputs a term tree r such that $L_\Lambda(r) = L_\Lambda(r_*)$ and halts, after it uses some queries and additional information. In order to show the exact learnabilities of the classes $\mathcal{OTT}_\Lambda^{\mathcal{H},1}$ and $\mathcal{OTT}_\Lambda^{\mathcal{H}}$, we give algorithms which exactly identify any term tree in $\mathcal{OTT}_\Lambda^{\mathcal{H},1}$ and $\mathcal{OTT}_\Lambda^{\mathcal{H}}$ in polynomial time by using membership queries and one positive example.

As our previous works, in [6], we showed that any finite set of linear term trees having single-child-port variables only is exactly identifiable in polynomial time using queries. Moreover, we showed that any finite set of nonlinear term trees having single-child-port variables only is exactly identifiable in polynomial time using queries [8]. In [10,12], we showed the class of linear term tree languages is polynomial time inductively inferable from positive data for any Λ with $|\Lambda| \geq 1$. Further, we proposed a tag tree pattern, which is an extension of a term tree, as a tree structured pattern in semistructured data and gave a

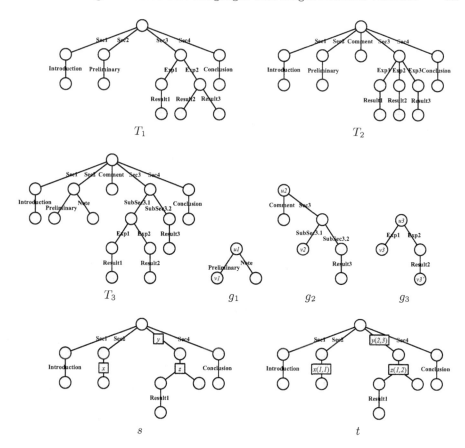

Fig. 1. Trees T_1, T_2, T_3, term trees s and t having height-constrained variables. A vertex and an edge are denoted by a circle and a line, respectively. A variable is denoted by a square connecting to all vertices in the list which represents the variable. Notations x and $x(i, j)$ in squares show that the square is a variable with a variable label x and an (i, j)-height-constrained variable with a variable label x, respectively.

data mining method from semistructured data, based on a learning algorithm for term trees [9]. In [11], we showed that a subclass of $\mathcal{OTT}_\Lambda^{\mathcal{H},1}$ is polynomial time inductively inferable from positive data for any Λ with $|\Lambda| \geq 2$. As other related works, the works [2,4] show the exact learnability of tree structured pattern in the exact learning model.

This paper is organized as follows. In Section 2 and 3, we explain term trees and our learning model. In Section 4, we show that the classes $\mathcal{OTT}_\Lambda^{\mathcal{H},1}$ and $\mathcal{OTT}_\Lambda^{\mathcal{H}}$ are exactly learnable in polynomial time using membership queries and one positive example. In Section 5, we give hardness results which indicate that one positive example is necessary to identify a target term tree.

2   Preliminaries

Let $T = (V_T, E_T)$ be an ordered tree with a vertex set V_T and an edge set E_T. A list $h = [u_0, u_1, \ldots, u_\ell]$ of vertices in V_T is called a *variable* of T if $u_1, \ldots, u_\ell$ are consecutive children of u_0, i.e., u_0 is the parent of $u_1, \ldots, u_\ell$ and u_{j+1} is the next sibling of u_j for any j with $1 \leq j < \ell$. We call u_0 the *parent port* of the variable h and $u_1, \ldots, u_\ell$ the *child ports* of h. Two variables $h = [u_0, u_1, \ldots, u_\ell]$ and $h' = [u'_0, u'_1, \ldots, u'_{\ell'}]$ are said to be *disjoint* if $\{u_1, \ldots, u_\ell\} \cap \{u'_1, \ldots, u'_{\ell'}\} = \emptyset$. For a set or a list S, we denote by $|S|$ the number of elements in S.

Definition 1 (Ordered term trees). Let $T = (V_T, E_T)$ be an ordered tree and H_T a set of pairwise disjoint variables of T. An *ordered term tree obtained from T and H_T* is a triplet $t = (V_t, E_t, H_t)$, where $V_t = V_T$, $E_t = E_T - \bigcup_{[u_0, u_1, \ldots, u_\ell] \in H_T} \{\{u_0, u_i\} \in E_T \mid 1 \leq i \leq \ell\}$ and $H_t = H_T$. For two vertices $u, u' \in V_t$, we say that u is the *parent* of u' in t if u is the parent of u' in T. Similarly we say that u' is a *child* of u in t if u' is a child of u in T. In particular, for a vertex $u \in V_t$ with no child, we call u a *leaf* of t.

We define the order of the children of each vertex u in t as the order of the children of u in T. We often omit the description of the ordered tree T and variable set H_T because we can find them from the triplet $t = (V_t, E_t, H_t)$. We denote by $|t|$ the number of vertices in t.

For any ordered term tree t, a vertex u of t, and two children u' and u'' of u, we write $u' <^t_u u''$ if u' is smaller than u'' in the order of the children of u. We assume that every edge and variable of an ordered term tree is labeled with some words from specified languages. A label of a variable is called a *variable label*. Λ and X denote a set of edge labels and a set of variable labels, respectively, where $\Lambda \cap X = \phi$. An ordered term tree $t = (V_t, E_t, H_t)$ is called *linear* (or *regular*) if all variables in H_t have mutually distinct variable labels in X.

Note. In this paper, we treat only linear ordered term trees, and then we call a linear ordered term tree a *term tree*, simply. In particular, an ordered term tree with no variable is called a *ground term tree* or *tree* and considered to be a tree with ordered children.

For a term tree t and its vertices v_1 and v_i, a *path* from v_1 to v_i is a sequence $v_1, v_2, \ldots, v_i$ of distinct vertices of t such that for any j with $1 \leq j < i$, v_j is the parent of v_{j+1}. The *height* of a term tree g is the length of the longest path from the root to a leaf, and the height of a vertex v of g is the length of the longest path from v to a leaf.

In this paper, we deal with height-bounded variables only, which is a restricted height-constrained variable. Therefore here we give only the definition of height-bounded variables. The general definition of height-constrained variables are given in [11].

Definition 2 (Height-bounded variables). Let $X^{\mathcal{H}}$ be an infinite subset of a variable label set X. For an integer $i \geq 1$, let $X^{\mathcal{H}(i)}$ be an infinite subset of $X^{\mathcal{H}}$. We assume that $X^{\mathcal{H}} = \bigcup_{i \geq 1} X^{\mathcal{H}(i)}$ and $X^{\mathcal{H}(i)} \cap X^{\mathcal{H}(i')} = \emptyset$ for $i \neq i'$. A variable label in $X^{\mathcal{H}}$ is called a *height-bounded variable label*. In particular, a variable label in $X^{\mathcal{H}(i)}$ is called an *i-height-bounded variable label*. For a variable e, we denote by $e^{(i)}$ a variable with an i-height-bounded variable label, and call it an *i-height-bounded variable*. For an i-height-bounded variable e, we say that the value i is the *size* of the variable e, and denote it by $size(e)$.

Let $f = (V_f, E_f, H_f)$ and $g = (V_g, E_g, H_g)$ be term trees. We say that f and g are *isomorphic*, denoted by $f \equiv g$, if there is a bijection φ from V_f to V_g such that (i) the root of f is mapped to the root of g by φ, (ii) $\{u, v\} \in E_f$ if and only if $\{\varphi(u), \varphi(v)\} \in E_g$, $\{u, v\}$ and $\{\varphi(u), \varphi(v)\}$ have the same edge labels, (iii) for $i \geq 1$, $[u_0, u_1, \ldots, u_\ell]^{(i)} \in H_f$ if and only if $[\varphi(u_0), \varphi(u_1), \ldots, \varphi(u_\ell)]^{(i)} \in H_g$, and (iv) for any internal vertex u in f which has more than one child, and for any two children u' and u'' of u, $u' <_u^f u''$ if and only if $\varphi(u') <_{\varphi(u)}^g \varphi(u'')$.

Definition 3 (Substitutions). Let f be a term tree with at least $\ell+1$ vertices, x a variable label in $X^{\mathcal{H}(i)}$ for $i \geq 1$, and g a tree with at least $\ell + 1$ vertices. Let $h = [v_0, v_1, \ldots, v_\ell]$ be a variable in f with the variable label x and $\sigma = [u_0, u_1, \ldots, u_\ell]$ a list of $\ell + 1$ distinct vertices in g, where u_0 is the root of g and $u_1, \ldots, u_\ell$ are leaves of g. The form $x := [g, \sigma]$ is called a *binding* for x if the height of g is at most i.

A new term tree $f' = f\{x := [g, \sigma]\}$ is obtained by applying the binding $x := [g, \sigma]$ to f in the following way. Let $e = [v_0, v_1, \ldots, v_\ell]^{(i)}$ be an i-height-bounded variable in f with the variable label x. Let g' be one copy of g and $w_0, w_1, \ldots, w_\ell$ the vertices of g' corresponding to $u_0, u_1, \ldots, u_\ell$ of g, respectively. For the variable $e = [v_0, v_1, \ldots, v_\ell]^{(i)}$, we attach g' to f by removing the variable e from H_f and by identifying the vertices $v_0, v_1, \ldots, v_\ell$ with the vertices $w_0, w_1, \ldots, w_\ell$ of g', respectively. We define a new ordering $<_v^{f'}$ on every vertex v in f' in the following natural way. Suppose that v has more than one child and let v' and v'' be two children of v in f'. We note that $v_i = u_i$ for any $0 \leq i \leq \ell$. (1) If $v, v', v'' \in V_g$ and $v' <_v^g v''$, then $v' <_v^{f'} v''$. (2) If $v, v', v'' \in V_f$ and $v' <_v^f v''$, then $v' <_v^{f'} v''$. (3) If $v = v_0(= u_0)$, $v' \in V_f - \{v_1, \ldots, v_\ell\}$, $v'' \in V_g$, and $v' <_v^f v_1$, then $v' <_v^{f'} v''$. (4) If $v = v_0(= u_0)$, $v' \in V_f - \{v_1, \ldots, v_\ell\}$, $v'' \in V_g$, and $v_\ell <_v^f v'$, then $v'' <_v^{f'} v'$. A *substitution* θ is a finite collection of bindings $\{x_1 := [g_1, \sigma_1], \cdots, x_n := [g_n, \sigma_n]\}$, where x_i's are mutually distinct variable labels in $X^{\mathcal{H}}$ and g_i's are trees. The term tree $f\theta$, called the *instance* of f by θ, is obtained by applying the all bindings $x_i := [g_i, \sigma_i]$ on f simultaneously. The root of the resulting term tree $f\theta$ is the root of f.

For example, let T_4 be a term tree and $\theta = \{x_1 := [T_5, [u_1, w_1]], x_2 := [T_6, [u_2, w_2]], x_3 := [T_7, [u_3, w_3, w_4]]\}$ a substitution, where T_5, T_6 and T_7 are trees in Fig. 2. Then, the instance $t'\theta$ of the term tree t' by θ is the tree T_4.

We write $f \preceq g$ if there exists a substitution θ with $f \equiv g\theta$. If $f \preceq g$ and $f \not\equiv g$, then we write $f \prec g$. We define the *size* of the term tree t as the sum of the number of vertices and the size of variables in t, and denote it by $size(t)$. More precisely, for a term tree $t = (V_t, E_t, H_t)$,

$$size(t) = |V_t| + \sum_{i \geq 1} i \times |\{e \in H_t \mid e \text{ is an } i\text{-height-bounded variable}\}|.$$

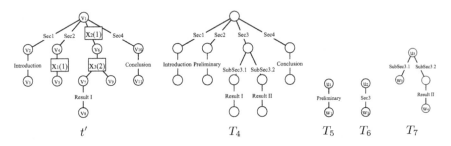

Fig. 2. A square with a notation $x(i)$ shows that the square is an i-height-bounded variable with a variable label x.

By the definition, it is clear that $|t| \leq size(t)$ for any term tree in which all variable have height-bounded variable labels.

We denote by $\mathcal{OT}_\Lambda$ the set of all trees. We define $\mathcal{OTT}_\Lambda^{\mathcal{H}}$ as the set of all term trees in which all variables have height-bounded variable labels. The *term tree language* $L_\Lambda(t)$ of a term tree $t \in \mathcal{OTT}_\Lambda^{\mathcal{H}}$ is $\{s \in \mathcal{OT}_\Lambda \mid s \preceq t\}$. In particular, we denote by $\mathcal{OTT}_\Lambda^{\mathcal{H},1}$ the set of term trees in $\mathcal{OTT}_\Lambda^{\mathcal{H}}$ of which all variable have one child port. When it is clear from the context, the notation $\mathcal{OTT}_\Lambda^{\mathcal{H}}$ (resp. $\mathcal{OTT}_\Lambda^{\mathcal{H},1}$) is abused to stand for the class of languages $\{L_\Lambda(r) \mid r \in \mathcal{OTT}_\Lambda^{\mathcal{H}}\}$ (resp. $\{L_\Lambda(r) \mid r \in \mathcal{OTT}_\Lambda^{\mathcal{H},1}\}$).

3   Learning Model

Let Λ be a set of edge labels and $\mathcal{TT}_\Lambda$ a class of term trees. In this paper, let r_* be a term tree in $\mathcal{TT}_\Lambda$ to be identified, and we say that the term tree r_* is a *target*. A term tree r is called a *positive example* of $L_\Lambda(r_*)$ if r is in $L_\Lambda(r_*)$. We introduce the exact learning model via queries due to Angluin [3]. In this model, learning algorithms can access to *oracles* that answer specific kinds of queries about the unknown term tree language $L_\Lambda(r_*)$. We consider the following oracles.

1. *Membership oracle* Mem_{r_*}: The input is a tree r. The output is "*yes*" if r is in $L_\Lambda(r_*)$, and "*no*" otherwise. The query is called a *membership query*.
2. *Subset oracle* Sub_{r_*}: The input is a term tree r in $\mathcal{TT}_\Lambda$. The output is *yes* if $L_\Lambda(r) \subseteq L_\Lambda(r_*)$. Otherwise, it returns a *counterexample* $t' \in L_\Lambda(r) - L_\Lambda(r_*)$. The query is called a *subset query*.
3. *Equivalence oracle* Equiv_{r_*}: The input is a term tree r in $\mathcal{TT}_\Lambda$. If $L_\Lambda(r) = L_\Lambda(r_*)$, then the output is *yes*. Otherwise, it returns a *counterexample* $t \in L_\Lambda(r) \cup L_\Lambda(r_*) - L_\Lambda(r) \cap L_\Lambda(r_*)$. The query is called an *equivalence query*.

A learning algorithm $\mathcal{A}$ may collect information $L_\Lambda(r_*)$ by using queries and outputs a term tree in $\mathcal{TT}_\Lambda$. We say that a learning algorithm *exactly identifies* a target r_* if it outputs a term tree r in $\mathcal{TT}_\Lambda$ with $L_\Lambda(r) = L_\Lambda(r_*)$ and halts after it uses some queries and additional information. We consider the above three oracles for $\mathcal{OTT}_\Lambda^{\mathcal{H},1}$ and $\mathcal{OTT}_\Lambda^{\mathcal{H}}$.

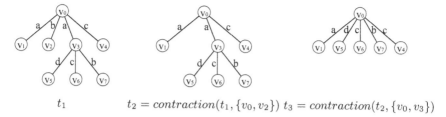

t_1 $t_2 = contraction(t_1, \{v_0, v_2\})$ $t_3 = contraction(t_2, \{v_0, v_3\})$

Fig. 3. A term tree t_2 is obtained by the contraction of the edge $\{v_0, v_2\}$ from t_1. Moreover, t_3 is obtained by the contraction of the edge $\{v_0, v_3\}$ from t_2.

4 Learning Using Membership Queries

In this section, we show that any ordered term tree in $\mathcal{OTT}_\Lambda^{\mathcal{H}}$ is exactly identifiable using membership queries and one positive example. In this section, we assume that $|\Lambda| \geq 2$.

Let $t = (V_t, E_t, H_t)$ be a tree and $e = \{u, v\}$ an edge in E_t. We define the *contraction* of e to t as the following operation: If v has children $v_1, \ldots, v_\ell$, then the operation removes v from V_t and replaces $\{u, v\}, \{v, v_1\}, \ldots, \{v, v_\ell\}$ in E_t with new edges $\{u, v_1\}, \ldots, \{u, v_\ell\}$, that is, $E_t = E_t \cup \{\{u, v_1\}, \ldots, \{u, v_\ell\}\} - \{\{u, v\}, \{v, v_1\}, \ldots, \{v, v_\ell\}\}$. Otherwise, the operation removes v from V_t and e from E_t. We denote by $contraction(t, e)$ the tree obtained from t by applying the contraction of e to t.

We use contractions to t to decrease the number of vertices in t. For example, in Fig. 3, t_2 is the tree obtained by the contraction of the edge $\{v_0, v_2\}$ from t_1, and t_3 is obtained by the contraction of the edge $\{v_0, v_3\}$ from t_2.

Lemma 1. *Let t be a term tree in $\mathcal{OTT}_\Lambda^{\mathcal{H}}$ and $t' = (V_{t'}, E_{t'}, H_{t'})$ a tree such that $t' \in L_\Lambda(t)$. If $contraction(t', e) \notin L_\Lambda(t)$ for any $e \in E_{t'}$, then $|t| = |t'|$.*

Let $t = (V_t, E_t, H_t)$ be a term tree in $\mathcal{OTT}_\Lambda^{\mathcal{H},1}$ and $e = [u, v]$ a variable in H_t. We define the *extension* of e to t as the following operation: The operation replaces the variable e with variables $[u, w], [w, v]$, that is, $V_t = V_t \cup \{w\}$ and $H_t = H_t \cup \{[u, w], [w, v]\} - \{[u, v]\}$. The variables are new 1-height-bounded variables. We denote by $extension(t, e)$ the term tree obtained from t by applying the extension of e to t.

Let $t = (V_t, E_t, H_t)$ be a term tree. We call t a *chain term tree* if $V_t = \{v_0, v_1, \ldots, v_k\}$, $E_t = \emptyset$, $H_t = \{[v_0, v_1], \ldots, [v_{k-1}, v_k]\}$ ($k \geq 1$), and v_0 is the root of t. Moreover, we call t a *chain tree* or *k-chain tree* if $V_t = \{v_0, v_1, \ldots, v_k\}$, $E_t = \{\{v_0, v_1\}, \ldots, \{v_{k-1}, v_k\}\}$ ($k \geq 1$), $H_t = \emptyset$, and v_0 is the root of t. For a k-chain tree $t = (V_t, E_t, H_t)$ and each vertex $v_i \in V_t$ ($0 \leq i \leq k - 1$), we attach a $(k-i)$-chain tree to both sides of v_i respectively, and call such a tree a *k-triangle tree*. For example, in Fig. 4, t_4 is a 3-chain tree and t_5 is a 3-triangle tree.

Let $t = (V_t, E_t, H_t)$ be a term tree in $\mathcal{OTT}_\Lambda^{\mathcal{H},1}$. Let $S = [u_\ell, u_{\ell-1}, \ldots, u_0]$ ($\ell \geq 1$) be a sequence of vertices in t such that $[u_i, u_{i+1}] \in H_t$ ($i = 0, \ldots, \ell - 1$)

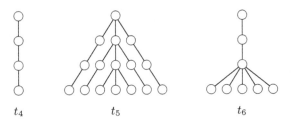

Fig. 4. t_4 is a 3-chain tree, t_5 is a 3-triangle tree and t_6 is a (3,5)-broom tree.

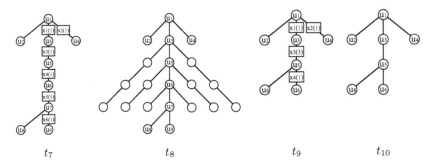

Fig. 5. For $S = [u_7, u_6, u_5, u_3]$, $t_8 = triangle(t_7, S)$, $t_9 = replace(t_7, S)$ and $t_{10} = tree(t_9)$.

and each vertex u_i $(1 \le i \le \ell-1)$ has only one child. We denote by $triangle(t, S)$ a tree obtained from t by replacing variables which consist of vertices in S with an ℓ-triangle tree, and other variables with edges. Moreover, we denote by $replace(t, S)$ (resp. $tree(t)$) a term tree (resp. a tree) obtained from t by replacing variables which consist of vertices in S (resp. each variable in t) with an $|S|$-height-bounded variable (resp. an edge). For example, in Fig. 5, for $S = [u_7, u_6, u_5, u_3]$, we have $t_8 = triangle(t_7, S)$, $t_9 = replace(t_7, S)$ and $t_{10} = tree(t_9)$.

Theorem 1. *The algorithm LEARN_OTT1 of Fig. 8 exactly identifies any term tree $r_* \in \mathcal{OTT}_\Lambda^{\mathcal{H},1}$ in polynomial time using at most $O(n^2)$ membership queries and one positive example t, where $|\Lambda| \ge 2$ and $n = \max\{|t|, size(r_*)\}$.*

Proof. (Sketch) By Lemma 1, we can get a tree t such that $|t| = |r_*|$ by using the procedure *Edge_Contraction* in Fig. 6. In the procedure *Variable_Extension* of Fig. 6, we can get a term tree which is isomorphic to a term tree obtained from r_* by replacing each variable with the longest substitutable chain term tree, which consists of 1-height-bounded variables only.

Let $e_1^{r_*}, e_2^{r_*}, \ldots, e_i^{r_*}, \ldots$ be the sequence of variables in r_* by post-order traversal. For the term tree r outputted by the algorithm *LEARN_OTT1*, let $e_1^r, e_2^r, \ldots, e_i^r, \ldots$ be the sequence of variables in r by post-order traversal. We assume that

Procedure *Edge_Contraction(t)*;
Given: The oracle Mem_{r_*} for a target $r_* \in \mathcal{OTT}_\Lambda^{\mathcal{H},1}$ and one positive example t;
begin
   repeat
     foreach edge e in t **do begin**
       Let $t' := contraction(t, e)$;
       if $Mem_{r_*}(t') = yes$ **then begin** $t := t'$; **break**; **end**;
     end;
   until t does not change;
   return t;
end.

Procedure *Variable_Extension(t)*;
Given: The oracle Mem_{r_*} for a target $r_* \in \mathcal{OTT}_\Lambda^{\mathcal{H},1}$
       and a tree $t \in L_\Lambda(r_*)$ with $|t| = |r_*|$;
begin
   $s := t$;
   foreach edge e_s in s **do begin**
     Let s' be a term tree obtained from s by replacing the edge label
       with another edge label;
     if $Mem_{r_*}(s') = yes$ **then begin**
       Replace the edge e_t in t corresponding to e_s
         with a new 1-height-bounded variable;
     end;
   end;
   repeat
     foreach variable e in t **do begin**
       $t' := extension(t, e)$;
       $t'' := tree(t')$;
       if $Mem_{r_*}(t'') = yes$ **then begin** $t := t'$; **break**; **end**;
     end;
   until t does not change;
   return t;
end.

Fig. 6. Procedure *Edge_Contraction* and **Procedure** *Variable_Extension*

there exists a positive integer i such that $size(e_i^{r_*}) \neq size(e_i^r)$. Let k be the minimum integer satisfying the above condition, ℓ_* the size of $e_k^{r_*}$ and ℓ the size of e_k^r. We assume $\ell < \ell_*$. Let r' be a term tree obtained from r by replacing each variable e_j^r with a chain term tree which consists of α 1-height-bounded variables for any $j \geq k$, and $[w_0, w_1], \ldots, [w_{\ell-1}, w_\ell]$ variables in r' with which e_k^r is replaced, where $\alpha = size(e_j^r)$. Let u_0 be the parent of w_0 and $S = [w_\ell, w_{\ell-1}, \ldots, w_0, u_0]$. In the repeat-loop of the procedure *Variable_Replacing* in Fig. 7, for a tree $triangle(r', S)$, the membership oracle outputs "no". But, $triangle(r', S)$ is in

Procedure *Variable_Replacing*(t);

Given: The oracle Mem_{r_*} for a target $r_* \in \mathcal{OTT}_\Lambda^{\mathcal{H},1}$ and a term tree t obtained from r_*
  by replacing each variable with the longest substitutable chain tree which
  consists of 1-height-bounded variables;

begin
  Let $V = [v_1, v_2, \ldots, v_\ell]$ be the sequence of vertices in t by post-order traversal;
  $r := t$;
  while $V \neq [v_\ell]$ **do begin**
    Let u be the first element in V;
    $S := [u]$;
    repeat
      Let v be the parent of u;
      if $[v, u] \in H_t$ **then begin** $S := S + [v]$; **end**
      else begin break; end;
      $t' := triangle(t, S)$;
      if $Mem_{r_*}(t') = yes$ **then begin** $u := v$; **end**
      else begin $S := S - [v]$; **break; end**;
    until u has more than one child;
    if u has more than one child **and** $|S| \geq 2$ **then begin**
      Let R be the sequence of vertices in r corresponding to S;
      Let u_r be the vertex in r corresponding to u;
      $r' := tree(replace(r, R))$;
      if $Mem_{r_*}(r') = yes$ **then begin**
        $r := replace(r, R)$;
      end else begin
        $R := R - [u_r]$; $r := replace(r, R)$; $S := S - [u]$;
      end;
      Let w be the vertex which is added in S at last;
      Remove vertices in $S - [w]$ from V;
    end else if $|S| \geq 2$ **then begin**
      Let R be the sequence of vertices in r corresponding to S;
      $r := replace(r, R)$;
      Let w be the vertex which is added in S at last;
      Remove vertices in $S - [w]$ from V;
    end else if $|S| = 1$ **then begin**
      Remove the vertex u from V;
    end;
  end;
  return r;
end.

Fig. 7. Procedure *Variable_Replacing*

$L_\Lambda(r_*)$. This is a contradiction. For $\ell > \ell_*$, we can show in a similar way. For any $i \geq 1$, $size(e_i^{r_*}) = size(e_i^r)$. Thus, the algorithm outputs a term tree r with $r_* \equiv r$.

Algorithm *LEARN_OTT1*
Given: The oracle Mem_{r_*} for a target $r_* \in \mathcal{OTT}_\Lambda^{\mathcal{H},1}$ and one positive example t;
Output: A term tree $r \in \mathcal{OTT}_\Lambda^{\mathcal{H},1}$ with $r \equiv r_*$;
begin
   $t := Edge\_Contraction(t)$;
   $t := Variable\_Extension(t)$;
   $r := Variable\_Replacing(t)$;
   output r;
end.

Fig. 8. Algorithm *LEARN_OTT1*

Let t be a given positive example. The procedure *Edge_Contraction* uses at most $O(|t|^2)$ membership queries. In the procedure *Variable_Extension*, the first foreach-loop uses at most $O(|r_*|)$ membership queries, and the repeat-loop uses at most $O(size(r_*)^2)$ membership queries. The procedure *Variable_Replacing* uses at most $O(size(r_*))$ membership queries. Thus, the algorithm uses at most $O(n^2)$ membership queries in total, where $n = \max\{|t|, size(r_*)\}$.   □

Next, we show that any term tree in $\mathcal{OTT}_\Lambda^{\mathcal{H}}$ is exactly identifiable using membership queries and one positive example.

Let $t = (V_t, E_t, H_t)$ be a term tree in $\mathcal{OTT}_\Lambda^{\mathcal{H}}$ and $e = [v_0, v_1, \ldots, v_\ell]$ ($\ell \geq 2$) a variable in H_t. We define the replacement of e to t as the following operation: The operation replaces the variable e with variables $[v_0, v_1], \ldots, [v_0, v_\ell]$, that is, $H_t = H_t \cup \{[v_0, v_1], \ldots, [v_0, v_\ell]\} - \{e\}$. If e has an i-height-bounded variable label, then each variable $[v_0, v_j]$ ($j = 1, \ldots, \ell$) has an i-height-bounded variable label. We denote by $varRep(t, e)$ the term tree obtained from t by applying the replacement of e to t.

Lemma 2. *Let $t = (V_t, E_t, H_t)$ be a term tree in $\mathcal{OTT}_\Lambda^{\mathcal{H}}$ and e a 1-height-bounded variable in H_t which has k child ports, where $k \geq 2$. Then, $L_\Lambda(t) = L_\Lambda(varRep(t, e))$.*

Let k and ℓ be positive integers. We say that a term tree t is a (k, ℓ)-*broom tree* if $V_t = \{u_0, \ldots, u_{k-1}, v_1, \ldots, v_\ell\}$, $E_t = \{\{u_0, u_1\}, \ldots, \{u_{k-2}, u_{k-1}\}, \{u_{k-1}, v_1\}, \{u_{k-1}, v_\ell\}\}$ and $H_t = \emptyset$. For example, in Fig. 4, a tree t_6 is a $(3, 5)$-broom tree.

Theorem 2. *The algorithm LEARN_OTT of Fig. 9 exactly identifies any term tree $r_* \in \mathcal{OTT}_\Lambda^{\mathcal{H}}$ in polynomial time using at most $O(n^2)$ membership queries and one positive example t, where $|\Lambda| \geq 2$ and $n = \max\{|t|, size(r_*)\}$.*

Proof. (Sketch) By Lemma 2, we pay no attention to variables of which the sizes are 1. Let $e_1^{r_*}, e_2^{r_*}, \ldots, e_i^{r_*}, \ldots$ be the sequence of variables of which the size are more than 1 in r_* by breath-first search order. For the term tree r outputted by the algorithm *LEARN_OTT*, let $e_1^r, e_2^r, \ldots, e_i^r, \ldots$ be the sequence of variables

Algorithm *LEARN_OTT*

Given: The oracle Mem_{r_*} for a target $r_* \in \mathcal{OTT}_\Lambda^\mathcal{H}$ and one positive example t;

Output: A term tree $r \in \mathcal{OTT}_\Lambda^\mathcal{H}$ with $L_\Lambda(r) = L_\Lambda(r_*)$;

begin

    $s = (V_s, E_s, H_s) := LEARN\_OTT1(t)$;

    $r := s$;

    flag:=false;

    Let $E = [v_1, \ldots, v_\ell]$ be the sequence of vertices in s

      by breath-first search order except the root;

    $i := 1$;

    while E is not empty **do begin**

      $S := [v_i]$;

      repeat

        Let u_i be the parent of v_i and u_{i+1} the parent of v_{i+1};

        if $[u_i, v_i] \notin H_s$ or $[u_{i+1}, v_{i+1}] \notin H_s$ **then begin break; end**;

        $e_i := [u_i, v_i]$;

        $e_{i+1} := [u_{i+1}, v_{i+1}]$;

        if v_{i+1} is the next sibling of v_i and $size(e_i) = size(e_{i+1}) > 1$ **then begin**

          $S := S + [v_{i+1}]$;

          $m := size(e_i)$;

          Let r' be a tree obtained from r by replacing variables

            which consist of vertices in S with an $(m, |S|)$-broom tree,

            and other variables with the substitutable longest chain trees;

          if $Mem_{r_*}(r') = yes$ **then begin**

            flag:=false;

            $i := i + 1$;

          end else begin

            flag:=true; $S := S - [v_{i+1}]$;

          end;

        end else flag:=true;

      until flag;

      if $|S| = 1$ **then begin** Remove vertices in S from E; **end**

      else begin

        Let R be the sequence of vertices in r which corresponds to vertices in $S + [u_i]$;

        Replace variables which consist of vertices in R

          with a variable which has $|R| - 1$ child ports;

        The variable has m-height-bounded variable label;

        Remove the vertices in S from E;

      end

      $i := i + 1$;

    end;

    output r;

end.

Fig. 9. Algorithm *LEARN_OTT*

of which the size are more than 1 in r by breath-first search order. We assume that there exists a positive integer i such that the number of child ports of $e_i^{r_*}$

is different from the number of child ports of e_i^r. Let k be the minimum integer satisfying the above condition, n_* the number of child ports of $e_k^{r_*}$ and n the number of child ports of e_k^r. Let $e_k^r = [w_0, w_1, \ldots, w_n]$ and w_{n+1} the next sibling of w_n, where w_0 is the parent port of e_k^r and $w_1, \ldots, w_n$ are the child ports of e_k^r. We assume $n < n_*$. Let r' be the term tree obtained from r by replacing each variable e_j^r ($j \geq k$) with α_j variables having one child port and an ℓ_j-height-bounded variable label and $S = [w_1, \ldots, w_n, w_{n+1}]$, where α_j is the number of child ports of e_j^r and ℓ_j is the size of e_j^r. In the repeat-loop of the algorithm *LEARN_OTT*, let r'' be a tree obtained from r' by replacing variables which consist of vertices in S with an $(m, |S|)$-broom tree, and other variables having β (≥ 1) child ports with β substitutable longest chain trees, where m is the size of e_k^r. For a tree t'', the membership oracle outputs "no". But, the tree r'' is in $L_\Lambda(r_*)$. This is a contradiction. For $n > n_*$, we can show in a similar way. For any $i \geq 1$, the numbers of child ports of $e_i^{r_*}$ and e_i^r are the same. Thus, the algorithm outputs a term tree r with $L_\Lambda(r_*) = L_\Lambda(r)$.

Let t be a given positive example. By Theorem 1, the algorithm *LEARN_OTT1* uses at most $O(n^2)$ membership queries, where $n = \max\{|t|, size(r_*)\}$. In the algorithm *LEARN_OTT*, the while-loop uses at most $O(size(r_*))$ membership queries. Therefore, the algorithm uses at most $O(n^2)$ membership queries in total. $\qquad\square$

5   Hardness Results on the Learnability

In this section, we show the insufficiency of learning of $\mathcal{OTT}_\Lambda^{\mathcal{H},1}$ and $\mathcal{OTT}_\Lambda^{\mathcal{H}}$ in the exact learning model. We uses the following lemma to show the insufficiency of learning of $\mathcal{OTT}_\Lambda^{\mathcal{H},1}$ and $\mathcal{OTT}_\Lambda^{\mathcal{H}}$.

Lemma 3. *(László Lovász [5]) Let W_n be the number of all rooted unordered unlabeled trees which have exactly n vertices. Then, $2^n < W_n < 4^n$, where $n \geq 6$.*

From this lemma, if $|\Lambda| \geq 1$, then the number of unordered trees which have exactly n vertices is greater than 2^n. Thus, the number of ordered trees which have exactly n vertices is greater than 2^n. The following lemma is known to show the insufficiency of learning in the exact learning model.

Lemma 4. *(Angluin [3]) Suppose the hypothesis space contains a class of distinct sets $L_1, \ldots, L_N$, and there exists a set $L_\cap$ which is not a hypothesis, such that for any pair of distinct indices i and j, $L_\cap = L_i \cap L_j$. Then any algorithm that exactly identifies each of the hypotheses L_i using equivalence, membership, and subset queries must at least $N - 1$ queries in the worst case.*

By Lemma 3 and 4, we have Theorem 3 and 4.

Theorem 3. *Any learning algorithm that exactly identifies all term trees which have exactly n vertices in $\mathcal{OTT}_\Lambda^{\mathcal{H},1}$ using equivalence, membership and subset queries must make greater than 2^n queries in the worst case, where $|\Lambda| \geq 1$ and $n \geq 6$.*

Table 1. Our results and future works

	Exact Learning		Inductive Inference from positive data
$\mathcal{OTT}_\Lambda$	Yes [7] membership & a positive example $|\Lambda| \geq 2$		Yes [10,12] polynomial time $|\Lambda| \geq 1$
$\mathcal{OTF}_\Lambda$	Yes [6] restricted subset & equivalence $|\Lambda|$ is infinite		Open
$\mathcal{OTT}_\Lambda^{\mathcal{H},1}$	sufficiency [This work] membership & one positive example $|\Lambda| \geq 2$	insufficiency [This work] membership equivalence subset $|\Lambda| \geq 1$	A subclass of $\mathcal{OTT}_\Lambda^{\mathcal{H},1}$ Yes [11] polynomial time $|\Lambda| \geq 2$
$\mathcal{OTT}_\Lambda^{\mathcal{H}}$	sufficiency [This work] membership & one positive example $|\Lambda| \geq 2$	insufficiency [This work] membership equivalence subset $|\Lambda| \geq 1$	Open
$\mathcal{OTF}_\Lambda^{\mathcal{H}}$	Open		Open

Proof. For a tree r, we have $L_\Lambda(r) = \{r\}$. We denote by $\mathcal{S}_n$ the class of singleton sets of a tree in $\mathcal{OTT}_\Lambda^{\mathcal{H},1}$ which has exactly n vertices. The class $\mathcal{S}_n$ is a subclass of $\mathcal{OTT}_\Lambda^{\mathcal{H},1}$. For any L and L' in $\mathcal{S}_n$, $L \cap L' = \phi$. The empty set is not a term tree language. Thus, by Lemma 3 and 4, any learning algorithm that exactly identifies all the term trees in $\mathcal{OTT}_\Lambda^{\mathcal{H},1}$ which have exactly n vertices using equivalence, membership and subset queries must make $\Omega(2^n)$ queries in the worst case, where $|\Lambda| = 1$ and $n \geq 6$. □

Since we can prove Theorem 4 in a similar way to Theorem 3, we omit it.

Theorem 4. *Any learning algorithm that exactly identifies all term trees in $\mathcal{OTT}_\Lambda^{\mathcal{H}}$ which have exactly n vertices using equivalence, membership and subset queries must make greater than 2^n queries in the worst case, where $|\Lambda| \geq 1$ and $n \geq 6$.*

6   Conclusions

We have discussed the learnabilities of $\mathcal{OTT}_\Lambda^{\mathcal{H},1}$ and $\mathcal{OTT}_\Lambda^{\mathcal{H}}$ in the exact learning model. In Section 4, we have shown that any term tree r_* in $\mathcal{OTT}_\Lambda^{\mathcal{H},1}$ and $\mathcal{OTT}_\Lambda^{\mathcal{H}}$ is exactly identifiable using at most $O(n^2)$ membership queries and one positive example t, where $|\Lambda| \geq 2$ and $n = \max\{|t|, size(r_*)\}$. In Section 5, we have shown the insufficiency of learning of $\mathcal{OTT}_\Lambda^{\mathcal{H},1}$ and $\mathcal{OTT}_\Lambda^{\mathcal{H}}$ in the exact learning model.

As future works, we will study the learnability of finite unions of term trees with i-height-bounded variables for any $i \geq 1$, denoted by $\mathcal{OTF}_\Lambda^\mathcal{H}$, in the exact learning model. We can define width-constrained variables in a similar way to height-constrained variables. We will also study a tree structured pattern which can give precious knowledge to us, by combining constraints of *height* and *width* of trees. We summarize our results and future works in Table 1. We denote by $\mathcal{OTT}_\Lambda$ the set of all term trees in which no variable has a height-bounded variable label, by $\mathcal{OTF}_\Lambda$ the class of all finite sets of term trees in which no variable has a height-bounded variable label.

References

[1] S. Abiteboul, P. Buneman, and D. Suciu. *Data on the Web: From Relations to Semistructured Data and XML*. Morgan Kaufmann, 2000.

[2] T. R. Amoth, P. Cull, and P. Tadepalli. On exact learning of unordered tree patterns. *Machine Learning*, 44:211–243, 2001.

[3] D. Angluin. Queries and concept learning. *Machine Learning*, 2:319–342, 1988.

[4] H. Arimura, H. Sakamoto, and S. Arikawa. Efficient learning of semi-structured data from queries. *Proc. ALT-2001, Springer-Verlag, LNAI 2225*, pages 315–331, 2001.

[5] L. Lovász. *Combinatorial Problems and Exercises*, chapter Two classical enumeration problems in graph theory. North-Holland Publishing Company, 1979.

[6] S. Matsumoto, T. Shoudai, T. Miyahara, and T. Uchida. Learning of finite unions of tree patterns with internal structured variables from queries. In *Proc. AI-2002, Springer LNAI 2557*, pages 523–534, 2002.

[7] S. Matsumoto, T. Shoudai, T. Miyahara, and T. Uchida. Learning unions of term tree languages using queries. In *Proceedings of LA Summer Symposium, July 2002*, pages 21-1 – 21-10, 2002.

[8] S. Matsumoto, Y. Suzuki, T. Shoudai, T. Miyahara, and U. Tomoyuki. Learning of finite unions of tree patterns with repeated internal structured variables from queries. In *Proc. ALT-2003, Springer-Verlag, LNAI 2842*, pages 144–158, 2003.

[9] T. Miyahara, Y. Suzuki, T. Shoudai, T. Uchida, K. Takahashi, and H. Ueda. Discovery of frequent tag tree patterns in semistructured web documents. In *Proc. PAKDD-2002, Springer-Verlag, LNAI 2336*, pages 341–355, 2002.

[10] Y. Suzuki, R. Akanuma, T. Shoudai, T. Miyahara, and T. Uchida. Polynomial time inductive inference of ordered tree patterns with internal structured variables from positive data. In *Proc. COLT-2002, Springer-Verlag, LNAI 2375*, pages 169–184, 2002.

[11] Y. Suzuki, T. Shoudai, S. Matsumoto, and T. Miyahara. Polynomial time inductive inference of ordered tree languages with height-constrained variables from positive data. In *Proc. PRICAI-2004, Springer-Verlag (to appear)*, 2004.

[12] Y. Suzuki, T. Shoudai, T. Uchida, and T. Miyahara. Ordered term tree languages which are polynomial time inductively inferable from positive data. In *Proc. ALT-2002, Springer-Verlag, LNAI 2533*, pages 188–202, 2002.

Learning Tree Languages from Positive Examples and Membership Queries

Jérôme Besombes and Jean-Yves Marion

LORIA - INPL
Ecole Nationale Supérieure des Mines de Nancy
615, rue du jardin botanique
54602 Villers-lès-Nancy, France
{Jerome.Besombes, Jean-Yves.Marion}@loria.fr

Abstract. We investigate regular tree languages exact learning from positive examples and membership queries. Input data are trees of the language to infer. The learner computes new trees from the inputs and asks to the oracle whether or not they belong to the language. From the answers, the learner may ask further membership queries until he finds the correct grammar that generates the target language. This paradigm was introduced by Angluin in the seminal work [1] for the case of regular word language. Neither negative examples, equivalence queries nor counter examples are allowed in this paradigm.

We describe an efficient algorithm which is polynomial in the size of the examples for learning the whole class of regular tree languages. The convergence is insured when the set of examples contains a representative sample of the language to guess. A finite subset $\mathcal{E}$ of a regular tree language $\mathcal{L}$ is representative for $\mathcal{L}$ if every transition of the minimal tree automaton for $\mathcal{L}$ is used at least once for the derivation of an element of the set $\mathcal{E}$.

1 Introduction

1.1 Some Linguistic Motivations

The most astonishing discovery of Chomsky is the universal grammar which is a model of how the human language works. The universal grammar is an innate combinatorial system from which every language, french, english, japanese, can be derived. What is the implication of Chomsky's universal grammar on grammatical inference? We think it gives a strong intuition on the mathematical modeling of language learning. Before going further, let us focus on the linguistic aspect of language acquisition processes.

Several recent works of psycho-linguists like Pinker [20] or Christophe [9] advocate that the universal grammar plays the role of a learning device for children. A child is able to determine whether or not a sentence is grammatically correct, even if we don't know the meaning of each word. Of course, semantics speed up the learning process, but it is not necessary. And, it is fascinating

S. Ben-David, J. Case, A. Maruoka (Eds.): ALT 2004, LNAI 3244, pp. 440–453, 2004.

to see that a child needs only few informations in order to learn a language (poverty-of-stimulus hypothesis).

Another important feature is our capacity to guess a mental tree structured representations of phrases. How a child is able to do that is beyond the scope of this paper. However the child language acquisition process is not based on the construction of a huge finite automaton with probabilistic transitions, because there is an infinity of valid sentences and we have the ability to generate them.

To sum up this brief discussion, we take as hypothesis that a child computes a grammar from tree structured sentences.

1.2   A Mathematical Model

Can we give a mathematical model of the language acquisition which corroborates this theory? The grammatical inference paradigm of Gold [16] is a good candidate. Indeed, the inputs of the learning process are just examples of the target language. And there is no interaction with the environment. But this paradigm is too weak to be plausible. For this reason, we add to Gold paradigm an oracle which answers to membership queries. Hence, the grammatical inference is based on positive examples and membership questions of computed elements, as introduced by Angluin in [1]. This learning model agrees with the poverty-of-stimulus hypothesis. Indeed the interaction with the environment is very weak. For example, a child asks something, but nobody understands. From this lack of reaction from the environment, he may deduce that the sentence is wrong, and so not in the language. We insist on the fact that membership queries are a minimal information which can be inferred from a dialog.

On the other hand, negative examples are not necessary because a parent does not say incorrect sentences to a child. One might think about other kind of queries like equivalence queries as suggested by Angluin [2]. But there are not necessary as we shall see and there are unrealistic in a linguistic context. In conclusion, our learning model seems quite adequate with respect to our initial motivation.

Now, we have set the learning paradigm, we have to say what's kind of language are targeted. As we have said, we can assume that a child has a kind of parser which transforms a (linear) sentence into a tree representation. So, we learn tree languages. Regular tree languages are the bare bone of several linguistic formalisms like classical categorial grammars for which learnability has been studied in [18,7], dependency languages [11,4,6] or TAG derivations.

1.3   The Results

We establish that the whole set of regular tree languages is efficiently identifiable from membership queries and positive examples. The running time of the learning algorithm is polynomial in the size of the input examples. The efficiency is a necessary property of our model. The difficulty is to construct trees to ask membership queries and which give useful information to proceed in the inference process. As far as we know, this result is new.

1.4   A Web Application

There are other applications of our result. For example, an XML document is a tree, if we forget links. The style-sheet defines a regular tree grammar. Now, say that we try to determine a Document Type Definition (the grammar which generates XML documents). For this, we can read correct XML documents from a server which forms a set of positive examples. Then, we can build a XML document and make a membership query by sending it to the server. If no error occurs then the the document is in the language, otherwise it is not.

1.5   Related Works

Learning from positive examples and membership queries. Angluin considers the same learning paradigm in [1] for the class of regular word languages. The notion of observation table which is defined in [2] is already implicitly used in [1]. However, we can not extend in a straight forward way the algorithm of [1] as it is explained by Sakakibara in [22]. In Section 4.3, we shall compare more precisely these works with our approach.

Other paradigms. Sakakibara studied grammatical inference of languages of unlabeled derivation trees of context free grammars. In [23], he extends the result of [2] by learning with membership queries and equivalence queries. The possibility of asking the teacher whether a calculated hypothesis corresponds to the target language seems not to be relevant for the aim of construct a model of natural language process. In [22,21] Sakakibara uses positive and negative examples with membership queries. At the end of the paper [21], it claims that the second algorithm is polynomial time (without proofs), but the main one is exponential in the function symbol arity. Compare with [21], we have showed that negative examples are not necessary and that the running time of our learning algorithm is polynomial. It is worth noticing that the set of all unlabeled context free derivation tree languages is a strict subclass of the set of regular tree languages. Therefore, we learn more and in a weaker setting since negative examples are not necessary in our work. This is important when we are learning from structured examples. Indeed, the language of structured examples may not come from a context free grammar but still the word language is context free.

Inference of regular tree languages from positive examples only, has been studied in [15,17], in [5] and [14] learnable subclasses have been defined and in [8], learning is studied from a stochastic point of view.

Inference of regular tree languages with queries has been studied in [12]; the learning algorithm is based on membership queries and equivalence queries and this result constitutes an extension of Sakakibara's works. In [13], a polynomial version of the former learning algorithm has been developed.

2   Regular Tree Languages

We present the general definitions of regular tree languages based on the Tata book [10]. A ranked alphabet $\mathcal{V}$ is a finite set of symbols with a function *arity* from $\mathcal{V}$ to $\mathbb{N}$, which indicates the arity of a symbol. The set $\mathcal{T}(\mathcal{V})$ of terms is inductively defined as follows. A symbol of arity 0 is in $\mathcal{T}(\mathcal{V})$, and if f is a symbol of arity n and $t_1, \ldots, t_n$ are in $\mathcal{T}(\mathcal{V})$, then $f(t_1, \ldots, t_n)$ is in $\mathcal{T}(\mathcal{V})$. Throughout, labeled ordered trees are represented by terms.

Subterms of a term t are defined by : t is a subterm of t and if $f(t_1, \ldots, t_n)$ is a subterm of t, then $t_1, \ldots, t_n$ are subterms of t. For a set of terms $\mathcal{E}$, $S(\mathcal{E})$ is the set of subterms of elements of $\mathcal{E}$.

A *context* is a term $c[\diamond]$ containing a special variable $\diamond$ which has only one occurrence. The variable $\diamond$ marks an empty place in a term. In particular, $\diamond$ is a context called the *empty context*. The substitution of $\diamond$ by a term s is noted $c[s]$. We write $\mathcal{E}[\diamond]$ for the set of contexts obtained by replacing exactly one occurrence of a $\mathcal{E}$-subterm by $\diamond$ ($\mathcal{E}[\diamond]$ contains the empty context $\diamond$).

A *bottom up non-deterministic tree automata* (NFTA) is a quadruple $\mathcal{A} = \langle \mathcal{V}, \mathcal{Q}, \mathcal{Q}_F, \underset{\mathcal{A}}{\rightarrow} \rangle$ where $\mathcal{V}$ is ranked alphabet, $\mathcal{Q}$ is a finite set of states, $\mathcal{Q}_F \subseteq \mathcal{Q}$ is the set of final states, and $\underset{\mathcal{A}}{\rightarrow}$ is the set of transitions. A transition is a rewrite rule of the form $f(q_1, \ldots, q_n) \underset{\mathcal{A}}{\rightarrow} q$ where q and $q_1, \ldots, q_n$ are states of $\mathcal{Q}$, and f is a symbol of arity n. In particular, a transition may be just of the form $a \underset{\mathcal{A}}{\rightarrow} q$ where a is a symbol of arity 0.

The single derivation relation $\underset{\mathcal{A}}{\rightarrow}$ is defined so that $t \underset{\mathcal{A}}{\rightarrow} s$ if and only if there is a transition $f(q_1, \ldots, q_n) \underset{\mathcal{A}}{\rightarrow} q$ such that for a context $u[\diamond]$, $t = u[f(q_1, \ldots, q_n)]$ and $s = u[q]$. The derivation relation $\underset{\mathcal{A}}{\overset{*}{\rightarrow}}$ is the reflexive and transitive closure of $\underset{\mathcal{A}}{\rightarrow}$.

A tree language $\mathcal{L}$ is recognized by $\mathcal{A}$ if $\mathcal{L} = \mathcal{L}_\mathcal{A}$ where

$$\mathcal{L}_\mathcal{A} = \{t \in \mathcal{T}(\mathcal{V}) \; : \; t \underset{\mathcal{A}}{\overset{*}{\rightarrow}} q_f \text{ and } q_f \in \mathcal{Q}_F\}$$

A tree language is regular if and only if it is recognized by a NFTA.

A state q is *reached* by term t if $t \underset{\mathcal{A}}{\overset{*}{\rightarrow}} q$. A state q *accepts* a context $c[\diamond]$ if $c[q] \underset{\mathcal{A}}{\overset{*}{\rightarrow}} q_f$. A NFTA is trimmed if and only if each state is reached by a term and accepts at least a context. In other words, there is no useless transition nor useless state. Notice that a trim automaton has a partial transition relation.

A finite tree automaton is *deterministic* (DFTA) if there are no two rules with the same left hand side. It is well known that NFTA and DFTA recognize the same class of languages. Therefore, each regular language is recognized by a trim DFTA.

The Myhill-Nerode congruence $\equiv_\mathcal{L}$ of a tree language $\mathcal{L}$ is defined by $t \equiv_\mathcal{L} s$ iff for every context $c[\diamond]$, $c[t] \in \mathcal{L}$ iff $c[s] \in \mathcal{L}$. Kozen in [19] has written an elementary proof of Myhill-Nerode Theorem and has told the story behind. The Myhill-Nerode congruence $\equiv_\mathcal{L}$ defines the minimal automaton for $\mathcal{L}$ (up to a renaming of states) and inversely. The minimal automaton of $\mathcal{L}$ noted $\mathcal{A}_m$ is defined as follows:

- the state set $\mathcal{Q}_{\mathcal{A}_m}$ is the set of non-empty equivalence classes of the Myhill-Nerode congruence,

- the set of final states $\mathcal{Q}_{F_{\mathcal{A}_m}}$ is the set of states such that $[t]$ is contained in $\mathcal{L}$,
- the transition rule $\underset{\mathcal{A}_m}{\longrightarrow}$ is the smallest relation such that

$$f([t_1], \ldots, [t_n]) \underset{\mathcal{A}_m}{\longrightarrow} [f(q_1, \ldots, q_n)].$$

Throughout, we note $[t]$ the equivalence class of t wrt $\equiv_{\mathcal{L}}$.

Example 1. Consider the DFTA $\mathcal{A} = \langle \{a, b, c\}, \{q_F, q_1, q_2, q_3, q_4\}, \{q_F\}, \underset{\mathcal{A}}{\longrightarrow} \rangle$, where $\underset{\mathcal{A}}{\longrightarrow}$ is the following set of transitions:

$$a(q_2, q_3) \underset{\mathcal{A}}{\longrightarrow} q_F$$

$$b(q_2) \underset{\mathcal{A}}{\longrightarrow} q_1 \qquad c(q_4) \underset{\mathcal{A}}{\longrightarrow} q_3$$

$$b(q_1) \underset{\mathcal{A}}{\longrightarrow} q_2 \qquad c(q_3) \underset{\mathcal{A}}{\longrightarrow} q_4$$

$$b \underset{\mathcal{A}}{\longrightarrow} q_1 \qquad c \underset{\mathcal{A}}{\longrightarrow} q_3$$

The tree $a(b(b), c(c(c)))$ belongs to $\mathcal{L}_\Gamma$. Indeed we have:

$$a(b(b), c(c(c))) \underset{\mathcal{A}}{\longrightarrow} a(b(q_1), c(c(c))) \underset{\mathcal{A}}{\longrightarrow} a(q_2, c(c(c)))$$

$$\underset{\mathcal{A}}{\longrightarrow} a(q_2, c(c(q_3))) \underset{\mathcal{A}}{\longrightarrow} a(q_2, c(q_4)) \underset{\mathcal{A}}{\longrightarrow} a(q_2, q_3) \underset{\mathcal{A}}{\longrightarrow} q_F$$

$\mathcal{L}_{\mathcal{A}}$ is the tree language $\{a(b^{2n+2}, c^{2m+1}) : n, m \in \mathbb{N}\}$.

An *automaton homomorphism* between the NFTA $\mathcal{A} = \langle \mathcal{V}, \mathcal{Q}, \mathcal{Q}_F, \underset{\mathcal{A}'}{\longrightarrow} \rangle$ and $\mathcal{A}' = \langle \mathcal{V}', \mathcal{Q}', \mathcal{Q}'_F, \underset{\mathcal{A}'}{\longrightarrow} \rangle$ is a mapping ϕ from $\mathcal{Q}$ and $\mathcal{Q}'$ such that :

- for each transition $f(q_1, \ldots, q_n) \underset{\mathcal{A}}{\longrightarrow} q$ of $\mathcal{A}$, $f(\phi(q_1), \ldots, \phi(q_n)) \underset{\mathcal{A}'}{\longrightarrow} \phi(q)$ is a transition of $\mathcal{A}'$.
- $\phi(\mathcal{Q}_F) \subseteq \mathcal{Q}'_F$.

This implies that $\mathcal{L}_{\mathcal{A}} \subseteq \mathcal{L}_{\mathcal{A}'}$. If ϕ is bijective, it consists in a renaming of the states and $\mathcal{L}_{\mathcal{A}} = \mathcal{L}_{\mathcal{A}'}$.

3   Learning Regular Tree Languages

3.1   The Learning Paradigm

The goal is the identification of any unknown regular tree language $\mathcal{L}$ with help of a teacher. The teacher is an oracle which answers to membership queries. The learning process begins with a set of positive examples. The a dialogue is established between the learner and the teacher. Then learner asks whether or not a new tree belongs to the unknown language. The teacher answers by "yes" or "no" to this query. This learning process halts after a finite number of queries.

We shall provide a necessary and sufficient condition to guess the unknown language and so to construct a DFTA which recognizes it.

3.2   Representative Samples

Informally, a representative sample of a language $\mathcal{L}$ is a finite subset $\mathcal{E}$ such that each transition of the minimal automaton is used to produce a term of $\mathcal{E}$. The set $\mathcal{E}$ is a *representative sample* of $\mathcal{L}$ if for each transition $\mathbf{f}(q_1, \dots, q_n) \xrightarrow[\mathcal{A}_m]{} q$, there is a term $\mathbf{f}(\mathbf{t}_1, \dots, \mathbf{t}_n)$ in $\mathcal{S}(\mathcal{E})$ such that $\forall 1 \leq i \leq n,\ \mathbf{t}_i \xrightarrow[\mathcal{A}_m]{*} q_i$.

Example 2. This example illustrates the fact that several distinct languages can have identical representaive samples. Let $\mathcal{A}$ be the **DFTA** defined in Example 1 and $\mathcal{A}'$ the **DFTA** defined by:

$$a(q_1, q_2) \xrightarrow[\mathcal{A}']{} q_F$$
$$b(q_1) \xrightarrow[\mathcal{A}']{} q_1 \qquad c(q_2) \xrightarrow[\mathcal{A}']{} q_2$$
$$b \xrightarrow[\mathcal{A}']{} q_1 \qquad c \xrightarrow[\mathcal{A}']{} q_2$$

where q_F is the unique final state of $\mathcal{A}'$. From this definition, we have

$$\mathcal{L}_{\mathcal{A}'} = \{a(b^n, c^m) :\ n, m \in \mathbb{N}^*\}$$

and the singleton set

$$\{a(b(b), c(c(c)))\}$$

is a representative sample for both $\mathcal{L}_\mathcal{A}$ and $\mathcal{L}_{\mathcal{A}'}$.

Remark 1. The question of the size of a minimal representative sample relatively to the size of the minimal automaton $\mathcal{A}$ of a language $\mathcal{L}$ is interesting to be discussed. In the contrary of the case of word language, there is no polynomial relation between the size (the total number of nodes) of a minimal characteristic sample and the size (the number of states) of the minimal **DFTA**. For instance, for two integers n and m, the singleton language containing the following tree:

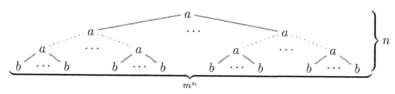

where the arity of a is m and the arity of b is 0, is a regular tree language recognized by the above minimal **DFTA**.

$$a(q_n, \dots, q_n) \to q_F$$
$$\vdots$$
$$a(q_1, \dots, q_1) \to q_2$$
$$b \to q_1$$

The size of the representative sample which the singeton language above, is $m^{n+1} - 1$.

3.3 Observation Tables

Following the method of Angluin [3], informations obtained from the queries are stored in a table. Let $\mathcal{L}$ be a tree language, $\mathcal{E}$ be a finite set of terms and F be a finite set of contexts. The *observation table* $T = T_{\mathcal{L}}(\mathcal{E}, F)$ is the table defined by:

- rows are labeled with terms of $\mathcal{S}(\mathcal{E})$,
- columns are labeled with contexts of F,
- cells $T_{\mathcal{L}}(t, c[\diamond])$ are labeled with 1 or 0 in such a way that

$$T_{\mathcal{L}}(t, c[\diamond]) = \begin{cases} 1 \text{ if } c[t] \in \mathcal{L} \\ 0 \text{ otherwise} \end{cases}$$

We call row(t) the binary word corresponding to the reading from left to right of the row labeled by t in T.

Example 3. Consider the tree language $\mathcal{L}_\Gamma$ defined in Example 1, $\mathcal{E}$ the set of terms:

$$\mathcal{E} = \{a(b(b), c(c(c)))\}$$

and F the set of contexts:

$$F = \mathcal{E}[\diamond] = \{\diamond, a(\diamond, c(c(c))), a(b(\diamond), c(c(c))), a(b(b), \diamond), a(b(b), c(\diamond)), a(b(b), c(c(\diamond)))\}$$

The corresponding observation table $T = T_{\mathcal{L}}(\mathcal{E}, F)$ is the following:

	$\diamond$	$a(\diamond, c(c(c)))$	$a(b(\diamond), c(c(c)))$	$a(b(b), \diamond)$	$a(b(b), c(\diamond))$	$a(b(b), c(c(\diamond)))$
$a(b(b), c(c(c)))$	1	0	0	0	0	0
$b(b)$	0	1	0	0	0	0
b	0	0	1	0	0	0
$c(c(c))$	0	0	0	1	0	1
$c(c)$	0	0	0	0	1	0
c	0	0	0	1	0	1

An observation table $T = T_{\mathcal{L}}(\mathcal{E}, F)$ defines a NFTA

$$\mathcal{A}_T = \langle \mathcal{V}_T, \mathcal{Q}_T, \mathcal{Q}_{F,T}, \underset{T}{\rightarrow} \rangle$$

where:

- $\mathcal{V}_T$ is the set of symbols occurring in $\mathcal{E}$,
- $\mathcal{Q}_T = \{\text{row}(t), t \in \mathcal{S}(\mathcal{E})\}$,
- $\mathcal{Q}_{F,T} = \{\text{row}(t), t \in \mathcal{L}\}$,
- the transition $\underset{T}{\rightarrow}$ is the smallest relation such that

$$f(\text{row}(t_1), \dots, \text{row}(t_n)) \rightarrow \text{row}(f(t_1, \dots, t_n)),$$

for each $f(t_1, \dots, t_n) \in \mathcal{S}(\mathcal{E})$.

Example 4. The table T of the Example 3 defines the NFTA $\mathcal{A}_T$ as:

- $\mathcal{V}_T = \{a, b, c\}$
- $\mathcal{Q}_T = \{100000, 010000, 001000, 000101, 000010\}$
- $\mathcal{Q}_{F,T} = \{100000\}$
- $\underset{T}{\longrightarrow}$ is the following set of transitions

$$a(010000, 000101) \underset{\mathcal{A}_T}{\longrightarrow} 100000$$

$$b(010000) \underset{\mathcal{A}_T}{\longrightarrow} 001000 \qquad c(000010) \underset{\mathcal{A}_T}{\longrightarrow} 000101$$

$$b(001000) \underset{\mathcal{A}_T}{\longrightarrow} 010000 \qquad c(000101) \underset{\mathcal{A}_T}{\longrightarrow} 000010$$

$$b \underset{\mathcal{A}_T}{\longrightarrow} 001000 \qquad\qquad c \underset{\mathcal{A}_T}{\longrightarrow} 000101$$

We remark that $\mathcal{A}_T = \phi(\mathcal{A})$, where $\mathcal{A}$ is the DFTA introduced in Example 1 and ϕ is the renaming defined by: $\phi(q_F) = 100000$, $\phi(q_1) = 001000$, $\phi(q_2) = 010000$, $\phi(q_3) = 000101$, $\phi(q_4) = 000010$.

Remark 2. In general, $\mathcal{A}_T$ is not complete and non deterministic.

An observation table $T = T_{\mathcal{L}}(\mathcal{E}, \mathsf{F})$ is said to be *consistent* if for any terms $f(t_1, \ldots, t_n)$ and $f(t'_1, \ldots, t'_n)$ in $\mathcal{S}(\mathcal{E})$, if $\forall 1 \leq j \leq n$ we have :

$$\mathrm{row}(t_j) = \mathrm{row}(t'_j)$$

then

$$\mathrm{row}(f(t_1, \ldots, t_n)) = \mathrm{row}(f(t'_1, \ldots, t'_n))$$

Lemma 1. $\mathcal{A}_T$ *is deterministic if and only if the table T is consistent.*

Proof. This equivalence is straightforward from definitions of consistency of T and of $\mathcal{A}_T$.

Lemma 2. *If $\mathcal{E}$ is a representative sample for a regular tree language $\mathcal{L}$, F any finite set of contexts and T the observation table $T_{\mathcal{L}}(\mathcal{E}, \mathsf{F})$, then we have $\mathcal{L} \subseteq \mathcal{L}_{\mathcal{A}_T}$.*

Proof. We exhibit an automaton homomorphism ϕ from the minimal automaton $\mathcal{A}_m$ onto $\mathcal{A}_T$. For each subterm t of $\mathcal{E}$, we set $\phi([t]) = \mathrm{row}(t)$. It is clear that if $[t] = [t']$ then we have $\mathrm{row}(t) = \mathrm{row}(t')$ and so ϕ is so well defined. Since $\mathcal{E}$ is a representative sample, the range of ϕ is $\mathcal{Q}_T$. Finally, for each transition $f(q_1, \ldots, q_n) \underset{\mathcal{A}_m}{\longrightarrow} q$, we have $f(\phi(q_1), \ldots \phi(q_n)) \underset{\mathcal{A}_T}{\longrightarrow} \phi(q)$.

Remark 3. The number of states of the automaton $\mathcal{A}_T$ is lower or equal to the number of states of $\mathcal{A}_m$.

Remark 4. If the automaton homomorphism ϕ defined in the proof of Lemma 2 is bijective, then $\mathcal{L} = \mathcal{L}_{\mathcal{A}_T}$. Consequently, if $\mathcal{L} \neq \mathcal{L}_{\mathcal{A}_T}$, then there are two subterms t and t' of $\mathcal{E}$ such that $row(t) = row(t')$ and $[t] \neq [t']$.

The next lemma is central for the construction of an algorithm that solves the learning problem. The consistency of the table constructed from a representative sample $\mathcal{E}$ implies that the corresponding automaton is minimal. So when the table is consistence then $\mathcal{L}$ is learned with the proviso that the inputs are representative.

In other words, when the table is not consistent, there are two subterms t and t' of $\mathcal{E}$ for which the rows are equal in the table, but $[t] \neq [t']$.

Lemma 3. *Let* $T = T_{\mathcal{L}}(\mathcal{E}, \mathsf{F})$ *be an observation table where* $\mathcal{L}$ *is a regular tree language,* $\mathcal{E}$ *a representative sample for* $\mathcal{L}$*,* F *a set of context containing* $\mathcal{E}[\diamond]$*.*
If $\mathcal{L}_{\mathcal{A}_T} \neq \mathcal{L}$*, then there are two terms*

$$f(t_1, \ldots, t_n) \text{ and } f(t'_1, \ldots, t'_n)$$

in $\mathcal{S}(\mathcal{E})$ *such that there is an index i satisfying*

- $row(f(t_1, \ldots, t_{i-1}, t_i, t_{i+1}, \ldots, t_n)) \neq row(f(t'_1, \ldots, t'_{i-1}, t'_i, t'_{i+1}, \ldots, t'_n))$,
- $[t_j] = [t'_j], \forall 1 \leq j \neq i \leq n$,
- $row(t_i) = row(t'_i)$.

The proof of Lemma 3 will appear in the full version of the paper. The first consequence is algorithmic. Indeed, Lemma 3 implies that a context $c[\diamond]$ can be constructed in order to separate t_i and t'_i. By adding $c[\diamond]$ to the table, the corresponding rows of t_i and t'_i will be then different. Such a context is called *separating-context*. Moreover, this separating context is obtained by plugging $f(t_1, \ldots, t_{i-1}, \diamond, t_{i+1}, \ldots, t_n)$ to a context of F. This observation restricts drastically the number of separating contexts to consider which leads to a polynomial time learning algorithm.

The second consequence is that the learning problem is solved when the table is consistent as we have already claimed.

Lemma 4. *Let* $\mathcal{L}$ *be a regular tree language,* $\mathcal{E}$ *a representative sample for* $\mathcal{L}$ *and* F *a set of contexts including* $\mathcal{E}[\diamond]$*. If the table* $T = T_{\mathcal{L}}(\mathcal{E}, \mathsf{F})$ *is consistent, then* $\mathcal{L}_{\mathcal{A}_T} = \mathcal{L}$*.*

Proof. The Lemma 3 means that if a table is consistent then two equivalent terms wrt Myhill-Nerode congruence have the same row. From this, we define an automaton homomorphism from $\mathcal{A}_T$ onto $\mathcal{A}_m$. So, $\mathcal{L}_{\mathcal{A}_T} \subseteq \mathcal{L}$. The conclusion follows by Lemma 2.

4   Identification of Regular Tree Languages

4.1   The Algorithm ALTEX

The algorithm ALTEX is defined in Figure 1. ALTEX first receives a finite subset $\mathcal{E}$ of an unknown language $\mathcal{L}$. ALTEX constructs the first observation table $T =$

$T_{\mathcal{L}}(\mathcal{E}, \mathcal{E}[\diamond])$ with help of queries. Then, it checks the consistency of the table. Each time ALTEX finds the table non-consistent, new contexts constructed from the terms that contradict the consistency are added in the table which is then completed with queries. The process stops when the table is consistent and the automaton $\mathcal{A}_T$ is output.

Input: a finite set of terms $\mathcal{E}$
Initialization: $\mathsf{F} = \mathcal{E}[\diamond]$;
Construct the table $T = T_{\mathcal{L}}(\mathcal{E}, \mathsf{F})$;
while there is $\mathsf{f}(t_1, \dots, t_n)$ and $\mathsf{f}(t'_1, \dots, t'_n)$ in $\mathcal{S}(\mathcal{E})$ such that
$\mathrm{row}(\mathsf{f}(t_1, \dots, t_n)) \neq \mathrm{row}(\mathsf{f}(t'_1, \dots, t'_n))$
and $\forall 1 \leq i \leq n,\ \mathrm{row}(t_i) = \mathrm{row}(t'_i)$ **do**
   Find a context $\mathsf{c}[\diamond]$ in F such that
   $\mathsf{c}[\mathsf{f}(t_1, \dots, t_n)] \in \mathcal{L}$ and $\mathsf{c}[\mathsf{f}(t'_1, \dots, t'_n)] \notin \mathcal{L}$;
   $\mathsf{F} = \mathsf{F} \cup \{\mathsf{c}[\mathsf{f}(t_1, \dots, t_{i-1}, \diamond, t_{i+1}, \dots, t_n)], 1 \leq i \leq n\}$;
   Construct $T = T_{\mathcal{L}}(\mathcal{E}, \mathsf{F})$;
end while;
Return the automaton $\mathcal{A}_T$.

Fig. 1. The learning algorithm ALTEX

4.2 Correctness and Termination

From the definition of consistency, ALTEX can easily verify whether the table T constructed with help of membership queries is consistent or not. In the case where T is not consistent, the problem is that the algorithm has to find by itself (no counter example is allowed) a new context that will separate two equivalent rows. The key point is that the input set of terms $\mathcal{E}$ is representative provides the ability of determining such separating context.

Lemma 5. *Assume that the inputs of* ALTEX *is a representative sample. If the table* $T = T_{\mathcal{L}}(\mathcal{E}, \mathsf{F})$ *is not consistent,* ALTEX *calculates a separating-context.*

Proof. ALTEX collects every couple of terms $\mathsf{f}(t_1, \dots, t_n)$ and $\mathsf{f}(t'_1, \dots, t'_n)$ in $\mathcal{S}(\mathcal{E})$, such that there is a context $\mathsf{c}[\diamond]$ in F with

- $\forall 1 \leq i \leq n,\ \mathrm{row}(t_i) = \mathrm{row}(t'_i)$,
- $\mathsf{c}[\mathsf{f}(t_1, \dots, t_n)] \in \mathcal{L}$,
- $\mathsf{c}[\mathsf{f}(t'_1, \dots, t'_n)] \notin \mathcal{L}$.

Among the couples gathered as above, Lemma 3 states that there is an index i such that
$$\forall 1 \leq j \neq i \leq n,\ [t_j] = [t'_j]$$
and
$$[t_i] \neq [t'_i]$$

So, $c[f(t_1, \ldots, t_{i-1}, \diamond, t_{i+1}, \ldots, t_n)]$ is a separating context which is added to F. The rows of t_i and t'_i are now different in

$$T_{\mathcal{L}}(\mathcal{E}, \mathsf{F} \cup \{c[f(t_1, \ldots, t_{i-1}, \diamond, t_{i+1}, \ldots, t_n)]\})$$

Theorem 1. *The algorithm* ALTEX *identifies the class of regular tree languages in polynomial time.*

Proof. The algorithm ALTEX starts with the construction of $T_{\mathcal{L}}(\mathcal{E}, \mathcal{E}[\diamond])$ and enters the loop. If the program leaves this loop, the observation table is consistent and by Lemma 4, the automaton given as output is correct. It remains to show that ALTEX terminates. From Lemma 5, each time the loop is processed, a new separating-context is added to the table. Since two rows that were different, are still different in the new table, the number of states of the automaton $\mathcal{A}_T$ is strictly increased. From Lemma 3, this number is always lower or equal to the number of states of the minimal automaton for $\mathcal{L}$. This implies that the loop may be processed only a finite number of times and by consequence, ALTEX terminates.

We noticed that any finite set containing a representative sample is also a representative sample. This implies that if we consider an incremental version of *Altex* (the table is completed as the set of positive examples increases during the process), the algorithm converges. Now, if the input set doesn't contain a representative sample yet, the algorithm calculates a sub-automaton (the recognized language is strictly contained in the target language). The algorithm terminates on any input and the success of learning is guaranteed if a representative sample is presented as input, that constitutes a weak hypothesis.

The time complexity of ALTEX depends on the size n of a representative sample $\mathcal{E}$ (The size is the sum of the size of terms in $\mathcal{E}$.) and the size m of the minimal automaton (number of states) for the language $\mathcal{L}$ to identify. The first observation table has n^2 cells. Then, the number of rows doesn't change and the number of columns increases until the table is non-consistent. At each step, there is at most n new contexts which are added to the table. And the loop is bounded by m. Now, since we have $m \leq n$, we conclude that the runtime is bounded by a polynomial in n.

4.3   Why Does It Not Blow Up?

In [1], Angluin studies the paradigm of learning regular (word) languages from positive examples and queries and in [3], the idea of observation table is introduced. It's interesting to see whether these results may be applied in the case of tree languages. Angluin's algorithms try any possible transition by considering the set of words $w\alpha$, where w is a prefix and α is an element of the alphabet. To apply this technique in the case of trees, we have to construct, for any subterm t of $\mathcal{E}$, all terms of the form $f(t_1, \ldots, t, \ldots, t_n)$, for each subterm t_j of $\mathcal{E}$ and each element f of arity n in the alphabet. This straight generalization leads to an exponential procedure in the maximum arity of the alphabet.

ALTEX proceeds in a different way. It determines efficiently from the non-consistent table a small set of contexts in which one is separating.

5   Examples

In Example 2, we saw that the tree $a(b(b), c(c(c)))$ is a representative sample for the tree language

$$\mathcal{L}_{\mathcal{A}} = \{a(b^{2n+2}, c^{2m+1}) \ : \ n, m \in \mathbb{N}\}$$

Now suppose that the above singleton is given to ALTEX ; the constructed table with help of membership queries is the table of example 3. This table is consistent and then, ALTEX output the automaton of example 4. This automaton is a renaming of $\mathcal{A}$ and the language is learned. If we suppose that, with the same input, the language to learn is

$$\mathcal{L}_{\mathcal{A}'} = \{a(b^n, c^m) \ : \ n, m \in \mathbb{N}^*\}$$

($\{a(b(b), c(c(c)))\}$ is representative for this language too), the table is now:

	$\diamond$	$a(\diamond, c(c(c)))$	$a(b(\diamond), c(c(c)))$	$a(b(b), \diamond)$	$a(b(b), c(\diamond))$	$a(b(b), c(c(\diamond)))$
$a(b(b), c(c(c)))$	1	0	0	0	0	0
$b(b)$	0	1	1	0	0	0
b	0	1	1	0	0	0
$c(c(c))$	0	0	0	1	1	1
$c(c)$	0	0	0	1	1	1
c	0	0	0	1	1	1

ALTEX checks again that this table is directly consistent and output the automaton $\phi'(\mathcal{A}')$, where ϕ' is the automaton homomorphism defined by:
$\phi'(q_F) = 100000$, $\phi'(q_1) = 011000$, $\phi'(q_2) = 000111$.
ALTEX is defined as an iterative algorithm; if during the process, the observation table is found not to be consistent, the minimal automaton for the target language must have some particular rules: rules which are identical except in a single state of its left hand side If the minimal automaton has no such rules, the first table constructed by ALTEX is consistent and the language is learned immediately. With the aim of illustrating the iterative behavior, we now propose an automaton specially constructed for having this property. Let so be $\mathcal{L}_{\mathcal{A}''}$ the language defined by the following minimal automaton $\mathcal{A}''$:

$$a(q_1) \underset{\mathcal{A}}{\longrightarrow} q_F \quad d(q_3, q_5) \underset{\mathcal{A}}{\longrightarrow} q_1 \quad e(q_7) \underset{\mathcal{A}}{\longrightarrow} q_3 \quad g \underset{\mathcal{A}}{\longrightarrow} q_7$$

$$a(q_2) \underset{\mathcal{A}}{\longrightarrow} q_F \quad d(q_4, q_5) \underset{\mathcal{A}}{\longrightarrow} q_1 \quad e(q_8) \underset{\mathcal{A}}{\longrightarrow} q_4 \quad h \underset{\mathcal{A}}{\longrightarrow} q_8$$

$$b(q_1) \underset{\mathcal{A}}{\longrightarrow} q_F \quad d(q_3, q_6) \underset{\mathcal{A}}{\longrightarrow} q_1 \quad f(q_9) \underset{\mathcal{A}}{\longrightarrow} q_5 \quad i \underset{\mathcal{A}}{\longrightarrow} q_9$$

$$c \underset{\mathcal{A}}{\longrightarrow} q_1 \quad d(q_4, q_6) \underset{\mathcal{A}}{\longrightarrow} q_2 \quad f(q_{10}) \underset{\mathcal{A}}{\longrightarrow} q_6 \quad j \underset{\mathcal{A}}{\longrightarrow} q_{10}$$

where q_F is the unique final state. From this definition, we establish that $\mathcal{L}_{\mathcal{A}''}$ is the finite language corresponding to the following set of terms:

$$\mathcal{L}_{\mathcal{A}''} = \{a(c), b(c), a(d(e(g), f(i))), a(d(e(h), f(i))), a(d(e(g), f(j))),$$

$$a(d(e(h), f(j))), b(d(e(g), f(i))), b(d(e(h), f(i))), b(d(e(g), f(j)))\}.$$

Let suppose that a teacher constructs the representative sample:

$$\mathcal{E} = \{b(c), a(d(e(g), f(i))), a(d(e(h), f(i))), a(d(e(g), f(j))), a(d(e(h), f(j)))\}.$$

The learner ALTEX starts with the construction of $F = \mathcal{E}[\diamond]$ and $T = T_{\mathcal{L}_{\mathcal{A}''}}(\mathcal{S}(\mathcal{E}), F)$.

ALTEX now notices the three problematics couples of terms

$$d(e(h), f(i)) \text{ and } d(e(h), f(j)),$$

$$d(e(g), f(i)) \text{ and } d(e(h), f(j))$$

and

$$d(e(g), f(j)) \text{ and } d(e(h), f(j)).$$

Indeed

$$\text{row}(e(g)) = \text{row}(e(h)) \text{ and } \text{row}(f(i)) = \text{row}(f(j))$$

but

$$b(d(e(g), f(i))) \in \mathcal{L}, b(d(e(g), f(j))) \in \mathcal{L}, b(d(e(h), f(i))) \in \mathcal{L}$$

and

$$b(d(e(h), f(j))) \notin \mathcal{L}.$$

ALTEX adds $b(d(e(g), \diamond))$, $b(d(e(h), \diamond))$, $b(d(\diamond, f(i)))$ and $b(d(\diamond, f(j)))$ to F and complete the table T with help of the teacher.

ALTEX now remarks that

$$b(d(e(h), f(i))) \in \mathcal{L}, b(d(e(h), f(j))) \notin \mathcal{L} \text{ but } \text{row}(i) = \text{row}(j)$$

and that

$$b(d(e(g), f(j))) \in \mathcal{L}, b(d(e(h), f(j))) \notin \mathcal{L} \text{ but } \text{row}(g) = \text{row}(h).$$

The new contexts $b(d(e(\diamond), f(j)))$ and $b(d(e(h), f(\diamond)))$ are added in F and the table T is completed one last time with help of the teacher.

T is now consistent and ALTEX output $\mathcal{A}_T$ which verify $\mathcal{L}_{\mathcal{A}_T} = \mathcal{L}_{\mathcal{A}''}$.

6   Conclusion

We have showed that the whole class of regular tree languauge is learnable from positive examples and membership queries, that extends Angluin's works. We gave a polynomial algorithm for this learning model and proved its correctness. It is worth noticing that, with the same proofs, ALTEX is able to learn from partial examples, that is subtrees of positive examples. Indeed, in the definition of representative samples, we stipulate that a representative sample must be a subset of the language; there is no need for this restriction and the property that any transition of the minimal automaton is necessary is enough. This constitutes a new paradigm that can be even more realistic for the problem of natural language acquisition modeling. A part of a sentence can be used by a child, even if the sentence in which it appears is not totally understood. Moreover, this may partially answer the problem of noise in the signal processing.

References

[1] D. Angluin. A note on the number of queries needed to identify regular languages. *Information and Control*, 51:76–87, 1981.

[2] D. Angluin. Learning regular sets from queries and counter examples. *Information and Control*, 75:87–106, 1987.

[3] D. Angluin. Queries and concept learning. *Machine learning*, 2:319–342, 1988.

[4] J. Besombes and J.Y. Marion. Identification of reversible dependency tree languages. *Proceedings of the third Learning Language in Logic workshop*, pages 11–22, 2001.

[5] J. Besombes and J.Y. Marion. Apprentissage des langages réguliers d'arbres et applications. *Conférence d'Apprentissage, Orléans 17, 18 et 19 juin 2002*, pages 55–70, 2002.

[6] J. Besombes and J.Y. Marion. Learning dependency languages from a teacher. In *Proceedings of Formal Grammar 2004*, pages 17–28, 2004.

[7] J. Besombes and J.Y. Marion. Learning reversible categorial grammars from structures. In *Proceedings of the international IIS:IIPWM'04*, Advances in Soft Computing, Springer Verlag, pages 181–190, 2004.

[8] R.C. Carrasco, J. Oncina, and J. Calera. Stochastic inference of regular tree languages. *Lecture Notes in Computer Science*, 1433:185–197, 1998.

[9] A. Christophe. L'apprentissage du langage. In *Université de tous les savoirs*, volume 2, pages 41–51. Odile Jacob, 2000.

[10] H. Comon, M. Dauchet, R. Gilleron, F. Jacquemard, D. Lugiez, S. Tison, and M. Tommasi. Tree automata techniques and applications. Available on: http://www.grappa.univ-lille3.fr/tata, 1997.

[11] A. Dikovsky and L. Modina. Dependencies on the other side of the curtain. *Traitement automatique des langues*, 41(1):67–96, 2000.

[12] F. Drewes and J. Högberg. Learning a regular tree language from a teacher. In Z. Ésik and Z. Fülöp, editors, *Proc. Developments in Language Theory 2003*, volume 2710 of *Lecture Notes in Computer Science*, pages 279–291. Springer, 2003.

[13] F. Drewes and J. Högberg. Learning a regular tree language from a teacher even more efficiently. Technical Report 03.11, Umea University, 2003.

[14] H. Fernau. Learning tree languages from text. 2375:153–168, 2002.

[15] H. Fukuda and K. Kamata. Inference of tree automata from sample set of trees. *International Journal of Computer and Information Sciences*, 13(3):177–196, 1984.

[16] M.E. Gold. Language identification in the limit. *Information and Control*, 10:447–474, 1967.

[17] K. Kamata. Inference methods for tree automata from sample set of trees. *IEEE International Conference on Systems, Man and Cybernetics*, pages 490–493, 1988.

[18] M. Kanazawa. *Learnable classes of Categorial Grammars*. CSLI, 1998.

[19] D. Kozen. On the myhill-nerode theorem for trees. *EATCS Bulletin*, 47:170–173, June 1992.

[20] S. Pinker. *The language instinct*. Harper, 1994.

[21] Y. Sakakibara. Inductive inference of logic programs based on algebraic semantics. Technical Report ICOT, 79, 1987.

[22] Y. Sakakibara. Inferring parsers of context-free languages from structural examples. Technical Report ICOT, 81, 1987.

[23] Y. Sakakibara. Learning context-free grammars from structural data in polynomial time. *Theoretical Computer Science*, 76:223–242, 1990.

Learning Content Sequencing in an Educational Environment According to Student Needs

Ana Iglesias, Paloma Martínez, Ricardo Aler, and Fernando Fernández

Computer Science Department
University Carlos III of Madrid
Avda. de la Universidad, 30, 28911- Leganés (Madrid), SPAIN
Tel: 34-91-624{9917, 9454, 9418, 8842} Fax: 34-91-6249430.
{aiglesia, pmf, aler, ffernand}@inf.uc3m.es

Abstract. One of the most important issues in educational systems is to define effective teaching policies according to the students learning characteristics. This paper proposes to use the Reinforcement Learning (RL) model in order for the system to learn automatically sequence of contents to be shown to the student, based only in interactions with other students, like human tutors do. An initial clustering of the students according to their learning characteristics is proposed in order the system adapts better to each student. Experiments show convergence to optimal teaching tactics for different clusters of simulated students, concluding that the convergence is faster when the system tactics have been previously initialised.

1 Introduction

Web-based education (WBE) is currently a hot research and development area. Traditional web-based courses usually are static hypertext pages without student adaptability, providing the same page content and the same set of links to all users. However, since the last nineties, several research teams have been implementing different kinds of adaptive and intelligent systems for WBE.

The Web-based Adaptive and Intelligent Educational Systems (Web-based AIES) use artificial intelligence techniques in order to adapt better to each student. One of the AIES main problems is to determine which is the best content to show next and how to do it.

RLATES (Reinforcement Learning Adaptive and intelligent Educational System) is a Web-based AIES. This proposal provides intelligence and student adaptability in order to teach *Database Design* topics. RLATES is able to adapt the hypermedia pages contents and links shown to the students (adaptive presentation and adaptive navigation support) based on the Reinforcement Learning (RL) model [5] in order to provide the student an "optimal" curriculum sequence according to his/her learning characteristics in each moment of the interaction. This approach forms part of the

S. Ben-David, J. Case, A. Maruoka (Eds.): ALT 2004, LNAI 3244, pp. 454–463, 2004.

PANDORA project [3], whose main goal is to define methods and techniques for database development implemented in a CASE tool.

System learning begins with a clustering of the students according to their characteristics. A different pedagogical tactical (action policy from the Reinforcement Learning point of view) is learned for each of those clusters. The goal of this paper is to study how many students are necessary to interact with the system until an optimal pedagogical sequence of contents is learned. Experiments will show that it depends on the student clusters homogeneity, so if all the students belonging to the same cluster have similar learning characteristics, the system adapt his curriculum sequence faster and better for each student. Furthermore, we will show that initializing the action policy improves the learning convergence to a very reduced number of students, even when the initialization is done assuming student with different learning characteristics.

The paper is organized as follows: first, the proposal architecture is described in Section 2. Section 3 shows how to apply Reinforcement Learning to educational systems. Next, the functional phases are defined in Section 4. Experiments and main results are presented in Section 5. Finally, the main conclusions and further research of this work are given in Section 6.

2 Proposal Architecture

RLATES is composed of four well differentiated modules shown in Figure 1. The *student module* contains all important information about the student in the learning process: goals, student background knowledge, personal characteristics, historical behavior, etc. Experiments in section 5 show the importance of constructing a good student model and clustering the learners according their critical learning characteristics. A great variety of student models and techniques have been studied [8], and any clustering technique could be used to assort students according to their learning characteristics.

The *domain module* contains all characteristics of the knowledge to teach. For the experimentation analysed in this paper the Database Design domain has been used. The hierarchical structure of topics is used for the domain knowledge, where each topic is divided in other topics and tasks (sets of definitions, examples, problems, exercises, etc.) in several formats (image, text, video, etc.).

In the *pedagogical module,* the educational system finds the best way (the sequence of contents) to teach the *knowledge items,* corresponding with the internal nodes of the tree (topics), to the current student. The definition of this problem as a Reinforcement Learning problem is explained in Section 3.

Finally, the *interface module* facilitates the communication between the AIES and the student. This module applies intelligent and adaptive techniques in order to adapt the content and the navigation to the students, leaning on the pedagogical module, that decides which is the next task to be shown to the student and in which format the knowledge is going to be taught.

3 Application of Reinforcement Learning

Reinforcement learning problems [7] treat agents connected to their environment via perception and action. On each step of the interaction, the agent observes the current state, s, and chooses an action to be executed, a. This execution produces a state transition and the environment provides a reinforcement signal, r, that indicates how good the action has been to solve a defined task. The final goal of the agent is to behave choosing the actions that tend to increase the long-run sum of values of the reinforcement signal, r, learning its behavior by systematic trial and error, guided by a wide variety of algorithms [7].

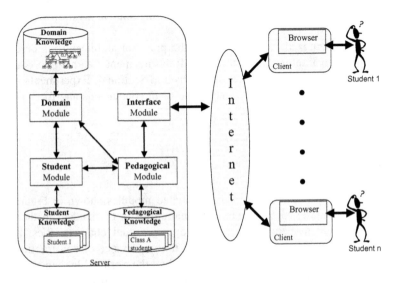

Fig. 1. Proposal Architecture

In RLATES, a *state* is defined as the student knowledge. It is represented by a vector of values related to domain knowledge items (internal nodes of the domain knowledge tree). The i-th value of the vector represent the knowledge level of the student about the i-th topic. In this work we present a simple example and, in order to limit the size of the state space, possible values of the student knowledge are limited to 0 (the student does not know the item) and 1 (the student knows the item). Sometimes, educational systems need to know how good the student learns a topic. This information can be easily added to our system by extending the possible values of the knowledge vector. Furthermore, RLATES perceives the current student state (the values of the knowledge vector) by evaluations (*tests*). The system *actions* correspond with the hypermedia pages that the educational system shows to the student (the *tasks* of the knowledge tree: *definition, exercise, problem*, etc.). The *reinforcement signal* (*r*), supplies a maximum value upon arriving to the goals of the tutor; i.e., when the student learns the totality of the contents of the educational system. This signal is used to update the system's action policy. The system behavior, B, should choose the actions that tend to maximize the long-run sum of values of the reinforcement signal, choosing in this way the optimal tutoring strategy (what, when, and how to teach; the best sequence of contents and how to teach them) to coach the current learner. The action-value function, $Q(s,a)$, estimates the usefulness of executing one action, a, (showing leaves of the knowledge tree to a student) when the system is in given knowledge state, s. This function provides an action policy, defined as is shown in equation (1).

$$\Pi(s)=\arg \max_{ai} Q(s,a_i).$$
(1)

The goal of the learning process is to find the policy such that it maximizes this function, i.e., to obtain the optimal value-action function, denoted by $Q^*(s,a)$, such that $Q^*(s,a) \geq Q(s,a) \ \forall\, a \in A, s \in S$. There are several ways to learn this function, from dynamic programming [2] to model-free methods [9]. The algorithm implemented in RLATES is the Q-learning algorithm [10], where its value-action function is defined in the equation (2).

$$Q(s,a)=(1-\alpha)\, Q(s,a)+ \alpha\{r+ \gamma\, max_{a'}\, Q(s',a')\}$$
(2)

This equation requires the definition of the possible states, s, the actions that the agent can perform in the environment, a, and the rewards that it receives at any moment for the states it arrives to after applying each action, r. The γ parameter controls the relative importance of future actions rewards with respect to new ones, and α parameter is the learning rate, that indicates how quickly the system learns.

In Table 1, how the *Q-learning* algorithm has been adapted to educational system is shown.

The Boltzmann exploration policy has been used in RLATES, because it has been demonstrated previously that it improves the system convergence in relation to the *e-greedy* exploration policy [5]. This exploration policy estimates the probability of choosing the action a according to the function defined in equation (3), where τ is a positive parameter called the *temperature*. If the temperature is high, all the probabilities of the actions have similar values and if the temperature is low, it causes a great difference in the probability of selecting each action.

$$P(a) = \frac{e^{\frac{Q_t(a)}{\tau}}}{\sum_{b=1}^{n} e^{\frac{Q_t(b)}{\tau}}}$$
(3)

4 System Functional Phases

The use of RLATES requires three phases in order to adapt better to each student in every moment of the interaction: *student clustering*, *system training*, and *system use*.

4.1   Student Clustering

RLATES is able to adapt to each student individually, updating its $Q(s,a)$ function according to the interaction with the student.

If the system maintains only one Q table for all the students that could interact, RLATES adapts to the set of all the students. However, they could have very different learning characteristics and the adaptation could be low.

Table 1. Adaptation of the *Q-learning* algorithm to Educational Systems

Q-learning adapted to AIES domain
- For each pair ($s \in$ S, $a \in$ A), initialize the table entry $Q(s,a)$.
- Do for each student of the same cluster
o   Test the current student knowledge, obtaining s
o   While the student has not finished learning (*s* is not a goal state)
• Select a knowledge tree leaf, *a*, to show to the student, following a exploration strategy.
• Test the current student knowledge, *s'*
• Receive the immediate reward, *r*. A positive reward is received when the AIES goal is achieved. A null reward is obtained in any other case.
• Update the table entry for Q(s,a), that estimates the usefulness of executing the *a* action when the student is in a particular knowledge state:
• $Q(s,a)=(1-\alpha) \, Q(s,a) + \alpha \{ r + \gamma \, max_{a.} \, Q(s',a') \}$
• Let us *s* the current student knowledge state, *s'*.

The solution is to cluster the students according to their learning characteristics before the interaction with RLATES. In this sense, the system maintains one Q table for each cluster of students. This allows the system to adapt better to each student cluster.

This phase is not necessary, but it is recommended for better adaptation to each user interacting with the system.

In this paper, a comparison of the system convergence when students of different clusters interact is presented. Two different kind of clusters have been defined based on the homogeneity of the students in the cluster (how similar their learning characteristics are). Only two learning characteristics have been used in order to define the population of students: the kind of task (*introduction* or *definition*) and the format of the hypermedia page (*video* or *text*) that they require to learn, as defined in Table 2.

In the *cluster1*, all the students learn only with *definition* tasks. They will learn the task with a probability of 0.95 if the task has *video* format, while if the task has text format, it will be learnt only with a probability of 0.05.

The *cluster2* students, on the other hand, require *definitions* and *introductions*, both with a percentage of 50%. They will learn the task in the *video* format with a percentage of 75% and the tasks in the *text* format with a probability of 0.25.

It is hypothesized that the RLATES would adapt better to the *cluster1* students individually, because they have very similar learning characteristics and the *cluster2* students are more heterogeneous.

Table 2. Students Cluster Types

Student Clusters	Tasks	Formats
Cluster Type 1 (more heterogeneous cluster)	Definitions (100%)	Video (95%) & Text (5%)
Cluster Type 2 (the most heterogeneous cluster)	Definitions (50%) & Introductions (50%)	Video (75%) & Text (25%)

4.2 System Training

In this phase, the proposal explores new pedagogical alternatives in order to teach the system knowledge, sequencing the domain content in different ways. At the same time the system interacts with the students and updates the appropriate Q table.

In this way, the system is able to converge to good teaching strategies based only in previous interaction with other students. This is related to the exploration/exploitation strategies in Reinforcement Learning. In [6], the advantages of the *Boltzmann* exploration strategy are demonstrated. That is why the RLATES system uses this exploration policy.

In this phase, the students that interact with the system could not be learning in the best way, because the system has not learned yet the optimal pedagogical policy. So, it is desired to minimize this phase as possible. This phase finishes once an near optimal action policy has been learned.

4.3 System Use

When the system has converged to a good pedagogical strategy, it is time to use this information to teach other students with similar learning characteristics. From the Q-learning algorithm point of view, that means to set the *learning rate (α)* parameter to zero and to select a greedy strategy for action selection. These students will achieve their knowledge goals in the best way the system has learned.

Although the system interaction with students has been divided in two phases (*System Training* and *System Use*), the system never stops learning, adapting its *value-action function, $Q(s,a)$*, in each step of the interaction with each student. It is said that the system is in this phase when it has learned a near optimal teaching sequence of contents.

5 Experimentation

The motivation of the experimentation in this work is to analyze how quickly the system is able to adapt its behavior to the students needs (the size of the *System Training* phase, measured in number of students needed to converge).

All the experimentation has been performed over simulated students in order to theorize about the system behavior when interacting with real students. How the behavior of the students has been simulated is explained in section 5.1. We have empirically tested with a variety of clusters types, from very homogeneous to heterogeneous. Therefore, we believe our conclusions are quite general.

5.1 Simulated Students

In order to obtain general conclusions, a great amount of experiments are necessary, and, then, lots of students are needed to interact with the system.

Most of researchers in educational systems use simulated student in order to prove the applicability of their systems, as was done in Beck's seminal work [1], based in two important motives:

First, it is difficult to persuade one person to use an application that could not be optimized, moreover when the application is an educational system that requires a high concentration (the application tests the knowledge of the person). To persuade a hundred of persons is unthinkable.

Second, the experimentation with real students has a high cost, because they spend a lot of time at the interaction and sometimes they abandon when they get bored or they notice that the system does not teach the content in the best way.

In this paper we want to test the system under very different conditions in order to draw general conclusions. We have use simulated students taking into account only two parameters in order to define the behavior of the simulated students: the student hypermedia format preference (text, video, image, etc.) and the student type of content preference (definition, introduction, etc.) as it has been defined in section 4.1.

Moreover, expert knowledge (knowledge of a database design teacher at the Carlos III University of Madrid) has been used in order to define the prerequisite relationships between the topics and the elements (tasks) of the topics. In this sense, when an hypermedia page of a certain topic, A, is shown to a student that do not knows the prerequisite topics of A, the student is not able to pass the exam associated to this topic (he could not learn this topic). Every simulated student uses this prerequisite table so that simulation results are reasonable and similar to what could be obtained from current students.

5.2   Experimentation Method

Although simulated students are used in these experiments, real situations are going to be studied: when the system interacts with different students and learns in each interaction according to the *Q-learning* algorithm.

The experiments are going to study three important issues: First, the number of students needed in order for the system to learn the action policy for a kind of cluster without initial pedagogical knowledge, i.e. initializing all the entries of the *Q* table to zero. Second, if the number of student required could be reduced by initializing the action policy with pedagogical knowledge. This could be done by training the system with simulated students which are supposed to model real students. The third issue is what should happen if the model does not represent the real student characteristics. This is equivalent to a situation where the system has been trained with students assumed to belong to *Cluster Type 1* and the real students belong to *Cluster Type 2*.

For the experiments, the *learning rate* parameter (α) of the *Q-learning* function has been fixed to 0.9 and the *Boltzmann* exploration/exploitation policy is followed. Notice that initially the system has no knowledge at all about teaching strategies.

Due to the stochasticity of the domain, experiments have been carried out ten times, and the average produced when the system learns to teach with simulated students has been shown.

5.3   Results

In Figure 2.A, the system convergence is shown when 200 *cluster1* students interacts with RLATES without initializing the *Q* table, for different *temperature* values. It is shown that the system only needs around 50 students in order to learn the optimal policy, obtaining the best result when the *temperature* parameter value is 0.01. With this value, an average of only 20 actions are required to teach the 11 topics of the domain module when *cluster1* students interact with RLATES.

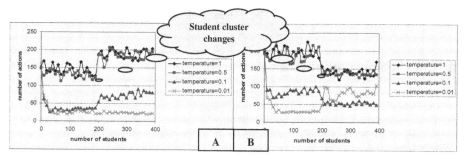

Fig. 2. A: *cluster1* to *cluster2* system convergence; B: *cluster2* to *cluster1* system convergence.

Figure 2.B shows the system convergence when 200 *cluster2* students interact with the system. The convergence property is only achieved when the *temperature* parameter is 0.01, requiring around 60 students. RLATES needs an average of 30 actions to teach only 11 topics, given the high heterogeneity of the students learning characteristics of this cluster type.

Although this results are reasonable, we are interested in reducing the number of students needed in the *System Training* phase by initializing the Q table with the pedagogical knowledge learned interacting with other students. If the initialization is correct according to the learning characteristics of the real students, *Training* phase will be eliminated. Obviously, this assumption is very strong and usually, a pedagogical policy adaptation could be required in order to achieve the best curriculum sequence for current users. This is illustrated in Figure 2.A, where *cluster2* students begin to interact with RLATES when it has previously learned the optimal teaching policy for *cluster1* students, and vice versa in Figure 2.B. In these figures, it can be observed how only 20 students are needed for the *Training* phase, even when this initialization was not good for the current students' learning characteristics. In figure 2.B, we can observe the system does not converge when the temperature is 0.01, because it behaves almost greedy.

Figure 3 summarizes all these results when the temperature is 0.1, showing the *Training* phase length for each cluster of students when no initialization is performed and when a bad initialization is done. Notice that if a correct initialization is performed, *Training* phase length is zero. This situation is the best situation for RLATES.

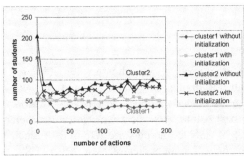

Fig. 3. Experiments summary

6   Conclusions and Further Research

This paper presents the application of the reinforcement learning model in an intelligent and adaptive educational environment. Moreover, experiments that prove the convergence of RLATES, the importance of a previous student clustering and the initialization of the pedagogical strategies have been presented and analyzed.

Simulated students have been used because it is necessary to tune all the learning parameters before using the system with real students. Also, we intended to draw general conclusions for RLATES acting under different conditions.

The experiments prove three important issues. First, the system automatically adapts its teaching tactics according to the current student learning characteristics, whatever the initial situation was. Second, RLATES adapts to the set of all the students, adapting better to the students when all of them have similar learning characteristics. This motivates a previous student clustering, although it is not necessary for the system. And third, the system reduces its *Training* phase (interacting with fewer number of students) when a initialization of the pedagogical strategies has been done, even for bad initializations (with simulated students with different learning characteristics than real ones). This can be achieved by using simulated students, before the system is put to real use with actual students. Even bad initializations (with students with different learning characteristics) will be better than no initialization at all.

Nowadays, we are involved in the evaluation of the proposal with real students, initializing the pedagogical knowledge with simulated students. It is believed that this initialization will reduce the interaction time with real students until the system convergence. For this validation we are designing an experiment with students of our Faculty belonging to different courses (intermediate and advanced courses of database design) in the Computer Science degree.

References

1. Beck, J. *Learning to Teach with Reinforcement Learning Agent*. In Proceedings of the Fifteenth National Conference on Artificial Intelligence, 1998.
2. Bellman, R. (1957). Dynamic Programming. Princeton University Press. Princeton, NJ.
3. Castro, E., Cuadra, D., Martínez, P., and Iglesias, A. Integrating Intelligent Methodological and Tutoring assistance in a CASE platform: the PANDORA experience. In Proceedings of the Informing Science & IT Education Conference. Cork, Irland, 2002.
4. De Bra, P. and Calvi, L. *An open Adaptive Hypermedia Architecture*. The New Review of Hypermedia and Multimedia, pp. 115-139 (4), 1998.
5. Iglesias, A., Martínez, P. & Fernández, F. (2003). An experience applying Reinforcement Learning in a Web-based Adaptive and Intelligent Educational System. Informatics in Education International Journal. Vol. 2, Pp. 1-18.
6. Iglesias, A., Martínez, P., Aler, R. & Fernández, F. (2003). Analising the Advantages of Using Exploration and Exploitation Strategies in an Adaptive and Intelligent Educational System. Second International Conference on Multimedia and Information & Communication Technologies in Education (m-ICTE 2003), Pp. 489-493, Vol. 1.
7. Kaelbling, L.P., Littman, M.L. & Moore, A.W. (1996) Reinforcement learning: A survey. *Int. J. of. Artificial Intelligence Research*, 237-285.
8. Sison, R. & Shimura, M. (1998). Student Modeling and Machine Learning. *International Journal of Artificial Intelligence in Education*, 9, 128-158.
9. Sutton, R.S. (1988). Learning to Predict by the Method of Temporal Difference. *Machine Learning*. Vol. 3, Pp. 9-44.
10. Watkins, C.J.C.H. *Learning from Delayed Rewards*. PhD thesis, King's College, Cambridge, UK, 1989.
11. Wenger, E. (1987). *Artificial Intelligence and Tutoring Systems*. Los Altos, CA: Morgan Kaufmann.

Statistical Learning in Digital Wireless Communications

Toshiyuki Tanaka

Department of Electronics and Information Engineering,
Tokyo Metropolitan University, Tokyo 192-0397, Japan,
tanaka@eei.metro-u.ac.jp

Abstract. Digital wireless communication systems can be regarded as solving a statistical learning problem in real time. The sender-side process of encoding and/or modulating information to be sent can be viewed as generation process of training data in the statistical learning point of view, while the receiver-side process of decoding and/or demodulating the information on the basis of possibly noisy received signals as the learning process based on the training data set. Based on this view one can analyze digital wireless communication systems within the framework of statistical learning, where an approach based on statistical physics provides powerful tools. Analysis of the code-division multiple-access (CDMA) user detection problem is discussed in detail as a demonstrative example of this approach.

1   Introduction

Various information processing tasks naturally fit into the framework of statistical inference. Nevertheless, this view was not considered seriously in many occasions in the past because formulation of a problem based on statistical inference often leads to a prohibitively large amount of computation required to solve the problem. However, recent advances in information technology allow us to reconsider the framework of statistical inference to apply to problems of information processing.

Digital wireless communications consist of various information processing tasks, many of which are best treated within the probabilistic framework. This is because digital wireless communications have to deal with various types of noise which are hard to characterize, so that they should be treated as stochastic processes. Rapidly expanding markets of various applications of digital wireless communications, including mobile phones and wireless LANs, are demanding analysis and design of larger-scale digital wireless communication systems.

An objective of this paper is, first of all, to demonstrate that communications based on the code-division multiple-access (CDMA) technology, which is increasingly adopted in several third-generation commercial mobile-phone services, can be viewed as an instance of statistical learning problem. One can expect that this view is efficient in analyzing systems' performance theoretically, as well as in deducing design policies to be used in formulating an algorithm to

S. Ben-David, J. Case, A. Maruoka (Eds.): ALT 2004, LNAI 3244, pp. 464–478, 2004.

solve a problem in CDMA communication systems, since it allows us to make use of knowledge accumulated so far in the field of statistical learning. The most nontrivial contribution to the field of statistical learning would be that from statistical mechanics [1], which suggests that various statistical-mechanical tools and concepts might be efficiently applied as well to problems of analysis and design in the field of CDMA communications. The second objective of this paper is to show that it is indeed the case, by reviewing an analysis on CDMA systems using the replica method, a tool for analysis originally developed in statistical mechanics.

This paper is organized as follows. In Sect. 2 we briefly review the basic framework of statistical learning theory. In Sect. 3 we introduce CDMA channel model and user detection problem, which are to be dealt with in the rest of the paper. The link between user detection problem and statistical learning is also established in this section. Section 4 is devoted to giving a brief explanation as to the fact that communications using error-control coding can also be linked to the framework of statistical learning. Returning to the main subject of CDMA, Sect. 5 first introduces Bayesian framework for the user detection problem, and then describes performance analysis of the optimum user detection scheme for the CDMA channel model. Appendix is devoted to give a more detailed description as to how the replica method is applied to the analysis of the optimum user detection scheme.

2   Statistical Learning Theory

We briefly review the basic framework of statistical learning theory. The basic setup of statistical learning consists of a "teacher" system, a "student" system, and a training data set. The student system is supposed to "learn" the teacher's behavior, by only observing the training data set, which is generated by the teacher.

Assume that the teacher has a stochastic input-output relation, which is characterized by a conditional distribution $p_0(y|x)$, where x and y denote input and output of the system, respectively. One may wish to deal with a deterministic teacher whose input-output relation is not stochastic but deterministic, but we can "stochastify" such a deterministic system by adding small noise to it, so that the deterministic-teacher case can be treated within the same framework by regarding it as a zero-noise limit of such stochastified teachers.

A training data set $T = \{(x_\mu, y_\mu)|\mu = 1, \ldots, N\}$ consists of N pairs of input x_μ and output y_μ. The output y_μ is assumed to be generated by the teacher system according to the conditional distribution $p_0(y|x_\mu)$. The inputs $x_1, \ldots, x_N$ are assumed to be realizations of independent and identically distributed (i.i.d.) random variables following a distribution $p_0(x)$. We also let $T_x \equiv \{x_\mu; \mu = 1, \ldots, N\}$ and $T_y \equiv \{y_\mu; \mu = 1, \ldots, N\}$.

The student system also has a stochastic input-output relation, which is characterized by another conditional distribution $p(y|x)$. The conditional distribution $p(y|x)$ is assumed to be of a parametric form with a parameter, denoted by b in this paper, so that the student can vary its behavior by adjusting it. The task of "learning from examples," which the student is supposed to perform, is to find a value of the parameter b which best approximates the teacher's behavior in view of the training data set T.

Bayesian framework is best suited to treat the problem of learning from examples. Let us assume that the student has a prior distribution $p(b)$ for the parameter b. Then, applying Bayes' theorem, one obtains the posterior distribution of b conditioned on the training data set T, as

$$p(b|T) = \frac{p(T_y|T_x, b)p(b)}{\sum_b p(T_y|T_x, b)p(b)}. \tag{1}$$

The conditional distribution $p(T_y|T_x, b)$ is given by

$$p(T_y|T_x, b) = \prod_{\mu=1}^{N} p(y_\mu|x_\mu, b), \tag{2}$$

where the notation $p(y|x, b)$ is used in order to explicitly show that the conditional $p(y|x)$, characterizing the student's input-output relation, depends on the parameter b. Based on the posterior $p(b|T)$, one can construct various estimators for b. They include:

– Maximum a posteriori (MAP) estimator:

$$\hat{b}^{(\text{MAP})} \equiv \arg\max_b p(b|T)$$

– Marginal posterior mode (MPM) estimator if b is a vector $(b_1, \ldots, b_K)$:

$$\hat{b}_k^{(\text{MPM})} \equiv \arg\max_{b_k} \sum_{b \backslash b_k} p(b|T), \quad k = 1, \ldots, K$$

– Posterior mean estimator:

$$\hat{b}^{(\text{PM})} \equiv \sum_b b\, p(b|T)$$

In order to quantify how good an estimator is, one needs a model for the teacher system. Let us assume that the teacher's conditional distribution is also parametrized by b as $p_0(y|x, b)$, and that the true prior distribution of b is $p_0(b)$. It should be noted that we make distinction between the true prior $p_0(b)$ and that assumed by the student $p(b)$, as well as between the true conditional $p_0(y|x, b)$ and that assumed by the student $p(y|x, b)$, in order to deal with situations in which the student's assumptions about the teacher are incorrect (i.e., $p(b) \neq p_0(b)$ and/or $p(y|x, b) \neq p_0(y|x, b)$). Let $\ell(\hat{b}^{(\cdot)}, b)$ denote a loss function defining a loss incurred by estimating b as $\hat{b}^{(\cdot)}$. The expected loss of an estimator $\hat{b}^{(\cdot)}$ for a given input set T_x is

$$L(\cdot|T_x) = \sum_{b, T_y} p_0(b)p_0(T_y|T_x, b)\ell(\hat{b}^{(\cdot)}, b). \tag{3}$$

Since we assume inputs T_x of the training data set to be generated randomly, one can further take its average over T_x, which is given by

$$L(\cdot) = \sum_{T_x} p_0(T_x) L(\cdot | T_x), \tag{4}$$

where $p_0(T_x) \equiv \prod_{\mu=1}^{N} p_0(x_\mu)$ denotes the distribution generating T_x. It should be noted that in evaluating the expected loss the expectation should be taken with respect to the true distributions, not those assumed by the student. It is known that the MAP estimator $\hat{b}^{(\mathrm{MAP})}$, the MPM estimator $\hat{b}^{(\mathrm{MPM})}$, and the posterior mean estimator $\hat{b}^{(\mathrm{PM})}$ are optimum if one takes $\delta_{\hat{b},b}$, $\delta_{\hat{b}_k,b_k}$, and $(\hat{b}-b)^2$ as the loss functions, respectively, and if the student's assumptions about the teacher are correct.

3   Code-Division Multiple-Access Communication Channel

In digital wireless communications, such as mobile phones and wireless LANs, it is not unusual to have more than one agent which communicates with the same receiver (a base station in cellphone systems or a wireless access point in wireless LAN systems). The term *multiple-access* refers to such a situation. The multiple-access interference (MAI) naturally occurs in a multiple-access environment, so that it is necessary for the receiver to have some means to mitigate the MAI.

CDMA is one of the technologies to alleviate the MAI. The basic fully-synchronous K-user CDMA channel model [2] (see Fig. 1) is represented by

$$y_\mu = \frac{1}{\sqrt{N}} \sum_{k=1}^{K} A_k b_k s_{k\mu} + n_\mu, \quad \mu = 1, \dots, N. \tag{5}$$

b_k is an information symbol of user k ($k = 1, \dots, K$), which is assumed to follow a prior distribution $p_{0k}(b_k)$. The information symbol undergoes the so-called spreading modulation, in which it is multiplied by the signature sequence $\{s_{k\mu}; \mu = 1, \dots, N\}$. The modulated sequence, $\{b_k s_{k\mu}; \mu = 1, \dots, N\}$, is then transmitted to a receiver. The received sequence, denoted by $\{y_\mu; \mu = 1, \dots, N\}$, is a superposition of K signals, each coming from each user. A_k denotes the amplitude of the signal sent by user k at the receiver. We also take into account additive channel noise, which is denoted by $\{n_\mu; \mu = 1, \dots, N\}$. Instances of the channel noise are assumed to be i.i.d. random variables following a distribution $\rho_0(n)$. The factor $1/\sqrt{N}$ placed at the right-hand side of (5) is to normalize the power of the signature sequence to unity. Equation (5) is also expressed in a vector form as

$$\boldsymbol{y} = S A \boldsymbol{b} + \boldsymbol{n}, \tag{6}$$

where $\boldsymbol{y} \equiv (y_1, \dots, y_N)^T$, $S \equiv (1/\sqrt{N})(s_{k\mu})$, $A = \mathrm{diag}(A_k)$, $\boldsymbol{b} \equiv (b_1, \dots, b_K)^T$, and $\boldsymbol{n} \equiv (n_1, \dots, n_N)^T$. The information symbol vector $\boldsymbol{b}$ follows the prior distribution $p_0(\boldsymbol{b}) \equiv \prod_{k=1}^{K} p_{0k}(b_k)$. The channel noise vector $\boldsymbol{n}$ follows the distribution $\rho_0(\boldsymbol{n}) = \prod_{\mu=1}^{N} \rho_0(n_\mu)$. At this point, without loss of generality we absorb the prefactor A_k into b_k and accordingly redefine the prior $p_0(\boldsymbol{b})$. The CDMA channel model therefore becomes

$$\boldsymbol{y} = S\boldsymbol{b} + \boldsymbol{n}. \tag{7}$$

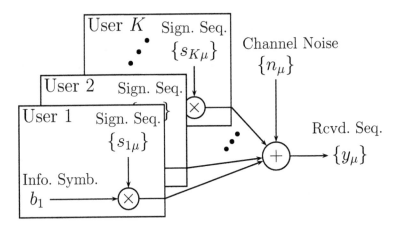

Fig. 1. CDMA channel model

The receiver has to solve the *user detection* problem. The user detection is a problem to estimate the information symbols $\boldsymbol{b}$ based on the received sequence $\boldsymbol{y}$. In performing the user detection, the receiver is assumed to have perfect knowledge about the signature sequences S. A justification to this assumption is that real CDMA systems use pseudorandom sequences as signature sequences, so that the receiver, knowing who are transmitting signals, can regenerate the same signature sequences as those used by the users sending signals, by using the same generators as the users do.

The key observation is that the user detection problem can be cast into the framework of learning from examples discussed in the previous section. Equation (7) can be further rewritten as

$$y_\mu = \frac{1}{\sqrt{N}} \boldsymbol{s}_\mu^T \boldsymbol{b} + n_\mu, \quad \mu = 1, \ldots, N, \tag{8}$$

where $\boldsymbol{s}_\mu^T \equiv (s_{1\mu}, \ldots, s_{K\mu})$. At this point, one can regard that (8) is defining a "teacher" system with input $\boldsymbol{s}_\mu$, output y_μ, and parameter $\boldsymbol{b}$, whose stochastic input-output relation is characterized by the conditional distribution $p_0(y|\boldsymbol{s}, \boldsymbol{b})$ as

$$p_0(y|\boldsymbol{s}, \boldsymbol{b}) = p_0\left(y - \frac{1}{\sqrt{N}} \boldsymbol{s}^T \boldsymbol{b}\right), \tag{9}$$

and regard $T \equiv \{(s_\mu, y_\mu); \mu = 1, \ldots, N\}$ as a training data set, which is generated by the teacher. The receiver's task of user detection is to estimate b based on T, which is equivalent to what is done by the student in the framework of learning from examples. A receiver in CDMA systems can therefore be regarded as solving the problem of learning from examples. It should be noticed as well that a receiver not only solves the learning problem, but also does it in almost *real time*, and with acceptably *high quality* of solutions, both of which should be certainly fulfilled in any commercial communication service.

4 Error-Control Coding

In this section we briefly explain that communications using error-control coding can also be cast into the framework of statistical learning. Let us consider a linear block code and a memoryless channel. A linear block code is characterized by its generator matrix G, which operates on an information block b to yield a codeword $w = G^T b$ mod 2, of length N. This relation can equivalently be rewritten as $w_\mu = g_\mu^T b$ mod 2, $\mu = 1, \ldots, N$, where w_μ and g_μ denote μ-th member of the codeword w and μ-th column of the generator G, respectively. The input-output characteristics of a memoryless channel is defined by a conditional distribution $\rho_0(y|w)$, where y and w denote an output alphabet and an input alphabet of the channel, respectively.

One can let

$$p_0(y|g, b) = \rho_0(y|w), \quad w = g^T b \quad \text{mod } 2, \tag{10}$$

and

$$T \equiv \{(g_\mu, y_\mu); \mu = 1, \ldots, N\}. \tag{11}$$

The task of decoding is to estimate the original information block b based on the received word $y \equiv (y_1, \ldots, y_N)^T$ with the knowledge of the code, i.e., G. This is equivalent to saying that the decoder should estimate b based on a "training data set" T, which, once again, can be regarded as an instance of the problems of learning from examples.

Having established the relation between error-control coding and statistical learning, it is natural to expect that various research fields, which have contributed to the field of statistical learning, will contribute to studies of error-control coding as well. In fact, statistical-mechanical approach to analyzing error-control coding is possible, yielding several nontrivial results. In this paper, we do not go into details any further about this subject: See [3] for a comprehensive review on statistical-mechanical approach to a family of error-control codes called low-density parity-check codes.

5 Performance Analysis

One can pose several questions regarding the user detection problem of CDMA systems. Since the optimum user detection problem has been proved to be NP-hard [4], efforts have been mainly directed toward designing efficient sub-optimal user detection algorithms which allow operation in nearly real time. However, from a theoretical point of view, it is important to ask the theoretical information transmission capability of the CDMA channel model. Answering this question turns out to be difficult, however: Although writing down formulas which give performance measures is not difficult, the amount of computation required to evaluate them typically scales exponentially as the system size increases, so that it soon becomes prohibitively large. Moreover, those formulas provide us with little theoretical insights into the structure of the user detection problem. Researchers have therefore sought a way of resolving this difficulty, and one important observation along this line is that the performance exhibits *self-averaging*, that is, if one adopts the so-called *random spreading assumption*, in which one regards the signatures S as randomly generated and considers averages over the randomness of the signatures, then the performance of a system with a particular realization of S does not deviate much from its average over S, and the former converges in probability to the latter in the *large-system limit*, in which one considers the limit K, $N \to \infty$ while their ratio $\beta \equiv K/N$ is kept finite. Although the approach based on the random spreading assumption as well as the large-system limit is expected to be promising, until recently there were almost no theoretical results as to the optimum user detection scheme. A notable exception is the work by Tse and Verdú [5], in which they analyzed performance of the optimum user detection, but only in the zero-noise limit.

Performance evaluation for the case of finite noise has become possible by applying tools and notions originally developed in statistical mechanics. In particular, application of the *replica method* to the performance analysis of the optimum user detection scheme has successfully resolved the difficulty mentioned above, further providing insights into the problem [6]. It should also be noted that approaches on the basis of statistical mechanics are efficient not only for theoretical performance evaluation but also for designing algorithms operating nearly real time and at the same time achieving close to theoretical performance bounds. The issue of designing algorithms on the basis of statistical mechanics will be discussed in [7].

In the following, we review the replica analysis of the optimum user detection scheme for the CDMA communication. We first introduce the Bayesian framework to the user detection problem. The receiver, acting as a student, assumes a conditional distribution, parametrized by b, as

$$p(y|s, b) = \rho\left(y - \frac{1}{\sqrt{N}} s^T b\right), \tag{12}$$

where $\rho(n)$ denotes the student's assumption about the channel noise distribution, which may be different from the true noise distribution $\rho_0(n)$. The receiver also has a postulated prior $p(b)$ of the parameter b, which is assumed factorized as $\prod_{k=1}^{K} p_k(b_k)$. One can then construct the posterior distribution of b conditioned on $T = (S, y)$ as

$$p(b|T) = \frac{p(y|S, b)p(b)}{\sum_b p(y|S, b)p(b)}. \tag{13}$$

which is to be used to estimate the parameter b based on T.

The basic quantity for evaluating the information transmission capability of a CDMA channel is the mutual information $I(b; y)$ between the information symbols b and the received sequence y. The mutual information is decomposed into two terms, as

$$I(b; y) = H(y) - H(y|b), \qquad (14)$$

where $H(y)$ is the entropy of the received sequence y and where $H(y|b)$ is the conditional entropy of y conditioned on the information symbols b. $H(y|b)$ is nothing but the entropy of channel noise n,

$$H(y|b) = NH(n) = -N \int \rho_0(n) \log \rho(n)\, dn, \qquad (15)$$

so that what remains is to evaluate $H(y)$. In view of the random spreading assumption and the large-system limit, we instead evaluate the per-user entropy averaged over S in the limit $K \to \infty$:

$$\mathcal{H} \equiv \lim_{K\to\infty} E_S\left[\frac{1}{K} H(y)\right] = -\lim_{K\to\infty} \frac{1}{K} E_S\left[\int \rho_0(y|S) \log p(y|S)\, dy\right]. \qquad (16)$$

Application of the replica method yields the following proposition:

Proposition 1. *The averaged per-user entropy in the large-system limit, $\mathcal{H}$, is given by*

$$\mathcal{H} = -\frac{1}{\beta} \iint \bar{\rho}_0\left(y - \sqrt{\frac{\beta m^2}{q}}t\right) \log \bar{\rho}(y - \sqrt{\beta q}t)\, Dt\, dy$$
$$+ \frac{1}{2}Gr + Em - \frac{1}{2}Fq$$
$$- E_{p_0,p}\left\{\sum_{b_0} p_0(b_0)\right.$$
$$\left. \times \int \log \sum_b p(b)\exp\left[\frac{G-F}{2}b^2 + (\sqrt{F}z + Eb_0)b\right] Dz\right\}, \qquad (17)$$

where $\bar{\rho}_0(n)$ and $\bar{\rho}(n)$ are defined as

$$\bar{\rho}_0(n) = \int \rho_0\left(n - \sqrt{\beta\left(r_0 - \frac{m^2}{q}\right)}u\right) Du, \qquad (18)$$

$$\bar{\rho}(n) = \int \rho(n - \sqrt{\beta(r - q)}u)\, Du, \qquad (19)$$

and where the values of $\{r_0, r, m, q, G, E, F\}$ are to be determined by solving the RS saddle-point equations:

$$r_0 = \mathrm{E}_{p_0}\left[\sum_{b_0} p_0(b_0) b_0^2\right], \qquad r = \mathrm{E}_{p_0,p}\left[\sum_{b_0} p(b_0) \int \langle b^2 \rangle\, Dz\right],$$

$$m = \mathrm{E}_{p_0,p}\left[\sum_{b_0} p(b_0) \int \langle b_0 b \rangle\, Dz\right], \qquad q = \mathrm{E}_{p_0,p}\left[\sum_{b_0} p(b_0) \int \langle b \rangle^2\, Dz\right],$$

$$G = \iint \bar{\rho}_0\left(y - \sqrt{\frac{\beta m^2}{q}}\,t\right) \frac{\bar{\rho}''(y - \sqrt{\beta q}t)}{\bar{\rho}(y - \sqrt{\beta q}t)}\, Dt\, dy,$$

$$E = \iint \bar{\rho}_0'\left(y - \sqrt{\frac{\beta m^2}{q}}\,t\right) \frac{\bar{\rho}'(y - \sqrt{\beta q}t)}{\bar{\rho}(y - \sqrt{\beta q}t)}\, Dt\, dy,$$

$$F = \iint \bar{\rho}_0\left(y - \sqrt{\frac{\beta m^2}{q}}\,t\right) \left(\frac{\bar{\rho}'(y - \sqrt{\beta q}t)}{\bar{\rho}(y - \sqrt{\beta q}t)}\right)^2 Dt\, dy.$$

$Dz \equiv (1/\sqrt{2\pi})e^{-z^2/2}dz$ denotes the Gaussian measure. $\mathrm{E}_{p_0,p}(\cdot)$ denotes taking average over distribution of $\{p_{0k}(b_k), p_k(b_k)\}$. The symbol $\langle \cdots \rangle$ denotes average of the form:

$$\langle \cdots \rangle \equiv \frac{\sum_b (\cdots) p(b) \exp\left(\frac{G-F}{2}b^2 + (\sqrt{F}z + Eb_0)b\right)}{\sum_b p(b) \exp\left(\frac{G-F}{2}b^2 + (\sqrt{F}z + Eb_0)b\right)}. \tag{20}$$

Derivation of the result is briefly described in Appendix.

The replica analysis also leads to a quite interesting consequence that, under the random spreading assumption and in the large-system limit, the optimum user detection scheme effectively reduces the problem into an equivalent single-user problem. The discussion in the following is an extension to that due to Guo and Verdú [8]. Let us consider a single-user problem in which the information symbol b is generated according to the true prior distribution $p_0(b)$ and is transmitted via a Gaussian channel so that the received signal y is given by

$$y = \frac{E}{\sqrt{F}}b + z, \qquad z \sim N(0, 1). \tag{21}$$

The signal-to-noise ratio (SNR) of the Gaussian channel is $(E^2/F)\sum_b b^2 p_0(b)$. In the Bayesian framework the receiver is also equipped with a postulated prior as well as a postulated channel model. The postulated prior is denoted by $\bar{p}(b)$ and the postulated channel is again a Gaussian channel described by

$$y = \sqrt{F}b + z, \qquad z \sim N(0, 1). \tag{22}$$

Furthermore, the signal-to-noise ratio (SNR) of the postulated Gaussian channel is $F \sum_b b^2 p(b)$. The posterior mean estimator based on the postulated model is defined as

$$\hat{b}^{(\mathrm{PM})} = \sum_b b\, p(b|y) = \frac{\sum_b b\, \bar{p}(b) \exp\left[-\left(y - \sqrt{F}b\right)^2/2\right]}{\sum_b \bar{p}(b) \exp\left[-\left(y - \sqrt{F}b\right)^2/2\right]}. \tag{23}$$

Identifying $y = (E/\sqrt{F})b_0 + z$ in view of the true channel model (21), and $\bar{p}(b) \equiv p(b)e^{Gb^2/2}$, one finds that the posterior mean (23) is equivalent to (20). This correspondence can be established in a more rigorous way, so that we have the following proposition:

Proposition 2. *Under the random spreading assumption and in the large-system limit, the optimum user detection scheme is equivalent, as far as one user out of the K users is concerned, to the estimation problem on a single-user Gaussian channel characterized by a true and a postulated priors, $p_0(b)$ and $\bar{p}(b) = p(b)e^{G^2b^2/2}$, as well as a true and a postulated Gaussian channel models, as described in (21) and (22), where $p_0(b)$ and $p(b)$ are the true and postulated priors for the user under consideration in the original CDMA channel model.*

It should be noted that the reduced single-user channel is Gaussian even though the channel noise distributions in the original CDMA channel model, $\rho_0(n)$ and $\rho(n)$, are *not* Gaussian.

As a simple corollary to Proposition 2, one obtains the following result, which reproduces a result reported by Guo and Verdú [9]:

Corollary 1. *Let $p_{0k}(b_k) = p_k(b_k) = (1/2)(\delta(b_k - A_k) + \delta(b_k + A_k))$, $A_k > 0$. Then the probability of error P in estimating b_k, the information symbol of user k, is given by*

$$P = Q\left(\frac{A_k E}{\sqrt{F}}\right), \tag{24}$$

where

$$Q(z) \equiv \int_z^{\infty} D x. \tag{25}$$

An example of performance evaluation is shown in Fig. 2, in which the same Gaussian distribution $N(0, \sigma^2)$ is assumed for both $\rho_0(n)$ and $\rho(n)$, and the probability of error P is plotted versus channel SNR $E_b/N_0 \equiv 1/(2\sigma^2)$. A nontrivial aspect observed in the result is that the performance curve becomes S-shaped as β increases. See [6] for discussion about the significance of this observation.

6   Summary

We have shown that the user detection problem can be regarded as an instance of problems of "learning from examples" in statistical learning theory. Next,

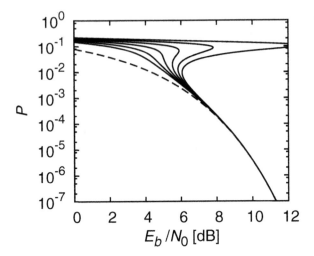

Fig. 2. Probability of error P versus SNR E_b/N_0, evaluated by replica analysis. Results for $\beta = 1$, 1.2, 1.4, 1.6, 1.8, and 2 are shown. Dashed line represents single-user bound.

we have given a brief description as to how the replica method of statistical mechanics can be applied to analysis of the optimum user detection scheme for CDMA communications. We have finally mentioned the consequence, deduced from the replica analysis, that, under the random spreading assumption and in the large-system limit, the optimum user detection scheme effectively reduces the problem of user detection into a problem of estimating an information symbol in an equivalent single-user Gaussian channel.

Acknowledgement. Support by the Ministry of Education, Culture, Sports, Science and Technology (MEXT), Japan, under the Grant-in-Aid for Scientific Research on Priority Areas, No. 14084209, is acknowledged.

References

[1] Watkin, T. L. H., Rau, A., Biehl, M.: The statistical mechanics of learning a rule. Rev. Mod. Phys. **65** (1993) 499–556
[2] Verdú, S.: *Multiuser Detection.* Cambridge Univ. Press (1998)
[3] Kabashima, Y., Saad, D.: Statistical mechanics of low-density parity-check codes. J. Phys. A: Math. Gen. **37** (2004) R1
[4] Verdú, S.: Computational complexity of optimum multiuser detection. Algorithmica **4** (1989) 303–312
[5] Tse, D. N. C., Verdú, S.: Optimum asymptotic multiuser efficiency of randomly spread CDMA. IEEE Trans. Inform. Theory **45** (2000) 171–188
[6] Tanaka, T.: A statistical-mechanics approach to large-system analysis of CDMA multiuser detectors. IEEE Trans. Inform. Theory **48** (2002) 2888–2910
[7] Kabashima, Y.: Article in this book (2004)

[8] Guo, D., Verdú, S.: Randomly spread CDMA: asymptotics via statistical physics. Submitted to IEEE Trans. Inform. Theory (2003)
[9] Guo, D., Verdú, S.: Mimimum probability of error of many-user CDMA without power control. Proc. 2002 IEEE Int. Symp. Inform. Theory, Lausanne, Switzerland (2002) p. 188
[10] Dembo, A., Zeitouni, O.: *Large Deviations Techniques and Applications*. 2nd ed., Springer (1998)

A   Replica Analysis

In this appendix we give a brief description as to how the replica calculation goes in evaluating $\mathcal{H}$ as defined in (16). Our starting point is the identity

$$\mathcal{H} = -\lim_{n \to 0} \frac{\partial}{\partial n} \lim_{K \to \infty} \frac{1}{K} \log \Xi_n, \tag{26}$$

where we let

$$\Xi_n \equiv \mathrm{E}_S \left\{ \int p_0(\boldsymbol{y}|S) \left[p(\boldsymbol{y}|S) \right]^n d\boldsymbol{y} \right\}. \tag{27}$$

First, we evaluate $\lim_{K \to \infty} K^{-1} \log \Xi_n$, under the assumption that n is a positive integer. Under the assumption, one can rewrite the integrand of (27) as

$$p_0(\boldsymbol{y}|S) \left[p(\boldsymbol{y}|S) \right]^n = \sum_{\boldsymbol{b}_0, \dots, \boldsymbol{b}_n} p_0(\boldsymbol{b}_0) p_0(\boldsymbol{y}|S, \boldsymbol{b}_0) \prod_{a=1}^{n} \left[p(\boldsymbol{b}_a) p(\boldsymbol{y}|S, \boldsymbol{b}_a) \right]. \tag{28}$$

Using this expression, Ξ_n is rewritten as

$$\Xi_n = \sum_{\boldsymbol{b}_0, \dots, \boldsymbol{b}_n} p_0(\boldsymbol{b}_0) \prod_{a=1}^{n} p(\boldsymbol{b}_a) \int \mathrm{E}_S \left[p_0(\boldsymbol{y}|S, \boldsymbol{b}_0) \prod_{a=1}^{n} p(\boldsymbol{y}|S, \boldsymbol{b}_a) \right] d\boldsymbol{y}. \tag{29}$$

Since $\boldsymbol{s}_\mu$, $\mu = 1, \dots, N$, are i.i.d., the integral in (29) can be evaluated for each μ separately, to yield

$$\int \mathrm{E}_S \left[p_0(\boldsymbol{y}|S, \boldsymbol{b}_0) \prod_{a=1}^{n} p(\boldsymbol{y}|S, \boldsymbol{b}_a) \right] d\boldsymbol{y} = e^{N\mathcal{G}}, \tag{30}$$

where we let

$$e^{\mathcal{G}} \equiv \int \mathrm{E}_{\boldsymbol{s}} \left[p_0(y|\boldsymbol{s}, \boldsymbol{b}_0) \prod_{a=1}^{n} p(y|\boldsymbol{s}, \boldsymbol{b}_a) \right] dy. \tag{31}$$

Let us assume that $e^{\mathcal{G}}$ depends on $\{\boldsymbol{b}_a\}$ only through an empirical mean

$$Q \equiv \frac{1}{K} \sum_{k=1}^{K} \mathcal{Q}(b_{0k}, b_{1k}, \dots, b_{nk}) \tag{32}$$

of a function $\mathcal{Q}(b_0, b_1, \ldots, b_n)$ (which is typically vector-valued, but may be an infinite-dimensional functional). This is indeed the case because, for fixed $\{b_0, \ldots, b_n\}$ and under the random spreading assumption, the quantities

$$v_a \equiv \frac{1}{\sqrt{K}} s^T b_a, \quad a = 0, 1, \ldots, n, \tag{33}$$

can be regarded, in the limit $N \to \infty$, as Gaussian random variables with $E(v_a) = 0$ and $\mathrm{Cov}(v_a, v_b) = K^{-1} \sum_{k=1}^{K} b_{ak} b_{bk}$, so that one can take

$$\mathcal{Q}(b_0, b_1, \ldots, b_n) \equiv \begin{pmatrix} b_0^2 & b_0 b_1 & \cdots & b_0 b_n \\ b_0 b_1 & b_1^2 & \cdots & b_1 b_n \\ \vdots & \vdots & \ddots & \vdots \\ b_0 b_n & b_1 b_n & \cdots & b_n^2 \end{pmatrix}, \tag{34}$$

which makes Q the covariance matrix of the Gaussian random variables $v \equiv (v_0, v_1, \ldots, v_n)^T$. The expectation with respect to s in (31) now corresponds to that with respect to the Gaussian random variables v, so that the result will be a function of Q, which is denoted by $e^{\mathcal{G}(Q)}$. The quantity Ξ_n is thus expressed as

$$\Xi_n = \int e^{N\mathcal{G}(Q)} \mu_K(Q) \, dQ, \tag{35}$$

where

$$\mu_K(Q) \equiv \sum_{b_0, \ldots, b_n} p_0(b_0) \prod_{a=1}^{n} p(b_a) \, \delta \left(\sum_{k=1}^{K} \mathcal{Q}(b_{0k}, \ldots, b_{nk}) - KQ \right) \tag{36}$$

is a probability weight, with respect to the measure $p_0(b_0) \prod_{a=1}^{n} p(b_a)$, of a subshell specified by Q,

$$S(Q) = \left\{ (b_0, \ldots, b_n) \, \middle| \, Q = \frac{1}{K} \sum_{k=1}^{K} \mathcal{Q}(b_{0k}, \ldots, b_{nk}) \right\}. \tag{37}$$

If the probability measure $\mu_k(Q)$ follows the large-deviation principle in the limit $K \to \infty$, with a rate function $\mathcal{I}(Q)$, one can apply the saddle-point method, or Varadhan's theorem [10], to obtain

$$\lim_{K \to \infty} K^{-1} \log \Xi_n = \sup_{Q} \left[\beta^{-1} \mathcal{G}(Q) - \mathcal{I}(Q) \right]. \tag{38}$$

We further assume that the cumulant generating function, defined as the limit

$$\Lambda(\tilde{Q}) \equiv \lim_{K \to \infty} \frac{1}{K} \log \sum_{b_0, \ldots, b_n} p_0(b_0) \prod_{a=1}^{n} p(b_a) \, e^{\tilde{Q} \cdot \sum_{k=1}^{K} \mathcal{Q}(b_{0k}, \ldots, b_{nk})}, \tag{39}$$

exists. Then, from Gärtner-Ellis theorem [10], the rate function $\mathcal{I}(\boldsymbol{Q})$ is given by the Fenchel-Legendre transform of $\Lambda(\cdot)$, as

$$\mathcal{I}(\boldsymbol{Q}) = \sup_{\tilde{\boldsymbol{Q}}}\left[\boldsymbol{Q} \cdot \tilde{\boldsymbol{Q}} - \Lambda(\tilde{\boldsymbol{Q}})\right]. \tag{40}$$

Summarizing these results, one obtains

$$\lim_{K \to \infty} K^{-1} \log \Xi_n = \sup_{\boldsymbol{Q}} \inf_{\tilde{\boldsymbol{Q}}}\left[\beta^{-1}\mathcal{G}(\boldsymbol{Q}) - \boldsymbol{Q} \cdot \tilde{\boldsymbol{Q}} + \Lambda(\tilde{\boldsymbol{Q}})\right] \tag{41}$$

The saddle-point equations, determining a saddle-point solution $(\boldsymbol{Q}, \tilde{\boldsymbol{Q}})$, are given by

$$\tilde{\boldsymbol{Q}} = \beta^{-1}\frac{\partial\mathcal{G}(\boldsymbol{Q})}{\partial\boldsymbol{Q}}, \quad \boldsymbol{Q} = \frac{\partial\Lambda(\tilde{\boldsymbol{Q}})}{\partial\tilde{\boldsymbol{Q}}}. \tag{42}$$

Let

$$\mathcal{R}(y, \boldsymbol{v}) \equiv \rho_0(y - \sqrt{\beta}v_0) \prod_{a=1}^{n} \rho(y - \sqrt{\beta}v_a), \tag{43}$$

then one can write $\mathcal{G}(\boldsymbol{Q})$ as

$$e^{\mathcal{G}(\boldsymbol{Q})} = \int \mathrm{E}_v\left[\mathcal{R}(y, \boldsymbol{v})\right] dy, \tag{44}$$

where $\mathrm{E}_v[\cdot]$ denotes taking average over Gaussian random variable $\boldsymbol{v} \sim N(\boldsymbol{0}, \boldsymbol{Q})$. Defining operators D_a, $a = 0, \dots, n$, as

$$D_0\mathcal{R}(y, \boldsymbol{v}) = \frac{\rho_0'(y - \sqrt{\beta}v_0)}{\rho_0(y - \sqrt{\beta}v_0)}\mathcal{R}(y, \boldsymbol{v}),$$

$$D_a\mathcal{R}(y, \boldsymbol{v}) = \frac{\rho'(y - \sqrt{\beta}v_a)}{\rho(y - \sqrt{\beta}v_a)}\mathcal{R}(y, \boldsymbol{v}), \quad a = 1, \dots, n, \tag{45}$$

one obtains, as saddle-point equations,

$$\tilde{Q}_{aa} = \frac{1}{2}e^{-\mathcal{G}} \int \mathrm{E}_v\left[D_a^2\mathcal{R}(y, \boldsymbol{v})\right] dy,$$

$$\tilde{Q}_{ab} = e^{-\mathcal{G}} \int \mathrm{E}_v\left[D_a D_b\mathcal{R}(y, \boldsymbol{v})\right] dy, \quad a \neq b. \tag{46}$$

Another set of saddle-point equations is

$$Q_{ab} = \mathrm{E}_{p_0, p}\left[\langle\!\langle b_a b_b \rangle\!\rangle\right], \tag{47}$$

where

$$\langle\!\langle \cdots \rangle\!\rangle \equiv \frac{\sum_{b_0, \dots, b_n}(\cdots)p_0(b) \prod_{a=1}^{n} p(b_a)e^{\sum_{a \leq b} \tilde{Q}_{ab}b_a b_b}}{\sum_{b_0, \dots, b_n} p_0(b) \prod_{a=1}^{n} p(b_a)e^{\sum_{a \leq b} \tilde{Q}_{ab}b_a b_b}}, \tag{48}$$

and where $\mathrm{E}_{p_0, p}(\cdot)$ denotes taking average over distribution of $\{p_{0k}(b_k), p_k(b_k)\}$.

To proceed further, we assume the replica symmetry (RS), which amounts to assuming that the saddle-point solutions are invariant under exchange of replica indexes $a = 1, \ldots, n$. Specifically, we let

$$Q_{00} = r_0, \qquad Q_{aa} = r, \qquad Q_{0a} = m, \qquad Q_{ab} = q,$$

$$\tilde{Q}_{00} = \frac{G_0}{2}, \qquad \tilde{Q}_{aa} = \frac{G}{2}, \qquad \tilde{Q}_{0a} = E, \qquad \tilde{Q}_{ab} = F, \tag{49}$$

where $a, b \neq 0$ and $a \neq b$. Under the RS assumption, the following representation can be introduced to define the Gaussian random variable v with the desired covariance structure:

$$v_0 = \sqrt{\left(r_0 - \frac{m^2}{q}\right)} u_0 + \sqrt{\frac{m^2}{q}} t,$$

$$v_a = \sqrt{r - q} u_a + \sqrt{q} t, \tag{50}$$

where t and u_a, $a = 0, \ldots, n$, are standard Gaussian random variables. Introducing $\bar{\rho}_0(n)$ and $\bar{\rho}(n)$ as defined in (18) and (19), one obtains

$$e^{\mathcal{G}(\boldsymbol{Q})} = \iint \bar{\rho}_0\left(y - \sqrt{\frac{\beta m^2}{q}} t\right) \left[\bar{\rho}(y - \sqrt{\beta q} t)\right]^n Dt \, dy. \tag{51}$$

The cumulant generating function $\Lambda(\tilde{\boldsymbol{Q}})$ is evaluated under the RS assumption, by making use of the so-called Hubbard-Stratonovich transform to linearize exponents. As a result, one has

$$e^{\Lambda(\tilde{\boldsymbol{Q}})} = E_{p_0,p}\left\{\sum_{b_0} p_0(b_0) e^{G_0 b_0^2/2}\right.$$

$$\left. \times \int \left[\sum_b p(b) e^{(G-F)b^2/2+(\sqrt{F}z+Eb_0)b_a}\right]^n Dz\right\}. \tag{52}$$

Putting these results together, and then taking derivative with respect to n and the limit $n \to 0$, we arrive at the final result, as summarized in Proposition 1.

A BP-Based Algorithm for Performing Bayesian Inference in Large Perceptron-Type Networks

Yoshiyuki Kabashima and Shinsuke Uda

Tokyo Institute of Technology, Yokohama 2268502, Japan,
kaba@dis.titech.ac.jp, uda@sp.dis.titech.ac.jp

Abstract. Although the Bayesian approach provides optimal performance for many inference problems, the computation cost is sometimes
impractical. We herein develop a practical algorithm by which to approximate Bayesian inference in large single-layer feed-forward networks
(perceptrons) based on belief propagation (BP). Although direct application of BP to the inference problem remains computationally difficult,
by introducing methods and concepts from statistical mechanics that are
related to the central limit theorem and the law of large numbers, the
proposed BP-based algorithm exhibits nearly optimal performance in a
practical time scale for ideal large networks. In order to demonstrate
the practical significance of the proposed algorithm, an application to a
problem that arises in a mobile communications system is also presented.

1   Introduction

Learning and inference in probabilistic models are important in research on machine learning and artificial intelligence. In a general scenario, a probabilistic
relationship between an N-dimensional input vector $\boldsymbol{x}$ and output y, which may
be discrete or continuous, and sometimes multi-dimensional, is obtained by a
conditional distribution $P(y|\boldsymbol{x}, \boldsymbol{w})$, where $\boldsymbol{w}$ denotes a set of adjustable param-
eters. Prior knowledge concerning $\boldsymbol{w}$ may be represented by a prior distribution
$P(\boldsymbol{w})$. Under such circumstances, a learner is required either to infer the machine
parameter $\boldsymbol{w}$ or to predict the output y^{p+1} of the $p+1$-th input $\boldsymbol{x}^{p+1}$ based on
a set of p training data (or examples) $D^p = \{(\boldsymbol{x}^1, y^1), (\boldsymbol{x}^2, y^2), \dots, (\boldsymbol{x}^p, y^p)\}$.

The Bayesian formula for evaluating the posterior distribution

$$P(\boldsymbol{w}|D^p) = \frac{P(D^p|\boldsymbol{w})P(\boldsymbol{w})}{P(D^p)} = \frac{P(\boldsymbol{w}) \prod_{\mu=1}^{p} P(y^\mu|\boldsymbol{x}^\mu, \boldsymbol{w})}{\int d\boldsymbol{w} P(\boldsymbol{w}) \prod_{\mu=1}^{p} P(y^\mu|\boldsymbol{x}^\mu, \boldsymbol{w})} \tag{1}$$

is important in such tasks. If the goal of the learning is to accurately estimate
the machine parameter $\boldsymbol{w}$, then the optimal estimator $\hat{\boldsymbol{w}}^{\text{Bayes}}$ can be designed
for a given loss function $L(\boldsymbol{w}, \hat{\boldsymbol{w}})$, which represents the deviation between $\boldsymbol{w}$ and
its estimation $\hat{\boldsymbol{w}}$, so as to minimize the expected loss as

$$\hat{\boldsymbol{w}}^{\text{Bayes}} = \operatorname*{argmin}_{\hat{\boldsymbol{w}}} \left\{ \int d\boldsymbol{w} P(\boldsymbol{w}|D^p) L(\boldsymbol{w}, \hat{\boldsymbol{w}}) \right\}, \tag{2}$$

S. Ben-David, J. Case, A. Maruoka (Eds.): ALT 2004, LNAI 3244, pp. 479–493, 2004.
© Springer-Verlag Berlin Heidelberg 2004

utilizing the posterior distribution (1) [1]. Predicting the output for a new input x^{p+1} is another possible goal of the learning. In such cases, a loss function $L(y^{p+1}, \hat{y})$ is defined for y^{p+1} and its estimation $\hat{y}$, to which the machine parameter w is not directly related. However, the optimal predictor $\hat{y}^{\mathrm{Bayes}}$ can also be constructed by minimizing the expected loss as

$$\hat{y}^{\mathrm{Bayes}} = \operatorname*{argmin}_{\hat{y}} \left\{ \int dy P(y^{p+1}|x^{p+1}, D^p) L(y^{p+1}, \hat{y}) \right\}, \tag{3}$$

where the Bayesian predictive distribution [2]

$$P(y^{p+1}|x^{p+1}, D^p) = \int dw P(w|D^p) P(y^{p+1}|x^{p+1}, w), \tag{4}$$

is evaluated from the posterior distribution (1) as well.

Equations (2)-(4) indicate that performing averages with respect to the posterior (1) is fundamental in such optimal strategies. Unfortunately, this becomes computationally difficult as the dimensionality of w increases. Therefore, previously, the Bayesian approach was considered to be impractical except with respect to small models that contain only a few parameters, despite being recognized as optimal. However, recent cross-disciplinary research in areas such as machine learning [3,4,5,6], error correcting codes [7,8,9], and wireless communications [10,11], has revealed that methods from statistical mechanics (SM) can be useful in developing efficient approximation algorithms for computing averages and that the difficulty associated with the application of Bayesian inference can be practically overcome for several applications [12].

The purpose of the present study is to demonstrate one example of such an application. More specifically, we develop an efficient algorithm that approximates Bayesian inference on a practical time scale for single-layer feedforward networks (perceptrons). The algorithm is based on belief propagation (BP), which was developed while researching graphically represented probabilistic models [14]. Belief propagation can be carried out on a practical time scale when the posterior distribution is pictorially represented by a sparse graph. Unfortunately, the posterior distribution of the learning problem of perceptrons corresponds to a dense graph, which implies that the direct application of BP is still computationally difficult. However, we demonstrate herein that this difficulty can be overcome using methods and concepts from SM and that the performance of the proposed BP-based algorithm is nearly optimal for ideal cases of large networks.

The present paper is organized as follows. In the next section, we introduce the learning problem for perceptrons that will be considered in the present study. In Section 3, the proposed learning algorithm based on BP is developed using techniques from SM. The properties of the proposed algorithm are also examined in this section. In Section 4, an application to a problem that arises in a mobile communications system is presented in order to demonstrate the significance of the proposed algorithm to real-world problems. The final section summarizes the present study.

2   Learning of Perceptrons

In the present study, we focus on a learning machine (probabilistic model) of the single-layer-perceptron-type that is specified by a conditional distribution

$$P(y|\boldsymbol{x}, \boldsymbol{w}) = g(y|\frac{\boldsymbol{w} \cdot \boldsymbol{x}}{\sqrt{N}}), \tag{5}$$

where $\boldsymbol{w} = (w_1, w_2, \dots, w_N)$ denotes the adjustable machine parameters. The parameters can be either continuous or discrete. However, in the present study we assume a factorized prior distribution

$$P(\boldsymbol{w}) = \prod_{i=1}^{N} P(w_i), \tag{6}$$

for computational tractability. For simplicity, we also assume that the input vectors $\boldsymbol{x}^{\mu}$ ($\mu = 1, 2, \dots, p$) of the training set are independently generated from an identical uniform and uncorrelated distribution that is characterized by $\overline{x_i} = 0$ and $\overline{x_i x_j} = \delta_{ij}$, where $\overline{(\cdots)}$ denotes the average of $(\cdots)$ over a certain distribution of examples. Extension to correlated distributions that have non-diagonal covariance matrices is possible at the expense of a slight increase in computational cost [4,16,17].

In many cases, the averages relevant to the optimal inference strategy can be easily computed from the marginal posterior distribution

$$P(w_i|D^p) = \int \prod_{j \neq i} dw_j P(\boldsymbol{w}|D^p). \tag{7}$$

Notice that the evaluation of this distribution is still computationally difficult in spite that several assumptions are introduced. Therefore, we develop an algorithm by which to efficiently evaluate Eq. (7). For this task, we select belief propagation (BP) [14], or the sum-product algorithm [15], as a promising candidate, since BP exhibits excellent performance in several applications [7,8,9, 18].

3   A BP-Based Algorithm

3.1   Graphical Representation

For the application of BP to the present learning problem, we graphically represent the dependences of $\boldsymbol{w}$ on the training set D^p in the posterior distribution (1), as shown in Fig. 1 (a). In this figure, each component of parameters w_i ($i = 1, 2, \dots, N$) is denoted by a node (circle) and each output of the training examples y^{μ} ($\mu = 1, 2, \dots, p$) is represented by a different type of node (square). The components of input vector x_i^{μ} are represented by lines, since w_i and y^{μ} are directly related through Eq. (5). Since, generally, none of the individual input vectors x_i^{μ} vanishes, this construction scheme implies that the posterior distribution of the current perceptron learning is represented as a *complete bipartite graph*.

(a)
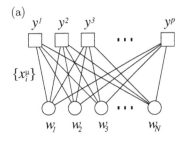

(b)
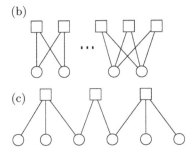

(c)

Fig. 1. Graphical representations of Bayesian inference problems. In the above graphs, variables to be estimated are denoted as circles and observed data are denoted as squares. Each line represents a direct relation between the unobserved variable and the data. (a) The inference problem in a perceptron is represented by a complete bipartite graph, the lines of which correspond to the components of input vectors x_i^μ. (b) A graph containing loops. (c) A loop-free graph.

3.2   Direct Application of BP and Computational Difficulty

In Fig. 1, BP is expressed as an iterative algorithm in order to compute Eq. (7) by passing certain positive functions $m_{i\to\mu}(w_i)$ and $\hat{m}_{\mu\to i}(w_i)$, which are often termed *messages*, between the two types of nodes [14]. In the current system, the messages are updated as

$$\hat{m}_{\mu\to i}^{t+1}(w_i) = \hat{\alpha}_{\mu\to i} \int \prod_{j\neq i} dw_j\, g(y^\mu | \Delta^\mu) \prod_{j\neq i} m_{j\to\mu}^t(w_j), \tag{8}$$

$$m_{i\to\mu}^t(w_i) = \alpha_{i\to\mu} P(w_i) \prod_{\nu\neq\mu} \hat{m}_{\nu\to i}^t(w_i), \tag{9}$$

where $\Delta^\mu = \frac{\boldsymbol{w}\cdot\boldsymbol{x}^\mu}{\sqrt{N}}$ and $t = 0, 1, 2, \ldots$ is the number of updates. Here, $\hat{\alpha}_{\mu\to i}$ and $\alpha_{i\to\mu}$ are constants such that the normalization condition $\int dw_i \hat{m}_{\mu\to i}(w_i) = \int dw_i m_{i\to\mu}(w_i) = 1$ holds. Rather than a sequential update (in which only a single variable is changed per single update), we employ a parallel update (in which all of the variables are changed for each update). Using the messages $\hat{m}_{\mu\to i}^t(w_i)$, the marginal posterior distribution (7) is approximately evaluated as

$$P(w_i | D^p) = \alpha_i P(w_i) \prod_{\mu=1}^{p} \hat{m}_{\mu\to i}^t(w_i), \tag{10}$$

at the t-th update.

If a graph is free from loops, then iteration of Eqs. (8) and (9) leads to the exact marginals (7) [14,8] (see Fig. 1 (b) and (c)). The required computational cost is practically tractable because the number of variable nodes linked to each example node is $O(1)$ and the evaluation of Eq. (8) is the most time-consuming task in BP. On the other hand, for general loopy graphs, BP can work as an approximation algorithm, although the convergence properties of Eqs. (8) and (9) have not yet been fully clarified. However, excellent experimental approximation performances have been reported for randomly constructed sparse graphs [7,8, 18,19], for which the BP updates are computationally feasible as well. This result may appear reasonable since the typical length of loops in randomly constructed sparse graphs diverges as $O(\ln N)$ with respect to the number of nodes N [20], and the properties of such graphs are therefore expected to approach those of loop-free graphs when N is large.

In contrast, dense graphs, including the complete bipartite graph of the present system, contain many short loops, which may cause the properties of the system to be very different from those of loop-free graphs. Furthermore, as all of the parameter nodes are connected to each example node, the evaluation of Eq. (8) is computationally difficult. As a result, the present attempt to develop an approximation algorithm based on BP does not appear to be promising for the current learning problem of perceptrons.

3.3   Gaussian Approximation and Self-Averaging Property

However, the computational difficulty of BP in the present problem *when the size of network N is large* can be resolved by applying methods and concepts from SM to obtain an algorithm that exhibits a nearly optimal performance with practical computational cost for ideal cases. This approach is similar to that introduced for characterization of the equilibrium state in [3,4,21]. Here, we show that a similar scheme is also useful for developing an efficient algorithm having a low computational cost that seeks the equilibrium state.

We first expand the conditional distribution of each example μ up to the first order of w_i as

$$g(y^\mu|\Delta^\mu) \simeq g(y^\mu|\Delta_i^\mu) + g'(y^\mu|\Delta_i^\mu)\frac{x_i^\mu w_i}{\sqrt{N}}, \qquad (11)$$

where $\Delta_i^\mu = \Delta^\mu - N^{-1/2}x_i^\mu w_i = N^{-1/2}\sum_{j\neq i} x_j^\mu w_j$. Next, we note that the integral over $w_{j\neq i}$ in Eq. (8) has an intuitive implication of the average with respect to $w_{j\neq i}$ over a factorial multi-dimensional distribution $\prod_{j\neq i} m_{j\to\mu}^t(w_j)$. Equation (9) indicates that $m_{j\to\mu}^t(w_j)$ can be regarded as a marginal distribution that is determined by a data set from which $(\boldsymbol{x}^\mu, y^\mu)$ is absent. Since inputs $\boldsymbol{x}^\mu$ are assumed to be generated independently of each other, $w_{j\neq i}$ is typically not correlated with $\boldsymbol{x}^\mu$ when $w_{j\neq i}$ is generated from $\prod_{j\neq i} m_{j\to\mu}^t(w_j)$ and, therefore, Δ_i^μ can be treated as a Gaussian random variable due to the central limit theorem. The average of the Gaussian variable is obtained as $\langle\Delta_i^\mu\rangle_\mu^t = N^{-1/2}\sum_{j\neq i} x_j^\mu \langle w_j\rangle_\mu^t$, where $\langle\cdots\rangle_\mu^t$ represents the average of $(\cdots)$ with respect to the factorized probability $\prod_{j\neq i} m_{j\to\mu}^t(w_j)$. On the other hand, evaluating the variance $\langle(\Delta_i^\mu)^2\rangle_\mu^t - \left(\langle\Delta_i^\mu\rangle_\mu^t\right)^2 = N^{-1}\sum_{j,k\neq i} x_j^\mu x_k^\mu \left(\langle w_j w_k\rangle_\mu^t - \langle w_j\rangle_\mu^t \langle w_k\rangle_\mu^t\right)$ is nontrivial. However, research in the area of statistical mechanics of disordered systems indicates that such variance converges to its expectation with respect to the sample $\boldsymbol{x}^\mu$ in various systems as

$$
\begin{aligned}
\left\langle (\Delta_i^\mu)^2 \right\rangle_\mu^t - \left(\langle \Delta_i^\mu \rangle_\mu^t \right)^2 &\simeq \left\langle (\Delta^\mu)^2 \right\rangle_\mu^t - \left(\langle \Delta^\mu \rangle_\mu^t \right)^2 \\
&\to \frac{1}{N} \sum_{j,k} \overline{x_j^\mu x_k^\mu} \left(\langle w_j w_k \rangle_\mu^t - \langle w_j \rangle_\mu^t \langle w_k \rangle_\mu^t \right) \\
&= \frac{1}{N} \sum_{i=1} \left(\langle w_i^2 \rangle_\mu^t - \left(\langle w_i \rangle_\mu^t \right)^2 \right),
\end{aligned}
\tag{12}
$$

in the 'thermodynamic limit' $N, p \to \infty$ with $\alpha = p/N$ fixed, which is referred to as the *self-averaging* property [3,4,21]. Therefore, we employ this property as an approximation for sufficiently large networks and further approximate the variance as $\left\langle (\Delta_i^\mu)^2 \right\rangle_\mu^t - \left(\langle \Delta_i^\mu \rangle_\mu^t \right)^2 \simeq \Xi^t$, where

$$
\Xi^t = \frac{1}{N} \sum_{i=1}^N \left(\langle w_i^2 \rangle^t - \left(\langle w_i \rangle^t \right)^2 \right),
\tag{13}
$$

neglecting the $O(N^{-1})$ difference, where $\langle (\cdots) \rangle^t$ denotes the average of $(\cdots)$ with respect to Eq. (10).

Substituting Eq. (11) into Eq. (8) and replacing the multi-dimensional integral with the average over the single Gaussian variable yields

$$
\begin{aligned}
\hat{m}_{\mu \to i}^{t+1}(w_i) &\propto 1 + \frac{\partial \ln \left[\mathcal{G} \left(y^\mu \,|\, \langle \Delta^\mu \rangle_\mu^t ; \Xi^t \right) \right]}{\partial \langle \Delta^\mu \rangle_\mu^t} \frac{x_i^\mu w_i}{\sqrt{N}} \\
&\simeq e^{\frac{\partial \ln \left[\mathcal{G} \left(y^\mu | \langle \Delta^\mu \rangle_\mu^t ; \Xi^t \right) \right]}{\partial \langle \Delta^\mu \rangle_\mu^t} \frac{x_i^\mu w_i}{\sqrt{N}}} \equiv e^{\hat{h}_{\mu \to i}^{t+1} w_i},
\end{aligned}
\tag{14}
$$

where

$$
\mathcal{G}(y^\mu \,|\, \langle \Delta_i^\mu \rangle_\mu^t ; \Xi^t) = \int Dz\, g(y^\mu \,|\, \langle \Delta_i^\mu \rangle_\mu^t + \sqrt{\Xi^t} z),
\tag{15}
$$

and $Dz = \frac{dz}{\sqrt{2\pi}} e^{-\frac{z^2}{2}}$. Inserting Eq. (15) into Eq. (9) yields

$$
m_{i \to \mu}^t(w_i) \propto P(w_i) e^{h_{i \to \mu}^t w_i},
\tag{16}
$$

where $h_{i \to \mu}^t$ is obtained as

$$
h_{i \to \mu}^t = \sum_{\nu \neq \mu} \hat{h}_{\nu \to i}^t = \sum_{\nu \neq \mu} \frac{x_i^\nu}{\sqrt{N}} \frac{\partial \ln \left[\mathcal{G} \left(y^\nu \,|\, \langle \Delta^\nu \rangle_\nu^t ; \Xi^t \right) \right]}{\partial \langle \Delta^\nu \rangle_\nu^t},
\tag{17}
$$

for each update t. Finally, the approximate marginal posterior distribution (10) is evaluated as

$$
P(w_i | D^p) = \mathcal{Z}^{-1}(h_i^t) P(w_i) e^{h_i^t w_i},
\tag{18}
$$

where

$$h_i^t = \sum_{\mu=1}^{p} \hat{h}_{\mu \to i}^t = \sum_{\mu=1}^{p} \frac{x_i^\mu}{\sqrt{N}} \frac{\partial \ln \left[\mathcal{G}\left(y^\mu | \langle \Delta^\mu \rangle_\mu^t ; \Xi^t \right) \right]}{\partial \langle \Delta^\mu \rangle_\mu^t}, \tag{19}$$

and the normalization factor

$$\mathcal{Z}(h_i^t) = \int dw_i P(w_i) e^{h_i^t w_i}, \tag{20}$$

can be used to evaluate the approximate posterior average $\langle w_i \rangle^t$ and macroscopic parameter Ξ^t as

$$\langle w_i \rangle^t = \frac{\partial \ln \left[\mathcal{Z}(h_i^t) \right]}{\partial h_i^t}, \tag{21}$$

and

$$\Xi^t = \frac{1}{N} \sum_{i=1}^{N} \frac{\partial^2 \ln \left[\mathcal{Z}(h_i^t) \right]}{(\partial h_i^t)^2}, \tag{22}$$

respectively.

3.4 Further Reduction of Computational Cost

Equations (14) and (16) constitute the fundamental component of the approximation algorithm. The necessary cost for computing these equations is $O(N)$ and $O(p)$ for each pair of indices i and μ, which means that the computation of $O(N^3)$ is required for each update in the 'thermodynamic situation' in which $\alpha = p/N$ is $O(1)$. Although this may already be practically tractable, the computational cost can be reduced further.

Here, we use the perturbation expansion

$$\langle w_i \rangle_\mu^t \simeq \langle w_i \rangle^t - \frac{\partial^2 \ln \left[\mathcal{Z}(h_i^t) \right]}{(\partial h_i^t)^2} \hat{h}_{\mu \to i}^t, \tag{23}$$

which is derived from Eqs. (17), (19) and (21). In addition, this implies

$$\langle \Delta_i^\mu \rangle_\mu^t \simeq \langle \Delta^\mu \rangle^t - \Xi^t a_\mu^t - \frac{x_i^\mu}{\sqrt{N}} \langle w_i \rangle^t, \tag{24}$$

where $a_\mu^t \equiv \frac{\partial \ln[\mathcal{G}(y^\mu | \langle \Delta^\mu \rangle_\mu^t ; \Xi^t)]}{\partial \langle \Delta^\mu \rangle_\mu^t}$. Inserting these into Eqs. (14) and (21) and omitting the negligible terms for large N and p yields update rules for $\langle w_i \rangle^t$ and a_μ^t as

$$a_\mu^{t+1} = \frac{\partial \ln \left[\mathcal{G}\left(y^\mu | \langle \Delta^\mu \rangle^t - \Xi^t a_\mu^t ; \Xi^t \right) \right]}{\partial \langle \Delta^\mu \rangle^t}, \tag{25}$$

and

$$\langle w_i \rangle^t = \frac{\partial \ln \left[\mathcal{Z} \left(\theta_i^t - \Gamma^{t-1} \langle w_i \rangle^{t-1} \right) \right]}{\partial \theta_i^t}, \tag{26}$$

respectively, where $\theta_i^t = \sum_{\mu=1}^{N} \frac{x_i^\mu}{\sqrt{N}} a_\mu^t$. In these equations, the macroscopic variables Ξ^t and Γ^t are evaluated as

$$\Xi^t = \frac{1}{N} \sum_{i=1}^{N} \frac{\partial^2 \ln \left[\mathcal{Z} \left(\theta_i^t - \Gamma^{t-1} \langle w_i \rangle^{t-1} \right) \right]}{\left(\partial \theta_i^t \right)^2}, \tag{27}$$

and

$$\Gamma^t = \frac{1}{N} \sum_{\mu=1}^{p} \frac{\partial^2 \ln \left[\mathcal{G} \left(y^\mu | \langle \Delta^\mu \rangle^t - \Xi^t a_\mu^t; \Xi^t \right) \right]}{\left(\partial \langle \Delta^\mu \rangle^t \right)^2}, \tag{28}$$

respectively, from $\langle w_i \rangle^t$ and a_μ^t. Equations (25)-(28) denote the general expression of the above-developed approximation algorithm.

We would now like to discuss a number of important points. The first is concerning the cost of computation. Equations (25) and (26), which are the heart of the developed algorithm, can be performed with $O(N)$ and $O(p)$ computations for each index μ or i, respectively, which indicates that the necessary computational cost per update is reduced from $O(N^3)$ to $O(N^2)$. This is because the number of variables to handle can be reduced from $O(N^2)$ to $O(N)$ by using the perturbation expansions (23) and (24) for large systems. The second point of discussion is the link to the Bayesian inference. The Bayesian predictive distribution (4) for a novel $p + 1$-th example can be computed as

$$P(y^{p+1}|\boldsymbol{x}^{p+1}, D^p) = \int Dz g \left(y^{p+1}| \langle \Delta^{p+1} \rangle^t + \sqrt{\Xi^t} z \right)$$
$$= \mathcal{G}(y^{p+1}| \langle \Delta^{p+1} \rangle^t; \Xi^t), \tag{29}$$

from the estimates at the t-th update, which indicates how the developed algorithm can be utilized for high-performance inference. The third point of discussion is the extensibility. The developed algorithm can be extended to the cases of the correlated distribution in which the covariance matrix $C = (\overline{x_i x_j} - \overline{x_i} \overline{x_j})$ is not diagonal. In such cases, a similar algorithm is obtained for continuous parameters by modifying the factorized prior distribution (6) to a correlated Gaussian distribution $P(\boldsymbol{w}) = (2\pi)^{-N/2} (\det FC)^{1/2} e^{-F \boldsymbol{w}^{\mathrm{T}} C \boldsymbol{w}/2}$ $(F > 0)$, as proposed in [4] while the linear response relation $\langle w_i w_j \rangle^t - \langle w_i \rangle^t \langle w_j \rangle^t = \frac{\partial \langle w_i \rangle^t}{\partial \theta_j^t}$ [16,17] offers another possibility of extension for other priors. Finally, as mentioned below, in developing the current algorithm, we have assumed that the distribution (covariance) of input vectors is known. In addition, we have utilized the self-averaging property under the assumption that the size of the network is sufficiently large. However, these assumptions are not necessarily both satisfied for real-world problems, for which the developed algorithm may not exhibit a sufficient approximation performance. For such cases, an alternative scheme termed the *adaptive TAP* approach has been developed [5]. This alternative scheme can be adapted to the given examples without knowledge of the properties of the background distribution from which the examples are generated. In addition, this scheme uses the same equilibrium solution as the current algorithm when the above two assumptions are satisfied. However, since the efficient scheme has not been fully examined yet, the necessary computational cost of this method is typically $O(N^3)$, which may limit its applicability to relatively small networks. Therefore, the present algorithm of computational cost $O(N^2)$ is still competitive for large networks.

3.5   Macroscopic Analysis in a Teacher-Student Scenario

In order to examine the properties of the proposed BP-based algorithm, let us assume a teacher-student scenario in which each output y^μ ($\mu = 1, 2, \ldots, p$) is labeled by a teacher network that is a perceptron-type probabilistic model (5) of a true parameter $\boldsymbol{w}^0 = (w_1^0, w_2^0, \ldots, w_N^0)$ ($|\boldsymbol{w}^0|^2 = N$). In such situations, the properties of the algorithm can be analyzed by monitoring several macroscopic variables. For comparison with the existing results from SM [22], we assume a factorizable Gaussian prior $P(w_i) = \sqrt{\frac{F}{2\pi}} e^{-\frac{F w_i^2}{2}}$, where F is adaptively determined from the *spherical constraint* $\sum_{i=1}^N \langle w_i^2 \rangle = N$.

For the macroscopic analysis, we assume that signal/noise separation is possible in $\hat{h}_{\mu \to i}^t$ as

$$\hat{h}_{\mu \to i}^t \simeq \frac{\hat{R}^t}{p} w_i^0 + \sqrt{\frac{\hat{Q}^t}{p}} z_{\mu i}, \tag{30}$$

where $\hat{R}^t$ and $\hat{Q}^t$ represent the signal and noise strengths, respectively, and $z_{\mu i}$ is modeled as an independent normal Gaussian random number for each pair of indices μ and i. Inserting Eq. (30) into Eq. (16) and neglecting statistical fluctuations and small differences yields $\boldsymbol{w}^0 \cdot \langle \boldsymbol{w} \rangle_\mu^t / N \simeq \boldsymbol{w}^0 \cdot \langle \boldsymbol{w} \rangle^t / N \equiv R^t$ and $|\langle \boldsymbol{w} \rangle_\mu^t|^2 / N \simeq |\langle \boldsymbol{w} \rangle^t|^2 / N \equiv Q^t$ hold for $\mu = 1, 2, \ldots, p$, and the macroscopic variables R^t and Q^t can be evaluated as

$$R^t = \frac{\hat{R}^t}{F^t}, \tag{31}$$

$$Q^t = \frac{\hat{Q}^t + (\hat{R}^t)^2}{(F^t)^2}, \tag{32}$$

where $F^t = \frac{1}{2}\left(1 + \sqrt{1 + 4(\hat{Q}^t + (\hat{R}^t)^2)}\right)$ is obtained from the spherical constraint. This constraint also yields the relation $\Xi^t = 1 - Q^t$.

Next, we examine the update of the strengths $\hat{R}^t$ and $\hat{Q}^t$. Equations (16) and (30), in conjunction with the self-averaging property, indicate that $\hat{R}^t$ and $\hat{Q}^t$ are updated as

$$\hat{R}^{t+1} \simeq \sum_{\mu=1}^{p} \frac{\sum_{i=1}^{N} w_i^0 \hat{h}_{\mu \to i}^{t+1}}{\sum_{i=1}^{N} (w_i^0)^2} \simeq \alpha \int dy^\mu g(y^\mu | \Delta_0^\mu) \Delta_0^\mu \frac{\partial \ln \left[\mathcal{G}(y^\mu | \langle \Delta^\mu \rangle_\mu^t ; \Xi^t) \right]}{\partial \langle \Delta^\mu \rangle_\mu^t}, \tag{33}$$

$$\hat{Q}^{t+1} \simeq \sum_{\mu=1}^{p} \frac{\sum_{i=1}^{N} (\hat{h}_{\mu \to i}^{t+1})^2}{\sum_{i=1}^{N} z_{\mu i}^2} \simeq \alpha \int dy^\mu g(y^\mu | \Delta_0^\mu) \left(\frac{\partial \ln \left[\mathcal{G}(y^\mu | \langle \Delta^\mu \rangle_\mu^t ; \Xi^t) \right]}{\partial \langle \Delta^\mu \rangle_\mu^t} \right)^2 \tag{34}$$

where $\sum_{i=1}^{N} (w_i^0)^2 = N$, $\sum_{i=1}^{N} z_{\mu i}^2 \simeq N$ and $\overline{(x_i^\mu)^2} = 1$. In addition, statistical fluctuations and small differences between $\langle \Delta_i^\mu \rangle_\mu$ and $\langle \Delta^\mu \rangle_\mu$ were neglected. In order to evaluate Eqs. (33) and (34), let us suppose that the relative position of $\langle \boldsymbol{w} \rangle_\mu^t$ to $\boldsymbol{w}^0$ is characterized by R^t and Q^t. In such cases, the central limit theorem implies that $\langle \Delta^\mu \rangle_\mu^t = N^{-1/2} \langle \boldsymbol{w} \rangle_\mu \cdot \boldsymbol{x}^\mu$ and $\Delta_0^\mu = N^{-1/2} \boldsymbol{w}^0 \cdot \boldsymbol{x}^\mu$ can be regarded as zero-mean correlated Gaussian random numbers, the second moments of which are obtained as

$$\overline{\left(\langle \Delta^\mu \rangle_\mu^t \right)^2} = Q^t, \quad \overline{\Delta_0^\mu \langle \Delta^\mu \rangle_\mu^t} = R^t, \quad \overline{(\Delta_0^\mu)^2} = 1, \tag{35}$$

because each component of $\boldsymbol{x}^\mu$ is generated from a distribution of the zero mean and unit variance, independent of other inputs $\boldsymbol{x}^{\nu \neq \mu}$. This allows us to represent these variables as

$$\langle \Delta^\mu \rangle_\mu^t = \sqrt{Q^t} u_\mu, \quad \Delta_0^\mu = \sqrt{1 - \frac{(R^t)^2}{Q^t}} v_\mu + \frac{R^t}{\sqrt{Q^t}} u_\mu, \tag{36}$$

using independent normal Gaussian random numbers u_μ and v_μ. Next, by applying the formula $\int Dz z f(z) = \int Dz f'(z)$, we obtain

$$\hat{R}^{t+1} = \frac{\alpha}{R^t} \int dy Du \frac{\partial \mathcal{G} \left(y | \frac{R^t}{\sqrt{Q^t}} u; \tilde{\Xi}^t \right)}{\partial u} \frac{\partial \ln \left[\mathcal{G}(y | \sqrt{Q^t} u; \Xi^t) \right]}{\partial u}, \tag{37}$$

$$\hat{Q}^{t+1} = \frac{\alpha}{Q^t} \int dy Du \mathcal{G} \left(y | \frac{R^t}{\sqrt{Q^t}} u; \tilde{\Xi}^t \right) \left(\frac{\partial \ln \left[\mathcal{G}(y | \sqrt{Q^t} u; \Xi^t) \right]}{\partial u} \right)^2, \tag{38}$$

where $\tilde{\Xi}^t \equiv \frac{(R^t)^2}{Q^t}$, which, in conjunction with Eqs. (31) and (32), describe the macroscopic behavior of the BP dynamics.

Note that these equations represent only the natural iteration of the saddle point equations of the *replica analysis* under the replica symmetric (RS) ansatz for the present teacher-student problem [22]. Since it is widely believed that the RS solution correctly predicts the behavior of the exact solution in the

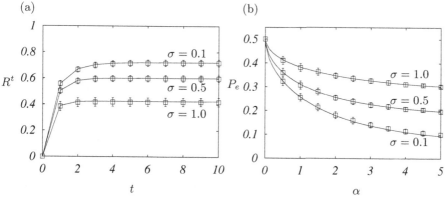

Fig. 2. (a) Trajectories of the overlap R^t. Symbols and error-bars represent the average and standard deviation, respectively, obtained from 100 experiments for $N = 100$ and $p = 200$. The horizontal axis indicates the number of updates t. The lines were obtained by Eqs. (31), (32), (37) and (38). (b) Prediction error $P_e = \text{Prob}\{y^{p+1} \neq \hat{y}^{p+1}\}$ obtained for the Bayesian inference based on Eq. (29) plotted with respect to $\alpha = p/N$ for $N = 100$ and varying p. Symbols and error-bars are based on the results of 100 experiments, whereas the lines were obtained from the convergent solution of Eqs. (31), (32), (37) and (38).

thermodynamic limit if the architectures of the teacher and student are of the same type [13], the proposed algorithm is thought to provide a solution very close to the exact solution when the size of the network is sufficiently large.

In order to verify this supposition, we performed numerical experiments for the case of a binary output $y = \pm 1$. In the experiments, the conditional distribution was obtained as $P(y|\boldsymbol{x}, \boldsymbol{w}) = g(y|\Delta) = \int_{-y\Delta/\sigma}^{+\infty} Dz$. In Fig. 2 (a), the symbols denote the trajectories of R^t experimentally obtained from 100 experiments using Eqs. (25) and (26) for $N = 100$, $p = 200$ and $\sigma = 0.1, 0.5, 1.0$, whereas the lines denote the theoretical predictions obtained using Eqs. (31), (32), (37) and (38). Figure 2 (b) plots the prediction error as a function of the ratio $\alpha = p/N$, varying p while maintaining $N = 100$, when the Bayesian inference is performed based on Eq. (29) using the equilibrium solution. The excellent correspondence between the experimental results and theoretical predictions shown by these figures strongly supports our supposition.

4   Application to CDMA Multi-user Detection

In the preceding section, we developed a BP-based approximation algorithm of computational cost $O(N^2)$ per update for the Bayesian inference in perceptron-type networks. Although this algorithm may be competitive for large networks, since several of the assumptions adopted herein are somewhat artificial, the significance of the proposed algorithm with respect to real-world problems is suspect. Therefore, we next present an application to the multi-user detection problem that arises in a code division multiple access (CDMA) scheme. Code division multiple access is a core technology of the current wireless communications system [10,11,23].

In the general scenario of a CDMA system, the binary signals of multiple users are modulated by spreading codes assigned to each user beforehand, and these modulated sequences are then transmitted to a base station. The base station (BS) receives a mixture of the modulated sequences and possible noise. Thereafter, a detector at the BS extracts the original binary signals from the received real signals using knowledge of the users' spreading codes.

Multiuser detection is a scheme used in the detection stage. By simultaneously estimating multiple user signals following the Bayesian framework, this scheme suppresses mutual interference and can minimize the rate of detection error. However, as following the Bayesian framework is computationally difficult, the development of approximation algorithms is necessary for practical implementation.

The technique developed in the preceding section is a promising method for addressing this problem. In order to demonstrate the potential of this technique, we next examine an N-user direct-sequence binary phase shift-keying (DS/BPSK) CDMA using random binary spreading codes of spreading factor p with unit energy over an additive white Gaussian noise (AWGN) channel[1]. For simplicity, we assume that the signal powers are completely controlled to unit energy, while extension to the case of distributed power is straightforward. In addition, we assume that the chip timing, as well as the symbol timing, are perfectly synchronized among users. Under these assumptions [11], the received signal can be expressed as

$$y^\mu = \frac{1}{\sqrt{p}} \sum_{i=1}^{N} x_i^\mu w_i + \sigma n_\mu, \tag{39}$$

where $\mu = 1, 2, \ldots, p$ and $i = 1, 2, \ldots, N$ are indices of samples and users, respectively. $x_i^\mu \in \{-1, 1\}$ is the spreading code independently generated from the identical uniform distribution $P(x_i^\mu = +1) = P(x_i^\mu = -1) = 1/2$, which yields $\overline{x_i^\mu} = 0$ and $\overline{x_i^\mu x_j^\nu} = \delta_{\mu\nu}\delta_{ij}$. $w_i \in \{+1, -1\}$ is the bit signal of user i, n_μ is a Gaussian noise sample with zero mean and unit variance, and σ is the standard deviation of AWGN. In the following, we assume that both N and p are sufficiently large, maintaining $\alpha = p/N$ finite, which may not be far from practical, since a relatively large spreading factor of up to $p = 256$ is possible in "cdma2000", one of the third-generation cellular phone systems [23].

The goal of multiuser detection is to simultaneously estimate bit signals $w_1, w_2, \ldots, w_N$ after receiving the signals $y^1, y^2, \ldots, y^p$ when all components of the spreading codes x_i^μ are known. The Bayesian approach offers a useful framework for this case. Assuming that the bit signals are independently generated from the uniform distribution, the posterior distribution from the received

---

[1] The notation used here differs from the conventional notation in order to emphasize the link to the perceptron learning problem argued in the previous section.

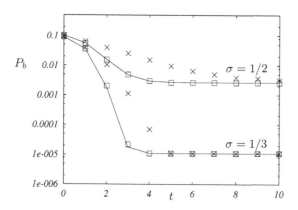

Fig. 3. Time evolution of BER for $N = 1000$ and $p = 2000$. $\square$ and $\times$ represent the experimental results obtained from 10000 simulations for the developed algorithm and the multi-stage detection [24], whereas the lines represent certain macroscopic equations corresponding to Eqs. (31), (32), (37) and (38).

signals is obtained as

$$P(\boldsymbol{w}|D^p) = \frac{P(\boldsymbol{w}) \prod_{\mu=1}^{p} P(y^\mu|\boldsymbol{x}^\mu, \boldsymbol{w})}{\sum_{\boldsymbol{w}} P(\boldsymbol{w}) \prod_{\mu=1}^{p} P(y^\mu|\boldsymbol{x}^\mu, \boldsymbol{w})}, \tag{40}$$

where D^p indicates the set of all received signals y^μ and spreading codes x_i^μ, $P(\boldsymbol{w}) = 2^{-N} \prod_{i=1}^{N} [\delta(w_i - 1) + \delta(w_i + 1)]$ is the uniform prior distribution for the transmitted signals, $(x_1^\mu, x_2^\mu, \dots, x_N^\mu)$ is denoted as $\boldsymbol{x}^\mu$ for each μ, $\Delta^\mu \equiv \frac{1}{\sqrt{N}} \sum_{i=1}^{N} x_i^\mu w_i$ and

$$P(y^\mu|\boldsymbol{x}^\mu, \boldsymbol{w}) = \frac{1}{\sqrt{2\pi\sigma^2}} \exp\left[-\frac{1}{2\sigma^2} \left(y^\mu - \alpha^{-1/2} \Delta^\mu\right)^2\right] \tag{41}$$

represents the AWGN channel. The Bayesian optimal estimator that minimizes the bit error rate (BER), which is the probability of occurrence of bitwise estimation error, is evaluated based on the posterior distribution (40) as

$$\hat{w}_i^{\text{Bayes}} = \underset{w_i \in \{+1, -1\}}{\text{argmax}} \sum_{w_{l \neq i}} P(\boldsymbol{w}|D^p) = \text{sgn}\left(\langle w_i \rangle\right), \tag{42}$$

where $\text{sgn}(x) = 1$ for $x > 0$, and 0 otherwise.

Note that this problem can be regarded as a Bayesian inference problem in a large perceptron, the parameters of which take only binary values $w_i = \pm 1$. Therefore, we can utilize the technique developed in the preceding sections for this problem by regarding Eq. (41) as $g(y^\mu|\Delta^\mu)$ and employing the uniform binary prior $P(w_i) = \frac{1}{2}(\delta(w_i - 1) + \delta(w_i + 1))$. This yields an approximation algorithm for the multi-user detection problem as

$$a_\mu^{t+1} = \frac{1}{\alpha\sigma^2 + 1 - Q^t}\left(\sqrt{\alpha}y^\mu - \sum_{i=1}^{N}\frac{x_i^\mu}{\sqrt{N}}\langle w_i\rangle^t + \Xi^t a_\mu^t\right), \tag{43}$$

$$\langle w_i\rangle^t = \tanh\left(\sum_{\mu=1}^{p}\frac{x_i^\mu}{\sqrt{N}}a_\mu^t - \Gamma^{t-1}\langle w_i\rangle^{t-1}\right), \tag{44}$$

where the macroscopic variables Ξ^t and Γ^t are evaluated as $\Xi^t = 1-Q^t$ and $\Gamma^t = \alpha\left(\alpha\sigma^2 + 1 - Q^t\right)^{-1}$, respectively [10]. Equations (43) and (44), which correspond respectively to Eqs. (25) and (26) of the previous section, can be performed in $O(N^2)$ computations per update when $\alpha = p/N \sim O(1)$.

Figure 3 shows the time evolution of BER obtained from Eqs. (43) and (44) in comparison with the multi-stage detection (MSD) algorithm, which is one of the conventional approximation schemes for the current problem [24]. This indicates that the proposed BP-based algorithm exhibits a considerably faster convergence rate than MSD, which is preferred for practical purposes.

5   Summary

In summary, we have developed an algorithm that approximates the Bayesian inference in a single-layered feed-forward network (perceptron) based on BP. Although the direct application of BP in perceptrons is not computationally tractable, we have shown that this difficulty can be overcome by using techniques from SM under certain assumptions, which leads to an iterative algorithm that can be performed in $O(N^2)$ computations per update when the numbers of examples and parameters, p and N, are of the same order. Examination of the properties of the algorithm for a simple teacher-student scenario indicated that a nearly optimal solution can be obtained using this algorithm for ideal situations. In order to demonstrate the practical significance of the proposed algorithm, we have presented an application to the CDMA multi-user detection problem that arises in a digital wireless communications system.

Extending the applicability of the proposed algorithm to multi-layered perceptrons is one of the challenging future works.

Acknowledgement. The present study was supported in part by a Grant-in-Aid (No. 14084206) from MEXT, Japan (YK).

References

[1] Iba, Y.: The Nishimori line and Bayesian statistics. J. Phys. A **38** (1999) 3875–3888
[2] Berger, J.O.: Statistical Decision Theory and Bayesian Analysis (2nd Ed.). Springer-Verlag (New York) (1985)

[3] Opper, M., Winther, O.: A mean field algorithm for Bayes learning in large feed-forward neural networks. Advances in Neural Information Processing Systems **9**, M.C. Mozer et al., Eds., MIT Press (Cambridge, MA) (1997) 225–231

[4] Opper, M., Winther, O.: A mean field approach to Bayes learning in feed-forward neural networks. Phys. Rev. Lett. **76** (1996) 1964–1967

[5] Opper, M., Winther, O.: Tractable approximation for probabilistic models: The adaptive TAP mean field approach. Phys. Rev. Lett. **86** (2001) 3695–3699

[6] Kappen, H.J., Rodríguez, F.B.: Efficient learning in Boltzmann Machines using linear response theory. Advances in Neural Information Processing Systems **11**, M.S. Kearns et al., Eds., MIT Press (Cambridge, MA) (1999) 280–286

[7] MacKay, D.J.C., Neal, R.M.: Near Shannon limit performance of low density parity check codes. Electronics Letters **32** (1996) 1645–1646

[8] MacKay, D.J.C.: Good error correcting codes based on very sparse matrices. IEEE Trans. Infor. Theor. **45** (1999) 399-431

[9] Kabashima, Y., Saad, D.: Belief Propagation vs. TAP for decoding corrupted messages. Europhys. Lett. **44** (1998) 668-674

[10] Kabashima, Y.: A CDMA multiuser detection algorithm on the basis of belief propagation. J. Phys. A **36** (2003) 11111–11121

[11] Tanaka, T.: A Statistical-Mechanics Approach to Large-System Analysis of CDMA Multiuser Detectors. IEEE Trans. Infor. Theor. **48** (2002) 2888–2910

[12] Opper, M., Saad, D.: Advanced Mean Field Methods. MIT Press (Cambridge, MA) (2001)

[13] Nishimori, H.: Statistical Physics of Spin Glasses and Information Processing. Oxform Univ. Press (New York) (2001)

[14] Pearl, J.: Probabilistic Reasoning in Intelligent Systems (2nd Ed.). Morgan Kaufmann (San Francisco) (1988)

[15] Gallager, R.G.: Low Density Parity Check Codes. MIT Press (Cambridge, MA) (1963)

[16] Tanaka, K.: Probabilistic Inference by means of Cluster Variation Method and Linear Response Theory. IEICE Trans. Inform. & Syst. **E86-D** (2003) 1228–1242

[17] Welling, M., Teh, Y.W.: Linear Response Algorithms for Approximate Inference in Graphical Models. Neural Compt. **16** (2004) 197–221

[18] Murayama, T.: Statistical Mechanics of the data compression theorem. J. Phys. A **35** (2002) L95–L100

[19] Murayama, T., Okada, M.: One step RSB scheme for the rate distortion function. J. Phys. A **36** (2003) 11123–11130

[20] Vicente, R., Saad, D., Kabashima, Y.: Statistical physics of irregular low-density parity-check codes. J. Phys. A **33** (2000) 6527–6542

[21] Mezard, M., Parisi, G., Virasoro, M.A.: Spin Glass Theory and Beyond, World Scientific (Singapore) (1987)

[22] Watkin, T.L.H., Rau, A., Biehl, M.: The statistical mechanics of learning a rule. Rev. Mod. Phys. **65** (1993) 499–568

[23] Ojanpera, T., Prasad, R. (Ed.): WCDMA: Towards IP Mobility and Mobile Internet, Artech House (Boston, MA) (2001)

[24] Varanasi, M.K., Aazhang, B.: Near Optimum Detection in Synchronous Code-Division Multiple-Access Systems. IEEE Trans. on Commun. **39** (1991) 725–736

Approximate Inference in Probabilistic Models

Manfred Opper[1] and Ole Winther[2]

[1] ISIS
School of Electronics and
Computer Science
University of Southampton
SO17 1BJ, United Kingdom
mo@ecs.soton.ac.uk
[2] Informatics and
Mathematical Modelling
Technical University of Denmark
DK-2800 Lyngby, Denmark
owi@imm.dtu.dk

Abstract. We present a framework for approximate inference in probabilistic data models which is based on free energies. The free energy is constructed from two approximating distributions which encode different aspects of the intractable model. Consistency between distributions is required on a chosen set of moments. We find good performance using sets of moments which either specify factorized nodes or a spanning tree on the nodes.
The abstract should summarize the contents of the paper using at least 70 and at most 150 words. It will be set in 9-point font size and be inset 1.0 cm from the right and left margins. There will be two blank lines before and after the Abstract. . . .

1 Introduction

Probabilistic data models explain the dependencies of complex observed data by a set of hidden variables and the joint probability distribution of all variables. The development of tractable approximations for the statistical inference with these models is essential for developing their full potential. Such approximations are necessary for models with a large number of variables, because the computation of the marginal distributions of hidden variables and the learning of model parameters requires high dimensional summations or integrations.

The most popular approximation is the *Variational Approximation* (VA) [2] which replaces the true probability distribution by an optimized simpler one, where multivariate Gaussians or distributions factorizing in certain groups of variables [1] are possible choices. The neglecting of correlations for factorizing distributions is of course a drawback. On the other hand, multivariate Gaussians allow for correlations but are restricted to *continuous random variables* which have the entire real space as their natural domain (otherwise, we get an infinite relative entropy which is used as a measure for comparing exact and approximate

S. Ben-David, J. Case, A. Maruoka (Eds.): ALT 2004, LNAI 3244, pp. 494–504, 2004.

densities in the VA). In this paper, we will discuss approximations which allow to circumvent these drawbacks. These will be derived from a Gibbs Free Energy (GFE), an entropic quantity which (originally developed in Statistical Physics) allows us to formulate the statistical inference problem as an optimization problem. While the true GFE is usually not exactly tractable, certain approximations can give quite accurate results. We will specialise on an *expectation consistent* (EC) approach which requires consistency between *two* complimentary approximations (say, a factorizing or tree with a Gaussian one) to the same probabilistic model.

The method is a generalization of the *adaptive TAP* approach (ADATAP) [16,15] developed for inference on densely connected graphical models which has been applied successfully to a variety of relevant problems. These include Gaussian process models [17,14,10,11], probabilistic independent component analysis [6], the CDMA coding model in telecommunications [4], bootstrap methods for kernel machines [7,8], a model for wind field retrieval from satellite observations [3] and a sparse kernel approach [12]. For a different, but related approximation scheme see [10,9].

2   Approximative Inference

Inference on the hidden variables $\mathbf{x} = (x_1, x_2, \dots, x_N)$ of a probabilistic model usually requires the computation of expectations, ie of certain sums or integrals involving a probability distribution with density

$$p(\mathbf{x}) = \frac{1}{Z} f(\mathbf{x}) \ . \tag{1}$$

This density represents the *posterior* distribution of $\mathbf{x}$ conditioned on the observed data, the latter appearing as parameters in p. $Z = \int d\mathbf{x} f(\mathbf{x})$ is the normalizing *partition function*.

Although some results can be stated in fairly general form, we will mostly specialize on densities (with respect to the Lebesgue measure in R^N) of the form

$$p(\mathbf{x}) = \prod_i \Psi_i(x_i) \ \exp\left(\sum_{i<j} x_i J_{ij} x_j\right) \ , \tag{2}$$

where the Ψ_i's are *non-Gaussian* functions. This also includes the important case of Ising variables $x_i = \pm 1$ by setting

$$\Psi(x_i) = (\delta(x_i + 1) + \ \delta(x_i - 1)) \ e^{\theta_i x_i} \ . \tag{3}$$

The type of density (2) appears as the posterior distribution for all models cited at the end of the introduction chapter.

$p(\mathbf{x})$ is a product of two functions $p(\mathbf{x}) = f_1(\mathbf{x}) f_2(\mathbf{x})$, where both the factorizing part $f_1 = \prod_i \Psi_i(x_i)$ and the Gaussian part $f_2 = \exp\left(\sum_{i<j} x_i J_{ij} x_j\right)$

individually are simple enough to allow for exact computations. Hence, as an approximation, we might want to keep f_1 but replace f_2 by a function which also factorizes in the components x_i. As an alternative, one may keep f_2 but replace f_1 by a Gaussian function to make the whole distribution *Gaussian*. Both choices are not ideal. The first completely neglects correlations of the variables but leads to marginal distributions of the x_i, which may share non Gaussian features (such as multimodality) with the true marginal. The second one neglects such features but incorporates nontrivial correlations. We will later develop an approach for combining these two approximations.

3   Gibbs Free Energies

Gibbs free energies (GFE) provide a convenient formalism for dealing with probabilistic approximations. In this framework, the *true, intractable* distribution $p(\mathbf{x})$ is *implicitly* characterized as the solution of an *optimization problem* defined through the the the relative entropy (KL divergence)

$$KL(q,p) = \int d\mathbf{x}\, q(\mathbf{x}) \ln \frac{q(\mathbf{x})}{p(\mathbf{x})} \tag{4}$$

between p and other trial distributions q. We consider a *two stage optimization* process, where in the first step, the trial distributions q are constrained by fixing a set of values $\boldsymbol{\mu} = \langle \mathbf{g}(\mathbf{x}) \rangle_q$ for a set of generalized moments. The Gibbs Free Energy $G(\boldsymbol{\mu})$ is defined as

$$G(\boldsymbol{\mu}) = \min_q \{ KL(q,p) \mid \langle \mathbf{g}(\mathbf{x}) \rangle_q = \boldsymbol{\mu} \} - \ln Z \ , \tag{5}$$

where the term $\ln Z$ is subtracted to make the expression independent of the intractable partition function Z. In a second stage, both the true values $\boldsymbol{\mu} = \langle \mathbf{g}(\mathbf{x}) \rangle_p$ and the partition function Z are found by relaxing the constraints ie by minimizing $G(\boldsymbol{\mu})$ with respect to $\boldsymbol{\mu}$:

$$\min_{\boldsymbol{\mu}} G(\boldsymbol{\mu}) = -\ln Z \qquad \text{and} \qquad \langle \mathbf{g} \rangle = \operatorname*{argmin}_{\boldsymbol{\mu}} G(\boldsymbol{\mu}) \ . \tag{6}$$

A variational upper bound to G is obtained by restricting the minimization in (5) to a subset of densities q.

It can be easily shown that the optimizing distribution (5) is of the form

$$q(\mathbf{x}) = \frac{f(\mathbf{x})}{Z(\boldsymbol{\lambda})} \exp \left(\boldsymbol{\lambda}^T \mathbf{g}(\mathbf{x}) \right) \ , \tag{7}$$

where the set of *Lagrange parameters* $\boldsymbol{\lambda} = \boldsymbol{\lambda}(\boldsymbol{\mu})$ is chosen such that the conditions $\langle \mathbf{g}(\mathbf{x}) \rangle_q = \boldsymbol{\mu}$ are fulfilled, i.e. $\boldsymbol{\lambda}$ satisfies

$$\frac{\partial \ln Z(\boldsymbol{\lambda})}{\partial \boldsymbol{\lambda}} = \boldsymbol{\mu} \ , \tag{8}$$

where $Z(\boldsymbol{\lambda})$ is a normalizing partition function.

Inserting the optimizing distribution eq. (7) into eq. (5) yields the *dual representation* of the Gibbs free energy

$$G(\boldsymbol{\mu}) = -\ln Z(\boldsymbol{\lambda}(\boldsymbol{\mu})) + \boldsymbol{\lambda}^T(\boldsymbol{\mu})\boldsymbol{\mu} = \max_{\boldsymbol{\lambda}} \left\{ -\ln Z(\boldsymbol{\lambda}) + \boldsymbol{\lambda}^T \boldsymbol{\mu} \right\} , \qquad (9)$$

showing that G is the *Legendre transform* of $-\ln Z(\boldsymbol{\lambda})$ making G a convex function of its arguments.

We will later use the following simple result for the derivative of the GFE with respect to a parameter t contained in the probability density $p(\mathbf{x}|t) = \frac{f(\mathbf{x},t)}{Z_t}$. This can be calculated using (9) and (8) as

$$\frac{dG_t(\boldsymbol{\mu})}{dt} = -\frac{\partial \ln Z(\boldsymbol{\lambda}, t)}{\partial t} + \left(\boldsymbol{\mu} - \frac{\partial \ln Z(\boldsymbol{\lambda}, t)}{\partial \boldsymbol{\lambda}} \right) \frac{d\boldsymbol{\lambda}^T}{dt} = -\frac{\partial \ln Z(\boldsymbol{\lambda}, t)}{\partial t} . \qquad (10)$$

Hence, we can keep $\boldsymbol{\lambda}$ fixed upon differentiation.

3.1   Simple Models

We give results for Gibbs free energies of three tractable models and choices of moments $\langle \mathbf{g}(\mathbf{x}) \rangle$. These will be used later as building blocks for the free energies of more complicated models.

Independent Ising variables. The Gibbs free energy for a set of independent Ising variables each with a density of the form (3) and fixed first moments $\boldsymbol{\mu} = \langle \mathbf{x} \rangle = \mathbf{m} = (m_1, m_2, \dots, m_N)$ is $G(\mathbf{m}) = \sum_i G_i(m_i)$ where

$$G_i(m_i) = \frac{(1 + m_i)}{2} \ln \frac{(1 + m_i)}{2} + \frac{(1 - m_i)}{2} \ln \frac{(1 - m_i)}{2} - \theta_i m_i . \qquad (11)$$

It will be useful to introduce a more complicated set of moments for this simple noninteracting model. We choose a tree graph $\mathcal{G}$ out of all possible sets of edges linking the variables $\mathbf{x}$ and fix the second moments $M_{ij} = \langle x_i x_j \rangle$ along theses edges as constraints. In this case, it can be shown that the free energy is represented in terms of single- and two-node free energies

$$G(\mathbf{m}, \{M_{ij}\}_{(ij)\in\mathcal{G}}) = \sum_{(ij)\in\mathcal{G}} G_{ij}(m_i, m_j, M_{ij}) + \sum_i (1 - n_i) G_i(m_i) , \qquad (12)$$

where $G_{ij}(m_i, m_j, M_{ij})$ is the two-node free energy computed for a single pair of variables, and n_i is the number of links to node i.

Multivariate Gaussians. The Gaussian model is of the form (2) with $\Psi_i(x_i) \propto \exp[a_i x_i - \frac{b_i}{2} x_i^2]$. Here, we fix $\boldsymbol{\mu} = (\mathbf{m}, \mathbf{M})$ where $\mathbf{m}$ is the set of all first moments and $\mathbf{M}$ is an arbitrary subset of second moments $\langle x_i x_j \rangle = M_{ij} = M_{ji}$. We get

$$G(\mathbf{m}, \mathbf{M}) = -\frac{1}{2}\mathbf{m}^T \mathbf{J} \mathbf{m} - \mathbf{m}^T \mathbf{a} + \frac{1}{2}\sum_i M_{ii} b_i \qquad (13)$$

$$+ \max_{\Lambda} \left\{ \frac{1}{2} \ln \det(\Lambda - \mathbf{J}) - \frac{1}{2} \operatorname{Tr} \Lambda (\mathbf{M} - \mathbf{m}\mathbf{m}^T) \right\} ,$$

where Λ is a matrix of Lagrangemultipliers conjugate to the values of $\mathbf{M}$.

3.2   Complex Models: A Perturbative Representation

We will now concentrate on the more complex model (2) together with a suitably chosen set of moments. We will represent the Gibbs free energy of this model as the GFE for a tractable "noninteracting" part $f_1 = \prod_i \Psi_i(x_i)$ plus a correction for the "interaction" term $f_2 = \exp\left(\sum_{i<j} x_i J_{ij} x_j\right)$. We fix as constraints all the first moments $\mathbf{m}$ and a subset of second moments $\mathbf{M}$ which is chosen in such a way that the Gibbs free energy for f_1 remains still tractable. Different choices of second moments will allow later for more accurate approximations. If *all second moments* are fixed, our result will be exact, but for most models of the form (2) this leads again to intractable computations.

We define $f_2(\mathbf{x}, t)$ to be a smooth *interpolation* between the trivial case $f_2(\mathbf{x}, t = 0) = 1$ and the "full" intractable case $f_2(\mathbf{x}, t = 1) = f_2(\mathbf{x})$. For the model (2) we can set

$$f_2(\mathbf{x}, t) = \exp\left(t \sum_{i<j} x_i J_{ij} x_j\right) .$$

Differentiating the Gibbs free energy with respect to t, using eq. (10), we get

$$G(\boldsymbol{\mu}, 1) - G(\boldsymbol{\mu}, 0) = -\int_0^1 dt \left\langle \frac{d \ln f_2(\mathbf{x}, t)}{dt} \right\rangle_{q(\boldsymbol{x}|t)} . \tag{14}$$

where $q(\mathbf{x}|t) = \frac{1}{Z_q(\boldsymbol{\lambda}, t)} f_1(\mathbf{x}) f_2(\mathbf{x}, t) \exp\left(\boldsymbol{\lambda}^T \mathbf{g}(\mathbf{x})\right)$. For the model (2) this can be written as

$$G(\mu) \equiv G(\boldsymbol{\mu}, 1) = G(\boldsymbol{\mu}, 0) - \int_0^1 dt \sum_{i<j} J_{ij} \langle x_i x_j \rangle_{q(\boldsymbol{x}|t)} . \tag{15}$$

4   Approximations to the Free Energy

4.1   Mean Field Approximation

If we restrict ourselves to fixed diagonal second moments M_{ii} only, the simplest approximation is obtained by replacing the expectation over $q(\boldsymbol{x}|t)$ by the factorizing distribution $q(\boldsymbol{x}|0)$ giving

$$G(\mu) \approx G(\boldsymbol{\mu}, 0) - \sum_{i<j} J_{ij} m_i m_j . \tag{16}$$

This result is equivalent to the *variational mean field* approximation, obtained by restricting the minimization in (5) to densities of the form $q(\mathbf{x}|0)$. Hence, it gives an *upper bound* to the true GFE.

4.2   Perturbative Expansion

One can improve on the mean field result by turning the exact expression (15) into a series expansion of the free energy in powers of t, setting $t = 1$ at the end. It is easy to see that the term linear in t corresponds to the mean field result. The second order term of this so-called Plefka expansion can be found in [18], see also several contributions in [13]. While the second order term seems to be sufficient for models with random independent couplings J_{ij} in a "thermodynamic limit", more advanced approximations are necessary in general [16,15].

4.3   A Lower Bound to the Gibbs Free Energy for Ising Variables

This was recently found by Wainwright & Jordan [20,19] and can be obtained by specifying *all second moments* $\mathbf{M}$. Then it is easy to see from the definition of the free energy that

$$G(\boldsymbol{\mu}) + \sum_{i<j} J_{ij} M_{ij} = -H[\mathbf{x}] ,$$

where $H[\mathbf{x}]$ equals the (discrete) negative entropy of the random variable $\mathbf{x}$. Wainwright and Jordan construct a *continuous random variable* $\tilde{\mathbf{x}}$ (a noisy version of $\mathbf{x}$) which has the same *differential entropy* $h[\tilde{\mathbf{x}}] = H[\mathbf{x}]$. Now they can apply a Maximum -Entropy argument and upper bound $h[\tilde{\mathbf{x}}]$ by the differential entropy $h_{\mathrm{Gauss}}[\tilde{\mathbf{x}}]$ of a Gaussian with the same moments:

$$- H[\mathbf{x}] = -h[\tilde{\mathbf{x}}] \geq -h_{\mathrm{Gauss}}[\tilde{\mathbf{x}}] = \frac{1}{2} \log \det[\mathrm{Cov}(\tilde{\mathbf{x}})] + \frac{N}{2} \log(\frac{ne}{2}) \qquad (17)$$

$$= \frac{1}{2} \log \det[\frac{1}{4}\mathrm{Cov}(\mathbf{x}) + \frac{1}{3}I_N] + \frac{N}{2} \log(\frac{ne}{2}) .$$

The approximate free energy comes out a convex function of its arguments.

4.4   Bethe–Kikuchi Type of Approximations

These are usually applied to discrete random variables and become exact if the graph which is defined by the edges of nonzero couplings $J_{ij} \neq 0$ is a tree or (for the Kikuchi approximation) a more generalized cluster of nodes. For tree connected graphs, the joint density of variables can always be expressed through single and two node marginals (similar to (12)). Using this structure within the optimization (5), one can calculate the Gibbs free energy exactly and efficiently when all first moments and the second moments along the edges of the graph are fixed. The approximation [21,22,5] is obtained when the graph of nonzero couplings is not a tree, but the simple form of the tree type distribution is still used in the optimization (5). Although the variation is over a subset of distributions, the Bethe–Kikuchi approximations do not lead to an upper bound to the free energy. This is because the constraints are no longer along trees and are thus not consistent with the distribution assumed.

5   Expectation Consistent Approximations

Our goal is to come up with another approximation which improves over the mean field result (16) by making a more clever approximation to $q(\mathbf{x}|t)$ in (15). We will use our assumption that we may approximate the density (2) by alternatively discarding the factor $f_1(\mathbf{x})$ as intractable, replacing the density $q(\mathbf{x}|t)$ by

$$r(\mathbf{x}|t) = \frac{1}{Z_r(\boldsymbol{\lambda}, t)} f_2(\mathbf{x}, t) \exp\left(\boldsymbol{\lambda}^T \mathbf{g}(\mathbf{x})\right) , \tag{18}$$

where the parameters $\boldsymbol{\lambda}$ are chosen to have *consistency for the expectations* of $\mathbf{g}$, i.e. $\langle \mathbf{g}(\mathbf{x})\rangle_{r(\boldsymbol{x}|t)} = \boldsymbol{\mu}$.

$r(\mathbf{x}|t)$ defines another Gibbs free energy with a dual representation eq. (9)

$$G_r(\boldsymbol{\mu}, t) = \max_{\boldsymbol{\lambda}}\left\{-\ln Z_r(\boldsymbol{\lambda}, t) + \boldsymbol{\lambda}^T \boldsymbol{\mu}\right\} . \tag{19}$$

We will use $r(\mathbf{x}|t)$ to treat the integral in eq. (14), writing

$$\int_0^1 dt \left\langle \frac{d \ln f_2(\mathbf{x}, t)}{dt} \right\rangle_{q(\boldsymbol{x}|t)} \approx \int_0^1 dt \left\langle \frac{d \ln f_2(\mathbf{x}, t)}{dt} \right\rangle_{r(\boldsymbol{x}|t)} . \tag{20}$$

Using the relations eqs. (10) for the free energy eq. (19) we get

$$\int_0^1 dt \left\langle \frac{d \ln f_2(\mathbf{x}, t)}{dt} \right\rangle_{r(\boldsymbol{x}|t)} = G_r(\boldsymbol{\mu}, 1) - G_r(\boldsymbol{\mu}, 0) . \tag{21}$$

and arrive at the *expectation consistent (EC)* approximation:

$$G(\boldsymbol{\mu}) \approx G(\boldsymbol{\mu}, 0) + G_r(\boldsymbol{\mu}, 1) - G_r(\boldsymbol{\mu}, 0) \equiv G^{\mathrm{EC}}(\boldsymbol{\mu}) . \tag{22}$$

6   Results for Ising Variables

We will now apply our EC framework to the model (2) with Ising variables $x_i = \pm 1$. We will discuss two types of approximations which differ by the set of fixed second moments M_{ij}. By fixing more and more second moments, we reduce the number of interaction terms of the form $J_{ij}x_i x_j$ which are not fixed and have to be approximated.

Since $r(\mathbf{x}|t)$ is a multivariate Gaussian, we have

$$G^{\mathrm{EC}}(\mathbf{m}, \mathbf{M}) = G(\mathbf{m}, \mathbf{M}, 0) - \frac{1}{2}\mathbf{m}^T \mathbf{J} \mathbf{m} \tag{23}$$

$$+ \max_{\Lambda}\left\{\frac{1}{2}\ln\det(\Lambda - \mathbf{J}) - \frac{1}{2}\operatorname{Tr}\Lambda(\mathbf{M} - \mathbf{m}\mathbf{m}^T)\right\}$$

$$- \max_{\Lambda}\left\{\frac{1}{2}\ln\det\Lambda - \frac{1}{2}\operatorname{Tr}\Lambda(\mathbf{M} - \mathbf{m}\mathbf{m}^T)\right\} .$$

To obtain estimates for the second moments which are not fixed in the free energy, we take derivatives of the free energy with respect to coupling parameters J_{ij} yielding

$$\langle \mathbf{xx}^T \rangle - \langle \mathbf{x} \rangle \langle \mathbf{x}^T \rangle = (\Lambda - \mathbf{J})^{-1} . \tag{24}$$

This result is also consistent with the fixed values $\mathbf{M}$ for the second moments.

6.1 Diagonal Approximation

When we fix only the trivial diagonal second moments $M_{ii} \equiv \langle x_i^2 \rangle = 1$ (Ising constraints), $\mathbf{M}$ does not appear as a variable in the free energy. The EC approximation eq. (23) is then given by

$$G^{\mathrm{D}}(\mathbf{m}) = G^{\mathrm{Is}}(\mathbf{m}) - \frac{1}{2}\mathbf{m}^T \mathbf{J} \mathbf{m} \tag{25}$$

$$+ \max_{\Lambda} \left\{ \frac{1}{2} \ln \det(\Lambda - \mathbf{J}) - \frac{1}{2} \sum_{i=1}^{N} \Lambda_i (1 - m_i^2) \right\}$$

$$+ \frac{1}{2} \sum_{i=1}^{N} \ln(1 - m_i^2) + \frac{N}{2} ,$$

where $G^{\mathrm{Is}}(\mathbf{m})$ is given by eq. (11) and Λ is a diagonal matrix of Lagrange parameters. This result coincides with the older *adaptive TAP approximation* [16, 15].

6.2 Tree Approximation

A more complex, but still tractable approximation is obtained by selecting an arbitrary tree connected subgraph of pairs of nodes and fixing the second moments of the Ising variables along the edges of this graph. The free energy is again of the form eq. (23) but now with $G(\mathbf{m}, \mathbf{M}, 0)$ given by eq. (12), the Lagrange parameters Λ_{ij} are restricted to be non-zero on the tree graph only. If the tree is chosen in such a way as to include the most important couplings (defined in a proper way), one can expect that the approximation will improve significantly over the diagonal case.

7 Simulations

We compare results of the EC approximation with those of the Bethe–Kikuchi approaches on a toy problem suggested in [5]. We use $N = 10$ nodes, constant "external fields" $\theta_i = \theta = 0.1$. The J_{ij}'s are drawn independently at random, setting $J_{ij} = \beta w_{ij}/\sqrt{N}$, with Gaussian w_{ij}'s of zero mean and unit variance. We study eight different scaling factors $\beta = [0.10, 0.25, 0.50, 0.75, 1.00, 1.50, 2.00, 10.00]$. The results are summarized in figures 1 and 2. Figure 1

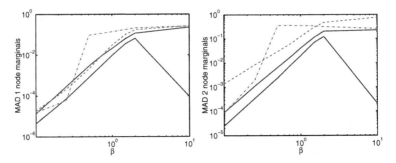

Fig. 1. Maximal absolute deviation (MAD) for one- (left) and two-variable (right) marginals. Blue upper full line: EC factorized, blue lower full line EC tree, green dashed line: Bethe and red dash-dotted line: Kikuchi.

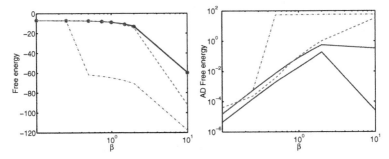

Fig. 2. Left plot: free energy for EC factorized and tree (blue full line), Bethe (green dashed line), Kikuchi (red dash-dotted) and exact (stars). Right: Absolute deviation (AD) for the three approximations, same line color and type as above. Lower full line is for the tree EC approximation.

gives the maximum absolute deviation (MAD) of our results from the exact marginals for different scaling parameters. We consider one-variable marginals $p(x_i) = \frac{1+x_i m_i}{2}$ and the two-variable marginals $p(x_i, x_j) = \frac{x_i x_j C_{ij}}{4} + p(x_i)p(x_j)$ with the approximate covariance $C_{ij} = \langle x_i x_j \rangle - \langle x_i \rangle \langle x_j \rangle$ given by eq. (24). Figure 2 gives estimates for the free energy. The results show that the simple diagonal EC approach gives performance similar to (and in many case better than) the more structured Bethe and Kikuchi approximations.

For the EC tree approximation, we construct a spanning tree of edges by choosing as the next edge, the (so far unlinked) pair of nodes with strongest absolute coupling $|J_{ij}|$ that will not cause a loop in the graph. The EC tree version is almost always better than the other approximations. A comparison with the Wainwright–Jordan approximation (corresponding to (17)) and details of the algorithm will be given elsewhere.

8   Outlook

We have introduced a scheme for approximate inference with probabilistic models. It is based on a free energy expansion around an exactly tractable substructure (like a tree) where the remaining interactions are treated in a Gaussian approximation thereby retaining nontrivial correlations. In the future, we plan to combine our method with a perturbative approach which may allow for a systematic improvement together with an estimate of the error involved. We will also work on an extension of our framework to more complex types of probabilistic models beyond the pairwise interaction case.

References

[1] H. Attias. A variational Bayesian framework for graphical models. In T. Leen et al., editor, *Advances in Neural Information Processing Systems 12*. MIT Press, Cambridge, 2000.

[2] C. M. Bishop, D. Spiegelhalter, and J. Winn. VIBES: A variational inference engine for Bayesian networks. In *Advances in Neural Information Processing Systems 15*, 2002.

[3] Dan Cornford, Lehel Csató, David J. Evans, and Manfred Opper. Bayesian analysis of the scatterometer wind retrieval inverse problem: Some new approaches. *Journal Royal Statistical Society B 66*, pages 1–17, 2004.

[4] T. Fabricius and O. Winther. Correcting the bias of subtractive interference cancellation in cdma: Advanced mean field theory. *Submitted to IEEE trans. Inf. Theory*, 2004.

[5] T. Heskes, K. Albers, and H. Kappen. Approximate inference and constrained optimization. In *Proceedings of the 19th Annual Conference on Uncertainty in Artificial Intelligence (UAI-03)*, pages 313–320, San Francisco, CA, 2003. Morgan Kaufmann Publishers.

[6] P. A.d.F.R. Hojen-Sorensen, O. Winther, and L. K. Hansen. Mean field approaches to independent component analysis. *Neural Computation*, 14:889–918, 2002.

[7] Dórthe Malzahn and Manfred Opper. An approximate analytical approach to resampling averages. *Journal of Machine Learning Research 4*, pages 1151–1173, 2003.

[8] Dórthe Malzahn and Manfred Opper. Approximate analytical bootstrap averages for support vector classifiers. In *Proceedings of NIPS2003*, 2004.

[9] T. Minka and Y. Qi. Tree-structured approximations by expectation propagation. In S. Thrun, L. Saul, and B. Schölkopf, editors, *Advances in Neural Information Processing Systems 16*. MIT Press, Cambridge, MA, 2004.

[10] T. P. Minka. Expectation propagation for approximate bayesian inference. In *UAI 2001*, pages 362–369, 2001.

[11] T. P. Minka. *A family of algorithms for approximate Bayesian inference*. PhD thesis, MIT Media Lab, 2001.

[12] Qui nonero Candela and Ole Winther. Incremental gaussian processes. In *Advances in Neural Information Processing Systems 15*, pages 1001–1008, 2003.

[13] M. Opper and D. Saad. *Advanced Mean Field Methods: Theory and Practice*. MIT Press, 2001.

[14] M. Opper and O. Winther. Gaussian processes for classification: Mean field algorithms. *Neural Computation*, 12:2655–2684, 2000.

[15] M. Opper and O. Winther. Adaptive and self-averaging Thouless-Anderson-Palmer mean field theory for probabilistic modeling. *Physical Review E*, 64:056131, 2001.

[16] M. Opper and O. Winther. Tractable approximations for probabilistic models: The adaptive Thouless-Anderson-Palmer mean field approach. *Physical Review Letters*, 64:056131, 2001.

[17] Manfred Opper and Ole Winther. Mean field methods for classification with gaussian processes. In *Advances in Neural Information Processing Systems 11*, pages 309–315, 1999.

[18] T. Plefka. Convergence condition of the tap equation for the infinite-range ising spin glass. *J. Phys. A*, 15:1971, 1982.

[19] M. Wainwright and M. I. Jordan. Semidefinite relaxations for approximate inference on graphs with cycles. In S. Thrun, L. Saul, and B. Schölkopf, editors, *Advances in Neural Information Processing Systems 16*. MIT Press, Cambridge, MA, 2004.

[20] M. J. Wainwright and M. I. Jordan. Semidefinite methods for approximate inference on graphs with cycles. Technical Report UCB/CSD-03-1226, UC Berkeley CS Division, 2003.

[21] J. S. Yedidia, W. T. Freeman, and Y. Weiss. Generalized belief propagation 13. In T. K. Leen, T. G. Dietterich, and V. Tresp, editors, *NIPS*, pages 689–695, 2001.

[22] A. L. Yuille. Cccp algorithms to minimize the bethe and kikuchi free energies: convergent alternatives to belief propagation. *Neural Comput.*, 14(7):1691–1722, 2002.

Author Index

Lecture Notes in Artificial Intelligence (LNAI)